.. nda Sternquist, Ph.D.
Professor of Marketing
Broad College of Business
632 Bogue Street, Room N305
East Lansing, MI 48824
sternquis@msu.edu 517-432-6378

MODERN RETAILING
Theory and Practice

Joseph Barry Mason

Board of Visitors Research Professor
and Chairman
Faculty of Management and Marketing

and

Morris Lehman Mayer

Professor of Marketing

both of
The University of Alabama

MODERN RETAILING
Theory and Practice

1978

BUSINESS PUBLICATIONS, INC.   Dallas, Texas   75243
Irwin-Dorsey Limited   Georgetown, Ontario   L7G 4B3

ISBN 0-256-02072-8
Library of Congress Catalog Card No. 77–085786
Printed in the United States of America

1 2 3 4 5 6 7 8 9 0 MP 5 4 3 2 1 0 9 8

To Linda and Judy

PREFACE

Retailing is exciting, dynamic, and extraordinarily diverse! *Picture*—the glamour of Neiman-Marcus; "Avon Calling"; Macy's, Gimbels, and Bloomingdale's (with it's own "Bloomies" cult) in New York City; B. Dalton's large chain of book stores; the discount giant of the country, K mart; Safeway's supermarkets, Kroger's superstores, and Carrefours 250,000-square-foot hypermarches; dramatic multilevel regional shopping centers with stunning boutiques, trendy decor, skating rinks, Magic Pans, see-through elevators, magnificent plantings, people movers, six separate cinemas, and a boat show; mom-and-pop grocery stores; Wilson's catalog show rooms; Levitz furniture and Toy City; 7–11s; and home improvement centers. *Remember?*—general stores; nickelodeons; five-and-dime stores; record stores with soundproof booths for listening; ice cream parlors with dime sodas; grocery delivery; singing telegrams; hanging out at the drug store with the other "cowboys" (or "girls"); jackpot night at the movies even before 3-D and Cinerama; Grants; New York City's Wanamakers, Hechts, James McCreery, and Sterns; Detroit's Kerns; the Automat; and the days *before* fast food places. *Consider*—predictions as to the future of electronic funds transfer systems (EFTS); point of service terminals (POS); Universal Product Code (UPC); metrication; unit pricing; governmental impacts on operations; energy shortages and costs; consumerism; quality of life concerns; inflation; and grocery and furniture warehouses.

Such are the present, past, and future dynamics and decisions of the retailing field, and for those with proper knowledge and background skills a challenging and successful career opportunity exists. Many of the chapters in this text have a decision orientation. This enables students to become comfortable with the many decisions that retail managers must make on an almost daily basis. Also the text has a strong environmental flavor which reflects the influences of consumers and competitors as well as the various economic, social, legal, and technological forces on retailing decisions. The focus is on the future and the kinds of decisions that can be made *now* to insure a successful business in the years ahead.

The perspective of the text is both middle- and upper-level management and the decision-making tasks that face these persons. The text shows the student how retail managers establish goals and objectives, define problems, evaluate alternative courses of action, and develop optimal strategies to insure the success of the firm. Specifically, the objectives set for the text are:

1. To instill awareness of and appreciation for the complex environmental forces that affect retailing decisions.

2. To instill an appreciation for the institutional structure of retailing, its past and probable future patterns.
3. To help students master the numerous decision areas facing retailing managers and to introduce a frame of thought for dealing with them.
4. To help the student develop a lasting understanding of the fundamental concepts and practices in retailing.

The student is introduced to retailing management via a consumer-oriented philosophy of management. Traditional retailing activities are described in an up-to-date, topically illustrated discussion which makes the material live and relevant.

As the title suggests, the text is a blend of theory and practice—there is a substantial base of retailing theory. However, the most pragmatic will find sufficient attention paid to the "practice" of retailing. The approach is one of substance and practicability.

The purposeful career orientation of the text adapts successfully to all potential audiences—most students are either disoriented as to career objectives or actively seeking out potentials. This book clearly defines just what a career in retailing will involve—and students at any level or institution and having any educational background or major can relate to the career dimensions of this text.

ORGANIZATION OF THE TEXT

Chapter 1, The Retailing Management Concept, of Part One provides the student with a framework and a philosophy for studying retailing, moving from the general to the specific. In this chapter students are introduced to the retailing management concept—the central focus of the text—which expresses a point of view and philosophy that is compatible with the society of the 1970s and 1980s. Continuing reference to the framework is encouraged so that the student may constantly fit the pieces together and in addition be ever aware of the central theme.

The framework provides the guidelines and philosophy for Part Two. The highly visible, vast, complex, and dynamic retailing structure is introduced in Chapter 2 wherein the student is shown the different ways in which retailing can be classified. Chapter 3 is concerned with the evolution, explanations, and conjectures about the firms comprising the retail structure. Chapter 4 introduces the reader to the basic organizational structures possible in organizing resources to accomplish agreed-upon management goals.

Part Three, Customers and Markets, emphasizes the foundation of the retailing management concept—namely the market. Chapters 5 and 6 stress the dependence of retailing on the customer. The emphasis here is on using what we know about the consumer to develop strategies appropriate for retail segmentation.

The five chapters of Part Four, The Environments of Retailing, stress those forces that cannot be controlled by the retail manager. The alert manager must be constantly monitoring uncontrollable forces outside the firm which can affect store operations. Chapters 7 through 11 investigate the economic, social, competitive, legal, and technological factors which are constantly changing and always affecting the strategy of retailers. A critical study of this part of the text provides the student with an appreciation for important areas of concern for all citizens. Awareness of the environments of retailing, which surround the framework, is a vital part of a person's total education.

After covering the above material, the student is prepared for the essential nuts and bolts of retailing management presented in Part Five. Chapters 12 through 20 address topics which are faced daily by retail management. The chapter topics are pragmatic and heavy on how-to-do-it and provide critical information about managing a retail business. Students are introduced to such points as: (1) a broad outline of how to merchandise (how to buy and project sales accurately) through planning and control techniques; (2) determination of profitability by utilizing either cost or retail methods of accounting; (3) factors affecting price setting, pricing strategies, and pricing mathematics; (4) choosing merchandise resources, market contact with vendors, methods of buying, terms of sale, and the need for good vendor relationships; (5) communications strategy, media selection and types, and personal selling; (6) trading area analysis; (7) store design and layout, credit, delivery, shoplifting problems; (8) expense classification, allocation, budgeting, and control; and (9) recruiting, selecting, training, compensation, union-management relations, and motivation.

In Part Six, Retailing Tomorrow, the focus is on the dynamics of retailing as a potential career opportunity and upon the future as the forecasted changes might affect the career opportunities as well as the institutions and strategies of management. In Chapters 21 and 22, the cycle is complete and the framework achieves closure.

NOTE TO THE STUDENT

Let us tell you about some plusses that will help *you* in the process of learning about retailing. Each of the six major parts of the text begins with an overview of what that part will include as well as how the material relates to what has preceded it. Always refer back to the framework and to see the interrelations among the parts of the book.

Each chapter is introduced by a direct quotation from a leading practitioner in the field who speaks from experience, concern for the practice of retailing, and a sincere interest in the student who will read this text. These outstanding businesspeople represent a most diverse group—areas of the country; types of retailing; functions; ages; and perceptions. You will be getting real concerns and commitments from people who have spent their careers in or serving the retailing industry. Consider their words carefully as they will help you appreciate the topics which are introduced by their statements.

Watch how each chapter is organized. The topical headings, tied in with the outline at the beginning, will make it easy to study and put the material into a simple perspective. Also note that in each chapter the purposes or objectives are spelled out. In this way you know why that topic is included and what you should gain from studying the material. The summary at the conclusion of each chapter will provide a ready reference when reviewing the material in connection with the questions which appear in each chapter for your self-testing and before-examination reviews.

We are strong believers in involvement by students in the real world of retailing. Consequently, we have included in most of the chapters short, realistic case situations which have direct application to the material in the chapter. Regardless of whether your instructor assigns any of these cases, we suggest that you read them and come up with some answers for yourself regarding the issues in the situations. They are fun to think about and are good for applying the theoretical concepts to a real world situation.

An even more "hands-on" experience is provided by the projects which are suggested in most of the chapters. Many of them will force you into the field to see how it really happens out there. Again, even if such projects are not required in your course, you will benefit greatly by attempting to do some of the things suggested in these projects. We have tested them with our students and have found them to be meaningful learning experiences which complement their other activities.

Two other features of our text should be brought to your attention as you begin this new experience. A comprehensive appendix on the Government Regulations Affecting Retailing will provide you with a ready reference to the laws that affect decisions and that must be understood by retailers.

Finally, in Appendix B we have the most comprehensive Glossary of Retailing Terms available in any text today. It is a most convenient reference source and will add to your total education as you use the words.

Enjoy your first retailing course. Based upon the visibility of retailing alone, it may be one of the most valuable courses you take as a part of your college career. It provides a good opportunity to evaluate retailing as a career path and at the very least, *Modern Retailing: Theory and Practice* will provide new insights into the dynamics and challenges of today's retail marketplace and that of the future.

ACKNOWLEDGMENTS

Numerous persons from both business and academics have made valued contributions to our thinking. Specifically, numerous prominent business persons have reviewed portions of the material and have provided valuable introductory statements at the beginning of each chapter to help students see the material from the perspective of today's sophisticated business person.

Among our academic friends and colleagues at Alabama who have evaluated portions of the material, we particularly would like to thank the following: Arthur Thompson, Harold Janes, William Bearden, Richard Durand,
Harry Lipson and Robert Robicheaux.

Special thanks go to Hazel Ezel who has taught the material for a year and
provided numerous valuable suggestions while we were preparing the man-
uscript. Also, she helped prepare the teacher's guide, glossary, index,
legislation appendix, and several of the cases and projects.

The following colleagues at other institutions were gracious in reviewing
and commenting upon one or more chapters of the material: Mark Alpert,
University of Texas, Austin; Dale Achabal, The Ohio State University; Danny
Bellenger, Georgia State University; Carl Block, University of Missouri-
Columbia; Bixby Cooper, Michigan State University; Ben Doddridge, Mem-
phis State University; O. C. Ferrell, Illinois State University; Walter Gorman,
University of Tennessee-Martin; Mary Harrison, Louisiana State University;
Jarrett Hudnall, Jr., Louisiana Tech University; Fred Langrehr, Marquette
University; Robert Lusch, University of Oklahoma; Claude Martin, The Uni-
versity of Michigan; Phillip McVey, University of Nebraska-Lincoln; Fred
Reynolds, University of Georgia; John Robbins, Loyola University; Tom
Speh, Miami University; P. Ronald Stephenson, Indiana University-
Bloomington; John Strubel, Troy State University-Montgomery; Howard
Thompson, Eastern Kentucky University; Charles Treas, University of Missis-
sippi; C. Glen Walters, Southern Illinois University-Carbondale; Robert
Wilkes, Texas Tech University; Robert Witt, University of Texas, Austin.

Also, Management Horizons, National Cash Register Company, Men's
Wear Retailers, and the National Retail Merchants Association have been
particularly generous with their material and assistance in helping us to
prepare the text.

December 1977   *Joseph Barry Mason*
                                                             Morris Lehman Mayer

CONTENTS

Consumers and retailing: *Why do people shop? Shopper typologies.* Consumer decision making: *Information search and retail shopping behavior. Information sources. The processing of information.* The consumer decision: *Evaluative criteria. Decision assessment.* Major consumer decisions. Where to buy: *Downtown versus the shopping center. Store choice. Out-shoppers and new arrivals. Composite influences on store choice.* What to buy: *Private versus national brands. The consumer and retail prices. Packaging. Coupons. Open code dating. Stockouts and merchandise unavailability. Unit pricing. Shelf space.* How consumers shop: *Attitudes toward time and distance. How far are shoppers willing to travel? Nonstore shopping.* When to buy: *Sunday openings. The effects of working wives. The effects of environmental changes. Effects of technological change. Consumer segments.*

The nature of segmentation: *The requirements for segmentation. Similarities among consumers. Partial segmentation. Uniqueness. Strategy dimensions.* Bases for segmentation: *Demography. Subcultures and minorities. Income. Education. Sex. Segmentation on social and psychological bases. Segmentation over time. Geographic location. Brand loyalty. Benefit segmentation.* The allocation of resources by market segments.

The economic environment: *Economic uncertainties and the retailer. The economy and consumer expenditures. Demography and consumer expenditures.* The social environment: *Cultural and life-style changes. Leisure preferences. Violence. The American family of the 1970s. The legal environment.*

The competition facing independent retailers: *Intratype competition. Intertype competition. Vertical marketing systems (VMS) competition. Total corporate systems competition. Free-form competition.* The new face of retailing: *Polarity in establishment types. Supermarket retailing. Store positioning. Nonstore retailing. Market intensification.* Changing channel structures: *Reasons for the emergence of VMS. Types of VMS.* The status of vertical marketing systems: *Legal problems. Management problems.* Managerial implications of vertical systems competition: *For the independent retailer. For resource markets.* Channel control: *Small retailers. Large retailers. Manufacturer control. Wholesaler leadership.* The use of power in channel management. Channel conflict:

width and support of assortments: *Model stock. Width plan. Support plan. Fashion goods. Staple goods. The act of planning.* Unit control: *Perpetual. Nonperpetual.*

can expect. Site evaluation: *Features of importance. Site evaluation in a shopping center. Rental agreements.*

Design objectives: *Consumer behavior and retail store space. How retail space affects behavior. Effects of crowding.* The basics of design: *Interior lighting. Store equipment. Counters and display cases. Signs. Store dividers.* Store layout: *Grid. Free flow. Boutique. Other considerations.* The allocation of space: *The sales productivity method. The buildup method. Gross margin influences.* Services offered: *Credit. Delivery. Extended shopping hours. Check cashing. Complaint policies.* Shoplifting and pilferage. Product recalls. The cost effectiveness of services offered. Operating policies and productivity.

Expense classification: *Natural. Functional.* Expense center accounting. The allocation of expenses: *The contribution plan. The net profit plan. The contribution/net profit combination.* Expense budgeting and control: *The expense-budgeting process. Break-even analysis.*

The development of human resources. Human resources planning: *The costs of improper selection. Forecasting human resources needs. Job design and analysis.* Recruiting, selecting, and training employees: *Recruiting. Selection. Training.* Employee evaluation. Employee compensation: *Job evaluation. Methods of compensation. Indirect compensation.* Union-management relations: *The Wagner and Taft-Hartley Acts. Grievance procedures. Disciplinary actions.* Motivation.

PART SIX

Characteristics of careers in retailing: *Security. Decentralized job opportunities. The diversity of retail institutions. Opportunities for advancement. Salaries in retailing. Nonmonetary rewards. The diversity of job skills. Working conditions. Typical employment categories.* Student perceptions of retailing: *Social status. Job opportunities. Bases of career choice.* Training programs in retailing: *Department stores. Chain stores.* Employment opportunities in small retail establishments. Business ownership: *Risks of ownership. Think about franchising.* An old or new business?

Monitoring social change: *The three American frontiers. Consumer attitudes in the late 1970s. The environment from the business leader's perspective.* Specific components of change: *Population growth rates. Regional shifts.* Projecting the retail operating environment: *Productivity increases. Energy. The environment. Materials shortages. Smaller stores. Remote retailing. Design changes for the future.* Forecast changes in various categories of retailing: *Drugstores. Mass merchandising outlets. Discount department stores. The food service industry. Shopping centers.* Retail strategies for the 1980s. Environmental uncertainties. Discussion.

MODERN RETAILING
Theory and Practice

PART ONE

INTRODUCTION

1

THE RETAILING MANAGEMENT CONCEPT

Retailing, unlike many other social science subjects, needs no introduction in terms of "proving" its importance to society. It is much too visible to every person everyday to need a typical introduction. Because of its visibility, however, the average citizen may mistakenly view retailing as a simple business—it must be simple because there are so many retail stores serving the public.[1]

Our first chapter departs from providing a rationale for the study of retailing, as is done by many texts, and focuses on providing the student with a framework and a philosophy for studying retailing management. A text without an organized framework to help students understand it is analogous to a person living in Tennessee and setting off on a winter skiing vacation with summer clothing, heading south toward New Orleans, without a road map and without any knowledge of highway systems between the points. That person might well see a lot of scenery en route and would undoubtedly gain some vital information about the countryside and places visited. The traveler might even reach the desired destination. Such an approach to a trip, however, is unsound, inefficient, and unprofitable.

THE FRAMEWORK

Figure 1–1 provides the framework for the text, but don't let the chart frighten you. Its point of view is simply that of the *retailing management concept.* As you have probably guessed, this concept is an outgrowth of the marketing concept. Because retailing is in part marketing, let's review briefly what we know about the changing attitudes toward marketing in the 1970s as an introduction to our study of retailing management.

CHANGING ATTITUDES ABOUT MARKETING

For many years it was accepted that marketing was the same as selling. Thus the task of marketing was to sell and distribute items which were produced. Consumers were viewed as buying whatever was offered.

A significant change in the prevailing point of view occurred in 1964, when marketing was defined as "the business process by which products are matched with markets and through which transfers of ownership are effected."[2] Marketing management was thus finally recognized as a significant function in business firms.

Explanations of the "marketing management concept" of the 1960s which followed from such definitions as that given above varied, but virtually all persons included the following components: (1) a consumer orienta-

---

[1] Approximately 1.9 million retail establishments exist in the United States. *1972 Census of Retail Trade,* Miscellaneous Subjects, (Washington, D.C.: U.S. Government Printing Office), table 1, p. 7.

[2] Edward W. Cundiff and Richard R. Still, *Basic Marketing* (Englewood Cliffs N.J.: Prentice-Hall, 1964), p. 2.

FIGURE 1–1
FRAMEWORK

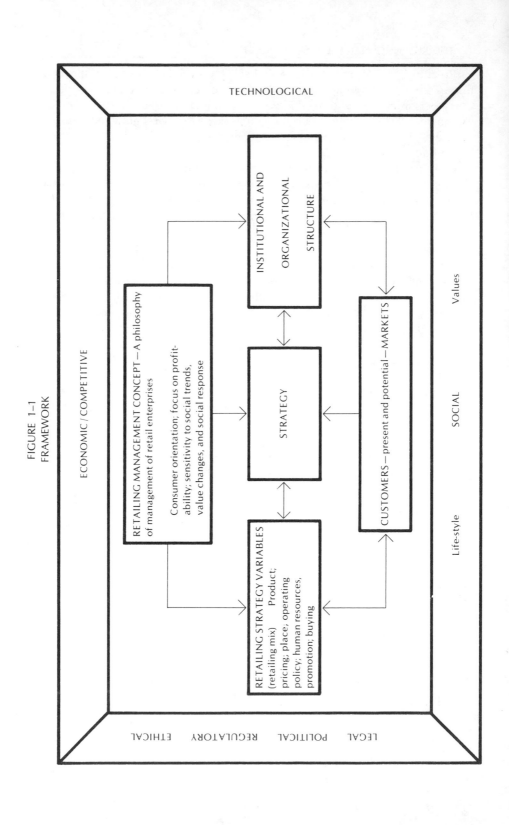

tion, (2) a profit objective, and (3) integration of the marketing functions under a key corporate executive.

In the late 1960s and the early 1970s, however, "the concept . . . faltered to the point where it [was] no longer an adequate statement."[3] Why?

Especially at the outset during the 1960s, firms had accepted the marketing concept in word but not in deed. It was impossible to implement the concept without clearly established objectives from management; these objectives could not be forthcoming without an acceptance of the key ingredient of the concept—a total consumer orientation. Thus, the "faltering" of the concept occurred because of the lack of a total consumer orientation—a point which is analyzed in the retailing management framework of this text.

THE RETAILING MANAGEMENT CONCEPT

Because sufficient time has passed to reveal the shortcomings of the marketing philosophy of the late 1960s and early 1970s, a point of view can now be developed which expresses the elements of a retailing management philosophy which is compatible with the society of the 1970s and 1980s. That is the aim of this text.

Components of the concept

Profitability.   Profitability remains very important for persons in retailing. Historically retail management has too often been "sales volume" oriented instead of having a strong profit orientation. Classic examples exist in retailing where management attempted to improve operating results by dramatic sales increases. The results have often been increases in sales but losses in net profit because of a failure to develop a business plan to accommodate the sales increases. This appears to have been one of the major problems of the now bankrupt W. T. Grant chain. The stores were urged to push credit and actually had credit quotas to fill. Lamented one Grant executive, "We gave credit to every deadbeat who breathed."[4] Likewise, Abercrombie and Fitch, traditionally upper-class merchants, suddenly tried to shift to serving both the upper classes and the masses and thus greatly increase sales volume. In 1976 the company filed for reorganization under the federal bankruptcy laws, primarily because it was serving neither group satisfactorily.[5] Finally, the frantic efforts of A&P to restore its image and profitability after several disastrous years also illustrate this point.

Consumer orientation.   Management historically has too often failed to have a *true consumer orientation*. This failure accounts in part for the rise in

[3] Martin L. Bell and William Emory, "The Faltering Marketing Concept," *Journal of Marketing*, vol. 35 (October 1971), p. 37.

[4] "Investigating the Collapse of W. T. Grant," *Business Week*, July 19, 1976, p. 61.

[5] "Abercrombie's Misfire," *Time*, August 23, 1976, p. 55.

consumerism. Consumerism can only occur if dissatisfied consumers exist. As noted by Senator Warren G. Magnuson:

"Consumerism" is a word used to describe the phenomenon whereby purchasers of goods and services are trying to attain a marketing system which makes the consumer sovereign—which guarantees to him the right to safety, the right to be informed, the right to choose, and the right to be heard. Consumerism is based upon that basic tenet of the free enterprise system which says that the consumer [rather than the government] should control, through rational purchasing decisions in the marketplace, which goods and services are produced. But consumerism looks to government to control producers [retailers] who would interfere with rational choice and thereby destroy the free enterprise system.[6]

One of the causes of the lack of a *true* consumer orientation can be traced to management's failure to look at the consumer (market) as part of our social environment (shown in the framework as including life-styles and values and discussed in detail in Chapter 5). As has been stated:

. . . the marketing concept as commonly conceived is not sufficiently adequate to reflect a subtle and yet fundamental transition now underway in the discipline. The transition in question is that of marketing changing from being mostly concerned with the firm's relationship to the customer to being concerned with the organization's . . . relationship to the societies in which it operates, including, but not restricted to, the organization's attempts to attract the customer. . . . while it (the marketing concept) stresses customer satisfaction (as it rightfully should), it does not stress social responsibility.[7]

It is impossible for an individual's *consumer-self* to be separated from the *social-self.* Consequently, in order to develop a successful consumer orientation, a sensitivity to the changing values of society must be developed— hence this component of the retailing management concept, as shown in Figure 1–1.

Responsible social relationships.   Further, business must accept a more responsible posture in its relationships with society. The following passages embody a thoughtful retail management response which presents the issues as clearly as any we have heard.

The traditional role of corporate business has been to produce the wealth which provides the basic support for our economic, social, and governmental activities. To fulfill this role, business must make a profit and attract and create capital in support of its mission. Yet the single-minded pursuit of profits is rather unpopular in today's times. Society . . . will not accept the proposition that the bigger the profit, the better the business. But just how far is modern corporate man to stretch himself and his vision of purpose?

---

[6] "What Is Consumerism?" *Dupont Context,* vol. 1 (1975), p. 2.

[7] Leonard L. Berry, "Marketing Challenges in the Age of the People," *MSU Business Topics,* Winter 1972, p. 8 Reprinted by permission of the publisher, Division of Research, Graduate School of Business Administration, Michigan State University.

It should be no surprise that there is little agreement about the answers to the questions being raised about the interrelationship of business and society. Questions which pertain to economic institutions are difficult to answer, for they involve a number of variables that all depend on each other. Business has failed to make a concerted response to its critics on the matter of the limits of business's responsibility, simply because business is divided on its own feelings about it. And so are its critics. Business should operate in the "public interest," but the public interest is a composite of competing and conflicting aims.

Businessmen today must be ever sensitive to the forces for change at work in our society. Whether these forces are positive or negative, constructive or destructive— whether they are based on hostility to the business system or a desire to improve the system—they present us with a formidable challenge.

This challenge (opportunity if you will) needs all the attention that . . . businessmen can give it.

We need to demonstrate our sensitivity to the issues affecting the quality of life of our citizens—equal employment, inflation, environmental affairs, adequate housing for the poor, energy shortages, education, law enforcement, welfare, health and safety, community improvement, etc.

We need to increase our involvement as corporate citizens in the affairs of the community, state, and nation, bearing our share of the financial and moral support of the institutions and organizations which cater to the well-being of the people. . . . We can no longer devote our efforts solely to . . . "tending the store." Our modern society demands that management play a leading role in all the action going on in the world about us. At the same time we must, of course, continue to make our business profitable. Companies which show no profit have no worries about their social responsibility. They cease to exist.[8]

In summary, the retailing management concept is a philosophy of management for the retail enterprise which focuses on profitability as the goal of the firm but is based on a true consumer orientation which includes sensitivity to social trends, value changes, and societal responsibilities. A philosophy of this kind is not only socially beneficial but often yields increased profitability. Such companies as Giant Foods and Stop and Shop have been particularly successful with programs based on the retailing management concept.[9]

The institutional and organizational structures

The institutional and organizational structures of retailing are also an integral part of our framework (Figure 1–1). The institutional structure at the macro level includes the various outlets through which goods and services are offered to the market. The institutional structure both affects and is affected by the management philosophy and the customer markets.

---

[8] Excerpts from a speech given to Sales and Marketing Executives International, Birmingham chapter, June 1971, by Don Graves, public relations, Sears, Roebuck, Atlanta office.

[9] Leonard L. Berry, James S. Hensel, and Marian C. Burke, "Improving Retailer Capability for Effective Consumerism Response," *Journal of Retailing*, vol. 52 (Fall 1976) pp. 3–14.

The same relationships noted above exist for the organizational structure of individual retailing outlets. This aspect of structure reflects the relationships established to carry out the goals of the firm.

The retailing mix

The central placement of *strategy* in the framework dramatizes the critical relationship between the retailing management concept and the market. Strategy is the posture assumed by management as it attempts to accomplish the objectives of the firm by manipulating the various elements of the retailing mix.

A major portion of this text is devoted to an in-depth analysis of the retailing mix variables: (1) the *product variable,* which includes merchandise management and accounting for merchandising effectiveness (Chapters 12 and 13); (2) *buyer and supplier relationships* (Chapter 15); (3) *pricing* (Chapter 14); (4) *promotion* (Chapter 16); (5) *place,* which includes location and site analysis (Chapter 17); (6) *operating policies* and accounting for operating effectiveness (Chapters 18 and 19); and (7) *human resources management.*

The arrows in Figure 1–1 show the interrelationships among the retailing mix, the retailing management concept, and customer markets. Likewise, the way the mix is manipulated for market effectiveness affects management's basic philosophy. These interrelationships among the various elements within the framework become more apparent as the material is covered in the following chapters of the text.

The environments of retailing

Surrounding the managerial elements of the framework are environmental forces which can dramatically affect the operations of the retail enterprise and the entire retail structure. In Chapters 7 through 11, these environmental forces are dealt with in detail. In addition to the social environment, Chapters 7 through 11 take up the competitive/economic forces which affect retailing, including vertical marketing systems; the effects of legal, political, and regulatory processes on retailing management decisions; and the dramatic impact of technological and environmental conditions on retailing.

OVERVIEW

This chapter has presented the framework for the text (with the exception of the final two chapters, which focus on the future of retailing and careers in retailing). In effect, the framework presents both the rationale and the organization of our presentation. Continuing reference to Figure 1–1 is encouraged so that the student may continually "fit the pieces together" and in addition be ever aware of the central theme of this book—the retailing management concept. The framework has applicability as a guideline for every kind and size of retail enterprise and for persons with any degree of interest in the subject matter. The subject of retailing management knows no bounds—size of the firm is only important as it affects specialization and potential service to the market. The same problems, opportunities, and decisions exist in any retailing situation—our framework allows for application to the entire spectrum of retailing.

Our framework also recognizes that "marketing is a pervasive societal activity that goes considerably beyond the selling of toothpaste [and] soap."[10] Marketing principles are transferable to the marketing of organizations, persons, and ideas. As a part of the marketing process and as an element in the distribution channel, the broadening logic can be applied to retailing management. The student is encouraged to see implications of the managerial principles of retailing for enterprises other than retail stores selling tangible goods. It is common today to hear bankers speak of "retail banking" when referring to their demand deposits and to the savings accounts of customers. Certainly an exterminator who markets pest control services to households is engaging in retail activities, as are persons offering janitorial contracting, office equipment repair, and nursing home care. Real estate firms that sell or rent to families or individuals are engaging in retailing; the insurance agent who deals directly with the ultimate consumer is a manager of retail activities. Students of retailing should broaden their focus to include all of the possibilities which can come within the retailing umbrella and fit within our framework. For example, one of the latest examples of growth in retail services is that of furniture rentals to newlyweds, divorced persons, and transients, among others. It is a $200 million a year business.[11]

Carrying the logic somewhat farther, when a university enters into student recruiting, the person responsible for that activity is a retailer in the broadened context. So is the business development manager of a bank, the fund raiser for the Heart Fund, and the person who is attempting to attract an audience to an art event, such as a symphony concert, a theatrical performance, or a museum showing.

WHAT IS RETAILING?

Within the modern retailing management concept, with its customer orientation and its sensitivity to environmental pressures, can we agree upon a single definition of retailing? Certainly every text will offer its own definition and careful investigation will show that the definitions advanced during the 1950s suggested that retailing was selling goods in small quantities to householders. We have made a great deal of progress since then, and with

---

[10] Philip Kotler and Sidney J. Levy, "Broadening the Concept of Marketing," *Journal of Marketing*, vol. 33 (January 1969), pp. 10–15.

[11] "Rented Furniture: A New Design for Living," *Business Week*, March 14, 1977, pp. 107–9.

the dynamics of our environmental, philosophic, and institutional parameters, we prefer to define retailing from three points of view.

The discipline of retailing.   As a social science discipline, retailing is the study of the interaction of consumers and their social institutions as they conduct transactions (that is, exchanges of goods, services, ideas) in the marketplace (broadly defined).

The science of retailing.   Retailing as a science is the attempt to organize our knowledge about retailing through observation, study, and experimentation and to use this information in broadening our base of knowledge.

The managerial point of view.   For the manager, retailing is the attempt to manage transactions at the point of ultimate consumption for the benefit of the organization and society.

Depending upon the subject being discussed, the approach necessary in treating that subject, and the breadth of the particular discussion, we will use one or more of the above points of view. In some sections of this book, the general discipline of retailing is of major concern; in others, the scientific method is of major concern. Perhaps, however, in the final analysis, our most substantial focus is upon retailing management. We stress, however, that looking at retailing "conventionally" in the 1970s and 80s will not provide a competitive edge for the aggressive entrepreneur and/or manager.

KEY CONCEPTS

The retailing management concept
The marketing concept
The teaching framework
  Consumer orientation
  Strategy
  The retailing mix
  The institutional and organizational structures
  Environments
    Economic/competitive
    Social
    Legal
    Technological
Retailing
  As a discipline
  As a science
  As a business/management activity

DISCUSSION QUESTIONS

1.   Why is it important for any subject to have a philosophic and teaching framework?

2. Discuss the changing attitudes about marketing.

3. Prepare a diagram of the text's framework and show the interrelationships among the various components.

4. After reading the various developmental definitions of marketing, attempt to put in your own words what you believe the discipline is all about.

5. What is the marketing concept? Why did it evolve? Has it been successful?

6. Describe the components of the retailing management concept.

7. How can sales of a company increase and profits decrease?

8. Explain the relationship between consumer orientation and consumerism.

9. Explain the relationship between the consumer and society.

10. Illustrate your interpretation of a "sensitivity" to changing life-styles.

11. Comment on retail management's social responsibilities.

12. Explain strategy and the retailing mix and the interrelationships between the two concepts.

13. Why is a study of the environments of retailing important?

PART TWO

THE RETAILING
STRUCTURE

The retailing management concept and the framework presented in the first part of the text provided you with the guidelines and the philosophy for what is to follow.

Retailing is highly visible. Its structure (the complex of outlets through which goods and services move to the ultimate consumer) is vast, complex, and dynamic. The purpose of Chapter 2 is to introduce you to the nature of that structure and to make it easier for you to understand it by showing you the different ways in which it can be studied. Thus you will be able to evaluate long-term trends in the growth of different kinds of establishments, to make informed decisions about various issues related to retailing, and to generalize about the future of the various types of establishments which make up the retail structure.

Chapter 3 is concerned with the evolution of and explanations and conjectures about the firms comprising our retail structure. From your point of view, this material is of assistance in determining the direction of your careers. Managerially, such an analysis is important in evaluating long-term trends in the various retail sectors.

The final type of retail structure, organizational structure, is the focus of the discussion in Chapter 4. In that discussion you will gain an appreciation of the complexities inherent in organizing retail establishments and of the various alternatives which exist for their organization. You will also be able to zero in on career opportunities if you read the material from a career point of view. We suggest that you take this approach in addition to the managerial perspective whenever doing so will assist in your career development.

2

THE RETAILING STRUCTURE: CLASSIFICATIONS AND ALTERNATIVES

*S*tructural analysis is a necessary first step in beginning to understand retailing. Classifications provide frames of reference, points of view, and vocabulary that collectively form part of the foundation for comprehension and insight.

Classifications can be used to create exciting new businesses. For example, Dayton Hudson created a multi-million-dollar chain of book stores—called B. Dalton—because book distribution was one of the fastest growing forms of nonrationalized retailing in America. Competition was at best mediocre; strategies and operating methods were feeble.

Used blindly, classifications often conceal more than they reveal. For example, the growth of food stores in total has been unexciting—yet we have witnessed dramatic growth in certain segments, such as jumbo food stores, convenience food stores, and fast-food and thematic restaurants. Similarly, general merchandise sales conceal the proliferation of discount department stores which have provided growth vehicles for such premiere companies as Wal Mart, Mervyn's, and Kresge.

Part of the rationale underlying these innovations is a strategic reevaluation of retailing options for product categories. Structure and classifications do not, in and of themselves, generate these strategies, but they are often useful in providing the underlying perspective.

David T. Kollat, Vice President
Limited Stores, Inc.
Columbus, Ohio

QUANTITATIVE MEASUREMENTS OF THE STRUCTURE

Retail employment

Retail stores constitute approximately 18 percent of all businesses in the United States. They outnumber manufacturing and wholesaling establishments and are one of the largest employers in the United States.[1] Retailing is the third largest employer in the nation, with over 13 million employees, as compared to approximately 19 million in manufacturing (Table 2–1).

TABLE 2–1
NONAGRICULTURAL EMPLOYMENT, FEBRUARY 1976
(seasonally adjusted)

Employment field	Number employed (000)
Contract construction	3,541
Federal government	2,739
Finance	4,419
Manufacturing	19,194
Mining	814
Retailing	13,662
Service	15,004
State and local government	12,317
Transportation and public utility	4,550
Wholesaling	4,313
Total	79,465

Source: *Survey of Current Business*, vol. 57, no. 2 (February 1977), S–14.

Retail sales are distributed among the various regions of the United States in approximately the same manner as is the population. Historically, retail sales have increased approximately three times as fast as population and approximately as fast as income.[2]

Number of retail outlets

The number of retail outlets has not increased significantly since 1929 (Table 2–2). However, between 1929 and 1975 population increased by 76 percent and personal income by over 1,300 percent (Table 2–3). Thus, the average sales per retail establishment increased significantly during this period, partly because of inflation and partly because of increasing

---

[1] *Statistical Abstract of the United States* (Washington, D.C.: U.S. Department of Commerce, 1975), table 801, p. 490.

[2] Douglas Dalrymple and Donald N. Thompson, *Retailing: An Economic View* (New York: Free Press, 1969), p. 11.

TABLE 2–2
NUMBER OF RETAIL ESTABLISHMENTS (000) BY MERCHANDISE GROUPS, 1929–1972

	1929		1948		1958		1972	
Merchandise group	No.	Per-cent	No.	Per-cent	No.	Per-cent	No.	Per-cent
Lumber..............	90	6.1	99	5.6	108	6.0	84	4.4
General merchandise	159	10.8	74	4.2	87	4.9	56	2.9
Food	482	32.7	504	28.5	357	19.9	267	14.0
Automotive	68	4.6	86	4.9	94	5.2	121	6.3
Gasoline	122	8.3	188	10.6	207	11.5	226	11.8
Apparel	114	7.7	115	6.5	119	6.6	129	6.8
Furniture	59	4.0	86	4.9	104	5.8	117	6.1
Eating, drinking	134	9.1	347	19.6	346	19.3	360	18.8
Drugs	58	3.9	56	3.2	57	3.2	52	2.7
Other	188	12./	214	12.1	241	13.4	338	17.7
Nonstore	*		*		75	4.2	162	8.5
Total	1,476	—	1,770	—	1,795	—	1,912	—

Percentages may not add to 100 because of "rounding".
* Prior to 1954, nonstore sales were not enumerated separately but included in the appropriate merchandise group.
Source: U.S. Bureau of the Census for the indicated years.

economies of scale. Per capita sales also increased, from $392 in 1929 to $2,726 in 1975, even though retail sales as a percent of personal income have consistently declined. This reflects the rising standard of living in the United States and the increasing level of discretionary income available to consumers.

TABLE 2–3
ECONOMIC IMPACT OF RETAILING AS INDICATED BY SELECTED MEASURES

Year	Population	GNP (in $billions)	Sales by retail establish-ments (in $billions)	Per capita sales (in current dollars)	Personal income (in $billions)	Retail sales (as percent of personal income)
1976	215,870,000	1,691.4	651.7	3,019	1,375.3	47.0
1975	214,400,000	1,516.3	584.4	2,726	1,249.7	46.6
1974	212,530,000	1,441.3	537.8	2,530	1,154.7	46.6
1973	210,400,000	1,294.9	503.3	2,392	1,035.4	48.6
1972	208,840,000	1,155.2	448.4	2,147	939.2	47.7
1970	205,820,000	989.9	364.6	1,769	801.0	45.5
1969	204,000,000	932.1	357.6	1,720	747.2	47.0
1968	201,000,000	865.7	339.3	1,688	687.9	49.3
1963	188,658,000	583.9	244.2	1,254	464.1	52.6
1958	173,320,000	444.5	199.6	1,152	360.3	55.4
1954	161,164,000	363.1	169.9	1,055	289.8	58.7
1948	146,093,000	259.4	128.8	882	210.4	61.2
1939	130,880,000	91.1	41.4	317	72.9	56.9
1929	121,770,000	104.4	47.7	392	85.5	55.7

Sources: 1929–73 data—Carl M. Larson et al., Basic Retailing (Englewood Cliffs, N.J.: Prentice-Hall, 1976), p. 18, 1974, 1975, and 1976 data—Survey of Current Business, vol. 57, no. 2 (February 1977), various pages.

There are many reasons for the relatively constant number of retail stores and the increasing size of each store. Of major importance are increasing productivity and greater managerial expertise. However, the failure rate for selected types of retailing still remains high. Failures are highest for eating and drinking places, followed closely by outlets in the automotive and apparel and accessories groups (Table 2–4).

TABLE 2–4
FAILURES BY TYPE OF RETAIL BUSINESS
(first ten months of 1976)

	Number	Percent
Food and liquor	364	10.3
General merchandise	108	3.1
Apparel, accessories	496	14.1
Furniture, and home furnishings	468	13.3
Lumber, building materials, and hardware	190	5.4
Automotive group	509	14.4
Eating and drinking places	660	18.7
Drugstores	88	2.5
Miscellaneous	644	18.3
Total	3,527	100.1

Source: Dun and Bradstreet, Inc., Business Economics Division, *Monthly Business Failures*, January 29, 1977, p. 2.

We are not able to tell specifically what has happened to trends in retail establishments since 1972, the latest year for which data are reported by the U.S. Bureau of the Census. However, we can look at trends in retail employment for the 1967–76 period.[3] The total number of employees increased by approximately 27 percent during the ten-year period for the categories of retail trade shown (Table 2–5). The fastest-growing category of retail trade shown is eating and drinking places, which increased by almost 57 percent during the period, probably because of the rapid growth of franchising. Other areas showing rapid growth in employment are department stores, food stores, and men's and boys' apparel stores. Variety stores continued to decrease in importance, and furniture stores were growing at a relatively slow rate, as were drugstores.

The compound annual rate of growth in retail sales for the ten-year period was 8.3 percent, and the annual increase in employment was 2.7 percent (Table 2–6). Convenience stores grew at the rapid pace of 15 percent per year and now number more than 27,500. At a time when supermarket chains have been opening fewer outlets, the convenience stores, which stock about 3,000 fast-moving items, have been gaining greater favor with consumers.[4]

---

[3] For further information see John F. Cady, "Structural Trends in Retailing: The Decline of Small Business?" *Journal of Contemporary Business,* Spring 1976.

[4] "Convenience Stores: A $7.4 Billion Mushroom," *Business Week,* March 21, 1977, p. 61.

TABLE 2–5
RETAIL TRADE EMPLOYMENT 1967–1976
(in 000)

	1967	1969	1970	1971	1972	1973	1974	1975	1976*	Percent change, 1967–1976
Total retail trade	10,081	10,907	11,102	11,333	11,705	12,209	12,751	12,771	12,834	27.3
Department stores	1,324	1,483	1,511	1,545	1,594	1,676	1,769	1,658	1,658	25.2
Variety stores	313	318	312	319	330	339	334	309	294	–6.1
Food stores	1,405	1,517	1,561	1,585	1,651	1,709	1,752	1,774	1,791	27.5
Men's and boys' apparel stores	114	126	131	131	132	133	135	137.4	140.2	22.8
Women's ready-to-wear stores	252	270	269	276	287	296	289	292.1	295.0	19.1
Furniture stores	271	288	288	289	297	308	328	313	313	15.5
Household appliances	84	88	88	89	92	95	101	101	101	20.4
Eating and drinking places	2,191	2,420	2,488	2,569	2,684	2,818	3,145	3,298	3,430	56.6
Drugstores	426	446	453	456	470	481	467	470	475	11.5

* Estimated by Bureau of Domestic Commerce.
Source: U.S. Department of Commerce, *U.S. Industrial Outlook, 1977, with Projections to 1985* (Washington, D.C.: U.S. Government Printing Office, 1977), p. 212.

TABLE 2–6
1976 PROFILE OF RETAIL TRADE

SIC codes	52–59
Sales ($ billions)	643
Number of establishments* (000s)	1,913
Compound annual rate of growth, 1967–76 (percent)	
Value of sales	8.3
Employment	2.7

* 1972.

Source: U.S. Department of Commerce, *U.S. Industrial Outlook, 1977, with Projections to 1985* (Washington, D.C.: U.S. Government Printing Office, 1977) p. 212.

Levels of retail sales

The total level of retail sales approximated $704 billion in 1977 (Table 2–7). By far the largest single category is grocery stores. The second largest category (not shown in Table 2–7) is automobile dealers, followed closely by department stores and eating and drinking places.

As measured in current dollars, the greatest increases in retail sales during the past ten years have occurred in eating and drinking places, followed by department stores and grocery stores. The smallest percentage increases have occurred in variety stores, women's apparel and accessory stores, furniture stores, household appliance stores, and drugstores.

Data limitations

The merchandise groups as defined by the census, however, do not necessarily reflect the types of merchandise which are actually sold in the various types of outlets. Determining the types of merchandise sold within a particular establishment is especially difficult in this era of scrambled merchandising. For example, Table 2–8 shows the volume of nonfood items sold in food stores. These nonfood sales in supermarkets totaled over 8 million dollars in 1975.

Moreover, regardless of the line of retail trade, corporations which are employing such mainstream retail strategies of the 1970s as supermarket retailing (Standard Brands), expansion into secondary markets (Bi-Lo—operators of discount supermarkets in small rural communities), market intensification (Lowes in the Southeast), product specialization (Child World), and nonstore retailing (Mary Kay Cosmetics) are likely to have experienced rapid growth even though in the aggregate the merchandise category into which these corporations fall may have experienced slow growth.[5]

Another potential source of distortion of the data is that the definitions utilized by the Bureau of the Census may change from one census to the

---

[5] Albert Bates and Bert McCammon, Jr., "Reseller Strategies and the Financial Performance of the Firm," paper presented at the Structure, Strategy, Performance Conference, Indiana University, 1975.

TABLE 2–7
RETAIL TRADE: TRENDS AND PROJECTIONS, 1967–1977
(sales in millions of current dollars)

SIC code		1967	1972	1973	1974	1975	1976*	Percent change, 1967–1976	1977*	Percent change, 1967–1977
52–59	Total retail trade	313,809	448,379	503,317	537,561	584,423	642,865	10	703,899	124.3
5311	Department stores	32,344	46,302	52,292	55,855	60,719	66,200	9	72,800	125.1
5331	Variety stores	5,407	7,756	8,212	8,715	9,120	9,700	6	10,300	90.5
5411	Grocery stores	65,074	88,340	98,392	111,347	122,666	130,000	6	139,100	113.8
5611	Men's and boys' apparel stores	3,385	5,198	5,609	5,665	6,085	6,300	4	6,678	97.3
5621–31	Women's apparel accessory stores	6,290	8,386	9,119	9,563	10,396	11,200	7	11,872	84.4
5712	Furniture stores	6,564	9,321	10,439	10,982	10,087	12,100	9	12,900	96.5
5722	Household appliances	3,014	4,634	5,124	5,222	5,083	5,540	9	5,928	96.7
5312–13	Eating and drinking places	23,843	33,891	37,925	41,821	47,514	52,700	11	58,000	143.3
5913	Drugstores	10,930	14,523	15,474	16,745	18,014	19,900	10	21,342	95.3

* Estimated by Bureau of Domestic Commerce.
Source: U.S. Department of Commerce, U.S. Industrial Outlook, 1977, with Projections to 1985 (Washington, D.C.: U.S. Government Printing Office, 1977), p. 211.

TABLE 2–8
SUPERMARKET NONFOOD SALES BY CATEGORIES FOR 1975

Categories	Sales	Percent of total nonfood sales	Percent of total store sales
Health and beauty aids	$4,135,000	50.5	2.9
Housewares, hardware	1,726,000	21.1	1.2
Soft goods, panty hose	640,000	7.8	0.4
Magazines and books	455,000	5.5	0.3
Stationery, school supplies	221,000	2.7	0.2
Sewing notions, yarns	107,000	1.3	*
Greeting cards	79,000	0.9	*
Photo films, flash, finishing	145,000	1.8	0.1
Pet supplies	165,000	2.0	0.1
Continuity, seasonal, and all other	522,000	6.4	0.4
Total all nonfoods	$8,195,000	100.0	5.6

* Less than 1 percent.
Source: "43rd Annual Report of the Grocery Industry," *Progressive Grocer*, April 1976, p. 173.

FIGURE 2–1

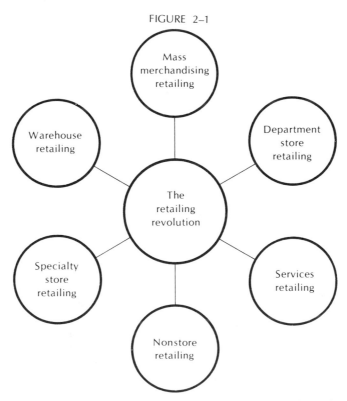

Source: Management Horizons, *Retail Intelligence System* (Columbus: n.d.), p. 13.

FIGURE 2–2

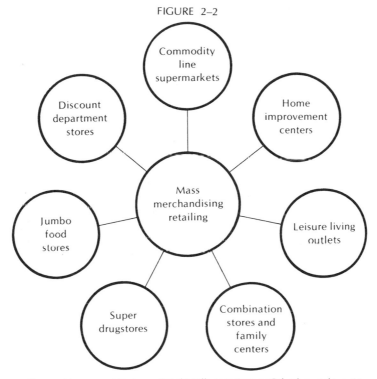

Source: Management Horizons, *Retail Intelligence System* (Columbus: n.d.), p. 14.

next. In addition, establishments may be reclassified between reporting periods. For such reasons, Management Horizons, a nationally recognized management consulting firm, has introduced the retail classification concept shown in Figure 2–1 as its basis of analysis. Its argument for the new approach is that "traditional methods of classifying retailers and retail activity no longer reflect market realities." For analysis, Management Horizons breaks down each of the six major categories shown in Figure 2–1 into the types of retailing most descriptive of the category. As examples, the primary types of retail outlets encompassed in mass merchandise retailing and specialty store retailing are shown in Figures 2–2 and 2–3, respectively. This approach has many advantages. However, the costs of acquiring and analyzing data in this fashion are substantial.

CLASSIFICATION OF THE STRUCTURE

Given the magnitude and complexity of the retailing structure in the United States, a careful study of that structure is in order. Two objectives are sought:

1. To present a classification format which has application to all types of retail enterprises.
2. To present the various alternatives which exist for the classification of retail structure.

The retailing structure can be viewed under many different headings, including type of merchandise offered, type of ownership, geographic location, and level of sales. Accordingly, a classification of the various components of structure is desirable for an understanding of retail evolution, growth, and change.

A rational classification of structure facilitates communication among students interested in retailing, aids government officials in analyzing the impact of retailing on the economy, and assists managements in the development of strategies for increasing the profits of their establishments. Also, analysis of the size, growth record, and future outlook of the various components of the retailing structure can enable managements to evaluate the present and potential competitive position of their outlets.

The study of structure reveals that the various components work together to serve the needs of consumers. Structure includes the different types of retail organizations. It also includes the persons and the facilitating agencies

FIGURE 2–3

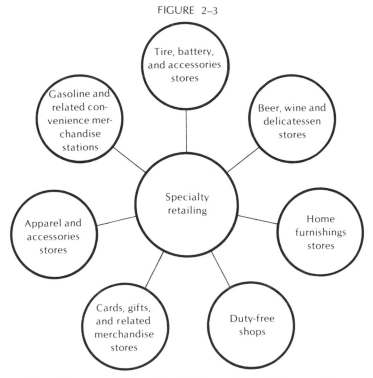

Source: Management Horizons, *Retail Intelligence System*, (Columbus: n.d.), p. 16.

that have a role in distribution at the retail level. Classification of structure is a first step to generalized hypotheses and, subsequently, to predictions about institutional structure.

The margin-turnover classification

Ronald Gist has introduced a general conceptual framework for retail structure which has application to all types of outlets. The framework, based on margin and turnover, is useful in retail strategy formulation rather than in data reporting and analysis.[6] In Gist's analysis, margin is defined as the percentage markup at which the inventory in a store is sold. Turnover is the number of times the average inventory is sold in a given year. Turnover and margin are discussed further in Chapters 12 and 14, respectively. Figure 2–4

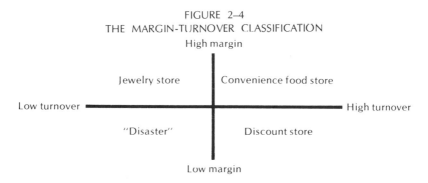

FIGURE 2–4
THE MARGIN-TURNOVER CLASSIFICATION

diagrams four quadrants defined by margin and turnover into which any retail outlet can be placed. These outlets can then be described in terms of the strategies which should be followed in serving consumers. The strategies depend on the quadrant in which a given retail outlet is most logically located. The key elements of retail strategy, as shown in Table 2–9, are the types of merchandise sold, varieties and assortments offered, services offered, price level, type of personal selling, type of promotion, complexity of organizational structure, and locational requirements.

Gist describes the differing retail philosophies as follows:

While customers "bought" in the low-margin/high-turnover operation, customers are "sold" in the high-margin/low-turnover enterprise. . . . In the same way that the low-margin/high-turnover prototype assumed that low prices were the most important patronage determinant, the high-margin/low-turnover enterprise assumes that service, distinctive merchandise, and sales skill are the most important patronage determinants. While promotional efforts on the part of the low-margin/high-turnover enterprise will emphasize price, promotion materials for the high-margin/low-

---

[6] Ronald R. Gist, *Retailing: Concepts and Decisions* (New York: John Wiley and Sons, 1968), pp. 37–40.

TABLE 2–9
PROTOTYPES OF THE MARGIN-TURNOVER
APPROACH TO THE CLASSIFICATION
OF RETAIL INSTITUTIONS

Low margin—high turnover
   Merchandise presold or self-sold.
   Few services or "optional charge" services.
   Isolated locations.
   Simple organizational characteristics.
   Variety large, assortments small.
   Prices below the market.
   Promotional emphasis on price.
High margin—low turnover
   Merchandise sold in-store.
   Many services.
   Cluster locations.
   Complex organization.
   Variety smaller, assortments larger.
   Prices above the market.
   Promotion institutional and merchandise oriented.
   Location in proximity to other institutions.

turnover operation will tend to dwell on merchandise offerings. The low-margin operation will almost never employ institutional (nonmerchandise) promotion; the high-margin counterpart will almost never feature a "clutter" ad or an advertisement that features an extremely large number of items in a small space.[7]

High-margin/high-turnover outlets. Let us think for a moment about the strategy implications for the various types of outlets which can be placed in the four quadrants of Figure 2–4. The convenience food outlet, such as a Seven-Eleven, is an example of a high-margin/high-turnover organization. Typically it is in a relatively noncommercial location in relation to other retail outlets but is in proximity to a major thoroughfare. It features a narrow line of grocery items which turn over rapidly. Because of locational convenience it can charge above the market prices. Overhead costs may be high because of the long hours that the store is open. Moreover, the lack of economies of scale that result from its small size require that it charge above the market prices to ensure profitability. Promotion is likely to be on the basis of locational and time convenience.

High-turnover/low-margin outlets. A discount store which is characterized by high turnover and low margins, such as K-Mart, is likely to be in an isolated location and to feature a wide variety of the fastest-moving items in many different merchandise lines. The merchandise is often confined to national brands, presold by the manufacturer through national advertising. Local promotion is likely to be entirely on the basis of price.

[7] Ibid., p. 40.

High-margin/low-turnover outlets. A full-line jewelry store, characterized by high margins and low turnover, is typically located in either a
downtown metropolitan area or a major shopping center. A wide variety and
assortment of jewelry, particularly rings, are carried. These items are rarely
sold on the basis of national brands or national advertising. Sales are likely to
occur on the basis of the expertise of the sales personnel and the overall
reputation of the outlet. Prices are high, but not higher than those of similar
outlets.

Low-margin/low-turnover outlets. We often encounter establishments
which can best be characterized as low margin/low turnover. Such outlets
have been forced by price competition to maintain low margins, but because
of a poor location, incompetent management, or undercapitalization are not
selling a high volume of merchandise. This type of outlet is a candidate for
bankruptcy.

The various margin-turnover classifications are not mutually exclusive. A
single store may have all of the traits identified as characterizing all four
margin-turnover classes.

The margin-turnover concept can assist managers in planning their marketing strategy. It shows that different strategies can lead to similar levels of
profitability, but that profitability is achieved in different ways. Further, it
assists in the conceptual placement of retail organizations within the total
competitive environment. Admittedly the classification is inexact and somewhat crude, but it can serve as a starting place for structuring competitive
models and for helping students to understand the dynamics of retail structure.

A variety of other classification schemes have been developed as approaches to the analysis of structure. They are more descriptive in name than
is the margin-turnover concept. Table 2–10 depicts some of the alternative
bases which can be used to classify retail establishments.

Ownership of establishment

The most common classification is based on ownership. The independent
operator with a single store continues to dominate the retailing structure.
This ownership class comprised 94 percent of all retail establishments in
1972. Sales by single-unit establishments constituted 57 percent of total retail
sales.[8] Single-unit organizations tend to be small businesses which are operated by family members.

Independents. Among the advantages which allow the small independent store to compete with larger chains are the following: (1) the store's cost
of doing business is usually low because of low rents, location in a somewhat isolated neighborhood or a rural area, and ownership by the proprie-
tors; (2) the store is usually located closer to customers than is possible for a

---
[8] *Statistical Abstract*, table 1315, p. 775.

TABLE 2–10
ALTERNATIVE BASES FOR THE CLASSIFICATION OF RETAIL ESTABLISHMENTS

A. By ownership of establishment.
   1. Single-unit independent stores.
   2. Multiunit retail organizations.
      a. Chain stores.
      b. Branch stores.
   3. Manufacturer-owned retail outlets.
   4. Consumer cooperatives.
   5. Farmer-owned establishments.
   6. Company-owned stores (industrial stores) or commissaries.
   7. Government-operated stores (post exchanges, liquor stores).
   8. Public utility company stores (for sale of major appliances).
B. By kind of business (merchandise handled).
   1. General merchandise group.
      a. Department stores.
      b. Dry goods, general merchandise stores.
      c. General stores.
      d. Variety stores.
   2. Single-line stores (for example, grocery, apparel, furniture).
   3. Specialty stores (for example, meat markets, lingerie shops, floor coverings stores).
C. By size of establishment.
   1. By number of employees.
   2. By annual sales volume.
D. By degree of vertical integration.
   1. Nonintegrated (retailing functions only).
   2. Integrated with wholesaling functions.
   3. Integrated with manufacturing or other form-utility creation.
E. By type of relationship with other business organizations.
   1. Unaffiliated.
   2. Voluntarily affiliated with other retailers.
      a. Through wholesaler-sponsored voluntary chains.
      b. Through retailer cooperation.
   3. Affiliated with manufacturers by dealer franchises.
F. By method of consumer contact.
   1. Regular store.
      a. Leased department.
   2. Mail order.
      a. By catalog selling.
      b. By advertising in regular media.
      c. By membership club plans.
   3. Household contacts.
      a. By house-to-house canvassing.
      b. By regular delivery route service.
      c. By party plan selling.

G. By type of location.
   1. Urban.
      a. Central business district.
      b. Secondary business district.
      c. String street location.
      d. Neighborhood location.
      e. Controlled (planned) shopping center.
      f. Public market stalls.
   2. Small city.
      a. Downtown.
      b. Neighborhood.
   3. Rural stores.
   4. Roadside stands.
H. By type of service rendered.
   1. Full service.
   2. Limited service (cash-and-carry).
   3. Self-service.
I. By legal form of organization.
   1. Proprietorship.
   2. Partnership.
   3. Corporation.
   4. Special types.
J. By management organization or operational technique.
   1. Undifferentiated.
   2. Departmentalized.

Source: Theodore N. Beckman, William R. Davidson, and W. Wayne Talarzyk, *Marketing*, 9th ed., p. 239. Copyright © 1973, The Ronald Press Company, New York.

larger chain store; (3) a personal relationship between customers and the manager is more likely to occur, allowing the smaller store to develop a unique personality. Nevertheless, the failure rate among small independent retail stores remains high. Such failures can be attributed to inexperience, incompetence, or other management inadequacies.

Chains. A chain is characterized by (1) the sale of similar merchandise by more than one store, (2) stores usually having a similar architectural format, (3) centralized buying, and (4) common ownership. The key to distinguishing a chain from other outwardly similar organizations is centralization of buying, which allows economies of scale and lower prices.

Typically, chains will feature staple merchandise for which there is little variation in customer preference. The chain store manager is primarily involved with selling and has little influence over the merchandise carried. The most typical chain organizations are such food outlets as Safeway and the Atlantic and Pacific Tea Company. The chain store suffers the following disadvantages as compared with the independent store: (1) higher overhead expenses, (2) less flexibility in operations, (3) lack of owner contact with consumers, and (4) greater legislative regulation.

Manufacturer owned.   Some manufacturers have practiced forward integration by owning their retail outlets. Such outlets contribute 2 to 3 percent of all manufacturers' sales.[9] Forward integration by manufacturers is practiced for such reasons as: (1) a belief that this is the most profitable distribution alternative, (2) the desire to have total control over distribution, and (3) the possibility of experimenting with various merchandising methods and product innovations. The limitations on expansion of this type of ownership include the high capital requirements. Also, other members of the channel on whom the manufacturer may depend, such as retailers and wholesalers, will probably object to this type of competition as being unfair.

Government owned.   Occasionally, governments may operate retail establishments. The most typical example is state-owned stores that sell liquor for off-premises consumption. Here the primary purpose of government-ownership is to achieve the social objective of limiting the distribution of alcoholic beverages. The other principal type of government-owned retail organization is the military commissary or post exchange, which is maintained as a fringe benefit for military service personnel.

Farmer owned.   A limited number of retail outlets are operated by farmers. Often these are seasonal roadside establishments. Farmer-owned retail outlets which are operated on a more permanent basis typically reflect purchases by a farmer of products from many persons or from regular wholesale outlets.

Public utility owned.   For many years public utilities sold stoves, refrigerators, and other types of appliances. These sales were designed to boost the consumption of gas or electricity. Recently, energy shortages have made it less acceptable for public utilities to expand the consumption of their products. Thus the retail sale of appliances, including gaslights and barbecue grills, by utility companies has become less popular.[10]

Consumer cooperatives.   Consumer cooperatives are retail stores which are owned by consumers and managed by a hired retailer. In the United States, co-ops have not been important in the retail structure because the advantages of membership have not proven to be important except in isolated instances where the populace has some strong reason—in many cases primarily social—for wanting to associate for mutual benefit. Where there is a heavy concentration of Scandinavians, (for example, the upper Mississippi Valley area), the cooperative has been more significant. This type of institution is based on the one-person, one-vote principle, regardless of the number of shares of ownership stock held. In addition, prices are supposedly competitive and the member benefits at year-end by receiving dividends based on the amount of patronage during the year. The Harvard Cooperative in Cambridge, Massachusetts, perhaps the best-known cooperative, carries a complete line of general merchandise and food.

---

[9] Theodore M. Beckman, William R. Davidson, and W. Wayne Talarzyk, *Marketing* (New York: Ronald Press, 1973), p. 240.

[10] "Marketing Observer," *Business Week*, October 27, 1975, p. 122.

Type of merchandise carried

Variety and assortment.   Retail establishments may also be classified on the basis of the variety and assortment of the goods they carry. Their size, location, and merchandising methods are often dictated by the lines of merchandise which are featured. *Variety* refers to the number of lines of merchandise carried—hence the term *variety store. Assortment* refers to the choice of products offered within a particular line. For example, a retail store specializing in the sale of television sets will not have as large a variety of other electrical appliances as would be found in a discount department store. However, the assortment of TVs would be greater than that available in the discount department store. The consumer would be able to choose among many different prices, cabinet styles, sizes, and other features.

General merchandise stores.   General merchandise stores can be viewed in a variety of ways. So-called general stores are often found in small, nonurban communities and feature a variety of product lines, including groceries, basic items of apparel, farm supplies, tools, and related merchandise items. Department stores are more likely to exist in major metropolitan areas and offer a wide variety of product lines, including apparel and accessories, home furnishings, housewares, and piece goods. Variety stores, such as Morgan and Lindsey or Ben Franklin, feature a wide variety of low-unit-value merchandise which is either presold or self-sold.

Single-line stores.   An outlet featuring an extensive variety within a single merchandise line having a common theme or use is known as a single-line store. Examples are furniture stores, jewelry stores, pharmacies, grocery stores, and hardware stores. Larger single-line stores feature a wide assortment in addition to a wide variety of items.

Specialty stores.   Outlets which handle a very limited variety of goods, perhaps even one type of merchandise, are called specialty stores. Examples include flower shops, bookstores, gasoline service stations, and millinery. The extremely limited variety of goods distinguishes such outlets from single-line stores, such as grocery outlets.

Merchandise group

Outlets may also be classified by merchandise group. The classification of the merchandise groups in Table 2–11 is similar to that used by the Bureau of the Census. This classification is especially helpful to the retailer because it permits the use of census data to analyze historical trends in retail sales by merchandise groups to determine the long-term trend in the relative importance of selected merchandise lines.

Location

Another common basis for classification is geographic location. An analysis by geography is helpful in establishing long-term trends in regional levels of retail sales.

TABLE 2–11
RETAIL SALES BY KIND OF BUSINESS
(in $ millions)

	December 1976	January 1977
Automotive dealers		$ 9,304
Passenger car, other automotive dealers	$9,282	
Tire, battery, accessory dealers	931	
Furniture, home furnishings, and equipment		2,282
Furniture, home furnishings stores	1,721	
Household, appliance, TV, radio stores	1,087	
Building materials and hardware	2,418	
Lumber, building materials dealers	1,771	
Hardware stores	647	
Apparel group		2,105
Men's and boys' wear	1,016	
Women's apparel, accessory stores	1,513	
Shoe stores	510	
Drugstores and proprietary stores		1,587
Eating and drinking places		4,059
Food stores		11,616
Gasoline service stations		3,951
General merchandise group, including nonstores		6,440
Department stores		4,145
Mail-order houses (department store mechandise)	709	
Variety stores	1,335	
Liquor stores		1,360
Total		$49,113

Source: *Survey of Current Business*, February 1977, table S—12.

Retail facilities can be classified by the specific urban locations which they occupy. Figure 2–5 presents the various types of urban locations which are available to retailers. The nature and characteristics of the various types of shopping centers available to retailers are discussed in detail in Chapter 17. The remaining classifications shown are largely self-explanatory. The characteristics and trends of central business district locations versus non-central business district locations are also presented in Chapter 17. Data for central business districts and major retail centers are reported by the Bureau of the Census for Standard Metropolitan Statistical Areas (SMSAs).

Size of trading area

Size of trading area is a useful basis for classification. Typically convenience stores will draw trade from no more than three minutes in driving time from the outlet. On the other hand, major retail centers which have full-line department stores as anchor tenants will draw 75 percent of their trade from within 15 minutes' driving time, and some consumers may drive over an hour to reach such outlets. The complex concept of the trading area is discussed in greater detail in Chapter 17.

FIGURE 2–5

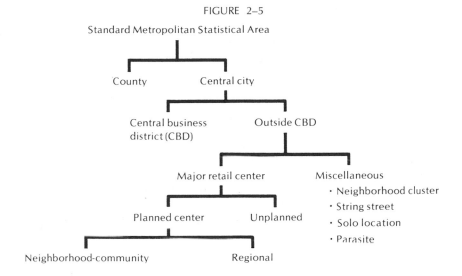

Standard Metropolitan Statistical Area

Size of establishment

The Bureau of the Census classifies retail establishments on the basis of number of employees and level of retail sales. These data provide descriptive insights into the magnitude and composition of the retail structure. In 1972, for example, 59 percent of all retail establishments had sales of less than $100,000; 30 percent had sales of less than $30,000. Only slightly more than 4 percent of these establishments had sales of more than $1,000,000. Almost 65 percent had fewer than four employees.[11]

Method of consumer contact

Retail sales outlets accounted for over 90 percent of retail sales in 1972 (Table 2–2). Thus, nonstore retailing categories, such as catalog outlets, door-to-door selling, and vending machines, account for a small percentage of total retail sales. The figures in Table 2–2 are somewhat misleading, however, because they do not reflect catalog order sales or in-home selling by many insurance companies, publishing companies, and similar organizations.

Mail order.   Historically, mail-order retailing has thrived where markets are not concentrated. Mail-order operations today, however, also serve the specialty needs of urban areas. These include general merchandise mail-order specialists such as Montgomery Ward and novelty retailers such as the Sunset House.

---

[11] *Statistical Abstract,* table 1315, p. 775.

Telephone shopping. Telephone shopping has become increasingly popular. General merchandise enterprises such as Wards and Sears maintain catalog desks at their local retail outlets. Catalog and telephone shopping have become increasingly important as a result of changes in the work force. For example, "11 billion hours of shopping time worth about $55 billion of retail trade have been dislocated as a result of U.S. women entering the work force."[12] This has had a highly positive impact on the mail-order business. Home cable TV and video discs are expected to be the greatest mail-order bonanzas of them all. Under this system consumers can choose from items displayed on the television screen and simply telephone their order to the retail outlet offering the items.

Household contact. Door-to-door household selling is also well known to most of us. It may occur by canvassing a neighborhood on a house-to-house basis, by advance prospecting over the telephone, or by party plan selling. This is a costly form of retailing because it involves almost a one-to-one contact with customers who may be in widely scattered locations. Such appliances as vacuum cleaners have long been effectively demonstrated and sold in homes. Some perishable products, such as ice cream, are sold door-to-door. Likewise, the products of such firms as Avon, Watkins, Fuller, and Stanley are often sold door-to-door by nonstore middlepersons who purchase the merchandise directly from the manufacturer.

Type of service rendered

Retail outlets, as noted under the section on margin and turnover, can be classified as either full-service or limited service outlets. Full-service outlets feature a variety of services, such as credit, delivery, installation, and repair. The limited service organization, on the other hand, offers few services and is typically a self-service or self-selection operation.

Degree of systems integration

Retail firms may exist as *independent outlets* which are not part of any affiliated group. The small single store may find it difficult to compete on the basis of volume purchasing and advertising with the chains or other organized groups.

Voluntary cooperatives consist of a group of retail outlets which have banded together to purchase or control a wholesale house so as to obtain the economies of large-scale purchases. Wholesalers may also take the initiative and induce a group of retailers to agree to centralized purchases and to participate in the other advantages of voluntary affiliation.

Administered systems involve manufacturer control of one or more lines of merchandise which are sold by the retailer. The special skills of manufac-

---

[12] "Marketing Briefs," *Marketing News*, April 23, 1976, p. 2.

turers enable them to induce retailers to participate in special merchandising plans.

Franchising is a type of contractual marketing. The franchisee operates as an independent business person but abides by the marketing plan and other policies established by the franchisor. The franchisee pays the franchisor a fee, such as a percentage of sales, for the use of the franchising plan.

SUMMARY

Retailing is the third largest employer in the United States. Its institutional structure is highly visible because each of us probably interacts with one or more retail institutions on a daily basis. The number of retail outlets has not increased greatly since 1929. However, the average sales per establishment have grown. The distribution of sales among the various regions of the United States approximates that of the population. Historically, retail sales have increased approximately three times as fast as population and approximately as fast as income.

As students of retailing, we need a framework for analyzing the institutional structure. Such a framework enables us to evaluate long-term trends in the growth of the various types of establishments, and to arrive at informed decisions about various facets of retail structure. It also enables us to make generalized hypotheses and predictions about the future of the various types of retailing.

One of the most comprehensive classifications, and one which aids in strategy development, is the margin-turnover classification introduced by Ronald Gist. Based on this classification all retail outlets can be placed into one of four quadrants, ranging from the high-margin/high-turnover outlet to the low-margin/low-turnover outlet. A variety of more specialized classifications have also been introduced. The U.S. Bureau of the Census classification by merchandise line is particularly useful. Other classifications are based on geography, size of establishment, and method of consumer contact.

An understanding of retail structure helps us to develop a better appreciation of the evolution of retail structure, explanations for that evolution, and conjectures about the future of the various types of establishments.

KEY CONCEPTS

A general classification of retail structure
    The classification may be based on margin and turnover
    Enterprises differ by
        Type of merchandise sold
        Variety and assortments offered
        Services offered
        Price level
        Kind of personal selling

Kind of promotion
Complexity of organizational structure
Locational requirements
Alternative bases for classification of retail structure
Ownership form
Degree of inventory specialization
Inventory variety and assortment
Merchandise group inventoried
Geographic region
Urban location
Extent of trading area
Size of establishment
Degree of systems integration
Method of customer contact
Type of service rendered

DISCUSSION QUESTIONS

1. What evidence may be cited in support of the claim that retailing is an important employer in the United States?

2. How would you describe the distribution of retail sales in the various regions of the United States?

3. What has been the trend in the number of retail outlets? Has this trend varied by type of outlet? If so, how?

4. What has been the trend in the level of sales per retail establishment? What has been the trend in the level of retail sales on a per capita basis?

5. What cautions should be observed by a person using census data to analyze retail structure?

6. What benefits from a study of retail structure in a given market area might be expected by an existing store owner?

7. Discuss the margin-turnover classification model. Give examples of various types of outlets which may exist in each of the four quadrants of the margin-turnover model.

8. What are some bases for the classification of retail outlets other than margin and turnover?

9. How might a manufacturer of consumer goods benefit from an analysis of trends in retail sales by kind of business?

PROJECTS

1. Take either a full city block or a shopping center, and classify each store according to the margin-turnover classification scheme.

2. Place five different stores in each of the quadrants of the margin-turnover figure, and explain the reasons for their placement.

3. Select an SMSA near your hometown or the one in which your school is located, and use census data to determine:

   a.   The retail classifications of businesses.
   b.   Which classification has the largest number of businesses.
   c.   Which classification has the largest dollar volume of sales.

4. Utilizing the classification schema in the text, choose the major stores in the retail structure in your community and make a complete classification chart of the structure. After you have done this, draw some strategy conclusions from your work.

CASES

Case 1. Mr. and Mrs. George Jones have just retired and have moved into a town of about 50,000 people. They plan to open a bookstore and to carry hardbound and paperback books, stationery, and greeting cards. A real estate broker has shown them three locations available for immediate occupancy. One is in a large mall, located on a main highway just outside of town. There are two anchor stores, a bank, a post office, several restaurants, and approximately 30 specialty stores. The rent is estimated to be $700 per month. A second location is in the downtown business district. Stores have been moving out of this area, but there is a program currently under way to promote the section. Many concessions are given tenants— free parking, wider sidewalks, landscaping, and extremely low rent ($250 per month)—but you must sign a lease for 12 months and join the Downtown Merchants' Association. The third site is in a small suburban shopping center. There are a large supermarket, a drugstore, a five-and-ten, and two small shops. This shopping center is located in a middle-class neighborhood, and the rent is $500 per month.

   Which location should Mr. and Mrs. Jones select? Why did you choose that location over the other two?

Case 2. Tom Redder has an idea for a new fast-food chain to be known as U-Grill-It. The chain will introduce a new concept in the steak line. Customers will select a cut of meat from an open freezer, pay for it, grill the meat themselves on a long grill at one end of the dining area, and take it to their table. Other foods to go with the steaks, such as baked potatoes, salads, and drinks, will also be available on a serve-yourself basis. Tom believes that this method will allow him to offer a price substantially below those being offered by the present steak chains.

   Evaluate the possibility of success for such a business in your community. How much below the price of existing steak businesses do you believe Tom's price would have to be in order to attract significant business away from them?

   Do you believe that price will be the only appeal of Tom's new procedure? What are some other attractions it may offer?

3

THE RETAILING
STRUCTURE:
EVOLUTION,
EXPLANATIONS, AND
CONJECTURE

*A*bove all else, retailing is an ever-changing and dynamic industry. Any serious student of the retailing phenomenon must have an adequate grasp of the many types of retailing enterprises and of the evolutionary processes which brought them about. Essentially, recognition of consumer needs and of changing consumer life-styles has produced today's unbelievably complex system of retail distribution. Indeed, more significant changes in the retail structure have occurred in the past 15 years than in the previous 150 years.

Richard Pizitz, President
Pizitz, Inc.
Birmingham, Alabama

THEORIES OF RETAIL INSTITUTIONAL CHANGE

The theories of retail institutional evolution provide insights into how retailers adapt to environmental changes. For students contemplating a career in retailing, it may also be possible to determine from these theories which components of the retailing structure are likely to increase in importance.

Each discipline seeks to describe, explain, and predict occurrences about the objects which are the foundation of the discipline. Thus, cause and effect relationships are sought. If the effects can be established, it may be possible to determine the causes.

In this chapter, we provide an overview of the theories of retail institutional change and of the innovations in structure which are part of such change. However, no single classification can explain the changes in all types of retail institutions.

The most common theories of change in retail institutional structure are (1) the wheel of retailing, (2) the retail accordion (general-specific-general), (3) the dialectical process, and (4) the adaptive behavior model (natural selection).

An ideal goal of the analysis of retail institutional change is a universal model for predicting such change. Such a goal appears unrealistic at this time. Although general trends can be predicted for some countries, among them countries in Western Europe, the models have to be modified to reflect different stages of economic development, different cultures, and different legal environments. Also, the lack of a generally accepted theory of consumer behavior makes a universal model almost impossible.

Given the admitted shortcomings of the various theories of retail evolution, why study them? The principal reason is that they give us a better after-the-fact understanding of events and of the reasons for their occurrence. Let's now look at the various theories.

The wheel of retailing

A more or less definite cycle appears to occur in American distribution. The cycle frequently begins with a bold innovation which experiences a period of growth during which it takes business from competitors who have not changed their operating methods. However, at some point the innovating institution enters a period of maturity characterized by slower growth and lower profit margins. For example, it develops

. . . a larger physical plant, more elaborate store fixtures and displays, and it undertakes greater promotional efforts. At this stage, the institution finds itself competing primarily with other similar institutions rather than old-line competitors. The maturity phase soon tends to be followed by topheaviness, too great conservatism, a decline in the rate of return on investment, and eventual vulnerability. Vulnerability to what? Vulnerability to the next revolution of the wheel, to the next fellow who has a bright idea and who starts his business on a low-cost basis, slipping in under the umbrella that the old-line institutions have hoisted.[1]

This theory tells us that innovative institutions initially offer lower prices than are available from competitive institutions. Low price gives the new method of doing business an initial hold in the marketplace. The new firm is able to earn a profit on a lower gross margin than is possible for the competitive institutions. One example is the hotel–motel–budget motel cycle.

How long it takes for an institution to reach maturity, that is, an increase in gross margins, depends on the institution. Why, however, do firms apparently become less efficient when they mature? A variety of explanations have been offered. These include the lack of competent management to ensure the perpetuation of the trend started by an innovative entrepreneur, the increasing conservatism of management, and a growing preference for nonprice competition, which necessitates large gross margins.

This theory has been criticized because not all institutions begin as low-margin outlets with a minimum of services.[2] For example, department stores, automatic vending and suburban shopping centers did not follow this model. Even if some outlets do begin as low-margin operations, the elimination of services is only a small factor. Goldman contends that the increasing size of the establishment and the changing nature of the product assortment are much more important reasons.[3]

The retail accordion

Several writers have suggested that retail institutions evolve from broad-based outlets with wide assortments to specialized narrow line store merchants and then return to the wide-assortment pattern (general-specific-general). This evolution suggests the term *accordion,* which reflects a supposed contraction and expansion of merchandise lines in retail outlets.[4]

In his history of Macy's of New York, Ralph Hower states:

Throughout the history of retail trade (as, indeed in all business evolution) there appears to be an alternating movement in the dominant method of conducting operations. One swing is toward the specialization of the function performed or the merchandise handled by the individual firm. The other is away from such specialization

[1] Reprinted from *Competitive Distribution in a High-Level Economy and Its Implications for the University,* A. B. Smith, ed., by permission of the University of Pittsburgh Press. © 1957 by the University of Pittsburgh Press.

[2] See, for example, Stanley Hollander, "The Wheel of Retailing," *Journal of Marketing,* vol. 25 (July 1960), pp. 37–42.

[3] Arieh Goldman, "The Role of Trading-Up in the Development of the Retail System," *Journal of Marketing,* vol. 39 (January 1975), p. 62; also, Goldman, "Institutional Change in Retailing: The 'Wheel of Retailing' Revisited," in Arch Woodside et al. (eds.), *Foundations of Marketing Channels* (Austin, Tex.: Lone Star Publishers, 1978).

[4] Stanley Hollander, "Notes on the Retail Accordion," *Journal of Retailing,* vol. 42 (Summer 1966), pp. 29–40.

toward the integration of related activities under one management or the diversification of products handled by a single firm.[5]

The supporters of this theory state that modern retailing in the United States began with general stores. These were in effect one-stop retail outlets which featured a wide assortment of merchandise. The vanishing rural general stores of today fit this description. These outlets carry everything from shoes to food to tractor parts. General stores usually occur when there is insufficient population to support a more specialized type of outlet.

The theory states that the department store, which was somewhat more specialized in its merchandise lines, emerged with an increase in population and industrialization. The mail-order store, which tended to be still more specialized in offering dry goods for sale, appeared shortly thereafter. As population became more concentrated in urban areas, it was increasingly possible to tailor merchandise offerings to specific market segments. Thus, through approximately the 1950s, increasing numbers of single-line and specialty outlets, such as bookstores, phonographic record stores, garden supply stores, and drugstores, were developed.

From the late 1950s on, we again saw the emergence of more generalized types of retailing, even though specialization had by no means been abandoned. The pressure on profit margins caused outlets to expand in order to spread fixed overhead costs over a wider assortment of merchandise.

Complementary merchandise lines were offered in what had previously been single-line outlets. For example, grocery outlets added produce and dairy products. The move continued, with firms selecting the fastest-moving merchandise lines of other types of outlets and adding them to the merchandise they sold. They sought to attract consumers by offering merchandise with higher than average margins. Discounting became increasingly popular. The consumer also benefited from the trend toward one-stop shopping.

In some instances full lines were "borrowed" from other outlets. Many supermarket chains now offer nonfood items, such as drugs and cosmetics; discount stores offer a variety of soft goods; and variety chains now sell big-ticket items, such as television sets and household appliances.

One must ask whether during the 1970s specialization will again increase in importance. Trends in this direction are evident. For example, we see highly specialized boutiques featuring very narrow varieties but deep assortments of highly specialized clothing, as well as toy supermarkets, tennis shops, and gourmet food outlets. As has been noted:

As consumer markets become more segmented, specialty stores will become increasingly important. This trend is already well advanced in a variety of product categories. Consider, for example, the explosive growth of such firms as Aaron Brothers (artist's supplies and picture frames); Hickory Farms (specialty foods); The Limited (junior apparel); and Mervin's (family apparel). In addition to these estab-

---

[5] Ralph Hower, *History of Macy's of New York, 1858–1919,* (Cambridge, Mass.: Harvard University Press, 1943), p. 73.

lished chains, a new wave of "super" specialists has emerged. Included in this latter movement are such companies as Athlete's Foot, County Seat, Calculators, Inc., and The Gap. In short, specialty store retailing has become a high-growth sector of the economy.[6]

The dialectical process

Dialectical materialism has also been offered as an explanation for the evolution of retail structure. The specific application to retailing has been outlined as follows:

In terms of retail institutions, the dialectic model implies that retailers mutually adapt in the face of competition from "opposites." Thus, when challenged by a competitor with a differential advantage, an established institution will adopt strategies and tactics in the direction of that advantage, thereby negating some of the innovators' attraction. The innovator, meanwhile, does not remain unchanged. Rather, as MacNair noted, the innovator over time tends to upgrade or otherwise modify products and institutions. In doing so, he moves toward the "negated" institution. As a result of these mutual adaptations, the two retailers gradually move together in terms of offerings, facilities, supplementary services, and prices. They thus become indistinguishable or at least quite similar and constitute a new retail institution, termed the synthesis. This new institution is then vulnerable to "negation" by new competitors as the dialectic process begins anew.[7]

The dialectical process for the supermarket is shown in Figure 3–1. Specific applications of this theory will be discussed later in the chapter.

FIGURE 3–1
THE DIALECTICAL PROCESS IN RETAILING
AS ILLUSTRATED BY THE SUPERMARKET

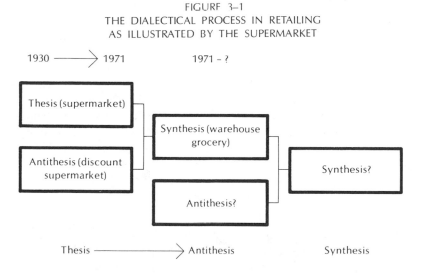

1930 ——→ 1971   1971 – ?

Thesis (supermarket)

Synthesis (warehouse grocery)

Antithesis (discount supermarket)

Synthesis?

Antithesis?

Thesis ——————→ Antithesis   Synthesis

---

[6] James M. Kenderdine and Bert C. McCammon, Jr., "Structure and Strategy in Retailing," in Henry W. Nash and Donald P. Robin (eds.), *Proceedings: Southern Marketing Association*, 1975, p. 119.

[7] Thomas J. Maronick and Bruce J. Walker, "The Dialectic Evolution of Retailing," in Barnett Greenberg (ed.), *Proceedings: Southern Marketing Association*, 1974, p. 147.

Natural selection (adaptive behavior)

The natural selection model is essentially that of adaptive behavior.[8] Dreesmann believes that the retailing institutions which can most effectively adapt to environmental changes are the ones most likely to prosper or survive. Thus, the retailer is continually faced with changes in consumer behavior and desires, in technology, in competitive behavior, and even in the legal environment which can affect chances of survival. For example, the removal of resale price maintenance laws by the federal government had major impacts on the distributive philosophy of a variety of vertical marketing systems. All retailing institutions feel the effects of environmental change.

The shopping centers of the late 1940s and the 1950s were seen as the ultimate answer to serving the needs of the ever-increasing numbers of consumers living in suburbia. Yet as consumers continued to move farther away from the central city, these older centers became vulnerable to still newer ones which were built even closer to the consumers. As new centers are constructed between the existing center and customers who live in the suburbs, the trading area of the older center decreases in size. Likewise, the degree of specialization in the older center decreases, as does the complexity of the merchandise lines offered.

The department store is often cited as an institution which has been slow to adapt to environmental changes. It remained in the central business district far too long. When it moved to a suburban location it failed to recognize the unique problems in serving this market segment. Indeed, the entire CBD appears to be having difficulty in surviving the rapidly changing conditions of the downtown areas of most cities.

Too often students of retailing tend to think only in terms of the economic environment (that is, sales, units sold, cost of sales, gross margin, and operating expenses) as explanations for retailing change, and fail to focus on other environments which are just as important. For example, technology will allow picture phone shopping in the near future. The so-called Green River ordinances placed restrictions on door-to-door selling which have hampered this type of retailing. Consumer demands for late evening hours and Sunday openings have also affected the institutions of retailing. The strategic profit models most successful in the 1970s and 1980s will be those that allow firms to adapt most readily to changing environmental conditions.

Summary

This section of the chapter has offered students a variety of theories or hypotheses which have been developed to explain the evolution of retail institutional structure. The primary underlying explanatory feature of each theory is different. For example, the adaptive behavior model reflects the necessity for adaptation to changes in the economic, social, technological,

---

[8] A. C. R. Dreesmann, "Patterns of Evolution in Retailing," *Journal of Retailing*, vol. 44 (Spring 1968), pp. 64–81.

and legal environments, emphasizing that the retailer must have institutional flexibility to respond to these changes.

The wheel of retailing also reflects the necessity of adapting to changes in the external environment, but in addition suggests the importance of management competence and foresight in institutional innovation. Less emphasis is placed upon the environment and more upon the farsighted behavior of pioneering innovators. Thus, the model places greater emphasis on controllable factors than does the adaptive behavior model.

The specific-general-specific retail accordion hypothesis places primary emphasis on the importance of merchandise lines in the evolution of retailing institutions. We have previously discussed different views on the variety versus assortment question in retailing.

Finally, the dialectical process was discussed as a way of explaining how retailers have adjusted to changes in the competitive environment.

These theories are not mutually exclusive. In combination they provide a more comprehensive understanding of the structural changes which have occurred and which are likely to occur in the future.

PATTERNS OF RETAIL EVOLUTION

Regardless of the shortcomings of our existing knowledge, it is appropriate to examine the evolution of selected types of our more familiar retailing institutions. In making that examination, we will provide our interpretation of the explanatory theory or hypothesis, focus on the life cycle of the institutions, and suggest appropriate firms which are illustrative of the various types. Our approach is admittedly subjective. Other students of the retail process may have ideas which differ from those we present.

The general store. The general store can perhaps best be explained by the concept of the retail accordion (general-specific-general) hypothesis. It was the first modern institution of retailing in the United States after the Yankee peddler. It featured a wide variety and limited assortment of many products. It began to decline in importance after the industrial revolution in the United States. The department store and the dry goods mail-order retailer then emerged.

The growth of cities and the increasing concentration of persons in urban areas allowed the development of market segmentation in merchandise offerings. Thus, single-line or specialty outlets evolved which served more narrowly defined groups of consumers.

However, profit pressures and the desire for growth caused the expansion of the merchandise lines of many of these stores. The stores began to take on complementary lines of merchandise. Also, the desire to carry merchandise with higher than average margins led to the scrambled merchandising which is familiar to all of us and is somewhat like the concept of the early general merchandise store. However, we again see evidence of a trend back to specialization in retailing.

Single-line/specialty stores.   These institutions are also an example of adaptive behavior. The family shoe store typifies our definition of a single-line store, whereas a store specializing in the sale of hats would be a specialty store. Single-line and specialty stores have continued to adapt over the years, primarily by trading up in terms of merchandise lines, quality of fixtures, and competence of personnel. The single-line stores have typically replaced the rural general stores whenever communities have grown enough in size to support more specialized outlets. The variety of merchandise offerings in the single-line store continues to remain greater than that of the specialty store but smaller than that of a general merchandise store.

The department store.   The department store is an example of the dialectical process. In the 1950s, the department store was a full-line outlet featuring a wide variety and assortment of merchandise, supplementary services, high prices, and high margins. The negation of the department store was the discount store, which featured low prices, high volume, low markup, few or no services, an isolated location, ample parking, and narrow assortments of hard and soft goods. Numerous developments are occurring in the general department store field, as shown in Figure 3–2, but it is still too early to determine the most probable next important development.

FIGURE 3–2

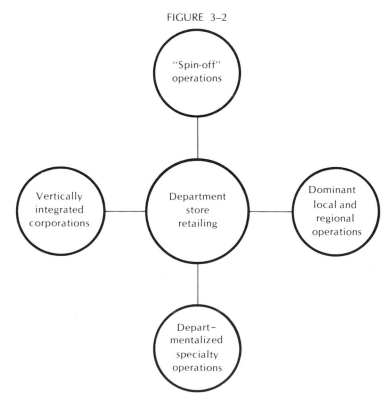

Source: Management Horizons, *Retail Intelligence System* (Columbus: n.d.), p. 14.

In a few years, the department stores had taken a variety of approaches to meeting discount competition. These included increasing self-service, longer business hours, and new merchandise lines.

During the late 1960s, discount stores began to locate in new and better buildings with better fixtures. They also began to offer credit and related services. With this increasing array of services, the markups increased. Thus the so-called promotional department store emerged. Korvettes, for example, reflects elements of the traditional department store and the discount store.

Variety stores.   Variety stores are an example of adaptive behavior. They have continued to trade up and to expand their merchandise lines without drastically changing their concept of merchandising. Over the years, they have become increasingly like the traditional department store.

Mail-order houses.   Mail order houses were among the earliest retail institutions to recognize the importance of the environment in affecting merchandising. The responses of mail-order houses have not been limited to opening retail stores. These organizations have also changed their methods of catalog selling by trading up in quality and variety of merchandise, improving their sales promotion, and adding private branded merchandise; yet they continue to stress price and a guarantee of satisfaction.

Recently, the solicitation of catalog customers by telephone has increased. In addition, mail-order houses have moved into the sale of insurance and mutual funds. If past behavior is any indication of the future, these outlets will continue to respond flexibly to changes in their environments.

The corporate chain.   The corporate chain is a relatively modern phenomenon which is present in virtually all merchandise lines. The corporate chain is characterized by central ownership and by central control over all retail units, including control of profit planning, losses, and merchandise planning.

The evolution of the corporate chain is an example of adaptive behavior. The corporate chain became an important factor in retailing in the 1920s because of the economic and social environments of that time. Distribution had not kept up with rapid advances in productive efficiency. However, the development of the automobile and a decent road structure made it possible for large numbers of nonurban residents to shop in cities frequently. Also, during the years immediately preceding the development of corporate chains, retail prices had almost doubled and consumers had become exceedingly price conscious.

The chains introduced the concept of self-service by shifting many of the functions traditionally performed by the retailer to the consumer. Also, volume purchases allowed further operating economies which allowed the chains to underprice most independents. The corporate chain as a method of merchandising has remained popular. Even today, corporate chains are preferred tenants in shopping centers.

Discount stores.   Controversy exists as to whether the discount house is an adaptation to changing environments or is primarily a result of entrepreneurial behavior. In any case, it is an important aspect of the evolution of retail structure. Discount retailers may be of various types. They have developed partly because of pressures in the economic environment for lower prices and partly because of the failure of department stores to respond to the needs of suburban markets.

A variety of features characterize the discount house, including self-service, low prices, convenience of location, and management skill in adapting merchandising strategies to the needs of consumers. Thus, the discount house is really as much a retail merchandising philosophy as it is an institution of retailing.

Discounting occurs primarily in the retailing of groceries, furniture, major appliances, and general merchandise. The discount house in general merchandising appeared initially as a direct challenge to the department store.

Supermarkets. Supermarkets as we know them today did not emerge until the late 1920s. Prior to that time, food had been sold in a variety of specialty shops, which were followed by mom and pop outlets with all types of services, including credit and delivery. The King Kullen supermarkets then emerged in abandoned warehouses, selling merchandise from the case on crude display benches. The outlets were in isolated, low-rent locations. They operated on high volume, low prices, and nationally branded merchandise. They were the antithesis of the small independent outlet, which tended to specialize in meat, produce, or dry goods.[9]

Gradually the two types of institutions blended, and the thesis emerged as the familiar neighborhood supermarket. The result was more equipment, larger buildings, and larger amounts of space to accommodate such products as delicatessen, liquor, cosmetics, nonprescription drugs, and a wide variety of services, including sacking and delivery to one's automobile.

The antithesis, which began to emerge in the late 1960s and early 1970s, has taken a variety of forms, one of which is the convenience store. This type of outlet features longer hours, self-service, narrow assortments, higher prices, and convenient location near residential subdivisions. Another form was the discount department store. More recently, warehouse grocery outlets have emerged. These are somewhat reminiscent of the supermarkets of the 1920s and represent a synthesis of the conventional supermarket and the discount supermarket. Customers mark their own merchandise, remove it from the crates, bag it, and carry it to their automobiles. The primary features are low price, high volume, and national brands.

Shopping centers. Shopping centers are an example of adaptive behavior. They began as high-margin/low-turnover clusters of basically nonfood operations under a single roof. It has taken a series of court cases to force developers of shopping centers not to discriminate against low-margin/high-turnover discounters in their tenant mix. Shopping centers evolved because

---

[9] David Appel, "The Supermarket: Early Development of an Institutional Innovation," *Journal of Retailing,* vol. 48 (Spring 1972), pp. 39–52.

of the decentralization of urban populations, the increasing popularity of the automobile, traffic congestion and parking problems in the CBD, a desire for more convenient and longer hours than were available downtown, and the aggregate convenience of one-stop shopping.

Some authors contend that the shopping center is not a new type of institution but rather, like the department store branch, an innovative response to changing environmental conditions. Whether or not this is so, shopping centers are an important response by some retailing institutions, especially department stores and variety chains, to changing economic and social environments.[10]

Cooperatives.   Cooperatives offer an example of adaptive behavior in retailing. The corporate chain of the 1920s greatly affected independent retailers and wholesalers.[11] Thus, they adapted their methods of operation to changing conditions. The primary change was the emergence of the voluntary chain, captained either by the wholesaler or the retailer. It was designed to provide purchasing and operating economies of scale to independent retailers and wholesalers. Subsequently cooperatives abandoned their initially defensive posture, and they are now adding a full array of services for their members. Cooperatives such as IGA can compete successfully with even the most modern vertical marketing system.

Gasoline service stations.   Gasoline was initially retailed through mom and pop outlets which offered a variety of products in addition to gasoline. Out of this, the full-service gasoline station emerged. It featured automotive parts, qualified mechanics, and lower prices because of the high volume of sales.

As often happens, the outlets gradually traded up by offering an increasing array of services. During the late 1960s, the discount gasoline station emerged as the antithesis. It offered self-service and provided no repair services or any other special features. The desire was to sell a high volume of gasoline as cheaply as possible while still making a profit. The synthesis has not yet emerged, although the self-service feature is likely to be retained, regardless of the final institutional product.

Convenience stores.   The convenience store, particularly in food, reflects elements of both the retail accordion and the dialectical process. Convenience stores are characterized by closeness of location, long hours, limited lines of fast-moving merchandise, and higher prices than are found in the typical supermarket. These outlets emerged because of the desire of consumers for the advantages which could be obtained through this method of operation. The convenience store can be viewed as the antithesis of the

[10] Delbert J. Duncan, "Responses of Selected Retail Institutions to Their Changing Environment," in Peter Bennett (ed.), *Marketing and Economic Development* (Chicago: American Marketing Association, 1965).

[11] William J Regan, "The Stages of Retail Development," in Reavis Cox, Wroe Alderson, and Stanley Shapiro (eds.), *Theory in Marketing*, 2d series (Homewood, Ill.: Richard D. Irwin, 1964).

supermarket. Likewise, if one thinks in terms of the specific-general-specific hypothesis of the retail accordion, the convenience store reflects elements of the single-line grocery outlets which existed in the 1920s prior to the emergence of the supermarket.

Fast-food outlets.   This institution exemplifies the dialectical process. So-called drive-in restaurants began with an extensive menu and provision for in-store eating. Typically the food was prepared after the order was taken. The antithesis of this kind of outlet emerged during the early 1960s. The new outlets featured a very limited menu, precooked food, and totally take-out operations. The thesis appears to be a combination of these two earlier types of outlets. Such combinations feature a somewhat broader menu than did the all take-out restaurant, but one which is less varied than that of the original drive-in. Also, even though the food is precooked and the service rapid, opportunities for eating it inside the outlet are again provided.

Hypermarkets.   The basic merchandising strategies of this new type of store have been described as follows:

Mix of food and nonfoods feeding through an up-front bank of 49 registers;

Extreme cherry-picking, reminiscent of discounters of the fifties, but on a more massive scale, with high-impact displays to selected classifications . . .

Wand reading of some 90 percent of nonfood items at . . . electronic terminals;

Credit via Master Charge for both food . . . general merchandise.[12]

A typical hypermarket is characterized by such features as:

Cost: $11 million;

Footage: Food and general merchandise 250,000 sq ft;
   Supermarket 42,000 sq ft;
   General merchandise 103,000 sq ft;

Parking: 3,000 cars;

Number of checkouts: 49 up-front, 11 department registers;

Opening-stock at retail: $5 million;

Estimated annual income: $35 million.[13]

The hypermarket—a combination discount store, supermarket, and warehouse under a single roof—is an example of adaptive behavior. Typically it sells both food and nonfood items at 10–15 percent below normal retail prices and stacks merchandise as high as ten feet. Hypermarkets may offer a major challenge to conventional retailing in the United States in the near future.

The superstore appears to be an example of adaptive behavior. The profits of food chains have been decreasing rapidly in the past 20 years. Many have

[12] Dick Groberg, "Hypermarche Splashes Down," *Discount Store News,* November 13, 1973; see also "An Overview: Europe's Hypermarkets," *Discount Store News,* December 10, 1973, p. 6.

[13] E. B. Weiss, "Department Stores and Hypermarche Competition," *Stores,* June 1974, p. 40.

tried to decrease distribution costs by diversifying their product lines both within the supermarkets and in other types of operations. For example, Safeway superstores sell "everything from $380 Sony television sets and $22 slow cookers to 8,000 different grocery items."[14] Also, consumer pressure for an ever-expanding variety of products and services in both food and nonfood under a single roof have prompted the emergence of this type of store. Chains need a more profitable merchandise mix and higher volume to remain financially viable. The superstore is the response. Lastly, changes in the technological environment, such as the uniform product code and the automatic front end, now provide the merchandising data which are necessary to make the complex decisions required in the successful operation of a superstore.

Home improvement centers. The volume of home improvement center sales increased from less than $3 billion to approximately $7 billion during the 1970–74 period.[15] Home improvement centers exemplify the general-specific-general retail accordion hypothesis. In the 1920s the general store offered an extensive variety of virtually all types of merchandise. The market potential was then insufficient to support specialized outlets featuring an extensive assortment of a few lines.

During the 1950s and 60s, some stores began to specialize in paint, lumber, wallpaper, or hardware. The 1970s saw the emergence of home improvement centers featuring all types of merchandise lines—from paint to nails to carpet to wallpaper—that the consumer needs for various home improvement projects. Thus the one-stop home improvement centers with a wide variety of merchandise lines and a reasonable assortment within the lines have emerged. Lowes is a typical example.

The boutique. The boutique is a highly specialized personality store which also exemplifies the general-specific-general retail accordion hypothesis. During the 1960s and early 70s, the consumer's quest for individuality and merchandise tailored to varying life-styles caused the emergence of single-line and even specialty shops with merchandise tailored to highly specific market segments. These outlets are similar in many ways to the single-line and specialty shops of the prechain era of the 1920s. Today we see outlets specializing in houseplants, gourmet foods, cut glass, greeting cards, bathroom accessories, kitchen accessories, and much more. These outlets provide an alternative for the consumer who wants the individuality and personal attention which simply aren't available in a large general merchandise department store.

Warehouse retailing. Warehouse retailing is an example of the wheel of retailing. It emerged in the 1920s with the introduction of supermarket merchandising of foods. Merchandise was sold in low-rent buildings with a

---

[14] "Safeway Selling Nongrocery Items to Cure the Supermarket Blahs," *Business Week,* March 7, 1977, p. 52; also Walter J. Salmon et al., *The Super Store—Strategic Implications for the Seventies* (Cambridge, Mass.: Marketing Science Institute, 1972), p. 9.

[15] Kenderdine and McCammon, "Structure and Strategy in Retailing," p. 117.

minimum of supplementary services. The supermarkets then gradually traded up with increasing profit margins and a wider array of services.

During the early 1970s, pressures on profit margins and rapidly rising prices caused a return to the warehouse retailing methods of the 1920s. Certain types of merchandise, particularly food and furniture, are again being retailed in isolated low-rent buildings. A minimum of services are offered. The consumer performs the bulk of the functions. This approach to merchandising allows profit margins to be maintained while offering low prices to the consumer. As shown in Figure 3–3, warehouse retailing is not

FIGURE 3–3

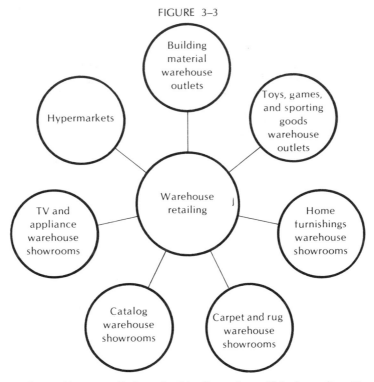

Source: Management Horizons, *Retail Intelligence System* (Columbus: n.d.), p. 16.

limited to a single category of merchandise but seems to represent a philosophy of merchandising as much as an institutional type.

The catalog showroom. The catalog showroom grew at a rapid rate during the late 1960s and early 70s. Let's consider the following projections:

For the calendar year 1972, it is estimated that some 1,300 catalog-showroom units accounted for sales of $1.3 billion. By 1976, it is projected there will be a minimum of 3,000 showrooms accounting for at least $40 billion annual volume. Certain key states such as Georgia will experience nearly a 2000 percent increase over the existing number of operating units by 1976. In the 18 key states it is expected that catalog-showrooms will swell to 2,282 units from the present 726 units with about a $2.1 billion increase over the 1971 level.[16]

The evolution of the mass merchandiser explains the current popularity of the catalog showroom. It exemplifies the retail accordion hypothesis. The mass merchandiser began as a low-cost/high-volume discount or chain store operation. However, it rapidly traded up from the low fixed and variable costs of the 1920s retailer. During the early 1960s, the management had to work exceedingly hard to earn a 1 or 2 percent net return on sales. Location, decor, and service had become almost as important as price. The catalog-showroom thus emerged, offering a wide assortment of merchandise, name brands, low prices, and the opportunity for a time-conscious consumer to make purchases from a catalog rather than having to travel to a series of individual outlets to purchase merchandise. The low overhead cost feature of these outlets is reminiscent of the discounters of the 1930s.

THE FUTURE

The retailing institutions of today must find ways of increasing their profitability and growth potential. Innovative strategies and innovative institutions will be needed if these institutions are to survive during the next decade. The aftertax profits of all retailing corporations declined by 50 percent during the 17-year period 1950–67.[17] This trend continued during the

TABLE 3–1
COMPOSITE GROWTH POTENTIAL RATIOS FOR
RETAILING CORPORATIONS: 1968–1974

Growth potential ratios	1968	1974
Net profits (after dividends) to net worth (percent)....................	6.7	5.6
Net profits (before interest and taxes) to total assets (percent)	8.2	7.8

Source: James M. Kenderdine and Bert C. McCammon, Jr., "Structure and Strategy in Retailing," in Henry W. Nash and Donald P. Robin (eds.), *Proceedings: Southern Marketing Association*, 1975, p. 118.

1968–74 period, as shown in Table 3–1, and it is forecast to continue into the 1980s. National Cash Register executives have stated:

Retail profit margins will be exposed to continuous pressure during the decade ahead. Gross margin percentages will be continuously threatened; payroll expenses will rise; and occupancy costs—given prevailing conditions in the construction and real estate markets—will assuredly escalate. Interest rates will also remain high. As a result of these and other factors, general merchandise executives will have to exper-

---

[16] Walter L. Schaffer, "The Catalog-Showroom: An Old Game With New Players," in Thomas V. Greer (ed.), *Combined Proceedings of the American Marketing Association* (Chicago: American Marketing Association, 1973), p. 128.

[17] *The Changing Economics of General Merchandise Retailing* (Dayton, Ohio: National Cash Register Company, 1970), p. 3.

iment aggressively and innovate relentlessly in order to maintain rather slender profit margins. To complicate matters further, it appears that leverage ratios cannot be significantly increased during forthcoming budget periods.[18]

The trends of the 1970s that can be expected to be most successful in the near future are as follows:

Furniture warehouse showrooms, catalog showrooms, and other warehouse outlets achieved explosive rates of growth between 1968 and 1974. . . . Thus, warehouse retailing will continue to be an important force in the marketplace. . . .

Retailers employing the supermarket concept have become a *major* and competitive reality in virtually all lines of trade. . . . These organizations have compiled an enviable record of growth over the past five years, which suggests that supermarket retailing will continue to be a mainstream thrust in the field of distribution.

Many analysts contend that direct marketing is the wave of the future.

As consumer markets become more segmented, specialty stores will become increasingly important. The trend is already *well advanced* in a variety of product categories. . . . In short, specialty store retailing has become a high-growth sector of the economy.

Retailers operating in secondary markets have consistently outperformed their metropolitan counterparts. . . . by focusing on secondary markets . . . organizations have achieved a position of competitive dominance at a relatively low cost. As competitive pressures intensify and as expenses continue to rise, a growing number of retailers will undoubtedly adopt a secondary market strategy.

TABLE 3–2
PERFORMANCE POTENTIAL OF SELECTED RETAILING INNOVATIONS: 1972–1975*

Retailing innovations	Net profits to net sales (percent)	×	Net sales to total assets	=	Net profits to total assets (percent)	×	Total assets to net worth	=	Net profits to net worth (percent)
Convenience food stores	2.9		3.6		10.4		1.7		17.7
Fast-food service outlets	4.7		1.8		8.5		2.2		18.4
Superstores	2.5		4.5		11.2		1.8		20.2
Hypermarkets	2.5		4.6		11.5		2.0		23.0
Bantam drugstores	3.4		2.7		9.2		1.6		14.7
Drug supermarkets	4.6		2.6		12.0		1.4		16.8
Super drugstores	3.6		4.1		14.8		1.3		19.2
Sporting goods supermarkets	4.9		2.1		10.3		1.3		13.4
Home improvement centers	2.8		3.0		8.4		2.4		20.2
Bantam discount stores	3.7		2.7		10.0		1.9		19.0
Bargain stores	4.0		2.6		10.4		1.8		18.7
Catalog-showrooms	4.7		1.5		7.1		2.2		15.6
Furniture warehouse showrooms	3.7		2.5		9.2		1.9		17.5

* The strategic profit model ratios may not multiply to the totals indicated because of rounding.

James M. Kenderdine and Bert C. McCammon, Jr., "Structure and Strategy in Retailing," in Henry W. Nash and Donald P. Robin (eds.), *Proceedings: Southern Marketing Association*, 1975, p. 118.

_____

[18] Ibid., p. 6.

By concentrating their efforts on a limited number of "core" markets, . . . companies have achieved single- and multiple-plant economies of scale, which suggests that market concentration programs will become increasingly important in the future. . . .

As consumer markets become more fragmented, a growing number of retailers will probably diversify their operations, despite the managerial problems and risks involved.[19]

Some retailers are beginning to respond with strategy models which are yielding sound growth and profits. A comparison of the operating results of the emerging retailing innovations shown in Table 3-2 with the performance of all retailing during 1968–74, shown in Table 3–1, reveals the success which the innovating institutions are experiencing. What are some of the innovations which are the keys to success?

1. The introduction of supermarket merchandising to a variety of new areas, such as drugs and sporting goods.
2. Merchandising efficiencies, such as those of the hypermarkets, which yield major economies of scale.
3. Reduced labor costs and high-volume economies in such categories of merchandising as furniture warehouses and catalog-showrooms.
4. Integrated merchandising around a concept, such as home improvement centers, which greatly outperform such traditional outlets as hardware stores and lumberyards.

All of these innovations in store types and merchandising strategies plus direct marketing and corporate diversification have led to superior market positions and major productivity increases which are reflected in increased profits.

OVERVIEW

Table 3–3 capsules the basic material which has been presented in this chapter. For each of the institutional types discussed, it presents the institution's period of fastest growth, the present stage of the institution's life cycle, what we perceive as the most appropriate explanatory hypothesis for the institution's development, and a representative example of the institution. The firms listed are simply examples of firms in the various classifications and do not necessarily have the characteristics specified for the institutional group as a whole.

Several generalized theories have emerged to explain the evolution of retail structure. These include the wheel of retailing; the retail accordion, or general-specific-general, hypothesis; natural selection or adaptive behavior; and the dialectical process. In their evolution many institutions exhibit characteristics of all of these theories. Further, no single theory can explain

---

[19] Kenderdine and McCammon, "Structure and Strategy in Retailing," p. 119.

TABLE 3-3

SUMMARY OF SELECTED ASPECTS OF RETAIL INSTITUTIONAL STRUCTURE

Institutional type	Period of fastest growth	Period from inception to maturity (years)	Stage of life cycle	Examples of explanatory hypotheses	Representative firms*
General store	1800–40	100	Declining	Retail accordion	A local institution
Single-line/specialty store	1820–40	100	Mature	Adaptive behavior	Hickory Farms
Department store	1860–1940	80	Mature	Dialectical process	Zayre
Variety store	1870–1930	50	Declining	Adaptive behavior	Morgan-Lindsay
Mail-order house	1915–50	50	Mature	Adaptive behavior	Sears
Corporate chain	1920–30	50	Mature	Adaptive behavior	Safeway
Discount store	1955–75	20	Mature	Adaptive behavior, dialectical process	K-Mart
Supermarket	1935–65	35	Mature	Dialectical process, wheel of retailing	A&P
Shopping center	1950–65	40	Mature	Adaptive behavior	Paramus
Cooperative	1930–50	40	Mature	Adaptive behavior	Ace Hardware
Gasoline station	1930–50	45	Mature	Dialectical process	Texaco
Convenience store	1965–75	20	Mature	Retail accordion, dialectical process	7–11
Fast-food operation	1960–75	15	Mature	Dialectical process	Shoney's
Hypermarket	1973–?	?	Early growth	Adaptive behavior	Laval (France)
Home development center	1965–80	15	Late growth	Retail accordion	Lowes
Boutique	1965–75	10	Late growth	Retail accordion	House of Nine
Warehouse retailing	1970–80	10	Late growth	Wheel of retailing	Levitz
Catalog-showroom	1970–80	10	Late growth	Retail accordion	Best Products

* These firms are representative of institutional types and are not necessarily in the stage of the life cycle specified for the institutional group as a whole.

the evolution of all types of retail institutions. At best, the existing theories are descriptive and perhaps somewhat explanatory. Certainly they are not predictive of institutional evolution. Also, they are not applicable without modification outside the retailing structure of the United States.

The retailing structure has experienced declining profit margins and increasing expenses during the past 20 years. Thus, major innovative approaches are called for in developing models which will insure adequate profitability and growth during the 1980s. Possible strategies are discussed in more detail in Chapter 12.

We might raise the question at this point, however, of the management activities which are appropriate at the various stages of the life cycle of retail firms. Three noted retailing persons have offered their views on the retailing strategies appropriate at each stage of the institutional life cycle. These are illustrated in Table 3–4.

The consensus of the marketing management literature is that, as is apparently true of the product life cycle, the institutional life cycle cannot be avoided but that it can be extended. Possible strategies for extension are discussed more fully in Chapter 22. Essentially, the mature institutions need to tap new market segments while holding existing customers, to become more innovative in merchandising strategies, and to adopt various risk reduction strategies. Suppliers of these firms are also particularly vulnerable to decline. For example, with the initial appearance of a new type of retail institution, suppliers may be hesitant to work with the institution for fear of affecting existing channel relationships. On the other hand, if they do not respond quickly enough, minor suppliers will enter and will adversely affect their market share.

One retailing expert maintains that the supermarket is in the declining stage of its growth and that strategies must be developed to extend its life cycle. "Since the supermarket's share of the total food dollar peaked at around 70 percent in 1965—declining to 64 percent and still falling in 1975—retailers have come up with at least a half dozen special types of stores in an effort to get growth out of a shrinking market."[20] He indicates that the viable alternative choices available for new outlets include a jumbo superstore, a combination store, a warehouse store, or a hypermarket.

Increasing attention is being given to secondary markets as opposed to a previous almost total concentration on major metropolitan areas. Warehouse showrooms, catalog-showrooms, and various approaches employing the mass merchandising supermarket concept appear to be having success even in such diverse lines as toys and recreation equipment. Specialty stores are becoming increasingly important, as is a market intensification strategy in contrast to the more traditional approach to corporate expansion. As has been noted, "Like other chains, Safeway is finding it harder to keep increasing its total selling space. Slower growth in the suburbs and a tight commer-

---

[20] "Supermarket Industry Must Deal with Its Decline," *Supermarket News*, March 28, 1977, p. 20.

TABLE 3-4
MANAGEMENT ACTIVITIES IN THE LIFE CYCLE

Area or subject of concern	Stage of life cycle development			
	1. Innovation	2. Accelerated development	3. Maturity	4. Decline
Market characteristics				
Number of competitors	Very few	Moderate	Many direct competitors Moderate indirect competition	Moderate direct competition Many indirect competitors
Rate of sales growth	Very rapid	Rapid	Moderate to slow	Slow or negative
Level of profitability	Low to moderate	High	Moderate	Very low
Duration of new innovations	3 to 5 years	5 to 6 years	Indefinite	Indefinite
Appropriate retailer actions				
Investment/growth/risk decisions	Investment minimization—high risks accepted	High levels of investment to sustain growth	Tightly controlled growth in untapped markets	Minimal capital expenditures and only when essential
Central management concerns	Concept refinement through adjustment and experimentation	Establishing a preemptive market position	Excess capacity and "overstoring" Prolonging maturity and revising the retail concept	Engaging in a "run-out" strategy
Use of management control techniques	Minimal	Moderate	Extensive	Moderate
Most successful management style	Entrepreneurial	Centralized	"Professional"	Caretaker
Appropriate supplier actions				
Channel strategy	Develop a preemptive market position	Hold market position	Maintain profitable sales	Avoid excessive costs
Channel problems	Possible antagonism of other accounts	Possible antagonism of other accounts	Dealing with more scientific retailers	Servicing accounts at a profit
Channel research	Identification of key innovations	Identification of other retailers adopting the innovation	Initial screening of new innovation opportunities	Active search for new innovation opportunities
Trade incentives	Direct financial support	Price concessions	New price incentives	None

Source: William Davidson, Albert Bates, and Stephen Bass, "The Retail Life Cycle," Harvard Business Review, November–December 1976, p. 92. Copyright 1976 by the President and Fellows of Harvard College, All rights reserved.

cial real estate market are forcing the big chains to rely more heavily on expanding existing stores."[21] The late 1970s and the 1980s will be an exciting time for retailers working to meet the challenges of a changing environment. The elements of change include high energy costs, the decay of the inner cities, lower population growth, an older population, more working women, continued inflation, and increasing concern for the environment.

KEY CONCEPTS

The wheel of retailing	Supermarkets
The retail accordion	Shopping centers
The dialectical process	Cooperatives
Natural selection	Gasoline service stations
Patterns of retail evolution	Convenience stores
The general store	Fast-food outlets
Single-line/specialty stores	Home improvement centers
The department store	The boutique
Variety stores	Warehouse retailing
Mail-order houses	The catalog showroom

DISCUSSION QUESTIONS

1. What is the value to you as students of retailing of studying the theories of retail institutional change?

2. Discuss the strengths and weaknesses of the following theories of change in the retail institutional structure: the wheel of retailing, the retail accordion, the dialectical process, and the adaptive behavior model.

3. What major environmental changes can affect the structure of retailing? Give current examples of each change and of its impact on retailing.

4. Discuss the evolution and current status of the general store, the supermarket, and the home improvement center.

5. Why did cooperatives emerge in the early 1930s?

6. What are the reasons for the rapid growth of warehouse retailing and catalog-showrooms?

7. What are the basic merchandising strategies of the hypermarkets which have emerged in Europe? Are these systems likely to be developed in the United States? Why or why not?

8. Do you believe that the corporate chain and discount mass merchandising are institutional types or merchandising philosophies?

9. Why have the net profits of most retailers continued to decline during the past two decades? What strategies can be adopted to offset the declining profit margins?

---

[21] "Safeway Selling Nongrocery Items," p. 56.

10. Why are the net profits of the various types of retailing innovations shown in Table 3–2 higher than those found for more conventional types of retailing?

11. Based on the discussion of the various theories of retail change, what is likely to happen to the institutions which are currently classified as innovators?

12. Are we likely to develop a universal theory of retail change? Why or why not?

PROJECTS

1. Show how two specific stores or store groups (for example, fast-food chains), are going through the developmental process using the theories discussed in the text, that is, the wheel of retailing, the retail accordion, natural selection, or the dialectical process.

2. Make a contact with a retail firm with which you can establish rapport. Explain that you want to trace the evolutionary development of the firm's organizational structure over the years the firm has been in existence (thus, the firm should have been in existence for a number of years). Show changes over time in functions, people, and approach to the market. Attempt to explain from the environmental conditions at the time of the changes why the changes occurred. Use organization charts to show the changes.

3. Some institutions about which little is known today seem to have moved through the institutional life cycle. One such institutional type is the Army-Navy Surplus store. Utilize one or more explanations of retail evolution to place this type of operation within a proper context. Try to find out when, why, how, and perhaps where the concept developed. What are such stores today? Have they changed? Are they viable in the present era? Try to come up with other examples of such institutions. What about the traditional "five-and-ten" store? You might do a similar analysis on this institution.

4. Use the current periodic literature to trace A&P's changing market penetration and image over the past few years. Assume a critical posture, and try to analyze how and why A&P has done what it has in each rather dramatic promotional change (for example, WEO, Price and Pride). If you are in an A&P market area, you might go farther and get customer and perhaps professional opinions on the occurrences of the last years.

5. One of the most (if not the most) dramatic business failures in history has been the demise of W. T. Grant. From the current publications find out as much as you can about "how and why." Then interview some professional retailers to get their opinions of what happened. After that, get the opinions of some consumers in an area where Grant had a store. Tie it all together in an evaluative essay on this tragic business debacle.

6. In retailing there are classic examples of companies which have grown, prospered, and become integral parts of their communities. We all know of those such as Sears, Penneys, and Marshall Field through books written about them. In your own hometown there may be a local store with a fascinating history. Look for one, and do a critical history of the evolution and impacts of a "local institution"—most likely it will be a department store. Bring the store's history up-to-date, and predict its future, based on any analytic tools at your disposal.

CASES

Case 1.   Bob Majors had just returned from Europe, where he was very impressed with the success of the hypermarkets. As the owner of a large shopping mall chain here, Bob decided to investigate the possibility of establishing a hypermarket in the United States. Bob has called his management team together to discuss this idea and is encountering some dissension. Joe Williams, Bob's operations manager, feels that the American public would not react favorably to a 250,000-square-foot store. Since there are currently no hypermarkets in the United States, Joe admits that he has no facts to back his conclusion. Bob Majors has commissioned Joe to develop and report on the major differences between the European hypermarket and the American shopping mall. In addition, Joe is to analyze these differences and to assess whether the concept will work in the United States. Assume you are Joe, and contrast shopping malls and hypermarkets. Do you think that the concept of the Hypermarket would work in the United States?

Case 2.   Cline Winston has been relatively successful in his convenience store chain. He has four stores in a trading area of approximately 80,000 people. His net profit as a percent of sales has run at approximately 2.3 for the last few years and his return to net worth has been around 17.5 percent. In the past few months his traffic has decreased and sales have dropped off slightly. It is clear to Winston what is happening. The major supermarket chains are staying open until midnight in many competitive locations. The supermarket prices are lower than his and the variety and assortment of merchandise are much more extensive than in his Quickie Marts. He wonders about the future of his (and *all*) convenience stores.

4

ORGANIZATION OF RESOURCES

Things happen through people!

The organizational structure allows for an efficient approach to accomplishing the established goals of a company.

As a practicing retail store manager for J. C. Penney, I believe that the authors have presented an accurate picture of retail organization: the way it has developed, the way it is today and the variations, and the current trends.

In my opinion the purposes of this chapter have been achieved.

H. P. Herbert, Store Manager
J. C. Penney Company, Inc.
Columbus, Ohio

All business activities must be organized to accomplish the objectives of the firm. But how should they be organized, and how should goals be set? The type of structure selected depends on a variety of factors, including the size of the establishment, the number of the firm's outlets, the type of goods or services sold, the availability of capital, and where the outlets are located. Retail organization, then, is simply the bringing together of productive resources to accomplish the goals of the firm. The overall objective is to satisfy customer needs while making a profit.

Organization is not a particularly important problem for small retailers, who may have only two or three employees. As stores increase in size and number, however, a more formalized approach to organization is necessary. Thus, a form of organization is always being sought that will lead to the most efficient operation and bring the greatest profits.

Because of the importance of organizational structure in retailing, the purposes of this chapter are to:

1. Acquaint students of retailing with the approaches to setting goals and objectives for the firm.
2. Present the basic principles of organizing to accomplish goals and objectives.
3. Introduce the basic patterns of organization in department and chain stores.
4. Review the current trends in retail organizational arrangements.

Typically, the same activities must be performed whether a retailer is large or small. These include the purchasing of merchandise and its preparation for resale, attracting customers, selling the merchandise, keeping proper records, and evaluating the organization's performance. Thus, the degree of specialization and not the functions performed distinguishes the small firm from the large one.

OBJECTIVES FOR RETAIL MANAGEMENT

How does one determine where an organization is headed and what employees are supposed to do? Answers to these questions help to set objectives for the firm and to suggest the appropriate organizational structure to carry out the objectives. The framework for this portion of the chapter is presented in Figure 4–1.

Situation analysis

The setting of goals and objectives and obtaining the necessary organizational resources are best accomplished by a situation analysis of the firm. The retailer needs to be able to answer such questions as where the firm is today, how the firm became what it is, and where it will go if existing policies and organizational structures are not changed. This type of analysis includes a

FIGURE 4–1

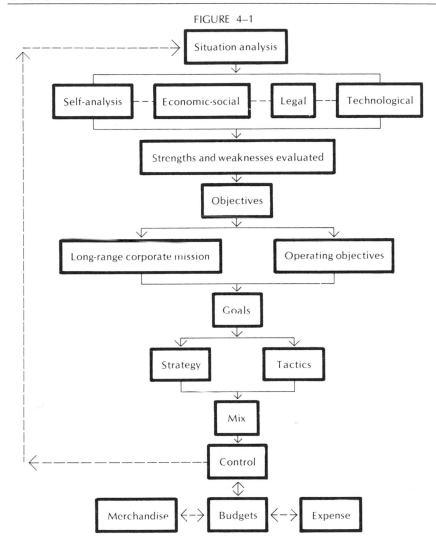

focus on the total environment for the firm as specified in Chapter 1—namely, the economic, competitive, legal, and technological environments. By this type of intensive analysis, the strengths and weaknesses of the firm can be identified. Thus, a situation analysis is simply an organized way to view the world.

In carrying out the situation analysis, the retailer begins with a *self-analysis* (or retail audit) internal to the firm, which includes information on the areas that have accounted for the firm's primary sales growth over the past several years, on the areas that have caused the greatest liabilities or been the greatest trouble spots, and on customers and noncustomers.

Necessary questions about the *competitive environment* center on a comparison of competitor performance to the performance of the firm in question. For example, who are the competitors and who are likely to be competitors in the near future? What is their share of the relevant market? How has their share changed over the past several years? How does their growth compare to that of our firm?

A focus on the *economic environment* includes an analysis of the basic characteristics and trends of the population in terms of age, income, occupation, race, and related dimensions. What dimensions of the population have accounted for the greatest share of the firm's growth in the past several years? What is the long-run outlook for the market segments and geographic areas being served?

The *legal and technological environments* are covered separately in Chapters 9 and 11. The legal dimensions include an analysis of the changes in the various regulations at the local, state, and national levels which will affect the firm. Examples include the so-called Sunday closing laws, the opportunities for price advertising of prescription drugs, and the legislative uncertainties about the status of electronic funds transfer systems.

The situation analysis thus identifies the *strengths and weaknesses of the firm*. By so doing, it also identifies problems and opportunities which can be addressed in the organization of the firm's resources.

After making this type of analysis, the retailer should be able to answer such questions as what quality of merchandise should be stocked, how complete the merchandise lines should be, what services or products will be needed by customers in the future, what opportunities appear to exist to serve new markets, and what products will be needed to capitalize on the potential markets. Other questions that the retailer should be able to answer concern the likely new forms of competition and competitors, the socioeconomic class of primary target consumers, the kinds of services that should be offered, the number and type of employees necessary to staff the organization, and the appropriate organizational structure.

For example, we might find that the overall market share of the firm has increased by 5 percent in the last eight years; that population, per capita income, and average level of education are stable in our market area; that the work force is increasing; that new and larger types of chain stores, particularly discounters, are likely to be in the area within the next five years; and that competitors have an advantage in hours of operation, location, and image. Further, the firm is not attracting enough newcomers; its customers don't know what services it offers; and upper-income consumers do not seem to believe that the employees have the expertise to meet their needs. Finally, organizational rigidities and overcentralization of functions may be found to prohibit rapid response to changing market conditions. What can the firm do in the face of such problems? Let's look at the options which are available in implementing a plan of action.

Setting objectives

The situation analysis enables management to establish realistic goals and objectives and to organize resources accordingly. Establishing such goals and objectives require many hours of management time. However, without them, no basis exists for evaluating the firm's past performance or its current position. It is not possible to know how you are doing without knowing specifically what you are trying to accomplish. Management must decide where it wants to go before it decides how to get there. Without specific objectives for the firm, the employees may pursue what *they* perceive to be the proper objectives.

Objectives may be viewed at several levels. Long-range corporate objectives are typically established by top management. These are really the so-called missions of the firm, and considerable latitude is allowed to personnel in carrying them out. They may indicate that the firm will (1) satisfy the merchandising needs of consumers at a profit; (2) grow through a market intensification and penetration program rather than by entering new geographic markets; (3) attempt to achieve before-tax profits of 20 percent.

Operating objectives are then set which are in harmony with the agreed-upon missions. The objectives are reviewed and revised periodically by management at various levels of the firm. Operating objectives may be to: (1) increase consumer awareness of the merchandising mix offered by the firm; (2) create an image of the sophisticated "with-it" outlet; (3) increase the penetration of higher income market segments; (4) become the dominant retail institution in the community for a given type of merchandise.

Finally, specific goals must be set. Goals involve all personnel within the retail organization. Further, they should be very specific and designed to accomplish corporate and operating-level objectives. Individuals within the organization should each have a personal goal toward which they are striving. The goals must be specifically related to marketing strategies. For example, goals might be to: (1) increase the number of charge accounts by 10 percent during the next 12 months among consumers with incomes of over $25,000 annually; (2) achieve a 40 percent recognition of the slogan of the firm during the next 12 months. Goals should be written, consistent with one another, realistic, flexible, and measurable.

From the retailer's perspective, the strategies and tactics selected to accomplish the goals involve the manipulation of products or services, prices, and communications to meet the needs of the agreed-upon target consumers.

Control

No plans will work exactly as expected. Competitors may not behave as anticipated; unexpected changes may occur in the economic environment;

and unexpected personnel problems may occur. Thus, we must have some method of keeping track of the firm's performance. Controls are necessary to make sure that the firm achieves agreed-upon objectives or to discover reasons why the objectives are not being accomplished so that action can be taken. Controls are established by the use of periodic reports which reflect the degree of progress toward such objectives as sales levels, amount of market penetration, and number of new charge customers. Questions must be answered about the desired frequency of reports, who gets them and their contents.

Thus, control is simply the managerial function of checking to determine whether agreed-upon objectives are being pursued. It involves setting measurable objectives and goals, checking and appraising performance, and taking corrective action when necessary.

The budget is a control device with which the manager will probably be in continuous contact. Management must learn to accept and live with budgets. Although the preparation of a budget is part of the planning process, budget application is part of the controlling function because budgets are simply preestablished standards against which the actual performance of a department or firm will be measured. Certainly whatever can be accomplished without a budget can usually be done in a much better fashion with one.

THE ORGANIZING FUNCTION

Employees are the major resource of any firm as it seeks to serve its customers. Thus, the organization and management of this resource in carrying out agreed-upon objectives occupy a key amount of management time. How do we organize human beings? In any organization, management must accomplish the following: achieve acceptance of agreed-upon goals; strike a balance between specialization and coordination; balance responsibility and authority; develop the proper span of control; and provide for organizational growth by balancing stability and flexibility. These organizational problems in carrying out the goals and objectives of the firm are among the greatest challenges faced by retailing management.

The classic organizational principles

Basically, four classic organizational principles have been developed over the years to help management coordinate material and human resources within the framework of a formal structure of tasks and authority in meeting agreed-upon objectives. These four principles are:

1. The principle of specialization of labor.
2. The principle of departmentalization.
3. The span of control principle.
4. The unity of command principle.

These principles answer such questions as the nature and content of each job, the way in which jobs should be grouped, the size of the various groups, and the distribution of authority within the organization.

Specialization of labor is the single most important principle of organization. All of us are affected by this principle every day. It guides us in determining the content of individual jobs. Generally, specialization of labor increases with the size of the firm.

Departmentalization carries the concept of specialization further and determines how jobs should be grouped. Should they be organized by type of customer served, on the basis of location of retail outlets in a multi-outlet firm or on the basis of operations performed? For example, if one thinks in terms of organizing by type of customer served, a home improvement center may have personnel who specialize in sales to contractors, whereas others specialize in sales to ultimate consumers. Grouping activities on the basis of location may lead to separate structures for the main store and for branch stores in the multi-unit firm. Finally, organization in terms of operations performed will yield specialists in such areas as finance and control, merchandising, and selling.

Span of control addresses the question of how many persons should report to a supervisor. Thus, in essence it determines the size of a department. Classical organization theory suggests that the span of control of a supervisor should be small because a limit exists to the number of persons with whom an individual can work at one time. Span of control, however, depends on a variety of factors, including the competence of the supervisor and subordinates, the extent to which the supervisor must carry out nonmanagerial tasks, the similarity of the various functions to be performed, the degree to which procedures are standardized, and the physical dispersion of persons and products.

The *unity of command* concept can be viewed as a series of superior/subordinate relationships. No person should be under the direct control of more than one supervisor in performing job tasks. Thus, the subordinate receives authority and decision-making power from and reports to one individual. An unbroken chain of command should exist from top to bottom, or unnecessary frustration and confusion will occur.

Organization charts, which are familiar to most of us, typically reflect elements of all of these principles of organization.

ORGANIZATIONAL STRUCTURE

Organization charts are simply pictures which depict the functions of a firm and its general lines of authority and responsibility. The charts should present a clear picture of the organization. Properly prepared, they contribute to good morale as well as specialization of functions and the delineation of tasks, both of which allow the fixing of responsibility and the delegation of routine duties.

The organization chart for a small retail store is simple. The extreme might simply be a one-person organization. In any case, the difference between large and small organizations is primarily one of specialization of employees. All retailers, regardless of size, endeavor to dispose of merchandise at a profit.

Typically the primary responsibility of all employees in a small firm is selling merchandise. Other duties are performed whenever time permits. Few communication problems exist, and the manager is able to maintain tight control over all employees.

Organizational possibilities

As a retail organization grows, the owner-manager cannot continue to perform all functions. Thus, efforts are made to divide the job responsibilities. Specialization begins to occur on a variety of bases. The most common organizational structures are based on functions, products, geography, or some combination of these possibilities.

The most typical specialization emerges along functional lines. Thus, separate persons may be appointed to assume responsibility for such functions as merchandising, operations, control, promotion, and personnel. Merchandising and operations will probably be the first specialities to emerge.

Likewise, some retail organizations, particularly supermarkets, tend to be organized on the basis of product lines. Thus, in supermarkets, department managers are appointed for groceries, meat, produce, and perhaps frozen foods. These classes of products define the various elements of the organization. Drugstores may also use this type of organizational structure.

A third organizational possibility is that of geography. The multi-unit or chain organization is a good example of organization on this basis. Here we may see the appointment of regional, divisional, and district managers. These appointments reflect the geographic relationships in the firm. Branch managers and downtown store managers may also be appointed. This type of organizational structure, since it refers to places, resembles organization on the basis of geography.

Finally, some stores may use a combination of the various organizational possibilities. Thus, even though a department store may be organized on the basis of functions, merchandising is likely to be based on product lines. Also, the store may have branch locations and thus some of its organizational dimensions may be based on geography.

In the organization charts in the following sections, the various types of structural possibilities are discussed.

The department store and the chain store organization probably have the two most distinctive types of organizational structures and therefore provide excellent examples of alternatives. Let's focus on these to refine our insights into patterns for organizing resources in retailing.

ORGANIZATION IN THE DEPARTMENT STORE

The department store was the first large-scale retailing institution in the United States. It emerged during a period when retailing consisted primarily of small single-line and specialty stores. Over time these stores were brought together under one roof, but they were still basically autonomous in buying and selling merchandise. For years, buying and selling remained the responsibility of each individual department manager. This arrangement allowed close contact with customers and the tailoring of merchandise offerings to customer needs. It also allowed the individual departments to operate as profit centers with a strong incentive to keep costs as low as possible.

Even today, smaller department store organizational charts depict relatively few separate functional responsibilities. Some division of labor does occur, however. Typically, two basic functions are recognized in the small, family-operated department store. These are (1) the functions which relate to the operation of the store itself and (2) the merchandising function. This simple organization is shown in the accompanying chart.

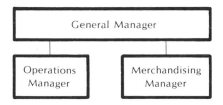

The operations function refers to responsibility for maintenance of the building, coordination of delivery, the stockroom, service, purchasing, and similar activities. The merchandising function includes buying and selling. Pricing is typically also a part of this function. The merchandising function also includes merchandising budget supervision; advertising, displays, and various other promotional activities; and inventory planning.

As a department store continues to grow in size, specialization is next typically introduced in the nonselling activities. Ordinarily, the third position to emerge is that of the controller. The controller handles the financial affairs of the organization. The position includes responsibility for such functions as expense budgeting and control; compliance with local, state, and national regulations; the preparation of reports for governmental and other public

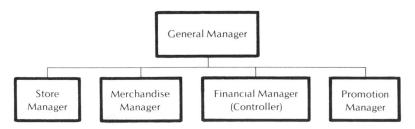

agencies; payroll; and payments to suppliers. The fourth function separated out is typically promotion.

Historically all of the persons who performed these functions typically reported to a general manager. The basic problem with this type of arrangement was the overlap in the supervision of the salespersons. The salesclerks were supervised by the various department managers and were also supervised by a general manager, defying the principle of unit of command. Conflicts often occurred as a result.

The Mazur plan

In a 1927 text on department store organization, Paul M. Mazur introduced the well-known Mazur plan. Under his plan, each department buyer-manager was given the responsibility for expenses and profit in the department. Thus, the supervision of both sales and merchandising resided solely with the department manager. The Mazur plan was the basic plan used in most department store organizations from the 1930s through the 1950s (see Figure 4–2).

The buying responsibilities of the departmental manager under the Mazur plan included preliminary merchandise plans and budgets, which were agreed upon with the division merchandise manager; knowledge of fashion trends and prices; and contacts with manufacturers and other sources of merchandise. The departmental manager's selling responsibilities included planning for the use of the salespersons in the department, providing salespersons with information about merchandise and fashion trends, merchandise display, and similar activities.

As the number of departments within the department store increased over the years, the span of control on occasion became too large for the merchandise manager to supervise effectively. Thus, an additional layer of management was introduced into the Mazur plan in the form of divisional merchandise managers. These persons supervised groups of departments and reported to the chief executive officer.

Modifications of the Mazur plan

A variety of changes have occurred in the Mazur plan during the past 20 years. Many of these address the problem of organization for multi-unit stores.

The primary controversy is over whether the major decisions for each of the units in the firm should be made centrally or whether decision making should be decentralized. Centralization and decentralization represent the extremes of possible organizational formats.

Advantages exist for both types of organizational structures. The centralized approach allows a high level of expertise and specialization within the organization. Also, significant economies of scale may accrue in pur-

FIGURE 4–2
THE MAZUR PLAN OF RETAIL ORGANIZATION

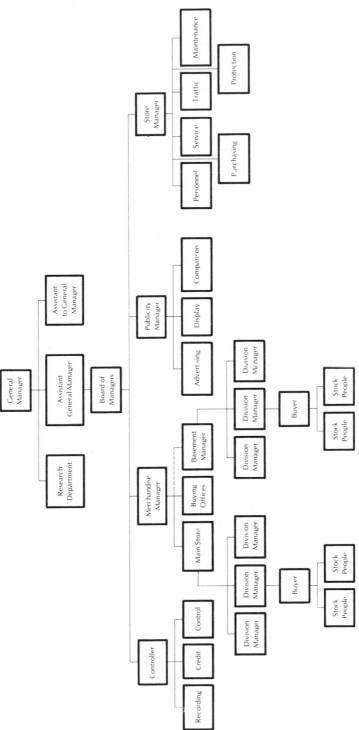

Source: Paul Mazur, *Principles of Organization Applied to Modern Retailing* (New York: Harper & Brothers 1927), frontispiece.

chasing and related activities. This philosophy is typified by the organization of Victoria Station restaurants. Right from the start "Victoria Station began building a system of controls and specifications that gives individual restaurant managers little to do but hire waiters and greet customers."[1] The same was true for Genesco, whose retail outlets include Bonwit Teller and S. H. Kress, when it unseated its chairman of the board in 1976, allegedly because "he centralized management to the point of frustrating the company's executives and causing red tape and delay. Operations were virtually paralyzed by paperwork."[2]

The decentralized, multi-unit operation may be particularly appropriate when decisions must be made at the local level. For example, merchandise requirements may differ widely for the various outlets in the group. Thus, merchandise may best be purchased locally. This is the philosophy of Carter Hawley Hale stores where divisions handle all their own buying, merchandising, and marketing. They consult headquarters only for yearly operating budgets, senior personnel changes, and long-range policy or expansion plans.[3]

Branch store arrangements

Branch stores account for a large portion of department store sales but present a variety of organizational difficulties for the parent firm. One approach is to have all major functions controlled centrally in the main store. Typically this approach is followed when a store has only a few branches. The centralized organization may also work well when the merchandise sold in the branches does not vary widely from that sold by the parent store. Also, when the branches are close and managerial talents would be expensive to develop, the centralized approach is usually followed, particularly if the branch operations are viewed as secondary in importance to those of the parent store.

As the number of branches increases, the highly centralized approach becomes difficult. The strain is particularly hard on buyers. Thus, each branch may eventually be viewed as a separate organization with its own management and buying staff. This allows flexibility in responding to local conditions, but may involve the duplication of management functions and costs. Some economies of scale may also be lost. The decentralized or separate store approach is most likely to be followed when major distinctions exist in types of merchandise sold in the various branches, when the branches are some distance from the main store, or when the branches are viewed as major parts of the organization.

---

[1] *Business Week,* August 9, 1976, p. 31.

[2] "What Undid Jarman: Paperwork Paralysis," *Business Week,* January 24, 1977, p. 67.

[3] "Carter Hawley Hale, Carriage-Trade Merchants," *Business Week,* October 4, 1976, p. 90; also Eleanor Carruth, "Carter Hawley Hale Acquires a Touch of Class," *Fortune,* December 1976, p. 116.

Under decentralized merchandising, only the merchandising function is decentralized to the branch store level. This occurs when the merchandise needs of the parent store and the branches differ widely. Also, the organizational approaches to sales promotion may be quite different. However, the merchandising and promotional functions for the various stores may still occasionally be brought together in a coordinated approach on a periodic basis.

It was recently noted that in a variation of this plan Gimbel had "brought in a complete new level of divisional group managers within the branch store. . . . The group managers supervise the presentation and supply of merchandise within a branch."[4]

Probably the predominant trend today is for department stores to view each unit in the firm as a separate outlet of a multi-unit organization. Under this approach, all major management responsibilities, including buying, reside at a single headquarters. All outlets have equal organizational status in the firm. Historically this has been true for Federated Department Stores, as noted by the president of Goldsmith's department store (in Memphis), a member of the Federated group. "Federated has . . . sought to maintain its stores' strong local family identification by keeping its distance."[5] Even this may be changing, however. "Divisional autonomy, a hallowed tradition for Federated and other department store groups, is gradually giving way to tighter control from central headquarters."[6]

The separation of buying and selling

Arguments go in both directions as to the desirability of separating the buying and selling responsibilities in the organization.

Persons opposing the separation of the two functions argue as follows:

1. The buyer must have contact with the consumer so as to be able to interpret the consumer's needs.
2. Persons who buy merchandise should also be responsible for selling it.
3. It's easier to pinpoint merchandising successes and failures when the two functions are combined.

Persons who argue in favor of the separation of the two functions make such arguments as the following:

1. If the two functions are combined, buying is likely to have more importance than selling.
2. Salespersons can be shifted more easily under this arrangement.

[4] "Kramer's Campaign to Rebuild Gimbel," *Business Week*, March 29, 1976, pp. 32–33.

[5] "Goldsmith's Is Tying a Ribbon on Oak Court Showpiece," *Memphis Commercial Appeal*, September 12, 1976, p. 5.

[6] "Federated: The Most Happy Retailer Grows Faster and Better," *Business Week*, October 18, 1976, p. 75.

3. Buying and selling require different types of job functions and different job skills.

The tendency today is to separate the buying and selling responsibilities in the department store. The growth of branches has been a major factor in this trend. Also, the increasing popularity of the discount department store and the selling of national brands through mass media advertising have caused a decline in the personal selling function in many outlets. Consumers are assuming greater initiative in informing themselves about merchandise.

In addition, trends toward the creation of specialized departments in the department store have made it necessary to separate the two functions. Historically, a dress department buyer would purchase dresses for sale in the dress department under the supervision of a different buyer. However, centralizing the buying function makes it easy to regroup merchandise to suit the needs of the consumer without regard for departmental buying rigidities. Thus, for example, a men's leisure-time boutique may feature such complementary merchandise as sportswear, tennis togs, and golf clubs. The merchandise mix must typically be purchased by several different buyers even though the merchandise is sold by the same salespersons.

The emergence of merchandising based on customer-oriented classifications also argues for the separation of buying from selling. This approach to merchandising focuses on homogeneous groups of merchandise as the most desirable units for control. The distinction between this classification and department merchandising is primarily one of size. Customer-oriented merchandising tends to represent units of selling responsibility, whereas departments represent units of buying responsibility. Customer-oriented classifications are much smaller than departments. They may be on such bases as price or customer use, age, or size. Thus merchandise can be regrouped to suit the needs of the customer. We have therefore seen the emergence of ski shops, bath shops, and kitchen shops, among others. Departmental barriers are broken down in this type of organization. The focus is on fitting merchandise lines together from a sales point of view without having to be unduly concerned about accounting and buying problems.

Various approaches may be taken to organization for separation of the two functions. One approach is to have a merchandise manager and a sales manager, both of whom report to the general manager. Other plans allow the buying and selling function to be separated but to remain under the control of the merchandise manager. Figure 4–3 shows the separation of the buying and selling functions. The general merchandise manager is responsible for merchandise buying, whereas selling is the responsibility of the vice president for the branch stores.

Still, the issue of separation of the two functions has not been totally resolved. "Today one of the major problems of a group department store is the effective coordination of the central buying organization with the store or regional selling organization. At the root of the problem is the division of

FIGURE 4-3
PIZITZ, INC.

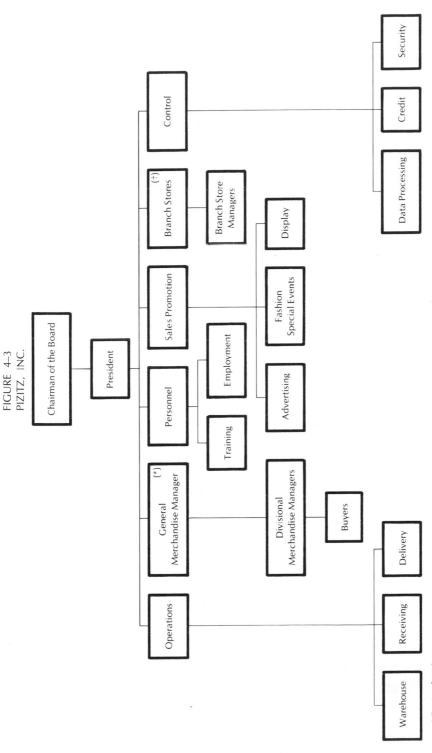

* Buying functions.
† Selling functions.

responsibility between buying and selling and the difficulties of coordination."[7]

Ownership groups

Many department stores which were once independently owned have been merged into such ownership groups as Federated Department Stores and Allied Stores. These differ from chain organizations such as Sears and Wards. Stores which are part of ownership groups typically retain their own name. Few customers are aware of their affiliation with the larger group. Also, most of the management functions which were performed at the store level prior to merger into the ownership group are retained locally. These functions include merchandising, operations, publicity, and control. For example, Goldsmith's of Memphis and Rich's of Atlanta are both part of the Federated ownership group.

Some centralized services are provided for the benefit of the ownership group so as to obtain economies of scale. These may include computer facilities, central buying opportunities, research, and similar functions. As noted earlier, the ownership groups are gradually exerting more control over the individual stores.

Examples of department store organizational structure

Small store. Figure 4–3 depicts the organizational structure for a relatively small department store which consists of the main store and seven branches. Six of the branches are in the same metropolitan area as the main store. Total sales for the firm are under $100 million. The organization chart depicts the functions of the main store. Vice presidents occupy the following positions: operations, merchandising, personnel, promotion, branches, and control. All management functions are decentralized to the branch level except that of merchandising, which is handled centrally. Occasionally, coordinated promotions may occur for all of the eight outlets. Buying and selling are separate at both the branches and the main store.

Since the chain store form of organization is not unique to the department store field, it is discussed in the following section. We must note, however, that most large department store organizations will be of a chain type. Indeed, it has been noted that "as the department store itself becomes a chain with centralized buying it can lose agility and attunement to local markets."[8]

Large store. Figures 4–4 through 4–7 depict the organizational arrangements at the various levels of the J. C. Penney organization. The organization charts for the department store range from the organization at corporate headquarters through successive layers of the organization to the organiza-

---

[7] D. S. Greensmith, "Productivity: Lewis/Selfridges Cites Yardsticks to Improve ROI," *Stores,* August 1976, p. 30.

[8] Carruth, "Carter Hawley Hale," p. 116.

FIGURE 4–4
ORGANIZATIONAL STRUCTURE—REPORTING TO THE CHAIRMAN OF THE BOARD:
J. C. PENNEY COMPANY, INC., MAY 1976

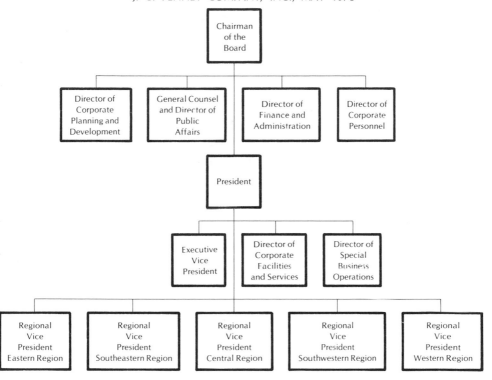

FIGURE 4–5
ORGANIZATIONAL STRUCTURE REPORTING TO THE EXECUTIVE VICE PRESIDENT:
J. C. PENNEY COMPANY, INC., MAY 1976

FIGURE 4–6
ORGANIZATIONAL STRUCTURE BY GEOGRAPHIC REGION:
J. C. PENNEY COMPANY, INC., MAY 1976

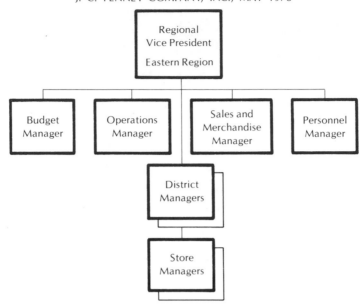

FIGURE 4–7
ORGANIZATIONAL STRUCTURE FOR A FULL-LINE DEPARTMENT STORE:
J. C. PENNEY COMPANY, INC., MAY 1976

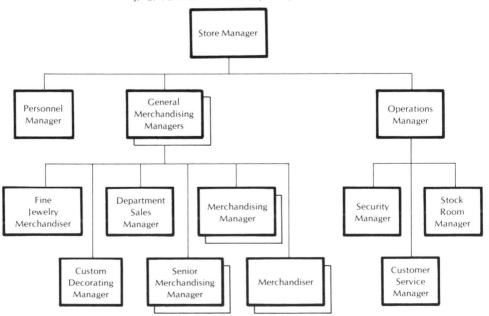

tion of a "typical" Penney's full-line department store. These organization charts typify the structure of large national department store organizations.

CHAIN STORE ORGANIZATIONAL STRUCTURES

Many of the functions which are performed by a department store organization are also performed by a chain store organization and do not need further discussion. However, a chain organizational structure is distinct from a department store organizational structure in several respects. These include the following: (1) In the chain organization responsibilities tend to be more centralized in the headquarters or home office. (2) The chain organization consists of more divisions than does the typical department store, especially real estate, transportation, and warehousing. (3) The chain store is characterized by tighter supervision and follow-up on store activities. (4) More up to date and frequent reports for control purposes are required by the chain organization so that top management can keep a constant eye on individual store operations.

Centralized management

The most distinguishing characteristic of the chain store is the tendency toward centralized management. The functions of buying, promotion, personnel, and control are typically performed in the central, or perhaps the divisional, headquarters. Selling is likely to be the only decentralized function. In addition, more layers of supervision exist in the chain store than in the department store. As has been noted of Sears:

> The even bigger push is on coordinating merchandising among the various stores. Inevitably, this means less autonomy for store managers and more centralized control in Chicago. In the past, more decision-making was left to the division managers within a store. But as Sears began changing its image and adding fashions, the people at the top assumed more responsibility.[9]

Woolco has also centralized more of its distribution and merchandising.[10] At Montgomery Ward, the policy of allowing local stores to override orders from headquarters has changed. The stores previously had the prerogative of vetoing recommended promotional pricing and advertising. Now a system of mutual cooperation has been established whereby the regional executives and buyers get together with the executive vice president for merchandising at quarterly meetings and agree on plans for action at the local level.[11]

In investigating the collapse of W. T. Grant Company, which may be the most significant bankruptcy in U.S. corporate history, we found a dramatic difference in centralization. Grant for many reasons adhered to the concept

---

[9] "Sears Identity Crisis," *Business Week*, December 8, 1975, pp. 55–56.

[10] "The Problems That Are Upsetting Woolworths," *Business Week*, June 29, 1974, p. 72.

[11] "Where Montgomery Ward Is Outpacing Sears," *Business Week*, January 19, 1974, p. 39.

that its store managers were entrepreneurs who should run their own stores. The managers were paid a salary plus a percentage of sales and profits as high as 8 percent after expenses. Grant top management allowed store managers to order 80 percent of their merchandise, price it, and then send the invoices to the central office for payment. As a result of this decentralized system, in the words of a former Grant executive, "We could have three stores within a ten-mile radius charging three different prices on the same item. We were competing with ourselves."[12]

Standardization

Standardization is a further distinguishing characteristic of chains. Both centralization and standardization by chains can contribute to operating efficiencies. For example, major savings accrue from centralized buying. Many chains are also integrated to the extent that they operate their own warehouses. This wholesaling function allows savings on transportation and distribution and savings from centralized marking and receiving. Some firms, such as A&P, may actually manufacture their own products. Control is thus assured from the factory to the consumer.

Standardization also assures similarity in merchandising, pricing, and layout. Thus in a chain such as A&P consumers may shop all over the United States and still feel at home because the fixtures and prices are basically the same. Equipment, supplies, and fixtures are likewise standardized to ensure maximum operating economies.

Despite the history of centralization in chains, increasing evidence of some decentralization can be observed in buying, selling, and even sales promotion. If authority is not decentralized to the level of the individual store, it may at least be decentralized to the level of the district manager. As a part of this decentralization effort by some chain stores, the position of store manager is being upgraded from that of an operating and personnel manager to include a wider range of functional and merchandising responsibility, as well as more freedom to adapt the store to local conditions. "To promote more management flexibility at the store level, Penney has decentralized a big chunk of decision-making on local merchandising, inventory, maintenance, advertising, and promotion."[13]

Trends

The desire of management is to achieve a balance between centralization and decentralization. Management is striving to achieve the advantages and economies of scale offered by centralization while allowing the individual stores to respond and adjust to local conditions. Thus, even though some

---

[12] "Investigating the Collapse of W. T. Grant," *Business Week,* July 19, 1976, p. 61.

[13] "J. C. Penney: Getting More from the Same Space," *Business Week,* August 18, 1975, p. 88.

decentralization is occurring, many of the functions will continue to be retained at the central level. At K-Mart, for example, the buying is done centrally. However, the K-Mart managers hire and train their own staffs, order all merchandise, and control their expenditures under the guidelines of corporate headquarters.[14]

Perhaps the most prevalent and honest approach is offered by Zales: "We give our people a great deal of latitude—but we also watch them like a hawk."[15]

Staff and management information services

Increasingly, large retail organizations are developing highly specialized staffs to furnish advice to top management, which is responsible for long-range planning and policy formulation. Such functions may include a research unit for analyzing the flow of information from within and without the organization, a long-range planning and development staff, and perhaps also a policy committee. For example, Sears added a corporate planning department in 1973. Consumer relations staffs have also increased in importance during the 1970s as a result of the increasingly organized and forceful consumerist movement. Merchandise testing and comparison shopping are also important staff functions, as is fashion coordination in department stores. These functions are becoming more important as competition in large-scale retailing intensifies.

SUMMARY

An organization is simply a group of individuals cooperating to achieve agreed-upon objectives or goals. In retailing, the overall objective is to satisfy consumer wants and needs while making satisfactory profits. All types of retailers must have an organization to carry out this mission. As a part of organizing, the retailer must establish goals and objectives for the firm. After these are stated, the retailer must carry on a continuous process of planning for the firm. This can be assisted greatly by a situation analysis which identifies problems and opportunities.

All retailers, regardless of size, perform certain functions, including selling, merchandising, financing, and staffing. The degree of specialization is the primary organizational difference between large and small stores. Organization to accomplish the mission of the outlet can be on the basis of function, products, geography, or a combination of the three.

For many years, the Mazur four-function organizational structure was the most widely used in retailing. Many firms have now modified this classic organizational structure. Many functions, for example, are being increasingly

---

[14] "The Orchestrated Growth of Kresge," *Dun's Review,* December 1975, p. 49.

[15] "Why Zale Glitters in More than Jewelry," *Business Week,* February 16, 1974, p. 101.

decentralized, with decision-making power residing at the regional and even the store level. Department stores are modifying their traditional organizational structure to reflect the increasing number of branches. Typically we see a separation of the buying and selling functions in department stores.

The distinguishing characteristics of organizational structures in chains are centralized control and standardization of virtually all other functions. This is still true to a large extent, even though some instances of decentralization can be found.

KEY CONCEPTS

Functions of retail management
Objectives for retail management
   Situation analysis
   Setting objectives
   Control
The organizing function
   Specialization of labor
   Departmentalization
   Span of control
   Unity of command
Organizational structure
   Functional
   Product
   Geographic
Department store organization
   The Mazur plan
   Branch store organization
   The separation of buying and selling
   Ownership groups
Chain store organization
   Centralization
   Standardization

DISCUSSION QUESTIONS

1. What do we mean by the retail organization?

2. What is a situation analysis, and what are its advantages for the retailer?

3. Discuss span of control and unity of command.

4. Why is control important?

5. How can the control function be carried out?

6. What are the advantages of separating the buying from the selling function in a large department store? What are the disadvantages?

7. What basic organizational patterns are available for branch–main store relationships?

8. Discuss the advantages of centralization and decentralization in the organization of department stores and chain stores.

PROJECTS

1. Visit a local department store and observe at least two separate departments. In each department, determine whether the merchandise is grouped according to consumer-oriented classifications or departmental classifications (for example, are sportswear and sports equipment grouped together according to use or carried in separate departments according to merchandise class?). Evaluate the store's strategy in selecting the particular policy it follows. Is the strategy effective?

2. Devise an organizational plan for a business that you would enjoy going into— one that would have more than five employees. Prepare a formal organizational chart depicting the personnel relationships, and explain how you have achieved efficiencies through span of control and unity of command. Prepare a merchandising schematic showing how you plan to lay out your business employing the concepts discussed in the text.

3. Prepare an in-depth report (approximately four pages) on one of the four organizational principles discussed in the text:
    a. The principle of specialization of labor.
    b. The principle of departmentalization.
    c. The span of control principle.
    d. The unity of command principle.

4. Locate a local merchant who has a downtown store and one or more branches in shopping centers. Indicate from interviews: (a) how the decision was made to move into the centers; (b) what happened to total business and the downtown volume; (c) what organizational plans were necessary to make the expansion possible (new functions, more people, training, and so on); (d) what kinds of contacts were made with the developers (for example, who made the contact and how the relationship was solidified); (e) how the merchandising for the branch(es) is carried out—the plans for servicing the branch(es). Draw a "before and after" organization chart of the organization and show changes over time if possible.

5. Do a field investigation of the similarities and differences among retail companies of differing types by kind of business, size, and number of units. See how the actual structures compare with what is "typical," and see how and why each type of company differs from the others.

CASES

Case 1. Sally Jones, a salesperson in linen and domestics, is told by the department buyer to push a certain towel combination, number 3440, since it is a high-margin item. A few days later the floor manager tells her she is spending too much time around the towels and directs her to circulate around the entire department. Later the same day, Sally is reprimanded by the personnel manager for violating the store's dress code by wearing slacks. (Sally had been told by the department's buyer that pantsuits were acceptable dress.) Sally becomes frustrated since she apparently can't do anything right and decides to quit.

What does this case say about the store's organizational structure?

Case 2. Allen Noble and John McPherson graduated from State University in May 1976 with degrees in marketing and accounting, respectively. They have been friends for years. Both are from Billings, and they attended the same high school. Billings is an industrial town of about 50,000 with a small junior college. While attending the university, Allen and John often ate lunch at a natural foods store called Sunflower Seeds. They returned home after graduation and decided to open their own health food store, organized as a partnership. Capital would be supplied by an inheritance received by Allen upon the death of his favorite uncle. They had scouted around and located what they considered an "ideal" site and had already lined up their suppliers. Their store, *Kelp Korner,* would be open from 11:00 A.M. to 2:00 P.M. and serve lunch only.

Which duties do you think each of the two should perform? Speculate on the outcome of this venture. Be sure to support your position.

PART THREE

CUSTOMERS AND MARKETS

The institutional and organizational structures of retailing exist to serve customers. Consequently, this part of the text emphasizes the focus of the retailing management concept—namely the market. Chapter 5 provides a broad macro view of the consumer and introduces you to the concept of market segmentation. It discusses the types of segmentation, the benefits of segmentation, and the strategy implications that result from an understanding of the various market segments. Chapter 6 focuses on the decision processes of consumers so that the retailer will be able to serve their needs more adequately.

5

THE CONSUMER

*A*lthough retailers have long appreciated the need to understand how and why consumers decide where to buy, they have often been puzzled about how such an understanding can be achieved. "Intuitive retailing" has, on occasion, led to brilliant retailing decisions, but all too often those who rely on unguided intuition are scarred by failure. Creative retailing is best served by a conceptual framework which guides and stimulates the retailer's efforts to develop strategies and tactics that will generate profitable sales volumes.

Not all conceptual frameworks serve this purpose equally well. Essential is the realization that consumer behavior is a dynamic motivated process. This involves, most importantly, the rejection of the notion that consumers are manipulable automatons, "things" that can be controlled by easily learned, mechanical rules. The application of the marketing concept to retailing requires treating consumers as individuals who selectively respond to their environments in terms of their self-determined (even if not always self-understood) goals and purposes. Consumers interact creatively with their environments as they weigh, however crudely or imperfectly, alternative courses of action—comparing benefits, costs, and risks. This decision-making process is structured by the individual consumer's past experiences and future expectations, giving it a "concreteness" that can easily be misunderstood as mindlessness or irrationality. That is to say, consumers make their purchase decisions in terms of immediate, highly personal obligations, aspirations, and purposes which may not seem to make sense from the retailer's perspective. The burden is on the retailer to learn how to adopt the variable perspectives that characterize different kinds of consumers. The conceptual framework developed in this chapter gives the retailer many of the tools necessary to accomplish this.

Irving Crespi, Vice President
Mathematica Policy Research, Inc.
Princeton, New Jersey

Edward Gorman, marketing consultant, J. C. Penney Co., has stated that "a retailer can get so busy that he takes his eyes off the consumer. Then he encounters trouble."[1]

The material presented in this chapter orients retailing activities within the framework of consumer decision making as the key to retail strategy formulation. In considering the consumer, retailers should bear in mind the following essential points:

1. Consumers are problem solvers. All retail activities should be designed to aid them in solving consumption-related problems.
2. Consumers seek to reduce the risk of wrong purchasing decisions by acquiring information.
3. Consumers shop for many and varied reasons in addition to the desire to buy, a primary reason for shopping. The retailer must respond to these consumer reasons for shopping.
4. Store choice is a function of many factors, such as location, image, hours, and prices. Variations in store choice, however, can be better explained by an understanding of consumer behavior.
5. Many variables affect in-store shopping behavior. The shopper responds to a series of cues which the retailer needs to understand in order to develop strategies that will trigger buying decisions. Further, the retailer may be the source of cues.
6. Nonstore shopping is growing in importance. Nonstore shoppers represent an affluent market, but special strategies are necessary to do an effective job of serving these consumers.

In covering the above points, the questions of *how* retail shoppers behave in the marketplace and *why* they behave as they do will be answered. The focus will be on decision making.

CONSUMERS AND RETAILING

Retail merchandising is sometimes defined as having the right goods at the right place, at the right time, and at the right price and quality to satisfy consumer wants. Ideally, then, consumer decisions on what, when, where, and how to buy will match the merchandise-offering decisions of the retailer. The materials in this chapter are presented with these thoughts in mind. The presentation follows the framework of Figure 5–1. You may wish to refer back to the framework periodically as you study these materials.

The behavior of consumers is often different from that of the so-called rational economic man even though consumers do seek to maximize utility. The difficulty is in defining the product and service characteristics that "rationally" lead to high utility. The retail manager's concept of rationality must include the recognition that consumers shop and buy for motives that may not

[1] "Consumers Seek Stores Where Clothes Match Current Changing Life-styles," *Marketing News*, February 25, 1977, p. 9.

FIGURE 5–1

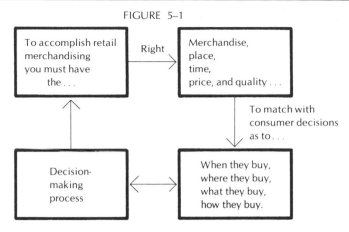

be as simple as price-quality relationships. Status consciousness is perfectly rational, for example, even though many economists would not predict that a consumer would be willing to pay more for the same diamond at Tiffany's than at Zales.

Why do people shop?[2]

Specifically, why do people shop? Motives for shopping are numerous and can be unrelated to the actual buying process. As a background for developing strategies to meet the needs of shoppers, we need to understand the satisfactions which are derived from shopping activities as well as the utility which is obtained from merchandise. Thus, we must understand not only how and where people shop but also why they shop and the variables which trigger problem-solving processes. The motives for shopping, other than buying, are typically labeled *personal* and *social*.

The process of shopping, especially for groceries, has utility for a large number of women who apparently view it as an integral part of their role. Shopping also offers an opportunity for diversion, a chance to escape from the routine of daily life. Shopping mall managers in particular can encourage shopping through various kinds of exhibits and traffic-generating attractions. For example, one study of shopping center patrons indicated that 63 percent would like to see art exhibits in the center and that 75 percent would be interested in musical events.[3] Many people keep up with the latest trends in fashions, styling, or product innovation by simply observing and not buying.

Shopping also provides many people with considerable exercise. Thus, some shoppers apparently welcome the opportunity to walk considerable

[2] This discussion is based upon Edward M. Tauber, "Why Do People Shop?" *Journal of Marketing,* vol. 36 (October 1972), pp. 46–49.

[3] "Successful Shopping Centers Will Hold Market Segments with Atmospherics," *Marketing News,* August 1, 1975, p. 8.

distances in shopping centers while examining the merchandise. Retailing institutions also provide many sensory benefits to shoppers. For example, noise in the form of background music, scent in the form of perfume or prepared food, and other sensory stimuli are very satisfying to many shoppers.

Shopping also provides opportunities for social experiences outside the home, encounters with friends, or simply people-watching. Common interests may be a major link for the retailer in stimulating communication among people. Stores that offer hobby-related items can serve as a focal point for people with similar interests.

Patronage of a store may reflect the desire to be with one's peer group or with a reference group to which one aspires to belong. Record shops, for example, are common attractions for teenagers.

A person may enjoy being waited on without having to pay for the service—the concept of status and authority. Store personnel compete for the favor of a potential buyer, especially where comparison shopping is involved. Also, some shoppers enjoy the process of bargaining and believe that goods and services can be obtained at more reasonable prices in this way.

Product- and store-related benefits, such as low price, credit, and quality lines, can be duplicated by competitors. Location can even be approximated. The development of a lasting differential advantage, however, may depend on catering to shopping motives that are not product related. Retailers are competing with other alternatives that provide similar benefits. In addition to providing product benefits, retailers may, for example, be competing with the social and recreational industry for the consumer's time and money.

Even if consumers are engaged in the buying process, they may still purchase for a variety of reasons other than price and quality, and they may value store characteristics in widely differing ways. Life-style research has disclosed a variety of different shopper profiles, knowledge of which can help retailers in appealing to specific segments of shoppers by means of merchandise and store characteristics.

Shopper typologies

Several studies have classified consumers into various groups on the basis of their attitudes toward the shopping and buying processes. The key findings help us understand how markets can be segmented and how different retailing strategies can be used to serve these groups of shoppers.

A study by William Darden and Fred Reynolds revealed several shopper typologies.[4] The *economic shopper* regards shopping as primarily buying.

---

[4] William R. Darden and Fred D. Reynolds, "Shopping Orientations and Product Usage Rates," *Journal of Marketing Research,* vol. 7 (November 1971), pp. 505–8; see also Gregory P. Stone, "City and Urban Identification: Observations on the Social Psychology of City Life," *American Journal of Sociology,* vol. 60 (July 1954), pp. 36–45.

The behavior of the economic shopper is directed primarily to the purchase of goods. Factors of importance in attracting this type of consumer are price, quality, and convenience. The relationships of such consumers with both chains and local stores are impersonal. These shoppers tend to be socially mobile and aspiring and have a high usage rate for socially visible products.

The *personalizing shopper* likes the opportunity for high levels of social participation and establishes primary relationships with local independent retail institutions. The *apathetic* shopper does not like to shop, dislikes chain stores, finds no satisfaction in personal relationships with local retail outlets, and feels no particular ties with these outlets. The *ethical* shopper feels the need to support local merchants and has personal ties with them. Further, this shopper tends to have high social status and long residence in the community.

The shopping orientations of consumers can be valuable inputs for understanding and influencing shopper patronage. These orientations can aid the retailer in successfully matching store strategies with one or more market segments since the satisfactions consumers derive from shopping can be used in developing retail strategies. This is especially true to the extent that shopping orientations as related to buying behavior can be generalized across products.

The benefits sought by consumers in each of the shopper profiles can provide the guidelines for strategy development. For example, the economic shopper is looking for bargains, and price and advertising can be utilized to appeal to this segment effectively. Likewise, the personalizing shopper is most likely to respond to friendly sales personnel. A key is to remember that shopping can be more than an economic activity.

Generally, a retailer should strive to appeal primarily to one or two of the shopper types discussed above and not attempt to attract all of the segments. Efforts to attract too many segments would lead to a confused store image in the minds of consumers and thus to an overall lowering of store patronage. The key from the retailer's point of view is to identify the percentage of shoppers with a particular orientation and to determine whether this group of shoppers is large enough to be a viable market segment. A good marketing research plan would be in order to accomplish this task.

CONSUMER DECISION MAKING

Thus far, we have noted that consumers shop for a wide variety of reasons and that store characteristics can be adjusted to appeal to various groups of shoppers once we understand the reasons for their behavior.

Fortunately, a body of theory has developed which is designed to offer explanations of behavior that we have already described in this chapter. A basic understanding of the reasons for this behavior can aid the retailer in offering better service to existing and potential customers.

The consumer behavior theories of particular use in understanding consumer decision making in the context of retailing are (1) information search and retail shopping behavior, (2) information processing, (3) consumer use of evaluative criteria, and (4) consumer learning.

Information search and retail shopping behavior

Communication involves the transmission, receipt, and interpretation of messages from the sender (the retail store) to the receiver (a consumer segment or store patrons). Consumers are exposed to about 150 messages each day, most of which are intended as persuasive communication. In retailing, a primary purpose of communication is to increase a shopper's tendency to purchase a product and/or shop at a particular store. The information provided is designed to affect the attitudes and beliefs of the shopper. Thus, we need to understand the role of the communication and dissemination of information in consumer behavior.

Information seeking takes a variety of forms, as consumers seek to reduce the social and economic risks and uncertainties in purchase decisions. When consumers perceive a need for information to aid them in reducing the risk of a wrong decision, they become actively involved in acquiring and evaluating information. The communications most effective at the retail level thus are those which help consumers reduce the risks of a wrong decision about products, services, conditions of sale, and credit terms.

Consumer behavior is essentially problem solving or uncertainty reduction. Thus, the information provided consumers should not only increase their awareness and understanding of a problem, but also their ability to solve it. Those products or services which are compatible with the solution of the consumer's problems are most likely to be purchased. When the product offered is unsatisfactory as a problem solution, other alternatives will be sought.

Information sources

Three types of information sources are available to the consumer who is seeking information:

1. Marketer-dominated sources.
2. Consumer-dominated sources.
3. Neutral sources.[5]

The primary marketer-dominated information sources are advertising, personal selling, and other vehicles of product information. The retailer exercises control over these sources. The shopper may use advertisements to obtain such information as price, product features, brands carried, and credit arrangements. The use of advertisements as an information source varies

---

[5] Rom Markin, *Consumer Behavior: A Cognitive Orientation* (New York: Macmillan Company, 1974).

considerably by product. Consumers also obtain information by shopping in retail outlets. They have the opportunity to compare price, quality, the conditions of sale, and related information.

Consumer-dominated information sources include product evaluations by other consumers. The consumer may seek information from friends, relatives, or others. Typically this information is perceived as more trustworthy than information provided by the retailers, because the retailer is trying to sell a product or service.

Neutral sources of information are likely to provide accurate and trustworthy information but may still be biased. *Consumer Research* and *Consumer's Union* are examples of neutral information sources. However, the information provided by neutral sources may not be sufficiently detailed to be used by the consumer for decision-making purposes.

Additional sources of information are persons who are known and respected by various groups of consumers [6] Consumers are likely to seek information from such persons. Retailers may therefore be able to utilize such diverse people as sports leaders, college class presidents, and other socially active persons in a community to convey product and store information to the public. Word-of-mouth information from such people is likely to be favorably received.

Many methods can be used to encourage shoppers to seek information about products. These include demonstrations, displays, coupons, and samples. In addition, advertisements which urge consumers to seek information should be used. The use of such appeals as "Ask the man who owns one" is a common approach aimed at stimulating consumers to seek information.

The processing of information

The retailer also needs to know how the information acquired by the consumer is processed, that is, how it is used in problem solving. All information received passes through the consumer's mind, where it is modified by such factors as experience, attitudes, and personality. The four phases of information processing are typically identified as exposure (to physical and social stimuli), attention (processing of the stimuli), comprehension (understanding), and retention (storing information for future use). It is through this process that the consumer gains knowledge and experience in the marketplace. Each phase of information processing is selective, and management must concern itself with all four phases.

The consumer is confronted with many stimuli each day. These are received by the senses. The consumer may modify his or her behavior as a result of the stimuli. This is the hope of the retailer. Adequate exposure is a realistic possibility through sound media management. However, actual processing of the information is another matter.

---

[6] J. Barry Mason and Danny Bellenger, "Analyzing High Fashion Acceptance," *Journal of Retailing*, vol. 49 (Winter 1973–74), pp. 79–88.

After the consumer has been exposed to a stimulus such as an ad, information processing begins. The consumer is now alert to various inputs which will help satisfy his or her needs. Attention, however, is selective, and will be directed toward the solution of a recognized problem. Because attention is selective, the retailer must design programs which provide stimuli with the greatest probability of getting the consumer's attention. These stimuli may include architecture, layout, lighting, color scheme, odor, temperature, location, access, noise, assortment, prices, and special events.

Attention does not necessarily mean comprehension. Consumers may misinterpret information or infer meanings which were never intended. This occurs because consumers are likely to interpret information in terms of their own attitudes and beliefs.

Information processing is selective in still another way. The stimuli stored for further use are smaller in number than those to which the consumer was initially exposed. Thus, not every comprehended message is retained for later use in the decision process.

Learning is at the root of all shopper behavior and is an integral part of risk reduction through information seeking. Consumer behavior is also adaptive behavior. Consumers may reappraise and reevaluate their purchase decisions. Adaptive behavior by the consumer may mean learning new goals and ways of adjusting because of economic, psychological, and social pressures. Such adaptive behavior is the primary means by which retailers attract new customers.

Consumers forget as well as learn. As a result of forgetting, they seek new information and may alter their response patterns. Consumers do not always remember products, brands, stores, or services. This information must be repeated regularly to bring about continued desired responses. Repetitive advertising is thus more effective than one-time advertising, arguing for a carefully planned and continuing media strategy by the retailer.

Consumers may learn that certain clerks in a store should be avoided, that private brands are not particularly desirable, or that the worst time to shop is on the weekend. Retailers must associate products with rewards, that is, sell benefits rather than tangible merchandise and induce satisfaction in consumers. This process creates customer loyalty and reduces decision-making time. Credibility is particularly important in the learning process. Devious selling methods, untruthful promotion, and other questionable practices should be avoided if the retailer wants to build repeat sales based on customer satisfaction.

THE CONSUMER DECISION

Evaluative criteria

In every buying decision, one or more criteria, such as price, brand, or style, are used as bases for comparing products or services. Consumers may use different criteria for comparing products or services and may disagree on the importance of those criteria. However, some basis is always used and information on consumer criteria must be reflected in the marketing mix of the retailer. Ideally research should also be conducted to determine the criteria most important to the groups of consumers the retailer seeks to serve.

The evaluative criteria of consumers may be grouped into the four general categories of cost, performance, suitability, and convenience for most products or services, as shown in Table 5–1. The evaluative criteria just for "cost"

TABLE 5–1
TYPES OF DECISION CRITERIA

Cost	Performance	Suitability	Convenience
Price	Durability	Brand	Store location
Repairs	Efficiency	Style	Store layout
Installation	Economy	Store image	Store atmosphere
Operating cost	Materials	Product image	Store services
Cost of extras	Dependability	Time factor	Product extras
Opportunity cost			

Source: C. Glenn Walters, *Consumer Behavior* (Homewood, Ill.: Richard D. Irwin, 1974), p. 548.

emphasize the complexity of the decision process in purchasing many products and the importance of communicating needed information through media programs. Further, the evaluative criteria also suggest the need for informed and articulate salespersons, especially for products or services which are not presold through mass media advertising.

Evaluative criteria may be either objective (cost, performance, suitability, or convenience) or subjective (symbolic values which products offer).

The number and importance of the various criteria vary from product to product. However, six or fewer criteria are generally used in evaluating products or services. Brand reputation and price tend to be the two most critical criteria or product attributes evaluated by the consumer.

Brand is typically used in judging quality. Reliance on a well-known brand can be an effective way to reduce risks. For example, some persons assert that blacks are risk avoiders and have preference for national brands.[7]

The importance of price varies by type of product and the nature of the decision process. Moreover, the perception of price-quality differentials may vary by income group.[8]

The decision-making process is the ordering of the importance of product and service attributes and the evaluation of the available alternatives. When evaluation occurs, how are the alternatives evaluated? Specifically, what are the important product attributes? What are the important store attributes? What role do reference groups and other persons play in the process? Evaluation is simply the ability of the consumer to effectively utilize all of the information which has been gathered about the how, what, when, and where

---

[7] Robert F. Dietrich, "Know Your Black Consumer," *Progressive Grocer,* June 1975, p. 46.

[8] Norman D. French, John J. Williams, and William A. Chance, "A Shopping Experiment on Price-Quality Relationships," *Journal of Retailing,* vol. 48 (Fall 1972), p. 16.

of the purchase. An alternative is acceptable only when it meets all of the criteria of importance to the consumer better than any other available alternative.

Decision assessment

Even after a purchasing decision has been made, consumers typically evaluate the effects of that decision. Thus, an understanding of dissonance and postpurchase evaluation will aid the retailer in providing the information necessary to help the consumer continue to be satisfied with the decision. Purchase evaluation is simply the consumer's estimate of the result of a particular purchase. Ideally, the consumer will think that a good product has been purchased, that it is of high quality, and that the warranty, if applicable, is good. Far too often, however, the consumer does not have sufficient information to make a meaningful postpurchase evaluation. Postpurchase evaluation may merely mean that a product has performed at least as well as expected. More often it may be based on new information, which is often simply experience which has resulted from the purchase. This type of information is utilized in adjusting behavior and in planning the next purchase. Retailer advertisements and other literature are often used to reassure the consumer who is assessing the results of a decision. The main selling points for the product or service should also be stressed in such advertisements and literature.

MAJOR CONSUMER DECISIONS

Key decisions facing the consumer in interacting with the retail institutional structure, as noted earlier, are the what, when, where, and how of shopping. The "what" question involves issues of price-quality relationships, the choice of private or national brands, and the consumer evaluation of new products. The "when" dimension focuses particularly on the timing aspects of shopping, including time of day, day of week, single- and multiple-purpose trips, and related information. "How" addresses such questions as store or nonstore shopping and distance traveled. "Where" involves the choice of downtown versus shopping center, the particular store from which the merchandise will be purchased, and in-store behavior dynamics. These facets of the consumer decision-making process are discussed in the following sections.

WHERE TO BUY

Downtown versus the shopping center

Why do some shoppers tend to shop downtown and others in the suburbs? One study focused specifically on this question. The reasons are shown in Table 5–2. Each central business district (CBD) location is unique, how-

TABLE 5–2
SHOPPERS' PERCEPTIONS OF THE CENTRAL BUSINESS DISTRICT VERSUS
SHOPPING CENTERS AS DESIRABLE PLACES TO SHOP
(percent)

	CBD	Shopping centers	Undecided
Better delivery service	23	9	68
Easier to establish charge accounts	22	19	59
Easier return and exchange of goods	28	28	43
Greater variety and range of prices and quality	39	44	17
Greater variety, styles, and sizes	28	48	24
More bargain sales	36	34	30
Better quality of goods	28	29	43
Cheaper prices	34	29	37
Less time to get there	61	26	12
Better place for combining different activities	38	49	13
Less walking required	25	62	13
Cost of transportation lower	52	23	25
More convenient to public transportation	50	13	37
Easier to take children shopping	13	49	42
Best place for a little outing away from home	24	59	17
Right people shop there	14	27	59
Best place to meet friends	19	55	26
Open more convenient hours	12	72	16
Better places to eat lunch	40	33	26

Percentages may not total to 100 percent because of rounding.
Source: Craig Frederick, Duna Norton, and Mary Lee Shannon, "Tuscaloosa CBD Redevelopment Feasibility Study," unpublished report, University of Alabama, 1975.

ever, and the patronage factors may differ from area to area. Research on this matter should be conducted prior to strategy formulation.

The perceived advantages of a shopping center location over the central business district as a desirable place to shop in the above study were:

It is easier to take children there.

It's the best place for a little outing away from home.

The "right" people go there.

It's the best place to meet friends.

It has more convenient hours.

Less walking is required.

The perceived major advantages for the CBD include:

It takes less time to get there.

It has better delivery service.

The cost of transportation is lower.

It is convenient to public transportation.

It is not likely that the reasons for CBD patronage can serve as major attractions for all shoppers. However, the reasons can be used to special advantage, even in the absence of downtown malls, in attracting such market segments as office workers, tourists, the elderly, and persons making multipurpose trips. Even so, "downtown market analysis must be highly attuned to special market demographics related to income, ethnicity, age, life style, and tastes, which can vary considerably from the standard citywide distribution."[9]

Some of the major department stores, such as Boston's Filenes and Jordan Marsh and New York's Bonwit Teller, Lord and Taylor, and Bergdorf Goodman, have invested major sums of money in revitalizing their downtown stores and have made them much more attractive to all classes of shoppers.[10]

Store choice

Apart from the question of whether consumers shop downtown or in a shopping center, there is still the question of how they choose the stores in

FIGURE 5–2
STORE-CHOICE PROCESSES

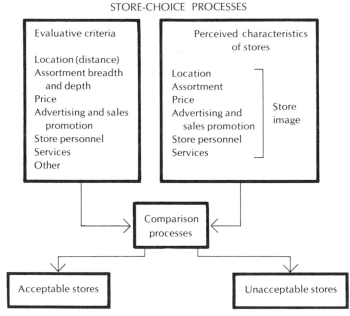

Source: *Consumer Behavior*, [2d ed., by James F. Engel, David T. Kollat, and Roger D. Blackwell.] Copyright © 1968, 1973 by Holt, Rinehart and Winston, Inc. Reprinted by permission of Holt, Rinehart and Winston.

---

[9] "Downtown Centers: Not Like Suburban Malls," *Chain Store Age*, January 1975, p. 5; also "Does Downtown Redevelopment Mean Revitalization?" *Stores*, March 1977, pp. 14–17; "Stores Analyzes What's Happening in Downtown," *Stores*, March 1977, pp. 18–20.

[10] "The Big Stores Vote for Downtown Again," *Business Week*, September 20, 1976, p. 38; see also "A Surge of Stores for Downtown Toronto," *Business Week*, January 31, 1977, p. 39.

which they shop. Further questions are the importance of a store's image in affecting patronage, the factors which image comprises, and the key factors in a consumer's choice of a particular location at which to shop.[11]

One well-known text conceptualizes the consumer's choice of retail outlets as shown in Figure 5–2. The evaluative criteria listed in the figure can be related to the discussion of the research findings which follow.

Supermarket choice.   Table 5–3 depicts the importance of 37 factors in affecting the shopper's choice of a supermarket. The table presents the ranking by all shoppers and by blacks. The assessments of blacks generally matched those of the population at large. Cleanliness was the most important factor for both groups. Convenience of location was ranked 11th and 10th, respectively, by blacks and by all shoppers. Good parking facilities and late hours were not rated high by either group.[12] A similar study of evaluative criteria in supermarket selection indicated that the major factors in order of importance were price, merchandise, location, and store appearance.[13] As a note of caution, it should be mentioned that lists of stated importance or various store selection factors are perhaps biased due to their direct questioning method and the lack of perceived differences among alternative stores in terms of some factors.

Department and specialty store choices.   Consumers with higher socioeconomic characteristics apparently prefer to patronize conventional department stores and specialty stores for products with high social risk. However, they are inclined to patronize discount stores for the large number of other products which have low social risk. Thus retailers may want to develop strategies which utilize a combination of discount and full-service selling methods, but vary by product line.[14] Perceived risk does play a role in the store selection process for such expensive and infrequently purchased items as draperies, furniture, and carpeting.[15]

In an analysis of persons who purchased audio equipment from a specialty shop versus a department store, it was found that the "specialty store customers were more self-confident, . . . perceived less risk, and considered the product area to be of greater importance than did those who shopped for similar items in a department store."[16] The specialty customer viewed an error in the purchase of equipment to be more serious than did the department store shopper. Thus, in promoting to the specialty store shopper, the authors

---

[11] For further information, see Joseph Barry Mason and William Bearden, "Consumer Images of Retail Institutions," in Arch Woodside et al. (eds.), *Foundations of Marketing Channels* (Austin, Tex.: Lone Star Publishers, 1978).

[12] Robert F. Dietrich, "Up-Date: Consumer Watch," *Progressive Grocer,* August 1975, p. 34.

[13] "Shifts in Supermarket Buying Patterns: 1975," *Nielsen Researcher,* no. 2, 1975, p. 6.

[14] V. Kanti Prasad, "Socio-Economic Product Risk and Patronage Preferences of Retail Shoppers," *Journal of Marketing,* vol. 39 (July 1975), p. 47.

[15] Robert D. Hisrich, Ronald J. Dornoff, and Jerome B. Kernan," Perceived Risk in Store Selection," *Journal of Marketing Research,* vol. 9 (November 1972), pp. 435–39.

[16] Joseph F. Dash, Leon Schiffman, and Conrad Berenson, "Risk and Personality-Related Dimensions of Store Choice," *Journal of Marketing,* vol. 40 (January 1976), p. 38.

TABLE 5–3
RANK ORDER OF FACTORS AFFECTING SUPERMARKET CHOICE

Factor	Importance to black shoppers Rank	Importance to black shoppers Index	Importance to all shoppers Rank
Cleanliness	1	98.0	1
Good meat department	2	97.8	7
All prices clearly labeled	3	97.0	2
Freshness date marked on products	4	96.6	6
Low prices	5	95.6	3
Good produce department	5	95.6	5
Accurate, pleasant checkout clerks	7	95.5	4
Good dairy department	8	93.8	11
Shelves usually well stocked	9	93.3	8
Helpful personnel in service departments	10	92.5	12
Convenient store location	11	91.1	10
Good layout for fast, easy shopping	12	90.5	13
Good parking facilities	13	89.6	9
Good frozen foods department	14	89.1	21
Good selection of nationally advertised brands	15	88.6	16
Short wait for checkout	16	87.6	15
Frequent "sales" or "specials"	17	87.5	14
Aisles clear of boxes	17	87.5	19
Good selection of low-priced "store brand" items	19	86.8	18
Don't run short of items on "special"	20	86.0	17
Pleasant atmosphere/decor	20	86.0	24
Baggers on duty	22	85.8	20
New items that I see advertised are available	23	85.1	23
Unit pricing on shelves	24	84.7	22
Manager is friendly and helpful	25	83.8	25
Check-cashing service	26	83.0	26
Not usually overcrowded	27	73.8	27
Open late hours	28	73.6	30
Good drugs and toiletries section	29	69.3	33
Good assortment of nonfoods merchandise	30	67.0	29
Carry purchases to car	31	65.8	28
Eye-catching mass displays	32	60.6	34
Has in-store bakery	33	59.6	31
Has delicatessen department	34	57.3	32
Trading stamps or other "extras"	35	52.0	36
People know my name	36	39.0	35
Sell hot foods to take out or eat in store	37	37.5	37

Source: Robert F. Dietrich, "Up-Date: Consumer Watch," *Progressive Grocer*, August 1975, p. 34.

suggested major emphasis on lenient exchange and specialized sales staff, quick and effective repairs, and a liberal trade-in policy. For department store customers, the recommended focus was on well-known major brands, the assistance available to shoppers, and customer satisfaction.

For products of high social risk, consumer choice of a retail store type is most susceptible to interpersonal influence from others of the same social class. For products of low social risk, even if economic risk is high, choices of a store type are based more on economic value, convenience, and product-related decisions than on the social influence of other people.[17]

Shopping center choice.   Consumers particularly like the convenience of a shopping center but will travel farther than is necessary or convenient if atmospherics are sufficiently attractive. Atmospherics draw customers more strongly than does convenience. The features most disliked about shopping centers are (1) poor access, (2) noise, and (3) high prices.[18]

Out-shoppers and new arrivals

Various research studies have shown that the frequent out-shopper (that is, a person from a smaller town traveling to a larger town to shop) tends to be better educated, to have a higher income level, to show a greater preference for evening shopping, and to spend more money out of town and by mail than do persons who are not out-shoppers. These out-shoppers also appear to be very active, are urban oriented, and have low store loyalty. Likewise, they tend to express overall dissatisfaction with local shopping conditions and to have a preference for urban shopping areas. Out-shopping behavior does not appear to be product specific.[19]

New arrivals are big buyers of household durables, including furniture, carpeting, and drapes.[20] However, clothing purchases are not as likely. In store selection, new arrivals place high reliance on impersonal sources of information, including the Yellow Pages and media advertising. Shopping trips rank second in importance, followed by personal sources of information and the reputation of a chain store. The length of time before store loyalty emerges is short. Most important decisions are made within a month after arrival. Typically no more than two stores are visited in this process. For shopping goods, a visit to only one store may result in a high level of confidence. Since new arrivals make many important decisions before establishing social contacts, formal search and impersonal information sources are of great importance to them. Welcoming services might be an effective strategy if contact is made with such consumers soon after their arrival in a community.

---

[17] Michael Perry and B. Curtis Hamm, "Canonical Analysis of Relations between Socio-Economic Risks and Personal Influence in Purchase Decisions," *Journal of Marketing Research,* vol. 6 (August 1969), pp. 353–54.

[18] "Successful Shopping Centers Will Hold Market Segments with Atmospherics," *Marketing News,* August 1, 1975, p. 8.

[19] A. Coskun Samli and Ernest B. Uhr, "The Outshopping Spectrum: Key for Analyzing Intermarket Leakages," *Journal of Retailing,* vol. 50 (Summer 1974) p. 75; and William R. Darden and William O. Perreault, Jr., "Identifying Interurban Shoppers: Multiproduct Purchase Patterns and Segmentation Profiles," *Journal of Marketing Research,* vol. XIII (February 1976), pp. 51–60.

[20] James M. Carman, "Selection of Retailing Services by New Arrivals," *Journal of Retailing,* vol. 50 (Summer 1974), p. 12.

TABLE 5–4

COGNITIVE DIMENSIONS AND COGNITIVE DETERMINANTS OF RETAIL STORE IMAGE

Low margin/High turnover → *High margin/low turnover*

None → *Store preference map* → *Complete*

Cognitive determinants

Cognitive dimensions	Convenience store—convenience goods	Convenience store—shopping goods	Convenience store—specialty goods	Shopping store—shopping goods	Specialty store—specialty goods
Locational convenience	Access route Traffic barrier Traveling time Parking availability	Access routes Traffic barriers Traveling time Parking availability	Access routes Traffic barriers Traveling time Parking availability	Traveling time Parking availability	—
Merchandise suitability	Breadth and depth of assortment	Quality of lines stocked Breadth and depth of assortment	Number of brands stocked Quality of lines stocked Breadth and depth of assortment	Quality of lines stocked Breadth and depth of assortment Number of outstanding department within store	Number of brands stocked Quality of lines stocked Breadth and depth of assortment
Value for price	Price of particular items in a particular store	Price of items in a competing store Prices on sale days Prices for substitutes in substitute stores Stamps and discounts	Prices of substitute products in substitute stores	Price of particular items in a particular store Price of items in a competing store Price of particular items in a particular store on sale days Prices of substitute products in substitute stores	Price of particular items in a particular store
Sales effort and store service	Very limited	Advertising, reliability and usefulness Billing procedures, adequacy of credit arrangements Delivery promptness and care	Courtesy of salesclerks Helpfulness of salesclerks Advertising, reliability and usefulness Billing procedure, adequacy of credit arrangements Delivery promptness and care	Courtesy of salesclerks Advertising, reliability and usefulness Billing procedure, adequacy of credit arrangements Delivery promptness and care	Courtesy of salesclerks Helpfulness of salesclerks Advertising, reliability and usefulness Billing procedures, adequacy of credit arrangements Delivery promptness and care
Congeniality of store	Store layout Merchandise display Store traffic and congestion	Store traffic and congestion	Store decor and attractiveness of merchandise display	Store layout Store traffic and congestion	Store layout Store decor and attractiveness of merchandise display Class of customers
Posttransaction satisfaction	Satisfaction with price and accessibility of store	Satisfaction with accessibility of store, price, return, and adjustments and merchandise in use	Satisfaction with merchandise in use, shopping experience, and accessibility of store	Satisfaction with merchandise in use, return, readjustments, and price paid	Satisfaction with merchandise in use Satisfaction with shopping experience in store

Source: Morris L. Mayer, J. Barry Mason, and Morris Gee, "A Reconceptualization of Store Classification as Related to Retail Strategy Formulation," *Journal of Retailing,* vol. 47 (Fall 1971), p. 35.

Composite influences on store choice

The consumer's patronage decision often depends upon perceptions of composite store characteristics and upon the way these perceptions match evaluative criteria. The consumer's perception may differ from objective reality. J. D. Lindquist examined 26 studies to determine the major groups of attributes which store image comprises. He determined that these were merchandise, service, clientele, physical facilities, convenience, promotion, store atmosphere, and institutional and posttransaction satisfaction.[21] Price level was not found to be a key variable. However, the images of individual departments rather than the image of the composite store may be more important in determining shopping patterns.[22]

Only limited analysis has been performed on shopping center images. However, one study has identified the following key dimensions of shopping center image: price, structure and design, ease of internal movement and parking, visual appearance, reputation, range of goods, service, shopping hours, and atmosphere.[23]

Mayer, Mason, and Gee have reconceptualized the work of several authors in the area of goods classification and retail image to develop a classification of consumer evaluative criteria as shown in Table 5–4. An analysis of the strategy variables suggested by the position of a particular outlet on the continuum enables one to develop strategies which reflect the behavioral and cognitive processes of the consumer in store selection.[24]

WHAT TO BUY

Price and brand are two of the most important factors influencing the consumer's purchase of products or services. Price is important because it is regarded as a measure of merchandise worth. Along with brand, it is one of the most important ways of estimating quality. The reaction to and reliance on prices and brands vary by product types, retail outlets, and socioeconomic classes. In addition to price and brand, such other factors as reliance on open code dating, nutritional labeling, packaging, shelf displays, and even the availability and use of coupons affect what is bought. These informational sources and cues are the focus of this part of the chapter.

---

[21] J. D. Lindquist, "The Meaning of Image," Journal of Retailing, vol. 50 (Winter 1974–75), pp. 31–32.

[22] R. N. Cardozo, "How Images Vary by Product Class," Journal of Retailing, vol. 50 (Winter 1974–75), p. 90.

[23] Richard M. Downs, "The Cognitive Structure of an Urban Shopping Center," Environment and Planning, June 1970.

[24] Morris L. Mayer, Joseph Barry Mason, and Morris Gee, "A Reconceptualization of Store Classification as Related to Retail Strategy Formulation," Journal of Retailing, vol. 47 (Fall 1971) pp. 27–36. See also Helmut Soldner, "Conceptual Models for Retail Strategy Formulation," Journal of Retailing, vol. 52 (Fall 1976), pp. 47–56.

Private versus national brands

In many purchase situations the consumer has a choice between national brands and private brands. The term *national brand* refers to a manufacturer's brand of merchandise which is supported by wide distribution and heavy advertising paid for by the manufacturer. *Private brands* are those sponsored or owned by a company whose primary business is distribution and/or selling the product line.

A *Woman's Day* survey revealed that over 60 percent of households buy some type of private brand during a 12-month period.[25] It is still unclear whether retailers can develop strategies based on private versus national brand preference or whether private brands affect quality perceptions. Clearly, the use of private brands in a retailing mix is important. However, price level, unavailability of private brands, and other structural variables may be more important than consumer characteristics in deciding whether the consumer will purchase a private brand. Typically, private brands are given better shelf positions, more advertising support in relation to sales, and more couponing support than national brands.

One study has revealed that the national brand appliance buyer regards in-store information sources quite highly, shops longer, and equates store with brand as a decision criterion. In addition, this purchaser has a relatively high socioeconomic status as measured by income, occupation, education, and housing patterns.[26] For beverages and paper products, blacks buy proportionately fewer private brands than all shoppers, but differences do not exist for other products.[27]

Additional research has revealed distinct differences between low- and middle-income consumers in their preferences for private and national brands in food products. The results of the findings are shown in Table 5–5. Lower-income consumers have a stronger preference for national brands than do middle-income consumers; middle-income respondents prefer private brands to a greater degree than do lower-income respondents; lower-income consumers exhibit a greater degree of brand loyalty than do middle-income consumers; middle-income consumers are more price conscious than lower-income consumers.[28] Thus, particularly among individuals in lower-income groups, "name" is associated with quality. This is a social problem because these individuals who are least able to pay show an in-

---

[25] Robert F. Dietrich, "Up-Date: Consumer Watch," *Progressive Grocer,* vol. 54 (March 1975), p. 55.

[26] James T. Rothe and Lawrence M. Lamont, "Purchase Behavior and Brand Choice Determinants for National and Private Brand Major Appliances," *Journal of Retailing,* vol. 49 (Fall 1973), p. 31.

[27] Donald Sexton, "Differences in Food Shopping Habits by Area of Residence, Race, and Income," *Journal of Retailing,* vol. 50 (Spring 1974), p. 43.

[28] Barbara Davis Coe, "Private versus National Preference among Lower- and Middle-Income Consumers," *Journal of Retailing,* vol. 47 (Fall 1971), p. 69.

TABLE 5–5
LOWER- AND MIDDLE-INCOME CONSUMERS' BRAND PREFERENCES FOR
INDIVIDUAL FOOD ITEMS

Item	National brand Lower (percent)	National brand Middle (percent)	Private brand Lower (percent)	Private brand Middle (percent)	Don't buy Lower (percent)	Don't buy Middle (percent)	N = 100 (percent)
Flour	36	27	12	20	2	3	100
Coffee	40	32	6	14	4	4	100
Milk (whole)	41	27	4	14	5	9	100
Milk (powdered)	34	10		1	16	39	100
Milk (canned)	46	16	2	6		28	100
Butter	34	10		4	16	36	100
Margarine	30	14	6	28	14	8	100
Bacon	33	13	10	26	7	11	100
Frankfurters	29	10		24	14	16	100
Eggs	35		10	58	5	1	100
American cheese	23	26		20	27	4	100
Cream cheese	15	19	6	21	29	10	100
Frozen orange juice	31	15	2	27	17	8	100
Frozen peas	6	4		14	44	32	100
Frozen corn	6	7		13	44	30	100
Canned green beans	37	18	3	20	10	12	100
Canned peaches	37	21	11	23	2	6	100
Cooking oil	35	30		10	15	10	100
Shortening	39	35	11	6		9	100
Cake mixes	38	20	3	11	9	10	100
Salt	44	40	6	10			100
Potato chips	45	31		8	5	11	100
Jams/jellies	44	18	3	24	3	8	100
Soft drinks	38	17		12	12	21	100
Soup	31	33	3	2	16	15	100

Source: Barbara Davis Coe, "Private versus National Preference among Lower and Middle Income Consumers," *Journal of Retailing,* vol. 47 (Fall 1971), p. 69.

ability to evaluate information sources other than price and "name." However, other socioeconomic groups also show evidence of a belief in a quality/brand relationship similar to that of price/quality.[29]

What change, if any, has occurred in brand preference as a result of the tumultuous environments of the 1970s? The opinion research firm of Yankelovich, Skelly, and White has indicated that loyalty to individual brands may be weakening. "As a result of the recession, inflation, and shortages, people became more open to experimentation and were willing to try other brands besides the single ones they had supported as a matter of custom."[30] Risk taking was reduced during this period, which resulted in a stronger shift

[29] David Gardner, "Is There a Generalized Price/Quality Relationship?" *Journal of Marketing Research,* vol. 8, (May 1971).

[30] "The Brand Power Study," *Progressive Grocer* vol. 55 (October 1976), p. 64.

to national brands. Low price is not necessarily synonymous with value, even when prices are rising and consumers feel the pinch.

The consumer and retail prices

Price knowledge. The response of consumers to price levels and price changes can also have a large influence on what is bought. Consumers, however, tend not to have a high level of absolute price knowledge about products.[31] This is true for both frequently purchased and less frequently purchased items. A study by *Progressive Grocer* provides information on the relative accuracy of consumers' price perceptions. As shown in Table 5–6, buyers' wrong estimates tend to be on the low side whereas nonbuyers tend to err on the high side. Shoppers had better recognition of private brand labels than of national labels. Likewise, buyers of private labels tended to show a better awareness of price than did buyers of national brands. Buyers in higher income stores were more likely to correctly recognize private label prices than were buyers in average income stores.[32] In summary, "consumer price perceptions tend to be imprecise about exact amounts, though reliable within well-defined ranges."[33]

One study found that price-conscious shoppers perceived prices more accurately than did less price-conscious shoppers, and that number of stores shopped, frequency of shopping trips, and automobile ownership were the best discriminators for accuracy of price perception. Persons displaying the greatest accuracy in price perception were: older persons, single persons, males, persons with higher income, and long-term residents of a community.[34] A more recent study of supermarket shoppers found that the following variables were not related to accuracy of price perception: price patronage motive, high response rates to food specials, patronage of more than one supermarket, and preparation of a shopping list prior to shopping.[35]

The importance of demographics. The response of consumers to price levels and price changes can have a large influence on what is bought. We know, for example, that some consumers are extremely price conscious, whereas others give very little consideration to price. Typically the higher income consumer is less price conscious than the low income consumer for the same product. Research has shown that the larger the fraction of a buyer's income spent on a commodity, the greater the savings to be derived

---

[31] J. B. Wilkinson, E. H. Bonfield, and J. Barry Mason, "Subjective Deception and Cue Effects in Food Advertisements," *Journal of Advertising*, vol. 4 (Fall 1975), p. 23.

[32] "What Shoppers Know and Don't Know about Prices," *Progressive Grocer*, vol. 53 (November 1974), p. 40.

[33] *Grey Matter*, vol. 48, no. 1 (New York: Grey Advertising, Inc., 1977), p. 4.

[34] F. E. Brown, "Who Perceives Supermarket Prices Most Validly?" *Journal of Marketing Research*, vol. 8 (February 1971), pp. 110–13.

[35] J. B. Wilkinson, J. Barry Mason, and Edward Bonfield, "Food Shopper Patronage Motives, Price Knowledge, and Shopping Behavior: Implications for Supermarket Strategy," in Barnett A. Greenberg (ed.), *Proceedings: Southern Marketing Association, 1974*.

from search, and hence the greater amount of search and price consciousness.[36]

The importance of price.   Prices are not as important to the nondiscount shopper as they are to the discount shopper. Thus, in effectively segmenting a grocery market the retailer can appeal either to the discount shopper with low prices or to the nondiscount shopper through the use of service-related store attributes.

It has also been found that price is not the most important factor in motivating pharmacy shoppers. Almost half of the respondents in one study did not have any idea which pharmacy had the lowest prices. The amount of money spent by the consumer had no relationship to whether the pharmacy with the lowest prices would be patronized. The consumer's perception of the pharmacy personnel was the most important factor in the patronage decision.[37]

Another study sought to determine the importance of price considerations to consumers in a town of under 25,000. Although the consumers felt that they were paying higher prices in their hometown, this did not bother them greatly. They were reasonably satisfied, particularly with the convenience of location and the friendliness of local merchants. It would seem that hometown loyalty and not price was the most important factor in their shopping behavior.[38]

Latitudes of price acceptance.   At the level of primary demand, consumers do appear to have ranges of acceptable prices for products; prices outside the acceptable range, either too low or too high, are objectionable. Demand appears to provide not only an upper constraint on pricing decisions (pricing what the market will bear) but also a lower constraint. Cost-plus pricing may lead to a pricing error even if it satisfies the cost and competition requirement. Optional price ranges for a product must be determined for the market segment to be served since the upper and lower price limits and the ranges are a function of market demand. Figure 5–3 illustrates the backward-bending demand curve which results from the price limit concept.[39] "Below certain price points, which vary widely from category to category, there is no elasticity of demand; lowering prices further does not have the classic effect of adding sales."[40]

Research has shown that when buyers are given a range of choices in

[36] Joseph Barry Mason and Morris L. Mayer, "Empirical Observations of Consumer Behavior as Related to Goods Classification and Retail Strategy," *Journal of Retailing,* vol. 48 (Fall 1972), p. 22.

[37] Richard A. Jackson, Michael R. Ryan, and Charles E. Treas, "A Study of Pharmacy Patronage Motives and Price Awareness," in Robert L. King (ed.), *Proceedings: Southern Marketing Association,* 1973, p. 186.

[38] Robert F. Hartley, "The Importance of Price in Small-town Shopping Behavior," *Southern Journal of Business,* vol. 5 (April 1970), pp. 24–32.

[39] Kent B. Monroe, "Measuring Price Thresholds by Psychophysics and Latitudes of Acceptance," *Journal of Marketing Research,* vol. 8 (November 1971), p. 463.

[40] *Grey Matter,* p. 3.

TABLE 5–6
HOW CUSTOMER'S ESTIMATES COMPARE WITH ACTUAL PRICES

	Buyers' estimates		
Product (ranked in order of buyers; correct estimates)	Correct price (± 5 percent)	Lower	Higher
Marlboro cigarettes (kings, carton)	71%	3%	26%
Land-O-Lakes butter (1 lb)	54	12	34
Scott paper towels (1 roll, 100 sq ft)	52	28	20
Fab detergent (giant 49 oz)	50	24	26
Private label coffee (1 lb)	47	35	18
Private label fruit cocktail (1ʹ6 oz)	46	37	17
Private label orange drink (46 oz)	42	47	11
Pillsbury Hungry Jack pancake mix (32 oz)	41	17	42
Carnation evaporated milk (13 oz)	38	42	20
Heinz catsup (14 oz)	37	34	29
Private label flour (5 lb)	36	32	32
Private label bleach (½ gallon)	36	39	25
Private label mayonnaise (quart)	36	46	18
Dole sliced pineapple (20 oz, 3 in.)	35	36	29
Ivory bar soap (large 9.5 oz)	33	41	26
Campbell tomato soup (10.75 oz)	33	32	35
Kleenex facial tissue (200 2-ply)	33	55	12
Domino sugar (5-lb bag)	33	54	13
SOS soap pads (10 count)	32	21	47
Private label canned milk (13 oz)..............	31	50	10
Morton chocolate cream pie	29	31	19
B & M baked pea beans (28 oz can)	28	29	43
Breck regular shampoo (11 oz)................	28	30	42
Kraft Miracle Whip salad dressing (quart)	28	57	15
Del Monte fruit cocktail (17 oz)	26	21	53
Coca-Cola (8-pack 12-oz cans)................	26	54	20
Dixie Cup 5 oz. refills (100 count).............	26	33	41
Armour bacon (1 lb sliced)	25	48	27
Tide XK detergent (giant 49 oz)	24	45	31
Kraft Soft Parkay margarine (1 lb)..............	24	56	20
Nestle Quik cocoa (1 lb)	24	40	36
Private label salad dressing (1 quart)	19	41	40
Crisco shortening (3 lb)	18	67	15
Clorox bleach (½ gallon)	18	48	34
Ken-L-Ration dog food (15.5 oz)...............	17	57	26
Private label apple sauce (25 oz)	16	57	27
Milk Bone biscuits (26 oz)	15	43	42
Green Giant niblets corn (12 oz)	15	19	66
Pillsbury's Best XXXX flour (5 lb)	14	33	53
Private label frozen orange juice (6 oz)	14	16	70
Kellogg's corn flakes (12 oz)	12	6	82
Crest toothpaste (3 oz)	10	43	47
Maxwell House instant coffee (6 oz)	9	66	25
Saran Wrap (100 sq ft)	8	43	49
Average of all items	29	38	33

* No comparison available.

Source: "What Shoppers Know and Don't Know About Prices," *Progressive Grocer*, vol. 53 (November 1974), p. 41.

	Nonbuyers' estimates		Estimates combined	
Correct price (± 5 percent)	Lower	Higher	Correct price (± 5 percent)	
36%	18%	46%	44%	54%
41	16	43	48	43
34	38	19	49	24
21	43	45	31	20
20	31	49	26	13
25	48	27	35	30
26	37	37	30	20
14	30	56	24	25
23	46	31	28	33
32	20	48	36	27
20	27	53	25	*
26	24	50	31	15
28	54	18	31	20
22	14	64	31	22
19	35	46	25	32
20	40	40	30	49
23	50	27	30	44
32	61	7	33	67
10	16	74	27	22
16	56	28	19	45
10	5	85	18	25
19	46	35	24	27
20	56	24	23	21
29	52	19	28	*
24	21	55	25	25
13	79	8	19	91
27	40	33	26	*
21	48	31	24	*
19	32	49	21	35
16	30	54	19	18
16	39	45	21	12
20	38	42	20	*
15	58	27	16	29
12	41	47	16	31
12	25	63	13	*
14	43	43	15	57
9	24	67	11	*
17	7	76	16	*
28	31	41	24	51
9	26	65	11	38
7	2	91	10	31
11	31	58	11	19
6	67	27	7	29
21	49	30	13	15
20	36	44	24	32

FIGURE 5–3
DEMAND CURVE IMPLIED BY THE
PRICE-LIMIT CONCEPT

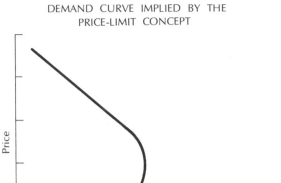

Median quantity demanded

prices, they are most likely to choose the middle-priced item. Retailers thus can influence the choice of products which are perceived as middle-priced. In particular, retailers who use price lists or price catalogs can influence the price perceptions of consumers.[41]

Store prestige interacts with price differentials in influencing consumer evaluations of brands. Consumers may assign a lower rating of quality to the low-price brand available in the high-prestige store than to the same low-price brand available in the low-prestige store. Price differentials among brands may be used by the consumer as a means of gauging whether wide quality differentials exist among the brands available in a product category.[42]

Customers who find it difficult to compare the prices of individual items directly tend to generalize from the overall price image of a store in judging prices. Price images tend to be relatively stable even in the face of special price promotions. In their pricing policies, stores should consider not only the pricing of individual items but also the need to develop a favorable overall price image.[43]

A store may not need to place low prices on every product in order to

[41] Kent B. Monroe and David M. Gardner, "An Experimental Inquiry into the Effect of Price on Brand Preference," in Kenneth L. Bernhardt (ed.), Marketing: 1776–1976 and Beyond (Chicago: American Marketing Association, 1976), p. 566.

[42] James E. Stafford and Ben M. Enis, "The Price-Quality Relationship: An Extension," Journal of Marketing Research, vol. 6 (November 1969), pp. 456–58.

[43] Harry Nystrom, Hans Tamsons, and Robert Thams, "An Experiment in Price Generalization and Discrimination," Journal of Marketing Research, vol. 12 (May 1975), p. 181; also John J. Wheatley and John S. V. Chiu, "The Effects of Price, Store Image, and Product and Store Characteristics on Perceptions of Quality," Journal of Marketing Research, vol. 14 (May 1977), pp. 181–85.

achieve a "low-price" image; only certain key items must be priced appropriately lower than expected. Information about a suggested price does influence the behavior of consumers in the purchase decision process. One experiment showed that when the retail selling price of an item was lowered to 15 percent below the manufacturer's suggested list price, there was a major increase in the attractiveness of the brand to consumers.[44]

Weber's Law.   Probably the two best-known theories of pricing are Weber's Law and the Fair Price Hypothesis. As applied to retail pricing, Weber's Law simply indicates that at higher price levels a greater change in price is required to influence consumer behavior. The Fair Price Hypothesis states that the consumer's perception of price is influenced more by the concept of a fair price for the product than by the degree of price difference. These two factors probably interact in influencing the consumer's perception of price.

"Retailers have long made use of the general rule of thumb that markdowns should amount to at least 20 percent of the old price to be in keeping with Weber's Law."[45] Even though many other variables intervene in affecting consumer perception, the use of Weber's Law can provide retailers with a better feel for the relationship between price changes and consumer perceptions. For example, if the retailer decides on a price reduction which is less than that which would be used under Weber's Law, the promotional emphasis should probably be on quality and other distinguishing features of the product rather than price. However, if the reduction in price is significant with respect to the absolute price as compared to the prices of competitive products, price probably should be emphasized in the retailer's advertising.

These findings on consumer perceptions of and reactions to retail prices reveal how far we still have to go in developing broadly based generalizations about these matters. Nevertheless, the findings do reveal that consumer reactions to price vary by market segment and that careful attention to this reality is essential in a demand-oriented pricing strategy. Simply following a cost-oriented approach to pricing or adding a predetermined percentage to the wholesale cost of a product ignores the realities of the marketplace.

Packaging

Packaging is only one element in a marketing program which operates at the point of sale. Packaging, however, is expected to perform at least three functions: (1) to identify the brand; (2) to identify the particular products of

---

[44] David C. Carlson, "Some Findings on How Demand May Be Affected by 'Suggested List Price' Cues," in Howard C. Schneider (ed.), *1976 American Institute for Decision Sciences Proceedings*, p. 581.

[45] Stewart Henderson Britt, "How Weber's Law Can Be Applied to Marketing," *Business Horizons*, February 1975, p. 24.

that brand; and (3) to differentiate the brand favorably from competition. A fourth function is to convey the proper image of the brand.[46]

Changes in technology and store features are causing packaging to play an increasingly important role. The retailer needs to be alert to whether packaging is making the shopper's search-and-find efforts easier and is helping the shopper to cope with in-store stress and tension.

In a pioneering study of packaging information, it was found that although the subjects felt better with more information, they actually made poorer purchase decisions. Instead of trying to provide more information to the consumer, the retailer should ask, "Just what specific information must or should the consumer have about the product, and how can we best organize and present that information?"[47]

Coupons

Approximately 30 billion cents-off coupons are distributed each year, according to a study by A. C. Nielsen. This figure includes regular cents-off coupons issued by manufacturers but not in-ad coupons in retailers' ads. More than half of the other coupons appeared in newspapers, approximately 13 percent in Sunday supplements, 7 percent in Sunday newspaper free-standing inserts, and almost 17 percent in magazines.[48] When all coupons are included, the annual total is approximately 50 billion. Only 10 percent of coupons are redeemed. The total cost of supporting all couponing is estimated to top $500 million.[49]

Coupons may be particularly useful in enabling retail management to draw new customers by attracting those loyal to other stores. Coupons may also be used to offset a particular negative attribute of the store—for example, by "drawing customers" to a less than ideal location.

Nine out of ten persons redeem coupons at one time or another.[50] One study of 96,000 consumer buying decisions indicated that "coupons were more effective for new products than for established products, that they were seldom useful in preventing a new competitive product from getting a foothold and that if a product was already in a sales skid, 'cents-off' usually did little to reverse the trend."[51]

As may be seen from the following quotation, the heaviest users of coupons are consumers with "upbeat profiles." Coupon users are big spenders whose transactions are above average in value.

[46] "Packaging Impact Test Finds Many Brands Are Not Noticed on Supermarket Shelves," *Marketing News,* October 10, 1975, p. 1.

[47] Jacob Jacoby, Donald E. Speller, and Carol A. Kohn, "Brand Choice Behavior as a Function of Information Load," *Journal of Marketing Research,* vol. 11 (February 1974), p. 68.

[48] *Marketing News,* April 11, 1975, p. 12.

[49] "What's behind the Coupon Boom?" *Progressive Grocer,* November 1974, p. 59.

[50] Ibid.

[51] Ibid.

Couponing's Biggest Boosters: Shoppers with Upbeat Profiles

More than nine out of ten housewives redeem coupons. Half (52%) use coupons frequently; 42% occasionally; 6% never, according to a recently released survey on coupon promotion by the Newspaper Advertising Bureau.

The report, based on studies by Foote, Cone & Belding and A. C. Nielsen, shows that those who frequently redeem coupons tend to live in highly urbanized areas. In rural areas, 42% use coupons often, 47% occasionally, 11% never.

Heavy users of coupons:

Are in higher income groups.

Live mostly in larger metropolitan areas.

Are better educated, frequently have college degrees.

Are from 39 to 49 years old.

Have more children than average.

Shop in ten different stores (compared to six for light users).

Make 14 trips per month to these stores (compared to 9 for light users).[52]

Open code dating

Open code dating is now taken for granted and expected in the super-market. Open code dating means that the consumer can tell the date after which an item of shelf stock should no longer be purchased. Most food shoppers use open code dating where it is available. The strongest users are the younger, the more affluent, and the more educated, and suburban residents. The benefits of open code dating to the retailer are (1) that it positions the firm as the friend of the consumer, and (2) that it increases the efficiency of stock rotation by employees. Clearly, open code dating can be a differential in-store advantage for the retailer in influencing what is bought.[53]

Stockouts and merchandise unavailability

One study investigated the effect of respondents' reactions to the un-availability of liquor on their shopping patterns. Approximately 40 percent of the shoppers indicated that they would shop at a different store to obtain the desired brand and size. These kinds of consumer decisions can have a major adverse impact on profit and revenue.[54] Product unavailability is a major source of consumer dissatisfaction and a frequent occurrence in such categories as food.[55] For food items, however, consumer response to a hypothetical case of product unavailability may be quite different from ac-

---

[52] Ibid.

[53] Prabhaker Nayak and Larry J. Rosenberg, "Does Open Dating of Food Products Benefit the Consumer?" *Journal of Retailing*, vol. 51 (Summer 1975), p. 19.

[54] C. K. Walter and John R. Grabner, "Stock-out Cost Models: Empirical Tests in a Retail Situation," *Journal of Marketing*, vol. 39 (July 1975), p. 59.

[55] J. Barry Mason and J. B. Wilkinson, "Mispricing and Unavailability of Advertised Food Specials," *Journal of Business of the University of Chicago*, vol. 49 (April 1976), pp. 219–25.

tual consumer behavior. Research, for example, has shown that even though 45 percent of shoppers indicated that they would change their place of patronage if they encountered unavailability, only 6 percent actually responded in this manner when the unavailability occurred.[56]

Unit pricing

Consumers have come to accept unit pricing as a guide in their in-store shopping. Unit pricing is primarily used by the younger, more highly educated consumer.[57] Unit pricing was initially established with the idea that it would provide more and better information to low-income consumers. Varying percentages of shoppers are reported to have switched brands because of unit pricing information. Two of the more rigorous studies have indicated switching rates of approximately 10 percent.[58] Friedman found that about half of the switching was to private brands. Similar findings have been reported elsewhere.[59]

Shelf space

The following generalizations relative to shelf space have been offered:

1. Impulse items are more responsive to space changes than are staples.
2. Manufacturers' brands are less space elastic than their private brand counterparts.
3. Shelf space changes have a greater effect on faster-selling products than on slower-selling products.
4. Shelf space changes seem to affect sales more in larger stores than in smaller stores.[60]

Generous space allocation is especially desirable for new products. It is likely to be perceived by the consumer as conveying the message that a product is well liked by other persons and that it is therefore OK to buy it.

A retailer may maximize profits by assigning the maximum facing to those products with the highest profit margins and the greatest shelf facing effects. Ideally, the increased sales that result from increased shelf facings increase

---

[56] J. Barry Mason and J. B. Wilkinson, "Insights into Supermarket Product Unavailability and the Consumer Response," paper presented at the Indiana University Conference on Consumer Satisfaction/Dissatisfaction and Complaining Behavior, April 1977.

[57] Jim Guin, "Shoppers' Perceptual Differences of Unit Pricing," in Henry Nash and Donald Robin (eds.), *Proceedings: Southern Marketing Association,* 1976, p. 44.

[58] Monroe Friedman, "Dual Price Labels: Usage Patterns and Potential Benefits for Shoppers in Inner-city and Suburban Supermarkets," *Congressional Record,* April 15, 1971; and C. E. Block, Robert Schooler, and David Erikson, "Consumer Reaction to Unit Pricing: An Empirical Study," *Mississippi Valley Journal of Business and Economics,* vol. 7 (Winter 1971–72).

[59] T. David McCullough and Daniel J. Padberg, *Unit Pricing in Supermarkets: Alternatives, Costs, and Consumer Reaction* (Ithaca: Cornell University Agricultural Experiment Station, 1971).

[60] Ronald C. Curhan, "Shelf Space Allocation and Profit Maximization in Mass Retailing," *Journal of Marketing,* vol. 37 (July 1973), p. 57.

the generic demand for the product category. The retailer may maximize total sales by allocating shelf facings to the products most responsive to additional facings.[61] Sales are reduced and consumer preference is adversely affected when shifts in store display and layout are too frequent.[62]

More research is needed on the effects of high or low shelf location and on end-of-aisle location and corresponding traffic patterns. Trade publications indicate that point-of-sale materials, even simple shelf signs, can increase item sales over 100 percent and that for end-of-aisle and special displays, "even dull displays can be expected to double or triple sales; tests show outstanding displays can increase sales by 700 percent or more."[63]

Shelf space is a major factor affecting shopping behavior. For example, Levi Strauss has begun distributing shoes through Brown Shoe Company. Instead of the usual way of displaying shoes on shelves, the shoes hang on rods (like ready-to-wear) for all 12 sizes to be displayed. "This gets the entire stock in each size out front so that the customer might be influenced to buy a second pair."[64] In one test market store, the shoes turned six times on an annualized basis as compared to an industry average of 1.9 times per year. Markups remained the same.

HOW CONSUMERS SHOP

Attitudes toward time and distance affect how consumers shop and are reflected in some of the shopper typologies mentioned earlier, for example, the apathetic shopper. Thus, retailers must understand how the search process for products and services is conducted and the distances consumers are willing to travel as part of that process.

Also, some consumers choose not to purchase from retail stores and may decide to purchase by catalog or telephone. Some even purchase from door-to-door salespersons. Thus, retailers need to understand the motives which prompt this type of behavior. They can then seek to adjust their strategies to attract the nonstore shopper, or if they are among the non-store retailers, they can stress the factors which are especially sought in nonstore shopping.

Attitudes toward time and distance

The costs of shopping. Consumers seek to minimize the costs incurred in shopping. These costs are money, time, and energy, and they greatly affect

---

[61] Jeffrey A. Cotzan and Robert V. Evanson, "Responsiveness of Drug Store Sales to Shelf Space Allocations," *Journal of Marketing Research*, vol. 6 (November 1969), p. 469.

[62] L. W. Jacobs, "The Continuity Factor in Retail Store Display," *Journal of the Academy of Marketing Science*, vol. 2 (Spring 1974), pp. 340–50.

[63] "The Brand Power Study: 13 Reasons for Welcoming Salesmen," *Progressive Grocer*, November 1976, p. 54.

[64] "Now Levi Puts Its Brand on Shoes," *Business Week*, November 10, 1975, p. 124.

how the consumer shops for goods and services. *Money costs* include the cost of goods purchased and the cost of transportation. *Time costs* include time spent traveling to and from the shopping place, time spent in moving from the auto to the store and back, and time spent in selecting and paying for goods. *Energy costs* include the energy spent in any normal period and to that extent are proportional to the amount of time involved in shopping. Extra energy, however, may be expended in carrying packages and in the frustration that results from such things as traffic difficulties, parking problems, and waiting in lines.

The importance of the above costs vary by consumer. However, for standardized products, such as staples, the time saved by purchasing at the most conveniently located store is probably more important than the small amount of money which could be saved by comparison shopping at several different outlets. Thus, the retailer needs to be particularly careful to locate as closely as possible to consumers seeking such goods. This is the location strategy of the neighborhood mini-marts.

Types of search.   As one moves along the continuum from standardized goods to specialized or shopping goods, location may become somewhat less important in attracting the consumer. The extent to which consumers are willing to search among stores varies with the amount of utility (money, time, or energy) which can be saved by shopping at additional stores. A *full search* by consumers involves shopping at several alternative stores in the expectation of saving a sizable amount of money. An example of full search would be the purchase of an automobile. *Casual search* occurs when the consumer is aware that little money will be saved by shopping at a variety of outlets. In such instances the consumer is likely to purchase from the nearest outlet.[65]

On each shopping trip some costs are fixed. The consumer has to expend a certain amount of time and energy, regardless of whether a purchase is made. The sophisticated retailer will try to help the consumer minimize the total costs of shopping by spreading the time and energy costs for a given trip over a larger "quantity of shopping." In other words, the retailer will try to help the consumer make as many purchases as possible on a single trip. The greater the returns which are enjoyed on a particular trip, the greater the cost the consumer is willing to bear in making it. The consumer is not likely to travel farther than is necessary to purchase goods or services, however, unless the more distant outlet has a better image, better atmospherics, or other psychological utilities.

Physical search patterns.   Less time is spent in physical search for merchandise today than in the past. The reasons include the increased affluence of consumers, which has made time saved more important than money, and the widespread access and exposure to mass media advertising which is a source of product information. In the selection of shopping goods, for

---

[65] Louis Bucklin, "The Concept of Mass in Intra-urban Shopping," *Journal of Marketing*, vol. 31 (October 1967), pp. 37–42.

example, it is unlikely that a person will visit more than two stores. Indeed, the typical consumer may visit only one store.[66] These patterns are true for a variety of shopping goods.[67] After an analysis of shopping behavior in Boston, Atlanta, Portland (Oregon), Omaha, and Erie (Pennsylvania), the Newspaper Advertising Bureau offered the following portrait of movement and search patterns of today's shopper:

. . . even though the shopper may go some distance, 64% of visits to a center are to only one store, both to look around and to buy, with only 16% of visits to three or more stores. Trips are generally not planned in advance; 71% are made to fill a definite need that same day, although 48% reported they almost always shop for sale items.[68]

This increasing consumer reluctance to physically compare merchandise offerings at several stores makes the location decision of increasing importance. The retailer needs to be centrally located to as many shoppers as possible, to have good atmospherics, to be located in proximity to complementary retail outlets so as to facilitate easy comparison shopping, and to carry nationally advertised—and thus presold—brands.

How far are shoppers willing to travel?

One major study of 18,000 shoppers found that shopping behavior is consistent, regardless of city size or region.[69] More than two thirds of the shoppers made half or more of their merchandise purchases outside their own neighborhood. As shown in Table 5–7, 61 percent traveled ten minutes or more to shop and 44 percent traveled five miles or more for general merchandise purchases. Such trips are typically made once a week. For convenience food stores, over 50 percent of shoppers travel less than one-half mile to reach the outlet.[70] The distance traveled for the purchase of general merchandise items increases with income. The willingness to travel greater distances decreases with age, however.

The retailer must attract shoppers from as wide an area as possible because not all shoppers are buyers. On a typical shopping day, only 95 women in 1,000 look at women's outerwear and only 37 in 1,000 actually make a purchase. Of these, 11 make the purchase even though they are not

---

[66] William P. Dommermuth and Edward W. Cundiff, "Shopping Goods, Shopping Centers, and Selling Strategies," *Journal of Marketing*, vol. 31 (October 1967), p. 33; see also Arno Kleimenhagen, "Shopping, Specialty, or Convenience Goods," *Journal of Retailing*, Winter 1966–67, p. 36.

[67] Joseph Barry Mason and Morris L. Mayer, "Empirical Observations of Consumer Behavior in the Marketplace: Implications for a Classification of Goods System and Retail Strategy Formulation," *Journal of Retailing*, vol. 48 (Fall 1972), pp. 22–23.

[68] "Shopping Habits," *Chain Store Age*, July 1975, p. 10.

[69] "Shoppers on the Move: Behavior Proves Consistent," *Stores*, March 1975, p. 6.

[70] "Who Shops Convenience Stores?" *Progressive Grocer*, November 1976, p. 69.

TABLE 5–7
SHOPPER PROFILES

Distance: Home to shopping area*

1 mile or less	22%
2–4 miles	34
5–9 miles	24
10 miles or more	20

* Visits for general merchandise.

Travel time: Home to shopping area*

Less than 10 minutes	39%
10–19 minutes	39
20 minutes or more	22

* Visits for general merchandise.

Distance: By income

	Under $10,000	$10,000– 14,999	$15,000 and over
1 mile or less	28%	22%	17%
2–4 miles	36	36	31
5 miles or more	36	42	52

Distance: By age

	18–34	35–64	65 and over
1 mile or less	18%	22%	32%
2–4 miles	33	35	32
5 miles or more	49	43	36

Source: Reprinted from "Shoppers on the Move: Behavior Proves Consistent," *Stores*, March 1975, National Retail Merchants Association, p. 6.

shopping for that particular item.[71] Some generalizations are also possible about the distances consumers are willing to travel to reach major shopping centers. For example, research has shown that approximately 75 percent of the patrons of a shopping center are likely to live within 15 minutes of the center.[72]

Nonstore shopping

Some consumers may choose to buy by the use of the catalog, by telephone, or by other nonstore means of purchasing. These in-home shoppers are not a captive market. Catalog and phone ordering are discretionary and

[71] James A. Brunner and John L. Mason, "The Influence of Driving Time on Shopping Center Preference," *Journal of Marketing*, vol. 32 (April 1968), pp. 57–61.

[72] L. A. Brown and J. Holmes, "Search Behavior in an Intra-urban Migration Context: A Spatial Perspective," *Environment and Planning*, 1971, pp. 307–26.

are based largely on convenience. In-home shoppers are less bound by shopping traditions and perceive less than average risk in buying by mail or phone. They are also more affluent and better educated than other shoppers. The results of over 40 research efforts on in-home shopping reveal that "the average in-home shopper tends to be more self-assured, venturesome, and cosmopolitan in outlook and in shopping behavior."[73]

Retailers can lower shopping costs and increase in-home sales by promoting the convenience and ease of shopping by mail or phone. Attention should also be given to merchandise quality, competitive prices, and store image. Themes based on the unpleasantness of store shopping are not likely to be effective since in-home shoppers are also frequent store customers and hold favorable attitudes toward stores.

Approximately 6,500 companies use mail order as a marketing vehicle. During the course of a year, one third of all Americans make at least one purchase from a mail-order organization.[74]

A major increase in mail-order sales has occurred as a result of a form of mail-order distribution known as syndication. This is a merger of the mail-order selling technique and the extension of consumer credit through credit cards. Most consumers are familiar with materials inserted into monthly credit statements which offer a variety of products for sale. The participating firms include such organizations as Diners Club, American Express, Shell Oil Company, and RCA Records.

Buying convenience, credit extension, and impulse factors are major reasons for the widespread acceptance of mail-order promotions. The quality of the promotional materials used and favorable prices are also important factors. In addition, liberal product guarantees have reduced risks and free bonus products have provided an extra incentive that induces many consumers to respond.[75]

In-home shoppers have been segmented into three groups. The first segment consists of people who shop from large catalog outlets, book clubs, and specialty outlets. These shoppers are higher income upper-class persons with high levels of education and white-collar occupations. They are also classified as venturesome. The second group consists of persons who patronize novelty outlets as opposed to specialty outlets. These persons tend to be distrusting, local in orientation, and in the early stages of the life cycle. The last group consists of persons who patronize specialty and credit card outlets. They resemble persons in the first segment except that they are less venturesome.[76]

[73] Peter Gillett, "In-home Shoppers—An Overview," Journal of Marketing, vol. 40 (October 1976), p. 86.

[74] "11 Publicly-Owned Consumer Mail Order Companies Outperform Major Retailers," Marketing News, November 19, 1976, p. 6.

[75] Jack M. Starling, "Syndication: Direct Merchandising to Credit Clientele," Journal of Retailing, vol. 49 (Winter 1973–74), p. 30.

[76] Isabella Cunningham and William H. Cunningham, "The Urban In-home Shopper: Socioeconomic and Attitudinal Characteristics," Journal of Retailing, vol. 49 (Fall 1973), p. 50.

WHEN TO BUY

Less research has been conducted on the "when" of consumer purchasing or shopping than on the other aspects of consumer behavior. Yet the decision on "when" is being affected increasingly by a variety of factors, including changes in the legal environment, the growing proportion of working wives, and even the emerging effects of the nation's energy policy.

Sunday openings

Traditionally, Sunday openings of retail outlets have been illegal in many states unless exceptions in state law allowed such businesses as pharmacists and gasoline stations to remain open. Such regulations vary widely from state to state and are often archaic and discriminatory. The laws are enforced only sporadically. More recently, however, concerted efforts have occurred in many states to eliminate the Sunday closing requirement. The proponents of both Sunday opening and Sunday closing have been highly vocal. Even many retailers are divided on the question. Small retailers in particular oppose Sunday openings. Nonetheless, increasing pressure by working wives and by families seeking a period of togetherness on a day away from work may cause Sunday openings to occur on a more frequent basis than has been true in the past.

The effects of working wives

Currently, over 45 percent of married women are employed outside the home. The constantly rising percentage of working wives has shifted significant amounts of shopping activity to either early morning or evenings. Thus, pressures are mounting to have shopping hours extended to allow for earlier openings, as with banks, and for later evening hours. Also, Friday evenings and Saturdays are becoming increasingly heavy shopping times. Thus, the retailer feels pressure for longer hours of business, but without much additional volume. This may affect profitability adversely. An increasing amount of the shopping in families where both the husband and wife work is performed by teenage members of the family. In addition, working wives have less time to spend in various types of information seeking and processing. Some studies have shown, as noted earlier in this chapter, that the result is a stronger tendency to purchase national brands as part of an overall risk reduction strategy to avoid a "wrong" decision made under the pressure of time constraints.

The effects of environmental changes

Changing conditions in the economic environment also affect the when of shopping. For example, the proposed peak-load pricing of electricity would set the highest rates for the daytime and the lowest for the late-night hours. "For retailers, the implications are obvious: stores are open during the peak daytime demand periods, and closed during the lowest demand periods."[77] If differences in the electricity rate structure by time of day become sufficiently large, shopping hours may be altered by retailers simply as a matter of profitability. Outlets might open later, for example at noon, and close much later in the evening. Outlets which are now open 24 hours a day for the convenience of customers might also begin to reduce their hours of operation. Perhaps both night and Sundays openings will be eliminated.

Research has also shown that partly as a result of the energy embargo and partly as a result of rapid inflation shoppers as a group are making fewer trips, making more multipurpose trips, and traveling shorter distances to shop. These behavior changes raise questions about the continued strength of the large regional shopping centers which draw traffic from a wide metropolitan area. Conversely, such trends may encourage the renewed vitality of downtown shopping areas and smaller neighborhood establishments. A resurgence in the bus as a mode of transportation would also affect both the when and the where of shopping. The stagflation economy of the early and middle 1970s made for an overall reduction in shopping activity. Fewer stores were shopped; driving times were shorter; retail traffic was down significantly, and price predominated over quality in product choice.[78]

Effects of technological change

Changes in the technology of shopping will also have major impacts on the when of shopping. By the late 1980s, remote retailing will probably be a reality, with most routine purchases made by consumers from their homes. "Retail outlets will offer only those products that the customer must feel or smell before making a buying decision."[79] Rapid advances in minicomputers, Picturephone availability, and the availability of cable television channels for continuous advertising will contribute to further flexibility in the when of shopping. These possibilities will cause yet-to-be-determined changes in consumer behavior and major shifts in the strategies of retailers as they strive to compete with the increasing options for nonstore shopping. Already, catalog shopping is rapidly expanding in popularity as a nonstore alternative, broadening the when of consumer shopping to 24 hours a day, seven days a week.

---

[77] Verrick O. French, "Proposed 'Peakload' Rate Structure Would Boost Retail Electric Bills," *Stores*, March 1977, p. 53.

[78] Richard T. Hise, Myron Gable, and Michael A. McGinnis, "Shopping Behavior in a Stagflation Economy: An Empirical Analysis," in Henry Nash and Donald Robin (eds.), *Proceedings: Southern Marketing Association*, 1976.

[79] Belden Menkus, "Remote Retailing: A Reality by 1985?" *Chain Store Age Executive*, September 1975, p. 42.

Consumer segments

As noted above for working wives, some segmentation on the basis of time is possible in developing retail strategies. Elderly persons prefer to shop in the mornings and particularly dislike evening shopping.[80] Thus, separate events can perhaps be arranged during the morning hours to attract such persons during these normally slow shopping times. Also, because of the time teenage shoppers spend in school, they are normally best served during the late afternoon or early evening hours.

Finally, 20 percent of the sales by some retail outlets occur during December. Other popular shopping times for some products include Easter, July 4, Thanksgiving, and Halloween. Also, such services as the tax counseling offered by H & R Block are sought primarily only during a few months of the year. Additional examples could be offered, but the rationale for focusing on the when of shopping as related to consumer behavior seems clear.

SUMMARY

Consumer behavior can be characterized as a series of decision processes. Consumers enter the marketplace seeking solutions to problems and the fulfillment of their needs or wants. Various processes (whether information seeking, information processing, or learning) are part of consumers' problem-solving behavior, as are the various evaluative criteria which consumers use. Thus, consumer behavior is an exercise in problem solving. Consumers recognize problems, search for and evaluate information, evaluate alternatives, and then make decisions to purchase or not to purchase.

Key decisions consumers make in shopping are what merchandise to buy, where and when to buy it, and how best to shop for it. The task of the retailer is to have the right merchandise at the right place, time, price, and quality to meet the needs of consumers.

KEY CONCEPTS

Why people buy
   Personal motives
   Social motives
Shopper typologies
Consumer decision making
   Information search
   The processing of information

---

[80] J. Barry Mason and Brooks E. Smith, "The Shopping Behavior of the Low Income Senior Citizen," *Journal of Consumer Affairs,* vol. 8 (Winter 1974–75), p. 205.

Consumer decisions
   Evaluative criteria
   Decision assessments
Major consumer decisions
   Where to buy
      Downtown versus the CBD
      Store choice
      Out-shopping
      Image
   What to buy
      Private brands versus national brands
      Reactions to prices
      Packaging
      Coupons
      Shelf space
      Open code dating
      Unit pricing
   How consumers shop
      Search patterns
      Distances traveled
      Nonstore shopping
   When to purchase
      Working wives
      Environmental influences
      Technological influences

DISCUSSION QUESTIONS

1. The urban in-home shopper is more highly educated and more mobile and has a higher income than the average consumer, and has a greater willingness to take risk than the non-in-home shopper. How would you use this information in developing a specific retailing strategy to attract this market segment?

2. Define evaluative criteria. Think back to your last purchase of an item of clothing. What criteria did you use in making that purchase? Are those criteria the same as the criteria you use in purchasing other products?

3. Many products which a consumer purchases do not involve a process of external search. Why is this so? Is it to the retailer's advantage to induce search on the part of the consumer?

4. List the features which you think characterize opinion leaders. How would you as a retailer identify opinion leaders? Do you ever seek information from opinion leaders? Why or why not?

5. Develop a research proposal which is designed to determine the influence of opinion leaders on the purchase of women's fashion dresses.

6. Assume that you are in the process of purchasing an automobile. Which sources of information would you seek? Would you seek information from

marketer-dominated information sources, consumer-dominated information sources, or neutral information sources? What types of information would you seek from these various sources?

7. What is the importance of image to the retailer? How does it affect the shopping behavior of consumers? Think of the two largest department stores in your community. How would you describe their image? What types of people do you think would shop in each of the two stores? What differences in consumer behavior do you think exist between these stores?

8. Outline plans for a research project which is designed to determine the image of two fashion specialty outlets in your community which cater primarily to college students.

9. What person do you know who frequently purchases private brands? Why does this person purchase private brands? How does the behavior of this person contrast with that of members of your own family?

10. Why is it important for the retailer to consider the effect of shelf displays, product unavailability, and brand loyalty on consumer behavior?

11. What would you expect the effect of unit pricing and open code dating to be on the behavior of consumers?

12. Think back to your last purchase of a consumer durable. Write an essay on the purchase which reflects all of the various dimensions of the where, when, what, and how of your behavior in making the purchase.

PROJECTS

1. Divide into groups, and have each group select five products which are currently very popular (for example, automatic coffee makers, such as Mr. Coffee). Have each member of your group visit a store and classify each product by its amount of shelf space and the location of shelf space in relationship to that of other products in the same merchandise class, and number of units of product displayed in relationship to the number of units of products displayed for other products in the same merchandise class.

2. Devise a questionnaire suitable for classifying shoppers into the shopper typologies discussed in the text. Interview at least ten shoppers, and classify them according to those typologies. Give your reasons for such classification.

3. Choose three completely different types of retail institutions in your area (for example, a conventional department store, a discount department store, and a women's sportswear boutique), and interview management as to the "image" it is attempting to create in the minds of its defined target market. Over a period of time, clip ads from each of the stores and evaluate the "image" depicted by these promotions relative to the objectives of the firm. If possible, some consumer interviews might be administered to see what their perception of the images of these same stores are. Critically evaluate the compatibility or dissonance created by these activities.

4. Select the stores in a shopping center (preferably a regional mall or at least one of community size), and identify those which carry a particular line of merchandise

(for example, junior dresses). Compose an observation sheet on which you will attempt to gather comparative data from each of the competitive stores (for example, price, colors, fabrics, styles, brands, and sizes, depending upon the line selected). Prepare a summary chart by store on the factors you considered, and then write up a narrative indicating the apparent strategy employed by each store to reach its markets. Also define what you consider to be the target market which each store appears to be aiming toward.

CASES

Case 1. A contemporary U.S. phenomenon has been the migration out of the inner city. As in so many towns in the United States, this has occurred in Factoryville. One project to revive the inner city has been Sunset Manor, a high-rise apartment complex for elderly retired people. Getting to the supermarket has become quite a problem for these people. There is a convenience store within walking distance, but it is not satisfactory to the tenants of Sunset Manor. There is a bus once a week, sponsored by a local civic group which transports these senior citizens to a suburban shopping center. If they want to go shopping, all they need do is call the group a couple of days before the day the bus runs. Lately there have been very few calls, and the members of the civic group are considering not sponsoring the bus. What has gone wrong in this situation? How would you suggest that the situation be corrected?

Case 2. The Bay City Bridge Club was having its usual Wednesday afternoon meeting. This particular Wednesday Mrs. Moore was late, so the other three ladies, Mrs. Young, Ms. Gilbert, and Mrs. Sanders, were having coffee—while they waited for her to arrive. The conversation turned to food stores, and it ran like this:

Ms. G: I usually shop at Quality Foods. The prices there are lower.

Mrs. S: I've found things high there, and I go to B&Q. The prices are much lower there, I've found.

Mrs. Y: I think you'll find that the new foodstore—what is its name?—anyway you mark and bag your own groceries. The prices are lowest there. And the produce is beautiful. The meats are red and fresh and cook so tender!

Mrs. S: Do you shop there often? How do you know the prices are lower?

Mrs. Y: Of course. I go there all the time. Besides, haven't you seen the commercials? They tell you all about it.

Ms. G: I never believe commercials. I always get the feeling they are trying to hoodwink me.

Describe these types of shopper behavior.

6

A MACRO VIEW OF CONSUMERS: MARKET SEGMENTATION

*L*ocated in one of the country's most affluent suburbs, our shop serves the segment of the market comprised of the upper upper-class. Customers travel from a number of prestigious residential areas, some distance away, where there are quality shops offering the same merchandise that we do. There is active competition among establishments serving this segment, inasmuch as there is the question whether a woman will select her Halston at Bonwit's, Saks Fifth Avenue, or Margaret Rice.

Trust and confidence are crucial in building any successful business. When an establishment caters to the wealthy, something more is required. These individuals are accustomed to obtaining maximum value for their money; they know quality; and they are not at all timid about expressing dissatisfaction.

We believe that the backbone of a small shop is a loyal clientele and that the only way to achieve that objective is an overworked but underutilized word in American business today—service. Our business grew by word of mouth because of the personal service which has always been our trademark and which, for us, assumes several dimensions. To illustrate several: (1) we buy merchandise with specific customers in mind, which requires knowing individual preferences vis-à-vis current fashion; (2) we buy very few numbers of any item in order to emphasize the exclusivity which our customers value; (3) salespersons are exceedingly skillful in suggesting coordinating items which enhance appearance and individuality while increasing sales; (4) a customer is discouraged from selecting an unsuitable item (based on age, figure, or because her best friend selected the same one and they belong to the same clubs) because she will soon regret her error and blame the mistake in judgment on the shop; (5) even the decor of the shop is planned to be exciting and is changed frequently to avoid boredom. Customers appreciate all of these personal touches, and these have paid off for us when other quality shops have offered identical merchandise. Our label has become a status symbol in its own right, and we believe that all of this has happened because the founder and proprietress is on the premises at all times. Even the most effective manager of a store in a chain would not have the same motivation as the person who has the most to gain or lose.

Margaret Rice, President
Margaret Rice, Inc.
Grosse Pointe Farms, Michigan

Retailers typically develop marketing strategies for aggregates of people. Market segmentation is a way of improving the retailer's ability to understand the various markets which are best served by particular locations or categories of merchandise. Segmentation involves subdividing the market and then tailoring products and/or messages for all or a subset of the segments thus identified.

As noted by the president of Federated Department Stores: "Customers don't fall into just a few broad groups. Markets are becoming increasingly fragmented as more people search for their own identity and answers. These attitudes are resulting in great diversity of desires, demands, lifestyles, and values."[1] Still, most segmentation studies usually identify five or six groups of consumers for a product or service. Thus, the purposes of this chapter are:

1. To introduce the concept of market segmentation and to illustrate the use of segmentation as a retail strategy.
2. To illustrate the key factors which must be considered in selecting a strategy of merchandise or store differentiation.
3. To illustrate the way in which market targets may be classified by retailers.
4. To provide an overview of selected research findings on the use of socioeconomic, demographic, and behavioral variables as bases for retail market segmentation.

THE NATURE OF SEGMENTATION

Differences in consumers affect distribution, media, and pricing decisions at the retail level. John Maynard Keynes introduced the concept of segmentation which is generally used to study consumption behavior. However, economists tend to assume a homogeneous market with a single demand schedule. Marketers recognize that markets and customers are not all alike. Nevertheless, retailers must still seek groups of customers with common features and not try to serve all people. The retailer desires to group consumers on some common basis so as to more effectively serve their needs.

Retailing strategy to accomplish this goal may be viewed as a two-stage process in which management (1) identifies the markets which it desires to serve and (2) develops a retailing mix which appeals to each segment. The goal is to offer the right product at the right price and place with the right promotion. Without segmentation it may not be possible to do a credible job of determining merchandise lines, establishing price policy, developing advertising objectives, and developing a proper location for a new outlet.

These points are clearly illustrated in the comments of persons knowledgeable about retailing. Let's look at a few of these comments as a backdrop for studying retail market segmentation.

---

[1] Presentation to the New York Society of Security Analysts, November 21, 1974, p. 6.

Bloomingdale's: According to the vice president, marketing, Bloomingdale's, "We segmented our thinking by life-style and developed physical areas for Via Europa, Peterborough Row, the Traditionalist, the Sportsman, the Polo Man, and Saturday's Generation. Our merchants work with suppliers here and abroad to find and develop clothing and furnishings to meet these specific customer profiles."[2]

Grey Advertising: "Increasingly the smart retailer is recognizing that he must communicate his 'positioning' with consumers through every single one of his contacts with them. . . . older 'class' stores once targeted at the carriage trade, for example, are finding that they must completely reeducate personnel to meet changing needs of new customers."[3]

Westinghouse Broadcasting Company: "Stores have to segment their messages as well as merchandise assortment. . . . it all goes back to knowing precisely who your customers are and understanding their lifestyles."[4]

Broadway Department Stores: Richard T. Hauser, president, in talking about a comprehensive and diversified research program for successful retailing, stresses the effectiveness of "a psychographic analysis of shoppers that relates people's attitudes about themselves and their life situations to the merchandising program of individual retailers."[5]

Eleanor G. May: "A long-established goal of being 'all things to all people' is not possible in today's consumer market. A store must decide which segments of the market it is serving, or wants to serve, and then attempt to match the store to the need of these consumers."[6]

The requirements for segmentation

The basic requirements for effective segmentation are:

1. . . . to identify and categorize actual or potential buyers into mutually exclusive groups (segments that have relatively homogeneous responses to controllable marketing variables).
2. . . . to identify certain characteristics of the mutually exclusive groups which can be used as a basis for directing specialized marketing efforts to the different groups.[7]

Further, segments must also represent sizable enough units in terms of sales and profit potential to warrant the effort.

---

[2] "Consumers seek stores where clothes match current changing life-styles, three retailers agree," *Marketing News,* February 25, 1977, p. 9.

[3] *Grey Matter* (New York: Grey Advertising, 1975), p. 7.

[4] "Department Stores Redefine Their Role," *Business Week,* December 13, 1976, p. 48.

[5] "Right Research Helps Stores Relate People to Selling Programs," *Marketing News,* November 19, 1976, p. 6.

[6] Eleanor G. May, "Practical Applications of Recent Retail Image Research," *Journal of Retailing,* vol. 50 (Winter 1974–75), p. 19.

[7] Harper W. Boyd, Jr., and William F. Massy, *Marketing Management* (New York: Harcourt Brace Jovanovich, 1972), p. 89.

In strategy development, customers can be viewed in terms of one of the following three bases, depending on the product or service offered:

Similarity—all consumers are basically similar. Although differences exist among consumers (for example, age, income, and so forth) these differences are not thought to be important in affecting the purchase of the specific product class. A standard product will essentially satisfy a large majority of consumers.

Unique—all consumers are unique. The differences among consumers (for example, age, income, needs, preferences, and so forth) make a standardized product unacceptable. Market offerings must be tailored specifically to the needs of each individual consumer.

Differences/Similarities—consumer differences and similarities exist and are important sources of influence in market demand. Such differences can be regarded as differences in consumer needs and wants. These differences and similarities facilitate the grouping of consumers in aggregates or segments according to their needs and wants and the degree to which they are present.[8]

Similarities among consumers

Aggregation as a retail strategy assumes that all consumers are alike. Many retailers follow such a policy. They do not recognize varying demand curves for different groups of consumers. The focus is on the common dimensions of the market, and the strategy is to attract the broadest possible number of buyers by an appeal to the universal themes of price or quality.

Aggregation, if followed by many retailers in the same market, creates intense competition for the largest market segments. Reliance is placed on mass distribution, mass advertising, and a universal theme of low price. This approach to retail strategy is probably the least expensive of the possible approaches to segmentation. On the other hand, all efforts at segmentation are expensive, but ideally such efforts have a high impact in terms of increased sales relative to costs. Aggregation appears to be the philosophy followed by such retailers as K-Mart and Woolco.

The concept of similarity also seems to have been followed by *Playboy* magazine for many years, but it is now causing the magazine some problems. As the advertising director for *Playboy* stated: "To move *Playboy* off its current circulation plateau, the publishers are narrowing the magazine's target market. . . . The plan is to present *Playboy* as an alternative to such magazines as *Time, Newsweek,* and *Sports Illustrated. . . .* Instead of focusing on males 14–64, *Playboy* will try to appeal to 18–34 upscale males in clerical, managerial, and professional jobs."[9]

---

[8] James F. Engel, Henry F. Fiorillo, and Murray A. Cayley, *Marketing Segmentation: Concepts and Applications* (New York: Holt, Rinehart and Winston, 1971), p. 4.

[9] "*Playboy* Fights Circulation Drop with Narrower Focus, New Content," *Marketing News,* March 25, 1977, p. 9.

Partial segmentation

A partial segmentation strategy recognizes that groups of consumers have differing needs. Goods and services are offered to most segments of the market, but different products and/or services are offered to each segment. This approach is designed to provide increased sales and better overall market penetration. For example, since the teenage market for records has peaked at a demand of 30 million annually, it is "imperative to have records that appeal to buyers of all ages and interests. Buyers are no longer simply bracketed in 'classical' and 'popular' markets, but are placed in a variety of categories: 'disco sound,' 'soul,' 'country,' or 'rockability,' and others."[10] The strategy represents an effort to sell small numbers of albums to many different markets, rather than try to develop a few million seller albums. Clearly this approach offers advantages to the retail music shop.

Partial segmentation seems to be the approach followed by Gold Circle, the discount department store affiliate of Federated Department Stores. As noted by its president: "We cater to young families, aged 20 to 35. You would find our customer is likely to be female with a moderate income. She is alert to taste, quality, and fashion trends. Her desires probably exceed her limited income and therefore she is responsive to honest value."[11] Similarly, Melville Shoe Corporation states that its "top customers are fashion-following shoppers under 35."[12]

Uniqueness

In extreme segmentation, the retailer concentrates primarily on a very narrowly defined segment. This approach enables the retailer to obtain greater knowledge of the consumer's needs and to handle more specialized product lines. Thus the outlet is likely to acquire a special reputation and strong customer loyalty. An example of this strategy is the retail outlet specializing in tall or stout persons' clothes. Likewise, a firm specializing in maternity wear fits this description, as does a boutique featuring only high-fashion women's wear.

The emphasis is on differentiated marketing whereby the outlet is characterized as providing personalized service and depth of product lines. Price as a strategy variable is of less importance than in the other strategies. For example, the philosophy of such outlets as Neiman-Marcus and Bergdorf Goodman is that "fashion retailers must offer more sales help and other costly customer services; above all, they must come up with the trendiest

---

[10] "The Record Industry Sounds a Note of Joy," *Business Week*, December 1, 1975, p. 54.

[11] Hal W. Ford, Published text of: *Presentation to the New York Society of Security Analysts*, November 21, 1974, p. 32.

[12] "Melville Steps into the Billion-Dollar Class," *Business Week*, April 11, 1977, p. 58.

items, which demands flexibility, eagle-eyed buying, and quick turnover of merchandise."[13] The risks of a strongly unique market appeal are highlighted in the problems of Marshall Field department stores: "The giant's drowsiness led Fields to retain what other retailers call its 'marble and mahogany' merchandising, instead of focusing on the changing tastes of its potential customers. . . . One of our problems is that Fields has the more mature, over-44 customer. . . . We don't want to alienate them but we want to attract the younger customer."[14]

Strategy dimensions

For the retailer to use market segmentation as a viable element of strategy, several questions must be answered:

1.   Upon what basis may markets be segmented?
2.   Can the segments be identified by measurable characteristics?
3.   Do the segments exhibit different demand elasticities for the products under consideration?
4.   Can retailing mix variables be altered to exploit these segments?

A variety of factors affect decisions in these matters. For example, if consumers do not perceive physical differences in such products as gasoline, market aggregation may be the best strategy to follow. A retailer with limited resources may want to concentrate on a particular subsegment. Likewise, if the firms with which a retailer desires to compete are following a strategy of segmentation, the retailer is almost forced to follow a similar policy. On the other hand, if the retailer is able to enter a market where the other firms are practicing aggregation, a strategy of differentiation can be very productive for both sales and profits.

BASES FOR SEGMENTATION

Markets may be segmented in a variety of ways. The more common bases for segmentation are: (1) individual consumer differences, such as demographic and socioeconomic differences, and life-style, personality, life cycle, and subcultural differences; (2) behavioral characteristics, including brand loyalty, attitudinal, and/or usage characteristics; (3) geography; (4) benefits.

Let us now look specifically at the various ways of developing basic segmentation classifications and at the relationship of segmentation to market planning at the retail level.

[13] Carter Hawley Hale Stores: Carriage Trade Merchants," *Business Week*, October 4, 1976, p. 90.
[14] "Why Profits Shrink at a Grand Old Name," *Business Week*, April 11, 1977, p. 67.

Demography

Demographic variables are among the most widely used bases for retail market segmentation. The demographic approach includes an analysis of markets in such terms as sex, age, occupation, income, education, and race. These data are easy to measure and are readily available from published government sources. Moreover, the segments defined in this manner are relatively large, and demographics provide the key to media selection. Crude measures of behavior can be inferred from these data. The ability to infer behavioral characteristics from demographic data is of value in establishing market potential estimates and in developing media strategy.

Age is one of the more commonly used variables in segmentation analysis. The purchase of many products is directly related to a person's age. Although age composition may be viewed in many different ways, the most common age classifications are children, young adults, older adults, and senior citizens.

Children. Adolescents comprise an easily identifiable and lucrative consumer goods market for retailers. One small-scale study, for example, found an average personal discretionary income of $4 per week among adolescent respondents.[15] Also, as discretionary income increases, the tendency for youngsters to make their own purchase decisions increases. Teenage boys 10–17 years of age spent $727 million in 1976 for sports equipment and clearly present a major market segment for the alert retailer. Even at this age, however, brand popularity is strong. For example, 23 percent of these youths prefer Schwinn bicycles.[16] The high spenders in the youth market, 16–19-year-olds, average $18.35 (males) and $19.50 (females) per week.[17] Also, over 70 percent of teenage girls now shop for food each week, spending over 38 percent of the total family dollars spent for food. Of these, more than 60 percent shop for specific brands and view taste and quality as more important than price in product selection.[18] Clearly these persons exert considerable force as initiators and influencers of purchase decisions.

Young adults. Young adults 20–34 constitute a large market for virtually all goods and services. Further, a high percentage of their income is discretionary prior to the birth of the first child. This is the fastest-growing market and will expand 14 percent in the next five years.[19] The material goals basic

---

[15] Lowndes F. Stevens and Roy L. Moore, "Consumer Socialization: A Communication Perspective," paper presented at the International Communication Association Student Summer Conference, Athens, Ohio, 1973.

[16] "Marketing Observer," *Business Week*, September 27, 1976, p. 65.

[17] Roy L. Moore and Lowndes F. Stevens, "Some Communication and Demographic Determinants of Adolescent Consumer Learning," *Journal of Consumer Research*, vol. 2 (September 1975), p. 80.

[18] "Marketing Observer," *Business Week*, December 6, 1976, p. 66.

[19] "Trends Affecting Drug and Grocery Retailing—An Update," *Nielsen Researcher*, no. 1, 1977, p. 4.

to the life-style of the young adult require items unknown or unavailable a few years ago. For example, the list of essentials may now include a color television set, a stereo set, and a tape recorder. The life-style of many of these persons represents a desire to participate immediately in standards of living which were achieved by their parents much later in life. Still others place a high value on financial security at an early age. A third group of young adults apparently see their own development as an investment in human resources. The young adults of today are marrying older, anticipating fewer children, moving more often, getting more education, and are reasonably prosperous.[20] One business executive stated that "this majority segment of young and middling young people has broadened its definition of success to include personal rewards, pleasure, adventure, fun, and a more genuine concern for physical self."[21]

Serving this market requires more skill in segmentation strategies than might be immediately obvious. In spite of the overall rapid growth projected, internal shifts in the composition of this age group may present problems for selected retailers. For example, 25 percent of all motorcycles are purchased by persons 15–25 years of age. This market will drop by 2 million persons by 1985. Unless retailers serving this market can attract older market segments, they face increasing problems.[22] On the other hand, for some retailers the growth forecasts are very good indeed. For example, 50 percent of all college students now buy wine at least once a week, typically spending between $3.50 and $5.00 per bottle. If these patterns of consumption continue later in life, this market will be increasingly fertile. As a result of this trend, Blue Nun now provides campus retail outlets with such Blue Nun items as T-shirts and posters.[23]

The unique life-styles of young adults have to be monitored carefully. In recent years, the department stores have lost major shares of furniture sales in this age group to discounters, warehouse chains, and specialty outlets. This age group comprises millions of single households that tend toward informal buffet dining. Since 1970 alone, the number of single households has increased 41 percent, compared to a 6 percent growth in husband-and-wife households.[24] These trends and others, such as smaller families, the do-it-yourself craze, and the popularity of garage and thrift sales, have been only belatedly recognized by the traditional furniture stores seeking to serve the young adult market.[25] This problem plagued Abercrombie and Fitch to such an extent that it finally filed for reorganization under the bankruptcy

---

[20] Lucile F. Mork, "Young Adults," *Family Economics Review,* Summer 1974, p. 16.

[21] "Successful Marketers Monitor Market" *Marketing News,* October 22, 1976, p. 9.

[22] "Motorcycles: The Dip Continues," *Business Week,* May 3, 1976, p. 85.

[23] "Marketing Observer," *Business Week,* June 7, 1976, p. 86.

[24] "Washington Roundup," *Marketing News,* October 22, 1975, p. 4.

[25] Norma Green, "Furniture Makers Adjust Marketing to Hit Less Home-Oriented Life Styles," *Advertising Age,* January 17, 1977, p. 3.

laws. Abercrombie and Fitch tried to merchandise to this age group while retaining the image and the merchandise approach of an upper-class "carriage trade" outlet.[26] As noted earlier, Marshall Field is trying to make the adjustment of serving this group while holding on to its prime market of customers over 44 years of age. Because the young adult group is forming new purchasing patterns, including changes in store and brand preferences, retailers must constantly press to make sure that they get their fair share of this expanding market.

Older adults.   Between now and 1985, the 35–44 age group will be the single most important consumer market segment. The real spending power of this group will increase by 85 percent over the next decade. By 1985, 38 percent of families in this group will have incomes of over $25,000 in 1975 constant dollars.

The 45–54 age group is not a particularly impressive market segment in longer term growth potential, but is a prime market for travel expenditures and for durable goods. By 1985, this age group will represent approximately 16 percent of the population and 20 percent of the income. It is a particularly affluent segment. By 1985, 46 percent of this income group is forecast to have incomes of more than $25,000.

Supermarkets in particular seek to attract the older adult market segment because older adults are perceived as the freest spending group of shoppers. As noted, "the presence of teenagers in these households, of course, is to consumption of groceries as oxygen is to fire. Any manager who can woo and win the 35-to-49's through merchandising and product selection targeted to them has one leg up on the competition."[27] Most of the households headed by persons in the 45–54 age group have five or more persons; over 90 percent of the persons in this group are married; and the average household income is almost $16,000.

Senior citizens.   The senior citizen market (composed of persons 65 years of age and older) is characterized by sharply lower incomes resulting from retirement. Two out of three families in this group have incomes of less than $10,000 yearly. Overall these persons comprise slightly more than 14 percent of the total population. The size of the senior citizen group will grow only moderately over the next decade. These consumers differ from other market segments in terms of demand for travel, housing, medical care, and other needs.[28] People today are retiring younger and have stronger income bases which allow continued purchasing power with more leisure time. This segment is not a prime market for new homes or furniture but is a good market for vacation travel and for hobby-related items. Further, this group is a concentrated retail market segment. According to the 1970 census, in

[26] "Abercrombie's Misfire," *Time*, August 23, 1976, p. 55.

[27] "New Index Shows Dangers of Taking Critical Shopper Habits for Granted," *Progressive Grocer*, March 1977, p. 40.

[28] Joseph Barry Mason and Brooks E. Smith, "An Exploratory Note on the Shopping Behavior of the Low Income Senior Citizen," *Journal of Consumer Affairs*, vol. 8 (Winter 1974), p. 205.

seven states the over-65 age segment represented at least 11.5 percent of the total population. Also, within such cities as Miami Beach, Port Charlotte, and St. Petersburg, Florida, the over-65 age group represents 30–50 percent of the total population. Thus, this market segment is easily identifiable and geographically segmented.

In summary, even though the population as a whole is moving toward zero population growth, real marketing opportunities still exist for the retailer who can adjust market strategies so as to better serve the market opportunities within the overall pattern.

Subcultures and minorities

For certain products, subcultures and minorities may represent distinct market segments. Perhaps the behavior of minorities is conditioned as much by such factors as low income, low education, and other demographic factors as by race. In any case, subcultures tend to cluster in groups. Thus, they are highly visible and are relatively easy to reach through the media.

There are 23.5 million U.S. blacks. Even though they comprise only slightly more than 11 percent of the population as a whole, they represent over 20 percent of the central city populations and over 19 percent of the population in the South. During 1970–74 they had a growth rate almost double that of the population as a whole.[29] In nine cities—Atlanta, Baltimore, Birmingham, Detroit, New Orleans, Newark, Richmond, St. Louis, and Washington, D.C.—they number over 40 percent of the total population.[30] Other demographic differences characterize this group. Approximately 34 percent of black families are headed by female heads, as compared to less than 10 percent of white families. Moreover, in husband-wife households only 40 percent of the white wives work as compared to 54 percent of the black wives.

These differences in demographics are reflected in shopping behavior. For example, blacks shop less frequently than whites; tend to be more loyal to national brands; and are particularly sensitive to quality merchandising. One study indicated that "Black families tend to be aware of brands and yet are also brand loyal. . . . Blacks are extremely race conscious and will switch brands if it can be demonstrated that it is in the interest of the black community to do so."[31]

Serving ethnic groups can present major merchandising problems. Detroit, for example, has 29 distinct ethnic groups, and most of the Detroit supermarkets serve more than one of these segments. As a result, shelf merchandising is geared carefully to neighborhood preferences, with many

---

[29] *Grey Matter,* vol. 45 (October 1974), p. 2.

[30] "Know Your Black Shopper," *Progressive Grocer,* June 1975, p. 45.

[31] Carl M. Larson and Hugh G. Wales, "Brand Preferences of Chicago Blacks," *Journal of Advertising Research,* vol. 13 (August 1973), p. 21.

end-of-aisle displays featuring favorites of specific groups.[32] Blacks tend to favor basic ingredients for food over convenience foods; and pork sales tend to be disproportionately high among blacks, as do Southern green vegetables.[33] A study of consumption among Southern households found that blacks spent more of their food dollar on meat, poultry, and grain products and less on milk products, vegetables, and fruits than did whites. Differences continued to exist when the households were grouped by urbanization, income, and quality of diet.[34]

These differences in product consumption levels translate to differences in product mixes and other merchandising elements at the level of the individual store. Thus, a focus on ethnic differences and product preferences can be particularly useful to supermarket management in planning shelf allocations. Table 6–1 lists sales by product category for supermarkets located in pre-

TABLE 6–1
SALES IN STORES IN BLACK NEIGHBORHOODS

Above average		Average		Below average	
Rice and rice		Powdered soft		Foil and plastic	
dinners	215%	drinks	101%	wrap	95%
Evaporated milk	187	Instant coffee	101	Frozen prepared	
All-purpose flour	153	Iced tea mixes	100	dinners	94
Salad and cooking		Margarine	100	Table syrups	92
oils	140	Canned green		Cake mixes	89
Toilet soaps	126	beans	100	Dry cereals	87
Strained baby		Carbonated		Canned tuna	87
foods	117	beverages	98	Powdered	
Tomato paste	116	Canned dog		puddings	87
Tea bags	116	food	98	Regular coffee	86
Catsup	111	Peanut butter	96	Prepared soups	82
Meal-type dog				Salad dressings and	
food	109			mayonnaise	80
Paper towels	108			Dishwashing	
Instant tea	105			detergents	57

Source: "Ethnic Marketing . . . Is It Necessary for Your Product?" *Nielsen Researcher*, no. 1, 1977, p. 21.

dominantly black neighborhoods. The first column, which shows heavy usage products, reveals that a store in a black neighborhood sells 115 percent more rice and rice dinners than does an average store of the same size. Overall 12 product categories sell at a disproportionately heavy rate in black neighborhoods. Six of these items are "ingredient" products, such as evaporated milk, flour, rice and rice dinners, perhaps reflecting greater creativity in

[32] "Making Good in the Ghetto," *Progressive Grocer*, June 1975, p. 51.

[33] "Black Products: There Is a Difference," *Progressive Grocer*, June 1975, p. 52.

[34] Constance Ward, "Food Spending Patterns of Southern Black Households," *Family Economics Review*, Fall 1975, p. 9.

cooking and menu planning. The last column lists products which blacks use at lower levels than does the population as a whole.[35]

Research has also compared various dimensions of behavior among whites, blacks, and Mexican-Americans (a market segment of over 8 million people).[36] The most frequent source of product and store awareness by blacks is radio. Recommendations by others and window and store displays are second and third, respectively. Among Mexican-Americans, window and store displays are the primary source of information. This is followed by personal recommendations and radio and television. Among whites, word of mouth (recommendations by others) ranks first, followed by window displays and television.

Among black respondents, good reputation and minority ownership are the two top-ranked reasons for patronizing a retail outlet. Among Mexican-Americans, good reputation and convenience are the primary factors. Ownership by a racial minority ranks third among Mexican-Americans. Among whites, good reputation, high quality, and convenient location rank first, second, and third, respectively.

Income

The consumer needs spendable income in order to satisfy wants and needs. The distribution of income among families and regions affects the type and amount of merchandise purchased. For example, it requires an income of $10,041 for an urban family of four to maintain a lower standard of living, $16,236 to maintain an intermediate standard, and $23,759 to maintain a higher standard, as shown in Table 6–2. The lower a family's income, the greater the proportion which must be spent on food, clothing, and medical care and the less which is available for discretionary spending.

Aggregate income shifts have a major impact on retailing strategy. For example, persons moving out of central cities to the suburbs earn more than do persons who move into the central cities from other parts of the United States. Almost 6 million more people moved out of the central cities during 1970–74 than moved into them. This represents a loss in purchasing power of the central cities of almost $26 billion.[37] The bulk of this purchasing power was thus absorbed by the suburban shopping centers.

---

[35] "Ethnic Marketing . . . Is It Necessary for Your Product?" *Nielsen Researcher,* no. 1, 1977, p. 21.

[36] These findings are based on Thomas E. Barry, Michael G. Harvey, and Richard W. Hansen, "Tri-Ethnic Attitudes toward Minority Entrepreneurs," in Robert L. King (ed.), *Proceedings: Southern Marketing Association,* 1973, pp. 269–74; see also John A. Geuren and Charles N. Weaver, "Media Consumption Habits of Mexican Americans," paper presented at the March 1977 meeting of the Southwestern Marketing Association, New Orleans; and Judy Greenwald, "Untapped Latin Market Outlined in N.Y. Seminar," *Supermarket News,* May 2, 1977, p. 5.

[37] "Washington Roundup," *Marketing News,* November 11, 1975, p. 11.

TABLE 6–2
ANNUAL BUDGETS AT THREE LEVELS OF LIVING FOR A FOUR-PERSON
FAMILY: URBAN UNITED STATES, AUTUMN, 1976

Component	Lower	Intermediate	Higher
Total budget	$10,041	$16,236	$23,759
Family consumption	8,162	12,370	17,048
Food	3,003	3,859	4,856
Housing	1,964	3,843	5,821
Transportation	767	1,403	1,824
Clothing	799	1,141	1,670
Personal care	265	355	503
Medical care	896	900	939
Other family consumption	468	869	1,434
Other items	451	731	1,234
Taxes and deductions	1,429	3,134	5,476
Social Security and disability tax	604	898	911
Personal income taxes	825	2,236	4,565

Source: "Autumn 1976 Urban Family Budgets and Comparative Indexes for Selected Urban Areas,"
U.S. Department of Labor, Bureau of Labor Statistics, April 27, 1977, p. 1.

The median incomes of black and white nonmetropolitan families are lower than the median incomes of either central city or suburban families. The median income of nonmetropolitan families is higher in counties containing major metropolitan cities.[38]

The importance of income combined with geography as a segmentation variable is clear from the differences between the central cities and the suburbs. The relationship between income and subculture segments is also evident. Income as a segmentation variable, however, is important in other ways. For example, reasons for store patronage differ by income levels, with low-income persons placing more emphasis on convenience of location. Further, the availability of credit and, for food items, delivery may be more important in the patronage decisions of low-income persons, as is the availability of bus transportation to serve the retail outlets. Also, the personalized attention available from small independent outlets appears to be important to low-income shoppers. For high-income shoppers time is likely to be more important than small monetary savings, and such shoppers are able to acquire and utilize information more quickly and efficiently than are low-income shoppers.[39] Thus, the media mixes necessary to effectively serve these two markets must be quite different.

Table 6–3 reveals the projected U.S. population and income composition

[38] *Social and Economic Characteristics of the Metropolitan and Nonmetropolitan Population: 1970–1974*, Current population Reports, series P–23, no. 55, September 1975, p. 15.

[39] J. Barry Mason and Charles Madden, "Food purchases in a Low Income Negro Neighborhood: The Development of a Socio-economic Behavioral Profile as Related to Movement and Patronage Patterns," in Fred Allvine (ed.), *Relevance in Marketing* (Chicago: American Marketing Association, 1971).

for 1985. These data show at a glance the projected upward income shifts over the next several years.

These aggregate income figures do not reveal disturbing trends in income levels which must be recognized by every retailer seeking to segment a market. The primary problem is the continuing plight of the lower-middle-class consumer with incomes of $5,000–$15,000. Both the poor and the upper income groups have been making gains at the expense of this group. As has been noted, "If you sell to the luxury market, the Rolls Royce drivers,

TABLE 6–3

DISTRIBUTION OF FAMILIES BY AGE OF HEAD AND EARNING BRACKETS

(all figures in 1975 dollars)

		Age of head					
	Total	Under 25	25–34	35–44	45–54	55–64	65 and over
1975							
Families							
Millions	56.7	4.4	13.2	10.8	11.2	8.9	8.2
Distribution	100.0%	7.8%	23.3%	19.1%	19.8%	15.7%	14.4%
Percent of total family income	100.0%	4.8%	22.0%	21.6%	24.8%	17.2%	9.6%
Families by income class							
Percent distribution	100.0%	100.0%	100.0%	100.0%	100.0%	100.0%	100.0%
Under $5,000	11.7	22.0	9.5	7.0	6.5	10.0	25.0
$ 5,000–10,000	21.1	34.0	18.5	15.5	13.5	18.5	39.0
$10,000–15,000	22.6	28.0	28.0	21.5	19.0	22.5	17.5
$15,000–20,000	18.5	12.0	23.0	22.0	20.0	18.0	8.5
$20,000–25,000	12.1	3.0	12.5	16.5	16.0	12.5	4.5
$25,000–35,000	9.0	1.0	6.5	11.5	15.5	11.0	3.0
$35,000–50,000	3.6	*	1.5	4.5	7.0	5.5	1.5
$50,000 and over	1.5	*	0.5	1.5	2.5	2.0	1.0
1980							
Families							
Millions	61.2	4.7	15.4	12.1	10.8	9.5	8.7
Distribution	100.0%	7.7%	25.1%	19.8%	17.7%	15.4%	14.2%
Percent of total family income	100.0%	4.7%	23.7%	22.6%	22.3%	17.1%	9.5%
Families by income class							
Percent distribution	100.0%	100.0%	100.0%	100.0%	100.0%	100.0%	100.0%
Under $5,000	8.5	17.0	7.0	5.5	5.0	7.0	16.5
$ 5,000–10,000	16.2	25.0	13.0	11.0	9.0	13.5	36.5
$10,000–15,000	18.9	29.0	20.0	15.5	15.0	19.5	20.5
$15,000–20,000	18.0	18.0	22.5	18.5	16.5	18.0	11.0
$20,000–25,000	14.4	7.0	18.5	17.5	15.5	14.0	6.0
$25,000–35,000	15.0	3.5	14.0	21.0	22.0	15.5	5.5
$35,000–50,000	6.2	0.5	4.0	7.5	11.5	8.0	2.5
$50,000 and over	2.8	*	1.0	3.5	5.5	4.5	1.5
1985							
Families							
Millions	66.3	4.6	17.1	14.9	10.8	9.7	9.2
Distribution	100.0%	7.0%	25.8%	22.4%	16.2%	14.6%	13.9%
Percent of total family income	100.0%	4.2%	24.4%	25.2%	20.5%	16.4%	9.4%
Families by income class							
Percent distribution	100.0%	100.0%	100.0%	100.0%	100.0%	100.0%	100.0%
Under $5,000	6.9	15.0	5.5	4.5	4.5	6.0	12.5
$ 5,000–10,000	14.7	22.5	12.0	9.5	8.0	12.5	34.5
$10,000–15,000	16.3	27.0	16.5	13.0	12.0	15.5	21.5
$15,000–20,000	17.0	19.5	20.5	17.0	15.0	16.0	12.5
$20,000–25,000	15.1	10.0	19.0	18.0	14.5	14.5	7.0
$25,000–35,000	18.2	5.0	19.0	24.0	24.0	19.5	7.0
$35,000–50,000	8.0	1.0	6.0	9.5	14.5	10.0	3.0
$50,000 and over	3.9	*	1.5	4.5	7.5	6.0	2.0

* Less than 0.05.

Note: The projections assume an average annual real growth in personal income of 4 percent between 1973 and 1980 and of 3.5 percent between 1980 and 1985.

Sources: U.S. Department of Commerce; The Conference Board.

or the poor, say baked beans, you'll do well. But the middle class is standing still or losing."[40] The implications for market segmentation at the retail level were summed up as follows: "A lot of department stores and big retailers are going for the Bloomingdale's-type customer, and I think there'll be a move back, in the other direction. As women have children and drop out of the labor force, they'll be going back to being price conscious."[41]

Let us now look at the specific use of income as a segmentation variable for one retailer so that we can better appreciate the importance of income at the store level in developing merchandising mixes. Consider Goldsmith's of Memphis:

. . . Goldsmith's, and Goldsmith's alone in Memphis, caters to middle, upper-middle and upper income brackets on a broad and aggressive scale—especially the latter two groups. Goldsmith's competition for these income groups, two of which are hardly fazed by either recession or inflation, is virtually nonexistent among Memphis mass retailers. Sears, for example, which vies for many of the same customers as Goldsmith's, was hurt more by the recession and inflation because its middle and lower income customers were feeling the pinch. Additionally, Sears in Memphis has had to cope with K mart.[42]

Finally, what more can one say than "Next week one million well-heeled Americans all over the country will receive that long-time symbol of elegance and snobbery: the Neiman-Marcus Christmas Catalog?"[43]

Education

Income and education are closely related. Income alone, however, cannot adequately explain purchasing patterns for all types of merchandise. For some types of purchases such variables as education may be better indicators than income alone. The incomes of blue-collar workers often equal or exceed the incomes of persons in such white-collar and higher education jobs as public school teaching and banking. However, the segments with the highest levels of education, regardless of income, are the best markets for such items as insurance, travel services, books, and magazines. Similarly, persons with lower levels of education comprise primary markets for fishing and camping equipment.

Sex

Several studies have investigated the usefulness of sex as a segmentation variable. Sex of respondent is significantly related to the use of trading

---

[40] "The New Two-Tier Market for Consumer Goods," *Business Week,* April 11, 1977, p. 80.
[41] *Ibid.,* p. 83.
[42] "Goldsmith's Is Tying a Ribbon on Oak Court Showpiece," *Memphis Commercial Appeal,* September 12, 1976, p. 5.
[43] "Carter Hawley Hale Stores," p. 90.

TABLE 6–4
WHO MAKES THE BUYING DECISIONS?

	Purchased by		Direct influence				Indirect influence			
			Product		Brand		Product		Brand	
	W	H	W	H	W	H	W	H	W	H
Cereals										
Cold (unsweetened)	84	16	74	26	71	29	65	35	67	33
Hot	84	16	67	33	67	33	63	37	59	41
Packaged lunch meat	73	27	60	40	64	36	56	44	57	43
Peanut butter	81	19	70	30	74	26	65	35	68	32
Scotch whisky	35	65	18	82	18	82	22	78	23	77
Bar soap	85	15	65	35	64	36	60	40	61	39
Headache remedies	67	33	67	33	67	33	64	36	65	35
Cat food (dry)	66	34	75	25	81	19	80	20	80	20
Dog food (dry)	76	24	60	40	59	41	60	40	61	39
Fast-food chain										
hamburgers	68	32	55	45	55	45	53	47	52	48
Catsup	75	25	68	32	68	32	60	40	62	38
Coffee										
Freeze-dried	68	32	57	43	62	38	56	44	59	41
Regular ground	74	26	65	35	65	35	58	42	60	40
Mouthwash	72	28	56	44	56	44	52	48	53	47

Share of Influence

	Purchase decision influence				Initiation				Information gathering			
	Product		Brand		Product		Brand		Product		Brand	
	W	H	W	H	W	H	W	H	W	H	W	H
Vacuum cleaner	60	40	60	40	80	20	69	31	66	34	65	35
Electric blender	59	41	53	47	67	33	50	50	53	47	52	48
Broadloom carpet	60	40	59	41	82	18	74	26	72	28	69	31
Automobiles	38	62	33	67	22	78	21	79	18	82	18	82

Source: Reprinted with permission from the March 17, 1975 issue of Advertising Age. Copyright 1975 by Crain Communications, Inc.

stamps,[44] and is also related to customer variations in the level of unplanned purchasing or "impulse purchasing."[45] Likewise, one study has classified the male clothing innovator as "youthful, sociable, educated, mobile, and active. He has a lack of family responsibility, higher income, and a relative indifference to price."[46] Clearly, retail promotion for some products should be devoted almost exclusively to one sex. For example, "women do approximately 85 percent of the selecting of foods, toiletries, paper goods, household cleaners and OTC drugs."[47]

The data shown in Table 6–4, based on a national probability sample of 2,480 respondents, indicate that husband-wife influence on purchase decisions and the actual purchases themselves vary widely between husband and wife. For example, approximately 60 percent of the wives purchase vacuum cleaners, electric blenders, and broadloom carpets, whereas approximately 62 percent of the automobiles are purchased by husbands. Most items of food or drink, except Scotch whisky, are purchased by the wife, even though the amount of the husband's direct and indirect influence is quite substantial.

Of increasing importance are the growing percentage of working wives and the steps to be taken by retail outlets in seeking to serve this large market segment. Over 44 percent of wives are now employed outside the home, compared to 24 percent in 1950. Limited research has shown that working wives may be more likely to purchase national brands so as to be able to make a product selection quickly and yet with confidence that a high-quality product is being purchased. Also, the increasing percentage of working wives means that the shift to convenience foods is likely to continue, as is the shift to eating more meals outside the home. Finally, evening hours are an asset in seeking to serve working wives. These consumers are likely to be particularly receptive to any offering of either products or services which will allow them to shop quickly, efficiently, with confidence, and at odd hours. Further, media mixes should be adjusted so as to reach them either early in the morning or in the early evening hours.

Segmentation on social and psychological bases

The life cycle. Most households pass through an orderly progression of stages:

1. The bachelor stage; young, single people.
2. Newly married couples; young, no children.

---

[44] J. G. Udell, "Can Attitude Measurement Predict Consumer Behavior?" *Journal of Marketing,* vol. 29 (October 1965), pp. 46–50.

[45] D. T. Kollat and R. P. Willet, "Customer Impulse Purchasing Behavior," *Journal of Marketing Research,* vol. 4 (February 1967), p. 21–31.

[46] Ibid.

[47] *Product Marketing,* news release, January 3, 1977, p. 1.

3. The full nest I; young married couples with dependent children.
    a. Youngest child under six.
    b. Youngest child six or over.
4. The full nest II; older, married couples with dependent children.
5. The empty nest; older, married couples with no children living with them.
    a. Head in labor force.
    b. Head retired.
6. The solitary survivor; older, single people.
    a. In labor force.
    b. Retired.[48]

After reviewing the life cycle literature, it was concluded that whether an item is a product or a service, a durable or a nondurable, life cycle is a meaningful way of classifying consumers.[49] The conclusion was based on a comparison of the consumption expenditures for some 400 products and services which were cross-classified by age and life cycle.

The usefulness of life cycle as a way of viewing retail markets is that it identifies which groups of persons are the heaviest users of, and thus the best customers for, particular groups of products. Examples of this approach to the segmentation of retail markets are shown in Table 6–5. By viewing markets in this way, strategies for each segment are readily identified.

Life-styles. The most widely used approach to life-style measurement is the AIO (activities, interests, and opinions) rating statement. Key life-style dimensions are shown in Table 6–6. Life-style segmentation measures people's activities in terms of: "(1) how they spend their time; (2) their interests, what they place importance on in their immediate surroundings; (3) their opinions in terms of their view of themselves and the world around them; and (4) some basic characteristics such as their stage in the life cycle, income, education, and where they live."[50]

Life-style segmentation recognizes that the markets for some products can be better defined in this manner than in terms of such variables as age or income, or even stage in the life cycle. For example, the retailer can more effectively serve consumers once the market segments are defined in such terms as "swinger," "fashion conscious," "bargain hunter," "hobbyist" or "risk taker." Indeed, Bonwit Teller's management has stated that it wants "to give Bonwit a swinger image through a careful mix of youth-oriented goods, an increased emphasis on design merchandise, lots of in-store events."[51]

---

[48] Reprinted from W. D. Wells and G. Gubar, "The Life Cycle Concept in Marketing Research," *Journal of Marketing Research* vol. 3 (November 1966), p. 355. Published by the American Marketing Association.

[49] Ibid., p. 360.

[50] Reprinted from Joseph T. Plummer, "The Concept and Application of Life Style Segmentation," *Journal of Marketing,* vol. 38 (January 1974), p. 33. Published by the American Marketing Association.

[51] "Bonwit's Turns Up the Heat," *Business Week,* October 11, 1976, p. 120.

TABLE 6–5
AN OVERVIEW OF THE LIFE CYCLE

Bachelor stage: young single people not living at home
    Few financial burdens
    Fashion opinion leaders
    Recreation oriented
    Buy: Basic kitchen equipment, basic furniture, cars, equipment for the mating game, vacations
Newly married couples: young, no children
    Better off financially than they will be in near future
    Highest purchase rate and highest average purchase of durables
    Buy: Cars, refrigerators, stoves, sensible and durable furniture, vacations
Full nest I: youngest child under six
    Home purchasing at peak
    Liquid assets low
    Dissatisfied with financial position and amount of money saved
    Interested in new products
    Like advertised products
    Buy: Washers, dryers, TV, baby food, chest rubs and cough medicine, vitamins, dolls, wagons, sleds, skates
Full nest II: youngest child six or over six
    Financial position better
    Some wives work
    Less influenced by advertising
    Buy larger sized packages, multiple-unit deals
    Buy: Many foods, cleaning materials, bicycles, music lessons, pianos
Full nest III: older married couples with dependent children
    Financial position still better
    More wives work
    Some children get jobs
    Hard to influence with advertising
    High average purchase of durables
    Buy: New, more tasteful furniture, auto travel, nonnecessary appliances, boats, dental services, magazines
Empty nest I: older married couples, no children living with them, head in labor force
    Home ownership at peak
    Most satisfied with financial position and money saved
    Interested in travel, recreation, self-education
    Make gifts and contributions
    Not interested in new products
    Buy: Vacations, luxuries, home improvements
Empty nest II: older married couples, no children living at home, head retired
    Drastic cut in income
    Keep home
    Buy: Medical appliances, medical care, products which aid health, sleep, and digestion

TABLE 6-5 *(continued)*

Solitary survivor in labor force
   Income still good but likely to sell home
Solitary survivor retired
   Same medical and product needs as the other retired groups; drastic cut in income
   Special need for attention, affection, and security

Source: Robert W. Haas and Leonard L. Berry, "Systems Selling of Retail Services," in Leonard Berry (ed.), *Marketing for the Bank Executive* (New York: Petrocelli Books, 1974), p. 202.

The more we know and understand about customers, the more effectively we can communicate and market to them. The advantage of life-style analysis is that it enhances our ability to develop adequate marketing appeals and promotional strategies. As noted by the vice president for sales promotion, Broadway Department Stores, "We've got to study what motivates people to buy. We have to target everything—from merchandise to advertising and displays—to a particular customer."[52] Life-style segmentation is simply an analysis of people from the retailing perspective instead of from a product perspective. A product orientation to segmentation focuses, for example, only on brand usage, product benefits, and perceived attributes. Typically two or three life-style segments account for 60 percent or more of the total business in a particular category.

Life-style analysis provides a unique opportunity to improve market planning because it provides a more lifelike portrait of the target consumer than does demographics alone. For example, the following life-style portrait was offered for the retail catalog shopper:

. . . retailers desiring to capture the segment of the catalog market which most frequently utilizes mail order catalogs would be wise to stress the ease and time-saving aspect of catalog purchasing in promotional campaigns. Furthermore, since frequent catalog shoppers also tend to be more innovative, these shoppers would be expected to perceive less risk associated with catalog buying. However, frequent catalog buyers would also be inclined to demand more variety and novelty in product lines offered by mail order retailers. On the other hand, since less frequent catalog buyers appear to be more store loyal and more likely to make credit purchases, retailers seeking to cultivate this market must develop marketing strategies unique to infrequent catalog shoppers.[53]

Opinion leaders.   Many questions have been raised about the usefulness of opinion leadership as a basis for retail market segmentation. The characteristics of opinion leaders appear to be dependent upon the product of

[52] "Department Stores Redefine Their Role," *Business Week*, December 13, 1976, p. 47.

[53] Christie Paksoy, "Life Style and Psychographic Analysis of Catalog Shoppers," in Karen Hull (ed.), *Consumers in an Era of Shortages and Inflation* (Kansas City, Mo.: American Council on Consumer Interests, 1975), p. 70.

TABLE 6–6
LIFE-STYLE DIMENSIONS

Activities	Opinions
Work	Themselves
Hobbies	Social issues
Social events	Politics
Vacation	Business
Entertainment	Economics
Club membership	Education
Community	Products
Shopping	Future
Sports	Culture
Interests	Demographics
Family	Age
Home	Education
Job	Income
Community	Occupation
Recreation	Family size
Fashion	Dwelling
Food	Geography
Media	City size
Achievements	Stage in life cycle

Source: Reprinted from Joseph T. Plummer, "The Concept and Application of Life Style Segmentation," *Journal of Marketing*, vol. 38 (January 1974), p. 34. Published by the American Marketing Association.

interest. For example, social status, income, and education have been identified with opinion leadership in such activities as community affairs. Further, young women are opinion leaders in fashion, whereas wives in large families are most likely to exhibit opinion leadership in various marketing practices.

Opinion leaders are important as a market segment beyond their individual purchases. For example, they may act as change agents in the diffusion of new products or services. Because of the greater visibility that results from their participation in social activities, they can have a major influence on the retailer's offering. They talk to more people and are more likely to provide data about stores and products than are non–opinion leaders. The use of these persons as members of a teen board, as community relations persons, or as salespersons will yield positive benefits for the retailer. By using them in such ways, the retailer can utilize peer group relationships, reference group concepts, and self-image concepts to great advantage as key variables in merchandising plans.[54]

---

[54] Joseph Barry Mason and Morris L. Mayer, "Insights into the Image Determinants of Fashion Specialty Outlets," *Journal of Business Research* vol. 1 (Summer 1973), p. 78.

Segmentation over time

Not all individuals respond alike to a new product or service. Some people may adopt the product or service early, some at a later date and some perhaps never. Thus, the market for a new product or a new retail outlet may be segmented in terms of time. Virtually all new products follow a rather uniform pattern of adoption. The same is probably true for a new type of outlet, such as a gourmet shop, or even for a new supermarket, which opens for the first time in a given community.

The adoption process refers to the decision of an individual to adopt a retail outlet for regular patronage. It consists of five stages. The first stage is awareness. The individual knows of the existence of the new outlet but does not seek information about it. At the interest stage, the individual begins to seek information in a very general way. At the evaluation stage, the person begins to judge the new outlet in relation to needs. If it appears that the outlet will meet unfulfilled needs, the individual enters the trial stage and is likely to visit it. Trial does not necessarily mean adoption. If the individual's experience with the firm is not satisfactory, patronage will probably not continue. People seek to minimize the risk involved in shopping at a new outlet. Special information, reduced prices, or demonstration of useful features, such as a self-service gasoline pump, may be a positive way to stimulate patronage. If the individual continues to patronize the firm, store loyalty has been established.

The speed with which consumers respond to a new firm depends entirely upon how they perceive its advantages in relation to existing outlets in terms of convenience, merchandise offerings, and price.

When time is used as a basis for segmenting individuals, five adopter categories are typically identified. The retailer would use a different set of strategies to attract each of the five categories. The categories are: innovators, early adopters, early majority, late majority, and laggards. Researchers on product adoption have grouped individuals into early and late adopters on the basis of age, income, education, social class, occupation, media and sources of information, and cosmopolitanism of contacts. The classification is shown in Table 6–7.

Innovators tend to be adventuresome, seek out and experiment with new ideas, and have a heavy reliance on informal communications. If an outlet is able to identify and market directly to these individuals, the probability of success for the new product or the new type of retailing service is greater. These persons may be the first to patronize a firm offering do-it-yourself auto repair services, for example. Early adopters, representing 13–14 percent of the population, are typically opinion leaders. The early majority and late majority account for 65–70 percent of adopters. The last group, the laggards, account for 15 percent of a community.

The differences among these groups provide the retailer with an opportunity to select media and an overall marketing strategy to reach each of the

TABLE 6–7
CHARACTERISTICS OF EARLY AND LATE ADOPTERS

Variables	Early adopters	Late adopters
Age	Younger	Older
Income	Higher	Lower
Education	Higher and more specialized	Lower and less specialized
Social class	Higher status	Lower status
Occupation	More prestigious	Less prestigious
Media and sources of information	Greater exposure to more media; variety of sources of information	Less exposure to fewer media and less variety of sources; more reliance on personal sources
Cosmopolitanism of contacts	More nonlocal contacts	Essentially local contacts

Source: Harper Boyd and William Massy, *Marketing Management* (New York: Harcourt Brace Jovanovich, 1972), p. 107.

groups. However, information as such is not sufficient to ensure the success of a new retail outlet. Mass media–dominated sources of information, for example, are important at the awareness stage of adoption, whereas the personal influence of opinion leaders tends to be more important at the evaluation stage. For example, we have heard such questions as "Have you tried Wendy's hamburgers yet?"

Geographic location

Geography is important for two reasons: (1) the pattern of population distribution, and (2) the notion that each location develops its own "culture" and hence may have different behavioral patterns.[55]

Frequently, geographic segmentation is used in terms of regions, such as the southeastern or northwestern portions of the United States. For example, much advertising in such magazines as *Time* or *Sports Illustrated* occurs in their various regional or metropolitan editions. Other segmentation breakouts may be on an urban-rural basis or in terms of standard metropolitan areas. At the aggregate level, these data are valuable only for firms screening likely areas for a new retail outlet.

One example of segmentation on the basis of geography is reflected in the mushrooming popularity of tennis. Cold weather drives many tennis enthusiasts to Florida, Arizona, or the Caribbean. However, indoor tennis is growing rapidly in importance for the enterprising retailer of this service to the public.

---

[55] Ronald E. Frank, William F. Massy, and Yoram Wind, *Market Segmentation* (Englewood Cliffs, N.J.: Prentice-Hall, 1972), p. 40.

TABLE 6–8
PROFILE COMPARISON OF SELECTED AMERICAN CITIES

	Ethnic profile— percent white	Effective buying income per household	Drug sales per household	Grocery sales per household
U.S. average	87.4	$11,333	$213	$1,332
Boise	98.1	9,436	333	1,255
Green Bay	98.5	11,534	171	1,330
Savannah	65.7	9,865	225	1,346
Tucson	93.5	10,454	274	1,398

Source: "Nielsen Data Markets . . . Middletown America They Are Not," *Nielsen Researcher*, 1975, p. 13.

Important differences also exist on a city-to-city basis. This is even true in test markets which have been designated as so-called Middletowns. Table 6–8 shows a profile comparison of four selected cities. Savannah, Georgia, offers a market which is over one-third nonwhite, as compared to Green Bay, Wisconsin, which is almost totally white. The "effective buying income" in Green Bay is above the U.S. average, whereas that of Boise, Idaho, is almost $2,000 below the average. Boise shoppers appear to have a particularly strong preference for shopping in drugstores, and shop more than half again as much in these outlets as does the average U.S. shopper. The reverse is true in Green Bay. Further evidence of these differences on a more macro basis are shown in Table 6–9. Thus, "the market" simply does not exist. Retailers with firms in more than one community must be alert to the need to view each market as different and to develop marketing strategies in terms of location, store personnel, hours, and promotion mixes which are optimal for each market.

Further, within any five-year period, approximately 41 percent of the population moves from one location to another. Of these, 17 percent move

TABLE 6–9
SELECTED CHARACTERISTICS OF THE POPULATION BY AREA OF RESIDENCE, 1974

	Central cities	Suburban areas	Nonmetropolitan areas
Population	61,650,000	80,394,000	65,985,000
Percent change since 1970	−1.9	8.4	8.0
Percent black	22.3	5.0	8.8
Percent of families headed by women	18.9	9.5	9.8
High school graduates as a percent of persons 25 years and over ...	59.8	68.5	53.9
Professionals as a percent of all employed persons	14.8	16.8	11.3
Median family income in 1973 ...	$11,343	$14,007	$10,327

Source: Current Population Reports, Special Studies, *Social and Economic Characteristics of the Metropolitan and Nonmetropolitan Population: 1970–1974*, series P–23, no. 55 (Washington, D.C.: U.S. Department of Commerce, 1975).

outside their existing county borders. Thus, even in an area in which population is not growing, the customer base is constantly shifting, which means that different buying patterns and preferences are being established. This simply means that programs to convert newcomers to steady customers can perhaps be identified and made ongoing on a continuous basis. The behavior characteristics of these persons were more fully discussed in Chapter 5.

Brand loyalty

A basic principle of retail strategy is to aim various brands of products at different groups of consumers. Brand perception depends on the information obtained from such marketer-dominated sources as mass media advertising, from such consumer-dominated sources as word of mouth, or from personal experience. Some brands do achieve major market shares. For example, one study found that the top 20 percent of all brands accounted for an average of 65 percent of the market share for all product categories studied.[56] Clearly, brands are important in some patronage decisions. Research has shown that over one half of the consumers seeking a man's dress shirt are seeking a particular brand,[57] whereas brands have been found to be of no importance in the purchase of diamond wedding rings.[58] As noted earlier in the chapter, Schwinn bicycles are particularly popular with teenage boys. Building brand loyalty is a means of repeating past success and minimizing future search and risks.

Advertising claims for uniqueness which are not supported by product attributes will not build brand loyalty for the retailer. Neither will such strategies as cents-off price reductions and other promotion efforts which are designed only to stimulate sales in the immediate future. These efforts do nothing for a brand except to stress price, which can be easily offset by competitive behavior. The retailer who is fortunate enough to secure distribution rights for nationally branded products is in a strong position. National retailers such as Sears go so far as to establish different private brands of the same product to sell to different market segments.

Benefit segmentation

Supporters of benefit segmentation state that the advantages people seek in a product or store are one of the best bases for segmentation. Benefit

---

[56] Wendell C. Hewett and Edward M. Smith, "Brand Behavior and the Development of Marketing Strategy for Low Cost Food and Household Products," in Robert L. King (ed.), *Proceedings: Southern Marketing Association, 1973*, p. 294.

[57] Joseph Barry Mason and Morris L. Mayer, "Empirical Observations of Consumer Behavior as Related to Goods Classification and Retail Strategy," *Journal of Retailing*, vol. 48 (Fall 1972), p. 24.

[58] Joseph Barry Mason and Harry A. Lipson, "A Case Study of a Consumer Durable: Diamond Wedding Rings," *Alabama Retail Trade*, vol. 39 (April 30, 1969), pp. 1–2.

segmentation appears to be particularly useful in a "fragmented product category with discernible brand/product preferences, such as cars."[59] Once the benefits sought have been identified, the various segments can then be profiled in such terms as demographics, life-style, and brand perceptions. In the case of autos, different segments may be interested in economy, performance, style, luxury, or a variety of other dimensions. Penneys appears to follow a form of benefit segmentation in merchandising its women's fashions. "J. C. Penney has analyzed its customer base and broken it down into three segments: young junior, who are highly fashion conscious; contemporaries, who spend more than any other segment on high-quality clothes; and conservatives, who are interested in comfort and value."[60]

The reverse of benefit segmentation is problem segmentation. The same approach is followed for this segment. The retailer focuses on ways of solving problems for the consumer and promoting accordingly. Such offerings as auto repair or carpet cleaning are often promoted in this way.

THE ALLOCATION OF RESOURCES BY MARKET SEGMENTS

How does the retailer allocate scarce resources? All customers cannot be treated alike. Neither should they all be treated differently. Decisions must be made, for example, as to the number of social classes at which to aim products or services, the primary income breakouts to use in analyzing market potential, and whether life cycle or life-style should be used as a segmentation strategy.

It is not easy to target markets at the local level. Probably the best way is through media channels. Each radio station in an area is likely to have a different socioeconomic listener profile. On the other hand, newspaper readership, particularly in small areas, provides broad overall market coverage. Selected targets can be specifically reached through stuffers in monthly statements or through direct mail.

The efficient allocation of resources is almost always going to require research. For example, if attitudinal segmentation is to be practiced, a knowledge of the attitudes of various segments toward product dimensions is important. Brand loyalty analysis will also require research, as will innovativeness and other perceptual measures. However, these types of data are likely to be very valuable in achieving an optimum allocation of resources among market segments.

SUMMARY

Market segmentation is at the heart of the retailer's efforts to divide customers and potential customers into a series of homogeneous groups. By

---

[59] "Marketing Researchers Examine the Practical Side of Segmentation Research," *Marketing News*, November 15, 1974, p. 8.

[60] "Department Stores Redefine Their Role," *Business Week*, December 13, 1976, p. 48.

viewing customers in groups, it is possible to make more effective use of such variables as promotion, pricing, and store location in serving customers. Market segmentation is a dynamic process. The shifts in consumer wants, needs, attitudes, and behavioral patterns require a constant reevaluation of the market.

Markets can be viewed in a variety of different ways, including demography, in which the retailer gives specific attention to such factors as the sex, age, income, and education of consumers. In other instances, such composite variables as social class, stage in the life cycle, or life-style may provide more viable bases for segmentation than can single-variable strategies alone. The most commonly used bases of segmentation are single-variable measures. However, such measures are largely descriptive and do not provide information about the probable responses of consumers.

Except in unusual circumstances, and probably in small communities, the retailer needs to adopt a strategy which recognizes that consumers are neither all alike nor all different. The key point is that consumer differences affect demand. All decisions about media, location, and pricing must recognize this fact.

KEY CONCEPTS

Possible segmentation strategies
   Market aggregation
   Extreme market segmentation
   Partial segmentation
The benefits of segmentation
Objectives of segmentation
Market segmentation as product differentiation
Market dimensions as bases for segmentation
   Socioeconomic
   Demographic
   Geographic
   Composite
   The life cycle
   Life-styles
   Social class
   Behavioral
      Attitudes
      Brand loyalty
      Usage characteristics
Allocation of resources by segments

DISCUSSION QUESTIONS

1. Explain what you understand market segmentation to mean.
2. Trace the origin of the concept of segmentation. Apply it to retailing. How does

retailing management look at the accomplishment of the goal of segmentation? Why is segmentation an important goal of retailing strategy?

3. Discuss the basic requirements for effective segmentation.

4. Explain how customers can be viewed in strategy development, depending upon the product or service offered. Discuss in some detail.

5. Discuss in detail how markets may be segmented.

6. Look at Table 6–3. Discuss the implications which you see in the data it contains.

7. Give as many examples as you can of the various segmentation bases (for example, income) in retail establishments which you have shopped or worked for.

8. Distinguish between life cycle and life-style.

9. Discuss life cycle in some detail.

10. Discuss the usefulness of opinion leadership as a basis for retail market segmentation.

11. How may the characteristics of early and late adopters of innovations differ?

12. Explain what is meant by the concept benefit segmentation. Evaluate the concept.

PROJECTS

1. Pick a product that has been developed within the last three years and is enjoying what you believe to be at least a modest amount of success. Visit a store that handles this product, and see whether you can pick out the retailer's marketing strategy. For example, has the retailer defined his or her market segment and focused on it adequately in advertising, in store promotion, and so on?

2. Most households pass through an orderly progression of stages which retailers have defined as the household life cycle. Visit a department store in your area, and pick out at least six products which typify the retailer's attempt to focus on each of the six stages in the household life cycle.

3. Use a recent purchase you have made, and fit your buying behavior into the adoption process discussed in the text. For example, explain how the product first came to your attention—the awareness state. Complete the adoption process for your product in this manner.

4. Are there really behavioral differences in the purchasing patterns of blacks? The text discusses some survey results on this matter. Determine whether there is a store in your area which attempts to serve the ethnic market. Interview management to see what specific segmentation devices it utilizes to attract this market. What types of advertising media have proved effective according to management? Compare the strategy of such a store with a similar store which projects its image to the white market. Draw any conclusions possible from this type of exploratory research.

5. Select a group of stores of the same type (for example, men's apparel stores, women's fashion boutiques, convenience stores, furniture stores) in a convenient

market area. Interview the managers of the selected stores, and determine the target market to which the manager of each store is appealing (attempt to define the market as completely as possible). Prepare a brief questionnarie for a customer interview to determine whether the "shoppers" are in fact the same as those management is attempting to attract. Compare the stores for differences in segmentation philosophies in goals and in fact.

6. In the transient-oriented lodging business certain companies stress "lower prices" to get their market segment. If one of these firms is conveniently located in your market area, establish contact with management and identify the market segment to which it appeals. Get permission to interview guests over a period of time, and profile these guests to validate the management's perception and target market. Then select a more "conventional" motel and do the same thing. Identify all the competing establishments; compare offerings and prices; see what strategies are employed; and determine whether distinguishable target markets do, in fact, exist.

7. Certain stores can be easily defined as appealing to a particular market segment (for example, the high school group; college students; young professionals). Select a type of store, for example a record store, and see whether you can determine from the assortment and variety of offerings what markets the competing stores carrying records are apparently trying to reach. Interview management, and determine its perception of the segment it is after. And finally get approval, and do some in-store interviewing to see how effective the strategy is in appealing to the defined market. (Other types of stores might be men's apparel stores, junior sportswear boutiques, shoe stores, and so on.)

CASES

Case 1. Stuart Pittman, the manager of the local outlet of So-Lo, one of the major discount chains, has been asked to speak to a Retailing Management class at the university. His presentation consisted of audiovisual segments in which his company was described. Included in the presentation were a historical portrait, an account of present operations, and goals and objectives for the future. When this ended, the floor was opened up for questions. Henry Grant, thinking of a previous class discussion of market segments, asked, "To which market segment do you appeal?" Mr. Pittman replied, "We at So-Lo have no concept of market segments. We believe that everyone is a potential customer, and we are out for their dollars." Continuing this line of questioning, Melissa Adams then said, "One of the points emphasized in our text and in our discussion was that every store has a target market, yet you just discounted it. Where does that leave us? Do stores have target markets, or don't they?" If you were Mr. Pittman, what would you say and why?

Case 2. After working ten years for a large grocery chain, Tom Liner decided that he would like to return to his hometown and open a grocery store there. Census data indicate that there are about 3,000 households in his hometown and that the average income per household is $8,000. Tom knows that there are already two supermarkets doing business there and that the gross sales of both of these stores are in excess of $1 million a year, which he feels is the minimum amount for a profitable supermarket. Tom is trying to decide whether there is a potential for another supermarket in his hometown. What advice would you give him? Why?

PART FOUR

THE ENVIRONMENTS
OF RETAILING

The five chapters composing this part of the text stress those forces which cannot be controlled by the retail manager. Managerial decisions are not made in a vacuum. Thus, the alert retailer is constantly monitoring forces outside the firm, shown in Figure 1–1, which can affect store operations but over which no store control exists. We attempt in Chapters 7 through 11 to make you aware of the importance of understanding these environmental forces as they impact upon the structures of retailing and the behavior of consumers.

We will investigate the economic, social, competitive, legal, and technological factors which are constantly changing and always affecting the short- and long-run strategies of retailers. We will help you to develop a concern and, perhaps more important, a curiosity about what goes on around you. Even if you never enter the field of retail management, as a citizen you will always be faced with decisions which can affect the world in which you live. You will have the opportunity to vote on issues which can have a dramatic impact not only on retailing but also on you as a human being in society. A critical study of this part of the book will provide you with an appreciation for some important areas of concern for all of us. We believe that awareness of this material is a vital part of your total education.

7

ECONOMIC AND SOCIAL ENVIRONMENTS

I think back a few years to the alarm with which I read Alvin Toffler's *Future Shock*. I suppose I felt that "it can't really happen" here—this is a futuristic dream! As I reflect about "our time" of the 1970s, I can only conclude that future shock is with us now. With the dramatic changes in the economic and social environment, the manager of the era of which I speak must be capable of anticipating the continuing changes to which he must adjust in order that his operation can continue to be among those of the future. I am firmly convinced that excesses to which our retailing structure has gone in the past few years will be limited by fiat! I see retailing affected directly by enforced limitations, for example, on the number of hours which will be allowed for openings because of the serious energy shortages of the present and the future. As the president of a relatively small chain, I have refused to open more than two nights a week, and the very idea of Sunday openings appears to be a gross miscalculation of the seriousness of our economic crises. Society, through government, will force the retailer to be responsive to the realities which must be faced head-on in the very short run. This chapter provides an appropriate framework for the consideration of these questions.

Emil Hess, President
Parisian Stores, Alabama
Birmingham, Alabama

The retailer has difficulty in predicting what will happen in the marketplace when conditions change rapidly. As Philip Kotler has stated:

The linear environment of the 1950–70 period has given way to a turbulent environment which produces new strategic surprises almost monthly. Competitors launch new products, customers switch their business, ad costs skyrocket, new regulations are announced, consumer groups attack.[1]

Consumer responses to such changing conditions are complex and are affected by many different economic and political forces. These in turn affect the consumer's emotional and behavioral responses. In a period of high inflation such as the early 1970s, consumers are faced with reduced disposable income, reduced confidence in the ability of the government to solve economic problems, and lower expectations about their future standard of living. These uncertainties are translated into changes in the consumption of goods and services.

In these circumstances, retailers need to be well advised on price elasticity for their brands and those of competitors. They must also give careful attention to the traditional indicators of the nation's economic health—GNP, employment rates, the retail price index, inventories—as well as consumers' real disposable and discretionary income.[2] High levels of economic activity produce a buoyant market in which it is much easier to sell goods and services. Conversely, in an economy constrained by high levels of unemployment, tight money, and inflation, market demand for many goods and services is lower.

Attention must also be given, however, to what remains stable in the consumer's mind. The danger of overlooking stability while studying economic and social change is real. Gross data can be particularly misleading. Unemployment may be increasing, and yet the demand for the product of a particular retailer may be unaffected. For example, the decline in the economy in the early 1970s did not alter the demand for Cadillacs between 1973 and 1974,[3] although the demand for Cadillacs was affected by the oil embargo.

However, signs do exist that retailers may soon be getting a smaller portion of total consumer expenditures. Because of rising prices, general economic uncertainty, and a growing conservatism among consumers, some economists predict that retailing's real growth in the 1980s will be less than the 4.2 percent annual rate of the past ten years. Retail sales slipped 4.2 percent in 1974 and approximately 2.0 percent in 1975.[4]

---

[1] "Kotler Presents Whys, Hows of Marketing Audits for Firms, Nonprofit Organizations," *Marketing News,* March 26, 1976, p. 12.

[2] "JWT Says U.S. Consumers Feel Like Infantrymen Walking through a Mine Field," *Marketing News,* November 11, 1975, p. 11.

[3] Ruth Ziff, "Conference Examines Stability, Changes in Consumer Environment," *Marketing News,* October 24, 1975, p. 9.

[4] "Sears' Identity Crisis," *Business Week,* December 8, 1975, p. 54.

Historically U.S. retailers have depended on rapidly increasing suburban population growth, a high level of home building, and a booming automobile market. They cannot continue to count on these factors as long-term props for their businesses. Family formation is slowing; the population is getting older, and inflation is pricing increasing numbers of people out of the single-family home. Thus, mass retailers who depend on volume economies are rethinking their retailing strategies in the face of these changes. As has been noted, "Stressing value, rather than choosing volume . . . strikes us as the best course of action. . . . as a policy it reflects present population, economic and societal trends. It is also a more positive and constructive way to improve the bottom line."[5]

The food industry exemplifies the effects of rapid environmental changes on the retail structure. Food manufacturers no longer assume that the economy will be stable in the future, and they react accordingly. In the early 1970s, costs spiraled because of rapid inflation and worldwide adverse weather conditions. At that time the food companies had been pushing for ever smaller market segments by introducing more and more products. This forced shorter processing runs and more handling at the warehouse and store levels. This in turn adversely affected productivity. Consumers simultaneously became increasingly skeptical about the proliferation of new products. As a result, food companies were compelled almost overnight to decrease emphasis on new flavors, new sizes, and other routine product line extensions.

Food salespersons are now calling on supermarkets more regularly, and the fight for shelf space is expanding. With a slowdown in the introduction of new products, wholesalers are trying to persuade retailers to keep existing products on the shelf for longer periods of time. This requires more attractive displays and better advertising support.[6]

In spite of these circumstances, new retailing firms, most of which are small, are started at the rate of more than 1,000 per day.[7] Given the complex environmental forces facing these entrepreneurs, the purposes of this chapter are to acquaint students of retailing with (1) the impact of economic conditions on market behavior, (2) the effects of population and related changes on retail markets, (3) the effects of the changing demographic composition of the population on retailing, and (4) the effects of the social environment on retailing.

Our interest must focus not only on the retailing organization but also on the interaction between the firm and the surrounding environments, which create new challenges and opportunities as they change. The retailer should

---

[5] "Volume Isn't Everything," *Progressive Grocer*, November 1976.

[6] "The Hard Road of the Food Processors," *Business Week*, March 8, 1976, pp. 50–54.

[7] Gerald Crawford and C. P. Rao, "An Analysis of Selected General, Operational, and Administrative Variables That Appear to Have a Relationship to Success and Failure in Small Retail Establishments," paper presented at the meeting of the Southwestern Marketing Association in San Antonio, Texas, March 1976, p. 2.

TABLE 7–1

MARKETING DECISIONS—MACRO-ENVIRONMENT RELATIONSHIPS

	Macro environment				
Marketing decision areas	Economic	Technological	Governmental	Social	Physical and natural
Market opportunity analysis	Effects of affluence on markets Demand for services given value of consumer's time	Means of fulfilling opportunities/needs Obsolescence	Government purchases as a market Effects of government action (e.g., pollution equipment industry) Legality of opportunities	Qualitative shifts in values and preferences Socioeconomic trends Subcultures Needs and wants of people Life-styles, classes	Effects on economic status of areas Needs related to physical environment changes (e.g., climate) New substitute products, given shortages
Marketing information systems/research	Economic conditions and effects on research expenditures Research costs Buying power index	Information processing approaches, methods (e.g., computer) Technological forecasting	Invasion of privacy laws Provision of secondary data, projections, etc.	Social issues of data banks–individual privacy Better information facilities, better serving of needs Social trends (predictions)	Effects on communications systems
Strategy Product	Demand for luxury items Production	Required servicing of increasingly complex products New and better products, innovations, inventions	Technology transfer from defense/space programs Product safety legislation Product Safety Commission Food and Drug Administration Patent laws	Materialism versus purchasing "experiences" Fads Convenience products	Product materials and costs—wood versus plastic (e.g., solid waste problem) Product-related pollutants

Pricing	Inflation psychology Consumer ability to pay prices Price elasticity—effect on volume by price changes	Costs of better technology Productivity increases and lower costs Costs of research and development	Illegal pricing constraints Executive branch "jawboning" against higher prices Price ceilings and regulatory pricing	Perceptions of pricing fairness—social issue Behavioral dimensions of pricing Effects of demographic changes on price elasticity	Cost of materials/resources given scarce supplies
Promotion	More important variable in economically advanced countries Promotion costs—efficient use of media	New techniques, media (e.g., color TV) Information about products change complex	Laws (e.g., Wheeler-Lea Act), cooling-off legislation Federal Trade Commission Federal Communications Commission	Shifts of promotional themes in response to social changes Truth in advertising Social desirability of promotion (advertising, personal selling)	Billboards—bad for environment
Distribution	Consumer willingness to pay for nicer outlets, more services Costs of distribution facilities	New marketing institutions Physical distribution methods New transportation modes (BART)	Legal constraints Regulation of transportation industry	Location decisions related to geographic mobility Efficiency of distribution system—social issue Ghetto marketplace structure	Land, water and other natural barriers to transportation Weather, acts of God

Source: David W. Cravens, Gerald E. Hills, and Robert B. Woodruff, *Marketing Decision Making: Concepts and Strategy* (Homewood, Ill.: Richard D. Irwin, 1976), pp. 88–89.

be seeking to develop a creative niche in the market. For example, when the federal regulatory authorities tighten the supply of money, the housing industry is adversely impacted. However, such a change creates additional opportunities for the sale of used homes for which interest rates are lower and results in increased apartment rentals. The tightening of the money market can thus increase the sale of various do-it-yourself items and increase the rental business for many items needed by the consumer in home repair. Thrift shops, garage sales, and the "secondhand" market expand.

The economic and social environments are only two of the major environments confronting the retailer, as shown in Table 7–1. The other environments will be discussed in later chapters.

THE ECONOMIC ENVIRONMENT

Economic uncertainties and the retailer

Shortages.   Shortages of various raw materials always have adverse impacts on retailing. For example, the increased price of oil and the oil embargo in the early 1970s created problems for retail service stations and drove many marginal stations out of business. Likewise, petroleum-based products were either unavailable or very costly. Many economists are forecasting some continuing raw materials shortages into the 1980s.[8] These shortages may cause some products to be unavailable or very expensive. Such effects can lead to severe price competition at the retail level and even to double-digit inflation.

Let us consider for a moment the specific effect of the gasoline shortage in the early 1970s. In 1973, 12,000 service stations were abandoned as compared to 4,000 in 1972. Virtually none of these stations later reopened as gasoline outlets.[9] Instead, abandoned buildings were used as units in franchised chains, as branches for banks, as used car lots, or as garden centers.

E. B. Weiss has offered the following probable occurrences for retailing wherever shortages occur:

1. The producer must cut lead times—and that means the retailer must place firm orders farther in advance.
2. Low-profit margin numbers will be discarded or cut back. . . . Price lining at retail is obviously buffeted by these changes.
3. More retailers will diversify as a result of shortages in inventory.
4. Shortages will accelerate the blurring of delineated seasons. A lengthening of the seasonal demand for a variety of merchandise categories, second seasons, and even third seasons evolve. . . .

[8] Jon Udell, Robert Lusch, and Gene Laczniak, "The Business Environment of 1985," *Business Horizons,* June 1976, p. 50.

[9] E. B. Weiss, "Retail History Repeats Itself—At the Gas Station," *Stores,* July 1974, p. 56, also Stephen Brown, Zohrab S. Demirdjian, and Sandra E. McKay, "The Consumer in an Era of Shortages," *M.S.U. Business Topics,* vol. 25 (Spring 1977), pp. 50–63.

5. The credit department of the manufacturer will be in seventh heaven during the shortage period. Clearly, the credit department wields an extra clout at such times.

6. The retail marketing role may tend toward actually managing shopper demand—either stimulating or discouraging customer demand for certain categories, brands, etc., depending on cost and supply problems.

7. The acceptable size of the minimum order will tend to increase.

8. Retailers will be compelled to scour the world for scarce inventory—new sources of supplies must be developed.

9. Keep a wary eye out for product liability suits. Alternate parts, substitute ingredients will increase the total number and costs of these suits.[10]

We have only to consider the effects of a coffee shortage in 1976 and 1977 and the reduction in the supply of some commodities because of the severe 1976 winter to recognize the effects of shortages on retailers. The fast-food chains were especially hard hit. As noted, "We're trying like heck to retain our prices. But we're taking a beating."[11]

A comparable problem is inadequate capital investment to support a sustained economic recovery. During recessions manufacturers cut back on capital investment, and as a result they may be unable to meet consumer demand for goods and services in periods of rapid economic recovery. Strikes in other industries can also have a major impact. For example, nationwide trucking strikes, such as the one which occurred in 1976, can severely disrupt the movement of merchandise from wholesalers to retailers.

Financial pressures. Financial worries often plague retail firms. Problems may occur because of overbuying as a hedge against anticipated inflation and the high cost of money. For example, bankruptcy petitions during the mid-1970s rose at a rapid pace because of a variety of problems, including high interest rates, high unemployment, and rapidly rising prices at a time when consumer wages were not increasing. The financial collapse of Interstate Stores was one of the largest ever to occur in retailing. W. T. Grant also went bankrupt.

Varying tactics are employed in such times. Retailers can engage in either cost-cutting or more aggressive marketing and merchandising policies. They can also streamline their operations by getting rid of unprofitable stores and getting out of nonretail lines. For example, A&P relied on drastic store pruning to turn the corporation around during the early 1970s.

Inventories. Inventory control is a major problem when a period of recession is followed by economic recovery. During 1973 and 1974, retailers experienced a massive buildup of stocks in the face of the shortage- and inflation-plagued days of that period. This in turn set the stage for a

---

[10] E. B. Weiss, "Retail Merchandising Problems Created by Shortages of Basic Resources." Reprinted from *Stores* magazine; May 1974; Copyright 1974; National Retail Merchants Association, p. 40.

[11] "Fast Food Chains Take a Beating on Breakfast," *Business Week*, February 21, 1977, p. 30.

major liquidation effort in 1975, which was evident in massive rebate programs on many items. Such programs allow an increase in the real rate of growth after stocks have been worked down. The memory of overstocking in such periods remains strong in the minds of retailers who vividly recall the carrying costs of excessive inventory. The result in an upturn, however, is that retailers often begin to scramble for stocks because they have been overly cautious in the initial phases of the economic upturn. Massive inventory buildups can also occur for reasons other than economic cycles, however. For example, in late 1976 massive inventories of CB radios occurred because 56 American importers were importing from more than 80 Japanese manufacturers. Also, consumer demand softened in the face of a government-announced change in the product from 23 channels to 40 channels.[12]

Accelerating competition.   The competitive environment is the one with which retailers are probably most familiar. Competition may take different forms, including competition on the basis of price, hours, and location. Increasingly, new types of retail institutions, product innovations, and changes in consumer expectations have been affecting the competitive environment.

Warehouse retailing became increasingly popular in the 1970s because of rapidly rising prices. The concept became particularly popular in food and furniture lines. Consumers buying from warehouses paid 20–25 percent less than they would have paid traditional retailers for the same merchandise. This concept of retailing has been filling a void left by the many retailers who traded up merchandise lines and services.

The number of retail outlets overall is not increasing substantially, but mergers, acquisitions, forward integration, and lower levels of population growth have contributed to increased competition. For example, firms such as Sherwin Williams and Dutch Boy have established home centers. Traditionally they had functioned as manufacturers and wholesalers.

Scrambled merchandising, in which firms such as supermarkets carry drugs and hardware, has also increased competition, as retailers have responded to consumer demands for aggregate convenience—that is, the ability to make many different types of purchases in one outlet. J. C. Penny opened catalog desks in over 46 Thrift Drug and Treasury Drug centers in an effort to increase customer traffic.[13] Another competitive innovation is the part-time shopping centers which have opened in abandoned discount stores. The individual outlets in the centers may be as small as 100 square feet and are often operated by housewives and retired persons. Most of these have failed miserably, however, because of poor merchandising skills and inexperience.[14]

Higher postal rates are causing a turn from the mail sampling of new

---

[12] "CB Radio Field Has Growing Pains, but Still Grows," *Marketing News*, December 17, 1976, p. 5.

[13] "Penny Catalog at Drug Stores," *Chain Store Age Executive*, June 1975, p. 2.

[14] "Part-time Malls: A Big Disaster," *Chain Store Age Executive*, September 1976, p. 44.

products to person-by-person sampling. Prior to self-service, retailers encouraged consumers to try samples of new products. When self-service became popular, emphasis was placed on ads and the mailing of samples to occupant addresses. Now, with high postal rates, door-to-door distribution of products is becoming increasingly popular.[15]

An entire new generation of specialty mass merchandisers has emerged. Toy supermarkets, outlets with up to 30,000 square feet of space devoted exclusively to toys, now account for over 6 percent of total toy sales and threaten to revolutionize toy sales in the same way that supermarkets revolutionized food distribution.[16] It has been pointed out that "these specialists offer everything from toys (Lionel Leisure City, Toys "R" Us) and sporting goods (Herman's) to furniture (Levitz, J. Homestock, Wickes), home electronics (Tandy Radio Shack Playback), home repair products (Handyman, Handy Dan), and ready-to wear (Gap, Casual Corner)."[17]

As an example of competition at the level of individual brands, Kodak has introduced a line of instant cameras to compete with Polaroid. Almost immediately, major changes in shelf space allocations occurred. Discount specialty stores indicated that they would devote 60–70 percent of existing space to Kodak, with only 35–40 percent for Polaroid. Among nondiscount specialty outlets, Kodak obtained 65–70 percent of the space.[18]

Even the automobile industry faces its uncertainties, as consumers move toward the purchase of smaller automobiles. Even though the shift to smaller cars is continuing, it has moved at a slower rate than the automobile makers predicted. The demand for subcompacts has lagged behind projected levels, whereas sales of larger cars have exceeded projections. This has caused problems not only in manufacturing, but also at the retail level.

Such situations can cause suicidal competition in retailing. An example of this type of competition has emerged in the food industry. Because population and total food consumption have leveled off, "the only way for food chains to grow is to bite into somebody else's market share and increasingly, that means price cutting."[19] As a result of tighter competition and full-fledged supermarket price wars in some parts of the country, the FTC launched an investigation into possible predatory pricing tactics. Price competition in supermarkets has been rougher than at any other time in the past 30 years. The situation is not likely to improve.

The economy and consumer expenditures

The cost of living has a major impact on the amount of money which is available for discretionary spending on such items as movies and recreation. As shown in Figure 7–1, it costs almost 23 percent above the national

---

[15] "Marketing Briefs," *Marketing News,* February 13, 1976, p. 2.

[16] "Toys Get Their Own Supers," *Progressive Grocer,* February 1976, p. 21.

[17] "Sears' Identity Crisis," p. 54.

[18] "Kodak: Set to Expose Its Instant Camera," *Business Week,* March 15, 1976, p. 28.

[19] "Supermarket Pricing: The Gloves Come Off," *Business Week,* April 5, 1976, p. 26.

FIGURE 7–1
LIVING COSTS*

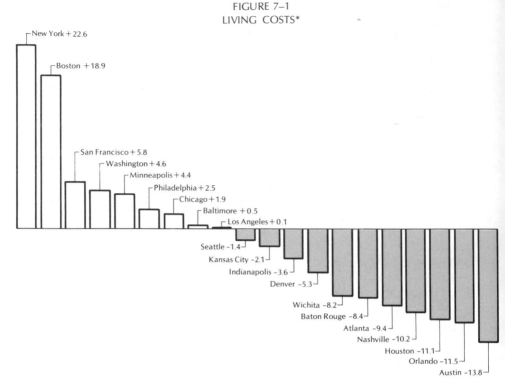

* Percent above and below the average spending necessary to maintain a high standard of living for an urban family
of four (national average in 1974: $20,777).
Source: Reprinted by permission from *Time,* The Weekly Newsmagazine, Copyright, Time, Inc., 1976.

average for a high standard of living for an urban family of four in New York
City, whereas it costs almost 14 percent below the national average to live in
Austin, Texas.[20] Thus, incomes alone do not tell the story of disposable
incomes available as a market potential for retailers.

The different sections of the country are also affected differently by
changes in the health of the economy. For example, during periods of recession the Southwest is likely to be less adversely affected than the Northeast.
Such jobs as wholesale and retail trade, services, and government comprise
the major sources of employment in the Southwest. The East North Central,
Middle Atlantic, and New England regions are more heavily industrialized
and are more likely to be faced with persistent unemployment during periods
of recession.

What are the effects of these problems on retailing? Research has shown
that during the stagflation economy of the early and middle 1970s, an overall
reduction in shopping activity occurred. Fewer stores were shopped; driving
times were shorter; retail traffic was down significantly; and price predomi-

---

[20] "Americans on the Move," *Time,* March 22, 1976, p. 159.

nated over quality in product choice.[21] These changes in consumer behavior necessitate shifts in marketing strategy by retailers to keep up their sales and profitability levels.

Income variations by market segment.   As income grows, shifts in the relative demand for different categories of goods and services occurs in accordance with Engel's laws. Engel determined that as income increases, the percentage spent on food declines, the percentage spent on housing and household operations remains constant, and the percentage spent on other categories (clothing, transportation, recreation, health, education) and reserved for savings increases.

Incomes are not evenly dispersed throughout the country. The median family income for Southern households in 1973 was approximately $1,400 below the national median. The medians in other parts of the country were as much as $800 above the national median. Nonwhite families had incomes almost $4,500 below the national median. Almost 42 percent of black families had incomes of less than $6,000 per year.[22]

Income trends must always be supplemented by a close watch on consumer credit. Consumer expenditures are a function not only of what consumers earn, but also of what they can borrow and of what assets they own. Increasingly, consumers have overcome their fear of credit. Any developments which increase the ease of credit or the amount obtainable have major effects on retailing.

All types of consumer installment credit and other types of consumer credit are increasing at a rapid rate. At the end of 1976, total consumer credit stood at $178,775 billion. The largest increase was for consumer goods other than automobiles. This is shown in Table 7–2.

During periods of economic uncertainty, consumers tend to cut back or postpone expenditures for major durables such as automobiles and appliances. The tendency is to repair existing items. This tendency causes severe adjustment problems for the retailer. However, consumers cannot postpone obligations to repay installment debt, which can go as high as several hundred dollars even for credit cards.

Installment buying also acts as a form of predetermined savings which can keep money from rapidly entering the income stream for the purchase of additional merchandise. Thus, even in an economic upturn consumers may feel pressure to repay installment debt and to delay major purchases until this is accomplished.

Purchasing power stabilizers.   Increasingly, state and federal governments are redistributing consumer wealth through a variety of programs that stabilize income. Funds are redistributed into lower income groups where they are more likely to be spent on consumer goods.

[21] Richard T. Hise, Myron Gable, and Michael A. McGinnis, "Shopping Behavior in a Stagflation Economy: An Empirical Analysis," in Henry Nash and Donald Robin (eds.), *Proceedings: Southern Marketing Association, 1976.*

[22] Helen McHugh, "The Current Situation and the General Economic Outlook for the Family," *Family Economics Review,* Winter 1976, p. 4.

TABLE 7–2
CONSUMER INSTALLMENT CREDIT: TOTAL OUTSTANDING
AND NET CHANGE, 1974–1976
(millions)

Holder and type of credit	1974	1976
Total	155,384	178,775
By holder		
Commercial banks	75,846	85,379
Finance companies	36,208	39,642
Credit unions	22,116	30,546
Retailers*	17,933	19,178
Others†	3,281	4,030
By type of credit		
Automobile	50,392	60,498
Commercial banks	30,994	35,313
Purchased	18,687	19,642
Direct	12,306	15,671
Finance companies	10,618	13,059
Credit unions	8,414	11,633
Others	366	493
Mobile homes		
Commercial banks	8,972	8,233
Finance companies	3,524	3,277
Home improvement	7,754	8,773
Commercial banks	4,694	5,381
Revolving credit		
Bank credit cards	8,281	11,075
Bank check credit	2,797	3,010
All other	73,664	83,910
Commercial banks, total	20,108	22,368
Personal loans	13,771	15,606
Finance companies, total	21,717	23,178
Personal loans	16,961	19,043
Credit unions	13,037	17,993
Retailers	17,933	19,178
Others	869	1,193

* Excludes 30-day charge credit held by retailers, oil and gas companies, and travel and entertainment companies.
† Mutual savings banks, savings and loan associations, and auto dealers.
Source: Board of Governors of the Federal Reserve System, *The Federal Reserve Bulletin,* February 1977, table 1.55, p. A42.

"In one way or another, all the government's social programs are equalizers. Social security transfers income from active workers to retired workers. Medicaid transfers income from the well to the sick."[23] The result has been a sharp decline in the level of poverty—except in recessions—as shown in Figure 7–2. Transfer payments account for 69 percent of the income of the bottom one fourth of all families.[24]

These types of support programs are rapidly built into the profit and volume expectations of retailers. Any efforts to change them have major

[23] "Egalitarianism: Threat to a Free Market," *Business Week,* December 1, 1975, p. 62.

[24] "Egalitarianism: Mechanisms for Redistributing Income," *Business Week,* December 8, 1975.

FIGURE 7–2
THE SHARP DECLINE IN POVERTY—EXCEPT IN RECESSIONS

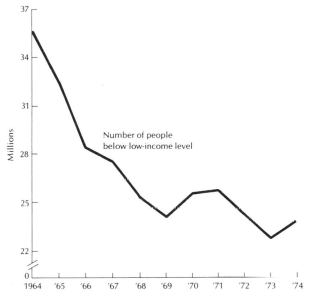

Source: "Egalitarianism: Mechanisms for Redistributing Income." Reprinted from the December 8, 1975, issue of *Business Week* by special permission. © 1976 by McGraw-Hill, Inc., p. 87.

effects on anticipated profit levels. For example, supermarkets are concerned about continuing efforts to revise the food stamp program. Approximately 20 million Americans now receive food stamps, and another 25 to 30 million are eligible. This program is one of the largest social benefit programs in the nation's history.

As shown in Figure 7–3, for fiscal 1975 the federal cost of food stamps came to nearly $5 billion. Food stamp sales in supermarkets are nearly half again the size of all convenience store sales. A spokesperson for the National Association of Food Chains points out that any cutbacks would have significance in an industry that counts on volume.[25] The association goes on to point out that "overall profit or loss in this business depends on that last marginal piece of business. Food stamps aim a greater proportion of income at food purchases; this is often the critical difference for us."

Such government support programs cushion the shock of recessions and unemployment. National economic stress is now less harmful to the retailer than at any time in history. However, these programs are conducted at the expense of higher income persons and cause less funds to be available for discretionary spending on higher priced items. Moreover, the programs do not completely cushion the effects of business cycles. During the heavy

---

[25] "Your Stake in the Fight over Food Stamps," *Progressive Grocer*, January 1976, p. 94.

FIGURE 7–3
FOOD STAMPS' FANTASTIC GROWTH

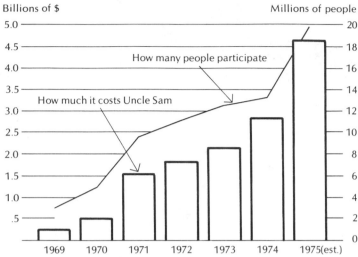

Although the food stamp program has been around for a dozen years, its spectacular growth is a story of the 70s. This composite chart shows the explosion in dollars and people served that has taken place over the six years from 1969 to 1975. For fiscal 1975, the federal cost of food stamps came to nearly $5 billion. Of that, some $4.4 billion represented the actual food stamp bonus paid to recipients. Administration and other program costs made up the rest. By adding this $4.4 billion to the $2.9 billion paid out for the stamps by participants, the total retail value of $7.3 billion is arrived at. Interestingly, only about half of the people participating in the program are public-assistance clients, a fact which underscores the massive increase in stamp use by middle-class families, largely as a result of inflation and the recession's high unemployment.

Source: "Your Stake in the Fight over Food Stamps," *Progressive Grocer,* January 1976, p. 94.

unemployment of 1974, for example, 55 percent of the unemployed did not receive unemployment benefits.[26]

Demography and consumer expenditures

Birthrate. The birthrate is declining. It dropped from 87 per 1,000 women aged 15 to 44 in 1971, to 67 per 1,000 in 1973. In 1975, it dropped to 62 per 1,000. This was the lowest birthrate ever recorded and was below the population replacement level. Further, the marriage rate has been declining. In contrast, divorces have been growing rapidly. For every two marriages, there is now one divorce.[27]

[26] McHugh, "The Current Situation," p. 3.

[27] "Birth Rate Is Declining Again," *Business Week,* March 8, 1976, p. 20.

The long-term trend for the growth of population is very important in retail planning. For example, by the year 2000 the concept of zero population growth (ZPG) will have a major impact on retailers who are specializing in the sale of prenatal wear and items for small children.

In the ZPG era the retailer must be better able to monitor targeted market segments in terms of the numbers, attitudes, and interests of people. The retailer will not be able to grow merely by opening new stores. Increased market share will be obtained only at the expense of competitors.

Geographic population shifts. The current growth in population appears to be occurring in what has been labeled the Southern rim. It extends from Virginia along the Gulf Coast to the southern half of California, as shown in Figure 7–4. This is an out-migration of primarily middle-class persons from other parts of the country. During 1970–74, almost 2 million more Americans left the major metropolitan areas, such as New York and Chicago, than moved into them. The rural areas of the nation, defined as counties with no communities of over 50,000 persons, are among the fastest growing. Overall, the population of the South increased by 5.3 million persons from 1970–75—almost 1 million more persons than for the combined growth of the three other regions.[28]

Age distribution. The population portrait in 1985 can be best described as one with "more babies, fewer teenagers, far more young adults, fewer middle-aged citizens and more oldsters than today,"[29] as was briefly discussed in Chapter 6. The forecasts for new households in 1990 range between 20 and 26 million, depending upon the forecast methodology utilized.[30] As shown in Figure 7–5, the major change in the age mix is the shift of post–World War II babies toward middle age. By 1985, the number of Americans between the ages of 35 and 39 will increase by 48 percent. Population will be leveling off by the mid-80s, as families continue to have only enough children to keep the population stable. Larger numbers of women will be in prime childbearing ages at that time, however, and total births will increase. This is good news for retailers of maternity and infant's wear.

By mid-1985, 40 percent of all babies will be first babies. The number of separate-person households will increase rapidly, whereas the number of husband-wife households will constitute a smaller proportion of the population.

The median age of Americans will move from the 20s to the early 30s by 1981. This change will have major effects. For example, the U.S. Forest Service says that this older population will mean less emphasis on skiing and hunting, since two thirds of all waterfowl hunters, for example, are under 35. This will have impacts on retailers of sporting goods wear. The older population, however, will provide opportunities for entirely new product lines.

---

[28] U.S. Bureau of the Census, "Estimates of the Populations of States, with Components of Change, 1970–75," no. 640, p. 25.

[29] "How the Changing Age Mix Changes Markets," *Business Week,* January 12, 1976, p. 72.

[30] "Washington Roundup," *Marketing News,* October 24, 1975, p. 11.

FIGURE 7–4
A BITTER STRUGGLE FOR JOBS, CAPITAL, AND PEOPLE—THE SOUTH AND
SOUTHWEST LEAD THREE WAYS: IN POPULATION, INCOME, AND
MANUFACTURING GROWTH

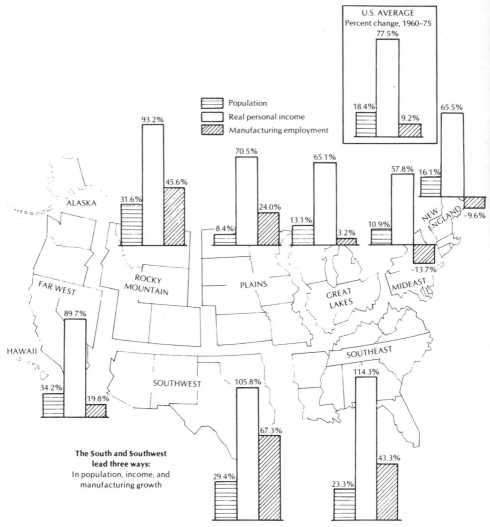

Data: Census Bureau, Bureau of Economic Analysis, Bureau of Labor Statistics.
Source: Reprinted from the May 17, 1976, issue of *Business Week* by special permission. © 1976 by McGraw-Hill, Inc., p. 93.

In the face of these changes, the following observations were recently offered for retailers thinking about declining age groups.

First . . . the bloom is off the youth market, at least for now. Items:

Newborns to pre-schoolers. Will continue down till 1980 when the late 50's and early 60's baby crop starts in on parenthood, peaking in 1985. Categories from baby

FIGURE 7–5
A LOOK AHEAD AT THE U.S. POPULATION: 1975–1985

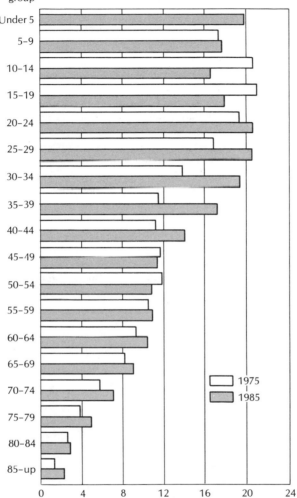

Shifting demographics: Population will grow from 213,446,000 to 234,067,000 during the next decade. The new mix will vitally affect markets for goods and services and alter the composition of the labor force.

Source: "How the Changing Age Mix Changes Markets." Reprinted from the January 12, 1976, issue of *Business Week* by special permission. © 1976 by McGraw-Hill, Inc., p. 74.

foods and furnishings to tot toys and apparel must fight to grow against population statistics. Worth a fresh look though, as we enter the 80's.

School agers and early teens, aged 5–14. No growth here till after 1985. In fact, the 10–14 group will be down 18 percent, or 3.6 million kids less from 1975–1985.

Tougher sledding for categories from sugared breakfast cereals, school equipment and supplies to bubblegum and teenybopper rock.

Teens. 1975 marks the last growth year for ages 15–19. After 1980, look for sharp declines in teen-oriented products from stereos to skin remedies.

Family formation (20–34). This group will expand 21% between 1975 and 1985—twice as fast as the total population. The affluent 30–34 age segment (up 42%) will be the fastest growing. Thus, despite later marriages and smaller families, record levels of new households (many with plural incomes) are going to be formed. Given a healthy economy with unemployment at manageable levels, this is good news for purveyors of home appliances, furnishings and all related household items.

But, meeting needs of this burgeoning market will require *astute understanding of their changing lifestyles.* More informal living and entertainment patterns, stress on convenience, leisure-orientation, fashion individuality and lack of concern for "lifetime" possessions—all point to reorganizing the way stores *select and present their wares.* More "instant" furniture and less formal housewares; more "boutiques" within a single store creating total "looks" for different style segments; perhaps an entire department with items from many categories organized around a lifestyle, say "leisure," rather than the more traditional merchandise orientation.

Peak income group (35–49). From 1975–1985 this well-heeled consumer group will grow by 8 million people (23%), making it a major growth segment during the period and an enticing retail prospect.

Discretionary spenders (50–64). Growth will slow, but they'll still represent nearly 14% of the population at 32 million in 1985. With more *discretionary dollars available than ever before* in their lives, they'll make a tempting target for travel, leisure, entertainment, retirement homes and furnishings.

Retirement (65 plus). Growing by 17% from 1975 to 1985—almost double the population's rate—retired oldsters must spend reduced buying power mainly on essentials. However, the group's size, its growing political power and geriatric needs, such as health care, open up *specialized opportunities.*[31]

THE SOCIAL ENVIRONMENT

The social environment is being subjected to increasingly close scrutiny by retail management. "More and more retail executives, in fact, appear to be talking about changing consumer attitudes than changing economic conditions—another key indication that retailers consider consumer attitudes the key factor regardless of economic conditions."[32] As noted by Edward Gorman, marketing consultant for J. C. Penney, "As retailers, we must be alert to changing values since they are the source of new lifestyles and, therefore, new consumer desires and new consumer demands.[33]

Cultural and life-style changes

Changes in life-styles always provide opportunities for the astute retailer. The trend back to nature provided opportunities for the sale of all types of

[31] *Grey Matter,* vol. 46 (October 1975), p. 3. Grey Advertising, Inc.

[32] "'77 Focus is on Changing Consumer Habits and Bottom Line," *Stores,* January 1977, p. 19.

[33] "Consumers Seek Stores Where Clothes Match Current Changing Lifestyles," *Marketing News,* February 25, 1977, p. 9.

camping and outdoor recreation equipment. Likewise, the boom in house-plant sales, greenhouses, and related items may also be attributed to this same desire.

Inflation and high energy costs are forcing many consumers to change their life-styles. Make-it-yourself and fix-it-yourself psychology is stronger than ever. Home sewing and gardening are forecast to increase in popularity as are various retail departments for do-it-yourself merchandise. Bikes are increasing as a way of travel for shopping and local movement. Many stores are introducing motorcycle parts in their automotive sections. With today's increasingly sedentary society, exercise and health are providing a good market for retailers selling everything from organic foods to jogging suits.

The consumer has become increasingly concerned about the quality of life. Evidence indicates that quality and durability may in some instances be more important than convenience. Likewise, concern over the environment is shown in increasing sales of organic foods. Recycling has become increasingly popular. In addition, legislation has emerged which is designed to eliminate throwaway bottles.

Leisure preferences

Many people no longer have to work long hours simply to buy the basic necessities of life. More discretionary time exists, but this is absorbed by factors other than leisure. Because of increasing pressures on time, many people now value time more than money. Thus, any effort to save the consumer time will give the retailer a competitive edge. We have seen the emergence of mail-order home shopping services, telephone shopping, shopping centers, mini-malls, late-night hours, and similar types of activities in response to these time pressures.

Violence

Crimes such as theft, shoplifting, and vandalism are on the increase in virtually all areas. Retailers are increasingly forced to reconsider store layout, design, and merchandise displays. For example, the 7–11 stores announced a plan for reducing robberies of their outlets.

The rise in robberies of stores which are open 24 hours a day is rapidly accelerating. Some chains of such stores have experienced a threefold increase in crime in three years. The 7–11 program, however, has enabled it to reduce the frequency of armed robbery by one third. Among the changes instituted were removing all store window advertising after dark so that outsiders could see into the store, posting signs which stated that the clerk could not open the safes, installing better lighting, placing chains across driveways to eliminate easy escape routes, and offering coffee to late-night visitors, such as policemen.[34]

Montgomery Ward, in citing internal thievery as the chain's biggest problem, dismissed 5,000 dishonest employees out of a work force of 100,000.

---

[34] "Holding Down the Hold-ups," *Business Week*, March 8, 1976, p. 60.

Shrinkage for Ward's had increased to $10 million annually. An investigation which included use of the polygraph revealed the dishonest workers.[35]

The American family of the 1970s

General Mills commissioned a nationwide study to determine the likely behavioral patterns of the American family of the 1970s.[36] The basic findings of its analysis reveal the problems and opportunities facing retailing executives as they respond to these changes in the family. The key findings were as follows:

Leisure time. For families the first step is to cut back on the "nice things of life"— eating out in restaurants (37 percent); entertaining friends for dinner (17 percent); certain hobbies and sports which cost money (21 percent). Overall, one out of two families reports that it now spends most of its free time at home rather than "going out."

Vacations. Families are not necessarily giving up vacations, but they now regard them differently. Annual vacations today are considered a luxury by more than half of all families. Among families with a lowered standard of living, almost two out of three look upon a vacation as a "real luxury."

Use of electricity. Most families are caught in a losing battle with their utility bills. Two out of three indicate that they are cutting back on the use of electricity, but the same percentage report that despite their efforts they are paying more for utilities than they did a year ago.

Food and eating patterns. Many of the changes in eating patterns reflect family efforts to hold the line on food costs—again with not much reported success. One out of four families is trying to cut back on its use of prepared and frozen foods; one out of five is not serving meat regularly; a small number of families are eliminating "seconds." A change is also indicated on items such as cookies and candies, with 45 percent of the families reporting that they are spending less this year on sweets and only 22 percent reporting that they are spending more.

Shopping patterns. An integral part of beating inflation is bargain hunting, especially among the 45 percent of families who report serious money problems. Many consumers now assume that inflation will get worse, not better, and that it is smarter to buy now, especially when items are on sale. The use of credit cards makes it especially tempting to buy now.

Health. Unfortunately, preventive health care is one area in which people are also trying to save money. Among the families surveyed, 18 percent indicated that they are already postponing regular medical and dental checkups; among families most impacted by the economy, 28 percent are putting off checkups.

Another method of coping with inflation may also have health implications; in 16 percent of the families, someone, usually the male head, is moonlighting or trying to do so.

Reading habits. Some families are considering cutting back on magazine and newspaper subscriptions as they try to pare down their expenses. This may mean a

---

[35] "Ward Axes 5000," *Chain Store Age Executive,* December 1975, p. 5.

[36] *The General Mills American Family Report, 1974–75.* Copyright General Mills, Inc. 1975. 9200 Wayzata Boulevard, Minneapolis, Minnesota 55440.

public less well informed and less exposed to badly needed money management help.

Gifts and charitable contributions. Gift giving is also a problem these days. Now almost one out of two families gives fewer gifts. In addition, 16 percent of families are economizing by reducing their charitable contributions.

Making do. Families are also learning that many objects in their homes are repairable, and that it is possible to do with less. Almost half say that they are wearing what clothes they have, rather than buying new ones, and 34 percent are repairing things that they would normally have thrown out. Among families whose standard of living is worse this year than last, over half are making fewer clothing purchases and almost half are repairing rather than replacing home appliances and equipment.

Car repairs. Car maintenance presents a special budget problem to most people. Repair costs are much higher than they were a year ago, and credit is not usually available. Most people meet these higher costs by trimming other expenses. But 10 percent have put off repairs until it is too late, and end up either with an accident or a permanently disabled car.

Working wives. Two incomes in the family are more and more common as a way of dealing with the family's finances. Among wives, 41 percent now work either full or part time, primarily to supplement the family budget. Working, however, presents its own problems: frustration rises as additional income does not produce major financial improvement; working wives lack time for bargain shopping, preparing meals, baking, preserving, canning, and getting things fixed; anger and bitterness grow as some men oppose their wives taking jobs. (Sixteen percent of the working women indicate that their husbands resent their working.)

A variety of marketing changes are forecast as a result of the above factors. For example, the growth of services at the retail level is forecast. These include such services as equipment rentals, home maintenance services (as apartment living accelerates rapidly), and home health services and leisure-time activities.[37]

Companies are thinking of innovative ways to appeal to consumers with changing life-styles. The ideas developed include insurance policies that would stay in force for one or two years without premium payments for persons who want to take occasional breaks from work, and life insurance coverage that would convert to a health insurance policy when the insured person reaches retirement age.[38]

The legal environment

It is beyond the scope of this chapter to focus on the legal environment as it affects retailing. The legal dimensions are covered in Chapter 9. However, in discussing the environmental dynamics of the marketplace, we would be remiss if we did not point out the speed with which changes in the legal environment can affect the retailer. Let us consider a few specific examples.

---

[37] "Study Forecasts Strong Service Industry Growth, Comments on Lagging Productivity, Rising Prices," *Marketing News,* November 11, 1975, p. 6.

[38] "How the Changing Age Mix Changes Markets," *Business Week,* January 12, 1976, p. 78.

By 1980, U.S. homeowners will buy an estimated 7.5 million smoke alarms a year. The reason for the growth of this market is that building codes are being amended to make the installation of smoke alarms mandatory in new houses. In addition, a new federal law which became effective on June 15, 1976, made smoke alarms mandatory in all mobile homes built after that date. Thus the boom in retail sales of this product has been tremendous.[39]

Noise regulations established by the Environmental Protection Agency have hit hard at motorcycles and are likely to have an adverse impact on sales of motorcycles by adding to their price. In addition, motorcycle manufacturers fear that cutting the noise level will turn off many potential customers.[40]

Consider the recent unexpected boom in the sale of women's wear for competitive sports now that schools have moved to comply with the new regulations calling for equality in sports programs.[41]

Finally, look at the tremendous increase in Sunday openings which has occurred in recent years, in spite of the fact that most merchants don't like Sunday openings. Yet consumer demand outweighs such problems as having to pay time and a half or double time to employees. It appears that the "blue laws" are basically dead.[42]

SUMMARY

The social and economic environments are having increasing significance for retailers. Problems with inflation, recession, unemployment, materials shortages, energy shortages, and so forth are a fact of everyday life. These problems are compounded by the emergence of new types of economic institutions. Increased intensity of competition is occurring among institutions as population growth slows and market shares can be expanded only at the expense of competitors.

Major shifts are occurring in the geographic distribution of population and in the age composition of the population. Increasing numbers of Americans are abandoning the inner cities of major metropolitan areas, whereas population is growing rapidly in nonmetropolitan areas of the United States, particularly in the Southern rim, or the so-called Sun Belt, which extends from the Carolinas to the southern half of California. Overall population growth is slowing down. In the years ahead, the population will become older. Births will be at a level approaching what is necessary to replace the population.

In the face of these changes, the retailer needs to be sensitive to shifting

[39] *Wall Street Journal*, Mid-East Edition, April 30, 1976, p. 1.

[40] "Motorcycles: The Dip Continues," *Business Week*, May 3, 1976, p. 80.

[41] "Sporting Goods Lose Some of Their Swing," *Business Week*, September 13, 1976, p. 37.

[42] " 'Never on Sunday' Is a Thing of the Past," *Business Week*, August 16, 1976, p. 51.

life-styles and their effects on behavior in the marketplace. Consumers seem somewhat uncertain about the future even though they have a basic confidence in the American economy. A make-it-yourself and do-it-yourself psychology is expanding. Increasing numbers of consumers are becoming more rational in their shopping, in that quality and durability are becoming more important in the purchase of goods and services. Increasing numbers of wives are working to maintain the family standard of living. This places increasing emphasis upon convenience in all aspects of American life.

We cannot be certain what the future holds for the economy and the American consumer. However, the close monitoring of all of the environments is a major requirement if students and practitioners of retailing are to be sensitive to the changes which are taking place.

KEY CONCEPTS

Economic uncertainties
   Disruptions of normal business
   Financial pressures
   Inventories
   Competitive behavior
The economy and consumer expenditures
   Credit
   Income stabilizers
Demography and consumer expenditures
   The birthrate
   Population shifts
   Age distribution
The social environment
   Cultural and life-style changes
   Leisure preferences
   The family of the 1970s

DISCUSSION QUESTIONS

1. Discuss the effects of inflation on the economic environment of the retailer. How can the retailer adjust to these effects? What about the effects of recession?

2. What are some steps which the retailer can take to anticipate and possibly control for such problems as materials and energy shortages?

3. What strategy alternatives are available to enable the retailer to achieve continued growth and expansion in the face of slowed population growth? Is increased competition for a decreasing market inevitable?

4. How are Americans adjusting their purchasing behavior to the turbulent environments of the 1970s? What can the retailer do to make a profit?

5. What elements of consumer demand are likely to remain inelastic even in the face of adverse changes in the economy? What elements of consumer demand would be hurt the most?

6. Such aggregate measures of economic change as GNP, unemployment levels, and the rate of inflation may present misleading information for a particular retailer. How can the retailer avoid being misled by these indicators of change? What types of information would the retailer find particularly useful at the store level? How can this information be obtained?

7. What types of products or services are likely to be adversely affected as the population gets older? What products or services will benefit?

8. Why is the major growth in population occurring in the Southern rim? Will this change greatly enhance the probable success of a given retail outlet in the areas comprised by the Southern rim? Why or why not? Does this mean that opportunities will not continue to remain good in other parts of the United States? Discuss.

9. What are the effects of income stabilizers on retailing? Do all segments of the retailing structure benefit from income stabilizers? Are these types of programs likely to increase or decrease in the future? Can the beneficiaries of the programs be viewed as a separate market segment to whom it is possible to direct promotion efforts?

10. What changes in the social environment of the 1970s have affected retailing most? What are some of the likely changes for the 1980s?

PROJECTS

1. Visit the downtown business district of your town and determine:

    a. How many vacant stores there are.
    b. Which particular types of stores are vacant.

    Discuss the factors leading to this situation. If the downtown area in your town has been revitalized, what strategy was followed to accomplish this, and how successful has the strategy been? If the downtown area has not been revitalized, are there any plans to do this?

2. Make a sketch of the floor plan of several different types of stores—for example, a grocery, a drugstore, a hardware store—and estimate how much space is devoted to original products. What new products are carried, and how much space do they have?

3. In the outside environment of retailing, the "energy" crisis facing the world (and the United States in particular) will impact on certain retailers. Set up a research project to investigate the concerns which you can uncover regarding how the retailer believes that he (she) may be affected by the energy crisis. What plans are being made to cope? In your estimation is the energy crisis being taken seriously by retailers? What do you predict will be the major long-run impact of the energy crisis on the retail structure in general? Be imaginative in this project.

CASES

Case 1.　Shirley and Frank Robertson own a food store in a low-income neighborhood. Recently there has been talk that Congress will replace the present food stamp program with a welfare program providing income supplements. The Robertsons realize that such a change will have a significant effect on the purchases made by the people in the area surrounding their store. They are not sure exactly how they should prepare for the change. What do you suggest, and why?

Case 2.　The Men's Shop in Mountainville, a highly industrial city of 75,000 population, had enjoyed several years of successful business. In anticipation of a continuation of these conditions the management had expanded the shop's offerings in both selection and depth. Then the economy took a sudden downturn which resulted in widespread layoffs at many local plants. Sales declined sharply, and the Men's Shop was left holding a rather large inventory. To make matters even worse, there were some major changes in men's fashions, and several new styles were introduced which soon became very popular. It was only by drastic reductions in price that the old stock was sold. For the last couple of years the Men's Shop has kept inventories at a low level by offering only a few styles in depth.

However, most economic indicators now predict a substantial upturn in the economy and many local plants are beginning to resume normal operations. The Men's Shop has been offered an excellent buy on a new line of good quality men's suits. However, in order to carry this line, the shop will have to make a substantial purchase, as the supplier expects retailers to offer the full line in depth.

After thinking it over, the management of the Men's Shop declined the offer and purchased a small selection of a less well known, but good, brand from another supplier.

1. What factors do you think caused the Men's Shop management to make the decision it made?
2. What are the major advantages and disadvantages of the decision?
3. Do you feel that the management was justified in making its decision?
4. Was the decision based more on historical experience or on future outlook? Which is more relevant for marketing decisions? Explain.

8

CHANNEL STRUCTURAL AND FUNCTIONAL CHANGES

*A*s a longtime independent retailer I would like to recommend the serious consideration of this chapter to anyone contemplating a career in retailing. The satisfactions of being your own boss are very real but are probably outweighed by the assistance in data processing, the financial resources, the technical assistance in advertising, merchandising, and site selection, and the other backup services available in the alternative channel structures, as explained in this chapter. For anyone already in the field of retailing, the vertical marketing systems described here open up several areas of operating expertise which may be available.

A. Joseph Wolf
Wolf Furniture Co.
Sayre, Pennsylvania

As a key member in the channel of distribution for consumer goods, the retailer must be continually attuned to the dynamics of distribution channel structuring. The past two decades have witnessed significant changes in the way products reach consumers. The channel has come to be viewed as a unit of competition, and vertically organized marketing systems have emerged. These systems are characterized by a willingness to shift marketing functions among manufacturers, wholesalers, retailers, and the other institutions and agencies responsible for making goods and services available to the public. For example, the manufacturer may be responsible for new product development and national promotion, the wholesaler may perform the inventory functions, and the retailer may perform the market research function in determining consumer needs and wants. Because these members of the channel are cooperating and each of the various marketing functions is performed by the member of the channel best qualified to perform it, greater efficiencies occur than would be obtainable if each level of the channel operated independently and sought to perform all of the functions itself.

Business executives are continually seeking to develop distribution structures which will maximize profits and consumer utilities and respond to competitive pressures. New members may be added to a channel and old members may be eliminated as such functions as pricing, financing, promotion, and product development are shifted to different levels within the channel. Clearly one of the member institutions must assume managerial leadership within the channel. This is known as channel control. Channel control depends on the locus of power within the channel. Power is the ability of one channel member to direct the activity of other channel members. For example, a channel member may possess that ability because of its size, financial resources, strong product research and development, strong consumer loyalty, market knowledge, or promotion skills. Depending on the circumstances, any member of the channel may obtain control.

Changes in channel structure and philosophy require revisions in marketing practices. Sometimes a firm's existence may be threatened by a major change in channel structure. Thus a new form of distribution or a new type of competition can impair existing institutional relationships. For example, until the early 1970s digital watches were sold only through conventional jewelers. Now they are sold in virtually every type of retail outlet from drugstores to supermarkets. Jewelers have been adversely affected by this change in distribution pattern. Consider the more recent situation of citizens band radios: "A yet immature industry that has not developed stable distribution patterns—be it the two-step wholesale distributor, the chain retail store, or the vertical market such as automotive, farm implement, recreational vehicle, truck, marine and many others is the CB radio."[1] The result is a major risk on the part of the various channel members if they guess wrong on

[1] "CB Radio Field Has Growing Pains, but Still Grows," *Marketing News*, December 17, 1976, p. 5.

what will be the dominant channel structure of the future. In addition, the question of whether major channel members will retain private brands is still largely unknown. Moreover, consumers may be hurt if they purchase a CB radio from an outlet which does not become part of the future channel structure for the radios.

The goal of this chapter is to provide a framework for understanding the forces that affect the structures and functions of the channel from the standpoint of retail management. Thus, the specific purposes of this chapter are to:

1. Analyze the basic types of competition facing retailers.
2. Focus on the new face of retailing.
3. Analyze changing structures.
4. Explain the emergence of vertical market systems.
5. Analyze the implications of vertical systems competition for retail management.
6. Examine the various dimensions of channel control, conflict, and power as they affect retailing.

THE COMPETITION FACING INDEPENDENT RETAILERS

The conventional marketing channel is a loosely aligned group of basically autonomous manufacturers, wholesalers, and retailers. Management at each level is likely to be concerned only with suppliers and customers and not with links at all levels of the channel. The managements of the various levels may aggressively bargain with one another, sever business relationships arbitrarily, behave in a highly independent manner, and have no strategic commitment to a channel system. For some managements, the choice of a channel is not open unless their firms have considerable freedom in market policies. In isolated areas, no choice may exist because only one middleman serves the area or agrees to serve the outlet. A small independent hardware store may deal with numerous suppliers in meeting customer needs, giving no thought to the sources of raw materials or to the manufacturer of the products. Such an outlet may have little influence with any one wholesaler because the volume it purchases from each wholesaler is limited. This type of situation exists in part because retailing, in spite of its increasing maturity, still has a large number of small businesses which are often led by untrained, undercapitalized managers who seek to maximize short-run profits at the expense of longer term profitability. Even the most sophisticated retailers, however, often behave arbitrarily and in their own interests.

As part of the conventional distribution structure, the manufacturer performs product research and development, much mass media advertising, and related functions. Wholesalers can best be characterized as intermediate distributors who provide inventory management, warehousing, delivery, product assortment, and often credit to the retailer. The third layer in this type of channel structure is the retailer, who provides promotion, distribution, and even inventory functions at the local level.

Lack of cooperation and even conflict are common. For example, the manufacturer may use free merchandise or special discounts to induce a supplier to push a new product aggressively with retailers even though the level of acceptance may be questionable. On the other hand, the retailer may be unwilling to share with the manufacturer customer information that would be valuable in new product development, packaging modifications, or national promotion. Likewise, the manufacturer may not give the middleman or the retailer advance information on a major promotional campaign because of a fear that the information will be leaked to competitors. Communication is bad because the various levels of the "channel" do not see themselves as pursuing common goals.

An example of such a channel is that used in the sale of gasoline and related products. In this area, each layer of activity—drilling, refining, and selling—is often not fully coordinated with the others unless the retail stations are operated by the refiner.[2] Role separation is emphasized in a variety of ways. Separate ownership of the product may occur at each layer of the channel. Moreover, the conventional wisdom discourages firms from performing functions historically reserved for other channel members.[3] For example, product promotion is handled only by the refiner, whereas prices are established by the supplier. A bulk distributor may operate retail stations and sell gasoline more cheaply than it can be sold by the other retail stations for which the distributor acts as a wholesaler. In addition, promotions may be offered by the supplier-owned stations which are not available at the other outlets.

Such situations have led to the emergence of several types of competitive behavior which are designed to resolve the problems of nonaligned channels. A careful analysis of each of these competitive models will help the student to appreciate more fully the ever-increasing complexity of the distribution structure.

Intratype competition

Competition among retailers is inevitable. The type of competition most familiar to students of retailing is intratype competition. This is competition between two independent retailers of the same type, such as two drugstores, as shown in Table 8–1. Most persons are familiar with intratype competition

---

[2] Most of the major oil companies operate fewer than 1 percent of their outlets with company employees. Fred C. Allvine and James M. Patterson, *Highway Robbery* (Bloomington: Indiana University Press, 1974), p. 25.

[3] James Constantin, Rodney Evans, and Malcolm Morris, *Marketing Management Strategy* (Dallas: Business Publications, Inc., 1976), pp. 259–60.

TABLE 8–1

Type of competition	Scope of competition	Corporate illustrations
Intratype competition	Competition between the same type of outlets	Thrifty versus Walgreen Ketchum versus McKesson-Robbins
Intertype competition	Competition between different types of outlets	Kroger versus K-Mart Belknap versus Garcia
Systems competition	Competition between different types of vertically integrated systems, including voluntary groups, cooperative groups, franchise networks, and corporate chains	A&P versus IGA Marta versus Silo
Free-form competition	Competition between free-form corporations, each of which operates multiple types of outlets to serve multiple market segments	Daylin versus Interco Bergen Brunswig versus American Hospital Supply

Source: Reprinted from Bert C. McCammon, Jr., "Future Shock and the Practice of Management," in Phillip Levine (ed.), *Attitude Research Bridges the Atlantic,* Marketing Research Series 16, 1975, published by the American Marketing Association.

since this type of competition is the model most frequently described in economics texts.

Intertype competition

A second type of competitive model is intertype competition, which is competition at the retail level among different types of firms selling the same product. Some persons view intertype competition as a subset of horizontal competition since all sales are at retail, even though they are made by different types of outlets. Intertype competition is probably the most representative model of retail competition today. For example, Firestone Tires may be sold through discount department stores; conventional department stores; tire, battery, and accessory dealers; independent garages; service stations; and other types of outlets. Also, as a result of the emergence of scrambled merchandising widely different types of products are sold in many different types of outlets. These outlets are all competing for the same customers.

Market segments have become narrower as firms have responded to consumer needs and sought to expand sales in an effort to lower costs. Thus, as part of the intertype competitive model, traditional lines of trade have been abandoned and wider assortments of merchandise have been offered to narrower market segments.

The economics of intertype competition are well illustrated in Table 8–2, which shows the high gross margins earned on health and beauty aids

TABLE 8–2
THE ECONOMICS OF INTERTYPE COMPETITION: HEALTH AND BEAUTY AIDS
GROSS MARGINS IN SUPERMARKETS, 1963–1973

Product category	Gross margin as a percent of sales						Percentage point change (1963–1973)
	1963	1965	1967	1969	1971	1973	
Baby needs	44.0	44.7	38.5	35.7	29.2	24.7	(19.3)
Cosmetics	42.8	41.6	37.5	34.5	30.9	32.2	(10.6)
Creams and lotions	40.1	38.4	35.9	33.1	32.5	32.1	(8.0)
First aid	43.2	43.0	39.3	36.3	33.6	33.6	(9.6)
Hair care	41.7	34.5	37.4	32.2	28.2	29.1	(12.6)
Hygiene needs	35.7	39.5	25.7	23.5	22.8	17.5	(18.2)
Medications	38.8	39.1	31.6	27.6	26.6	27.2	(11.6)
Men's toiletries and shaving preparations	37.6	36.8	33.6	31.4	26.5	26.6	(11.0)
Oral hygiene	35.9	33.7	28.7	26.7	29.7	27.4	(8.5)
Total	38.8	37.6	32.6	29.4	26.4	26.4	(12.4)

Source: Bert C. McCammon, Jr., Robert F. Lusch, and Bradley T. Farnsworth, "Contemporary Markets and the Corporate Imperative: A Strategic Analysis for Senior Retailing Executives," paper presented at a seminar for top management in retailing, Graduate School of Business Administration, Harvard University, 1976, p. 8.

featured in supermarkets. Historically, health and beauty aids were sold primarily by department stores or drugstores.

Vertical marketing systems (VMS) competition

The vertical marketing system is the form of competition which is growing most rapidly in retailing today. "Vertical marketing systems . . . consist of networks of horizontally coordinated and vertically aligned establishments which are managed as a system. Establishments at each level operate at an optimum scale so that marketing functions within the system are performed at the most advantageous level or position."[4]

Vertical systems competition is exemplified by the competition between Kentucky Fried Chicken and Burger King, or between General Motors Corporation and the Ford Motor Company. Vertical systems are capital-intensive networks which seek to provide maximum economies and efficiencies in promotion, technology, and management expertise. In such systems all marketing flows are coordinated from the point of production to the point of ultimate distribution, as shown in Figure 8–1. The same functions are performed by both the conventional marketing channel and the vertical marketing system. However, in the vertical marketing system the functions are performed for the channel as a unit of competition and not for each channel member. Figure 8–1 contrasts the differences between the conventional marketing channel and an integrated marketing system. Various types of vertical

---

[4] William R. Davidson, "Changes in Distributive Institutions," Journal of Marketing, vol. 34 (January 1970), p. 7.

FIGURE 8–1
THE CONCEPT OF FUNCTIONAL SHIFTABILITY

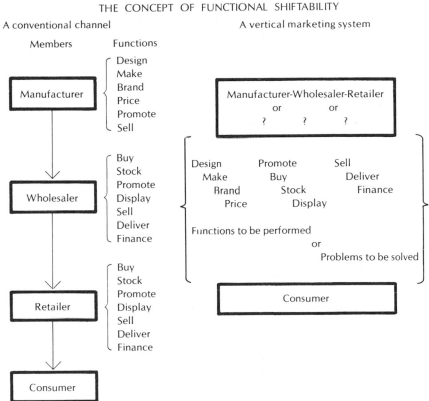

Source: Adapted from *Strategic Marketing* by David Kollat, Roger D. Blackwell, and James F. Robeson, p. 289. Copyright © 1972 by Holt, Rinehart and Winston. Reprinted by permission of Holt, Rinehart and Winston.

systems exist, and these will be discussed later in the chapter. Table 8–3 provides a more detailed description of the differences between the conventional channel and the integrated system.

Total corporate systems competition

Total corporate systems competition is the most sophisticated present form of competition. Corporate systems competition occurs when a single management ownership links resources, manufacturing capability, distribution networks, and strong customer loyalty. Corporate systems competition is distinguished from other types of vertical marketing systems on the basis of ownership. Many franchise systems may be viewed as vertical systems, but since ownership of the retail establishments is in different hands, control is not as absolute as that of the total corporate system. Well-known examples of corporate systems include Sears and Firestone. These firms manufacture

TABLE 8–3
SALIENT CHARACTERISTICS OF COMPETING DISTRIBUTION NETWORKS

	Type of network	
Network characteristic	Conventional marketing channel	Integrated marketing system
Composition of network	Network composed of isolated and autonomous units, each of which performs a conventionally defined set of marketing functions. Coordination achieved primarily through bargaining and negotiation.	Network composed of interconnected units, each of which performs an optimum combination of marketing functions. Coordination achieved through the use of detailed plans and comprehensive programs.
Economic capability of member units	Operating units frequently unable to achieve systemic economies.	Operating units *programmed* to achieve systemic economies.
Organizational stability	Open network with low index of member loyalty and relative ease of entry. Network therefore tends to be unstable.	Open network, but entry rigorously controlled by the system's requirements and by market conditions. Membership loyalty assured through the use of ownership or contractual agreements. As a result, network tends to be relatively stable.
Number and composition of decision makers	Large number of strategists supported by a slightly larger number of operating executives.	Limited number of strategists supported by a *significantly* larger number of staff and operating executives.
Analytic focus of strategic decision makers	Strategists preoccupied with cost, volume, and investment relationships at a *single* stage of the marketing process.	Strategists preoccupied with cost, volume, and investment relationships at *all* stages of the marketing process. Corresponding emphasis on the "total cost" concept accompanied by a continuous search for favorable economic trade-offs.
Underlying decision-making process	Heavy reliance on judgmental decisions made by generalists.	Heavy reliance on "scientific" decisions made by specialists or committees of specialists.
Institutional loyalties of decision makers	Decision makers emotionally committed to traditional forms of distribution.	Decision makers *analytically* committed to marketing concept and viable institutions.

Source: Bert C. McCammon, Jr. "Perspectives for Distribution Programming," from *Vertical Marketing Systems,* edited by Louis P. Bucklin. Copyright © 1970 by Scott, Foresman and Company. Reprinted by permission.

some of their merchandise, handle their own storage and distribution functions, and perform all management activities necessary for the sale of merchandise at the retail level.

Forward integration under this arrangement occurs whenever a manufacturer establishes its own wholesale and retail network, as has occurred for Goodyear, Singer, and Sherwin Williams. Backward integration occurs whenever retailers or wholesalers assume the functions normally performed before the merchandise reaches them at the retail level. Sears is an example of backward vertical integration.

Free-form competition

Keep in mind that none of these types of competition exists in isolation. Retail firms in any of the systems discussed face competition from retailers in any or all of the other systems. Also, the comments made above must be regarded only as broad generalizations about the nature of competition and the various types of channel systems, because numerous exceptions exist. This is particularly obvious when one examines the major multiplex or free-form retailers. As Bert McCammon has noted:

Dayton Hudson, an early proponent of the free form concept, currently operates conventional department stores, discount department stores, ready-to-wear boutiques, pants shops, cosmetic salons, book stores, jewelry stores, catalog show-rooms, automotive service centers, and warehouse outlets. In short, the company has embarked on an eclectic expansion program on the assumption that this is a logical response to market segmentation.[5]

As will be seen below in the discussion of managerial implications, the retailer's role, functional performance, constraints, and power position vary for each of the competitive model and channel systems discussed above. Thus, the managerial strategies in each situation necessarily differ.

THE NEW FACE OF RETAILING

Polarity in establishment types

Consumers are no longer willing to buy whatever is produced and offered to them in the marketplace. They demand merchandise which fits their life-styles, income levels, and household requirements. This has led to a fragmentation of retail markets as they are more carefully designed to offer products to ever smaller segments.

An emerging trend in the face of greater segmentation is the increasing diversity of retail outlets. A polarity in the prevailing types of retail establishments is occurring. Mass merchandising firms such as Lowes, with its home improvement centers and discount pricing, have made major inroads into the markets of traditional hardware stores. Other mass merchandising firms, such as Woolco and K-Mart, have brought supermarket merchandising practices to many types of retailing. The other high-growth market, at the opposite end of the scale from the mass merchandisers, is the specialty store "which carries a deep assortment of a very specialized line, often limited to a concept or 'look,' as opposed to commodity types."[6] An example is the Casual Corner shops. These are specialty shops which feature a well-coordinated assortment of women's sportswear. Other examples include Pier

---

[5] Bert C. McCammon, Jr., "Future Shock and the Practice of Management," in Phillip Levine (ed.), *Attitude Research Bridges the Atlantic,* 1975, published by the American Marketing Association.

[6] Davidson, "Changes in Distributive Institutions," p. 8.

1 and Radio Shack. The entire operation of such firms is programmed to a specific market segment and projects a sharply defined image.

Small independent retail establishments, such as a local hardware store, cannot effectively compete with a Lowes home improvement center or with a highly specialized paint and wallpaper shop because the management of such establishments do not have the merchandising or financial skills to compete with either the mass merchandisers or the specialty retailers. They are in the middle of the retail spectrum and cannot effectively compete on either a price or a nonprice basis.

Supermarket retailing

The supermarket concept, long familiar in the food field, is now being adapted to many other types of merchandising. The key elements are self-service and self-selection, large-scale but low-cost physical facilities, a strong price emphasis, simplification of customer services, and a wide variety of merchandise. This concept has been particularly successful in the drug, sporting goods, and home improvement fields. An example is Standard Brands, which operates over 55 paint and home decorating supermarkets. More than 40 percent of its volume is obtained from self-manufactured products.[7]

Store positioning

Increasing numbers of retailers are positioning themselves to capitalize on life-style and demographic markets, particularly in such areas of retailing as apparel, home accessories, and home furnishings. Customer preferences vary widely by life-style and social class. For example, The Limited, a chain of women's clothiers, serves primarily a market consisting of 18–35-year-old high-fashion female shoppers.

Nonstore retailing

Direct marketing is becoming an increasingly important method of distribution. Wards and Sears are continuing their direct marketing efforts, and such firms as Mary Kay Cosmetics and Unity Buying Service are making increasing inroads and will continue to do so as shoppers become more disenchanted with the shopping process.

Market intensification

Increasingly retail expansion is becoming a carefully programmed effort. Many retailers are focusing on a limited number of so-called core markets

[7] Albert D. Bates and Bert C. McCammon, Jr., "Reseller Strategies and the Financial Performance of the Firm," paper presented at the Structure, Strategy, and Performance Conference, Graduate School of Business, Indiana University, 1975, p. 15.

TABLE 8–4

MAINSTREAM STRATEGIES FOR IMPROVING PRODUCTIVITY IN DISTRIBUTION

Strategic thrust	Company and corporate profile
Warehouse retailing	*Carrefour* is the leading hypermarche chain in Western Europe. In fiscal 1973, the company operated on a gross margin of 16.4 percent, which enabled it to underprice conventional retailers by at least 10.0 percent. As a result of its underpricing strategy, Carrefour generates unusually high sales per employee and per square foot of selling area. In 1973, Carrefour announced that it plans to enter the North American market on a joint venture basis.
	Levitz pioneered the furniture warehouse showroom concept in North America. Available data suggested that the company underprices conventional furniture stores by 13.3 percent. In 1974, Levitz added carpets, consumer electronics, and major applicances to its merchandise mix by signing leased department agreements with Allen Carpet and Kennedy and Cohen, respectively.
	Consumers Distributing is the major catalog-showroom chain in Canada. In 1973, the company signed a joint venture agreement with May Department Stores to enter the U.S. market.
Supermarket retailing	*Handy Dan* operates 52 home improvement centers in six states. A typical center generates $1.8 million in annual sales, contains over 40,000 square feet of space, and carries an inventory of 30,000 items.
	Standard Brands Paint operates paint and decorating supermarkets in California and other Western states. At the present time, the company obtains 41 percent of its merchandise requirements from captive manufacturing facilities.
	Child World is a leading operator of toy supermarkets. A typical Child World unit contains 25,000 square feet of space and carries over 20,000 items in inventory.
Direct marketing	*Unity Buying Service* operates a unique direct mail program. Through the company's Factory Buying Club, consumers purchase merchandise from a 10,000-item catalog. The consumer's purchase price is factory cost plus a six percent service fee, taxes where applicable, and shipping costs. As of September 1973, the club's active membership consisted of 781,000 consumers.
	K-Tel is one of the leading direct response marketing organizations in North America. The company markets records and other specialty products through saturation TV campaigns. The products are distributed through 20,000 retail outlets on a consignment basis.
Vertical marketing systems	*Koffler Stores* is the largest franchiser of drugstores in North America. In 1972, the company signed a joint venture agreement with Steinberg's to open franchise stores in Quebec.
	Canadian Tire is a large voluntary group wholesaler that supplies affiliated stores with a variety of lines, including automotive parts and accessories, hardware, housewares, small appliances, and sporting goods. A typical Canadian Tire outlet contains approximately 25,000 square feet of space and carries over 20,000 items in inventory.
Corporate diversification	*Malone & Hyde* is a large voluntary group wholesaler in the food field. The company has pursued a vigorous diversification policy in recent years and currently obtains 34 percent of its earnings from company-owned stores and related ventures.
	Lucky Stores is the eighth largest food chain in the United States. The company also operates 115 discount department stores, 39 membership department stores, 39 home and auto stores, 29 drugstores, and 4 sporting goods stores.

Source: Bert C. McCammon, Jr., and William Hamner, "A Framework for Improving Productivity in Distribution," *Atlanta Economic Review*, September–October 1974, p. 12.

instead of expanding into geographically distant areas. Such retailers often perform better than do national firms. For example, Lowes primarily operates in the Southeast. Concentrating expansion in this way has produced attractive profitability results. The advantages of geographically concentrated outlets include a small number of distribution centers, greater customer awareness, and advertising economies made possible by the location of multiple outlets in a single market.

Other changes include warehouse retailing and corporate diversification. All of these are explained in greater detail in Table 8–4.

The life cycles for many types of retailing institutions are also becoming increasingly shorter. This may be observed in Table 8–5. Department stores have moved from a period of early growth to the stage of maturity in 80–100 years. However, more recent types of retailing institutions, such as furniture warehouse showrooms, have completed the same cycle in approximately a decade.

TABLE 8–5
TRENDS IN THE LENGTH OF LIFE CYCLES FOR U.S. RETAILING INSTITUTIONS

Type of retail institution	Examples	Early growth*	Maturity*	Elapsed time (in years)
Department stores	May Company Macy's I. Magnin	Mid-1860s	Mid-1960s	100
Variety stores	Woolworth Kresge S. S. Kress	Early 1900s	Early 1960s	60
Supermarkets	King Kullen Jewel Winn-Dixie	Mid-1930s	Mid-1970s	40
Discount department stores	Korvette K-Mart Arlans	Mid-1950s	Mid-1970s	20
Fast-food service	McDonald's Kentucky Fried Chicken Shakeys	Early 1960s	Mid-1970s	15
Home improvement centers	Channel Handy Dan	Mid-1960s	Late 1970s	15
Furniture warehouse showrooms	Levitz J. Homestock Wickes	Late 1960s	Late 1970s	10
Catalog showrooms	Best Products Wilson Service Merchandise	Late 1960s	Late 1970s	10

* The dates shown are valid for types of retail institutions, not for the particular companies used as examples.

Source: Adapted from Bert C. McCammon, Jr., "The Future of Catalog Showrooms: Growth and Its Challenges to Management," Working Paper P–69–C (Cambridge, Mass.: Marketing Science Institute, 1973), p. 3; also James Heskett, Marketing (New York: Macmillan Company, 1976), p. 286.

FIGURE 8–2
MARKET MATURITY AND PROFITABILITY
IN THE DISCOUNT DEPARTMENT STORE FIELD, 1964–1973

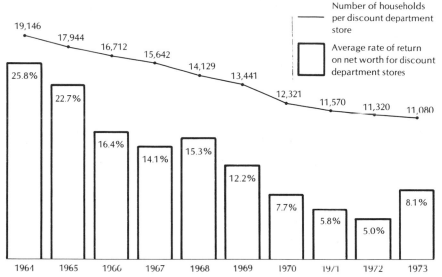

Source: Bert C. McCammon, Robert F. Lusch, and Bradley T. Farnsworth, "Contemporary Markets and the Corporate Imperative: A Strategic Analysis for Senior Retailing Executives," paper presented at a seminar for top management in retailing, Graduate School of Business Administration, Harvard University, 1976, p. 7.

TABLE 8–6
LIFE CYCLE CHARACTERISTICS OF FIVE RETAIL INSTITUTIONS

Institution	Approximate date of innovation	Approximate date of maximum market share	Approximate number of years required to reach maturity	Estimated maximum market share	Estimated 1975 market share
Downtown department store	1860	1940	80	8.5% of total retail sales	1.1%
Variety store	1910	1955	45	16.5% of general merchandise sales	9.5%
Supermarket	1930	1965	35	70.0% of grocery store sales	64.5%
Discount department store	1950	1970	20	6.5% of total retail sales	5.7%
Home improvement center	1965	1980 (estimate)	15	35.0% of hardware and building material sales	25.3%

Source: William Davidson, Albert Bates, and Stephen Bass, "The Retail Life Cycle," *Harvard Business Review*, November–December 1976, p. 94. Copyright 1976 by the President and Fellows of Harvard College. All rights reserved.

The maturity of institutions is related to the institutional life cycle. Typically, "expansion programs are vigorously pursued during the initial stages of the life cycle, administrative and operating issues are stressed during maturity, and greater emphasis is placed on strategic reprogramming toward the end of the cycle."[8] The effect of institutional maturity on profitability is vividly illustrated by the discount department store, as shown in Figure 8–2. A brief look at some other examples of the life cycle characteristics of retail institutions may also be useful. Table 8–6 depicts the approximate time of appearance of five different innovative institutions and the approximate time of their maximum market share. These dates roughly approximate those shown in Table 8–5. The estimated 1975 market share for the five institutions shown clearly reflects a decline in market share and indicates that this share appears to be accelerating increasingly for the newer types of institutions.

CHANGING CHANNEL STRUCTURES

Realistically, most retailers, even very small ones, are part of some type of system—whether it is a buying group or a voluntary association. Typically, however, they don't feel directed by manufacturers, and most manufacturers aren't capable of putting much effort into trying to "direct" numerous small retailers, except perhaps in the area of pricing. Still the constraints are greater in some types of channel system arrangement than they would be if the retailers acted in a totally independent fashion.

Reasons for the emergence of VMS

Vertical marketing will continue to grow in importance. As has been noted by McCammon:

The trend toward vertical marketing will continue, as corporate chains, cooperative groups, voluntary groups, and franchise networks steadily increase their market power. If present trends prevail, corporate chains will increase their market share of total retail sales from 29.6% in 1970 to at least 40.0% in 1981. Outlets affiliated with cooperative groups, voluntary groups, and franchise networks will experience equally rapid rates of growth, as their market share climbs from 27.6% in 1970 to approximately 45.0% in 1981. Thus, by 1981, vertically integrated networks will account for 85.0% of total retail throughput. As a consequence, the systems revolution which began in the 1920's will be substantially completed by the end of the decade.[9]

[8] Bert C. McCammon, Jr., "The Future of Catalog Showrooms: Growth and Its Challenges to Management," Working Paper P–69–C, (Cambridge, Mass.: Marketing Science Institute, 1973), p. 4.

[9] Bert C. McCammon, Jr., "Future Shock and the Practice of Management," in Phillip Levine (ed.), *Attitude Research Bridges the Atlantic,* 1975, published by the American Marketing Association.

The movement toward vertical marketing systems is an outgrowth of management efforts to achieve operating economies and to control costs. Vertical marketing systems also give the consumer more recognition in the development of marketing strategies. One prevailing philosophy under the channel concept is that such economic systems as marketing channels can be designed with the more explicit purpose of satisfying consumer needs. Thus, plans for the development of channels should begin with consumer needs and work backward from that point.[10] With this philosophy, consumer demand can be estimated more accurately and the system can respond accordingly. This process eliminates much inefficiency which would occur, for example, if the retailer were purchasing from several suppliers. Competition continues to occur, but it is between channels rather than between two different outlets on different levels in the channel. The concept requires compatibility between the strategies of all firms in the channel as they focus on the same consumer needs.

Let's briefly focus on one specific example of the emergence of vertically integrated market systems. In the 1940s and 1950s, food processors did not recognize food service and restaurants as a formal industry. They tended to focus on supermarkets only. During the 1960s, however, with the rapid growth of food franchising, many processors began moving into the food service field at the retail level.

Many added fast-food or family-style restaurant chains, including General Foods (Burger Chef), Pillsbury (Burger King and, pending stockholder and director approval, Steak and Ale), Heublein (Kentucky Fried Chicken), United Brands (A&W), Campbell Soup (Hurfy's, Clark's, Pietro's), Quaker Oats (Magic Pan), and Nestle (Stouffer's). Others entered food service distribution: Beatrice Foods (John Sexton & Co.), Consolidated Foods (Monarch Institutional Foods), and Clorox (Martin-Brower).[11]

Further, other types of manufacturers have also been moving into the retail field. "Texas Instruments, Dallas, has opened two outlets for its products; General Telephone and Electronics markets its equipment direct to consumers through 'Phone Marts.' Home improvement chains by paint marketers Sherwin Williams and Dutch Boy are off and running."[12]

Loosely aligned channels cannot compete against these total marketing systems. Consider the difficulties of a small independent hamburger outlet trying to compete with the McDonald's system or the difficulties of an independent hardware store competing with Lowe's or Montgomery Ward. The prices offered by members of vertical marketing systems are typically lower; the hours they are open for business may be longer; their promotional pro-

[10] Donald J. Bowersox and E. Jerome McCarthy, "Strategic Development of Planned Vertical Marketing Systems," in Louis P. Bucklin (ed.), Vertical Marketing Systems (Glenview, Ill.: Scott, Foresman and Co., 1970), p. 55.

[11] "America's Eating-out Splurge," Business Week, October 27, 1975, p. 45.

[12] Grey Matter vol. 46, no. 6, 1975, p. 5, Grey Advertising.

grams are more sophisticated; and the benefits and working conditions they offer employees are usually superior.

The concept of vertical marketing systems is not new. Automobile dealerships and gasoline service stations have been part of such systems for over 50 years. The new dimension is the tremendous recent growth which has virtually revolutionized the distribution structure. There are a number of reasons for this growth.

Capital requirements. The capital requirements for implementing new marketing programs are becoming increasingly higher. Thus, sales have to be maintained at high levels to assure profits. This encourages coordinated systems for marketing and distribution so as to achieve the economies of scale necessary to overcome the barriers of high fixed costs.

Declines in profitability. Many channel members are experiencing declines in operating margins and rates of return. These declines in profitability are occurring because of rising costs and increased competition. In order to achieve the economies of scale and the market impact needed to offset decreasing profit margins, mergers, acquisitions, and manufacturer or wholesaler ownership of retail institutions have become increasingly necessary.

The complexity of marketing systems. Marketing systems have become more complex in recent years as a result of advances in technology, increasing consumer sophistication, and increasing government regulation. This has led to the use of central data processing systems and other aids to central management, such as store location experts, corporate counsel, and other highly specialized staff functions.

System economies. Centrally coordinated systems of distribution have also made possible other economies which are difficult to maintain in the conventional channel structure. For example, economies of scale and economies of standardization are possible because storage and promotion can be programmed to achieve systematic economies. Economies can also be achieved through repositioning and eliminating some marketing activities. Such functions as ordering and financing are simplified or reduced by programmed routines and automatic reorder systems.

Figure 8–3 depicts the various types of vertical marketing systems with which students of retailing need to be familiar.

Types of VMS

Corporate systems. The corporate system was discussed earlier in the chapter. In this system all levels of the channel are under one ownership, assuring operating economies and absolute control over the channel. The centralization of power facilitates economies of scale through standardization and automation. There are some disadvantages to the corporate system. The financial investment is very high; the management problems may be more complex; other market opportunities often cannot be pursued; payroll and related costs are higher; inventory carrying costs are high; diseconomies of

FIGURE 8–3
TYPES OF DISTRIBUTION SYSTEMS

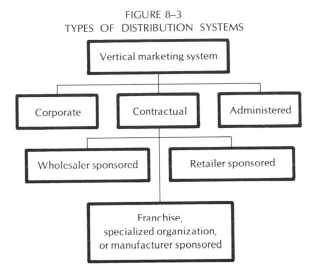

scale may occur in the larger systems; and unique legal restrictions exist in the case of mergers or acquisitions. Still the problems of pricing, product quality, promotion, and similar aspects of strategy are simplified under this arrangement, and on balance these advantages outweigh the disadvantages.

Administered systems. Administered systems are developed to control a line or classification of merchandise as opposed to an entire store operation, and are the vertical marketing systems which most closely resemble the concept of the conventional marketing channel. Such systems involve the development of comprehensive programs for specified lines of merchandise since the ultimate authority still resides with the individual channel member. Expertise as opposed to ownership is used to achieve system economies and control. In this type of system, vertically aligned companies, even though in a nonownership position, may work together on agreed-upon goals to reduce the total systems cost of such activities as advertising, transportation, and data processing.

The viability of many wholesalers depends on the administration of these types of programs for the retailers with whom they deal. Administered systems are often used for selling sewing machines, hearing aids, garden supplies, housewares, and appliances. In these systems, the dealer is viewed as an independent business person who desires to make a profit and yet remain independent. Manufacturers who choose to market through such dealership systems have thus delegated to their dealer "a large part of their competitive effort; a little product differentiation, some price competition, and much selling effort."[13] Manufacturer brands which enjoy national mar-

[13] Valentine F. Ridgeway, "Administration of Manufacturer-Dealer Systems," in Louis W. Stern (ed.), *Distribution Channels: Behavioral Dimensions* (Boston: Houghton Mifflin Co., 1969), p. 123.

ket acceptance have little difficulty in securing this kind of an arrangement with retailers.

Manufacturers in these systems typically seek to develop specialized programmed merchandising agreements for the retailers with whom they work. These include the following activities for each line of merchandise and each outlet featuring a manufacturer's brand:

1. Merchandising goals.
    a. Planned sales.
    b. Planned initial markup percentage.
    c. Planned reductions, including planned markdowns, shortages, and discounts.
    d. Planned gross margin.
    e. Planned expense ratio (optional).
    f. Planned profit margin (optional).
2. Inventory plan.
    a. Planned rate of inventory turnover.
    b. Planned merchandise assortments, including basic or model stock plans.
    c. Formalized "never out" lists.
    d. Desired mix of promotional versus regular merchandise.
3. Merchandise presentation plan.
    a. Recommended store fixtures.
    b. Space allocation plan.
    c. Visual merchandising plan.
    d. Needed promotional materials, including point-of-purchase displays, consummer literature, and price signs.
4. Personal selling plan.
    a. Recommended sales presentations.
    b. Sales training plan.
    c. Special incentive arrangements, including "spiffs," salesmen's contests, and related activities.
5. Advertising and sales promotion plan.
    a. Advertising and sales promotion budget.
    b. Media schedule.
    c. Copy themes for major campaigns and promotions.
    d. Special sales events.
6. Responsibilities and due dates.
    a. Supplier's responsibilities in connection with the plan.
    b. Retailer's responsibilities in connection with the plan.[14]

Contractual systems. Probably the most significant type of vertical marketing system today is the contractual system. In this arrangement, independent firms at different levels in the channel operate contractually to obtain economies and market impacts which could not be obtained by unilateral action. Thus, power in this arrangement is legal and is not based on ownership,

---

[14] Bert C. McCammon, Jr., "Perspectives for Distribution Programming," from *Vertical Marketing Systems* Louis P. Bucklin. Copyright © 1970 by Scott, Foresman and Company. Reprinted by permission.

as in corporate systems, or on expertise, as in administered systems. Arrangements under contractual marketing systems differ, but all such systems are trying to achieve the economies of scale which are offered by integrated systems without giving up the identity and autonomy of the individual firm. Contractual systems may be either wholesaler-sponsored voluntary groups, retailer-owned cooperatives, or franchised store programs. Participants in these types of organizations typically contribute to a common advertising fund; pool their buying power to lower the cost of merchandise; and have standardized merchandising programs, central data processing and warehousing facilities, and similar arrangements designed to increase their buying power.

Retailer-sponsored cooperatives. The retailer-sponsored cooperative is a voluntary association and an example of backward integration. One of the most familiar of the retailer-owned cooperatives is Associated Grocers. The primary aim of a retailer-sponsored cooperative is to give the cooperating retailers market power in dealing with suppliers. The retailers own and operate their own wholesale company. Stores organized in this fashion are able to obtain concessions and assistance from suppliers which would not be available to independent retail outlets acting alone.

Wholesaler-sponsored voluntary groups. Wholesaler-sponsored voluntary groups are best typified by the Independent Grocers' Alliance (IGA), which is an example of forward integration by a contractual system. The better-known voluntary groups in the drug and hardware field are shown in Table 8–7. In this arrangement, the wholesaler induces many retail organizations to purchase merchandise from the wholesaler. Typically the wholesaler will offer cooperating retailers standardized merchandising packages which may include financial assistance in opening a store; assistance in location, programmed advertising, price marking, storage, and central data processing; lower prices because of the volume discounts available; and other advantages.

Groups of this type are particularly appropriate for retail outlets in small communities where the lack of a large market precludes the advantages of sophisticated merchandising practices if each independent retailer acts alone. The wholesaler sponsored voluntaries may be large in size and highly sophisticated. In the food field, they rival even A&P.

The wholesaler-sponsored groups have been more successful than the retailer-sponsored groups, largely because the wholesaler can provide stronger leadership. Power is more highly centralized, and resource utilization is more efficient. In the retailer sponsored-cooperative, power is diffused among the various retail members, and they may therefore act in a more independent fashion.

Franchising. Franchising as a contractual system is simply a means that a firm uses to find a substitute for capital. The franchisor possesses a product or service but may lack the money to build and equip outlets. The franchisor therefore develops a way for other persons (the franchisees) to finance the

TABLE 8–7
MAINSTREAM RETAILING STRATEGIES:
CONTRACTUAL INTEGRATION

	Number of affiliated stores
Leading voluntary groups in the hardware field (1974)	
Western Auto	4,230
Sentry	4,200
Pro	2,650
Ace	2,500
Gamble-Skogmo	1,200
Coast-To-Coast	1,040
Trustworthy	800
Stratton & Terstegge	550
Farwell, Ozman, Kirk & Co.	495
American Wholesale Hardware	175
Total	17,840
Leading voluntary groups in the drug field (1974)	
Economist	5,000
Good Neighbor Pharmacies	1,400
Associated Druggists	1,132
United Systems Stores	744
Family Service Drug Stores	350
Triple A	300
Velocity	250
Community Shield Pharmacies	200
FIP	200
Sell-Thru Guild	200
Total	9,776

Source: Bert C. McCammon, Jr., Robert F. Lusch, and Bradley T. Farnsworth, "Contemporary Markets and the Corporate Imperative: A Strategic Analysis for Senior Retailing Executives," paper presented at a seminar for top management in retailing, Graduate School of Business Administration, Harvard University, 1976, p. 13.

stores. The franchisor then sells the product or service for a fee to the franchisees (the persons who own or operate the franchises). For example, McDonald's "sells a 20-year license for about $200,000, picks the site, buys the land, builds the store, equips and rents it for 8.5 percent of gross annual revenues plus a 3 percent annual franchise fee."[15] Franchisors may sell products, sell or lease equipment, and even sell or rent the site and premises, even though the legal limitations are carefully prescribed.

Types of franchises. Franchises can be developed in many different ways and exist in virtually all business fields. The conventional franchise is the traditional *dealership,* which grants the franchisee an exclusive marketing territory. *Mobile franchises* are similar to conventional franchises. However, business is done from a vehicle which moves about. Snap-On Tools is this type of franchise. *Distributorships* include systems in which franchisees

---

[15] "Horatio Hamburger and the Golden Arches," *Business Week,* April 12, 1976, p. 14; see also "There's More to Fast Food than Big Mac and Chicken," *Fortune,* March 1977, pp. 213–19.

maintain warehouse stocks to supply other franchisees. The distributor takes title to the goods and provides services to other customers. An example of this type of franchise is Bear Brand Automotive Equipment.

Ownership franchises are those in which the franchisor has an ownership interest in the operation. This holds true, for example, for the International House of Pancakes and the Travelodge system. *Service franchises* are those in which franchisors license persons to dispense a service under a trade name. Snelling & Snelling and H & R Block are examples of this type of franchise.

In general, franchisors can be placed in two basic categories. The first is that of the manufacturer-retailer franchise (automobile dealers) or the manufacturer-wholesaler franchise (Coca-Cola), both of which need retail outlets for products. The second consists of firms which have developed a unique method of performing a service or of doing business and wish to profit by selling the franchise to others. The wholesaler-retailer franchise is typified by Rexall Drugs; the service sponsor–retailer franchise is the arrangement followed by such firms as Holiday Inn, Avis, McDonald's, and Kelly Girl. These systems are more tightly defined since the use of power is legitimated by the contractual agreement, whereas expertise is the primary source of power in the administered system.

Reasons for franchising growth.   The tremendous growth in franchising since 1950 has occurred for a variety of reasons, including the growth of automobile ownership and usage, the continuing increase in disposable personal income, the continuing trend toward urbanization, the increase in the available quantity and variety of goods and services, and the development of computers and data processing equipment for management control.

Disadvantages for franchisors.   The advantages of contractual arrangements as part of a vertical marketing system are numerous, as noted above. However, distinct disadvantages also exist. For example, the franchisor is limited in the amount of control that can be exercised over the retail outlet, and thus has limited flexibility, because the franchisee is really an independent business person who has a contractual agreement with the franchisor. Even minor changes in contracts can involve lengthy negotiations and complex legal entanglements. It is also often difficult to get rid of undesirable franchisees. Another major problem is the screening, recruiting, and selection of franchisees. The motivation of franchisees is also a problem.

Decisions must be made by franchisors in several areas. Perhaps the most important is that of the type of income or revenue stream. Possibilities include initial franchise fees, royalties in the form of monthly fees or a percentage of sales, the rental or lease of premises, the sale or lease of equipment, the sale of finished goods for resale by franchisees, the sale of supplies or raw materials, and the sale of area distributorships.

Disadvantages for franchisees.   Disadvantages also exist for franchisees. The terms of a franchise are designed for a continuing relationship. Thus, the franchisee may find that it is difficult to get out of a franchise arrangement.

For franchisees to get help, they must be willing to give up much of the freedom which they sought in becoming franchisees. The franchisor has superior financial and management power, and thus is likely to defeat franchisees in any conflict of interest which may arise. Franchisees often complain that the franchisor is not sufficiently interested in their problems. In addition, the franchisor may own some of the retail outlets and compete with the ones owned by franchisees.

Franchisees may suffer when other franchises decrease in quality or when the parent company becomes involved in major difficulties. Finally, they may develop an overdependence on the franchisor and abandon their own good judgment and initiative.

Advantages for franchisees.   However, distinct advantages also exist for the franchisee, and these should not be overlooked. Franchising greatly increases the opportunity for an individual to become an independent business person. Research has shown that were it not for franchises over half of the owner-managers in franchising would not be self-employed.[16] Moreover, the failure rate in franchising is lower than in other types of businesses. Finally, financial and managerial expertise is provided by franchisors which would be unavailable otherwise.

Legal problems of contractual systems.   The numerous legal problems of contractual systems are beyond the scope of this chapter. Many of the legal problems of channels are discussed in Chapter 9 on the legal dimensions of retailing, particularly the section on channels of distribution.

The most frequent sources of litigation are the right to sell other products or services, the right to purchase equipment or supplies from sources other than those specified by the franchisor, territorial restrictions, resale price determination, the termination of a lease for cause, and violations of covenants not to compete.

Other sources of litigation include operating policies, lack of advertising and promotional support, profit limitations, and the supplier's support limitations. The laws most frequently involved are the Sherman Act, the Clayton Act, and Section 5 of the Federal Trade Commission Act.

Exclusive dealing agreements, which require a retailer to buy only the supplier's products, are not per se illegal, but Section 3 of the Clayton Act makes them illegal if the effect is to lessen competition substantially.

A practice related to exclusive dealing is tying agreements. Suppliers seek to have retailers purchase a particular good or line of merchandise if they want to purchase another more highly desired product or merchandise line. This activity is illegal if the seller has a monopoly on the market for the tying product. Here, as with exclusive dealing agreements detailed economic analysis is necessary before a decision as to the legality of the practice is possible.

Granting an exclusive territory to a retailer as part of a contractual system is not necessarily illegal. The courts have evaluated these practices on a

---

[16] Shelby D. Hunt, "The Socioeconomic Consequences of the Franchised System of Distribution," Journal of Marketing, vol. 36 (July 1972), p. 33.

case-by-case basis. An example is the related practice of customer restriction in sales territory, for example, prohibiting a retailer from engaging in fleet sales of automobiles. The supplier cannot prohibit such sales if title to the merchandise has passed to the retailer. However, if the retailer acts as an agent for the supplier, the sales may be prohibited because title to the merchandise is retained by the manufacturer until the sale of the merchandise.

A major legal problem has been that of fraud committed by franchisors who fail to provide adequate information to enable a franchisee to make an intelligent decision on whether to become affiliated with the franchisor. As a result of this practice, a variety of full-disclosure laws have been passed. All are designed to reduce the incidence of situations in which franchisors mislead prospective franchisees about the potential profitability of their franchises.[17]

THE STATUS OF VERTICAL MARKETING SYSTEMS

Vertical integration may occur either through forward integration, as when a manufacturer assumes wholesaling and/or retailing responsibilities, or through backward integration, as when a retailer such as Sears acquires wholesaling and manufacturing facilities. Wholesalers may integrate in either direction.

The process of integration may occur by internal expansion, as when an existing manufacturing firm creates its own wholesaling operation. It may also occur through a merger, by which one firm acquires the assets of another.

Legal problems

Internal expansion is regulated primarily by Section 2 of the Sherman Act. This section is designed to prohibit monopolies or attempts to monopolize. Internal expansion by the merger route is controlled by Section 7 of the Clayton Act as amended by the Celler-Kefauver Act. This legislation prohibits mergers if the effects are to lessen competition to a major degree or to create a monopoly in a particular line of business.

The courts seem to view internal expansion more favorably than they view mergers since it may increase competition rather than decrease it. The difficulties with the vertical mergers occur when supplies formerly available to independent firms are cut off.

Dual distribution, in which the wholesaler may operate retail outlets and also sell to other retailers, is not per se illegal. However, the courts have not yet fully defined legal and illegal practices in this area. Management must watch this type of distribution rather closely to make sure that the wholesalers are not selling to independent retailers at high prices and then undercutting the

---

[17] Shelby D. Hunt and John R. Nevin, "Full Disclosure in Franchising: An Empirical Investigation," *Journal of Marketing*, vol. 40 (April 1976), p. 61.

retailers by reselling merchandise at much lower prices through their own retail outlets.

Management problems

Vertical marketing systems face a variety of problems which must be resolved to insure the continued growth and expansion of this type of distribution. Independent retailers have long experienced difficulty in maintaining capable management. Affiliation with a vertical market system has not significantly changed this difficulty.

Standardization of operations is still a major problem of vertical marketing systems. This is particularly true for cooperative and voluntary groups. These organizations often differ greatly in terms of inventory policy, store layout, and other features. Persons in contractual networks have less control over such matters than they would if they were part of a corporate system.

Also, many firms affiliated with vertical marketing systems are still having difficulty in securing the type of financing necessary to remain viable. Capital for modernization and expansion is often in short supply. This problem is less troublesome for organizations in corporate systems.

A strong move is occurring toward company-owned chains as opposed to franchise operations. McDonald's owns 32 percent of its over 3,700 stores. Other organizations which are following the trend toward company ownership are Pizza Hut, Kentucky Fried Chicken, Hardees, and Wendys.[18] Why? "In one typical market, the average volume for a company-owned Shoney's Big Boy is $810,000, compared with $575,000 for franchised units. The average return on sales also runs higher on company units. At Denny's, Inc., a 1,090-unit chain that has stopped selling franchises, the return averages 60 percent higher . . . This difference in return takes only three years to offset the temporary gain from a franchise fee."[19]

Accompanying these trends are efforts by franchisors to organize true chains which are operated either by the franchisor or by large multi-unit franchisees. Many franchisors are now selling franchises only to existing franchisees or to investors who want to build chains of franchises. Among the reasons for the growth of company-owned units are that these operations permit greater control over the system, that they present fewer legal difficulties, and that further legislation is expected to make franchisor-franchisee relationships even more complicated.

The development of vertical marketing systems and the continued growth of such retail channel captains as Sears raise important questions. One of these is whether the new types of channels with highly systematized operations can continue to be responsive to changing market requirements.[20]

---

[18] "Fast Food Franchisers Squeeze Out the Little Guy," *Business Week,* May 31, 1976, pp. 42–48.

[19] "America's Eating-out Splurge," p. 61.

[20] These thoughts are based on M. S. Moyer, "Toward More Responsive Marketing Channels," *Journal of Retailing,* vol. 51 (Spring 1975), pp. 7–19.

Moyer argues that corporate systems channels led by retailers are not sufficiently responsive to changing market conditions. The trend toward vertical marketing systems has been characterized by increasing emphasis on the capital function, with exotic equipment for materials handling and data processing. The trend has also been toward self-service to save labor costs and offset equipment costs. The retail store is thus becoming a factory of distribution.

Accompanying increasing capitalization is a trend toward longer hours and Sunday openings with a requirement for shift workers.[21] Thus, increasingly retailing is characterized by immature salespersons.

Outlets have also become increasingly larger. The result may be isolation from consumers. Key decisions are increasingly removed from the sales floor and delegated to central staff specialists. Buying is done centrally. Central buyers know how other merchants are handling merchandise but are less in tune with the retail outlets of the systems with which they are affiliated. Rigid central buying organizations also run the danger of knowing little about the wants of customers and markets. (This problem is discussed in further detail in Chapter 15.) The result has been to create a market for small specialty stores that offer high levels of personal service, merchandise tailored specifically to local tastes and needs, and more depth in merchandise lines. These trends reflect the polarity in retailing discussed earlier.

A possible alternative is for the retailer to absorb much of the manufacturer's product planning function. This requires better communication with the consumer. Ideally the new point-of-sale systems, which include electronic cash registers, optical scanners, and similar features, can provide details on every purchase transaction. This timely information can overcome the retailer's traditional lack of information. However, if retailers are to grasp the full potential of vertical marketing networks, they must begin to engage in specification buying that moves beyond so-called me-too products, which far too often have been the result of private brand offerings at the retail level. All of these possibilities, however, assume more cooperation and sharing of information than that which typically exists in any vertical arrangement except that of the corporate ownership system.

MANAGERIAL IMPLICATIONS OF VERTICAL SYSTEMS COMPETITION

For the independent retailer

The small independent retailer will find it increasingly difficult to compete against channels which operate as a unit of competition. The independent retailer and affiliated agencies in conventional channel arrangement are not able to achieve economies of scale which are possible through central buy-

[21] Hazel F. Ezell, "A Critical Analysis of Sunday Closing Laws Utilizing Opinion Technology," unpublished doctoral dissertation, Graduate School of Business, University of Alabama, 1974.

ing, central data processing, centralized management training, programmed merchandising, store location assistance, and related crucial elements of effective retail operations. Since a locus of power is absent, the management of conflict is difficult.

However, the opportunity remains for the small retailer to provide a unique and specialized service which it would not be profitable for retailers to provide as part of a vertical marketing system. The independent retailer is better able to sense local market and consumer needs. Also, this type of retailer can respond more quickly to shifts in demand. This makes the need for accurate, up-to-date information on consumer markets more imperative than ever. To survive, the independent retailer must become an even more astute observer of the local marketplace and make the greatest possible use of management technology to obtain necessary information for quick decisions in responding to changing consumer markets.

For resource markets

Changes are also likely to occur in the resource markets. These markets will continue to seek affiliation with vertical market systems. Such affiliation will provide more stable market demand, greater economies of scale, and better programming of marketing efforts and resources.

Increasingly, retailers will also insist on such arrangements as ways of avoiding the uncertainties of materials shortages. This will give resource markets the opportunity to wrangle concessions from retailers. Increasingly, however, resource markets will have to supply more than products. They will have to become part of a process which is designed to assist the retailer in programming total marketing efforts. Thus, suppliers will work increasingly with retailers in efforts to improve volume, maintain the best merchandise assortments within financial investment limitations, and in general help the retailer run a more profitable business. Otherwise, resource suppliers may be looked upon as marginal and will be eliminated in times of difficulty. The activities in which the resource supplier will participate include sales promotion planning, sales training, display, inventory planning, and publicizing of merchandise. In short, we will witness more commitment and a more responsible buyer-seller relationship.[22]

CHANNEL CONTROL

Every channel system must have a leader—that is, a level in the organization which can get some degree of consensus on goals and can exercise power in achieving these goals for the organization. Power may be achieved either through coercive means, such as legislation or slow delivery of products, or noncoercive means, such as providing expert advice. The various

---

[22] Louis Carroll, "The Vendor Must Have a Plan," *Stores*, February 1974, p. 8.

uses of power in channel leadership will be discussed in the next section. However, from the point of view of retail management what generalizations are possible as to who can or should lead the channel?

Small retailers

Small retailers typically do not become channel leaders because they lack the resources. This is not always the case, however, since, particularly for convenience goods which are sold through numerous outlets, the small retailer may become highly valuable to a manufacturer who is seeking maximum shelf space. This is especially true for the manufacturer who is not able to establish a strong brand image. As has been noted, "Where the manufacturer selling through convenience outlets is unable to develop a brand image through advertising, . . . the retailer becomes very powerful and the manufacturer's ability to achieve product differentiation in the eyes of the consumer is severely limited."[23]

Small retailers may also be successful at channel control through legislative activity, particularly restrictive legislation. This may include licensing, Sunday closing laws, and price legislation.

The retail cooperative has also been viewed as a way for small retailers to overcome the limitation of diseconomies of scale. It is somewhat questionable, however, whether these cooperatives can ever compete with the major chains. Stanley Hollander has observed, "The retailer-sponsored cooperatives certainly do face some very serious problems. Membership turnover can be high. Coordination is difficult. Investment in manufacturing or processing facilities may be hazardous and inadvisable since acceptance of the output may not be assured. Financing problems may inhibit growth since the members have little interest in financing newcomers, and particularly in helping potential competitors."[24]

Large retailers

Large retailers are really multilevel merchandisers who have integrated wholesaling functions and even manufacturing functions. They may exercise considerable power as experts who have detailed knowledge of customer needs. Also, the larger the market served by retailers, the more important they become to manufacturers, particularly if, as multilevel retailers, they can obtain alternative sources of supply. This lessens their dependence on any one particular supplier. As Roger Dickinson has noted:

. . . the supplier has more to gain under most conditions by selling to the retailer than the retailer has to gain by buying from the supplier. This is a reasonable assump-

---

[23] Michael E. Porter, "Consumer Behavior, Retailer Power, and Market Performance in Consumer Goods Industries," *Review of Economics and Statistics,* vol. 56 (November 1974), p. 423.

[24] Stanley C. Hollander, "Channel Management by Small Retailers," in Robert L. King (ed.), *Marketing and the New Science of Planning* (Chicago: American Marketing Association, 1968), p. 135.

tion, since the manufacturers usually have (or think they will have) excess capacity, that is, a capacity to produce more than they are producing, and when they operate at full capacity it is only for a small part of the year. This is even truer of wholesalers. For manufacturers and wholesalers, then, no sale nearly always means no profit. Retailers, on the other hand, are sitting on a scarce resource whether they make a particular purchase or not. That resource is shelf space, the battle for which is so fierce that some suppliers even pay to have space reserved for them. Moreover, if a particular supplier does not sell to a particular retailer, the loss to the retailer is only relative, since there is always another supplier with other goods for a particular unit of space. In fact, it may be no loss at all, since in retailing most products can be replaced without great loss of profit by the retailer.[25]

Retailer dominance in a channel most often occurs when a strong consumer franchise has been developed through good promotion programs, wide consumer acceptance of private brands, and similar activities.

Robert Little offers the following generalizations about who should exercise channel leadership:

1. Multi-level merchandisers (MLM) are in the best position to lead channels because the value to the manufacturer of market access provided by each MLM far exceeds the value of one more product to the MLM merchandising mix.
2. The more product sources available to the MLM within a channel system, the more the locus of power will tend to shift toward the MLM.
3. Reciprocally, the wider the manufacturer's product line, the greater his economic significance to the MLM organization and the greater his potential power.[26]

Manufacturer control

"If the manufacturer can develop a brand image, the retailer has very little power because (1) the retailer is little able to influence the buying decision of the consumer in the store; (2) a strong manufacturer's brand image creates consumer demand for the product, which assures profits to the retailer from stocking the product and at the same time denies him the credible bargaining counter of refusing to deal in the manufacturer's goods."[27]

The manufacturer may also be able to dominate a channel by refusing to deal with certain middlemen or by restricting retailer territories. However, even if exclusive dealing, tying contracts, and similar arrangements are legal, they can only work when the manufacturer has a strong brand image. Thus, channel control by the manufacturer is more likely to exist for shopping goods and specialty goods. These are goods for which consumers will make

---

[25] From *Retail Management: A Channels Approach* by Roger A. Dickinson. © 1974 by Wadsworth Publishing Company, Inc., Belmont, California 94002. Reprinted by permission of the publisher.

[26] Robert W. Little, "The Marketing Channel: Who Should Lead This Extra-Corporate Organization?" *Journal of Marketing*, vol. 34 (January 1970), p. 36.

[27] Porter, "Consumer Behavior," p. 23.

a strong effort to compare competing brands or to seek a particular brand, and hence goods for which few substitutes are available.

Wholesaler leadership

Wholesaler dominance in a channel is likely to occur only when the manufacturers are weak and have few marketing skills and when both buyers and producers are large in number, small in size, and widely scattered.

One of the primary forms of organization for channel control by the wholesaler is the voluntary chain, particularly in groceries and hardware. This institution is somewhat newer than the closely aligned retailer cooperative. Well-known wholesaler cooperatives include Gamble-Skogmo, and Western Auto in the hardware field and Ben Franklin Stores and Butler Brothers in the variety store field. The voluntary chain concept has been successful because it provides the retailer with the advantage of group identity, large-scale buying, private labels, centralized promotion, and various management aids.[28]

Some wholesalers have achieved channel leadership through private brands. This is particularly the case for undifferentiated, frequently purchased products which have a stable demand. Also, private brands usually have a high gross margin. To be successful with private brands, however, the wholesaler must have them in all key product lines. It is difficult to establish a primary consumer demand for products which are commonly used and frequently purchased. Typically the differentiation in private brands is slight. Manufacturers' brands are often differentiated by heavy advertising which puts the marketing emphasis on the price appeal only.

THE USE OF POWER IN CHANNEL MANAGEMENT

The goals and objectives of channel members in any of the channel systems discussed are not necessarily compatible. For example, manufacturers may seek growth, whereas small retailers may be more interested in preserving the status quo. Further, conflict over role performance may occur. For example, manufacturers may compete with their wholesalers by selling to large retailers on a direct basis, thus precluding the wholesalers from making the sales.

Power is often used to specify the roles of channel members and to respond to channel conflict. In its general sense, power "refers to the ability of one individual or group to control or influence the behavior of another."[29]

---

[28] Edwin H. Louis, "Channel Management by Wholesalers," in Robert L. King (ed.), *Marketing and a New Science of Planning* (Chicago: American Marketing Association, 1968).

[29] Shelby D. Hunt and John R. Nevin, "Power in a Channel of Distribution: Some Sources and Consequences," *Journal of Marketing Research*, vol. 11 (May 1974), p. 186.

However, power may also be defined as the extent to which one channel member relies on another. Conflict is often defined as the frequency of disagreement among members of the channel on various issues.[30]

The clear specification of the functional roles of each channel member is important in increasing the efficiency of the channel structure. Channel members typically specialize in certain functions. Specifically, manufacturers may be responsible for production and promotion, whereas retailers may specialize in distribution at the consumer level. Whatever the specific situation, operational interdependence among the channel members is necessary.

What sources of power are available to the various channel members? These have been referred to throughout this chapter, but it might be well to evaluate them again. Power is typically viewed in coercive and noncoercive terms. In a study of automobile distribution, Robert Lusch specified the following six coercive sources of power: slow delivery of vehicles, slow payment on warranty work, unfair distribution of vehicles, turndowns of warranty work, threat of termination, and bureaucratic red tape.[31] He specified the noncoercive sources of power as: national advertising, local advertising, executive training, salesman training, mechanic training, sales promotion kits, salesman incentive programs, dealer incentive programs, bookkeeping assistance, manufacturer service representatives, manufacturer sales representatives, tools and equipment, product warranty, inventory rebates, floor plan assistance, and service manuals.[32]

In a study of power in franchising, Hunt and Nevin specified the following five sources of coercive power by the franchisor: (1) control of the building—the franchisor's right to sell the franchisee's facility; (2) control of the land—similar to control of the building; (3) the threat to revoke the franchise—the franchisee's right to sell the franchise; (4) the need for legislation; and (5) the fairness of the agreement.[33]

Noncoercive sources of power exercised by the franchisor include on-the-job training, local advertising, pricing assistance, deletions and additions to product lines, product preparation, field supervisors, formal training, suppliers, operating manuals, bookkeeping, and day-to-day advice.

CHANNEL CONFLICT

The use of power, particularly coercive power, can often lead to channel conflict. Such conflict may occur over any of a number of issues. In his investigation of power and conflict relationships between automobile manufacturers and dealers, Robert Lusch identified the various conflict issues

---

[30] Robert F. Lusch, "Sources of Power: Their Impact on Intrachannel Conflict," *Journal of Marketing Research*, vol. 13 (November 1976), p. 384.

[31] Ibid., p. 386.

[32] Ibid., p. 385.

[33] Hunt and Nevin, "Power in a Channel of Distribution", p. 188–89.

TABLE 8–8
AREAS OF MANUFACTURER-DEALER CONFLICT

Area of disagreement	Percentage of dealers who frequently or very frequently disagree with manufacturer
Vehicle availability	72.0
Parts availability	65.6
Product quality	58.4
Factory sales contests	53.9
Warranty work	52.1
New vehicle inventory	47.8
Minimum sales responsibility	34.4
Parts purchases from factory	30.6
Sales promotion displays	28.7
Tool and equipment purchases	26.0
Promotional allowances	25.0
Customer relations	23.6
Factory competition	22.8
Local advertising	16.9
Parts inventory	16.6
Number of salesmen	14.1
Retail price discounting on new vehicles	13.2
Remodeling and expansion	8.3
Number of mechanics	4.7
Hours of operation	1.4

Source: Robert F. Lusch, "Sources of Power: Their Impact on Intrachannel Conflict," *Journal of Marketing Research,* vol. 13 (November 1976), p. 385, published by the American Marketing Association.

shown in Table 8–8. The most frequent areas of conflict were vehicle unavailability, parts availability, and product quality. Many of the areas of conflict identified in this investigation—specifically, local advertising, hours of operation, sales promotion, promotional allowances, and customer relations—are potential sources of conflict in all areas of retailing.

Causes of channel conflict

Glen Walters has reported several causes of channel conflict. These are: (1) roles, (2) issues, (3) perceptions and expectations, (4) decisions and goals, and (5) communications among the institutions in the channel.[34] These difficulties can occur in any of the channel structures described above.

Each member of the channel has a separate view of channel performance. Each institution in the channel also has a set of role prescriptions. If all members of the channel agree on the roles of each member, consensus is

[34] C. Glen Walters, *Marketing Channels* (New York: Ronald Press, 1974), p. 417. See also Michael Etgar, "Effects of Administrative Control on Efficiency of Vertical Marketing Systems," *Journal of Marketing Research,* vol. 13 (February 1976), pp. 12–24.

likely to occur and to be reflected in cooperation and coordination in the performance of the marketing functions.

Channel issues often involve territorial rights, product lines carried, shelf space allocated, and similar issues. Another frequent issue is that of dual distribution. The manufacturer may sell direct to large customers, such as contractors, at more attractive prices than the prices that are available to small retail outlets which perhaps had previously sold to the contractors.[35]

Conflict also arises over differences in the perceived needs, motives, and attitudes of the various channel members. For example, wholesalers may perceive themselves as having the primary responsibility for product distribution and storage. The manufacturer, however, may view the wholesaler's function as promoting the manufacturer's products. Differences in expected rewards, policies, and procedures at each channel level can also lead to conflict.

Each level of the channel has certain expectations in terms of products offered, populations served, and services rendered; however, each level may have different expectations. For example, the wholesaler may expect consistent product quality from the manufacturer and may expect retailers to be responsible for forecasting consumer needs. Deviation from role prescriptions can occur for many reasons, such as a price war or inadequate return on investment.

Conflict is likely to occur over many of the decisions made by channel members. This is particularly true when two channel members want to control the decision-making process. Differences in opinion may occur over the relative amount of shelf space to be allocated to a product, over the promotion which is to be developed for a product, and perhaps even over the pricing structure for a product.

Conflict may also arise because of differences in the goals pursued by the various channel members.[36]

Lack of good channel communications is a major source of conflict in many marketing channels. Manufacturers may fail to communicate plans for promotional campaigns, price changes, and similar situations to other members of the channel, who thus feel left out. Conversely, retailers and perhaps even wholesalers often fail to give manufacturers basic information about market conditions and operating problems.

Constructive and destructive conflict

Not all channel conflict is bad.[37] Conflict is as natural as cooperation. The result of conflict may be changes in selected policies or procedures within

---

[35] Thomas J. Murray, "Dual Distribution versus the Small Retailer," in Bruce J. Walker and Joel B. Haynes (eds.), *Marketing Channels and Institutions* (Columbus, Ohio: Grid, 1973), pp. 12–23.

[36] F. Kelly Shuptrine and J. Robert Foster, "Monitoring Channel Conflict with Evaluations from the Retail Level," *Journal of Retailing,* vol. 52 (Spring 1976), pp. 55–74.

[37] Lusch, "Sources of Power," p. 388.

the channel. These changes can bring about improvements in the efficiency of channel operations. Thus, constructive conflict in a process of goodwill "give-and-take" can make for change and innovation. Destructive conflict, on the other hand, is likely to destroy the channel system if it develops in an atmosphere of distrust and ill will. The channel leader must recognize when conflict is constructive. Undue control may stifle constructive criticism, reduce efficiency, and perhaps retard innovation.

Indicators of channel conflict include reports of salespersons, contacts with the various channel members, the return of merchandise orders, and similar types of data. Each member should act after having analyzed the available information.

Conflict management

Louis Stern has suggested a variety of potential conflict management mechanisms which depend on the various degrees of perceived vertical interdependence among channel members. His model is shown in Figure 8–4. Stern perceives vertical interdependence on a continuum from high to low, and specifies means for conflict management at each of these levels.

FIGURE 8–4
DEGREE OF PERCEIVED VERTICAL INTERDEPENDENCE

| | High ← | | | → Low |
	Supraorganizational	*Interpenetration*	*Boundary*	*Bargaining and negotiation*

Specific mechanisms	Superordinate goals
	Conciliation and
	  mediation
	Arbitration
	Special-purpose
	  mechanisms
	  (1) Commissions of
	     inquiry
	  (2) Observers
		Membership:
		  exchange-of-persons
		  programs
		Ideological
		  (1) education
		  (2) propaganda;
		Membership and
		  ideological:
		  cooptation
			Diplomacy	Bargaining
				strategy

Source: Reprinted by permission of the publisher, from *Contractural Marketing Systems,* edited by Donald N. Thompson (Lexington, Mass.: Lexington Books, D. C. Heath and Company).

Supraorganizational means of conflict management refer to management of the entire channel as opposed to a single organization. The primary ways of conflict management under these circumstances are to establish agreed-upon goals for the entire channel, to employ conciliation and mediation, to submit to arbitration, or to establish special-purpose mechanisms, such as commissions of inquiry.

Interpenetration conflict management mechanisms consist of membership in trade associations, such as the Grocery Manufacturers of America. These associations create a network of relations among channel members. The processes employed by the associations may include an exchange of persons among channel members during a training program and various informational, educational, and propaganda activities.

Cooptation means the inclusion of channel members at various levels in the decision-making apparatus so that channel members at all levels have a clearer understanding of common problems in the distribution of goods. Firms may also seek to resolve channel conflicts through such diplomatic procedures as negotiation, persuasion, and pressure upon various members of the channel.

Regardless of the conflict management mechanism, resolution is always likely to be the result of bargaining. This may involve commitments, the offering of rewards, or threats of punishment between members of the channel. In this context, channel members are viewed as interest groups in opposition over scarce resources. Key questions become (1) the amount of control that it is necessary to concede and (2) the way in which the other party can be induced to accept less favorable terms than it initially set out to achieve.

THE FUTURE OF CHANNEL SYSTEMS

Future directions in channel systems and institutional structure are discussed in detail in Chapters 3 and 22. Briefly, free-form retailing, warehouse retailing, and nonstore retailing are likely to expand as alternative forms of distribution. More emphasis will be placed on organizations instead of individuals in final buying decisions. Already, 40 percent of all life insurance is in the form of group policies, approximately 20 percent of all automobiles manufactured are fleet vehicles and over 43 percent of all carpet produced goes into contract markets.[38]

Retailers affiliated with contractual systems, whether wholesaler-sponsored voluntaries, retailer-sponsored cooperatives, or franchises, account for more than 40 percent of retail sales, and their share of total retail sales is growing. Corporate chains represent another 32 percent of the retail market.[39] As noted earlier McCammon predicts that by 1981 vertically integrated networks will account for 85 percent of total retail sales. Chains will continue to characterize the institutions of retailing.

SUMMARY

A distribution channel is a structure of organizational units through which a product, a service, or an idea is marketed. Rights and responsibilities of ownership as well as related activities involving the transfer of title to the goods are part of this channel. Historically, each channel member felt that its role started and ended when the merchandise was obtained and sold. Under this situation, the channel members did not think of themselves as a system.

[38] McCammon, "Future Shock and the Practice of Management," p. 80.

[39] McCammon and Hamner, "A Framework for Improving Productivity in Distribution," p. 13.

During the last two decades, major changes have occurred in distribution. Entirely new forms of distribution have emerged. These are typically vertically aligned and are characterized by a willingness to practice functional shiftability. Functional shiftability is designed to improve the performance of the total system so that functions are performed at the most advantageous level in the channel.

The most common vertical marketing systems are corporate systems, contractual systems, and administered systems. Corporate systems are characterized by manufacturer ownership of retail outlets. Conversely, such major retailers as A&P or Holiday Inns may also own part of their manufacturing and warehousing facilities. Contractual systems are typified by wholesaler-sponsored voluntary groups, retail cooperatives, and various types of franchising organizations. Administered systems typically involve control over a single line of merchandise in an outlet as opposed to interest in or control of the entire operation.

Conflict is a natural part of vertical marketing systems because of the interdependence which exists among the channel members. Conflict is thus a result of continuing power struggles among channel members. Such conflict may be either constructive or destructive. Conflict issues in vertical marketing systems arise from the differing perceptions of members' roles, differences in members' goals, lack of communication among channel members, and differences in performance expectations among members.

KEY CONCEPTS

Types of competition
  Horizontal
  Intertype
  Vertical systems
  Total systems
Functional shiftability
New dimensions of retailing
  Dual distribution
  Polarity
  Multiple brands
  Shortened life cycles
The marketing channel concept
Types of vertical marketing systems
  Corporate
  Administered
  Contractual
Channel conflict
  Constructive and destructive conflict
  Conflict management

DISCUSSION QUESTIONS

1. What are the basic changes which have occurred in the retailing structure during the past 20 years?

2. Distinguish between the three types of vertical marketing systems, and discuss the strengths and weaknesses of each.

3. At what level in the distribution channel should planning occur?

4. Are planned channels better than evolutionary channels?

5. How does the structure of a distribution channel serve to create power?

6. What is the most familiar type of market competition today? What distinguishes it from the more conventional types of competition discussed in economics?

7. What has been the rationale for the development of vertical marketing systems? What of total systems competition?

8. What is the concept of functional shiftability?

9. Discuss the meaning and implications for the retailer of the marketing channel concept.

10. What is the likely future for franchising as a method of distribution?

11. What are the implications of vertical systems competition for the various members of the channel?

12. What are the key causes of channel conflict? How can such conflict be managed?

PROJECTS

1. Visit a wholesale, retail, or consumer cooperative, and find out why the cooperative was developed, what products it carries, and what pricing method is followed.

    In your opinion, what effect has the cooperative had on either the prices or the pricing policies of competitors carrying similar merchandise?

    What restrictions does the cooperative impose on its customers or members? Is membership limited? If so, what is the purpose?

2. Visit a manufacturer's outlet, a franchise operation, and a conventional retailer. Compare and contrast the operations of these three stores, including such things as breadth of product offerings, price policies, specialization of labor, efficiency of design and layout, and customer services offered.

3. Establish a contact with a VMS which is a wholesaler-sponsored voluntary group, such as IGA or Western Auto, and gain interviews with the management of the wholesale sponsor. Find out exactly what services are offered to the retail dealers, and focus on assistance in the area of accounting. Are there facilities for on-line computer inventory control, automatic replenishment of inventory, and so on? If the wholesale contact is difficult, you may interview retail dealers who are members of voluntaries for the other side of the coin. You may want to do both if possible.

4. Franchising is a very important type of vertical marketing system. In your local area, select one franchise type (for example, fast food) and interview the franchisee (or the franchisor if possible) and compare and contrast the different "brands" on such bases as: training programs for franchisees, financing required, financial assistance provided, promotional assistance, fixtures and equipment provided, locational analyses assistance, and other elements that you deem to be important. Evaluate each franchise in terms of the others, and come up with a ranking for potential success based on your criteria.

5. Scrambled merchandising is a fact of life. Select a product line (for example, tires); determine all of the different types of retail establishments which carry that product line (for example, service stations, tire stores, department stores); and compare the types of stores in terms of prices for comparable quality, brands (national versus private), services offered, information given, degree of professionalism in the selling situation, and assortments and varieties of goods offered in addition to the product line you have selected. Draw conclusions from your analysis. (This project can be done with many types of products other than tires.)

CASES

Case 1.   Several years ago Suzanne Kramer opened Accessories Unlimited, a shop dealing with shoes, handbags, belts, and other accessories. Since then she has expanded twice. She was very successful at selling but found buying and control tedious and boring. Wampum, a national manufacturer of turquoise jewelry, contacted her about becoming their exclusive outlet in the city. In return they agreed to perform financing, inventory control, and advertising functions for her. This arrangement worked well until a large department store chain built an outlet in the same city. It too carried Wampum's products. All of a sudden Suzanne was no longer pleased with the agreement. Why not? What problems are connected with agreements such as this between small, independent merchants and nationwide manufacturers which provide such a vast array of services?

Case 2.   The Fashion Shop began as a high-fashion specialty store. After a period of time and as the manager, Jo Ann Thompson, acquired experience in the field and grew in confidence, she added more lines. Jo Ann also decided to expand selling space and leased the store next to the Fashion Shop. But soon afterward Jo Ann found that she could no longer control all of the operations herself. About this time she ran into another woman, Mrs. Merit, who had a noncompetitive specialty operation. Mrs. Merit suggested that Jo Ann let her do Jo Ann's buying and handle Jo Ann's credit operations, saying that this would free Jo Ann to spend most of her time with her customers. Jo Ann was excited about the suggestion and accepted it. After a while, however, Jo Ann began to feel that Mrs. Merit was running her business.

What should Jo Ann do?

9

THE LEGAL ENVIRONMENT AND RETAILING

Restraint of trade
Unfair methods of competition
Trade regulation rules
Pricing
   Price-fixing
   Predatory pricing
   Fair trade (resale price maintenance)
   Sales below cost
   Price discrimination
Promotion
   False advertising allowances
   Deceptive advertising
   Advertising substantiation
   Bait and switch
Distribution
   Exclusive agreements
   Exclusive territories
   Elimination of competitors
   Tying agreements
The product
   Warranties
   Product liability
Monitoring potential legal problems
Costs of complying with government regulations
Discussion

*A*s our society becomes more complex, there is increasing governmental control over the free marketplace. And while the philosophy of marketplace protection is both noble and necessary, a fine line separates what is too much governmental interference from what is too little governmental concern.

The legal aspects of retailing grow as this philosophy is debated and decided by state and national governments. A historical perspective of marketplace regulation by which proposed changes can be measured is therefore vital to retail management.

Charles McDonald, Executive Director
Alabama Retail Association
Montgomery, Alabama

"Government regulation is probably *the* issue on retailers' minds today."[1] Government regulations affect retail pricing, advertising, competition, products carried, channels of distribution, and much more. The economic system of the United States is based on a free marketplace. However, absolute freedom in the marketplace is not in the best interest of either consumers or suppliers. Complete economic freedom may lead to monopoly, may restrict competition, and may allow price-fixing. Historically, much of the regulation of retailing has been designed to encourage and maintain competition and to limit deceptive or unfair business practices.

This chapter outlines in broad terms the following dimensions of retailing which are most strongly affected by legal constraints:

Restraint of trade	Promotion
Unfair methods of competition	Distribution (place)
FTC trade rules	Product regulations
Pricing	

RESTRAINT OF TRADE

The oldest approaches to consumer protection are found in the federal antitrust laws. The theory behind the antitrust laws is that prices will be kept at competitive levels if unreasonable restraints on trade are removed.[2] Antitrust theory also recognizes that nonprice competition, such as product and service improvements, will also benefit the consumer if firms must compete to survive.

The Sherman Antitrust Act of 1890 was the first legislation designed to maintain competition. Section 1 of the Act states that every contract, combination, or conspiracy in restraint of trade is illegal, and Section 2 states that monopoly and attempts to monopolize are illegal. The act was designed to curb efforts by large organizations to drive smaller ones from the marketplace.

Because of the vagueness of certain provisions of the Sherman Act, the Clayton Act was passed in 1914. The Clayton Act made it illegal to engage in specific practices which might lessen competition. These practices are discussed later in the chapter.

Enforcement of the production and marketing aspects of the Clayton Act rests primarily with the Federal Trade Commission (FTC), which was created almost simultaneously with the passage of the Clayton Act.

The above laws are the principal federal restraint-of-trade statutes. They declare price-fixing and market-sharing agreements to be per se illegal. Price

---

[1] "Chains Struggle with Government," *Chain Store Age Executive*, October 1976, p. 35; see also "Government Rules, Other Changes Make Life Chancy for Marketers," *Marketing News*, May 6, 1977, p. 8.

[2] Marshall C. Howard, "Government, the Retailer, and the Consumer," *Journal of Retailing*, vol. 48 (Winter 1972–73), p. 49.

discrimination, various forms of exclusive dealing, and mergers may also be declared illegal where their effect is to substantially lessen competition or create a monopoly. Since federal statutes are not always effective in controlling restraint of trade at the local level, most states have some form of regulation against restraint of trade.

The primary restraint-of-trade features for retailers are:

1. Retailers cannot put pressure on manufacturers to prevent them from selling products to competitive retailers.
2. Retailers cannot acquire other retail firms if the intent is to substantially lessen competition or if this tends to create a monopoly.
3. Retailers cannot conspire to fix the prices of the goods they sell. In other words, retailers cannot agree to eliminate price competition among themselves.
4. Retailers cannot undersell other retailers to gain control of a market. This prevents a large chain, for example, from lowering prices to drive smaller competitors in one area out of business while the chain maintains high prices in other areas.[3]

All four of the above activities are frequently encountered in practice, as is pointed out later in the chapter. (For persons seeking the details of the legislation discussed in this chapter, the appendix entitled "Government Regulations Affecting Retailing" provides an overview of the relevant materials.)

Certain exemptions to the antitrust laws are allowed. The Capper-Volstead Act allows persons engaged in farming to band together as associations in processing and marketing their goods. The Cooperative Marketing Act allows farmers to act as a group in collecting, acquiring, and disseminating crop and market information. Voluntary export trade associations are exempted from antitrust regulations by the Webb-Pomerene Export Trade Act as long as they do not fix prices in domestic trade. Finally, the Fisherman's Collective Market Act allows fishers or growers of aquatic products to form associations to permit bargaining in selling to dealers and processors.

UNFAIR METHODS OF COMPETITION

The expression "unfair methods of competition" refers to unethical busitrust theory also recognizes that nonprice competition, such as product and for regulating unfair business practices resides with the FTC. Section 5 of the FTC Act prohibits unfair methods of competition and unfair or deceptive acts or practices in interstate commerce.

Many unfair or deceptive acts or practices in retailing occur at the local level, particularly in door-to-door selling. Thus, state and local laws against

---

[3] R. Ted Will and Ronald Hasty, *Retailing: A Mid-Management Approach* (San Francisco: Canfield Press, 1973), p. 306.

unfair and deceptive selling exist in most states and localities. For example, salespersons selling door-to-door may be required to obtain a license to sell.

Another common method of unfair competition is shipping merchandise which has not been ordered by a retailer. Consumers are not obligated to pay for unordered merchandise mailed to them.

Another common practice in retailing which may be an unfair method of competition is the use of "push money" which encourages sales of certain products by rewarding salespersons for selling those products. The practice is not per se illegal, even though it is a likely candidate for FTC regulation. From the retailer's point of view, allowing suppliers to pay push money to retail salespersons may cause some loss of control over the merchandise which is sold. On the other hand, the retailer may elect to offer push money to salespersons who move merchandise sold by the retail outlet. From the suppliers' point of view, the use of push money provides an opportunity to increase sales of their products.[4] An example of this dilemma has been noted in connection with Revlon's use of sales promotion contests: " 'The cosmetician becomes a Revlon girl, instead of selling what is best for the customer, which is what we want her to do.' For months, this discounter rejected all Revlon contests. 'But they kept coming back and making it more attractive and finally wore me down.' "[5]

Some forms of push money are clearly illegal. For example, the FTC has issued decrees which prohibit payola by record distributors to disc jockeys in return for playing certain records. The FTC position is that this practice leads people to believe that the records which are played the most frequently are the most popular. But does the practice really differ from the use of "push money" to increase sales of cosmetic items?

TRADE REGULATION RULES

For many years the FTC has issued codes of conduct for retailers through trade rules which cover a variety of products and services. In 1976, the FTC issued a rule that requires firms selling merchandise by mail to state definite delivery dates for the merchandise. If the merchandise cannot be delivered by the promised date, the buyer must be given the means and the option to cancel the order or to agree to the delay.[6] The courts have also upheld an FTC order which requires door-to-door retail sellers of encyclopedias to identify themselves as salespersons when seeking admission to a person's home. The FTC ruled, for example, that Encyclopaedia Britannica used deceptive practices in recruitment, sales, and debt collection.[7]

---

[4] Dale Varble and L. E. Bergerson, "The Use of PM's—A Survey of Retailers," *Journal of Retailing*, vol. 48 (Winter 1972), p. 40.

[5] "Management Realists in the Glamour World of Cosmetics," *Business Week*, November 29, 1976, p. 48.

[6] William M. Hannay, "Merchandising Subject to New Mail Order Rule," *Stores*, February 1976, p. 21.

[7] *American Council on Consumer Interests Newsletter*, May 1976, p. 29.

The FTC has also issued a trade regulation rule regarding the mispricing and unavailability of advertised food products. Numerous firms such as A&P and Kroger have been charged by the FTC with such practices. In spite of the rule, the practices have continued to occur. For example, the FTC signed consent orders with two Northwest retailers requiring them to sell items at or below advertised prices and charged another with not having advertised food items available for sale and/or selling items at higher than advertised prices.[8] Research has shown that the unavailability of advertised food products may range from 25–45 percent[9] and under varying assumptions may cost consumers $18,000 per year in a single store.[10]

Agencies other than the FTC also issue trade regulation rules which affect retailing. For example, the Food and Drug Administration has issued rules to guide retail pharmacists who publicly post or advertise prescription prices, since at least 15 states now permit or require public price posting.[11]

The most frequent contact of the retailer with the legal environment probably occurs in the manipulation of the retailing mix to achieve the profitability goals of the firm and still render consumer satisfaction. Thus, let us look now at the key legal dimensions affecting retail decisions about the four p's—price, promotion, place, and product.

PRICING

Pricing is one of the most important elements of the retailing mix. It may affect profitability and share of market, and it can serve as a differential advantage over competition. Cutthroat pricing on the part of some retailers may even drive smaller or less efficient firms out of business. Thus, pricing is carefully regulated at both the state and federal levels by a variety of laws. Let us examine some of these regulations.

Price-fixing

Regardless of the approach taken to establish prices in retailing, retailers cannot agree with competitors on the price of goods or services which will be sold. Price-fixing is per se illegal. Retailers engaging in this practice may be prosecuted under the Sherman Act or under the Federal Trade Commission Act. For example, the executive vice president of Bergdorf Goodman was fined $25,000 for conspiring to fix prices on women's apparel in violation of the Sherman Act. Earlier, Bergdorf Goodman and Genesco had been indicted for price-fixing and had pleaded no contest to the charges.[12]

---

[8] "FTC: Let Credit Companies Beware," *Chain Store Age Executive,* January 1976, p. 8.

[9] J. Barry Mason and J. B. Wilkinson, "Mispricing and Unavailability of Advertised Food Products," *Journal of Business,* vol. 49 (April 1976), pp. 219–25.

[10] J. B. Wilkinson, J. Barry Mason, and Carl E. Ferguson, "Economic and Opportunity Losses as a Result of Advertised Food Specials," paper presented at the 1975 Fall Educators Conference of the American Marketing Association, Rochester, N.Y.

[11] *American Council on Consumer Interests Newsletter,* February 1976, p. 2.

[12] "Exec Fined $25 G," *Chain Store Age,* September 1975, p. 10 (a).

Likewise, in 1976 a federal grand jury indicted Saks Fifth Avenue and I. Magnin and Company on charges of conspiring to fix prices on women's clothing from 1963 to April 1974. Each company was subsequently fined $50,000 after pleading no contest.[13] In a separate situation, "Bergdorf Goodman, Bonwit Teller and Saks Fifth Avenue have agreed to put up some $5.2 million to settle a series of price-fixing class-action suits brought by credit card customers.[14]

Retail price-fixing appears to be far too common. As noted by Owen M. Johnson, Jr., director of the Bureau of Competition for the Federal Trade Commission, "You can find it just about anywhere you look. . . . We could fill the office with these cases alone, and 95 percent of the time price maintenance has the effect of raising prices."[15]

Predatory pricing

Charging different prices in various communities is also illegal if it is not cost-justified and if the intent is to eliminate competition. Such activities are labeled predatory pricing. The FTC's Bureau of Competition in 1976, for example, investigated a complaint by a group of independent supermarkets in San Antonio, Texas, that a competing chain's pricing policy, which existed only in its San Antonio stores, was predatory.[16]

Fair trade (resale price maintenance)

Many states enacted fair-trade laws during the depression era. Such legislation allowed manufacturers to set minimum retail prices for their products. Stores which attempted to sell the designated items below the specified minimum price faced prosecution and fines. Appliances, watches, cosmetics, and entertainment equipment were among the products covered by resale price maintenance laws.

The first fair-trade laws were enacted by states during the 1930s to protect brand-name manufacturers and small stores from price-cutting competition by large retail organizations. These state fair-trade agreements were exempted from antitrust prosecution by the Miller-Tydings amendment, which was enacted under pressure exerted by independent wholesalers and retailers. By 1941 resale price maintenance laws existed in 45 states.

Most of the laws included a "nonsigner" provision which meant that if a manufacturer wanted to operate a vertical price fixing program, only one retailer had to be contracted with in order to bind all other retailers in the

---

[13] "Saks, I. Magnin Hit on Pricing," *Chain Store Age Executive*, June 1976, p. 4.

[14] "Price-Fixing Suit Accord?" *Chain Store Age Executive*, August 1976; see also "Three Chains' Pricing Woes," *Chain Store Age Executive*, February 1977, and "Saks Is Sued on Price-Fixing," *Chain Store Age Executive*, March 1977, p. 18.

[15] "FTC's Retail Role Grows," *Chain Store Age Executive*. October 1976, p. 38.

[16] "FTC Probes Texas Price War," *Chain Store Age Executive*, August 1976.

state. The nonsigners' clause was declared illegal by the U.S. Supreme Court, but, in 1951, Congress eliminated the loophole in the Miller-Tydings law by passing the McGuire amendment to the Federal Trade Commission Act which legalized the nonsigner clause in interstate commerce. By early 1975, however, the nonsigners' clause, after having been slowly but persistently voided or repealed in state after state, was still fully operative in 13 states. President Ford signed federal legislation repealing the fair-trade laws in November 1975, and legal resale price maintenance came to an end in March 1976 in those states with fair-trade laws still on their books.

What made "fair trade" such a tempting target for consumer groups and price-cutting discounters was the notion that it greatly increased the costs of products to the American consumer. Nullifying fair trade would save consumers $2 billion annually, according to some estimates.

Even though there was fear that the repeal of fair trade would result in a "bloodbath" of price cuts among chains in which the small retailer would be the principal victim, the impact of repeal on prices was in fact not large, though there was an initial flurry of price cutting which was mainly limited to loss leaders and items sold by low-overhead retailers. Essentially the prediction that the end of fair trade would result in more pricing competition has not come true.

Certain impacts have occurred as a result of the repeal of resale price maintenance, however. For example, although "fair trade legally imposed" is no longer with us, "resale price maintenance" as a philosophy cannot be legislated away. Many manufacturers are continuing to stress "suggested retail prices" within their channels and are encouraging dealers to maintain the suggested prices because these prices provide customers with some yardstick of value.

Also, retailers who preferred the environment of protection under legalized fair trade may attempt to get exclusive dealerships so that comparison shopping on the brands they carry will be impossible. Other dealers may resort to stressing service and to positioning themselves as providers of services superior to those of their competitors. Finally, some manufacturers may offer two lines of products—one for the "non–price cutter" and one for the discount operation.

Sales below cost

In addition to fair-trade laws, several states have sales-below-cost laws. These laws provide that the prices at which items are sold must at least cover the cost of the items. Cost may be interpreted in a variety of ways, or what is meant may be stated in very specific terms. State sales-below-cost laws are typically restricted to specific product lines, such as milk and dairy products, cigarettes, and gasoline. Several states permit sales below cost if this is necessary to meet the price of a competitor. Unclear areas of the state sales-below-cost laws include the questions of whether it is legal to give away free merchandise and whether prizes or premiums constitute price reductions.

Price discrimination

The bulk of price discount legislation which affects retailers is found in the Robinson-Patman Act, which is enforced by the FTC. Sellers do not always charge the same prices to retailers. Situations exist in which quantity discounts may need to be given because some retailers purchase in larger quantities than do others. Likewise manufacturers may grant wholesalers larger discounts than they grant retailers because of the functions wholesalers perform. Finally, it may be necessary to charge lower prices in one market area than in another to meet competition or to keep potential competitors from entering a market. Not all price discrimination is illegal, since charging different prices to different ultimate consumers is not always covered by legal restraints.

Section 2(a) of the Robinson-Patman Act applies to goods of like grade and quantity, and states that price discrimination is unlawful where its effect is to lessen competition substantially or to tend to create a monopoly. For example, in 1976 the FTC ruled that A&P had violated the Robinson-Patman Act by "knowingly receiving discriminatory prices for milk and other dairy products" from Borden.[17] Price differentials may be allowed where there are differences in the cost of manufacturing or delivery, or because of changing marketability for merchandise.

Section 2(b) of the Robinson-Patman Act permits the seller to discriminate in price "in good faith to meet an equally low price of a competitor, or the facilities furnished by a competitor." Section 2(d) requires that services or facilities rendered to a retailer by a supplier to aid in the sale of merchandise must be available to all retailers on "proportionally equal terms." Section 2(f) indicates that it is unlawful for a firm to knowingly receive a discrimination in price over that available to competition or to pressure a seller to grant such a discrimination in price. Overzealous retailers in particular may have problems with this portion of the act whenever they push for excessive concessions from suppliers. For example, Fred Meyer Company "has paid a $200,000 fine in the settlement of an FTC complaint that it allegedly obtained funds from certain suppliers to cover employee product demonstration costs. Similarly, the Thrifty Drug Stores, a large California chain, accepted an FTC consent order in which it agreed not to seek preferential treatment from suppliers or overcharge them for promotional activities."[18]

The FTC may also establish quantity limits for certain classes of merchandise "where it finds that available purchasers in larger quantities are so few as to render differentials unjustly discriminatory or promotive of monopoly."

[17] "FTC Sours on A&P Milk," *Chain Store Age Executive,* July 9, 1976, p. 9.
[18] "Three Chains Rapped by FTC," *Chain Store Age Executive,* March 1976, p. 4.

Essentially, price differentials must not exceed the savings which the supplier realizes in selling to the retailer. Also, both the buyer and the seller must provide justification for discounts granted and received.[19]

The Robinson-Patman Act has long been controversial. Joe Sims, special assistant to the chief of the Justice Department's Antitrust Division, has argued that the Robinson-Patman Act hurts both the consumer and the small retailer, two groups whom the act was specifically designed to help. Sims pointed out the following ways in which the pricing inflexibilities of the act have adversely impacted businesses and consumers:

1. The Act prevents businesses from maximizing their sales by preventing them from engaging in price competition for the resale customers of another firm. Under the Robinson-Patman Act, a small business person can only match, but not beat, the price of a large corporation whose customers he seeks unless he offers the same price to his existing customers who compete with the prospective customers. The small business person may not be able to afford to cut his prices across the board, and he may not be able to make inroads on a large, established corporation's customers unless he can offer them a lower price.

2. The Act may prohibit a company doing business in one region from offering promotional prices in order to enter a new area. Thus, firms may be blocked by the Act from entering new geographical areas since promotional prices are usually necessary if entry is to be made.

3. The Act reinforces monopoly pricing. An oligopolist uses the Act as an excuse for not granting a customer's request for a lower price.

4. The Act makes it more expensive and more difficult to be a small business person. [The small business person] must seek frequent, and often costly, legal advice before he changes pricing practices. All too often, the ultimate pricing strategy must be decided by lawyers and not by those with marketing expertise.[20]

PROMOTION

False advertising allowances

A variety of local, state, and federal statutes are designed to regulate retail advertising. One of the key provisions of the Robinson-Patman Act makes false advertising allowances illegal. Section 2(e) states that any services or facilities furnished to a retailer must be made available to all retailers on a proportionately equal basis. This provision is designed to ensure that such allowances or services are not a form of reduced prices to a few select customers. Revlon promotions are typical of those which must meet the proportionately equal requirement. "In a new joint promotion called Retail Partners, Revlon

---

[19] Morris L. Mayer, Joseph Barry Mason, and Einar A. Orbeck, "The Borden Case—A Legal Basis for Private Brand Price Discrimination," *MSU Business Topics*, Winter 1970, pp. 56–63.

[20] Burk Tower, "Depression Era Robinson-Patman Act Hurting Consumers, Small Businesses, May Be Re-examined," *Marketing News*, October 24, 1975, published by the American Marketing Association.

helps merchants stage everything from in-store musicals, magic shows, and makeup and hair styling clinics to fashion shows."[21]

Deceptive advertising

False or deceptive advertising and labeling for merchandise which is sold in interstate commerce is an unfair method of competition under Section 5 of the Federal Trade Commission Act. The FTC has jurisdiction over a wide variety of promotional activities in which false or deceptive advertising or labeling is involved. This includes advertisements placed through the media, promotional items sent through the mails, price lists, and similar types of material. For example, in 1976 Levitz Furniture entered into a consent agreement with the FTC to stop making "false and misleading representations concerning price savings, comparable value, warranties and furniture composition." The firm also agreed to provide refunds on defective and damaged merchandise which could not be repaired.[22]

The FTC also has jurisdiction over laws which are designed to remedy special problems involved in the labeling of textile and fur products. These are the Wool Products Labeling Act, the Fur Products Labeling Act, and the Textile Fiber Products Identification Act. These acts are designed to protect the consumer, since typically only an expert is able to tell the true content of items made from these products.

Misrepresentation under Section 5 of the Federal Trade Commission Act is difficult to prove because the limits between puffery and deception are vague. Puffery is not illegal, but deception is illegal. The FTC has introduced a variety of means of regulating unfair methods of competition which occur because of false or misleading advertising claims.

Advertising substantiation

The FTC is also concerned with the substantiation of advertising claims to avoid misleading the public. Thus, advertisers may be required to submit data to the FTC supporting advertising claims about a product's safety, performance, or quality.[23] Retailers carrying the products of firms which are required to engage in corrective advertising may be at a disadvantage because of the unfavorable publicity. In addition, large national retailers may also be subject to corrective advertising for the private label products that they may carry.

Bait and switch

Various other deceptive promotion techniques are also controlled by the FTC. One of these is bait and switch advertising. In such advertising, products

---

[21] "Management Realists in the Glamour World of Cosmetics," *Business Week,* November 27, 1976, p. 44.

[22] "FTC Hits Levitz," *Chain Store Age Executive,* August 1976.

[23] Robert E. Wilkes and James B. Wilcox, "Recent FTC Actions: Implications for the Advertising Strategist," *Journal of Marketing,* vol. 38 (January 1974), p. 55.

are advertised to the consumer at an unusually attractive price. The retailer then endeavors to "switch" the consumer to a higher priced product once the consumer enters the store. For example, in 1976 Sears agreed to an FTC order forbidding it from using bait and switch advertising of home appliances. Specifically, the complaint was "that Sears used 'bait and switch' tactics to sell appliances, advertising low-priced products and inducing customers to buy higher priced goods by not stocking enough or disparaging the lower priced product once customers were in the store."[24]

DISTRIBUTION

Exclusive agreements

Suppliers may enter into agreements with retailers whereby the retailers agree to handle the products of the suppliers but not the products of competitors. This is known as exclusive dealing. Exclusive dealing is not illegal. Section 3 of the Sherman Act makes these agreements illegal only where the result may be the lessening of competition. When entered into in good faith, these agreements provide opportunities for both the supplier and the retailer. From the retailer's perspective, such agreements make it possible to have a stable source of supply. For the supplier, they assure a continuing market for the products being sold.

Exclusive territories

A supplier may indicate to a retailer that a product or service can be sold only within a certain geographic area. The supplier then agrees not to sell to any other retailer within the area. Thus, the retailer is protected from competition by firms which might be selling products of the same supplier. Such an arrangement is likely to ensure that the retailer will devote sufficient time and attention to selling the product.

Recent antitrust decisions have revealed, however, that many territorial or customer restriction agreements are in violation of the law. As a result of recent court restrictions, it appears that the only reliable control technique which apparently would not be subject to antitrust violation is an agency distribution system. Under this system, a supplier would maintain title over the product until it was transferred to the ultimate consumer. In this way, retail control over prices and customer or territorial restrictions can be maintained. However, this arrangement can cause major cash flow problems for the supplier. The alternative is for the supplier to lose some of the control previously exercised over the distribution of the product.[25]

---

[24] "FTC Fights Sears Settlement," *Chain Store Age Executive*, April 1976, p. 3; see also "Three Consent Orders Issued," *FTC News Summary*, May 6, 1977, p. 3.

[25] James R. Burley, "Territorial Restriction and Distribution Systems: Current Legal Developments," *Journal of Marketing*, vol. 39 (October 1975), pp. 52–56.

Elimination of competitors

The FTC has ruled that the big "anchor stores" in shopping centers no longer have a say over which other tenants can be admitted into the shopping center, nor can they place price or quality limitations on the other tenants or limit their promotional activities.[26] The FTC is also considering ways of limiting the power of developers to unilaterally limit competition in a center.

Tying agreements

Tying arrangements are likely to be the type of distribution problem with which the retailer has the greatest difficulty. In this type of arrangement, a supplier agrees to sell a retailer a line of products only on the condition that the retailer purchase other products. Occasionally the supplier may force the retailer to carry an entire line of items if the retailer is to get the one product desired. Tie-in sales may be illegal under the Clayton or the Sherman acts if the supplier has sufficient economic power to restrain trade. For example, the FTC has indicted Levi Strauss for fixing prices on its jeans and other items and for forcing retailers to purchase other lines of clothing in return for being allowed to sell its jeans.[27]

The franchisor-franchisee arrangements of such outlets as Shakey's Pizza, H&R Block, and 7–11 stores have been heavily hit with both legislation and litigation because of tie-in provisions. Some legal experts consider these types of problems with franchisors to be of crisis proportions.[28] Tying agreements may be necessary to ensure proper standards of quality control among the franchises. In addition, tie-in agreements may offer franchisees the opportunity to participate in bulk volume purchases which will lower overall prices. The argument against tying agreements in franchising is that the franchisors seek to secure revenue through the sale of supplies to the franchisees at inflated prices.

THE PRODUCT

Warranties

A warranty is simply an affirmation by a seller as to the quality or performance of the goods which are being sold. *Express warranties* are written affirmations. The distinction between statements of fact and mere sales talk in relation to warranties is often vague. Retailers have to be particularly careful in distinguishing between puffery and promise in promotional efforts, or they may be charged with an unfair competitive practice. Moreover, according to

[26] Joseph Barry Mason, "Power and Channel Conflicts in Shopping Center Development," *Journal of Marketing*, vol. 39 (April 1975), pp. 28–35.

[27] "Saks, I. Magnin Hit on Pricing," *Chain Store Age Executive*, June 1976, p. 4.

[28] Shelby D. Hunt and John R. Nevin, "Tying Agreements in Franchising," *Journal of Marketing*, vol. 39 (July 1975), p. 20.

the Uniform Commercial Code every sale has an implied warranty that the merchandise being offered is fit for the purpose for which it is being sold.[29]

In 1975, the Magnuson-Moss Warranty Act became law for all consumer products manufactured after July 4, 1975. The law is applicable to written warranties covering consumer products and concerns the presale availability on the sales floor of warranty information for consumers. Whenever products are sold with a written warranty as to a level of performance or the absence of certain defects, the warranty is covered by the act. The distinction between written warranties, which are covered, and statements of consumer satisfaction, which are not covered, is not precise. However, if written warranties are used in advertising they are likely to be covered by the act.

Many warranties are technically those of a manufacturer. However, if the retailer offers any type of warranty, such as a warranty for parts and labor for a stated period of time, this warranty also comes under the act. The general merchandise categories most likely to be covered by a written warranty are "personal care electrics; some men's, infants', boys' and girls' wear; major and small appliances; some home furnishings; consumer electronics; and housewares."[30]

In addition, no written warranty may be based on the requirement that a consumer use only a certain brand or trademarked product or service. Thus, the retailer can no longer require the consumer to use only "genuine Delco parts."

Other dimensions of the Magnuson-Moss Warranty Act are of importance to retailers. The act amended the Federal Trade Commission Act to read "in or affecting commerce" in place of "in commerce." Thus, the FTC now has the authority to regulate some aspects of local commerce.[31] It is also authorized to develop rules for warranties in the sale of used automobiles. The commission cannot require a warranty to be given, but it may require sellers to disclose their lack of obligation for repairs once the sale is made. In general, retailers will find it necessary to scrutinize all media advertising for any written affirmations of fact which might be interpreted as constituting a legal written warranty.

The first three regulations issued by the FTC under the Magnuson-Moss Warranty Act required retailers to:

1. Reveal warranty information to consumers before they buy the product.
2. Fully disclose warranty terms in "simple and readily understood language."
3. Establish a procedure to handle consumer complaints.

---

[29] C. L. Kendall and Frederick A. Russ, "Warranty and Complaint Policies: An Opportunity for Marketing Management," *Journal of Marketing*, vol. 39 (April 1975), p. 37; also Richard Moellenberndt, "Product Warranty Policy," *Atlanta Economic Review*, May–June 1977, pp. 29–34.

[30] "The ABC's of Warranties: Here Are the Do's and Don'ts," *Stores*, August 1976, p. 26.

[31] Robert E. Wilkes and Walter Jensen, Jr., "Protecting the Rights of the Reasonable Average Consumer: The Consumer Product Warranty Act of 1975," *The Barrister*, Fall 1975, p. 84; also "Consumer Lawsuits Allowed if Disputes Can't Be Settled," *Hardware Retailing*, April 1976, p. 78.

The first two regulations were effective January 1, 1977, and the third was effective July 4, 1976. Under the third regulation, suppliers may choose to have their dispute heard by a consumer business arbitration panel.

Warranties must be available to consumers in one of four ways: (1) in text material near the product; (2) in a binder available for inspection; (3) on a product package and visible; or (4) on a sign displaying the warranty text.

Product liability

Unsafe consumer products are being distributed in unacceptable numbers, and consumers are frequently unable to guard themselves against the risk of using such products. Suppliers are being pressed to find more and better ways of informing consumers about this hazard.

Retailers often make implied or express warranties to consumers about the safety of products. Thus, consumers may be entitled to recover damages which result from a breach of warranty or of misrepresentation by retailers. The National Consumer Product Commission was formed to prescribe mandatory safety standards for all consumer products except those which are already covered by safety legislation, and it is being active in carrying out its responsibilities.[32]

Confusion exists as to whether the retailer can be held liable for the unforeseen or abnormal use of a product by consumers. If such a possibility is reasonably foreseeable, apparently the retailer and/or the supplier can be held liable.[33] Whatever the facts of the case, "when a consumer makes good on the threat and names your firm in a product liability suit, odds are that you'll lose."[34] What can the retailer do about this? Careful records should be kept; brand product liability protection insurance should be obtained; and sales personnel should be instructed not to overstate the capability of the products being sold.

MONITORING POTENTIAL LEGAL PROBLEMS

The legal environment within which the retailer operates is becoming increasingly complex. Thus, the need exists for monitoring potential legal problems. The retailers may be able to avoid such problems through a periodic evaluation of the internal operating records of the firm. James Stafford and William Staples have developed a checklist for use by the retailer in spotting potential legal problems (see Table 9–1).[35] For example, the retailer

---

[32] Paul Busch, "A Review and Critical Evaluation of the Consumer Product Safety Commission: Marketing Management Implications," *Journal of Marketing*, vol. 40 (October 1976), pp. 41–49.

[33] William L. Trombetta and Timothy L. Wilson, "Foreseeability of Misuse and Abnormal Use of Products by the Consumer," *Journal of Marketing*, vol. 39 (July 1975), pp. 48–55.

[34] "Product Liability: You Better Watch Out," *Hardware Retailing*, June 1976, p. 74; also "Product Liability Crisis Grows," *Chain Store Age Executive*, March 1977, p. 9.

[35] James E. Stafford and William A. Staples, "Retailing: Potential Legal Problems in the Selling Process," *Tennessee Survey of Business*, September–October 1975, p. 27.

TABLE 9-1
POTENTIAL LEGAL PROBLEMS IN THE SELLING PROCESS

Selling stages	Activities	Potential legal problems	Internal indicators of potential legal problems
Presale	Media advertising	Deceptive advertising Nondisclosure of material facts Unfair advertising Deceptive pricing	Refunds and/or exchanges (if product purchased)
	Credit practices	Unfair credit practices Deceptive credit representations	Bad debts expense—customer failure to meet credit payment installments (if product purchased)
Point-of-sale	Selling practices	Deceptive packaging, labeling Nonavailability of advertised items Oral misrepresentations regarding product/service Unfair or deceptive games and contests	Retailer failure to fulfill customer product/service request
	Contracts	Unfair contract terms Unclear contracts Deceptive contract terms Unfair or deceptive lease contracts	Number of contract cancellations by customer
	Product performance	Unreasonable consumer safety hazard Unsatisfactory performance/quality of product	Refunds and/or exchanges by customer
	Service adequacy	Failure to perform delivery Failure to perform refund/exchange Repair problems (guarantees/warranties)	Number of guarantee/warranty options used by customer
	Credit practices	Unfair or incorrect billing Unfair creditor's remedies Unfair methods of debt collection	Accounts receivable and bad debts expense accounts

Note: The type and frequency of complaints may indicate problems in any of the above areas.
Source: James E. Stafford and William A. Staples, "Retailing: Potential Legal Problems in the Selling Process," *Tennessee Survey of Business*, September-October 1975, p. 27.

may evaluate the adequacy of service by studying the number and type of guarantee and warranty options which are used by customers. Further, an analysis of accounts receivable records and bad debt expenses may pinpoint potential problem areas with credit practices. In addition, continuing close contact with Better Business Bureaus may help the retailer to ascertain the nature of consumer complaints received about the firm. The retailer may also receive information about potential legal problems by keeping in touch with local and state consumer protection agencies.

COSTS OF COMPLYING WITH GOVERNMENT REGULATIONS

Until recently, government regulation was not a major problem for most retailers. However, during the 1960s and 1970s the regulations have become increasingly numerous and costly. Perhaps one reason is simply the visibility of retailing.

What does increasing regulation mean for the retailer? It means increased costs to hire staff to fill out the forms, interpret various regulations, and fight those that are unfair, plus the increased costs of complying with the forms. Table 9–2 shows the annual federal forms and the estimated annual time needed to fill them out for a typical food chain. Fifteen separate agencies require 56,000 filings per year. Some of the agencies noted in the table have been discussed in this chapter. Others are discussed in the chapters on consumer activism, pricing, and human resources management.

TABLE 9–2
ANNUAL FEDERAL FORMS FOR A TYPICAL FOOD CHAIN

Agency	Number of filings per year	Estimated annual time needed	Agency	Number of filings per year	Estimated annual time needed
Securities and Exchange Commission	77	1,023	Department of Justice	460	1,875
Internal Revenue Service	42,642	6,068	International Trade Commission	1	5
Department of Labor	25	4,750	Food and Drug Administration	7	111
Environmental Protection Administration	57	355	Federal Trade Commission	5	5
Department of Agriculture	725	4,664	Department of Transportation	25	25
Department of Commerce	108	495	Customs Service	1	5
Department of the Treasury	12,001	1,005	Equal Employment Opportunity Commission	1	320
Wage and Hour Division	168	90			

Source: "Chains Struggle with Government," *Chain Store Age*, October 1976, p. 35.

Richard George, executive vice president—finance for Jewel Companies, noted that "not counting tax filings, we estimate a typical supermarket chain spends 13,700 man-hours a year filling out federal forms. At an average cost of $7.50 per hour, the direct cost to the chain for labor only is $100,000 per year."[36]

Table 9–3 presents the costs of government regulations to the food chains. Inevitably, the increase in costs must be passed on to the consumer in the

TABLE 9–3
WHAT GOVERNMENT REGULATION COSTS FOOD CHAINS

Regulation	Dollar cost per store per year for each firm					
	Firm A	Firm B	Firm C	Firm D	Firm E	Firm F
Sanitation inspections	$232	$ 831	$ 180	$ 894	$ 280	$ 13
Weights and measures	13	266	7,182	269	73	360
OSHA	12	87	17	15	4	7
Labor regulations	29	29	5	19	12	3
Environmental protection	n.a.	6,500	n.a.	n.a.	n.a.	n.a.
Clear meat packaging	0	0	0	0	0	1,850
Open code dating	0	0	0	0	0	0
Unit pricing.................	0	2,117	1,576	8,242	0	1,265
Chopped meat standards	121	105	2,820	3,209	308	47
Returnable bottle law	0	0	0	0	7,280	0
Corporation costs	450	677	1,292	1,000	n.a.	196*
Total costs	857	10,612	13,102	13,648	7,957	3,741

n.a. = not available.
* Does not include all appropriate corporation costs.
Source: "Chains Struggle with Government," Chain Store Age, October 1976, p. 37.

form of higher prices. Retailers must become more aggressive in having input into government regulations so that they can "live with them." In addition, they may have to enlist the support of their shareholders and become more active in letting their congressional representatives know of the stifling effects of these regulations.

DISCUSSION

Retailers, suppliers, and consumers are all part of a complex legal environment. Various regulations impact on pricing, promotion, and distribution decisions at the retailer level. The increasing wave of consumer activism has also spurred the passage of increasing numbers of laws which are designed to provide the consumer with additional information.

Retailers must be concerned with the rights and responsibilities which they have when selling a product, the liabilities they may incur, and the options for consumer redress against them. They need to work with competent attorneys on a continuing basis to lessen the possibility of litigation. For

---

[36] "Chains Struggle with Government," Chain Store Age Executive, October 1976, p. 36.

example, as a result of an FTC provisional rule, retailers may be liable, under certain circumstances, for advertising prepared by others. Under the provisional order retailers are prohibited from making advertising claims for products unless they obtain a written certification from a reliable source that a reasonable scientific basis exists for the claims.[37] Also the retailer can be held liable in some instances for claims made in advertising prepared by the manufacturer.

The retailer who is interested in serving the public by providing complete and accurate information and products at fair prices is not likely to encounter difficulties. All legal actions are designed to ensure fairness and equity in competitive behavior and to protect the consumer from unscrupulous sellers.

KEY CONCEPTS

Regulation of monopolistic methods
  Sherman Act
    Prohibits monopolies or attempts to monopolize
    Prohibits contracts, combinations, or conspiracies in restraint of trade
  Federal Trade Commission Act (1914)
    Establishment of the commission
    Section 5 declares that unfair methods of competition in commerce are
      unlawful
Regulation of price
  Miller-Tydings Resale Price Maintenance Act (1937)—allowed manufac-
  turers in interstate commerce to enforce resale price maintenance laws in
  states having such laws
  Robinson-Patman Act (1936)
    Forbids discrimination in price between different purchases of
      commodities of like grade and quality if the effect is to lessen
      competition
    Instances of legal price discrimination
    Key issues
      Quantity discounts
      Quantity limits
      Functional discounts
      Brokerage discounts
  Unfair trade practices acts
Promotion
  Robinson-Patman Act—Sections 2(d) and 2(e). Necessity of making
    promotional allowances and services available to all customers on
    proportionately equal terms

---

[37] Nancy L. Buc, "Retailers Liable for Ads Prepared by Resources," *Stores,* December 1975, p. 26.

Guidelines against bait and switch advertising
Trade regulation rules
Better Business Bureaus—concern themselves with a variety of unfair
  advertising and sales practices
Current issues of interest
  Diminishing limits of puffery
  Advertising substantiation
Regulation of channels of distribution
  Exclusive dealing (Section 3 of the Clayton Act)—the agreement whereby a
    seller requires the outlets featuring his products not to carry those of a
    competitor
  Horizontal market distribution
  Tie-in agreement (Section 3 of the Clayton Act)—not per se illegal but
    becomes illegal if the effect is to substantially lessen competition
Product warranties, product liability
Positive stances available to the retailer

DISCUSSION QUESTIONS

1. What was the basis for the initial introduction of fair-trade legislation? Why was fair-trade legislation finally repealed?

2. Why do some states have sales-below-cost laws which set prices below which it is illegal to sell certain merchandise?

3. Discuss the conditions under which price discounts are legal as defined by the Robinson-Patman Act.

4. What is meant by the term *good faith defense?*

5. Is exclusive dealing illegal? Can suppliers designate exclusive territories for a product or service to be sold by a particular retailer?

6. What is meant by the term *tie-in agreement?*

7. What precautions must a retailer take in advertising warranties on merchandise?

8. What are some steps which management can take in monitoring potential violations of the law?

9. What are the primary federal restraint-of-trade statutes? What are the key elements of the statutes?

10. What is included in the term *unfair methods of competition?*

11. May a retailer legally engage in price-fixing? Explain.

PROJECTS

1. Study the provisions of the Robinson-Patman Act, and imagine that you are a small retailer of drug items. Write your congressman a letter stating why you believe that the act should be repealed, amended, or remain intact. Imagine that

you are with a large chain such as A&P, and voice your opinion on the matter to your congressman.

2. Go to the library and read the most recent articles on substantiation of advertising, counter ads, and corrective advertising. How are these developments likely to affect the retail structure? Interview various retailers to get their opinions on these issues. What is their level of understanding and concern?

3. Do the same on product liability.

4. Determine the status of sales-below-cost laws and price discount laws in your state.

CASES

Case 1. In a relatively small (70,000) Southeastern university town, the issue of enforcement of Sunday closing "blue laws" was suddenly exploded by a local minister. He was not the only one opposed to stores being open on Sundays; indeed most store operators had normally closed on Sundays in observance of the law and because they felt that Sunday openings would probably not be highly profitable. Five arrests were made. Among those arrested were convenience store managers who were opening on Sunday.

The enforcers of the law claimed that this was a purely legal issue. Enforcement has apparently caused a lot of inconvenience for the citizens of the town. Many of them were surprised when they were unable to buy needed food items on Sunday.

Several weeks ago a three-judge panel in a neighboring county ruled that the state blue laws were constitutional. However, a city judge dismissed the charges against convenience store owners on the basis that the state law was unconstitutionally vague. That ruling will be appealed.

What implications does this situation have for the citizens, merchants, ministers, and others of the town? What should/can they do? What are the key issues? Assume that you are being asked to prepare a position paper for top management which discusses the various issues involved and the likely effects of the situation on the department store for which you are employed. What would you recommend as to Sunday openings and why, assuming that the law is held unconstitutional?

Case 2. In a recent congressional session, the Department of Justice recommended changes in the Robinson-Patman Act. The department transmitted a 320-page report to Congress in which its Antitrust Division stated that evidence "seriously undermines historic claims" that the statute offered "any substaining economic protection to small business." During early 1975 the department had recommended to President Ford that Robinson-Patman be repealed in part and otherwise modified. The proposal met with a solid wall of opposition from retailers and other small business groups.

Assume that you are a small retailer. Write a letter to your congressman stating your position on the proposal and giving the rationale for your position.

10

CONSUMERISM, PUBLIC POLICY, AND RETAILING

*R*etailers tend to feel that by the nature of their business they are and must be sensitive to the consumer; and, indeed, in many ways they are. The rationale is that the retail world is a very competitive place, and that for a retailer to be successful for any time he must necessarily satisfy the consumer.

The fact is that the relationship between the consumer and the retailer has become much more complex–just as life itself has become more complex. The relationship can no longer be covered by the old cliché "The customer is always right." Today the customer is always right except, for example, when the customer doesn't pay a bill on time, or when the customer trips a device in the store designed to prevent shoplifting.

On the other side, the customer becomes properly irritated when she feels that her credit information is being abused or that changes in account information are not being processed properly. These are legitimate complaints, as are complaints against marginal operators who are, in fact, out to cut corners and literally cheat the consumer. Add to all of this the consumer's experience with shoddy products, inadequate warranties and care information, inadequate information with respect to energy consumption, and we begin to see the whole complex world pressing the consumer.

It is in this context that we, as retailers, must increase our sensitivity and understanding of the issues which concern consumers, recognizing that they are legitimate issues and that they must be dealt with effectively. It is therefore important that retailers have a fundamental understanding of the problems presented in this chapter.

Stanley J. Winkelman
Chairman of the Board
Winkelman Stores, Inc.
Detroit, Michigan

We need to be familiar with and to understand the forces which give rise to consumerism. With this information the opportunity exists to structure programs and merchandise offerings which will respond to consumer needs and wants. The end result will be increased profitability, a differential advantage over competition, and a strong image in the minds of consumers.

Thus, the purposes of this chapter are to:

1. Provide a historical overview of consumerism and retailing.
2. Provide insights into consumerist concerns in the 1970s.
3. Profile consumer activists.
4. Focus on voluntary retailer action taken in response to consumerism.
5. Focus on actions taken at various levels of government.

Textbooks teach that the strategies of retailers should be consumer oriented. Thus, all of the business activities of retailers should center on maximizing consumer satisfaction in the marketplace. However, the behavior of retailers does not always reflect this professed belief. Too often business is busy prescribing remedies and cures for the consumer, and too often it fails to ask consumers what is bothering them about the marketplace. Thus, the consumers are often convinced that the efforts of retailers are primarily self-serving.

Consumerism as a social and economic movement of dissatisfied and militant consumers is not a new phenomenon. Further, the overt manifestation of dissatisfaction by a few consumers is probably indicative of the opinions held by a much larger number. For example, one nationwide study revealed that only 2 percent of dissatisfied consumers write the manufacturer about defective products.[1] Their behavior is a clear signal that all is not well with the marketplace. From the retailer's perspective, it is worthwhile to focus on selected aspects of consumerism for a variety of reasons: "(1) consumerism is a signal that *all* consumers are not docile, happy, well-satisfied customers of the marketplace; (2) the militant consumer is an unsatisfied consumer and, therefore, is probably worthy of special effort and attention from marketers; (3) militant consumers are usually characterized as the active, vocal, and semi-organized, participative *critics* of marketing systems and firm behavior."[2]

HISTORICAL ANTECEDENTS OF CONSUMERISM

Consumerist groups have been active in the United States throughout the past hundred years, and at various times they have pursued three sets of objectives with a direct bearing for retailers. These are: (1) nonconsumerist

[1] "Improving the New Products Equation," *Nielsen Researcher*, November 1, 1974, p. 11.

[2] Rom J. Markin, Jr., *Consumer Behavior: A Cognitive Orientation* (New York: Macmillan Company, 1974), p. 25.

goals; (2) the introduction or support of new retailing institutions; and (3) the modification of practices in existing retail establishments.[3]

Nonconsumerist goals. Over the years consumers have often tried to use purchasing power to bring about changes in political or economic institutions. For example, during periods of war, goods from particular countries have been boycotted. Goods produced or distributed under conditions deemed undesirable, such as by the use of prison workshop labor or nonunion labor, have also been the target for such action. In more recent times, boycotts of stores which discriminated in employment against blacks and other minority groups have occurred. Activities such as boycotts may place management in an untenable position. The retailer is likely to lose trade but may be unable to accede to the protesters' demands for a variety of reasons, including personal conviction or contractual requirements. For example, in 1976 the Amalgamated Clothing and Textile Workers Union launched the largest and most costly unionization campaign in the history of organized labor against J. P. Stevens and Company. It urged consumers not to buy Stevens sheets, towels, and blankets and "formed committees of unionists, church, and civil rights leaders and other social activists to bring pressure on retailers."[4]

The introduction of new retailing institutions. This aspect of consumerism has included the introduction of such establishments or features as consumer cooperatives and farm cooperatives. The aims of most of these activities have been to reduce the cost of distribution and to provide affected groups with a countervailing force against big business. Shopping services and Consumers Union are other examples of this type of consumer activity. Obviously, the recommendations forthcoming from these services may affect the sales of particular products in a retail outlet.

New types of retail businesses. Management in times past has been able to obtain support from consumer organizations for new retailing innovations or institutions. The best-known example was the efforts of consumer groups in fighting anti–chain store legislation during the 1930s and 1940s. Consumers have also been helpful in establishing various uniform grading and packaging practices.

TIME DIMENSIONS

Consumerism may also be viewed in terms of time spans. The first era is typically identified as the early 1900s. It was characterized by the publication of Upton Sinclair's *The Jungle*, which resulted in such regulations as the Meat Inspection Act. The second era was the mid-1930s. The Pure Food and

---

[3] Stanley C. Hollander, "Consumerism and Retailing: A Historical Perspective," *Journal of Retailing*, vol. 48 (Winter 1972–73), p. 6.

[4] "A Boycott Battle to Win the South," *Business Week*, December 6, 1976, p. 80; also "A Touch of Civil Rights Fervor," *Time*, March 14, 1977, p. 44.

Drug Act of 1938 was enacted after more than 100 people died following the use of a new sulfa drug which was lethal under certain conditions. The third era was the 1960s, which probably began with President Kennedy's consumer message in 1962. In his address, Kennedy listed the four rights of a consumer: The right to safety, the right to be informed, the right to choose, and the right to be heard.

Consumer activism is typically not detrimental to retailing. Most case histories follow a similar pattern: (1) initial retailer opposition to change because of perceived excessive cost and difficulty; (2) introduction of the change; (3) discovery that the change does not cost as much as anticipated, does not influence customer purchases to the extent feared, and does not yield the volume of benefits its advocates desired.[5]

CONSUMERISM IN THE 1970S

A new era in the history of consumerism may be emerging as a result of rising prices, materials shortages, and inflation. Americans abandoned the Protestant work ethic after World War II in favor of the so-called psychology of affluence. The move was away from a struggle for daily existence toward an increased emphasis on self, less structured life-styles, and a more compatible personal environment. The psychology of affluence is changing, and Americans are:

Cutting back on expenditures in areas that have little emotional value, such as the supermarket.

Committed to convenience and simplification.

Less willing to take risks—for example, by buying private labels.

Distrustful of a value-only store.

Chipping away at expenditures that give the "good life" but not eliminating them.

Controlling exposure to temptations—for example, by not shopping as often.

Supporting consumerism and the more information concept even if they don't use it.

More concerned about waste.

Returning to self-sufficiency projects, such as home sewing, gardening, and home maintenance.[6]

Retailers need, however, to keep these so-called changes in perspective. For example, will the trend for consumers to bake their own bread, raise their

---

[5] Robert O. Herrmann, "Consumerism: Its Goals, Organizations, and Future," *Journal of Marketing*, vol. 34 (October 1970), pp. 55–60.

[6] "Consumers Fight Inflation via New Shopping Habits," *Advertising Age*, March 17, 1975, p. 16.

own vegetables, and repair their own automobiles continue? Already we see the youth of the 1960s who chose to reject middle-class values and careers in favor of "more fulfilled lives" enrolling in business courses and engaging in similar conventional activities. Further, a reemergence of the psychology of affluence appears likely to occur in the near future.

Clearly today's consumer is not the consumer of the 1960s and early 70s. Consumers' faith in business has eroded, and their skepticism has increased. Specifically, in 1968 70 percent of the public felt that business struck a balance betwen profits and the public interest. Today, more than 70 percent feel that business is mostly concerned with profit at the expense of the public good and more than 50 percent feel in danger of being "ripped off" by the business community. Also, business executives are believed by only one in eight consumers, whereas Ralph Nader is believed by one in two consumers.[7]

FORCES BEHIND CONSUMER ACTIVISM[8]

Inflation. Inflation and recession have gone almost hand in hand for the past several years, and these factors have greatly affected the marketplace. The result is that consumers are increasingly suspicious of and hostile toward retailing institutions. For example, one study indicated that 83 percent of the women surveyed believed that stores raise prices on some items to offset specials.[9] Similarly, a research report prepared by Needham, Harper, and Steers reveals that consumers are angry about rising prices, "but nothing seems to infuriate them as much as knowing that the supermarket manager hikes prices on 'old stock.' " Also causing resentment are shrinking package sizes, which are seen as an insult to shoppers' intelligence. Consumers report that they have eliminated such things as purchases of cosmetics and trips to the hairdresser, as well as postponed the buying of automobiles, appliances, and household goods. Clearly, these kinds of reactions to inflation have a major impact on retailing institutions.[10]

Nutrition. Consumers have become increasingly angry about reports which reveal the nutritional deficiencies in many foods. They are "angry at sugar companies for disseminating nutritional misinformation, and their mistrust of these companies leads to a spill-over of mistrust to other com-

---

[7] Address by Satenig S. St. Marie, divisional vice president for J. C. Penney, at the annual meeting of the National Retail Merchants' Association, New York City, January 11, 1977, p. 2.

[8] For further reading, see Ralph L. Day, "Prescription for the Marketplace—Everyone Listen Better!" *Business Horizons*, December 1976, pp. 57–64.

[9] Lawrence Dogarty and Maurine Block, "Retailers Faced with Consumer Anger, Low Profits," *Advertising Age*, May 12, 1975.

[10] "Shopping Prices Report Shows Concern about Prices, Nutrition," *Marketing News*, August 1, 1975, p. 1. Also Joseph Barry Mason, "The Economics of Food Prices," paper presented at the annual meeting of the American Home Economics Association, Los Angeles, June 25, 1974.

panies."[11] Consumers are increasingly aware of additives, and many consider processing bad because it robs food of much of its natural nutrition. They appear to be cutting down on items containing sugar and to be serving more substitutes, such as fruit, raw vegetables, peanut butter, and other natural foods. They wonder why the government wants to ban such products as artificial sweeteners while it is trying to legalize marijuana and continues to allow the advertising of cigarettes and alcoholic beverages.

Increased expectancies. Society has witnessed tremendous breakthroughs in technology such as space walks, organ transplants, and supersonic transportation. The consumer wonders why, if we are able to develop technology which can speed an airplane at 600 miles per hour in the darkness of night to a perfect landing in New York City, we can't make a coffee pot that works. Consumers seems to be demanding better products than are presently available at the prices which society is willing to pay. They are also complaining increasingly about the poor quality of products.

Deceptive practices in pricing and advertising. Mispricing and unavailability have always been major problems for the consumer. As a result of supermarket abuses in these areas, the Federal Trade Commission has issued rules designed to regulate overpricing and unavailability in food distribution. However, the practices continue to cost consumers large amounts of money.

THE FREQUENCY OF CONSUMER COMPLAINTS

It is difficult to develop precise information on the nature and frequency of consumer complaints about retailing practices. However, some generalizations are possible. For example, one study found that 96 percent of the business persons reached had experienced dissatisfaction in the marketplace during the preceding 12 months and that 81 percent of the consumers reached had experienced dissatisfaction.[12] Similar studies have focused on consumers whose dissatisfaction was strong enough to prompt them to seek relief in the marketplace. One study found that 47 percent of consumers were sufficiently dissatisfied to seek relief.[13] Two additional studies place the percent of dissatisfaction sufficient to prompt a formal complaint at approximately 50%.[14] The Office of Consumer Affairs receives over 30,000 com-

[11] "Food Prices Have Altered Shopping Habits: NHIS," *Advertising Age,* May 26, 1975, p. 59.

[12] F. Kelly Shuptrine, Henry O. Pruden, and Douglas S. Longman, "Business Executives' and Consumers' Attitudes toward Consumer Activism and Involvement," *Journal of Consumer Affairs,* vol. 9 (Summer 1975), p. 91.

[13] William R. Thomas and F. Kelly Shuptrine, "The Consumer Complaint Process: Communication Problems and Complaint Resolution," in Barnett A. Greenberg (ed.), *Southern Marketing Association Proceedings,* 1974, p. 293.

[14] Joseph Barry Mason and Samuel H. Himes, Jr., "Consumer Action relative to Dissatisfaction following the Purchase of Selected Household Appliances," *Journal of Consumer Affairs,* vol. 7 (Winter 1973–74); and John R. Thompson, "Consumers, Complaints, and Cognition," paper presented at the annual meeting of the Southwestern Social Sciences Association, San Antonio, Texas, March 30, 1972, p. 2.

plaints per year, and the Consumer Product Safety Commission receives over 85,000 complaints per year—particularly about new cars and about problems with old ones.[15]

THE MOST COMMON CONSUMER COMPLAINTS

Table 10–1 lists the types of consumer dissatisfaction reported in four separate studies. The first study was based on an analysis of all articles published about various aspects of consumerism during a 12-month period by 14 general interest consumer magazines. The second consisted of an analysis of letters from consumers to Sidney Margolius, a syndicated colum-

TABLE 10–1
SELECTED SOURCES OF CONSUMER DISSATISFACTION
WITH RETAILING PRACTICES

Magazine article analysis*
  Complaints concerning energy
  Complaints against government
  Food complaints
  Complaints about dwellings
  Complaints about business
  Insurance complaints
  Banking complaints
  Pollution and environment complaints
  Advertising and promotion
  Health and medical complaints
  General product safety
  Automobiles
  Food additives
  Consumer groups
  Toys

Complaints to columnist Sidney Margolius†
  Insurance
  Food quality and prices
  Pyramid schemes
  Housing or renting
  Autos—equipment and repairs
  Vitamins and health foods
  Consumer materials and books
  Credit costs and problems
  Savings and investments

Calls to a consumer hot line‡
  Prepurchase
    Deceptive advertising
    Offensive advertising

Purchase/transaction/delivery
  Failure to deliver
  Wrong product delivered
  Product damaged
  Unsolicited advertising
  Excessive charge
Product performance
  Defective product
Guarantee/warranty/contract
  Deceptive or inadequate warranty
  Failure to honor guarantee/warranty
  Failure to honor contract
  Cancellation of contract
Service/repair
  Deposits, credit/collections

Voluntary organization responses§
  New automobiles—sales and servicing
  Appliance repair service
  Books, magazines, and/or newspaper
    subscriptions
  Mail orders
  Home improvements
  Used automobiles—sales and repairs
  Credit and/or loans
  Mobile homes

* James E. Haefner, "Indexing Consumerism Issues through the Mass Media," *Journal of Consumer Affairs,* vol. 9. (Summer 1975), pp. 84–86.
† Sidney Margolius, "What's Worrying the Consumer?" *Federationalist,* March 1974, p. 20.
‡ Steven L. Diamond, Scott Ward, and Ronald Faber, "Consumer Problems and Consumerism: Analysis of Calls to a Consumer Hot Line," *Journal of Marketing,* vol. 40 (January 1976), published by the American Marketing Association.
§ Ralph M. Gaedeke, "The Filing and Disposition of Consumer Complaints: Some Empirical Evidence," *Journal of Consumer Affairs,* vol. 6 (Summer 1972), p. 49.

---

[15] *U.S. News and World Report,* May 10, 1976, p. 56.

TABLE 10–2

TYPES OF CONSUMER COMPLAINTS AND TYPES OF BUSINESS FIRMS AGAINST WHICH COMPLAINTS ARE MADE

(no. of business firms)

Types of consumer fraud complaints	Finance and investment	Autos, auto parts, and fuels	Clothing, food, and miscellaneous retailing	Home furnishings, appliances	Home improvements and services	Housing	Non-store retailing	Personal and educational services	Miscellaneous services	Total No.	Total Per cent
Advertising fraud	102	203	116	112	44	115	92	151	51	986	18.4
Improper repairs or negligence with service	6	353	39	173	178	65	5	25	18	862	16.1
Misuse of contracts and warranties	76	135	137	83	105	86	40	105	26	793	14.8
Merchandise not delivered or faulty when received	13	209	91	64	65	28	184	51	69	774	14.4
Improper accounting or handling of accounts and bills	78	75	41	19	39	140	57	54	50	553	10.3
Deceptive sales practices	72	34	19	34	55	7	135	27	17	400	7.5
Dunning, repossessions, etc.	53	31	10	35	25	6	33	53	24	270	5.0
Specific Kansas law violation	12	45	2	3	9	2	4	109	1	187	3.5
General inquiry or provision of information by consumer (No fraud perceived)	130	45	35	36	31	17	36	67	143	540	10.1
Column total Number	542	1,130	490	559	551	466	586	642	399	5,365	
Percent	10.1	21.1	9.1	10.4	10.3	8.7	10.9	12.0	7.4		100.0

John R. Darling and Frederic B. Kraft, "Consumer Protection at the State and Local Level: A Case Study," in Henry Nash and Donald Robin (eds.), 1976 Southern Marketing Association Proceedings, p. 272.

nist. The third was based on calls to a consumer "hot line," and the fourth was based on consumer complaints received by consumer voluntary organizations, such as state consumer leagues. The various analyses were conducted under different conditions and for different purposes. However, the consumer complaints appear to be similar. For example, complaints about automobiles and automobile repair are important in all of the lists. Problems with repair and product safety are major, as are various complaints about home dwellings and home improvements.

Specific information on complaints is difficult to come by. One study of consumer durables does provide some insights, however. For example, 30 percent of the consumers expressed dissatisfaction with automobiles, 30 percent with motorcycles, 35.5 percent with color television sets, 25.9 percent with black-and-white television sets, 19.7 percent with stereotape decks, and 18.9 percent with lawn mowers.[16] Thomas and Shuptrine point out that the frequency of consumer complaints appears to be a function of what is paid for the product, how often it is used, how much the consumer depends on the product for the performance of an essential function, the newness of the product as a class, and the age of the product. As shown in Table 10–2, the type of complaint also appears to vary widely by type of retail outlet.

FROM WHOM DO CONSUMERS SEEK SATISFACTION?

The complaint resolution process often appears to be difficult and frustrating for the consumer. For example, one study found that over half of the consumers had to complain more than once before relief was obtained. Almost 29 percent of persons with complaints had to express dissatisfaction three or more times before achieving resolution.[17]

Allan Andreasen has noted, after analysis of the results of a national sample selected by Ralph Nader's Center for the Study of Responsive Law, that only one fourth of the problems people perceive with products are satisfactorily resolved.[18] Various reasons exist for these difficulties, including the failure to take the product to the proper outlet in the channel for repair, shoddy workmanship in the initial repair process, disagreement over whether a given problem is covered by warranty, and disagreement over which person in the distribution channel is responsible for repairs.

Consumers do seem to talk to other consumers in expressing their dissatisfaction. This can cause a major ripple effect when consumers are dissatisfied. The types of action taken by consumers in an effort to receive satisfaction in

---

[16] Thomas and Shuptrine, "Consumer Complaint Process."

[17] Mason and Himes, "Consumer Action," p. 124.

[18] "Andreasen Reports Only 25% of Problems Consumers See Are Satisfactorily Resolved," *Marketing News,* July 16, 1976, p. 9.

the marketplace vary widely. Table 10–3 depicts the results of one study. Apparently persons who get upset in the marketplace are most likely to complain personally to someone or else to do nothing. They appear to be least likely to boycott a store or product or to go through channel intermediaries. The most frequent action was a personal complaint to the store manager, salesperson, clerk, or similar person. However, approximately 25 percent of the consumers became frustrated and simply did nothing, feeling that they would be unable to get satisfaction. Andreasen, in the study noted above, found that less than 1 percent of complaints went to any unit of government.

TABLE 10–3
TYPES OF ACTIONS TAKEN TO RESOLVE MISTREATMENT AS A CONSUMER

Type of action	Number	Percent
Complained to store manager, salesman, clerk, president of corporation	145	31.7
Wrote a letter to the store, manufacturer, or company involved	35	7.6
Intend to write or contact firm and complain	4	0.9
Stopped shopping at store or changed stores	27	5.8
Returned product, exchanged product, or returned product for repair	14	3.1
Did not pay or stopped paying for product or service	9	2.0
Will not purchase product or service in future	25	5.4
Contacted Better Business Bureau, congressman, government official, TV station, or newspaper	15	3.3
Contacted a lawyer, filed suit, or went to small claims court	10	2.2
Complained to family, relatives, friends, or others	38	8.3
Nothing, just got mad and walked out, just went home, wasn't worth doing anything	115	25.1
Nothing I can do, poor can't do anything, or nothing because didn't know what to do	21	4.6
Total	458	100.0

Source: Rex H. Warland, Robert O. Herrmann and Jane Willits, "Dissatisfied Consumers: Who Gets Upset and Who Takes Action?" *Journal of Consumer Affairs*, vol. 9 (Winter 1975), p. 152; © 1975 by the Board of Regents of the University of Wisconsin System.

One study has profiled the chronic complainer as a person who typically contacts consumer protection agencies, newspaper and radio hot lines, Ralph Nader's group or similar organizations, and/or the FTC. The occasional or infrequent complainer is most likely to contact the retailer, the manufacturer, or the Better Business Bureau.[19]

Management seems to need a better system for communication with consumers. It appears that many consumers become frustrated but do not take any action. If they do take action, they either switch to another store or brand or make their complaint through an intermediary. Thus, management apparently experiences direct contact with only a small proportion of dissatisfied consumers. It must have a way of getting a better flow of information

[19] Joseph F. Hair, Jr., Rolph Anderson, and Paul Busch, "Profiling the Complaining Consumer: A Cluster Analysis Approach," in Howard C. Schneider (ed.), *1976 American Institute for Decision Sciences Proceedings*, p. 313.

so that it can respond to consumer problems. A "hot line" is one way to approach this problem. In any case, all complaint letters should be kept on file and made available in litigation because such files may be subject to discovery proceedings during the course of a lawsuit.

SOCIOECONOMIC PROFILES OF CONSUMER ACTIVISTS

One study has classified consumers into three groups: upset-action—consumers who experienced dissatisfaction and took action; upset–noaction—consumers who were dissatisfied with an experience in the marketplace but did nothing about it; not upset—consumers who had not experienced dissatisfaction with the marketplace during the preceding 12 months.[20]

Upset-action. The upset action group were dissatisfied with business practices overall and were either active in, or sympathetic to, the consumer movement. They were young, politically active and had a higher social status, higher incomes, more education, and a larger number of group memberships than did other consumers. This portrait of the upset-action-oriented consumer is similar to those which have emerged elsewhere. Other representative profiles are:

. . . evidence here indicates it is the younger, more mobile, more educated consumer with her higher expectations who is predominantly the "discontented consumer."[21]

. . . the average consumer complainer is a middle-aged, well-educated, affluent managerial-professional man or woman.[22]

. . . the demographic profile of discontented consumers indicates that these individuals most likely to operate efficiently in the market place are the least content with its operation.[23]

Anti-business consumers cannot be written off as a dissonant element among life's losers. They are more accurately described as an activist, avant-garde segment of society with both the motivation and the capacity to institute change . . . largely

---

[20] Rex H. Warland, Robert O. Herrmann, and Jane Willits, "Dissatisfied Consumers: Who Gets Upset and Who Takes Action?" *Journal of Consumer Affairs*, vol. 9 (Winter 1975). A similar effort at categorizing consumerists is reported in Gary M. Griksheit and Kent L. Granzin, "Who Are the Consumerists?" *Journal of Business Research*, vol. 3 (January 1975).

[21] John A. Miller, "Store Satisfaction and Aspiration Theory," *Journal of Retailing*, vol. 52 (Fall 1976), p. 82.

[22] J. P. Liefeld, F. H. C. Edgecombe, and Linda Wolfe, "Demographic Characteristics of Canadian Consumer Complainers," *Journal of Consumer Affairs* vol. 9 (Summer 1975), p. 73.

[23] William Lundstrom and Roger Kerin, "Psychological and Demographic Correlates of Consumer Discontent," in Howard C. Schneider (ed.), *1976 American Institute for Decision Sciences Proceedings*, p. 488.

through correcting what they perceive as the defects in current institutions and practices.[24]

. . . the image of the socially conscious consumer emerging from the research is that of a pre-middle-age adult of relatively high occupational attainment and socio-economic status. He is typically more cosmopolitan, but less dogmatic, less conserva-tive, less status conscious, less alienated, and less personally competent than his less socially conscious counterpart.[25]

. . . those who write complaint letters or take other action in response to dissatisfac-tion . . . tend to be younger, more affluent, better educated, and more active politi-cally than those who do relatively little complaining.[26]

Upset–no action.   The group portrait of these consumers is particularly disturbing for the retailer. They tend to be alienated from society and to have low social involvement, low incomes, low levels of education, and little political activism. Because of their lack of sophistication and their limited resources, they appear incapable of achieving satisfaction in today's marketplace.

Not upset.   Various studies have shown this group to represent approxi-mately half of the consumers. They are satisfied with business practices and optimistic about the future outlook for the economy. They have little interest in or knowledge of the consumerist movement. Their socioeconomic profiles tend to fall between the two extremes noted above.

VOLUNTARY ACTIONS IN RESPONSE TO CONSUMER DISSATISFACTION

Many different actions are taken by management in response to con-sumerism and in efforts to provide better service to the community. Often these actions also result in increased profit margins. Let's look at some of these actions. As you probably remember, the specific consumer reactions to these information sources were covered in Chapter 5.

Open dating of food

Open date labeling was long sought by many consumers. This type of information provides for a readable, understandable date on food packages.

---

[24] Thomas T. Hustad and Edgar Pessemier, "Will the Real Consumer Activist Please Stand Up?' An Examination of Consumers' Opinions about Marketing Practices," *Journal of Marketing Research,* vol. 10 (August 1973), p. 32.

[25] W. Thomas Anderson, Jr., and William H. Cunningham, "The Socially Conscious Con-sumer," *Journal of Marketing,* vol. 36 (July 1972), p. 30.

[26] Ralph L. Day and Muzaffer Bodur, "A Comprehensive Study of Satisfaction with Con-sumer Services," paper presented at the Indiana University Symposium on Consumer Satisfaction/Dissatisfaction and Complaining Behavior, April 21–22, 1977, p. 2.

Approximately 70 percent of food retailers carry open-dated food products.[27] Companies have been coding the freshness dates of products for many years, but these codes are still not understood by all consumers. Consumer advocates argue that consumers have a right to know how fresh food is. In response to such statements, a number of food manufacturers and supermarket chains have introduced open code dating programs. Typically the date on an item is the last day on which it can be sold in the store.

The dating of foods does not add significantly to retailer costs. Store managers for the most part appear to favor open dating of foods since it helps improve the rotation of stock.

Nutrition labeling

For most foods nutrition labeling is voluntary. However, if a product is fortified by the addition of a nutrient or if a nutritional claim is made in the labeling or advertising, the product label must then have full nutrition labeling.[28]

The intended benefit of these regulations is to allow value comparisons by consumers. Supposedly, the availability of product information at the point of purchase will help consumers to make more informed choices among brands. Ideally, consumers will shift demand away from brands with marginal nutritional value.

Management needs to be aware of the effects of nutritional labeling on brand shifts among consumers. Product offerings may become more limited as a result of such labeling. Thus, we may be entering a new era of food merchandising that will focus increasingly on the marketing of nutrition.[29]

Unit pricing

Many different factors, including price, influence a shopper in making choices in the supermarket. However, the increasing array of weights, sizes, and shapes of packages makes price and value comparisons difficult. Unit pricing is designed to help consumers compare prices more quickly and easily. Under unit pricing, products offered for sale include the price per unit, such as the price per pound or per quart, in addition to the price of the product. This approach takes the guesswork out of prices and makes comparisons easier for consumers. The New York City Department of Consumer Affairs has reported several studies which show that 40 percent of the time

[27] Eileen Taylor et al., "Food Retailers and Open Date Labeling," *National Food Situation*, May 1976, p. 30; and Charlene Price, "The Consumer and Open Date Labeling," *National Food Situation*, September 1976.

[28] "Food Labeling Regulations: The Official Summary of the Regulations Published in the Federal Register, January 19, 1973," *Nutrition Today*, January-February 1973, p. 14.

[29] Warren A. French and Hiram C. Barksdale, "Food Labeling Regulations: Efforts toward Full Disclosure," *Journal of Marketing*, vol. 38 (July 1974).

consumers make the wrong selections when asked to choose the package with the most quantity for the least money. The department estimates that these errors cost shoppers ten cents on each food shopping dollar.[30] Unit pricing has been voluntarily adopted by over 100 food chains and is required by law in some areas. Where not required by law, unit pricing benefits the retailer by providing greater promotional value over outlets not using it.

Value-conscious shoppers are using both unit pricing and open code/freshness dating in their shopping efforts. An investigation of the effects of unit pricing on price shopper behavior found that 94 percent of the users of unit pricing had switched package size within a product brand, that 86 percent shopped most frequently at a supermarket which used unit pricing, and that 44 percent had switched to stores where unit pricing indicated that the prices were lower.[31] Research has also shown that "when unit prices were posted on separate shelf tags in a supermarket, consumer expenditures decreased by 1 percent; when unit prices were also displayed on an organized list, consumer savings were 3 percent."[32]

Estimates of the frequency of use by shoppers of unit pricing, open code dating, and nutritional labeling vary considerably. Figure 10–1 presents the results of an analysis of use by a nationwide sample of 2,334 shoppers.

The universal product code

The universal product code (UPC) is a national coordinated system of product identification. It is designed to benefit the consumer through more efficient marketing practices. The linear bar symbols are familiar to most of us. A ten-digit number is assigned to every grocery product sold through retail grocery channels in the United States. The UPC is designed so that an electronic scanner will read the symbol on the product and automatically transmit the information to a computer which controls the cash register. The UPC will speed up checkouts by faster tabulation, reduce the cost of price-marking each item, provide instant inventory information, cut warehouse costs, decrease out-of-stock problems, and increase accuracy by reducing human error. Hopefully, these benefits will hold down prices.

Many consumer groups, however, are not happy with the idea of the UPC, since it would eliminate the necessity for price-marking individual items. The California state legislature passed and sent to the governor a bill which would require stores to put individual price markings on all items offered for sale. Connecticut, Rhode Island, and other states already have

---

[30] "Focus on the Food Markets: Unit Pricing Explained," Cooperative Extension Service for New York State, Cornell University, December 21, 1970, p. 1.

[31] "Unit Pricing: Its Awareness and Usage," in Howard C. Schneider (ed.), *1976 American Institute for Decision Sciences Proceedings*, p. 314.

[32] J. Edward Russo, "The Value of Unit Price Information," *Journal of Marketing Resarch*, vol. 14 (May 1977), p. 193.

FIGURE 10–1

	Open code dating	Nutritional labeling	Unit pricing
	LAST SALE DATE **JUNE 26** PEPPERIDGE FARM	NUTRITIONAL INFORMATION **Per Serving** SERVING SIZE 1 OUNCE SERVINGS PER CONTAINER 1 CALORIES 190	PATES **89¢** VARIETY PACK 540-724 9.25 OZ 12 9.6 PER OUNCE

FAMILIARITY

	Open code dating	Nutritional labeling	Unit pricing
	94% / **6%** Very familiar — Somewhat familiar	**57%** / **38%** / **5%** Very familiar — Somewhat familiar — Not familiar	**62%** / **26%** / **12%** Very familiar — Somewhat familiar — Not familiar

Almost everyone who shops has a nodding acquaintance with the "pull date" type of coding in common use on packaged perishables. Some critics contend that such clearly labeled dates are often replaced by "pack dates," "quality assurance dates," and "expiration dates," an assortment of systems which could lead to confusion.

Calories count, and calories are counted. Not too many shoppers know, or care about, the difference between thiamine and riboflavin. But they are aware that useful information on the quantities of dietetic elements they may be trying to increase or avoid is as near as the side of the package on the store shelf.

Familiarity naturally relates very closely with the opportunity for exposure. In New York City, where shelf tags are mandatory, 75% of shoppers are very familiar with them, a proportion which drops to only 47% in a midwestern location where the practice is optional. The less educated and less affluent demonstrate lowest awareness.

RATING

	Open code dating	Nutritional labeling	Unit pricing
	75% / **21%** / **4%** Essential — Very useful — Somewhat useful	**28%** / **36%** / **28%** / **8%** Essential — Very useful — Somewhat useful — Not useful	**41%** / **38%** / **15%** / **6%** Essential — Very useful — Somewhat useful — Not useful

Freshness dates provoke relative apathy from the less-educated and less-affluent shoppers. While only six out of ten shoppers who did not graduate from high school, or with household incomes under $7,000 a year, deem the system "essential," the proportion jumps to eight out of ten for the college-educated and $15,000+ sector.

Above-average marks are given to nutritional labeling by the college-educated (science majors?). The concept also finds more favor with diet-conscious women than with men. In addition to nutritional attributes of food, there is also interest in the presence of additives and preservatives.

Consumerists have advocated unit pricing as an easy way for tightly budgeted shoppers to pick through the maze of sizes and brands in a product category and — ignoring the reality of taste and quality differences — to make the most economical choice. The system finds least favor among these low-income shoppers.

USAGE

	Open code dating	Nutritional labeling	Unit pricing
	94% / **6%** Use frequently — Occasionally	**51%** / **35%** / **14%** Use frequently — Occasionally — Seldom or never	**70%** / **19%** / **11%** Use frequently — Occasionally — Seldom or never

Checking dates has become almost as important as checking prices. While most shoppers rely on this aid to ensure freshness, many would agree with a recent paper from Cornell University which points out the limitations of systems which do not control the ultimate catalyst of decay: improper regulation of storage conditions.

The most dedicated users are found in the 50-to-64 age bracket. Can this be related to medical problems which may first plague a family at that time of life? The lack of greater enthusiasm among younger shoppers might give rise to misgivings about nutritional consciousness-raising in today's home economics classes.

While claimed usage is high, particularly near the top of the socioeconomic ladder, some grumblings are heard. Specifically, the tags are sometimes found too illegible or confusing, out of date, or positioned improperly. Men show a slightly above-average predisposition to use the system.

Source: Robert Dietrich, "Some Signs of Our Time: On the Road to Smarter Shopping," *Progressive Grocer*, November 1976, p. 43.

such laws in effect. The consumer impacts of the technology are covered in greater detail in Chapter 11.

Retail advisory groups

Consumer advisers at the corporate level are becoming increasingly common. They represent management to the consumer and the consumer to management. Esther Peterson, adviser to the president of Giant Foods and probably the first official "consumerist," has stated, "I'm to protect the consumer's position and to tell the company what's on the consumer's mind . . . not to tell the consumer what's on the company's mind."[33]

In addition to corporate consumer advisers, in-store staff consumer consultants are also becoming popular. In-store consumer consultants operate on the sales floor. Their job is to "keep people happy" by giving straight answers. They also enable management to keep a constant finger on the pulse of the shopper.[34]

The idea of consumer advisory panels is also growing in popularity. Such panels consist of a cross section of community citizens, including average shoppers, senior citizens, men, women, and representatives of various ethnic groups.

Even though the payoff from consumer programs such as these can't be measured, evidence does show that some companies have achieved more favorable economic results because of their programs in response to consumerism.[35]

Each individual company program is different. However, let's focus on the various programs of two of the nations largest retailers to develop an idea of the diversity of programs which have emerged in responding to consumer needs.

First let's consider Federated Department Stores. Federated is an ownership group, as noted in Chapter four. The 20 divisions of Federated have autonomy in many of their consumer relations activities. Still, they all have certain common consumer relations strategies, including consumer advisory councils, buyer booklets, in-store warranties, and employee training on consumer rights. However, individual programs differ among some of the divisions, as noted below:

> Rike's, Dayton: A consumer ombudsman to elicit consumer likes and dislikes about Rike's. Seminars on cost adjustments and consumer rights.

---

[33] "The Consumer Adviser," *Progressive Grocer*, June 1974, p. 40; also "Consumer Advisors a 'Significant' Step in Improving Retailer-Shopper Relations," *Supermarket News*, March 28, 1977, p. 38.

[34] Audrey Allen, "See Who's Talking to the Customer Now," *Progressive Grocer*, February 1975, pp. 34–48.

[35] Leonard L. Berry, James S. Hensel, and Marian C. Burke, "Improving Retailer Capability for Effective Consumerism Response," *Journal of Retailing*, vol. 52 (Fall 1976), pp. 3–14.

Burdine's, Miami: Special on-location grooming sessions for senior citizens, the retarded, and the young.

Foley's Houston: Appeal to Spanish Americans through Spanish language signs, sales notices, and applications.

Shillitos, Cincinnati: Consumer groups in product areas to advise buyers on what people want in the area of fashion, personal tastes, and needs.

Gold Circle: Consumer surveys to judge consumer needs and tastes.

Ralph's supermarkets: Consumer groups to inform individual stores on the cultural tastes of the community. A nutritional education program headed by a full-time economist.

Lazarus, Columbus: Private appliance labels on how to better use small appliances to conserve energy.

The consumer affairs department of J. C. Penney focuses primarily on the company and not the consumers. The department seeks to make employees more sensitive to the needs of the consumer in every aspect of its program. The Penney education program includes:

A consumer feedback system to elicit articulated and nonarticulated concerns of consumers.

An extensive consumer education program which distributes educational materials in individual stores for community use.

Five field representatives in major metropolitan areas who present educational programs for individual stores to sponsor.

Consumer information programs to help consumers make buying decisions. One example is Penney's Christmas catalog toy section, which discusses how different toys contribute to the development of children of various ages.

An active consumer affairs forum—a week-long program at which representatives from higher education and business meet to discuss consumer concerns.

An active consumer advocate on the staff, whose responsibility is to sensitize the company to consumer concerns.[36]

Voluntary certification

Such agencies as the National Institute for Automotive Service Excellence (NIASE) are being created as independent nonprofit corporations for the primary purpose of improving the quality of performance to consumers. The NIASE was established in 1972, and since that time it has certified over 97,000 mechanics who have passed an aggregate total of more than 352,000 specialty examinations. The tests of competence are developed and

---

[36] "Convention '77—What Changing Consumer Attitudes Mean, and How to Cope," *Stores,* February 1977, p. 38.

administered by the Educational Testing Service of Princeton, New Jersey. The NIASE publishes a directory entitled "Where to Finde Certified Mechanics for Your Car." Other organizations are considering similar arrangements to upgrade the quality of services to consumers.

Voluntary action groups

An increasing number of voluntary action organizations have evolved. The following is a list of agencies which can be approached about particular product complaints:

Air travel: Civil Aeronautics Board, Office of Consumer Affairs, Washington, D.C. 20428.

Appliances: (air conditioner, dehumidifier, dishwasher, disposer, washer, dryer, range, or other nonportable appliance): Major Appliance Consumer Action Panel (MACAP), 20 N. Wacker Drive, Chicago, IL 60606.

Automobiles: Department of Transportation, National Highway Traffic Safety Administration, Washington, D.C. 20590, or Automobile Consumer Action Panel (AUTO CAP), 2000 K Street, N.W., Washington, D.C. 20006.

Carpet and rugs: Carpet and Rug Institute, Box 1568, Dalton, GA 30720.

Dry cleaning: International Fabricare Institute, Textile Approval Division, Empire State Building, 350 Fifth Avenue, New York, NY 10001.

Food and cosmetics: Food and Drug Administration, Office of Consumer Inquiries, PA–10, 5600 Fishers Lane, Rockville, MD 20852.

Furniture: Furniture Industry Consumer Action Panel (FICAP), Box 951, High Point, NC 27261.

Hazards of any kind: U.S. Consumer Product Safety Commission, Washington, D.C. 20207. Toll-free 1-800-638-2666.

Insurance: Federal Trade Commission, Pennsylvania Avenue and 6th Street, N.W., Washington, D.C. 20580.

Magazine subscriptions: Magazine Publishers Association, 575 Lexington Avenue, New York, NY 10022.

Mail orders: The Consumer Advocate, U.S. Postal Service, Washington, D.C. 20260, or Direct Selling Association, 1730 M Street, N.W., Washington, D.C. 20036.

Moving: Interstate Commerce Commission, Constitution Avenue and 12th Street, N.W., Washington, D.C. 20423.

Packages that are deceptive: Federal Trade Commission, Pennsylvania Avenue and 6th Street, N.W., Washington, D.C. 20580.

Photographic equipment and film: Consumer Affairs Department, Photo Marketing Association, 603 Lansing Avenue, Jackson, MI 49202.

Voluntary trade guidelines

From time to time various trade groups develop voluntary guidelines in response to emerging industry problems and consumer complaints. Such action may be taken only partly as a result of the desire to protect the consumer. Sometimes it is taken before new laws are passed to protect consumers from possible abuse. For example, voluntary industry sanitary guidelines for food distribution centers and warehouses were published because of deteriorating sanitary conditions in the food industry.[37] These guidelines were published jointly by the Association of Institutional Distributors, Cooperative Food Distributors of America, Grocery Manufacturers of America, International Food Service Manufacturers Association, National-American Wholesale Grocers Association, and National Association of Food Chains. Such voluntary action by industry groups heads off increasing government regulation. Government typically acts only after a failure on the part of private industry to regulate itself.

LEGISLATIVE AND REGULATORY EFFORTS AT CONSUMER PROTECTION

Regulatory agencies

Federal, state, and local governments constantly enact legislation to protect and enhance consumer rights. Also, as noted in Chapter 9, such agencies as the Federal Trade Commission regularly issue rules which are designed to regulate the business practices of retailers.

The U.S. Consumer Product Commission is charged with identifying and taking action against hazardous consumer products. It is also responsible for administering such consumer protection legislation as the Flammable Products Act and the Consumer Products Safety Act. For example, it asked seven retailers, including Macy's, to sign consent agreements because of possible violations of the Flammable Fabrics Act. They were accused of selling allegedly flammable clothing.[38]

Recent credit legislation

Two major pieces of credit legislation have been enacted which are designed to alleviate consumer abuses. The Fair Credit Act, which became effective in late 1975, is an amendment to the Truth-in-Lending Act. It re-

---

[37] Joseph Barry Mason and Morris L. Mayer, "Food Industry Sanitation Practices: Guidelines in Regulations," *MSU Business Topics*, Summer 1975, pp. 47–52; "U.S. Sanitation Checks Rated Stiffer than States," *Supermarket News*, March 28, 1977, p. 37.

[38] "Chains Accused in Clothing," *Chain Store Age Executive*, February 1976, p. 5.

quires department stores and other retailers extending open-end credit to include a statement with the monthly bill which informs the customer of his or her rights in questioning the statement and gives the address to which all inquiries should be sent. The act also provides that a seller may no longer be restricted by issuers of bank cards from offering cash discounts.[39] In addition, it reverses the doctrine of the "holder in due course" under which a third party holding a credit contract had no obligation for the merchandise received by the consumer.[40]

The second piece of legislation bars sex discrimination in judging a credit application. A 1977 amendment to the Equal Credit Opportunity Act opened the way for a married woman to establish a credit history in her own name. After June 1, 1977, lenders' reports to credit bureaus had to include the names of both spouses. These provisions were especially geared to the needs of divorced or widowed women. All reports to credit bureaus on accounts used by both husband and wife had been only in the husband's name—leaving a widow or divorcée with no credit rating. The wife now has the right to share in the credit rating that the couple built up together.[41]

The impact of these acts has been considerable. For example, an average of $1 per account has been necessary to administer the new acts. Small stores were hit the hardest by this legislation. Many smaller stores which have been doing their own billing are dropping individual accounts and going to bank credit cards.

Criticism is also growing against the retailer practice of retaining all amounts paid by a customer toward a layaway item when delinquency in payment of the account occurs. Steps have been taken to challenge this practice. Consumerists feel that the practice is unfair or illegal. Thus, retailers must make sure that their layaway policies are both legal and ethical.

These are only a limited number of examples of consumer legislation enacted after failure by manufacturers, wholesalers, and/or retailers to act positively in alleviating consumer abuses. Once such legislative acts are passed, they are hardly ever repealed, and they contribute to an ever-increasing burden of red tape with which the retailer must contend.

THE BROADER MEANING OF CONSUMERISM

Increasingly, consumerism has been concerned with more than the individual welfare of consumers in the marketplace. The 1960s were an era of turmoil in which society became painfully aware of problems of racial discrimination, increasing government intervention in a variety of economic and social issues, and increasing demands by citizens for input into the public decision-making process. Consumerist issues exploded with Rachel

---

[39] "Fair Credit Billing Act," *Family Economics Review*, Fall 1975, p. 36.

[40] "A New FTC Rule Irks the Banks," *Business Week*, May 24, 1976, p. 35.

[41] "Married Women Get a Credit Rating," *Business Week*, June 6, 1977, pp. 28–29.

Carson's *Silent Spring* (1962) and continued through Ralph Nader's *Vanishing Air* (1970) and beyond. As an outgrowth of this era, the retailer was confronted with federal and state regulations covering such matters as open space, land use, historic preservation, job safety and health, and much more. All of this appears to reflect society's belief that the material abundance we have known is coming to an end and that it is time to make a transition. These concerns were manifest at a meeting of the International Council of Shopping Centers in which the statement was made that "the shopping center industry is dealing with a great deal more than a fad, but instead a movement which will change the face of a nation."[42] Likewise, James Rouse, one of the largest developers of shopping centers in the nation, has called for an end to "careless, piecemeal construction."[43]

The general manager of the Operations Division of the National Retail Merchants Association has stated that the legislative enactments with the largest impacts on retailers are "the Clean Air Act of 1970, the National Environmental Policy Act of 1970, the Federal Water Pollution Control Act of 1972. . . . Land use policy and planning legislation is also expected to be an active issue."[44] The executive vice president of the International Council of Shopping Centers has identified the key concerns for retailers as "waste disposal, noise pollution, water pollution, land use controls, economic growth-control plans and coastal area management."[45]

The Clean Air Amendments. The Environmental Protection Agency is now requiring ten-year air quality maintenance plans for various areas of the nation. The strategies proposed by the EPA, which vary from area to area, include mass transit and traffic flow changes, bus/car pool lanes, street parking restrictions, management of parking supply, and employer mass transit incentives. The director of the Office of Transportation and Land Use Policy of EPA has stated that because of these regulations shopping center developers must change their notion that "so many square feet of retail space translate automatically into so many parking spaces."[46] Likewise, shopping centers are now labeled as major indirect sources of pollution. The final indirect source regulations have been postponed several times. However, retailers are rushing to start major projects such as shopping centers before it becomes necessary to comply with federal regulations.

The Federal Water Pollution Control Act. Of interest to retailers is the required regulation of nonpoint sources of pollution. Nonpoint sources relate specifically to runoff from various types of activities. Land use controls

---

[42] John H. Fulweiler, "Shopping Center versus the Environment," *Chain Store Age*, August 1973, p. E–6.

[43] "Environmental Pressures," *Environmental Comment*, October 1973, p. 7.

[44] Gordon L. Williams, "Environmental Legislation Affecting Retailers," *Stores*, April 1974, p. 19.

[45] ICSC State Environmental Action Committee Bulletin, July 23, 1974, pp. 1–2; also Verrick French, "The Land Use Hassle," *Stores*, August 1976, p. 37.

[46] "Malls Face EPA on Parking," *Chain Store Age*, December 1974, p. 15.

are envisioned as one control mechanism, and such controls can have a significant impact on the issuance of permits for the construction of parking lots and various building structures.

The Coastal Zone Management Act.   A total of 34 states and territories are eligible for participation in this program. It is designed to preserve, protect, develop, restore, or inhance the resources of the nation's coastal areas. The new philosophy of the Corps of Engineers is a public interest determination by corps officials. These officials are required to consider whether the proposed activities are *primarily* dependent upon the wet land resource and environment and whether feasible alternative sites are available.[47] Under this philosophy, the Corps of Engineers denied a permit to fill in approximately 13 acres of Gulf of Mexico submerged land in Florida which was to be used for a condominium and shopping complex.

The Noise Pollution Control Act.   This act recognized noise as a major environmental pollutant. Governments are required to set up noise limits for various kinds of equipment. These standards relate primarily to the quantity of noise emitted by products for sale and by transportation vehicles.

The National Environmental Policy Act (NEPA).   All proposals for legislation or federal action must include an environmental impact statement. Seventeen states now also require impact statements for all significant public actions. Several states require environmental impact statements for major private projects.[48] Essentially an environmental impact statement is a report on the potential environmental effects of a proposed land use. In the near future such statements may be required for any new construction project. The statements outline both the adverse and the beneficial effects of the proposed development on people, animals, fish and vegetation.

Low growth or no growth.   The philosophy of low growth or no growth is designed to limit growth and may totally prohibit development in some areas. Numerous examples of the effects of this emerging philosophy may be found. For example, one shopping center developer sued the town of Corte Madera, California, for $11 million, "charging that it reneged on an implied contract which called for the development of an 83-acre regional mall." The city council of Ithaca, New York, tried to block a proposed mall in suburban Lansing, New York, by cutting off water supplies to the project.[49]

A variety of techniques have emerged to control land use and growth, all of which will have a major impact on future location decisions by retailers. These techniques include flexible zoning, down zoning, and development

---

[47] William N. Hedeman, Jr., "The Role of the Corps of Engineers in Protecting the Coastal Zone," *Environmental Comment,* April 1975, p. 3.

[48] Robert Gladstone and Robert Witherspoon, "Environmental Impact Statements: A Current Overview," *Environmental Comment,* June 1974, p. 5.

[49] ". . . Meanwhile in Ithaca," *Chain Store Age,* March 1975, p. 11; also "No Growth Zoning," *Business Week,* July 5, 1976, p. 28.

[50] Harold A. Lubell, "Environmental Legislation and Real Estate," *Real Estate Review,* vol. 3 (Spring 1974), p. 94.

timing. It has been pointed out that "the burgeoning environmental concern reflects a shift in values of the last decade that has reoriented our common-law thinking that property rights are inviolate."[50] However, what are the constitutional limitations on the public control of private land?[51]

The Occupational Safety and Health Act (OSHA).   This act, which now covers 60 million workers and 5 million places, became law in 1970. It probably has had more impact on the American worker than any legislation since the Wagner Act of 1935. Society has now mandated that the cost of safety can no longer be balanced against the cost of accidents. The act has had a major impact on retailing and many other industries. Apparently the most common violations of OSHA by retailers pertain to the electrical code, portable fire extinguishers, means of egress, guarding the floor and wall openings and holes, power transmission apparatus, handling materials, and personal protective equipment.[52] It has been estimated that the cost of meeting the kinds of standards now required by OSHA will add $1 to $1½ per square foot to the construction of new retail stores.[53]

George Matwes, safety director for Bamburger, prepared the list shown in Figure 10–2 as a sort of OSHA self-inspection list for stores in the Bamburger chain. The checklist can prove useful for other types of retailing institutions, since a total of 660 inspections of department store/general merchandise retailers were conducted in 1975.[54]

FIGURE 10–2
SUGGESTED OSHA CHECKLIST FOR RETAILERS

1.   OSHA poster is posted in appropriate location.
2.   OSHA Form 100 (Record of Occupational Injury and Illness) maintained.
3.   Regular employee and customer accident reports, with any follow-up reports kept in orderly fashion.
4.   All new employees are being indoctrinated in safety by films, pamphlets, etc.
5.   Parking lot meets requirements of striping, speed limit signs posted, lighting maintained, snow and ice removal arrangements, hole repairs, and debris cleaning and removal.
6.   Stairways clear of any debris or obstructions.
7.   Exits are marked properly. Exit lights not hidden.
8.   Exits must not be blocked and must be clearly marked.
9.   All floor mats must not slide or be curled up and must be butted.
10.   Glass panels marked by decals.

---

[51] Victor Yannacone, "Land Use Crisis: Two Solutions," *Shopping Center World,* March 1974, p. 19.

[52] "OSHA Chief Does Not See It the Way Chains Do," *Chain Store Age Executive,* April 1975, p. 17; see also Joseph Barry Mason, "OSHA: Emerging Problems and Prospects," *California Management Review,* vol. 19 (Fall 1976), pp. 21–28.

[53] "The OSHA Man Is Coming and He Is Changing Your Buying Habits," *Progressive Grocer,* December 1972.

[54] "OSHA Shifts Its Emphasis," *Chain Store Age Executive,* October 1976, p. 39.

FIGURE 10–2 (continued)

11. All stairways more than 88 inches wide have a handrail down the middle.
12. Main aisles must be at least 36 inches wide; keep aisles clear of boxes, displays, wires, etc.
13. Fixtures should not have extensions which can trip people, or sharp corners.
14. All display counters should be free of nails, broken glass, or easily knocked over counter displays.
15. Stock drawers must be closed when not in use.
16. Check for open carpet seams, tears, or folds in carpet.
17. Check for holes in floor, floor tiles missing, slippery floor finishes.
18. There are no obstructions in or near elevators. Escalators are maintained properly.
19. Doors that are not exits must be marked "not an exit," "office," "basement," etc.
20. Any door which is an exit must be unlocked when employees are in the building.
21. All aisles must be properly striped; no stock, empty cartons, or debris piled in aisles.
22. Material or stock is not stacked within 18 inches of sprinkler head.
23. Hazardous and flammable material not stored properly.
24. Employees trained in use of power equipment; forklift operators properly trained.
25. All rolling ladders have wheel locks and rubber "crutch" tips.
26. All pulleys are guarded; all saw blades have guards.
27. All grinders have hood guards; "table" not more than one-eighth inch away from grinder.
28. All equipment designed with interlocks should not have interlocks made inoperable.
29. All electrical equipment, wall sockets, and plugs—three-prong types and grounded.
30. Extension cords not to be strung across walk areas without being properly covered.
31. All electrical hand tools should be grounded.
32. "Temporary wiring installations" are not acceptable.
33. Fan blades less than seven feet off the floor must be "mesh guarded."
34. Fire extinguishers readily accessible, charged within past year, hung properly.
35. Fire doors not blocked and work properly.
36. No-smoking signs posted where necessary; no-smoking rules enforced.
37. Monthly fire drills.
38. Emergency lighting system works properly.
39. Floors are clean and free of grease and spills.
40. Flues, ducts, and hoods are clean, relatively free of grease.
41. Meat-cutting and all other machines have guards on blades, pulleys, and cutting edges and are grounded.
42. Refrigerators and other food and storage areas are kept clean and at proper temperatures.
43. No excessive noise levels (over 90 decibels).

Source: "The OSHA Tangle," *Chain Store Age Executive*, April 1975, p. 16.

SUMMARY

Clearly the retailer's reaction to consumerism must reflect the new attitudes and demands of consumers. Retailers need to be increasingly sensitive to the needs of society and to practice better community relations. The
demands made by consumers are not unrealistic. Primarily consumers want
the retailer to provide more and better information and to be honest in
dealing with them. Systematic performance monitoring to regularly appraise
the nature of the consumer's experience with the store or its products can be
very beneficial.

A more positive approach needs to be developed by retailers. Obviously
retailers do not want to make money by selling products which would hurt
or kill people or drive people away. However, far too often retailers appear
to act as if this is what they do want. The result is increased government
regulation and unnecessary consumer hostility.

Specifically, consumers are seeking clearer labeling, proper disclosure of
the terms of credit, more honest advertising, and similar improvements
which would make it easier for them to function as informed buyers. Consumerism must be the hope of the retailer. Historically, when the retail
institutions of society have not served consumers adequately, new institutions have evolved. For example, the increasing popularity of warehouse
grocery outlets, flea markets, and similar institutions reminiscent of the
1930s reflect this fact. These institutions have evolved because of consumer
demands for quality products at lower prices than are available through
conventional retail outlets.

Consumerism is not a new phenomenon. However, the current wave of
consumerism is a cause of particular concern for the retailer. The consumerist
movement reflects the ravages of inflation, increased expectancies that resulted from the Great Society movement of the 1960s, the depersonalization
in the marketplace which has resulted in poor service or self-service, deceptive practices in pricing and advertising, changing life-styles, and sweeping
efforts to regulate business for social ends.

In spite of the increasing sophistication of consumers, however, on many
occasions they still appear to be at a loss as to how to seek proper resolution
of their dissatisfaction. This provides a major opportunity for the retailer to
establish better communication with the consumer. The use of in-store staff
consultants and of corporate-level consumer advocates exemplifies the ways
in which retailers are beginning to establish better communication with
consumers. Consumer boards of directors for retail outlets, unit pricing, and
open code dating are other examples of voluntary responses by retailers.

A major dilemma for the retailer is to resolve the extent to which management should go in meeting the stated demands of one group of consumerists while still having to compete with other stores in delivering an
acceptable line of products to various markets. A simple philosophy of
"better service to the consumer" ignores market segmentation and the vari-

ous needs and demands for quality and product choices. One point is clear, however—numerous trade-offs exist in the consumerist area. Often one group of consumers is not willing to subsidize the demands of another group. Whatever the specific situation, more attention must be given to consumer complaints. Indeed, a strong case can be made that retailers should actively solicit consumer complaints to better determine the difficulties consumers are having with their product or service. For example, nationwide studies by A. C. Nielsen indicate that only 2 percent of consumers with complaints about defects in a packaged product complained to the manufacturer. Further, complaint-handling departments are often merely window dressing, for too little executive concern is expressed about the policies and activities of such departments. This is a shortsighted view of store complaint policies if a company is really experiencing lost sales because of unhappy consumers and unfavorable consumer attitudes. In the final analysis, however, the actions of the retailer may be constrained to the extent that comparable policies are not followed by competition.[55]

KEY CONCEPTS

Historical antecedents of consumerism
Forces behind consumer activism
Who are the dissatisfied consumers?
Socioeconomic profiles
The most common consumer complaints
Voluntary actions taken by the retailing sector
Unit pricing
Open code dating
In-store staff consultant
Consumer advocates at the corporate level
Legislative and judicial effects
Legislative agencies
The new consumerism
The Clean Air Amendments
The National Environmental Policy Act
The Federal Water Pollution Control Act
The Coastal Zone Management Act
The Noise Pollution Control Act
The Occupational Health and Safety Act
No growth or low growth

---

[55] C. L. Kendall and Frederick A. Russ, "Warranty and Complaint Policies: An Opportunity for Marketing Management," *Journal of Marketing,* vol. 39 (April 1975), pp. 36–43.

DISCUSSION QUESTIONS

1. Why is consumerism an important issue for analysis by retailers?

2. Is the low-income consumer particularly disadvantaged in the marketplace? If so, how and why?

3. What are some of the activities that are being undertaken by consumer groups and businesses in your area in response to consumer dissatisfactions?

4. Develop your own definition of consumerism and defend it.

5. What do you believe to be the most pressing problems facing consumers in the United States today? Outline a research project which is designed to reveal the nature and frequency of consumer dissatisfaction with major durables in the area in which you live.

6. What are some of the broad issues of the so-called new consumerism which we as a society are likely to face in the next several years?

7. Why is the retailer typically so resistant to consumer demands for change in the marketplace?

8. Describe the basic conditions of society today which are contributing to the current rise in consumerism. How do these circumstances differ from those which were found to exist during the earlier waves of consumerism, for example, the consumerism of the 1930s?

9. What are some steps which the retailer can take to lessen the adverse impacts of consumerism?

10. It has often been stated that consumerism provides a unique opportunity for the retailer. What is meant by this statement? Do you believe that the statement is valid? Why or why not?

PROJECTS

1. Find out what office handles consumer complaints in your state and the branch of state government from which this office obtains its power.

    What is the procedure for making a complaint with this office? Does the consumer require the services of an attorney in order to take legal action against the party responsible for an alleged offense when using the services of the office? What limitations govern the nature of the complaints that the office will handle? What powers of settlement does the office have? Can its decisions be appealed?

2. Find out whether your county or city has a small claims court.

    Who is the presiding officer of the court? What limitations govern the complaints that the court can hear? Are the services of an attorney required for litigation in the court? Will the consumer be at great disadvantage if he is not represented by an attorney? What powers of settlement does the court have? Can its decisions be appealed?

3. There are numerous special interest groups which deal with specific areas in the consumer protection field. Identify one such group, and describe the process that is followed from the time that a complaint is filed to final disposition.

4. Select a local multi-unit organization. Interview store managers of each of the organization's local stores and find out what they perceive to be the most prevalent customer complaints. Then do a convenience sample of store customers to see whether the complaints perceived by customers conform with the managers' listing.

5. What are major consumer complaints? Get the cooperation of a shopping area within your community and conduct a survey among randomly selected "customers" to determine what they are most concerned about with regard to retailing practices in general. Then do a similar survey among management personnel of the stores in the shopping area. Compare the perceptions of the customers and the management personnel, and see whether there is conflict or concurrence in the perceived complaint areas. Make recommendations based on your findings.

6. Given the great interest in "consumerism," an attempt to investigate some of the realities within retailing could be a valuable experience. Ask the management of a major chain store unit in your area whether it might cooperate with you to determine the types of consumer opinions about that organization. In-store interviewing of customers concerning key issues developed by you in concert with management would provide an interesting point of departure. For such a project to be effective, the management would have to be quite interested in the results and most cooperative.

7. Do a survey of consumers to determine the negative impressions developed by them in connection with retail selling situations during the past years. Find out whether the particular incidents of concern (for example, rudeness of a salesperson) were reported. Was affiliation with the particular store affected? Was that employee just avoided? Did the "injured" party tell others? How did the store's reputation in the customer's mind change after the incident? Do some cross tabs to see whether behavior or opinions vary according to such factors as age, race, sex, education, and so on. Prepare a statistical analysis and a summary chart of your results. Draw conclusions from the results.

CASES

Case 1. Mrs. Ross and her daughter Alice, who has been informed that she needs glasses, go to a discount optical store that features low prices for fashion frames. Although no one in the store seems well informed about the selection of frames available, Mrs. Ross is finally able to locate a pair of frames that Alice likes. They inform the salesperson of their selection, but he tells them that the frames will have to be ordered, as the store carries only display samples, and that it will be several weeks before the frames arrive. They agree to this and tell him to order the frames. The salesperson asks for Alice's lense prescription, but Mrs. Ross explains that the appointment with the optometrist is still a couple of days away. He explains that the store must have the prescription before the frames can be ordered. So Mrs. Ross tells him that Alice will give him her prescription after she goes to the optometrist. Several days later Alice brings her prescription to the store and asks the salesperson to order the frames that she and her mother had selected. But the salesperson now informs Alice that he cannot order the frames until Alice makes a down payment of $10. Alice doesn't have that much money with her, so she has to leave disappointed. That night Alice's father phones the store and asks that it go ahead and order the glasses for Alice. However, he is informed that the store cannot order the glasses without having first received the $10 down payment. He tells them to simply charge it to him and explains that he has an excellent credit rating. He gives the names of several local stores at which he has charge accounts and also the numbers of his Bank Americard and Master Charge credit cards. However, the store insists that the only way that it can order the frames is for him to come by and make the down payment. Mr. Ross then asks why the store didn't get the down payment before, when his wife was there if it was so important, or at least tell them about it. The salesperson replies that he would have if they had asked about it, but since they didn't ask, he assumed that they already knew about it. Mr. Ross tells the salesperson that he thinks that that was a fairly risky assumption to make since the salesperson knew it was Alice's first pair of glasses. The salesperson replies that Alice could have heard about the downpayment policy from a friend. The conversation deteriorates further until Mr. Ross finally hangs up, slamming the phone down.

How do such instances lead to consumer complaints about the indifference of business to consumers needs? How could the difficulties have been avoided?

Case 2. A consumer group in Birmingham has been urging all grocery stores to put unit price information on the shelves. One large grocery chain did this. Afterward a college marketing class did a consumer survey to determine whether shoppers were using the unit prices and found that most were not. This caused the management some concern. It wondered whether it should continue to post unit prices, since extra costs were being incurred by doing so.

What advice would you give the management of this chain?

11

THE TECHNOLOGICAL ENVIRONMENT OF RETAILING

*A*ctionable information, on an exception basis, has never been more urgently needed by profitability-oriented retailing managements than it is today. Every improvement in point-of-service registers over the past 30 years has enabled retailers to get more information and to establish greater control over their operations and assets than was previously possible.

    Electronic data processing of store transactions at the store level, providing actionable information when and where it is most needed, became possible with the advent of microcircuitry and powerful minicomputers. Improved hardware and software applications are being developed and announced at a rapidly accelerating rate, and you will want to understand these improved systems in order to use them in effective management. This chapter clearly outlines the impact of the technology of retailing as it is today and as it is likely to be tomorrow.

Gordon R. Callihan
NCR Corporation, Retail Systems Education
Dayton, Ohio

We are taking the general systems view in this chapter, which focuses on technology as it affects the retailing mix. Essentially, advancing technology has improved methods of capturing accounting data which affect key decisions about each retail strategy variable. We look in particular at some of the effects of the new point-of-service technology on management and consumers.

Because of the rapid adoption of electronic point-of-service technology by retailing, the purposes of this chapter are to:

1. Evaluate the major electromechanical inventions in retailing.
2. Evaluate the penetration of point-of-service technology in all aspects of retailing.
3. Focus on the status of POS technology in food retailing and evaluate the futuristic electronic retail outlets.
4. Evaluate the issues of the universal product code (UPC) as adopted by the grocery industry and the optical character recognition (OCR) code advocated by the National Retail Merchants Association for general merchandise retailers.

SELECTED IMPACTS

Merchandise management.   The new technology is greatly assisting retailers, whose major problems historically have been a lack of timely and detailed information. An electronic point-of-service (POS) system can achieve 95 percent sales retrieval within three or four days.[1] Such a system provides a quick and accurate way to tell which merchandise, styles, and colors of which manufacturer are selling most rapidly. The identification of slow- and fast-moving items is a key to merchandise management. Information on merchandise flow is needed daily because a single wrong decision can mean thousands of dollars in lost profits at the end of a year.

Pricing.   Management control of gross margins is a major problem, particularly since gross margins have been dropping in many lines of retailing during the past ten years. One potential approach to the problem is variable pricing, which relates prices and margins to the sales and turnover of specific items. However, this type of price control requires information which historically has not been readily available to management and whose unavailability has unnecessarily decreased margins and net profits. The new electronic technology may soon allow variable pricing, an analysis of price elasticity by type and brand of merchandise, a quick evaluation of the effects of major price changes, and testing of the effects of different pricing levels.[2]

Operations.   Retailing thrives on a large variety of merchandise, minimal inventory, and rapid turnover. The new systems provide useful, frequent,

---

[1] "Point-of-Sale Recording Systems Benefit Both Retailers, Garment Manufacturers: Norman," *Marketing News,* May 23, 1975, p. 12.

[2] "POS: Good Medicine in Store," *Computer Decisions,* April 1974, p. 32.

up-to-date information on markup rates, stock outages, sales patterns, and similar information which can be grouped for buyers by department. It also includes item data, such as price, size, color, and supplier.[3]

Personnel.   Information on the effectiveness of salespersons can be developed by analyzing the volume of merchandise which passes through individual cashier stations. Standardization of sales procedures is possible, since training differences between departments in retail stores can be eliminated. There are major customer benefits at the sales level, including quicker completion of sales transactions, lessened opportunity for sales error, faster credit approval, and total departmental interselling.[4]

Buying.   The new technology is enabling retailers to reduce inventory levels and to obtain more accurate and faster information for use in modifying the inventory mix and for purchase order management. Given the fashion revolution and the increase in fashion seasons in retail clothing in particular, it has become increasingly important to have accurate, fast information about merchandise levels and movement so as to avoid unnecessarily high merchandise markdowns. Through such information, bad products can be discovered more readily and new products which will be a major hit ("runners") can be recognized more quickly.

Promotion.   The retailer can have more accurate data on the effects of couponing, cents-off, and variable levels of price reduction by merchandise line. Coupled with better data on price elasticity and product turnover, this information should help to increase the effectiveness of merchandise promotions and thus increase the profitability levels of the firm.

The A. C. Nielsen Company recently evaluated the effects of electronic technology on various aspects of the retailing mix. Its perceptions of these effects are shown in Figure 11–1.

FIGURE 11–1
IMPACT OF AUTOMATED CHECK STANDS
ON MARKETING FUNCTIONS

Major
    Store promotions—features, price merchandising
    Consumer promotions—price off, coupons

Minor
    Product—quality, need for improvement
    Advertising—level, copy

Uncertain
    Presence—product availability
    Price—compared to competition

Source: T. J. Sullivan, "Marketing in the Age of UPC," *Nielsen Researcher*, December 3, 1975, p. 18.

---

[3] "POS and the Retailer," *Computer Decisions*, April 1974, pp. 36–38.

[4] A. Richard Tash and Edward W. Wheatley, "Electronic Point of Sale Technology: Promises, Problems, and Prospects," paper presented at the annual Conference of the Southwestern Marketing Association, March 1976, San Antonio, Texas, pp. 6–7.

ELECTROMECHANICAL ADVANCES IN RETAILING

Three great electromechanical inventions have been applied in retailing. The first was the mechanical cash register. The second was the computer. The third is the point-of-service terminal.[5] The essence of the POS concept is that all sales data are captured through terminals at a single point in time on the sales floor. The data are then transmitted over a communications network for entry into a back office system for further processing. This technology represents a revolutionary development for retailers, whose traditional problem has been lack of timely detailed information. Timely sales data are badly needed to combat the steady erosion of profit margins which has been caused by the proliferation of branch stores, the lack of good inventory control, the rapid growth of credit, rising labor costs, and the expansion of various competitive forms of retailing.

Sales penetration

Figure 11–2 indicates that point-of-service systems are rapidly penetrating the general merchandise market. The total volume of sales for these systems exceeded $300 million in 1977. Sales to nonfood retailers were $78 million in 1975 and over $94 million in 1976. "By 1979 annual sales of POS equipment are expected to exceed $1 billion, with an additional $1 billion being spent for computer equipment needed to support the POS installations."[6] Electromechanical cash register sales in general merchandising dropped to virtually zero in 1977, whereas electronic cash registers, which were virtually unheard of in 1973, made rapid gains to a sales level of slightly less than $150 million in 1977. Electronic cash registers are popular in all sizes of retail outlets, whereas point-of-service systems are still confined to such large retailers as Sears and Penneys. POS sales in supermarkets have grown even more rapidly than in general merchandising, as shown in Figure 11–3.

The dropouts from the battle for the POS market have been major. These include Pitney Bowes, which has dropped its Alpex POS operation, and Motorola, who sold American Regital to General Instrument/Unitote. RCA sold its system to Sperry Univac. Singer has also dropped out of the race, and such firms as NCR, IBM, and Litton are continuing to battle for the market.[7]

The equipment manufacturers

The bulk of POS sales to the major general merchandise retailers were made by the end of 1976, but a huge market remains, especially among retailers other than such giants as Sears, Penneys, and Wards. NCR appears

---

[5] Irving Solomon, "The Future of Electronic POS," *Stores,* April 1974.

[6] Joseph S. Wilkinson and William G. Mitchell, "POS Systems Revolutionize Retailing," *Journal of Systems Management,* April 1976, p. 34.

[7] "TRW Tests Its Luck in a Tricky Market," *Business Week,* May 31, 1976, p. 24.

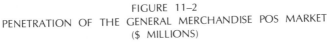

FIGURE 11–2
PENETRATION OF THE GENERAL MERCHANDISE POS MARKET
($ MILLIONS)

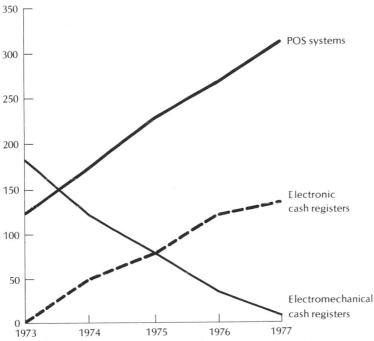

Source: "Key to POS Market . . . The Door Is Never Locked," *Electronic News*, section 2,
May 6, 1974, p. 20.

to be the overall leader in the field. By 1980 virtually all retailers will have
switched to point-of-service terminals.[8]

Reasons for rapid expansion

A major reason for this rapid expansion is the success of industry standardization programs. The food industry (manufacturers, suppliers, and retailers) has adopted the universal product code (UPC) as a standard
machine-readable code for source (producer) marking of merchandise to be
electronically read and recorded. The National Retail Merchants Association
(NRMA) has also adopted a standard code—OCR–A (optical character
recognition—A represents the font style used)—for use in point-of-service
systems. This voluntary standard of merchandise identification was reached
following 11 years of investigation and reports by task forces.[9] Its acceptance
by the general merchandise industry is less than that of the UPC in food

[8] "Chains Unlock Floodgates for POS Systems," *Chain Store Age*, February 1972, p. E-23.
[9] Morris L. Mayer, "Point of Sale Retailing: An Impending 'Identity' Crisis?" *Alabama Business*, February 1976, p. 23.

FIGURE 11–3
PROJECTED PENETRATION OF THE SUPERMARKET POS MARKET
($ MILLIONS)

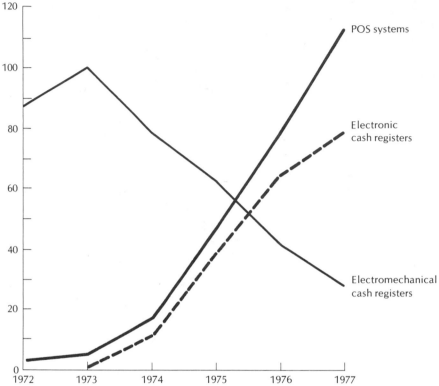

Source: "Key to POS Market . . . The Door Is Never Locked," *Electronic News,* section 2, May 6, 1974, p. 20.

retailing, at least in part because the system is newer. Another factor encouraging the growth of POS systems has been the development of the minicomputer and its use at the individual store level.

One factor which is hindering the faster adoption of POS equipment is the fear of the quick obsolescence of first-generation POS systems because of continuing rapid advances in design and technology. This has confused retailers as they are confronted with on-line systems, off-line systems, stand-alone systems, shared processor systems, different coding techniques, different credit authorization techniques, and different software management packages. Software continues to be a major problem in accomplishing the promises made by the equipment manufacturers. However, modular software, which is compatible with a variety of equipment, is being developed.

SEGMENTS OF RETAILING AND TYPES OF SYSTEMS

Let's take a brief look at the impacts of POS technology on the major types of retailing and at the systems necessary to meet the unique requirements of different retailers.

Segments of retailing

The largest department and specialty store general merchandisers, such as Sears and Wards, essentially cover the entire United States. These types of retailers are therefore developing national information system networks which consist of a series of data centers. The data centers range from a big corporate data center to regional centers to the individual store level. Each of the various levels is connected by a data communications network. The point-of-service system is linked with the point-of-receipt system, the personnel system, and warehouse control systems, which are connected at all levels of the organization.

The bulk of the department and specialty stores are part of ownership groups which operate as financial holding companies, such as Federated and the May Company. The ownership groups comprise separate groups of stores or divisions under different names. For example, the Federated group includes such stores or divisions as Bloomingdales, Lazarus, Shillitos, Foleys, Abraham and Straus, and Rich's. Each division typically consists of stores in the same general metropolitan area. The ownership group's corporate headquarters usually has its own data center. However, each division of the ownership group serves as a data center for the stores which are part of the division. Each of these stores, in turn, has its own in-store POS system which interfaces with the other stores of the division. Thus, for this type of organizational structure, the systems network extends over three levels: corporate, division, and store.

Discounters have networks which resemble those of the national department stores. However, the systems typically operate only at the store and corporate levels. Ordinarily they do not include credit files for retail credit authorization, which are a large part of general merchandise retailing.

The supermarket networks typically exist at the store, regional, and corporate levels. These systems have greater file capacities at the store level than do either the department or discount store systems. This situation occurs because the UPC supermarket system can store the price of each food item on discs and search the on-line file for the price of each item processed at the checkout counters.

Other large regional or national retailers in such lines as drugs, shoes, apparel, and furniture are implementing systems which resemble those of the discount store. Interfacing will occur at the corporate level whenever on-line communications are used. There are fewer terminals per store than in the giant department stores.

The stand-alone electronic cash register (ECR) is not tied to any data processor or communicator system. Such machines are typically replacements for electromechanical cash registers and are most likely to be used in outlets requiring fewer than ten terminals. They cost only one half to two thirds as much as the most sophisticated mechanical systems but capture many more totals and perform more functions. Further, they are faster, quieter, easier to operate, require less maintenance, and have a much longer life.[10] These machines do no data collection other than the normal cash register totals. They are not on-line and do not handle credit authorization or other large-scale file functions. However, modules can be added which permit data collection, and either on-line transmission or polling are possible. These features can make stand-alone electronic cash registers very similar to a regular point-of-service terminal.

Types of systems

Large general merchandisers. Personalized service is stressed by department stores, specialty stores, and other types of general merchandise retailers. Such service requires a wide range of transaction types, methods of payment, and return merchandise policies. These features affect the design of point-of-service terminals for general merchandise retailers. Because the transaction process is personalized, less pressure exists to speed up the transaction than exists in supermarkets, where faster transaction speed is the ultimate goal. However, the variety of services to be performed requires a more complex service terminal. Moreover, general merchandise retailers are beginning to use a hand-held wand reading device to ensure greater transaction accuracy. The wand is connected directly to the POS terminal. It reads tickets, labels, tabs, credit cards, and other symbols which are displayed directly on the merchandise or on packages.

The emphasis in general merchandise retailing is on timeliness and accuracy of reports, whereas the emphasis in food retailing is on front-end checkout economies. This is because of the huge number of stock-keeping units (SKUs), which may exceed 300,000 in a large department store. The number is so high because every item carried may have several SKUs, such as the assortment factors of sleeve length, size, and color in shirts.

The checkout counter typified by food retailing is greatly different from that of general merchandise retailing. The objective is to move the customer through the store as quickly as possible. As part of one system, for example, the customers place their UPC-marked merchandise with labels face down so that it can be moved rapidly across a laser beam omnidirectional scanner. The checker can use both hands to bag while the merchandise is automati-

---

[10] "Stand-alone Registers Used if Total EDP Not Needed," *Chain Store Age Executive,* February 1975, p. 27.

cally checked out. Based on the UPC code, a minicomputer identifies the price of the product, retrieves and displays the price, prints a receipt, and updates the store's inventory files with each product scan.

Discount checkout will probably move in the same direction as that of food retailing even though the current checkout systems are simpler versions of the department store terminals. Lack of standardization in merchandise coding, the absence of manufacturer marking of products, and a much larger number of products than those sold in food retailing have slowed the move to a laser scanning price lookup system.

Small stores. Some chains are too small to have a minicomputer in each store for price lookup or to have an on-line data communications link to a data center. These stores may use a stand-alone POS terminal which records all of the day's transactions on tape. The tape cassettes can then be transferred via WATS lines to the computer data center of the chain. Other chains may simply use the electronic cash register, to which a data communications module can be added if needed.

Shared systems may be attractive to small retailers, particularly those in shopping centers or major metropolitan areas. Such retailers could be served by larger retailers who have their own minicomputers. Thus small retailers would have access to merchandise control, credit authorization, and other on-line functions which are now available only to large retailers.

POS AND PROFITABILITY

Food retailing

The one-time investment in POS equipment is rather large—at least $6,000 to $10,000 for a terminal with a laser-optic scanner. However, the savings which are experienced in many aspects of store operation can rather quickly offset these costs. Table 11–1 presents the results of an analysis of the incremental aftertax return on investment in various types of electronic cash register and POS systems in food retailing under varying assumptions.

Cost savings can also be viewed in other ways. The elimination of price marking and cash register keypunching are hard savings which can be quickly measured. Stores using UPC coding and electronic scanning would not need to price-mark each item, since prices would be stored in the computer and automatically machine-read at the checkout. Shelf marking would continue to be used for shopper convenience.

Estimates are that these types of direct savings will exceed 0.5 percent of sales. This is a substantial amount, since the typical supermarket profit is less than 1 percent of sales.[11] Savings which are more difficult to measure include reduction in shrinkage or theft, fewer cash register errors, better evaluation of promotion, better scheduling of employees, detailed analysis of the move-

[11] Gordon F. Bloom and Ronald C. Curhan, *Technological Change in the Food Industry* (Cambridge, Mass.: Marketing Science Institute, 1974), pp. 26–27.

TABLE 11–1

SUMMARY OF RETURN ON INVESTMENT CALCULATIONS FOR ECR SYSTEMS

Type of equipment	Investment per store (no. of registers)	Annual operating savings (pretax)*	ROI (aftertax)†	Incremental investment	Incremental operating savings	Incremental ROI (aftertax)†
Electromechanical	$ 24,000 (ten @ $2,400)	—	—	—	—	—
Stand-alone electronic	$ 36,000 (ten @ $3,600)	$ 5,000 (0.1% of sales)	7%	$ 12,000	$ 5,000	27%
Electronic system	$ 45,000 (ten + computer)	$12,500 (0.25% of sales)	15	9,000	7,500	65
Electronic system with scanner	$140,000 (eight + computer)	$50,000 (1% of sales)	22	95,000	37,500	26
Electronic system over electromechanical				21,000	12,000	47
Scanner system over electromechanical				116,000	50,000	29
Scanner system over stand-alone electronic				104,000	45,000	29

* Assuming sales of $5 million annually per store.

† Calculations based on eight-year useful equipment life using accelerated depreciation schedule and current tax rates.

Source: Gordon F. Bloom and Ronald C. Curhan, Technological Change in the Food Industry, (Cambridge: Marketing Science Institute, December 1974), p. 31.

ment of key items, improved funds control, and perhaps automatic reordering in the future. Other savings may be obtained through improved price-margin and inventory-space management and better integrated chain communications.

Research has shown that labor scheduling alone can more than justify the automated front end "by potentially doubling an operator's profit."[12] A Marsh supermarket in Troy, Ohio, was used as a test store for scanning technology. The researchers found that scanner-equipped stores would need fewer checkout lanes. "For a hypothetical $120,000 work unit, . . . his rule-of-thumb is eight lanes for electro-mechanical registers, seven lanes for electronics and six lanes for scanning."[13] The results of research by Indiana State University and the U.S. Department of Agriculture revealed the following:

. . . an approximate 8 manhours savings per 100 orders . . . based on 13.3 grocery items per order. Translating this into dollar savings depends on labor rate and item movement for each store. Cashier and checking errors can also be reduced by approximately $12,000 per year for a store with $4,000,000 in annual sales.[14]

General merchandise retailing

The potentials for profit increases in merchandise retailing are numerous. Other possibilities, in addition to those listed above, include speeding stock data from the receiving dock to floor displays, pooling orders, and combining such functions as receiving and ordering. Also, performance between stores can more easily be compared; transactions can be speeded up and simplified; check authorization and the handling of exchanges, returns, and other courtesy functions become simpler; and the rescheduling of clerks is facilitated. Due largely to credit authorization via POS, general merchandisers have been able to reduce bad credit losses to less than 0.5 percent of annual sales.[15]

The new systems will also allow quick and accurate handling of the inventory data on the 200,000–300,000 stock-keeping units. This inventory needs to be analyzed daily to stay current on the quick turnover of fad, fashion, and seasonal items.

During clearance or sale days, the POS system is particularly valuable. Not only does the system help herd the typical jam of people far more easily through the checkout, but it also automatically adjusts for markdowns, credits, exchanges and final sales items. In addition, it calculates the impact of the clearances on inventory and the cash position of the store. Because the information is readily available in the back office the

---

[12] "How Scanning Will Boost Front-end Productivity—and Backroom Output," *Progressive Grocer*, May 1976, p. 39.

[13] Ibid.

[14] "Point of Sale: Registering Gains for Retailers," *Infosystems*, July 1974, p. 22.

[15] Randy L. Allen, "The Merchant's View," *Magazine of Bank Administration*, April 1974, p. 26.

day the sale ends, managers can determine whether the sale was successful, whether it should go on another day or whether other items should be included as loss leaders or promotional items to get the store traffic necessary for successful sales.[16]

Added major savings would be achieved by the source marking of goods by the manufacturer, which would eliminate most price marking by retailers. The total receiving and marking costs per $1 million of typical apparel merchandise is about $10,750 if the merchandise is opened, checked, and marked to the SKU level at the warehouse. Overall, $10,200 of this total amount could be saved if the merchandise were source-marked and sent unopened to the branch outlet. In this way the merchandise would also get to the selling floor more quickly.[17]

TABLE 11–2

ANTICIPATED IMPACTS OF POINT-OF-SALE SYSTEMS ON SELECTED ASPECTS OF RETAIL MANAGEMENT OPERATIONS

	Anticipated impact on selected activities (in percents)					
	Apparel stores*			Department stores†		
Category of activity	No change	Decrease	Increase	No change	Decrease	Increase
Labor costs						
Number of salespersons	85.4	7.3	7.3	57.6	37.6	4.7
Number of nonselling personnel...	34.1	55.3	10.6	29.6	60.9	9.5
Merchandise costs						
Merchandise carrying costs	37.9	56.9	5.2	27.3	47.3	25.5
Cost of merchandise controls	20.3	45.8	33.9	22.2	53.1	24.7
Systems support						
Number of registers or						
terminals	68.3	17.5	14.2	46.6	42.8	10.6
Physical space for systems						
support	57.7	15.4	26.8	32.5	16.2	51.2
Abuses or errors by employees						
Number of arithmetic errors at						
point of sale.................	14.5	74.2	11.3	16.0	76.3	7.7
Internal pilferage	66.4	32.8	0.8	60.1	36.2	3.7
Accounts receivables fraud	61.7	38.3	0.0	35.2	61.7	3.1
Customer abuses:						
Shoplifting....................	86.0	12.4	1.6	75.3	14.6	10.1
Bad debt losses	52.9	46.2	0.8	29.2	67.7	3.1
Losses from bad checks	72.4	26.8	0.8	56.8	40.7	2.5
Stolen credit card detection	59.8	24.8	15.4	27.3	47.3	25.5
Generalized overall expense						
impact	26.2	38.9	34.9	22.5	51.5	26.0

* N = 242.

† N = 262.

Source: Morris L. Mayer and Joseph Barry Mason, "The Status of Point-of-Sale Systems in Department and Apparel Stores—1975," paper presented at the American Marketing Association Educators Conference, fall 1976, Memphis, Tennessee.

---

[16] "Point of Sale: Registering Gains for Retailers," p. 22.

[17] "Point-of-Sale Recording Systems," p. 12.

Another "soft" but potentially major benefit is the probable change in merchandising attitudes and concepts which would be possible as the manager develops a more sophisticated view of the business. The manager can in effect model various possible changes in the merchandise mix, inventory levels, price, and promotion mixes to improve the profitability of the business.

Table 11–2 summarizes the results of research to determine the areas of greatest probable savings for apparel and department stores.[18]

THE POS EQUIPMENT DILEMMA

Retailers considering the possible adoption of a POS system must develop a broad master plan as a guide to their actions, regardless of whether a system is purchased. This starts with the desired objectives of the system. Possible objectives include check out speed, more accurate and up-to-date reports, and increased profitability. Quantitative performance measures must then be established to determine the extent to which the objectives have been achieved. Lastly, benefit/cost measures must be devised to include both "hard" and "soft" benefits as well as additional operating costs.

If the decision is made to purchase a system, it must then be designed. Management must determine the types of information needed from the system, the frequency of need, the reports required, how the data will be processed, and the data base.

The following checklist has been developed by one manufacturer as a guide to equipment selection:

1. What are the basic controls I cannot do without?
2. What added controls (important though not presently essential) can I afford now or plan for later?
3. What are the end results of the system and how does it jibe with my business objectives?
4. Am I wasting time trying to understand every intricacy of the hardware when I should be evaluating the kind of reports the system produces?
5. Will what I buy today be obsolete tomorrow?
6. What are the software capabilities? Can software modifications give me a system tailored to my various merchandising needs?
7. Will I have to extensively reprogram as I grow?
8. Will the software be compatible with the larger spectrum of hardware?
9. Will the system fit only high volume "A" stores or can it be scaled down to fit my "B" and "C" stores?
10. Does the product I am buying permit an orderly systems growth pattern? Can new stages be added?

---

[18] See also Morris L. Mayer and Joseph Barry Mason, "Point-of-Service Re-examined," paper presented at the annual meeting of the National Retail Merchants Association, New York City, January 9, 1977.

11. How will the system perform in regard to each of these vital areas?

                         Security
                         Accuracy
                         Productivity
                         Customer service
                         Information

12. Will my cashiers and other operators feel comfortable with the system?
13. Is the supplier's background retail-oriented?
14. How long has the supplier been in business? How long will he stay in business? What is the supplier's position in the marketplace? Does he commit large sums to research and development?
15. What kind of field technical support does he offer? Are his men where my stores are—capable of response within 24 hours? Or is it just a small task force covering the whole country?
16. What can the supplier teach me and my staff about software? How extensive is his educational program, and does he train at all levels: cashier, head cashier, store manager, district supervisor, middle management?
17. What is the supplier's track record in the industry?
18. Is his capacity truly total? Does it encompass main frames and the ability to interface with foreign main frames? Does the supplier have a data center for smaller retail operations?
19. How do other top executives at other retail companies rate the supplier? Which system have they chosen?[19]

PRODUCT MARKING TECHNOLOGY

Universal product code (UPC)—the food industry

Reducing costs through advances in technology appears to be one way in which the grocery industry can increase profit margins. This is particularly true as population growth continues to slow, with resulting lower food sales and intensified competition. In 1970 the Universal Product Code Ad Hoc Committee was appointed, with representatives from manufacturers, wholesalers, and retailers. The committee recommended that the grocery industry adopt a 12-digit all-numeric universal product code. The code is OCR—font B. It is shown in Figure 11–4.

Thus the food industry developed a code which is compatible with the needs of both manufacturers and retailers. It also accommodates the nonfood items sold by supermarkets. The code excludes price, expiration or manufacturing date, plant location, and other information. It is thus designed to provide a unique identification for each product. It assigns a five-digit manufacturer identification number, and requires that manufacturers assign and register five-digit numbers for each of their products. Retailers can use a modified version of the code to encode their own price information. This is particularly useful for handling non-source-marked packages.

---

[19] "Which System?" *Chain Store Age Executive*, September 1975, p. 136.

FIGURE 11–4
THE UNIVERSAL PRODUCT CODE SYMBOL FOR SUPERMARKETS

Number system
designator

Manufacturer ID

Item ID

Check character
(not in human
readable form)

The committee selected a bar code which is omnidirectionally machine-readable. The bar code is read using laser technology and is in the public domain. All manufacturers are requested to use it.

Approximately 75 percent of all supermarket products are marked with the UPC. Thus these products are ready for electronic checkouts. The use of electronic point-of-service cash registers in supermarkets is a well-established fact; scanning devices which take advantage of the UPC to ensure greater front-end productivity are being tested commercially.

Industry sources estimate that there are now 25,000 terminals in 2,500 supermarkets and that 350 stores will have scanners by the end of 1977, as contrasted to 42 in 1975.[20] The cost of this equipment is rather high, ranging from $80,000 to $120,000 for an eight-lane supermarket equipped with a POS system and scanning devises.[21] Hard data on productivity increases resulting from the use of the scanners are limited. On the basis of limited testing, supermarket executives have reported a 25 percent increase in front-end productivity through the use of scanning. In-store productivity gains are estimated to be in the 35–40 percent range once 80–90 percent of supermarket items are coded for the use of the UPC.[22]

A Marsh supermarket in Troy, Ohio, billed as the first commercial test of UPC scanning, experienced increases in productivity, improved labor scheduling, and a reduction in shrinkage.[23] In the 15 percent of items which

[20] "Scanning Gains More Ground," *Chain Store Age Executive*, February 1977, p. 21.

[21] "When Will Scanning Catch Up with EPOS?" *Chain Store Age Executive*, February 1976, p. 13.

[22] "Scanning Gains More Ground," p. 21.

[23] "UPC Scanner One and One-half Years Later," *Chain Store Age Executive*, February 1976, p. 16.

will probably not be UPC-coded, such as produce, deli, bakery, and store-weighed meat items, the store can use in-store symbol printing or can keyboard the information into the terminal at the checkout counter.

Finally, Giant Foodstores, on the basis of its tests, concluded that point-of-service registers equipped with UPC scanners "could save around $120,000 a year per store. These savings could possibly help stabilize prices, while doubling the stores' operating income to 1.4 percent of sales."[24]

Optical character recognition, font A (OCR–A)—general merchandise retailing

More than 120,000 terminals were in use in 1977 in over 10,000 nonfood establishments. Only 300–400 of these locations employ electronic wand readers. The costs of this equipment for department stores are tremendous. It requires approximately $550,000 to install a total POS system in an 80-register department store.[25]

Nonfood merchants lag behind supermarket management in the use of electronic reading of some type of UPC. Part of the problem is that the NRMA equivalent of the UPC, OCR–font A (an optical character recognition, machine- and human-readable code), is in competition with codes developed by such manufacturers as IBM and NCR. Another major problem is getting vendors to source-mark merchandise. In 1976 only 40 of the 300–400 stores using wands were reading OCR–A.[26] The basics of the OCR–A format are shown in Figure 11–5.

OCR–A was not accepted as the voluntary universal vendor marking (VUVM) system for nonfood retailers until mid-1975. Thus three or four years probably must pass before suppliers incorporate it into their labels.

OCR–A can be printed on price tickets, credit cards, and many other types of retail documents so that the information can be read by customers, retailers, vendors, and others. In talking about the need for a universal vendor marking system, Fred Lazarus, chairman of the board of Shillitos, recently stated the following:

Most retailers, in the past, have had inadequate records except in big ticket merchandise and apparel. Much of our merchandise has not been marked at all. We figured in our division, Shillitos, which does approximately 150 million in volume that it would cost us $250,000 a year to mark all of our merchandise down to style and color and size level. Should this become a part of the normal identification put on by the vendor, and we marked all merchandise with department, class and price—we wouldn't spend any more for marking than we are today. We could have records for everything as complete as our present ready-to-wear records. We could trace the sources of markdowns. We could automatically reorder much of our merchandise and do so more accurately than we do now. We could use the computer to measure our lost sales and tell us how much to reorder on a first reorder in order to avoid the

[24] "In a Fish Bowl," Forbes, December 1, 1975, p. 80.
[25] "When Will Scanning Catch Up with EPOS?" p. 13.
[26] Ibid., p. 14.

FIGURE 11–5
OCR–A FORMAT

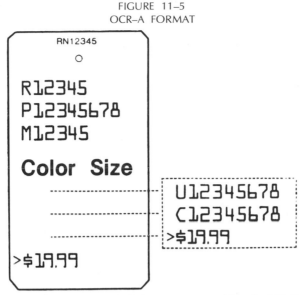

Sample ticket using OCR–A (optical character recognition, font A). From top, code R identifies merchandise class and season; P identifies vendor and style; M identifies color and size; U is a nondescriptive code; C identifies department, class, and season.

NRMA's Voluntary Retail Identification Standard Specification–A–1974 outlines the construction of the function codes as follows:

Function Code R—four numeric digits to identify NRMA's classification of merchandise; one numeric digit to identify the season.

Function Code P—three numeric digits representing the vendor; a five-digit code identifying the garment style.

Function Code M—two numeric digits for the color; three representing the size.

Function Code U—an eight-digit numeric nondescriptive code with the last position representing a modulus "10" check digit.

Function Code C or D—a variable-length field of two to eight numeric digits representing the store department, class, and season.

Function Code $—a five-digit numeric field representing the retail price.

Source: Lance G. Campbell, "SKUs: The Long and Short of It," *Stores* magazine, May 1976 p. 32; © 1976: National Retail Merchants Association.

lost sales between the first and second reorder. We could trace our customers' individual preferences and use this in publicity.[27]

Clearly, premarked merchandise which identifies the manufacturer, style, size, and color will speed merchandise through the retailer's receiving and marking functions. If a more complete merchandise stock record is required, the merchandise could be store-marked with information as to department,

[27] Fred Lazarus III, "Voluntary Universal Vendor Marking," *Retail Control,* March 1976, p. 50.

class, season, and price. However, this could be handled quickly with a small quick-stick.

J. C. Penney has tested the OCR–A system and is pleased with the results. These indicate that wand reading should cut down transaction time by 20 percent and provide a significant improvement in accuracy. Prior to the use of wands, merchandise information was approximately 80 percent accurate, whereas it is now 100 percent accurate on wand-read items.[28]

The producers of business machines and terminals will probably support the UPC and the OCR–A system since their own problems would not be complicated by these systems. Complications are occurring, however, because of decisions which must be made by several groups, including the scanning device manufacturers, vendors who must serve two markets and voluntarily code their merchandise for two different coding systems, and the "double-market retailers," such as the superstores which feature both food and general merchandise. One writer pinpointed the problem as follows: "Source marking of department store merchandise is far in the future. What's OK for the grocery store is inadequate for the department chain. At least 30 stripes will be needed for the necessary information."[29]

One of the major problems is the lack of standardization of coding systems between food and nonfood retailers. As noted above, the supermarket industry has endorsed OCR–B, whereas the National Retail Merchants Association has endorsed OCR–A. The OCR font B is slightly larger than the A font and is therefore a problem for the fixed supermarket scanners. A machine capable of reading both codes would be the answer, but none is commercially available at this time—primarily because of prohibitive costs.

The primary difference between the two segments of retailing is that the general merchandise retailer wants the dollar amount included on the tag. The grocery industry wants the price stored in the computer and marked on the supermarket shelves. The nonfood merchants are using a wand for reading the codes, whereas the supermarkets are using a scanner and a conveyer belt. Discussions are continuing between the two industry segments in an effort to resolve the differences.

In any case, industry standardization in general merchandise retailing is some time off because many of the merchandise wands are still in the demonstration stage and use merchandise codes which are unique to the equipment manufacturer. Thus, the general merchandise retailers will continue to use the fiber optic or magnetic wands for a while longer.

REACTIONS TO SOURCE MARKING

Consumers do not want to have prices removed from individual items. For the UPC program in food retailing to be most cost effective, prices would

---

[28] "Penney Tests Wand System," *Chain Store Age Executive,* February 1976, p. 15; also "General Merchandisers Don't Rush to Wands," *Chain Store Age Executive,* February 1977, p.22.

[29] "Marking Time/Again," *Retail Directions,* May–June 1975, p. 20.

only be displayed on shelves and not on individual items. Groups such as the Consumer Federation of America contend that the new checkout systems will enable grocers to pass higher prices on to unwary consumers. Further, these groups contend that consumers often will not know the price of an item until they have checked out and will be too embarrassed to return the item if its price is higher than the price they wanted to pay. Research on the UPC by the food industry's Public Policy Subcommittee showed that "some shoppers in 'prices off' stores do experience a measurable reduction in price awareness and consciousness."[30]

A test by Marsh supermarkets in Troy, Ohio, found mixed consumer acceptance of UPC and scanning, as noted in Table 11–3. Similar results

TABLE 11–3
CONSUMER REACTION TO UPC SCANNING IN SUPERMARKETS: MARSH
CUSTOMERS SAY SCANNING IS FASTER

How much faster has it made your transactions?		Have you had much trouble finding the prices on the shelves?	
Much faster	53%	Much trouble	20%
Not much faster	34	Some trouble	13
No difference	13	No trouble	60
		Not sure	7
Are you more afraid of errors with this type of system?		**Would the speed influence your decision on where to shop?**	
Yes	6%	Yes	20%
No	94	No	80
Do you object to the absence of price markers on items?		**Would you like to see these systems in more stores?**	
Strongly object	34%	Yes	46%
Object	46	No	34
Don't care	20	Not sure	20

Source: "UPC Scanner 1½ Years Later," *Chain Store Age Executive*, February 1976, p. 16.

were found in general merchandise retailing, as shown in Table 11–4. Approximately 87 percent of the supermarket consumers found that transactions were faster. On the other hand, 80 percent did object somewhat because the price was not marked on each item. Slightly less than half of the consumers wished to see the systems installed in more stores, and 20 percent indicated that speed in checkout would be a factor in determining where they shopped. Annual consumer savings in food stores using wand-read UPC scanning systems are $65–75.[31]

---

[30] "Universal Product Code and Item Pricing," *Focus on the Food Markets*, May 3, 1976, New York State Cooperative Extension Program, p. 2.

[31] John P. Hebert, "UPC Experiment Provokes Little Consumer Reaction," *Computer World*, February 2, 1976, p. 7.

TABLE 11–4
CONSUMER REACTION TO WAND READING IN GENERAL MERCHANDISE RETAILING:
MIDDLETOWN SHOPPERS RATE SCANNING

How much faster has it made your transactions?

Much faster 44%
Not much faster 12
No difference 32
Slower 12

Are you more afraid of errors with this type of system?

Yes 24%
No 72
Not sure 4

Would the speed influence your decision on where to shop?

Yes 24%
No 76

Would you like to see these systems in more stores?

Yes 52%
No 40
Not sure 8

Source: "Penney Tests Wand System," *Chain Store Age Executive*, February 1976, p. 15.

The preparation of consumers and union members for acceptance of the system seems to minimize problems. Steinberg's, one of Canada's largest supermarket chains, installed UPC scanning and eased customers into the system over a two-month period. Initially it used only two automated checkout lanes. Bag stuffers explained the benefits of the system. Customers were—and still are—provided with grease pencils at the entrance to the store to price-mark items if they so chose. They were also allowed to scan some items themselves by the use of a scanning device placed in the back of the store. By the end of the second month, price marking was discontinued with no adverse effects on sales or customer satisfaction. The same type of educational program was followed with unionized employees.[32]

Pressure from the federal government and from consumers now seems to be such as to force the supermarket industry to continue item marking all merchandise. The alternative is federal legislation which would require the industry to place the price on each item.[33]

CREDIT MANAGEMENT AND ELECTRONIC FUNDS TRANSFER (EFT)

Credit authorization can be handled almost automatically by large retailers who handle their own credit, such as Sears or Wards. However, for the smaller retailer, credit authorization is awkward and cumbersome unless some type of credit card is used. Even then, the customer may be over an authorized limit or perhaps using a stolen card. Generally only cash or a

---

[32] Nancy Farench, "Properly Prepare Customers, Employees for Scanning," *Computer World*, November 12, 1975, p. 8.

[33] "Grocers May Head Off Item Pricing Law, but the Cost Will Be Stiff," *Progressive Grocer*, May 1976, p. 40.

check can be used to pay for merchandise in food retailing. Any other method slows the checkout process. All retailers would like to reduce their float—the period of time between the presentation of a check and the debiting of funds to the retailer's account. Both automatic authorization of credit and electronic funds transfer (EFT) from one account to another are possible through an EFT/POS system.

EFT and POS are terms which are often used interchangeably. However, POS typically refers to retail activity, whereas EFT/POS refers to financial activity. To the retailer, point-of-service typically conjures up a vision of an electronic cash register which handles transactions on a sales floor and collects data as part of a financial merchandising system. To the banker, it means a subsystem of an EFT which uses a terminal at the point-of-service for credit authorization, credit card transactions, data capture, check verification, and funds transfer. Such an arrangement would eliminate credit management problems for the retailer.

EFT technology is operational on a limited scale. Glendale Federal Savings and Loan Corporation in southern California allows account customers to make deposits and withdrawals or to cash checks at several supermarkets. These customers can also have the amount of their purchase switched from their personal account to the stores account. On Long Island, Hempstead Bank customers can use their instant transaction cards in numerous stores to transfer funds from their personal account to a merchant's account.[34] Thus, the EFT concept is beginning to invade retail establishments by offering services ranging from check verification to a complete package of services.

The implementation of EFT has been slowed because of the argument that it is really a form of branch banking. The U.S. comptroller of the currency ruled in 1974 that EFT is not branch banking. However, the federal appeals court in Washington, D.C., has ruled that states can forbid the establishment of EFT installations at off-bank locations.[35] The controversy is continuing.

Ideally, if customer needs are to be met, retailers should be part of a network linking all financial institutions instead of being tied to a single institution. Indeed, Hinky Dinky supermarkets, a Nebraska-based food chain, now has full-service funds transfer terminals in many of its stores. Service on the same terminal is available from several savings and loan associations. The desire of the chain is to have access to any financial institution on one terminal.[36]

Other major problems are also impeding the implementation of EFT. For example, the major department stores already have their own credit card and do not want to use a bank's card. In addition, most supermarkets are hesitant to support any financial transaction other than cash or check verification. However, PDQ stores (in the Midwest) and the Buffalo-based Tops and Bells chain, among others, now allow the use of Master Charge in their

[34] "EFT Banking into Clouds," *Chain Store Age Executive,* February 1976, p. 19.

[35] "Key Court Round Is Bad News for EFT in Supers," *Progressive Grocer,* May 1976, p. 19.

[36] "Grocers May Head Off Item Pricing Law," p. 20.

supermarkets. Colonial accepts BankAmericard in its Atlanta-area stores.[37] The overall evidence indicates that EFT is making considerable headway among retailers. The primary gray areas include cost, effect on checkout time, impact on retailer-sponsored credit cards, technology, mandatory sharing of systems, and government regulation.[38] Research by the Food Marketing Institute indicates that the use of electronic funds transfer in supermarkets could lengthen checkout time by as much as 25 percent above the time needed for ordinary check or cash sales.[39]

The large retailers for the most part do not feel that they need banks to help attract customers or to handle retail sales. Bank linkups are most likely to be adopted by the small retailers so that they can compete on more nearly equal terms with the large retailers. Thus, the next generation of bank cards will probably start with the small retailers, as was true of the previous generation of cards. The process will greatly simplify the problem of credit for the small retailer. However, some evidence does exist that department store opposition is also softening.

Until a universal card for use in EFT is developed, the proliferation of terminals will continue. Retailers object to having several terminals linked to different financial institutions. They also fear that through an EFT system the banks will attract the best credit customers and leave the retailer to either finance or refuse credit to the marginal 25 percent of customers.

The benefits of an EFT/POS plan to consumers are numerous. These benefits include automatic payroll deposit, the elimination of delay in receiving a check in the mail and in getting a deposit to the bank, and the elimination of check writing and costs for mailing payments. Also, consumers will obtain greater security because payroll or other checks are not likely to be lost or stolen if an EFT/POS plan is used.

The major problem for the consumer is the loss of float that results from preauthorized payments. Under EFT/POS the transfer of money from the consumer's account to the merchant's account is instantaneous, whereas when the consumer writes a check it may be several days before the bank switches the money from the consumer's account into the merchant's account.[40]

ELECTRONIC INSTALLATIONS

Let's look at the nature of the electronic outlets of the near future. Numerous manufacturers offer equipment which can facilitate the flow of transactions in supermarkets and ensure greater productivity and accuracy. The National Cash Register (NCR) systems are chosen for illustrative pur-

---

[37] "What the Point-of-Sale Revolution Means to Banks," *Banking,* August 1974, p. 34.

[38] "EFT: The Unanswered Questions," *Chain Store Age Executive,* February 1977, p. 19.

[39] "Will EFT Up Checkout Time?" *Chain Store Age Executive,* March 1977, p. 10.

[40] Anthony M. Dilorio, "EFT Today," *Computer Decisions,* March 1976, p. 21.

poses in this part of the chapter. Other systems are currently available which are capable of performing many of the same functions.

The electronic supermarket

The NCR 255 food store system consists of NCR 255 terminals which operate under the control of an NCR 726 controller. The controller is connected to each terminal by a high-speed in-store communications system. The operating system consists of a software package which is developed specifically for retail food stores. Program changes can be made at modest cost to accommodate new requirements. The system also offers modular expandability. Store totals are also intact, as each terminal has stand-alone capability. Program loading is accomplished by the use of magnetic tape cassettes which can be easily handled and stored. The system is illustrated in Figure 11–6.

FIGURE 11–6
CONFIGURATION OF NCR 255 FOOD STORE SYSTEM

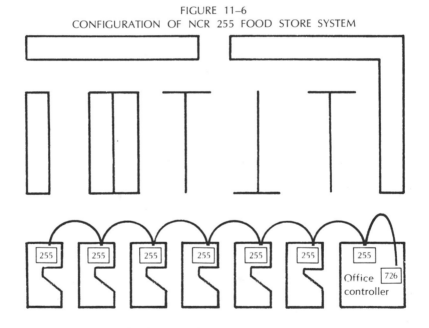

The system offers numerous advantages to the supermarket, including:

Accountability over all in-store funds	Sales analysis reports
Item price lookup ability	Front-end productivity reports
Price changes	Automatic checker balance reports
Product codes	Automatic store balance reports
Sales tracking	Universal product code adaptability
Coupon lookup	Augmented internal security
Check authorization	measures

Issuance of food stamp credits

Automatic computing of food stamp change

Floating cashiers

Automatic stamp computation

Automatic split-package pricing

Net department totals

Automatic food stamp sorting

Separate vendor and store coupon categories

Automatic price and quantity extensions

Billion-dollar accumulating capacity

Automatic computing of trading stamps

Flexibility for individual requirements

Let's focus for a moment on just one specific element of the above system and note the kinds of information which can be developed through the use of this new equipment. In the area of price, the following types of controls are possible:

Test of sales on new items

Track items subject to pilferage

Automatically establish current market prices of fluctuating items at the checkout

Promotional sales items by vendors

Effective shelf display planning

Most effective spots for special displays

Effect of sales items on related items

Pinpoint slow- and fast-moving items

Customer response on coupon items

Positive check on advertising media response

Inventory control of a specific item

To-date sales volume of a specific item

Sales of discounted merchandise

An example of the actual use of the NCR 255 system in the supermarket is illustrated in Case History 1, which was prepared for Publix Supermarkets.

The electronic mass merchandisers

The NCR 255 retail system for mass merchandisers consists of point-of-service terminals which are on-line to an in-store control processor. Sales, merchandise, and accounting information is recorded and transmitted to the processor. The data are then processed, updated, and stored for access when needed for the preparation of reports. Terminals are located wherever customer sales occur or wherever accounting entries must be posted. Data input can occur at checkout lanes, in selling departments, at the service desk, and even in the store office. If more than one store is part of the system, selected summary data from each of the stores can be transmitted by a central processor. Figure 11–7 shows the configuration of the NCR 255 system for mass merchandisers.

For stores which are part of a multiple-store system, data are collected at each store during the day and transmitted after-hours to a central processing

What does a 200-store Florida food chain have in common with a one-store Ohio independent?

Ask Gene Dampier, Construction and Maintenance Director of Publix, and Neil Frank, Owner/Manager of the Shiloh IGA market in Dayton, Ohio.

They'll tell you that the ways they've solved their electronic checkout needs have practically everything in common. The explanation is twofold:

1. Publix and the Shiloh IGA had the same basic objective when they decided to shift to Electronic Checkout (ECO). As Frank of IGA puts it, "We realized we needed better control to get the efficiency and productivity we must have in every department."

2. After intensively researching the problem, both Publix and the Shiloh IGA concluded that one ECO supplier had a clear edge above the rest in systems performance, systems responsibility, and supermarket experience.

The Solution

The solution Dampier of Florida and Frank of Ohio (and their colleagues) each came up with was the NCR 255 system.

Although it was a clear decision, it wasn't a quick one. The two food executives shopped around, asking hard questions every step of the way:

Would the system adapt to UPC scanning with a simple add-on rather than an overhaul?

How much would it cut labor costs, speed up registering and throughput?

Would information be available to the manager at all times without interrupting checker operations?

Would the system generate reports that were high in quality and practical value?

Would it significantly improve sales per man-hour?

Was the company behind the system reliable and genuinely intelligent about the supermarket business?

Dampier and Frank, in other words, each dealt from strength. They used their retailer's know-how to set tough standards for buying a technologically complex product. And they found, in the end, that the supplier with the longest and deepest experience in the food business offered the most sensible technology for food businessmen.

The Benefits

The benefits of an ECO system designed by a food-oriented computer company were quickly apparent at Publix . . . often in an unexpected way. Dampier says, for example, that checkers learn the new terminals so easily that new store openings can now be staffed *entirely* with inexperienced cashiers.

Publix and IGA management constantly receive the reports they need to compete profitably and maximize productivity:

Activity reports to help analyze customer shopping habits and schedule checkers, baggers, and carry-out personnel.

Check reports showing hourly production in dollars.

Store dollar reports summarizing current on-hand accountability of all checkers and the office. It's available at any time during the business day, without interrupting cashier operations.

Weekly checker settlement reports— weekly, because with the 255 only weekly balance is needed (unless a daily balance is desired).

CASE HISTORY 1 *(continued)*

Other operating controls are similarly improved. The system automatically alerts the checker to bad checks; provides high-low controls on every department key; has code lookups for markdowns and weekly specials; and the 255 automatically determines the eligibility of items for tax, food stamps, trading stamps, and coupons.

This, of course, is only a partial listing. It would take a book to detail every feature.

Conclusions

Dampier and Frank feel that the no-nonsense, bottom-line applicability of the 255 system proves that it's *essential* to choose an ECO supplier with a long history in the food industry.

Says Dampier: "We wanted to associate with a company we knew would be there for the future. We like the way we can buy and add to the 255 system as different things are de-

veloped. The adaptability to our operation was one of the leading factors in our selecting NCR. While we went to these terminals in anticipation of UPC scanning, we find that they already justify themselves economically."

Says Frank: "The reports supplied to us by this system throughout the day are invaluable. So is the reliability of the system. The system performance has been outstanding."

facility. Under this system, the NCR 726 processor is placed in an unattended transmission mode and is polled by an NCR 725 multiline receiver or other processing system. Data are then transmitted over regular dial-up telephone lines, as shown in Figure 11–7. An example of the use of the NCR 255 retail system in mass merchandising is illustrated in Case History 2, which was prepared for Gibson's Discount Stores.

FIGURE 11–7
THE USE OF THE NCR 255 RETAIL SYSTEM IN MASS MERCHANDISING
AS ILLUSTRATED BY GIBSON'S DISCOUNT STORES

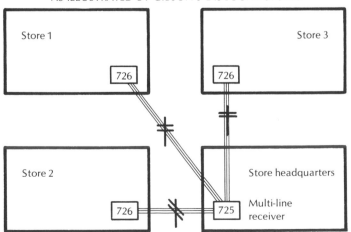

CASE HISTORY 2

Gibson's has long been a superstar of the discount industry. The massive Texas-based operation encompasses 640 company-owned and -franchised stores. The chain's merchandising style has remained true to the basic precepts of discounting: no frills, fast turnover, and heavy promotional artillery. Nevertheless, the chain has been bold to pioneer new applications of mass merchandising. One of these is the hypermarket concept. When Gibson's Discount Centers of Midland, Texas, a franchisee, decided to expand and remodel, management recognized the need for a new level of sophistication in POS equipment for its hypermarket concept.

Gibson Requirements

As Vice President David Hoelscher and Store Manager Ray Boulter tell it, their new expansion plans needed terminals which would permit:

Classification merchandising.

Price lookup capability which would accommodate a particularly wide range of advertised specials.

Full control over checks, charges, and coupons.

Higher sales per man-hour at the front end.

Close monitoring of cashier transactions.

Equipment the checkers would quickly feel comfortable with.

Hourly sales activity reports for personnel scheduling.

Automatic tax calculation.

Automatic food stamp change computation.

Readily available reports on sales data.

The Systems Choice

The Gibson's hypermarket game plan called for a sales breakdown of 14 major departments and 99 categories. The departments are: grocery, meat, produce, H&BA, pharmacy, housewares, hardware, sporting goods, cameras, tobacco, toys, women's wear, men's wear, and shoes. Gibson's began looking for equipment to replace its mechanical cash registers.

After exhaustively surveying the field, it decided that the best replacement was an NCR product—the 255 Mass Retailer System. Its new setup consists of 25 electronic POS terminals and an NCR 726 in-store minicomputer with 32K memory.

Results

In terms of the criteria they established, the two Gibson's executives feel that their choice was decidedly accurate. Their system has a 400-item price lookup file, automatic layaway records, a check authorization file, negative credit authorization, and many other features they sought. What's more, sales per man-hour have increased over 30 percent because of speed, ease of handling, and checker acceptance.

Hoelscher describes the hourly activity report as "invaluable" in efficient cashier scheduling and in getting a clear grasp of what's happening in a given 13-week cycle.

"We're talking about a store of 183 employees, a large store," he says. "We were apprehensive when we introduced the 255 system. But the ten-key is so easy to handle, the girls' acceptance of it was unbelievable. We're actually getting speeds of up to $500 an hour from them.

"And the information I get is absolutely fantastic. For the first time we're able to keep track of each checker's personal ac- countability, because the 255 has floating checker control. The checkers come and go at the various lanes, but all they have to do is take out their trays and move to a new terminal location.

"The end result is that I've got a far stronger mer- chandising arsenal, be- cause I can find out what really does go on during any day or during any hour."

In the complex world of the hypermarket, in- stinct and information are the keys to healthy sur- vival and a rewarding bot- tom line. Gibson's of Mid- land has both.

METRICATION

A chapter on technology would be incomplete without mentioning metri- cation, since a totally metric environment for the United States is inevitable. Multinational companies have long been involved in metrics even though the United States has not yet converted to the system. The rate of world adoption of the metric system has been so rapid that the United States is the only major trading nation officially uncommitted to it.[41]

Domestic consumer products will bear the biggest burdens in this change. Thus, the marketers of consumer goods can do the most to smooth the transition.[42] Effective January 1979, the domestic wine industry, soon to be followed by the liquor industry, will convert to metric packaging. The indus- try consensus is that only 7 package sizes will be offered, down from the current 16.

The simplicity of the metric system is that its units, subunits, and multiples of units for any given physical measure are based on factors of ten or tenths. Thus, one value can be quickly related to another and to the decimalized money systems of most countries in the world today.

Consumers fear that they will be victimized because they do not under- stand the metric system. The business community will have to work hard to overcome this distrust. One of the biggest aids which can be provided by the retailer is to develop, for example, metric portioned recipes for food products and reference guides for the various products which need mixing or measur- ing. Optimistic estimates are that the United States will have converted to metric by 1980. More realistic estimates appear to be 1985–90. The views of the various groups involved in the transition are depicted in Figure 11–8.

[41] "Metric Measures and the Consumer," *FDA Consumer,* December 1975–January 1976, p. 24.

[42] "Eight Steps Domestic Consumer Product Marketers Can Take to Make Metric Changeover 'Big Non-Event,' " *Marketing News,* August 1, 1975, p. 4.

FIGURE 11–8

MANUFACTURERS

Apparel manufacturers are
trying to devise a uniform
metric system of sizing.
Some manufacturers, such
as Levi Strauss, offer
merchandise tags in metric
and nonmetric sizes.

RETAILERS

Such large chains as Sears,
Wards and Penneys have established consumer and manu-
facturer metric informa-
tion centers.

STORE PLANNERS

Designers and store planners
view metrics as a mixed
blessing. Some feel it
will simplify computa-
tions; others are reluc-
tant to "start thinking
in metrics."

CONSUMERS

Consumer groups
strongly oppose metric
conversion, fearful
that packaging will
confuse shoppers.

Source: "Chains Disagree on U.S. Metrics Switch," *Chain Store Age Executive*, March
1976, p. 52.

LONGER RANGE DEVELOPMENTS

The emerging technological developments, other than those discussed in
this chapter, which are likely to have the greatest future impact on retailing
are discussed in greater depth in Chapter 22. However, it might be well at
this point to speculate on the technological impacts of automated retailing.
Can consoles be placed in homes for self-selection of standardized items,
picked by computer-controlled warehouse operations, and delivered to
homes? The energy-saving aspects for display and transportation in this
manner are massive, as are the laborsaving aspects, given consumer acceptance and efficient terminals.

In terms of somewhat longer range developments, experiments in automated retailing with in-store selections from consoles or IBM-type order

sheets are also a probability. Controversy does exist, however, as to whether technology really holds the key for still greater productivity increases in retailing or whether we already have the necessary technology but are not utilizing it to the greatest extent possible.

A virtual certainty is that computer fraud will become increasingly common in retailing. Already, for example, a group of employees at a Pennsylvania department store have used computer terminals to manipulate the records of a furniture store and misappropriate $200,000 in merchandise.[43]

SUMMARY

Three great electromechanical inventions have been applied in retailing. These are the cash register, the computer, and the point-of-service terminal. The new technology has impacts on virtually every aspect of retailing, including merchandise management, buying, pricing, promotion, location, operations, and personnel.

The point-of-service terminal allows all sales data to be captured through the terminals at the source of the sale and to be transmitted over an in-store communications network for entry into a back office system. It can then be recalled for processing and analysis. The resulting data give retailers timely, detailed information which is needed to combat a steady decline of profit margins caused by such factors as lack of inventory control, the rapid growth of credit, rising labor costs, and the proliferation of merchandise.

Keys to the acceptance of point-of-service terminals are the universal product code in the food stores and the OCR–A in general merchandise retailing. These are machine-readable codes which ensure greater productivity and efficiency at the point-of-service. They also allow merchandise to be source-marked by the manufacturer, thus eliminating the less efficient marking of merchandise at the retail level.

The expansion of POS systems and electronic scanners has been rapid. The terminals have been adopted by many different types of retailers, and adoption is approaching the point of saturation among large retailers. Electronic scanning in both food and general merchandising is still in the infancy stage. Problems associated with the EFT concept have not yet been resolved. Essentially this concept would allow for the automatic transfer of funds from the customer's account to that of the store.

Technological advances are likely to be the greatest challenge for retailing during the 1970s and 1980s. Indeed, the fully electronic outlet is a likelihood. The key questions which must always be before us, however, are, do modern computer systems make shopping easier and quicker for the consumer? Can sales be made more quickly and easily through the use of these systems?[44]

---

[43] "More on Computer Frauds," *Retail Control,* vol. 44, April–May 1976, p. 52.

[44] "Today's Fashion Customer," *Retail Directions,* March–April 1975, p. 18.

KEY CONCEPTS

Point-of-service system
Types of POS systems
POS and profitability
Keys in equipment selection
Product marking technology
Universal product code

OCR–B
OCR–A
Source marking
Credit management and POS
Metrication

DISCUSSION QUESTIONS

1. What are the key impacts of the point-of-service systems on retailing?

2. What have been the three major electromechanical advances in retailing?

3. What has allowed point-of-service systems to expand so rapidly in retailing?

4. What are the various types of point-of-service systems in existence for the different segments of retailing?

5. What is the effect of point-of-service systems on retail profitability?

6. What is the status of product marking technology?

7. How have consumers reacted to source marking?

8. How do the point-of-service systems affect credit management for the retailer?

9. How can the retailer best adjust to metric conversion?

PROJECTS

1. Interview the managers of a large department store, a local outlet of a supermarket chain, and a fast-food store. Determine the type of system (electromechanical cash registers, electronic cash registers, or POS) employed in each. How many terminals are there? Are there any plans to change the type of system currently used? Has such a change occurred already? If a store plans to change, to what type of system will it go? Why? What savings are associated with the change?

2. Assume that you are the operations manager for a department store chain located in one region of the country. Your boss has asked you to present to him and the board your evaluation of a POS system for the chain. Prepare a paper detailing the advantages and disadvantages to your company. You are free to use any data in the chapter or in the library.

3. Electronic funds transfer systems (EFTS) are "hot" topics for retail management today. The impetus for this interest is perhaps coming from the banking community. Make contacts with local banks and see what is going on in your area relative to "thinking" and "planning" for the era of EFTS. Has there been any impact yet? What forms have EFTS taken in general? Then go to the retail community and determine the status of retailers' knowledge about the issue. If they are knowledgeable, "pick their brains" about future plans. If they are relatively

naive about the entire situation, attempt to determine for yourself how this can be possible in an era when information is so readily available.

4.   What is the state of technological advances in retailing within your local community? Do a careful survey of the state of adoption of POS systems in the area. Find out from management what equipment is being used, what functions are being performed by the equipment on hand, what plans are being made for expanding the functions of the new technology or for adopting the new technology in any form. Make a summary chart, comparing companies by kind of business and other possible causal factors.

5.   Check in your area on the "state of the art" relative to technology in the specific area of vendor marking (UPC in the grocery trade and OCR–A in general merchandise). What plans for scanning are being made in the stores at this time? If plans are being made, when will implementation be accomplished? What problems are perceived in the scanning process? What uses will be made of the input? Do a convenience sample of customers to see what they know about vendor marking and how they react to the "nonhuman readable" portion of the code in grocery stores. How do they react to the detailed tape received from the new terminals? What general conclusions do you draw from your study?

CASES

Case 1.   After returning home from a recent trip to Europe, Eleanor and Marilyn Grey told their father of the hypermarkets they had seen. "You've never seen a store quite that big," said Eleanor. "They have *everything* you could possibly need—right under one roof," added Marilyn. When they had finished telling him all about it, their father, a wealthy Texas millionaire, decided to investigate the possibility of operating a hypermarket in the United States. He knew that there would be problems, but he figured that these could be resolved. The merchandise he planned to carry ranged from clothing to hardware to sporting goods to groceries. He had lined up suppliers and was about to begin construction of the building. One of his friends from the club contacted him and received an OK on installation of a POS system. The friend pointed out that such a system was a must for a store the size of a hypermarket.

What have Mr. Grey and his friend overlooked? How do you suggest that the problem be solved?

Case 2.   Mrs. J. W. Brown was visiting a major metropolitan city in the East. She was from the Midwest and had a charge card from her "favorite department store" at home, which had an Eastern affiliate. In the past when she visited the Eastern mecca she went to customer services and received a temporary shopping credit card which made it possible for her to be charged directly so that she did not have to carry cash with her. In addition, her major bank credit cards were not accepted, so that the only way she could take advantage of the elegant new gourmet department about which she had heard so much was to work out her usual arrangement.

She went to customer services, took a number from a spindle, and waited 30 minutes while other customers were involved in what appeared to be a series of confrontations with the service representatives. She wondered whether that was what "services" were all about. Finally her number came up and she presented her hometown card. After she had explained to the representative that the store was a member of the same ownership group, the rep disappeared behind a rather dismal-looking partition. After some 20 additional minutes, a temporary card was given to Mrs. Brown. Since it was getting rather late, Mrs. Brown dashed to the men's furnishings department to get her husband a wallet. She found just what she wanted and handed it to the salesperson together with her newly acquired temporary charge card. She was testily informed that the wallet could not be purchased since the store was in the midst of inventory taking and instructions had been given that nothing which had been counted and segregated could be sold. Mrs. Brown was annoyed but anxious to get to the gourmet section, so she left disgruntled but in anticipation of the pleasures to follow.

The visit to the new "shop" was a delight. The assortments of unusual gourmet foods and accessories were up to all expectations. Her cart was brimming with imported Brie, crackers from England, flat bread from Sweden—her hotel room would be a veritable food hall in a few minutes! At the checkout, she anxiously handed her temporary card to the checker—the items were entered in the shiny new POS terminal, and the clicks sounded like music to Mrs. Brown. As the card number was entered into the terminal, a red light flashed, the sale was voided, and the checker rather rudely said to Mrs. Brown, "Move the cart to the side and go up to customer services." Mrs. Brown was horrified and stated that she had no intention of going back to customer services since she had just come from there. The line behind her was growing, and the checker became rather adamant about the procedure. Mrs. Brown said that she wanted to see a management representative. The checker said that she was too busy to look for one, so Mrs. Brown asked the checker to call credit and see what was wrong. The checker very angrily picked up the store phone, dialed a number, and quickly slammed down the receiver. She said that she had been told that if a sale were voided, as Mrs. Brown's had been, the only recourse was to go to customer service. "Next customer, please," the checker said.

Mrs. Brown looked around the department for someone with an identifying tag which indicated that the person was "official." She finally found a young floor manager who was very pleasant, but after Mrs. Brown had calmly related her story, the floor manager said, "The only thing you can do is go to customer services and find out what is wrong. Credit won't answer me any better than they did the checker. 'I'm sorry, but that's the way the system works since we went on the 'new computer.' " Mrs. Brown was furious. She asked the store representative if there were not some higher authority to whom they could appeal. She was assured that nothing more could be done.

Normally, Mrs. Brown would have walked out of the store, never to return. Instead, because of the potential pleasures sitting against the far wall in an unattended cart, Mrs. Brown made the long trip to customer services. After taking her second number and waiting her 30 minutes, she got the same surly service representative who seemed never to have seen her before. She explained the occurrences of the past hour or so; the service representative again disappeared into the "back room," came out a short time later, and without a word of apology told Mrs. Brown, "Well, it was very simple. Someone, and it wasn't me, forgot to 'put your new number into the system,' so when you tried to charge, the sale was automatically voided. I don't know why you came back here! Why didn't you call credit?"

Analyze the above situation and see how many errors were caused by technology, misunderstanding, and lack of customer orientation. What should the floor representative have done? If you were the operating vice president of the store, what would you do if Mrs. Brown had got to you? What do you think Mrs. Brown did immediately after the last encounter, and what do you think she did subsequently?

PART FIVE

THE RETAILING
STRATEGY VARIABLES:
THE RETAILING MIX

W e suggest a review of the framework (in Chapter 1) at this time since the following chapters comprise the essential "managerial" focus of this text and include much of the nuts and bolts of a course in retailing management. We have introduced you to the general subject matter and provided you with its philosophic underpinnings, that is, the retailing management concept in Part One. Part Two included the structural components facing retailers as they accomplish their objectives; as the framework review indicates, these chapters focused on institutional and organizational structure. Crucial to the entire philosophy of this text is the customer orientation. The customers and markets were detailed in Part Three. Part Four examined the forces external to the organization. In that part we saw the myriad of impacts on the managers' decisions.

The following nine chapters provide the strategy components and take up matters which are faced daily by retail management in adjusting to the forces described in the chapters on the environments of retailing. As a consequence, the chapters in this part are heavy on "how to do it" and are the most pragmatic portion of this text. They are designed to provide the "nuts and bolts" of managing a retail business.

12

THE PRODUCT VARIABLE: MERCHANDISE MANAGEMENT

Planning the width and support of assortments
  Model stock
  Width plan
  Support plan
  Fashion goods
  Staple goods
  The act of planning
Unit control
  Perpetual
  Nonperpetual

There are many approaches to merchandise management. Good merchants are those who know when to gamble—to maximize sales. And just as important—when to recognize mistakes and correct them immediately by making the necessary decisions to accomplish the corrections.

This chapter will give you a broad outline of how to plan, how to buy, and how to project sales fairly accurately. A major thing it will tell you is that there is a method called "markdowns" to correct buying mistakes. Fear of markdowns has kept many potentially good merchandisers from being "top-flight." Use your six-month plans as a guide—a road map to get where you wish to go—but don't be afraid to get off the highway when necessary to get around the mistakes that are obstacles on your road to success.

Louis A. Baum, President
B. Siegel Company
Detroit, Michigan

The role of merchandise management is to ensure that the consumer receives the right merchandise at the right place, at the right time, in the right quantities, and at the right price. The four "rights" in addition to the merchandise "right" are the basic justification of retailing. As noted by the president of Burdines, Miami, Florida: "The strength of department store buying and merchandising lies in its sensitivity to its customers and its ability to be highly flexible—both in its approach to its customers and its approach to its suppliers."[1] Thus, the purposes of this chapter are:

1. To familiarize students with the key concepts utilized in the management of the merchandising function.
2. To illustrate the key components of the merchandise plan and of merchandise management.
3. To introduce students to the control function of merchandise management.

ESSENTIAL TERMS

A product is simply a tangible object, service, or idea, such as a suit of clothes or a suit-cleaning service. The product line consists of all the products or services offered by a retail organization.

Product lines are typically defined in terms of "variety" and "assortment." *Variety* refers to the different kinds of goods which may be present in a product line such as food. This product line may include such diverse products as bread, canned tomatoes, frozen peas, cheese, and so on. No natural relationship necessarily exists among the items. *Assortment* means the range of choices available for any given item in a product line. For example, bread may consist of a wide assortment of choices in terms of brands, size of package, and type of flour.

Let's look at an example of the common usage of these terms in retailing. A men's tie shop, for example, offers a single product line (ties) as well as a single variety, but the assortments may be extensive in terms of the elements of fashion.

The major focus of this chapter is the merchandise planning and control function. The function includes all of the activities that are carried on to plan and to maintain a balance between inventories and sales. Figure 12–1 presents a flowchart of the merchandise management process which provides a *total* framework for this section. We are primarily concerned with assortment planning and control. Figure 12–2 presents a schematic diagram of the assortment planning and control process which is the specific framework for the following discussion.

---

[1] Presentation to the New York Society of Security Analysts, November 21, 1974, p. 9.

FIGURE 12–1
FLOWCHART OF THE MERCHANDISE MANAGEMENT PROCESS

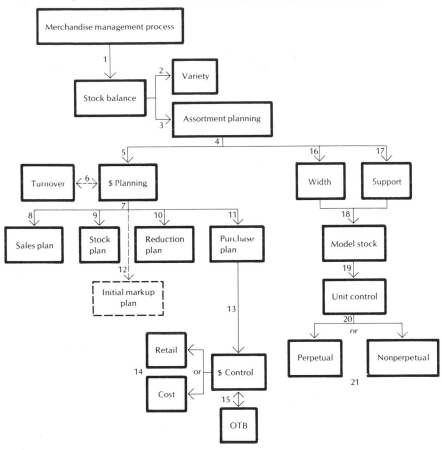

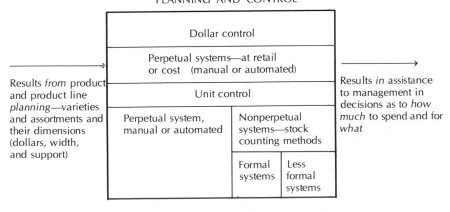

STOCK BALANCE

A critical decision is the extent of merchandise variety which a store will offer. As an example, assume that a men's store carries all of the components of a men's product line except shoes. Physical space limitations may have precluded the merchant from offering shoes. If shoes had been offered, then space would have been taken from another variety, such as men's furnishings. Thus, assortments of existing merchandise varieties would have been decreased. This might have affected customer attraction features, store image, and return on investment. Management decisions about variety thus directly affect assortment planning. Variety and assortment must be considered as joint decisions in merchandise planning.

Let's consider three cases which illustrate the importance of the merchandise mix and of good records in inventory planning. Top management of Robert Hall, a clothing chain, in its efforts to revitalize stated that the "biggest problem was the merchandise and the merchandise mix. . . . There was too much tailored clothing—suits and coats. There was a lack of infant's and children's wear, of leisure wear in the men's area, of jeans and tops for the younger people."[2]

Likewise, when new management came to Bonwit Teller, it began continuously evaluating "the classifications of the goods on all the shelves and making sure the stores carry each category in a wide range of prices. . . . In addition to weekly selling reports, each store now has to produce detailed reports on merchandise classifications, selling margins, and markdowns every six months."[3]

Difficulty with inventories was one of the problems which contributed to the failure of W. T. Grant. As has been noted, "Further complicating the inventory problem was Grant's lack of a sales classification system to indicate what specific items were selling. 'We relied on total store figures. . . . No one knew what was selling, and the buyers did not have any guidance as to what to promote.' "[4]

The merchandise investment must be balanced with expected sales. This is difficult because of the complicated, changing, and fickle environmental conditions which affect customer acceptance of the store's offerings. It must be done with careful attention to *planning* and *control*—the key components of merchandise management and the only means of maintaining healthy stock balance. One of the difficulties of City Stores, whose Lit Brothers 11-unit department store division was closed after a $19.5 million loss, was that it didn't "develop store-for-store merchandising strategies. . . . as City Stores began doing poorly, the divisions became more promotional in their merchandising without fully considering the effects on each store's reputation. They had a low comprehension of how to sell off-price goods. They compli-

---

[2] "The Major Alterations at United Merchants," *Business Week,* October 4, 1976, p. 29.

[3] "Bonwit's Turns Up the Heat," *Business Week,* October 11, 1976, p. 120.

[4] "Investigating the Collapse of W. T. Grant," *Business Week,* July 19, 1976, p. 60.

cated inventories with a lot of goods that had no value after the sale and which blurred the store's image."[5]

Ways to look at stock balance

The retailer may look at merchandise assortments in three ways. Each of the dimensions suggests different planning processes. To add concreteness to the discussion, let's assume that we are planning for the men's sport shirt classification in the furnishings department of a department store.[6] The three perspectives from which we can look at our stock balance are: (1) width, (2) support, and (3) dollars.

Width. Width of merchandise assortments refers to the assortment factors necessary to meet the demands of the market and to meet competition. Decisions must be made on the numbers of brands, sizes, colors, and the like. In our hypothetical classification for shirts, the following might be a planning process in terms of width:

Brand	3 Sku's
	×
Sizes (small, medium, large and X-large)	4 = 12 Sku's
	×
Prices	2 = 24 Sku's
	×
Colors	3 = 72 Sku's
	×
Fabric (knit, woven)	2 = 144 Sku's

Thus, we see that 144 stock-keeping units (Sku's) are necessary to meet customers wants and the offerings of competition.

Support. The next natural question is, How many units of merchandise do we need to *support* our expected sales of each assortment factor? This decision must be based on expectations of the sales importance of each of the assortment factors. To illustrate, "How many small shirts, in Brand A, at $10.95, in yellow knit do I expect to sell?" Such decisions as this involve the "art" of merchandising. Knowledge of the consumer market, the segment appealed to, the image of the store and/or the department, and other factors all enter into this subjective decision. Only actual experience in planning the composition of stock will give you any confidence in this activity.

Dollars. Middle management is heavily involved in planning the width and support dimensions of stock balance. Let us assume that all of the factors affecting width and support have been considered and that the buyer has decided that a total of 1,000 shirts is needed for model stock. This number, however, has no necessary relationship to the dollars which top manage-

---

[5] "Why the Pressure Is Still on City Stores," *Business Week*, April 25, 1977, p. 94.

[6] The men's furnishings department would include all shirts, ties, underwear, and so on. The planning can be in terms of classifications, subdepartmental units, or a small department. But for illustrative purposes, we will look at the sport shirt classification only.

ment will allow to be invested in the stock. Thus the total dollar investment in inventory is the final way to view stock balance. Management must strive for a merchandise turnover which is fast enough to provide an adequate return and yet not so fast that frequent out-of-stocks occur.

Merchandise turnover

Merchandise (or stock) turnover is a productivity ratio which is defined as the number of times average inventory[7] is sold annually (the normal period for which turnover is computed). It is typically computed by dividing dollar sales by the average dollar retail inventory (or the cost of goods sold[8] by the average inventory at cost), for example:

$$\frac{\text{Merchandise}}{\text{turnover}} = \frac{\text{Sales} \qquad (\$100,000)}{\text{Average inventory in retail dollars} \quad (\$25,000)} = 4$$

or

$$\frac{\text{Merchandise}}{\text{turnover}} = \frac{\text{Cost of sales} \qquad (\$60,000)}{\text{Average inventory in cost dollars} \quad (\$15,000)} = 4$$

Only through planning on the basis of homogeneous merchandise groupings (classifications or dissections) can turnover goals be meaningful. Planning on the basis of large, diverse groupings is unsound. Today, technology allows classification merchandise planning and thus provides, among other aids, better turnover information as a guide to dollar planning. Until recently Marshall Field department stores did not follow this method, and this failure contributed at least in part to their problem of shrinking profits. "In the past . . . each floor manager in each store was in charge of buying, pricing, displaying, and selling all the products on his floor. This merchandising method was abandoned years ago by most retailers. Now, . . . separate merchandise managers are in charge of different product groups, such as sportswear, boutique apparel, junior clothing, and women's shoes."[9]

It is impossible to say whether a particular turnover figure is good or bad;

---

[7] The average inventory is derived by adding together all the available inventory figures and dividing by the number of counts included. If a small retailer takes a fiscal inventory in January and a midyear inventory in July, for example, three inventory figures are used to compute an average (the January inventory at the beginning of the year, the July inventory; and the January inventory at the end of the year). The more inventories available, of course, the more accurate or representative in the "average." Stores maintaining perpetual or book inventories have monthly inventory figures for deriving the average inventory component of the turnover formula.

[8] Cost of goods sold is the cost value of the goods which move out of stock and is computed as follows: Beginning inventory + Purchases + Transportation charges = total cost dollars available for the sale − Ending inventory = Cost of goods sold. (In simple terms we determine what we had available and subtract from that what we had left to give us the dollars which moved out.)

[9] "Why Profits Shrink at a Grand Old Name," *Business Week*, April 11, 1977, p. 66.

TABLE 12–1
AVERAGE STOCK TURNOVER RATES FOR
VARIOUS BUSINESSES

Kind of business	Annual rates
Bars and taverns	13.7
Camera and photographic supplies	3.2
Confectioneries	13.8
Florists	11.5
Hardware	2.3
Grocery stores	11.8
Men's wear	2.7
Family shoe stores	1.8
Toys	3.0

Source: Adapted from R. Ted Will and Ronald W. Hasty, *Retailing: A Mid-Management Approach.* Copyright © 1973 by R. Ted Will and Ronald W. Hasty (Canfield Press Book). Reprinted by permission of Harper & Row, Publishers, Inc.

or whether a particular ratio is efficient or not. Table 12–1 indicates average stock-turnover rates for various businesses. It is apparent from the table that turnover goals must be based on the nature of the operation and that a "raw" turnover figure is virtually meaningless.

Returning to our men's sport shirt example, Table 12–2 shows turnover information for that classification and indicates the variance which can occur even within a narrow merchandise grouping.

TABLE 12–2
1975 INVENTORY TURNOVER BY MERCHANDISE CLASSIFICATION

Classification	All firms		Firms handling men's wear only		Firms handling women's wear	
	Range of common experience	Median firm	Range of common experience	Median firm	Range of common experience	Median firm
Men's sportswear sport shirts	2.60–4.00	3.45	2.57–4.14	3.30	2.65–3.68	3.54

Source: *1975 Menswear Retailers of America Annual Business Survey,* Men's Store Operating Experiences, 47th Annual Report by the Financial and Operations Group, Washington, D.C., p. 35.

Let us suppose that our firm is handling men's wear only and that our turnover goal is 3.30, the median for all firms of that type. Our operating results indicate that for the year our turnover was 2.57, the lowest figure in the range of common experience. After improvement in stock levels in relation to sales, we manage to improve our turnover the following year and to achieve the planned 3.30 turnover rate. This higher turnover rate alone does not mean a great deal. Real improvement occurs only when the improvement in turnover reflects a better profit performance.

Gross margin return on inventory investment (GMROI)

The consequence of this logic focuses the perceptive merchant's attention on a philosophy of merchandise management which puts the concept of merchandise turnover into a proper perspective and gives a sound direction to planning.

Gross margin return on inventory investment (GMROI)[10] can be stated as:

$$\text{GMROI} = \frac{\text{Gross margin dollars}}{\text{Average inventory investment}}$$

This single ratio does not indicate clearly the focus which we want to emphasize—that of the important relationship between profit return (margin) and sales–to–retail stock (turnover). Consequently it is more useful to express GMROI as the product of gross margin as a percent of sales and of the sales-to-average-retail-inventory ratio (turnover):[11]

$$\frac{\text{GMROI}}{\text{(Retail)}} = \frac{\text{Gross margin dollars}}{\text{Total sales}} \times \frac{\text{Total sales}}{\text{Average inventory investment}}$$

The value of the turnover and margin components of the GMROI concept can be seen in Table 12–3, where three different types of hypothetical retail classifications each produce the same GMROI with differing gross margin percents and turnover components.

TABLE 12–3
EXAMPLES OF DIFFERING CLASSIFICATIONS, MARGINS, AND
TURNOVERS RESULTING IN IDENTICAL GMROI

Type of store	Gross margin percent	× Turnover ratio =	GMROI percent (retail)
Discount store sport shirt classification	25.0	4.0	100.0
Specialty store sport shirt classification	40.0	2.5	100.0
Department store sport shirt classification	33.3	3.0	100.0

---

[10] The return on investment criterion has been suggested as an effective means of planning and controlling retailing operations, but substantial problems have existed over the years in determining "return" and "investment." When the planning is used exclusively for merchandising inventory investment, the average or EOM value of inventory as the investment component and gross margin dollars representing "return" provide unambiguous and easily measured variables. See Daniel J. Sweeney, "Improving the Profitability of Retail Merchandising Decisions," *Journal of Marketing,* vol. 37 (January 1973), pp. 60–68.

[11] Gross margin return on retail inventory is not, strictly speaking, a measure of return on *investment,* but since many retail managers with a planning focus maintain a retail book inventory figure perpetually, retail value GMROI can be calculated more frequently using the more common and more easily obtainable turnover component. (Sales-to-cost inventory ratios are more accurately described as ROI ratios.) In this discussion, however, the value of utilizing retail GMROI outweighs the slight inaccuracy of terminology. For a further discussion of the point, see Daniel J. Sweeney, "Improving the Profitability of Retail Merchandising Decisions."

The above illustration indicates the impact that turnover and margin planning has on the return on each dollar invested in inventory. Just for illustrative purposes, let's keep the gross margins constant at 40.0 percent and change only the sales-to-retail-stock (turnover) ratios, as in Table 12–4.

TABLE 12–4
EXAMPLES OF IMPACTS IN THOSE CLASSIFICATIONS
WITH CONSTANT GROSS MARGINS AND VARYING
TURNOVER RATES

Type of classification	Gross margin percent	Turnover ratio	GMROI percent
A	40.0	4.0	160.0
B	40.0	2.5	100.0
C	40.0	3.0	120.0

This hypothetical illustration dramatically indicates how turnover can affect profitability and stresses the importance of turnover goals in the total merchandise planning process. Store A in Table 12–4 emphasizes relatively higher turnover with a turnover rate of four times, and achieves a 160 GMROI. The four turns mean that for every dollar invested in inventory, $4 of sales are generated; the 40 percent gross margin says that of each dollar of sales, 40 cents is available to cover operating expenses and profit (see Chapter 14); and the 160 percent GMROI indicates that for each dollar invested in merchandise inventory, $1.60 is generated in gross margin.

Table 12–3 shows that management can focus on either turnover or gross margin in strategic planning to accomplish the identical GMROI results. It is not possible in a survey course to illustrate all of the strategy alternatives available within the GMROI concept. The student must, however, appreciate the importance of turnover to the entire process. The significance of gross margin is dealt with in more detail in Chapter 14).

To provide a complete perspective for the merchandise management process, we believe it is critical, particularly with the growing importance of financial strategy as a part of total competitive strategy, to introduce the reader to the strategic profit model (or total profitability model). GMROI is placed within the total model so that the student can see how critical merchandise management is as a part of total profitability planning. We also stress the importance of this emphasis within our retailing management concept, introduced in Chapter 1, wherein profitability is a key component of the philosophy of the text.

The strategic profit model

As shown in Figure 12–3, the strategic profit model combines the principal elements of a company's operating statement and balance sheet (see the

FIGURE 12–3
THE STRATEGIC PROFIT MODEL

$$\frac{\text{Net profit}}{\text{margin}} \times \frac{\text{Rate of}}{\text{asset}} = \frac{\text{Rate of}}{\text{return on}} \times \frac{\text{Leverage}}{\text{ratio}} = \frac{\text{Rate of}}{\text{return on}}$$
$$\text{turnover} \quad \text{(ROA)} \quad \text{(RONW)}$$

$$\frac{\text{Net profits}}{\text{Net sales}} \times \frac{\text{Net sales}}{\text{Total assets}} = \frac{\text{Net profits}}{\text{Total assets}} \times \frac{\text{Total assets}}{\text{Net worth}} = \frac{\text{Net profits}}{\text{Net worth}}$$

Measures amount of net profit produced by each dollar of sales	Measures dollars of sales volume produced by each dollar invested in total assets of business	Measure for managers of return on *all* funds invested in business by both owners and creditors	Dollars of total assets that can be acquired or supported for each dollar of owners' investment	Measure of profitability for owners who have provided net worth funds

Source: Based on ideas contained in: William Davidson, Alton Doody, and Daniel Sweeney, *Retailing Management,* 4th ed. (New York: The Ronald Press Co., 1975), pp. 127–28; and Bert C. McCammon, Jr., and Robert F. Lusch, "The New Economics of Hardware/Home Center Retailing: A Financial Profile of 17 Leading Hardware/Home Center Companies," *Hardware Retailing,* October 1976, p. 74.

following chapter for complete descriptions of these statements) into a single profit planning equation.[12]

The strategic profit model, in addition to providing the student with perspective for this section of merchandise management, also serves three significant purposes for the retailer:[13]

1. It specifies that a firm's *principal* financial objective is to earn an adequate or target rate of return-on-net-worth.
2. It identifies the three profit paths in a business: that is, a firm can improve its rate of return-on-net-worth by increasing its profit margin, by raising its rate of asset turnover or by leveraging[14] its operation more highly.
3. It dramatizes the principal areas of decision-making in the firm, namely margin management, asset management and financial policy or leverage management. Firms effectively interrelating their margin, asset and financial policy decisions may be described as high performance companies.

The strategic profit model also provides a basis for analyzing the financial strategies of different organizations. Consider, for example, the following comparison between Payless Cashways and Standard Brands Paint [see Figure 12–4].

---

[12] Bert C. McCammon, Jr., and Robert F. Lusch, "The New Economics of Hardware/Home Center Retailing: A Financial Profile of 17 Leading Hardware/Home Center Companies," *Hardware Retailing,* October 1976, p. 73.

[13] Ibid.

[14] "Leveraging" means that by borrowing some capital either from a bank or from suppliers in the form of trade credit, a retailer can acquire assets worth more than the amount of capital invested by owners.

FIGURE 12–4
STRATEGIC PROFIT MODELS FOR TWO
HIGH-PERFORMANCE HARDWARE/HOME
CENTER RETAILERS

A. Payless Cashways, Inc.

$$\frac{\text{Net profits}}{\text{Net sales}} \times \frac{\text{Net sales}}{\text{Total assets}} = \frac{\text{Net profits}}{\text{Total assets}} \times \frac{\text{Total assets}}{\text{Net worth}} = \frac{\text{Net profits}}{\text{Net worth}}$$

$$3.9\% \qquad 2.1\times \qquad 8.2\% \qquad 2.1\times \qquad 16.7\%$$

B. Standard Brands Paint Company

$$\frac{\text{Net profits}}{\text{Net sales}} \times \frac{\text{Net sales}}{\text{Total assets}} = \frac{\text{Net profits}}{\text{Total assets}} \times \frac{\text{Total assets}}{\text{Net worth}} = \frac{\text{Net profits}}{\text{Net worth}}$$

$$7.7\% \qquad 1.9\times \qquad 14.3\% \qquad 1.3\times \qquad 17.8\%$$

The strategic profit model may not multiply to the totals indicated because of rounding.

Source: Bert C. McCammon, Jr., and Robert F. Lusch, "The New Economics of Hardware/Home Center Retailing; A Financial Profile of 17 Leading Hardware/Home Center Companies," *Hardware Retailing*, October 1976, p. 76.

Both companies achieved excellent results, despite the fact that their financial strategies were different.

Payless Cashways, a leading home center chain in the Midwest, generated a profit margin of 3.9% of sales, and a rate of asset turnover of 2.1 times, while operating on a leverage ratio of 2.1. These ratios, when multiplied through, produced a rate of return-on-net-worth of 16.7%.

Standard Brands Paint, a leading operator of home decorating supermarkets, achieved similar results . . . a rate of return-on-net-worth of 17.8% . . . on a profit margin of 7.7% of sales, a rate of asset turnover of 1.9 times, and a leverage ratio of *only* 1.3.

So that the student can see even more clearly the relationship between the planning of turnover rates (essential to planning total investment in inventories which is one of the essential dimensions of stock balance), GMROI, and the strategic profit model, a "fan-out" of the total assets component of the model is presented in Figure 12–5.

Total assets are very important to our discussion; consequently, by indicating that total assets comprise fixed and current assets and that inventory is a current asset item, we can then focus on inventory as the unambiguous and easily measured "investment" component of the GMROI concept. GMROI provides a goal against which to measure a retailer's "performance in using the major asset under his control, merchandise inventories, to generate a merchandising profit stream, gross profit dollars."[15]

Finally, the relationship between turnover ratios, GMROI, and the strategic profit model can be seen most clearly when it is admitted that GMROI percent, one of whose two components is turnover, offers perhaps

[15] Sweeney, "Improving the Profitability of Retail Merchandising Decisions," p. 62.

FIGURE 12-5
A PRESENTATION OF THE COMPONENTS OF THE TOTAL ASSETS
COMPONENT OF THE STRATEGIC PROFIT MODEL

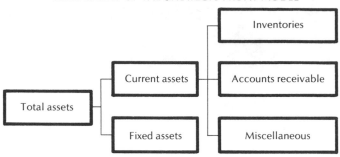

the most effective starting point for merchandising toward predetermined goals. A departmental or classification GMROI must be consistent with the general financial objective of the entire organization, and consequently the merchandiser can define the gross margin goals and turnover ratios which will produce the planned GMROI. Planned sales-to-inventory ratios (turnover) can be applied to planned monthly sales to produce beginning of month (BOM) inventory plans in accordance with the plans for the merchandise budget. The merchant can then "develop a complete merchandise budget based on a single unambiguous performance objective, a target rate of gross margin return on inventory investment."[16]

PLANNING INVESTMENT IN MERCHANDISE

As indicated in Figure 12-2, assortment planning and control begins with product and product line (merchandise) planning. The focus in this section is thus on planning from the total dollar perspective of stock balance. Subsequent sections take up the planning of the width and support components of stock balance.

The merchandise budget

Figure 12-6 is a schematic diagram of the components to be planned in the merchandise budget. Let us continue to use our sport shirt classification in this discussion to illustrate the actual implementation of a budget process.

Sales planning

By season. The beginning point in the merchandise budget is a sales plan. As noted in Figure 12-6, two kinds of information exist upon which the

---

[16] Ibid.

FIGURE 12–6
SCHEMATIC DIAGRAM OF THE MERCHANDISE BUDGET

| | Components to be budgeted | | | | | |
| | Sales | | | Reductions | | |
	Season	Month	Stock	Season	Month	Purchases
Concrete information available for planning						
Judgment must be applied in certain issues (environmental factors)						

merchandiser can base the forecasts for each component. The first consists of concrete information which the planner has available. Let's assume that the budget under consideration is for the spring season (February, March, April, May, June, and July) of 1978 and that the planning time frame is 60–90 days prior to the beginning of the season.

The starting point is last year's statistics for the same period, that is, the sales for the spring of 1977. Let's assume that the sales were $50,000. At this point too many retailers merely project the same sales volume as that obtained for the preceding year. To force thoughtful reflection, recent trends in sales should also be considered. For example, suppose that sales during the current fall season have been increasing over sales during the prior fall season at approximately 4 percent per month. Such a trend might well be expected to continue. If the company is a member of a trade association or has access to information from a university's economic and business research center, the company's sales trend can be compared with external statistics which reflect average performances. Assuming that our 4 percent increase looks reasonable in comparison with trade facts, we would project a spring 1978 sales figure of $52,000.

The budget process, however, cannot stop here, since factors other than internal and regional sales trends can affect our planning. Consequently, the merchandise planner must use expert judgment in evaluating environmental conditions which might affect sales in the planning period. Let us assume the following conditions: a new men's store is opening across the street and will carry competitive shirts; the new store is a part of a large chain of fine men's stores, and it has the latest in POS equipment and thus instant information for decision making; our store is in an area dominated by a particular industry whose union contracts are coming up for renegotiation, with a strike expected; and finally sport shirts are a major item in the fashion forecasts because of the increasing trends toward leisure wear. In addition to the external environmental issues cited, let us also assume that our store is contemplating moving the sport shirt classification from a less desirable location to a major traffic aisle near the main entrance.

It is impossible to quantify each of the above factors, but it is essential that each be considered for its potential impact on the forecast sales. In this case, let's say that the positive factors offset the negative factors and that we will go with the planned $52,000 for the season.

By month.   We must now plan the sales which have been forecast for the season by months. Our factual starting point is the sales percentages for 1977 on a month-by-month basis. It is also wise to check those percentages against the trade figures to see whether something unusual has been occurring in the store. For example, we might find from regional figures that May is the most important month in the season whereas our performance has been rather poor in that month. Such a finding would suggest planning adjustments or at least a situation which should be "flagged" for concern. Let's assume that our sport shirt sales distribution for the spring of 1977 was: February—10 percent; March—10 percent; April—25 percent; May—15 percent; June—30 percent; and July—10 percent. Based on the above monthly distribution, the season's sales plan would look like that shown in Table 12–5.

TABLE 12–5
FALL SALES PLAN, 1978

Month	Percent of total season's business in 1977	×	Season sales forecast	=	Planned sales for months of 1978 season
February	10%		$52,000		$ 5,200
March	10		52,000		5,200
April	25		52,000		13,000
May	15		52,000		7,800
June	30		52,000		15,600
July	10		52,000		5,200
Total	100%				$52,000

Referring again to Figure 12–6, we must consider any environmental factors which might suggest that our 1978 monthly distribution would differ from that of 1977. One consideration which might make a difference is that Easter fell on April 10 in 1977, whereas it falls on March 26 in 1978. The sport shirt classifiction would not be appreciably affected by the change in date, but if this were ladies' fashion merchandise, a late Easter would give a longer selling season for spring merchandise and would consequently affect our sales distribution. Let's assume that after consideration of the change in the date of Easter we decided to continue with the prior distribution.

The number of selling days per month can also affect the sales distribution by month. Monday is typically a big sale day because of Sunday advertising. The month of May 1977 had five Mondays, whereas May 1978 has only four Mondays. Such a factor could appreciably affect distribution relationships and must be considered.

To simplify our illustration, let's assume that after all pertinent factors are considered, we will stick to the monthly sales forecast indicated above. We are now ready to consider planning our stocks to support the planned sales.

Stock planning

Stock-sales ratios—average for the year. Tying in with the GMROI concept, planned average BOM stock-sales goals can be calculated directly from the goal sales–to–retail stock ratios (turnover) which we have previously defined as a component of the target GMROI. For illustrative purposes, let's refer to Table 12–4, Classification B, with a target turnover rate of 2.5. If the annual turnover rate is divided into the number of months in a year, an average BOM stock-sales ratio for the year can be computed (for example, $12 \div 2.5 = 4.8$; 4.8 is the average stock-sales ratio for the year, which becomes a goal for the budget period).

Stock-sales ratios—monthly. Monthly stock-sales ratios are valuable planning aids in stock planning because they relate inventories at the first of a month to the sales of that month and thus are more useful than average turnover figures for planning purposes. A retailer can use stock-sales ratios based on past performance or, (if the system is just being set up) trade data. Even if the store possesses information on its own past performance, trade statistics should be checked for comparison purposes. Sources of trade statistics include various publications of the Federal Reserve banks and trade associations. Tables 12–6 and 12–7 provide monthly stock-sales ratios of the

TABLE 12–6
BEGINNING OF THE MONTH STOCK-SALES RATIOS* BY EACH MONTH FOR
DEPARTMENT AND SPECIALTY STORES IN SPECIFIED SIZE CATEGORIES
(for fiscal year ended January 1976)

	Department stores					Specialty stores		
	Under $1 million†	$1–5 million	$5–10 million	$10–20 million†	Over $20 million	Under $1 million	$1–5 million	Over $5 million†
February	8.27	5.77	5.70	6.00	5.00	5.68	4.42	6.51
March	6.93	5.02	4.47	4.68	4.00	4.86	3.49	5.19
April	7.48	5.28	5.02	4.74	4.14	5.82	3.60	5.72
May	7.34	5.23	4.64	4.05	4.03	5.34	3.64	5.30
June	6.44	4.29	4.42	4.68	3.92	6.26	4.20	3.75
July	6.02	4.94	4.49	5.07	4.54	5.82	4.20	4.86
August	5.79	4.72	4.13	4.43	4.06	4.74	3.77	4.71
September	6.55	4.47	4.40	4.33	3.88	5.94	3.78	3.91
October	6.41	5.01	4.27	4.31	4.44	6.78	3.19	4.45
November	6.43	4.38	3.80	4.26	3.58	6.09	3.64	4.52
December	3.70	2.62	2.05	2.60	1.95	2.98	2.20	2.37
January	7.37	6.52	4.92	5.70	5.35	6.07	4.24	4.06

* Median figures.
† Less than ten stores.
Source: *Department and Specialty Store Merchandising and Operating Results of 1975* (New York: Financial Executives Division, National Retail Merchants Association, 1976), p. xix.

TABLE 12–7
BEGINNING OF THE MONTH STOCK-SALES RATIOS FOR 1975*

	All firms: Distribution of sales by month (119 firms)		All firms: Beginning of the month stock-sales ratio (79 firms)		Firms handling men's wear only Distribution of sales by month (85 firms)		Firms handling men's wear only Beginning of the month stock-sales ratio (54 firms)		Firms handling women's wear Distribution of sales by month (34 firms)		Firms handling women's wear Beginning of the month stock-sales ratio (25 firms)	
	Range of common experience	Median firm	Range of common experience	Median firm	Range of common experience	Median firm	Range of common experience	Median firm	Range of common experience	Median firm	Range of common experience	Median firm
January	6.3– 9.0%	7.6%	5.4– 7.9%	6.4%	6.2– 9.1%	7.7%	5.4– 8.8%	6.8%	6.6– 8.8%	7.4%	5.2– 6.6%	5.9%
February	4.6– 6.3	5.2	6.6–11.9	9.4	4.6– 6.1	5.2	7.6–12.4	9.8	4.7– 6.6	5.2	5.6–10.9	7.6
March	5.5– 7.1	6.3	6.5–11.0	8.4	5.4– 7.0	6.3	6.8–11.7	8.8	5.6– 7.4	6.2	5.6– 9.9	7.0
April	5.9– 7.2	6.5	6.9–10.9	8.6	6.2– 7.3	6.6	7.1–10.9	8.7	5.8– 6.8	6.2	6.5–10.7	7.7
May	7.3– 8.9	8.1	5.8– 8.8	8.8	7.4– 9.1	8.2	5.9– 9.3	7.3	7.2– 8.3	7.7	5.1– 7.7	6.6
June	7.3– 8.9	8.1	5.7– 8.5	6.8	7.3– 9.0	8.3	5.7– 9.0	7.2	7.2– 8.4	7.8	5.5– 7.9	6.3
July	6.8– 8.4	7.4	5.8– 9.2	6.9	6.4– 8.4	7.3	5.9– 9.3	7.7	7.0– 8.2	7.8	5.2– 7.1	6.2
August	6.0– 8.3	7.0	5.2– 9.3	7.4	5.8– 8.0	6.8	5.5–10.3	8.0	6.7– 9.2	7.8	4.6– 8.4	6.2
September	6.2– 8.3	7.2	5.3–10.0	8.0	6.1– 7.9	7.0	5.6–11.3	8.6	6.6– 8.7	7.5	5.0– 9.4	6.8
October	7.5– 8.8	8.1	5.7– 9.2	7.4	7.5– 8.8	8.2	6.1– 9.8	7.8	7.6– 8.8	8.0	5.2– 8.6	6.2
November	8.4–10.2	9.1	5.6– 7.9	6.9	8.4–10.6	9.3	5.9– 8.4	7.2	8.3– 9.8	8.7	4.7– 7.6	6.2
December	15.6–19.2	17.6	2.8– 4.4	3.6	15.4–19.0	17.7	2.8– 4.7	3.7	15.8–19.4	17.6	2.4– 3.8	3.2
Total		100.0%				100.0%				100.0%		

* The ratio of retail stock at the beginning of the month to sales for the month.
Source: *Menswear Retailers of America Annual Business Survey* (Washington: Financial and Operations Group, 1976), p. 38.

National Retail Merchants Association and the Menswear Retailers of America, respectively. Unusually high stock-sales ratios may be the result of stock buildup in anticipation of a major selling season, or it may be caused by limited opportunities in certain months.

Continuing with our sport shirt classification, we have already planned our sales and stock-sales ratios (see Table 12–8), which we can assume are

TABLE 12–8

Month	Planned sales	×	Stock-sales ratio	=	Planned BOM stocks
February	$ 5,200		9.8		$ 50,960
March	5,200		9.8		50,960
April	13,000		8.8		114,400
May	7,800		8.7		67,860
June	15,600		7.3		113,880
July	5,200		7.2		37,440
Total	$52,000				$435,500

derived from historical records and trade association data.[17] Using February as an example, with planned sales of $5,200 and a 9.8 stock-sales ratio, we calculate the planned BOM stock level of $50,960 for that month (5,200 × 9.8). Each month of the period is calculated similarly.

The planner next needs to check the effectiveness of the preliminary planning. At this point the turnover goal comes into play. Let's assume that a turnover goal of two was the target. In the above plan, the average inventory is $75,583 ($435,000 ÷ 6); thus the spring season's turnover with the planned figures is 0.72 ($52,000 ÷ $75,583). Expressed in annual terms, the turnover is 1.4 (0.72 × 2). At this point the retailer will see that the turnover figure is unsatisfactory. A rethinking of some of the planned stock-sales ratios may be undertaken, or perhaps some of the planned sales may be reconsidered, in adjusting the figures to reach the two turns which are desired.

The stock-sales ratio method is easy to apply and is appropriate under conditions where the turnover goal is realistic, stock-sales ratios are available, and planning inventories are appropriately done on a monthly basis. Such data are more likely to be available in a large multi-unit organization than in small, separate outlets.

The weeks' supply method. The weeks' supply method can be utilized in classification where it is advisable to plan for a supply that will cover sales for certain number of weeks. This method is appropriate, for example, in a staple grocery department. Let's assume that approximately ten turns per year are desired; thus, the stock should equal about five weeks' supply (52 ÷ 10 = 5.2). The retailer would then purchase enough inventory to cover

---

[17] In fact, the stock-sales ratios utilized in Figure 12–8 are median results from the 1975 annual survey of the Menswear Retailers of America and are utilized here to give reality to the example.

5.2 weeks of sales at the beginning of the first week of the season. The method is most useful for businesses with relatively stable sales. Operations with peaks and valleys within seasons are advised to use stock-sales methodology.

Reduction planning

The logic of planning reductions is that as the dollar value of inventory levels is reduced, the beginning of the month (BOM) stock planned to support a certain sales level is inadequate unless adjustments are made ahead of time. Thus, reductions must be built into the planned purchases formula so that anticipated reduction dollars are recognized in bringing the BOM stock to the proper level. Referring to Table 12–8, let's look at the February planned stock of $24,440 to support the planned shirt sales of $5,200. Suppose that during the month of January, markdowns in the amount of $3,000 were taken; if these dollars had not been replaced in inventory, the end of the month inventory (EOM) in January, which is the same as the BOM for February, would be $21,440, which is inadequate to do the merchandising job necessary to achieve the forecast sales.

The starting point for the planning of reductions is to look again at last year's performance for the spring season and to compare that performance with any available trade data. Next, the retailer must look at any factors in the environment which might affect the spring reductions. Such things as prior season carry-overs, price decreases at the wholesale level which may affect retail prices in the future, or any other variables which might affect reduction decisions must be recognized. Employee discounts are quite predictable and should also be considered as a planned reduction since when an employee receives a 20 percent discount on purchases, a $10 sport shirt will have only an $8 inventory value. Shortages have similar impacts and must be planned. The impact of reductions is discussed in further detail in the following chapter.

To conclude our illustration, let's assume that markdowns for the spring season in the sport shirt department are planned at 8 percent, or $4,160 ($52,000 × 0.08). Table 12–9 illustrates the monthly reductions which are planned on this basis because purchases are most often planned by the

TABLE 12–9

Month	Planned sales	Planned reduction	Amount of reduction
February	$ 5,200	30%	$1,248
March	5,200	—	—
April	13,000	—	—
May	7,800	—	—
June	15,600	30	1,248
July	5,200	40	1,664
	$52,000	100%	$4,160

month and reductions (that is, markdowns, employee discounts, and shortage) vary appreciably by month.[18]

Planned purchases

After sales, stocks, and reductions have been planned, the computation of the planned amount of dollars for purchases is routine and does not involve judgmental decisions, as do the other items in the budget process. The calculation of planned purchases follows naturally from the foregoing discussion of the planning process. In essence, planned purchases can be viewed as follows:

We *need* dollars of purchases to ──→ Make sure that we have enough retail EOM inventory to "be in business" the following month
Make sure that we have enough to cover our sales plan and
Take care of our planned reductions

and

We *have* dollars to contribute to the above needs in the form of ──→ Retail BOM inventory

Stated more concretely, planned purchases = planned EOM + planned sales + planned reductions − planned BOM inventory. Referring to Tables 12–8 and 12–9 in our sport shirt illustration, we can compute the planned purchases for February as follows:

Planned purchases = $50,960 (EOM February or BOM March at retail)
  +   5,200 (sales—February)
  +   1,248 (reductions—February)
  = $57,408 (dollars needed)
  −   50,960 (BOM February at retail)
  = $ 6,448

As we complete the dollar merchandise budget, it is appropriate to refer to Figure 12–2 and realize that we have set up our dollar requirements only—we have planned our dollar perspective of stock balance. Logically we now proceed to the control aspect of the dollars just planned. (See Figure 12–7 for a typical six-month merchandising plan which incorporates all of the factors just discussed.)

---

[18] In actual budgeting, the retailer would plan initial markups at this point. Such planning is essential prior to actual purchase of the merchandise. The reason we prefer not to discuss the details here is that such markup planning has no direct effect on planned purchases. Consequently we discuss markup planning in Chapter 14 as a part of the pricing component of the retailing mix. The planning involves considerations of the retail price which will be necessary to provide the retail firm with enough dollars to ·cover merchandise costs, expenses, and reductions, and to afford a profit.

FIGURE 12–7
SIX-MONTH MERCHANDISING PLAN

SIX-MONTH MERCHANDISING PLAN	Department name_____ Department no._____							
	·		PLAN (this year)			ACTUAL (last year)		
	Stock turnover							
	Workroom costs							
	Etc.							
SPRING 19—	FEB.	MAR.	APR.	MAY	JUNE	JULY	SEASON TOTAL
FALL 19—	AUG.	SEP.	OCT.	NOV.	DEC.	JAN.	
SALES	Last year							
	Plan							
	Percent of increase							
	Revised							
	Actual							
RETAIL STOCK (BOM)	Last year							
	Plan							
	Revised							
	Actual							
MARKDOWNS	Last year							
	Plan (dollars)							
	Plan (percent)							
	Revised							
	Actual							
RETAIL PURCHASES	Last year							
	Plan							
	Revised							
	Actual							
PERCENT OF INITIAL MARK-ON	Last year							
	Plan							
	Revised							
	Actual							
Comments								
Merchandise manager_____ Buyer_____								
Controller_____								

Source: *Retail Store System: Inventory Management Concepts,* International Business Machines Corporation, 1973, p. 35. Courtesy of International Business Machines Corporation.

DOLLAR CONTROL

Open-to-buy

Without a control process, planning is an exercise in futility. The planned purchase illustration just reviewed is a natural point of departure to an introduction of the subject of controls.

At the beginning of February, the buyer has a planned purchase figure of $6,448. In retailing, a process known as open-to-buy (OTB) exists to "control" the merchant's utilization of the planned purchase amount. At the beginning of the month, assuming no commitments against the planned purchase amount, OTB and planned purchases are identical. In the sport shirt classification, by February 10 the manager has ordered and received merchandise in the amount of $1,500 at retail and has placed merchandise orders for $500 which have not yet been received (these are "open orders"). At this point in time, the OTB is $4,448. By February 20, all of the OTB has been used up; in fact, the general merchandise manager informs our manager that he has "overcommitted" to the amount of $600—the situation is called "overbought" and is not a good position to be in.

The control system known as OTB must be used only as a guide in decisions and must not be allowed to actually dictate decisions to the merchant. A merchant, however, always wants to have OTB to take advantage of unique market situations. The system must also allow for budget adjustments. If the buyer needs more OTB for whatever purpose, management must be convinced. This can be done by: (1) convincing management of the importance of a contemplated purchase and thus obtaining a budget increase in planned sales which will give more OTB because of the way the system is programmed; (2) increasing the planned reductions or taking more markdowns than have been budgeted; or (3) increasing the planned EOM inventory because of anticipation of an upswing in the market. Each of these is a legitimate merchandising option and indicates that the OTB control system is flexible, as any budget control system must be.

All of the prior discussions of planning and OTB have been in retail dollars. The retailer who goes into the market with $6,448 must be aware that these are retail dollars and as such must be converted to cost dollars by applying the average cost complement to the retail amount (see the following chapter for further discussion on this topic). The inputs for OTB come from the perpetual book inventory system, which is essential if a firm employs dollar control. A perpetual book inventory system allows the merchant to know at all times the amount of ending inventory. Such a system may be maintained at retail or cost. Retail is more common because of the difficulties of maintaining a cost book inventory. Figure 12–8 illustrates a "back office" perpetual system with notations as to where each entry on the control statement came from.

Figure 12–8 indicates the typical items which are necessary to have a dollar control system perpetually maintained at retail. It is clear that the information on the statement (which should not be confused with the accounting statements discussed in the subsequent chapter) provides all that is needed to maintain an OTB system—namely, BOM and EOM inventories, sales, and reductions. (Markdowns, employee discounts, and shortages are included as retail reductions and are planned. See Chapter 14.)

FIGURE 12–8
BOOK INVENTORY—SPORT SHIRT CLASSIFICATION
FOR THE MONTH OF FEBRUARY

			Data obtained from:
Beginning inventory plus additions		$50,960	(EOM January audited inventory
Purchases	6,448		(Purchase records or invoices)
Less returns	(448)		(Vendor return records)
Net purchases		6,000	
Transfers in	1,000		(Interstore transfer forms in a
Less transfers out	(500)		multistore organization)*
Net transfers in		500	
Additional markups		1,000	(Price change forms)
Total additions		7,500	
Total available		58,460	
Deductions from stock			
Gross sales	5,400		(Daily sales reports)
Less customer returns	(200)		(Return forms)
Net sales		5,200	
Gross markdowns	2,000		(Price change forms at beginnin
Less markdown	(752)		of a sale)
Cancellations			(Price change cancellations at end of sale to bring back to regular price)
Net markdowns		1,248	
Employee discounts		200	(Form completed at time of sale
Total deductions		6,648	
EOM inventory (including shortages)		$51,812	

* A transfer *in* within a multifirm organization is handled like a purchase. Store A ships goods to Store B, where sales are more likely. A transfer *out* is like a purchase return.

Physical inventory

The only way that the shortage figure can be determined is by taking a physical inventory and comparing the physical inventory figure with the book figure obtained from the dollar control records. For example, assume that when a physical inventory is taken the on-hand count is $24,000 rather than the $24,292 which our perpetual figures say we should have. This indicates that we have experienced a shortage of $292; depending upon expectations as to *shortages,* this figure may or may not be alarming to management. If, on the other hand, the inventory is physically determined to be $25,292, then the retail classification has incurred an *overage.* In retailing such a situation is almost always due to clerical errors or miscounts, and would seldom have any meaningful implications for management.

The perpetual dollar control data may be either maintained manually or automated. The advantages of automated systems have been explored in

Chapter 11, and there is little doubt that technology will allow such systems to be operated with efficiency. The anticipated widespread acceptance of the point-of-service systems within which dollar control can be easily accommodated will also allow for quicker decisions than has been possible heretofore.

Whether maintained manually or by automation, retail book inventory systems can easily be extended to become retail accounting systems for determining company profits. (Chapter 13 makes this point clear and explains in some detail the retail method of accounting).

Cost dollar control

A perpetual dollar control system maintained at cost is less often found in retailing than one maintained at retail because of the major problem of "costing" each sale to build into the system. The same process illustrated in Table 12–5 is followed in a cost book inventory, except that no price changes are necessary. As indicated, instead of recording sales at retail, sales must be directly recorded at cost. Table 12–10 illustrates the kind of back

TABLE 12–10
DIRECT COST INVENTORY

Date	BOM inventory	Costs of receipts	Cost of items sold	Net change
February 1	$15,000	$1,500	$1,000	+$ 500
February 2	15,500	—	2,000	− 2,000
February 3	13,500	400	1,200	− 800
February 4	12,700	.	.	.
.	.	.	.	.
.	.	.	.	.
.	.	.	.	.

office information which would be necessary to maintain a perpetual inventory at cost.

Since the burden of costing each sale is great in many retail situations, it is reasonable to have a cost book inventory only under conditions when the burden is lessened, such as when the merchandise is of an unusually high unit value and there are relatively few transactions. A typical cost inventory situation exists in big-ticket classifications such as furniture or automobiles. Our sport shirt illustration would not be ideal for a cost book inventory.

PLANNING THE WIDTH AND SUPPORT OF ASSORTMENTS

Again referring to Figure 12–2, we have discussed the planning and control perspective of our dollar investment in merchandise. In other words, we have asked, "How much do we have to spend for stock?" and we have continually accounted for the amount remaining so as to maintain proper balance between stocks and planned sales.

We now ask the question, what do we want to spend our dollars for, and in what amounts?

Model stock

Returning to our sport shirt classification, we must set up a model stock which reflects the assortment plan that is our best prediction of the assortment factors which will satisfy our market.

For illustrative purposes, let's look at a sport shirt stock plan. Much judgment, inquiry, and fashion knowledge goes into setting up such a plan, and our illustration is not presented as an ideal sport shirt plan—it is merely for textbook illustration.

Width plan

Figure 12–9 is a simplified model stock representation of the classification. We are assuming that for the foreseeable future only two basic customer-attracting features are important, namely, that a customer will not take a knit shirt if a cut and sewn one is desired.[19] We are further assuming only four sizes (rather than collar and sleeve sizes, which would greatly complicate the problem). In addition, we are not bringing in any fashion designs other than solids and/or prints and we are assuming only four fashion colors (this number could easily be doubled). Lastly, we are not discussing brands—we can assume that either each price point is a separate brand or that we are carrying only one brand of cut and sewn sport shirts (and knit as well) with three qualities or price points.

Even in this simple example, it can be quickly calculated that to offer our customers only *one* shirt in each assortment width factor (in both knits and cut and sewn), we would need 384 shirts ($2 \times 4 \times 2 \times 2 \times 4 \times 3$).

Support plan

Our next problem is to decide on the support needed by each of the designated assortment factors. An ever-impacting parameter is the investment in stock (for example, February, $50,960), which is being planned simultaneously. Our support decision is based on the relative importance of each factor to the total sport shirt classification. Let us assume, as indicated in Figure 12–9, that cut and sewn shirts account for 60 percent of sales. Let us also assume that our average shirt retails at approximately $12. This means that we can invest in about 4,200 shirts for February stock ($50,960 ÷ $12) and that 60 percent, or 2,520, will be cut and sewn. Of those, 252 will be

---

[19] Knit shirts are constructed by a continuous-thread process, and cut and sewn are woven fabrics cut in patterns and sewn into a shirt.

FIGURE 12–9
MODEL STOCK—SPORT SHIRTS

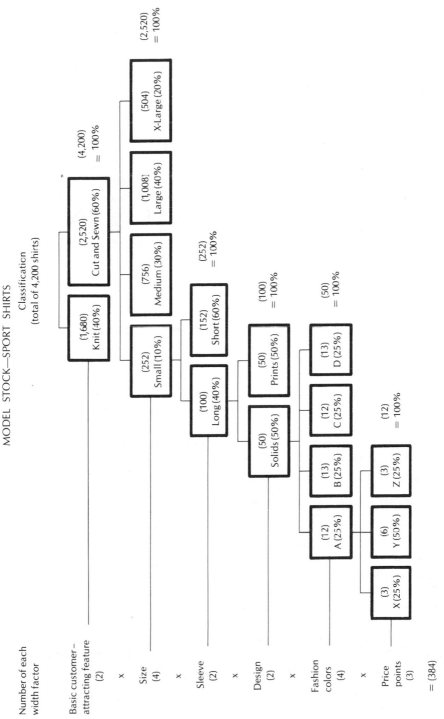

* Note: The percentage in each factor is the expected importance of that component. Numbers represent the percent share of the 4,200 total; for example, 60 percent × 4,200 = 2,520, 10 percent × 2,520 = 252, and so on.

small (10 percent); 100 will be long sleeves (40 percent); 50 will be solids; 12 will be in fashion color A (25 percent); and 6 will be at price point Y (50 percent).

Fashion goods

Classifications which have a fashion dimension, such as sport shirts, require a constantly changing model stock plan. Specific colors, fabrics, and styles may exist in the plan (for example, Figure 12–9 expanded) for one season only. In fashion goods, buying must often be accomplished well in advance of scheduled delivery. Consequently, a great deal of experience, intuition, and expertise is necessary to decide what proportion of the season's planned purchases should be dedicated to early commitments for assortment support.

Staple goods

Planning proper support for staple merchandise differs from planning support for fashion goods. Let's assume that we are planning the support for the canned vegetable classification in a supermarket. In such a plan it is necessary to have on hand and/or on order enough cans to cover the *review period* (the time that elapses between two "reviews" of an item to determine whether an order should be placed) and the *delivery period* (the time that elapses between the ordering and the receipt of merchandise). In actuality, of course, it is impossible to predict with absolute accuracy either the expected sales or the delivery period for the most predictable of items. Thus, it is necessary to add a *safety stock* to the basic stock necessary to cover sales and the delivery period.[20]

The act of planning

The foregoing illustration of the formulations of width and support (model stock in units) appears to be a rather routine approach to planning. In fact, the decisions as to the percentage relationships among the various assortment factors are based on many complex considerations relating to the "art" of retailing. Obviously in planning the assortment width factors, the entire merchandising philosophy of a particular store assumes critical importance. The factors would be significantly different for the sport shirt classification in a unit of Neiman-Marcus as compared with the sport shirt classification in a K mart outlet. The merchandiser in Neiman-Marcus would consider the most unusual styles and fashion colors. Also, the Neiman-Marcus price

---

[20] See William Davidson, Alton Doody, and Daniel Sweeney, *Retailing Management*, 4th ed. (New York: The Ronald Press Co., 1975), pp. 328–32 for a detailed discussion of operating stock levels with illustrations of computations of safety stock requirements.

points would greatly exceed those of K mart. In other words, the total image the store wishes to project affects decisions on width factors and the relative importance of each factor. Certainly the target market of the store as determined from customer analysis affects planning decisions. Environmental conditions during the particular planning period will also affect the width factors. For example, as technological advances in textile fibers allowed more vibrant color-fast materials to enter the men's wear industry, the widths of offering were expanded. The technological advances were, of course, a response to changing life-styles which dictated a more fashion-conscious male market for sportswear in general—the increased amounts of time devoted to such activities as tennis and golf, for example, were reflected in sportswear offerings.

Monitoring of the environment and the targeted customer is essential if the merchant is to do a proper job of planning the width and support of merchandise classifications. It must be stressed that percentages and numbers such as those given in Figure 12–9 are determined by a most complex and dynamic mix of variables of the kind alluded to in the foregoing discussion. The excitement and "crystal ball" aspects of merchandise management are always present and always complement the financial elements of planning and control.

Because of the artistic and creative nature of merchandising, the immense variability among differing types of merchandise classifications, and—primarily—the virtual impossibility of "teaching" the art of merchandising, we have focused on the "how to" rather than the "what" and "why." Experience is the only teacher here. Our major concern at this point is that you appreciate how the financial and the creative aspects of merchandise planning relate.

UNIT CONTROL

The final element of merchandise management to be discussed (see Figure 12–2) is the control of units planned. From the point of view of data complexity, unit control is simpler than dollar control. The factors which affect the number of units in stock are fewer than those which affect dollar investment. The major difference between the two types of control is price change. Since price changes do not affect units; thus the concept of unit control is less complicated.

As Figure 12–2 indicates, there are basically two types of unit control methods: (1) perpetual and (2) nonperpetual, or stock counting.

Perpetual

Perpetual unit control, like perpetual dollar control, is a book inventory. If you look at Figure 12–8, in which we illustrated dollar book inventory for our sport shirt classification, you have the basic framework for unit control.

As noted, the difference is in the fact that fewer items affect the unit investment.

Figure 12–10 continues the sport shirt illustration and shows a comparable February unit book inventory figure, which essentially reflects the dollar

FIGURE 12–10
PERPETUAL UNIT CONTROL DATA: SPORT SHIRT CLASSIFICATION
FOR THE MONTH OF FEBRUARY

BOM—inventory—units			2,000
Plus additions			
Purchases	500		
Less returns	(80)		
Net purchases		420	
Transfer in	83		
Transfer out	(40)		
Net transfer in		43	
Total additions			463
Total units handled			2,463
Deductions from stock—units			
Gross sales............................	450		
Less customer returns	17		
Net sales		433	
Total deductions			433
EOM inventory (including shortages)			2,030

operating results represented in Figure 12–8. Again, the ending inventory includes shortages which can be determined only by a physical inventory.

A perpetual book inventory for unit control is the most sophisticated of the systems in use. Since perpetual book systems demand continuous recording of additions and deductions from stock, they are expensive to operate and must be supported by a great deal of paperwork. The new technology (especially the point-of-service systems—see Chapter 11) offers great potential savings in cost and time, but there are also operational problems which must be worked out before unit control can be efficiently executed from the point of sale. The easiest and most efficient way to collect data is from a coded ticket affixed to the merchandise. The automated systems in which unit data are collected for control purposes involve manually inputting the control number into the POS terminal.

Where perpetual systems are maintained manually, it is likely that because of the high cost of recording the merchandise, the benefits derived may be outweighed by the costs associated with operating such a system. In a manual system, the information on sales can be written on sales checks and entered in a back office procedure; can be handled from stubs which are detached from the item sold (see Figure 12–11); or can be accommodated by deducting from a floor sample as items are sold.

FIGURE 12–11

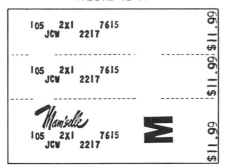

A three-part, punched ticket from which unit control information can be obtained. When the item is sold, one part of the three goes into a receptacle for later analysis. If the item is returned, there are still two parts of the ticket remaining so that the garment can be placed back into stock. Such an arrangement saves on marking and remarking costs.

Legend for notations on ticket:
a. 105   Product line (for example, blouse)
b. 2X1   Cost code (the store is operating on a cost accounting system)
c. 7615 Date of receipt of item
d. JCW   Code for manufacturer
e. 2217 Style number of item
f. M   Size "medium"—the ticket is also color-coded for ease in identification of size (for example, yellow is size "medium")

Nonperpetual

The nonperpetual systems consist of methods whereby the merchandise is formally or informally counted. These systems are obviously compromises by management, since a perpetual system is always more effective and current. The cost of perpetual systems dictates the use of another format—thus, the nonperpetual systems.

Formal systems. Formal nonperpetual systems involve a planned model stock, a periodic counting schedule, and definite, assigned responsibility for counting. In our sport shirt classification, we can assume that every item in stock is counted once a month, that the classification is broken down into knits and cut and sewns (Figure 12–9), and that the knits are counted on the first Tuesday of each month and the cut and sewns on the first Wednesday. Based on the stock on hand, the stock on order, and the stock sold, the buyer will place a reorder as the information is reviewed each count period. Figure 12–12 illustrates a type of count sheet that the salesperson in the department might utilize for counting and that the buyer can analyze to place the necessary order. The merchandiser must, of course, know the seasonality of the item and any other variables which must be considered before an order is placed.

A less formal system. Some types of merchandise, particularly where there is immediate delivery and no need to account for "on order amounts,"

FIGURE 12–12
FORMAL UNIT CONTROL COUNT SHEET

Department <u>Mens' Furnishings</u> Classification <u>Sport Shirts</u> Stock Number <u>5530</u>
Item Description <u>Short sleeve sport shirt</u>   Color <u>Blue</u>   Size <u>Medium</u>
Design <u>Print</u>   Cost <u>$7.20</u>   Retail <u>$12.00</u>   Vendor Number_____
Miscellaneous_____

Date of
Count_____On Hand_____On Order_____Received_____Sold_____

can be quite adequately controlled by a less formal system than the periodic counting method just illustrated. However, it is still important to have a planned model stock, a specific time for visually inspecting the merchandise, and an assigned responsibility for checking the stock. Under this less formal system there will be a certain shelf level or stockroom level below which the merchandise must not go. When the stock reaches that level, a reorder is placed. In a grocery classification of a supermarket, it is quite conceivable that this type of system will work.

SUMMARY

This chapter has focused on the product variable of the retailing management mix and has dealt with merchandise management; specifically, with merchandise planning and control, which includes all of the activities that are carried on to maintain a balance between inventories and sales. The control aspects of this chapter present a natural springboard from which we shall dive into the accounting effectiveness of our merchandising activities.

KEY CONCEPTS

Product
Product line
Variety
Assortment
Stock balance
  Width
  Support
  Total dollar investment
Merchandise turnover
Classifications or directions

Gross margin return on inventory investment (GMROI)

Strategic profit model
  Net profit margin
  Rate of asset turnover
  Rate of return on assets (ROA)
  Leverage ratio
  Rate of return on net worth (RONW)

Merchandise budget
  Sales plan
  Stock plan
    Stock-sales ratios
    Weeks' supply method
  Reduction plan
  Planned purchases

Open-to-buy

Physical and book inventories—dollars and units

Shortages and overages

DISCUSSION QUESTIONS

1. Place merchandise management within the teaching framework. Explain merchandising.

2. Distinguish among product, product line, variety, and assortment. Give specific examples of their interrelationships by selecting illustrations not included in the text.

3. Explain the relationship between management decisions about variety and assortment planning. Use a real example to illustrate this relationship.

4. Explain in detail the schematic diagram for assortment planning and control. Discuss all the perspectives of stock balance and the relevant factors which must be considered.

5. Discuss your reactions to the following statement made by the manager of a large men's and women's apparel store: "I am very pleased that my store had a 3.8 turnover rate for 1978."

6. Describe the logical relationship between merchandise turnover and GMROI; or explain how turnover planning impacts on the total merchandise planning process.

7. Describe the strategic profit model, and explain its value to retail management and students of retailing alike.

8. Explain the relationship between turnover, GMROI, and the strategic profit model.

9. Explain how planned average BOM stock-sales goals can be calculated from turnover goals.

10. Explain the logic of the merchandise budget format utilized in the text. Describe

the total process of dollar budgeting, including all the factors that should be considered in each element of the budget.

11. Why are stock-sales ratios better for planning BOM inventories than turnover ratios would be? How do turnover ratios relate to stock planning?

12. Why should reductions be planned? Can you give any argument against reduction planning?

13. Explain the reciprocal relationship between dollar planning and control.

14. Explain OTB. How can a buyer who is "overbought" make adjustments to get more OTB? Why should a retailer always attempt to have OTB available?

15. Distinguish between shortages and overages. How are these determined? What are their likely causes?

16. Explain why retail dollar control is more common than systems maintained at cost.

17. What is a model stock? Illustrate width and support considerations in a classification of your choice.

18. Explain why unit control is simpler than dollar control. Distinguish between perpetual and nonperpetual systems.

PROBLEMS

1. If net sales for the season are $640,000 and the average monthly retail stock on hand for the season is $350,000, what is the stock turnover rate?

2. Given the following figures, what is the stock turnover rate for the season?

	Retail stock on hand	Monthly net sales
Opening inventory	$342,000	
End of 1st month	339,000	$135,000
End of 2d month	345,000	127,400
End of 3d month	336,000	131,900
End of 4th month	328,000	128,700
End of 5th month	305,000	114,000
End of 6th month	294,000	106,500

3. If the average inventory at cost is $20,000 and the cost of goods sold is $100,000, what is the stock turnover rate?

4. What is the rate of stock turnover if the average inventory at cost is $15,000, net sales are $100,000, and the markup on retail is 40 percent?

5. What is the average stock if the stock turnover rate is three and net sales are $90,000?

6. A new store shows the following figures for its first three months of operation: net sales, $32,000; average retail stock, $64,000. If business continues at the same rate, what will the stock turn be for the year?

7. The merchandising executive in a retailing organization is continually thinking in terms of stock turnover rates. The following problems are illustrative of matters that receive frequent attention. Calculate the answers to the following problems:

	Given	Find
a.	Average inventory at cost, $20,000; cost of goods sold, $85,000	Rate of stock turn
b.	Average inventory at retail, $60,000; net sales, $280,000	Rate of stock turn
c.	Average inventory at cost, $30,000; net sales, $200,000; gross margin as percentage of sales, 25 percent	Rate of stock turn
d.	Stock turnover, 5; average inventory at retail, $140,000	Sales
e.	Stock turnover, 4; net sales volume, $160,000	Average retail stock

8. Last year a certain department had net sales of $60,000 and a stock turnover rate of five. A turnover rate of six is desired for the year ahead. If sales volume remains the same, how much must the average inventory be reduced in dollar amount and in percentage?

9. A hardware store has net sales for the year of $142,500. The stock at the beginning of the year is $45,000 at cost and $75,000 at retail. A stock count in July showed the inventory at cost as $47,500, and at retail as $72,500. End-of-year inventories are $50,000 at cost and $77,500 at retail. Purchase at cost during the year amounted to $97,500. What is the stock turnover rate (a) at cost? (b) at retail?

10. Assume that planned sales for August are $8,000, that planned reduction is $500, that planned BOM stock is $24,000, and that planned EOM stock is $18,000. Calculate the planned purchase figure for the month in question.

11. Given the following data for a certain department as of March 12, calculate the planned purchases and OTB for March 12.

Planned sales for the month	$11,000
Actual sales to date	5,400
BOM inventory	23,000
Planned reductions for the month	900
Actual reductions to date	600
Merchandise received to date	7,000
On order, March delivery	2,000
Planned EOM stock	25,000

12. With the following figures, find open-to-buy for January:

Stock on hand—January 1	$365,000
Planned stock on hand—February 1	342,000
On order for delivery in January	73,500
Planned sales for January	109,000

13. Find open-to-buy for August, given the following figures:

Stock on hand, July 31	$10,000
Merchandise purchased for delivery in August	8,000
Planned sales for August	5,000
Planned stock on hand, August 31	15,000

14. In a certain department the following figures have been planned for the month of October: sales, $70,000; markdowns and other retail reductions, $6,000; BOM retail stock, $280,000; EOM retail stock, $300,000; planned initial markup, 35 percent of retail. Calculate planned purchases at retail and at cost.

15. The following data represent conditions in a certain department as of February 12.

Planned sales for the month $14,000
Actual sales to date 6,500
BOM inventory 25,000
Planned reductions for the month 1,000
Actual reductions to date 500
Merchandise received to date 7,500
On order, February delivery 2,500
Planned EOM stock 27,500

Compute the OTB as of February 12.

16. Stock on hand at the beginning of week 1 is $5,000, and the planned sales for the next seven weeks are as follows:

Planned sales

Week 1 .... $1,180
Week 2 1,160
Week 3 750
Week 4 1,190
Week 5 720
Week 6 800
Week 7 1,050

Find the number of weeks supply.

17. The following weekly sales estimates have been prepared for a certain department:

Week beginning	Sales	Week beginning	Sales
January 5	$4,500	February 16	$5,000
12	3,250	23	5,500
19	3,750	March 2	5,000
26	3,500	9	6,000
February 2	3,750	16	5,500
9	4,500	23	7,500

The goal rate of stock turnover is eight. Using the weeks of supply method, calculate the planned stock for January 5, for February 9.

PROJECTS

1. Make a contact with a local buyer of a line in which you are interested. If you can work out such a relationship, allow the buyer to let you do a full six-months merchandise plan for a specific merchandise classification. Utilize the text format for your process of planning. You will need to get information from the buyer to do your job. If such information is not available from the store, you may have to make certain assumptions to come up with your planned purchase and to work out your OTB control.

2. An interesting "retail service" phenomenon of the 1970s is the "club" with disco entertainment or live bands. A product offering of most of these clubs is alcoholic beverages (beer, wine, whiskey, and liquors). One of the major problems in such establishments is "inventory control." Also, each of the clubs apparently has a rather unique "image" for the market. Investigate the establishments in your area and look for "the inventory control devices" (if any) employed; for the shortages believed to be experienced and how these are controlled; and finally, for the

"image" projected through pricing, promotion, or other elements of the retailing mix.

3. The text gives much attention to formal merchandise planning and control. Select certain stores which are available to you and find out how they handle these functions in reality. How much planning? Any control? Levels of sophistication? Does the degree of planning and control differ by merchandise lines! See whether you can develop some generalizations from your investigations.

CASES

Case 1. Mr. and Mrs. Catton own a small grocery store in a middle-income neighborhood in the central city of a Southwestern city of 100,000. Mr. Catton started the business many years ago and has run it as his "baby" ever since. Mrs. Catton, his ostensible "right hand," has in reality been the checker, bagger, and general greeter. She has not been involved in the "back office" procedures of the store, including buying merchandise.

Some months ago Mr. Catton had a slight, but frightening, heart attack. Mrs. Catton insisted that he "take it a bit easier," and since she too was not feeling completely fit, she begged her husband to hire a young man to come in and help with the business. The business had been very profitable for the Cattons, and he did not like the idea of bringing someone else in, but he finally agreed with his wife (and his doctor) that this was essential.

Jim Smith, a local young man and a recent graduate of the state university, was hired. Jim had a degree from the College of Business and specialized in Marketing/ Retailing. He was looking for a small retail opportunity rather than a large, multi-unit organization, and the Catton job appealed to him. His family was well respected in the neighborhood of the Catton store; he had good connections with the present customers; and his new bride was a neighborhood girl who wanted to "come back home." It all looked perfect, especially when Mr. Catton said that he was willing to work out a purchase plan for Jim since there were no Catton children to come into the business.

Jim's first challenge came during the first week. Mr. Catton could not come in at all, and the salesman for the wholesaler who was the major supplier came in for the wholesaler's regular order. Mrs. Catton knew nothing about how the order was placed and told Jim, "Let's see what you learned at that fine school of yours." She also implied that the salesman from the wholesale establishment was new and said that she had heard her husband complain that he was a "little high pressure for me." Jim gathered from that statement that the salesman overstocked the Cattons upon occasion. Mr. Catton kept no records except purchase invoices which were merely filed by date and supplier. He also had a daily sales record. His accountant kept the tax information. So Jim was "high and dry" as far as merchandise records were concerned.

Jim probably has no option now but to work with the salesman on the basis of past history in filling the orders. However, since the salesman comes by every two weeks, some type of plan is necessary. Suggest an outline of a control system that might work for Jim, at least in the short run, and that he could manage himself without hiring additional help.

Case 2.   Joe Williams has recently been hired as assistant buyer for men's wear in Oak Department Store. Oak's is actually a limited-line junior department store which is located in a new community mall in a medium-sized Southern city. The downtown store was recently closed, and plans for a new branch in another planned mall are on the drawing boards.

Williams had worked for the past three years as assistant store manager of Becks, a small, family-owned men's store in the deteriorating downtown area. He had also had previous, similar experience at another men's store in the downtown area. However, virtually all of the stores in the CBD have either branched to shopping centers or closed their downtown sites and moved to a center, making the mall store, in effect, the "main" store.

Joe's move to Oak Department Store as assistant buyer was actually a somewhat "lower status" job at essentially the same salary. Also, he had been in management in his past jobs, and this job was the first which could be considered merchandising specifically. Of course, he was knowledgeable about men's fashions, prices, display, and so on, but he had never had real buying authority or market contact.

Ransom Reese, the buyer of Oak's men's department, is an "old-timer" and has run the store's profitable men's area for over 30 years. Reese, as he admitted himself, "ran the whole show out of his hip pocket," and one could not argue with success. But with future plans for expansion and the fact that Reese wasn't getting any younger, management insisted that an assistant be hired in the large department, which included furnishings, clothing, and sportswear. Ran had never been interested in classification merchandising; he did not have any real controls, either dollar or unit. The controller of Oaks was making noises about putting in some system, but rumor had it that he feared the reactions of oldsters like Reese.

For the three months that Joe has been with Oaks he has followed Ran around, observed his working methods, and learned a lot about the customer market served. Most of the customers want special attention from Reese even though there are three good young salespersons in the department on a full-time basis and a part-time salesperson in furnishings who comes in during the evening hours. Reese told Joe that it was time for the old-timers to admit that fashions were moving rapidly and that his hip pocket was getting stuffed with too much information. Consequently, Joe's first assignment was to prepare the department for classifications or dissections and to make a report within a month as to what would be needed to set up a unit control system for each classification established. Reese didn't know much about dollar control—he had no open-to-buy even though some departments were experimenting with the system. Ran asked Joe to make a recommendation about that too, since Joe was working on all the merchandise.

Joe was somewhat shocked and frightened. He had been good at personnel relations in his prior jobs and he kept a neat, clean store! But this—he was beside himself and really didn't know where to start.

Advise Joe carefully, and make his job easy. Prepare the report and recommend what should be done about dollar control.

13

ACCOUNTING FOR MERCHANDISING EFFECTIVENESS

*T*oday's retailer, large or small, must have the tools required to make sound merchandising decisions in order to survive in the highly competitive marketplace.

One of the most important tools of the retailer is inventory control. Herein lies the secret of success. Inventories must be controlled in the areas of dollars, price lines, and departmental and subdepartmental classification. Inventories must be constantly reviewed in terms of turning over slow-moving items as well as further expanding fast-moving items. This can only be accomplished by the implementation of the retail method of inventory valuation and control.

John A. Chalmers
Chalmers & Kendall
Southfield, Michigan

Accounting is often characterized as "the language of business." The acceleration of change in our complex society has contributed to ever increasing complexities in the "language," which is used in recording and interpreting basic economic data for individuals, businesses, governments, and other entities. Sound decisions, based on reliable information, are essential for the efficient distribution and use of the nation's scarce resources. . . .

. . . Accounting is concerned with processes of recording, sorting, and summarizing data related to business transactions and events. . . .

The individuals most dependent upon and most involved with the end-products of accounting are those charged with the responsibility for directing the operations of enterprise . . . "management." The type of data needed by managers may vary with the size of the enterprise. The manager of a small business may need relatively little accounting information. As the size of a business unit increases, however, the manager becomes farther and farther removed from direct contact with day-to-day operations. He must be supplied with timely information.[1]

The above statements stress the importance of accounting to the retailer. The previous chapter showed how accounting information is utilized for the planning and control for merchandise operations within a retail enterprise. In this chapter our attention is focused on assuring the effectiveness, or indeed profitability, of the merchandise management activities discussed previously. Specifically, we will be examining the problems that arise in the determination of the cost and the value of merchandise inventory.

In determining the net income of a retailing firm, which reflects the effectiveness of operations, the cost of merchandise sold is the largest deduction from sales—the essential source of revenue. The importance of merchandise inventory is also reflected in other ways. It appears on the balance sheet as a current asset, and typically as the largest of the current assets. The cost of merchandise sold, reported on the income statement, is critical in determining gross profit. Thus an error in the determination of the inventory figure will cause an equal misstatement of gross profit and net income in the income statement. The amount for assets on the balance sheet will thus be incorrect by the same amount. The effects of understatements and overstatement of inventory at the end of a period are demonstrated in Figures 13–1 and Table 13–1, which are abbreviated income statements and balance sheets.[2]

KEY FINANCIAL STATEMENTS AND RATIOS

For the student who does not feel at ease with a discussion of financial statements and financial ratios, let's take a few pages to review basic information so that the following materials will have more meaning. Many business persons are often intimidated by the language of finance and accounting, so don't feel too bad if you need a brief reorientation.

---

[1] C. Rollin Niswonger and Philip E. Fess, *Accounting Principles,* 11th ed. (Cincinnati: South-Western Publishing Co., 1973), p. 1.

[2] Adapted from Niswonger and Fess, *Accounting Principles,* p. 186.

FIGURE 13–1
EFFECTS OF CORRECT STATEMENT, UNDERSTATEMENT, AND OVERSTATEMENT
OF INVENTORY ON NET PROFITS

Income statement—1978		*Balance sheet—1978*	
Net sales	$200,000	Merchandise inventory	$ 20,000
Beginning inventory .... $ 30,000		Other assets	80,000
+ Purchases 110,000		Total	100,000
= Available for sale 140,000		Liabilities	30,000
− Ending inventory 20,000		Net worth	70,000
= Cost of goods sold	120,000	Total	$100,000
Gross profit	80,000		
− Expenses	55,000		
= Net profit	$ 25,000 (correctly stated)		
Net sales	$200,000	Merchandise inventory	$ 12,000
Beginning inventory .... $ 30,000		Other assets	80,000
+ Purchases 110,000		Total	92,000
= Available for sale 140,000		Liabilities	30,000
− Ending inventory 12,000		Net worth	62,000
= Cost of goods sold	128,000	Total	$ 92,000
Gross profit	72,000		
− Expenses	55,000		
= Net profit	$ 17,000 (understated by $8,000)		
Net sales	$200,000	Merchandise inventory	$ 27,000
Beginning inventory .... $ 30,000		Other assets	80,000
+ Purchases 110,000		Total	107,000
= Available for sale 140,000		Liabilities	30,000
− Ending inventory 27,000		Net worth	77,000
= Cost of goods sold	113,000	Total	$107,000
Gross profit	87,000		
− Expenses	55,000		
= Net profit	$ 32,000 (overstated by $7,000)		

TABLE 13–1
EFFECT OF ERRONEOUS ALLOCATION OF MERCHANDISE COST ON
NET INCOME, ASSETS, AND CAPITAL

	Net income	Assets	Capital
Ending inventory understated $8,000	Understated $8,000	Understated $8,000	Understated $8,000
Ending inventory overstated $7,000	Overstated $7,000	Overstated $7,000	Overstated $7,000

FIGURE 13–2
THE BALANCE SHEET

This is how the business looks on a specific date.

Assets

What the business itself owns.

Current assets: In varying states of being converted into cash within the next 12 months.

Cash: Money on hand, in the bank.

Accounts receivable: What the customers owe the business for merchandise or services they bought.

Inventory: Merchandise on hand:
1. Ready to be sold.
2. In some stage of production.
3. Raw material.

Fixed assets: Used in the operation of the business. Not intended for resale.

Real estate: Land and buildings used by the business. Listed at original cost.

Leasehold improvements: Permanent installations—remodeling or refurbishing of the premises.

Machinery, equipment, vehicles: Used by the business. Listed at original cost.

Less accumulated depreciation: These assets (except land) lose value through wear, tear, and age. The business claims this loss of value as an expense of doing business. The running total of this expense is the accumulated depreciation.

Net fixed assets: Cost of fixed assets − Depreciation = Present value.

Liabilities

This side of the balance sheet shows the claims on the assets by both creditors and owners of the business. The claims of creditors are debts of the business—the *liabilities.* The owner's claim is his investment in the business—the *net worth.*

Current liabilities: Debts owed by the business to be paid within the next 12 months.

Notes payable: IOU bank or trade creditors.

Accounts payable: IOU trade and suppliers.

Income taxes: IOU government.

Long-term liabilities: Debts owed by the business to be paid beyond the next 12 months.

Mortgage: On property.

Net worth: Owner's (or stockholders') assets of the business; owner's investment; owner's equity in the business.

For proprietorship or partnership: *Mr. Owner, Capital:* Owner's original investment plus any profit reinvested in the business.

For corporation:

Capital stock: Value assigned to the original issue of stock by the directors of the corporation. If the stock sold for more than the assigned value, the excess will show as:

Surplus, paid-in: The difference between the assigned value and the selling price of the original issue of stock. (The subsequent selling price of the stock does not change the assigned value.)

Retained earnings: Profits reinvested in the business *after* paying dividends.

Balance sheet equation: Assets = Liabilities + Net worth

Source: Reprinted with permission from "Understanding Financial Statements," vol. 7, no. 11, *Small Business Reporter,* copyright © Bank of America, San Francisco, 1974.

In spite of appearances to the contrary, financial statements (income statement and balance sheets) merely list what you did and how you stand profitwise. They are a summary of the financial health of your firm for a given period of time.[3]

The balance sheet

Figure 13–2 indicates the components of the balance sheet—the financial health of a business on a specific date—and it is self-explanatory. The simplest expression of the balance sheet equation is: Assets = Liabilities + Net worth. Such a presentation places the prior discussion of the importance of cost in perspective. Figure 13–3 shows how the net worth can increase or decrease in the period covered by the income statement and indicates how this figure becomes a part of the balance sheet equation. Net worth is the owner's claim on the assets of the business—that is, the owner's investment or equity.

FIGURE 13–3
RECONCILEMENT OF NET WORTH
(shows how your net worth increased or decreased in the period
covered in the income statement)

Net worth at beginning of the period (as shown on the last balance sheet)	$
Add: Net profit after taxes (or subtract net loss)	$
Other additions (if any) For example: Sale of assets (net profit or loss) More capital (proprietorship: invested by owner; corporation: raised by sale of more stock)	$
Less: Dividends or withdrawals	$ ( )
Net worth as shown on balance sheet	$

Source: Reprinted with permission from "Understanding Financial Statements," vol. 7, no. 11, *Small Business Reporter,* copyright © Bank of America, San Francisco, 1974.

The income statement

The merchant is typically more interested in the income statement (Figure 13–4) than in the balance sheet because it presents the results of operations

---

[3] The information in this section comes in part from "Understanding Financial Statements," *Small Business Reporter,* vol. 7, no. 11 (1974), pp. 1–4.

FIGURE 13–4
INCOME STATEMENT

Also called profit and loss statement or statement of income and expenses. Here are the results of the business operation during a period of time.

Sales $ _____

Cost of sales   _____

Gross profit   _____

Expenses   _____

Net profit before taxes (or loss)   _____

Taxes   _____

Net profit after taxes   _____
    This is what's left for: Debt repayment
                        Withdrawal by owners
                        Dividends to stockholders
                        Reinvestment in the business

Source: Reprinted with permission from "Understanding Financial Statements," vol. 7, no. 11, *Small Business Reporter,* copyright © Bank of America, San Francisco, 1974.

during a prescribed period of time and gives a more dynamic picture of the effectiveness of merchandise operations.

Figure 13–5 is a formalized presentation of a business statement as it might be structured for analysis by management. Later in this chapter you will be more deeply involved with the income statement. There is no attempt here to teach the details of accounting, nor do we expect you to have more than an appreciation for the mechanics of these major statements at this point.

Ratios

The key ratios shown in Figure 13–6 provide the basis for a quick evaluation of how a business is doing in relation to similar businesses. Comparisons of ratios for similar businesses may cause management to ask some piercing questions. If most businesses in your line of trade are making more *profit on sales* than you are, which expenses may be causing you trouble? If your average *sales to working capital* is lower than that of comparable stores, you might question your operating efficiency—are your resources being used to their best advantage? The ratios are easy to calculate and are among the best guides to a firm's profitability and growth.

In 1975 a regional study revealed rather surprising findings concerning the use of accounting data for decision making.[1] Admittedly the retail firms

---

[1] Robert E. Stevens, "Using Accounting Data to Make Decisions," *Journal of Retailing,* vol. 51 (Fall 1975), pp. 23–28.

FIGURE 13-5
EXAMPLE OF HOW YOUR OWN FINANCIAL STATEMENT MIGHT LOOK

Individual, Partnership, or Corporation

Financial Statement of:

Name _____ Business _____

Address _____ At close of business _____

Statement of Income	Dollars		Financial Position Detail	Dollars	
Net sales			Receivables		
Cost of sales, buying, and occupancy expenses			Customer installment accounts receivable		
Selling and administrative expenses			Easy payment accounts		
Operating income from sales and services			Revolving charge accounts		
General expenses			Other customer accounts		
Interest expense			Miscellaneous accounts and notes receivable		
Contribution to employees' profit-sharing fund			Less—unearned finance charges		
Income taxes			Allowance for uncollectible accounts		
Net income			Property, plant, and equipment (at cost)		
Per share			Land		
Net income			Buildings and improvements		
Average shares outstanding			Furniture, fixtures, and equipment		
			Total property, plant, and equipment		
			Less accumulated depreciation		
			Accounts payable and accrued expenses		
			Accounts payable		
			Accrued expenses		
			Federal income taxes accrued		
			Other accrued taxes		
			Long-term debt		

Statement of Financial Position Assets			Statement of Shareholders' Equity		
Current assets			Common stock		
Cash			Balance, beginning of year		
Receivables			Stock options exercised		
Inventories			Issued to profit-sharing fund		
Prepaid advertising and other charges			Balance, end of year		
Total current assets			Retained income		
Investments			Balance, beginning of year		
Property, plant, and equipment			Net income		
Deferred charges			Balance, end of year		
Total assets			Total shareholders' equity		
Liabilities					
Current liabilities					
Notes payable					
Commercial paper					
Banks					
Accounts payable and accrued expenses					
Unearned maintenance agreement income					
Deferred income taxes					
Total current liabilities					
Deferred income taxes					
Long-term debt					
Total Liabilities					
Shareholders' equity					

FIGURE 13–6
RATIOS

Current Ratio

How calculated: Divide current assets by current liabilities.

What it shows: How the business can meet its current debt. Popular thought is that the higher the ratio, the better shape the business is in. However, a high ratio of itself does not tell:

1. Whether cash is being used to best advantage.
2. The distribution of current assets—receivables may be too high; inventory may be too high.

Worth to Debt Ratio

How calculated: Divide net worth by total debt. (Total debt = Current liabilities + Long-term liabilities.)

What it shows: What percentage of the total money invested in the business is the owner's; what percentage was contributed by creditors. The higher the ratio, the more money the owner has in the business and the safer the creditors. (They are safer because more owner's equity is there to cushion creditors against a loss.)

However, a high ratio may also show that the owner is too conservative—unwilling to take any risks, not using his funds to best advantage, not realizing the maximum potential of his business.

Profit on Sales

How calculated: Divide net profit (before taxes) for period by sales for period.

What it shows: What part of every sales dollar is profit. A higher percentage means greater efficiency of operation.

Inventory Turnover

How calculated: Divide cost of goods sold by inventory.

What it shows: How many times the inventory turns—or "sells out"—during the year. Normally, a high turnover rate means salable, fresh, and liquid inventory. Too slow turnover means too much inventory for the sales capacity of the business. However, too fast turnover can indicate a hand-to-mouth existence easily upset by a sales drop-off—the business is buying today what it is selling today; it is paying today out of today's sales.

Receivables Turnover

How calculated: Divide annual sales by accounts receivable.

What it shows: How fast the business is collecting from customers. The higher the turnover, the faster the collecting.

The average number of days it takes to collect the accounts receivable can be calculated by dividing the turnover rate into 360. The more days, the greater the chances of delinquent accounts.

Profit to Net Worth

How calculated: Divide profit by net worth.

What it shows: Return on investment. What yield—or "interest rate"—the investment in the business is getting, the percentage of the investment that is being returned yearly through profit. Divide this percentage into 100 to see how many years it will take to get back the total investment in the business.

Sales to Working Capital

How calculated: Net sales divided by working capital. (Working capital = Current assets − Current liabilities.)

What it shows: How many dollars of sales the company makes for every dollar of working capital it has. This ratio can be of great value when the business is expanding. It helps determine how much more working capital will be necessary to support higher sales.

Source: Reprinted with permission from "Understanding Financial Statements," vol. 7, no. 11, Small Business Reporter, copyright © Bank of America, San Francisco, 1974.

represented only one geographic area and a random sample design was impossible; nevertheless, the findings are interesting as we study this chapter.

It was found that only 58 percent of the retailers interviewed had income statements and balance sheets prepared for their use. The researcher anticipated a much higher usage rate since an income statement is virtually a by-product of a tax return.

Only 36 percent of the retail respondents used any kind of ratio analysis. The users were the younger managers of larger retail stores that were likely to be multi-unit and incorporated. The stores had a comparatively large number of employees and large sales volumes. The most common ratios computed by those who used any were measures of profitability, stockturn, and net profit as a percent of net worth.

DETERMINING THE COST OF INVENTORY

A major problem in determining inventory cost arises when identical units of a particular product are acquired over a period of time at various unit cost prices. To illustrate the problem, let's return to the sport shirts example used in the prior chapter. Assume the following purchases of sport shirts during the spring season:

	Knit sport shirts	Units	Unit cost	Total cost
February 1	Inventory	50	$ 9	$ 450
April 15	Purchases	40	13	520
May 1	Purchases	30	14	420
Total		120		$1,390
Average cost per unit				$11.58

In some departments and/or classifications it may be possible to identify units with specific expenditures. This can occur when assortments and varieties of merchandise carried and the sales volume and transactions are relatively small. More often, however, as in the sport shirt classification, specific identification procedures are too complex to justify their use. Consequently, one of the three accepted costing methods, each approved for income determination by the Internal Revenue Service, may be adopted to simplify the problem of inventory costing.

FIFO and LIFO

The assumption of the first-in, first-out (FIFO) method of costing inventory is that costs should be charged against revenue in the order in which they were incurred—that is, the first shirts purchased are the first ones sold. Thus, the inventory remaining at the end of an accounting period is assumed to be of the most recent purchases as follows:

February 1 inventory............	50 shirts @ $ 9	$ 450
April 15 purchases	40 shirts @ 13	520
May 1 purchases	30 shirts @ 14	420
October 1 purchases	100 shirts @ 16	1,600
Available for sale during year	220 shirts	$2,990

Let's assume that the physical inventory at the end of the fiscal year (January 31) is 130 shirts. Based on the assumption that the inventory is composed of the most recent purchases, the cost of the 130 shirts is as follows:

Most recent purchase (October 1)....................	100 shirts @ $16	$1,600
Next most recent purchase (May 1)	30 shirts @ 14	420
Inventory January 31.............	130 shirts	$2,020

If we deduct the end of period inventory of $2,020 from the $2,990 worth of shirts available for sale during the period, we get $970 as the cost of merchandise sold. FIFO is generally in harmony with the actual physical movement of goods in a retail firm. Thus, FIFO best represents the results that are directly tied to merchandise costs.

The costing method known as last-in, first-out (LIFO) assumes that the most recent cost of merchandise should be charged against revenue. Thus, the ending inventory under LIFO is assumed to be made up of earliest costs. Referring to the previous example:

February 1	50 shirts @ $ 9	$ 450
April 15	40 shirts @ 13	520
May 1	30 shirts @ 14	420
October 1	10 shirts @ 16	160
Inventory January 31.............	130 shirts	$1,550

If we deduct the inventory of $1,550 from the $2,990 of merchandise available for sale during the accounting period, we get $1,440 as the cost of merchandise sold.

In comparing FIFO and LIFO:

	FIFO	LIFO
Merchandise available for sale	$2,990	$2,990
Inventory January 31..............	2,020	1,550
Cost of merchandise sold	$ 970	$1,440

FIFO yields the lower cost of merchandise sold and thus yields higher gross profits and higher inventory figures on the balance sheet. On the other hand, LIFO yields a higher figure for cost of goods sold and a lower figure for gross profit, net income, and inventory.

It is not the purpose of this discussion to critically evaluate the two methods. The major point is to indicate how important the selection of the inventory costing method is to the retailer. Management may not change from method to method without a valid reason.

Conservative valuation of inventory

Cost or market, whichever is lower. Another problem in determining the cost of merchandise inventory is that of placing a conservative value on the inventory, that is, at cost or market, whichever is lower. This approach is an alternative to valuing inventory at cost. Under either course of action it is first necessary to determine the cost of inventory. "Market" means the cost required to replace the merchandise at the time of the inventory, whereas "cost" refers to the price of merchandise at the time of its purchase.

Table 13–2 demonstrates the impact on profits of valuing the ending inventory at (1) actual cost, (2) depreciated value, and (3) appreciated value. In addition, it provides a rationale for the acceptance of the conservative practice of valuation—at cost or market, whichever is lower. At any given time, some merchandise in stock may not be valued at the amount originally paid for it. The merchandise may have declined in value (because of obsolescence, deterioration, or a downward movement in wholesale market prices), or it may have increased in value (because of inflation, scarcity of materials, and the like). The first column in Table 13–2 indicates the profit to

TABLE 13–2

THE IMPACT ON PROFITS OF VALUATION OF ENDING INVENTORY AT ACTUAL COST, DEPRECIATED MARKET VALUE, OR APPRECIATED MARKET VALUE

	Actual cost*		Depreciation†		Appreciated‡	
Net sales		$100,000		$100,000		$100,000
Merchandise available						
for sale	$70,000		$70,000		$70,000	
Ending inventory	10,000*		4,000†		12,000‡	
Cost of goods sold		60,000		66,000		58,000
Gross profit		$ 40,000		$ 34,000		$ 42,000
Expenses		35,000		35,000		35,000
Net profit		$ 5,000		($1,000)		$ 7,000

be $5,000 after the valuation of inventory at its actual cost (determined by a method discussed earlier). The second column indicates that if the retailer were to replace that same inventory at the time of valuation, it would be depreciated to $4,000 (a $6,000 decline in value from the actual cost), and that instead of a $5,000 profit, a $1,000 loss has been incurred.

The information in the third column reflects a $12,000 valuation of the ending inventory, resulting in a $7,000 profit rather than the $5,000 profit based on actual cost.

The depreciated ending inventory value relative to the actual cost results in an increased cost of goods sold. This yields a reduced gross profit, and consequently, with the expense structure illustrated, a loss results.

The appreciated ending inventory relative to the actual costs results in a decreased cost of goods sold, an increased gross profit, and, with the same expense amount, an increased net profit. Comparing each method with the actual cost, the conservative rule would dictate that the inventory value should be taken at the depreciated value (column 2) and at actual cost (column 1) when compared with the market increase. Let's investigate the logic of such practice.

Rationale for the conservative rule. If management values the ending inventory at $4,000 rather than the cost of $10,000, the resulting loss will be taken in the period in which it occurs. This is logical because the ending inventory of one period becomes the beginning inventory of the next; thus, if a realistic depreciated market value is placed on ending inventory, the low-ered figure, which will be the next beginning inventory value, will give the merchant the opportunity to reflect a proper beginning inventory cost at the beginning of the next period. Consequently, the opportunity will exist to show a realistic, and perhaps profitable, performance in the next period. In addition, this ending inventory figure becomes an asset item on the balance sheet. A realistic valuation reflecting declining value is wise because other-wise the assets and, consequently, the net worth of the firm will be over-stated. Finally, if the market value was declining and the inventory was taken in at cost, the firm would show a profit (per our illustration in Table 13–2) and income taxes would be paid on "paper profits."

To emphasize the concept of "paper profits," let's look at what the results would be if the inventory were valued at an appreciated value (column 3) of $12,000 rather than a cost of $10,000. The $7,000 profit, rather than the $5,000, represents anticipated profits on merchandise which has not yet been sold and thus should not be reported.

In summary, retail inventories should be valued at cost or market, whichever is lower. As with the method chosen for the determination of inventory cost (LIFO or FIFO), the method elected for inventory valuation (cost or market, whichever is lower) must be consistently maintained from year to year. The Internal Revenue Service accepts either method for cost determination and for inventory evaluation for federal income tax purposes. However, when the LIFO method is used, the inventory must be stated at cost.[5]

THE RETAIL METHOD OF INVENTORY COSTING

The retail method of inventory costing is widely utilized in retailing, especially among general merchandise retailers. Simply stated, this method

---

[5] Niswonger and Fess, *Accounting Principles*, p. 195.

of inventory costing involves approximating the "cost or market value, whichever is lower" for homogeneous groups of merchandise without having to determine the market prices of individual items. If a store is operating on a cost method, the problem of determining inventory depreciation exists, and in many retail stores it is difficult, if not impossible, to solve this problem adequately. Determining market values by the retail method is more satisfactory. In a cost system, cost codes or some other complex system must be utilized to determine what was actually paid for each item in stock. Then a separate system must be set up to determine the market value at the same time that inventory is taken.[6]

Advantages of the retail method

As was pointed out in Chapter 12, the retail method of inventory is a logical extension of the retail book inventory utilized for dollar control. The advantages of the retail method over the cost (nonperpetual) method of inventory are as follows:

1. Accounting statements can be drawn up at any time, especially with the new technology. Income statement and balance sheets are normally available once a month.
2. Shortages can be determined. The retail method is a book inventory, and this figure can be compared to the physical inventory. Only with a book inventory can shortages (or overages) be determined.
3. The retail method, through its book inventory, serves as an excellent basis for insurance claims. In case of loss, the book inventory is good evidence of what *should* have been in stock. Records should be kept in a safe, fireproof vault or cabinet.

(Note: The three reasons given above are in actuality advantages which exist because the retail method is a perpetual book inventory method. The following two advantages are uniquely related to the retail method of inventory.)

4. The physical taking of inventory is easier with the retail method of inventory. The items are recorded on the inventory sheets at only their selling prices instead of their cost prices.
5. The retail method gives an automatic, conservative valuation of ending inventory because of the way the system is programmed. This means

---

[6] Cost codes are symbols or letters which represent numbers so that a coded cost figure can appear on price tickets for inventory purposes, and the customer does not know the actual cost of the merchandise. Determining present market prices is easier in big-ticket merchandise for which present price lists can be checked against manufacturers' stock numbers on the items. At best, however, this is a laborious process and less than satisfactory.

that the retail method gives a valuation of ending inventory at cost or market, whichever is lower.[7]

The retail method is in actuality an income statement which follows certain programmed steps in the final determination of net profits. These steps are illustrated in Figure 13–7. Virtually all of the items which affect the profit position have been discussed in Chapter 12 under the topic of dollar control. The methodology here, however, is somewhat different and this section provides a format for computing net profit through the retail method. The steps are as follows:

The steps of the retail method

1. *Determine the total dollars of merchandise handled at cost and retail.* As is indicated in Figure 13–7, we start with a beginning inventory which we assume is an actual, physical inventory from the end of the previous period. To this figure we add purchases (less vendor returns and/or allowances), any interstore or departmental transfers, and transportation charges (at cost only). The price change which can be a part of Step 1 is additional markups. Suppose that the retailer has a group of sport shirts in stock which have recently been received. They are carried in stock at $14.95. Since their delivery, wholesale costs have increased, and the wholesaler suggests that we take an additional markup of $3.00 per unit, bringing the retail price to $17.95. We take a physical count and find that we have 700 shirts in stock; thus, we take an additional markup of $2,100 to accommodate the price increase. Immediately after processing the price change, we find that the count was incorrect or that the amount of the additional markup was too high due to a misunderstanding. At any rate, the retailer wants to cancel $600 of the additional markup so that the mistake can be corrected. (See Step 1 in the statement for the handling of this situation.) Cancellation of an additional markup is *not* a markdown which reflects market depreciation. It is rather a procedure for adjusting an actual error in the original additional markup. Summing all the items which increase the dollar investment in inventory provides the total merchandise handled at cost and retail.

2. *Calculate the cost multiplier and the cumulative mark-on.* As is indicated in Figure 13–7, the computation of the cost multiplier (sometimes called the cost percentage or the cost complement) is derived by dividing the total dollars handled at cost by the total at retail (that is, $270,000 ÷ $435,000 = 62.069 percent). This is a key figure in the retail method, and in fact it is the major assumption of the system. This cost

---

[7] The actual mathematics utilized to prove *how* the method provides an automatic, conservative valuation of inventory is somewhat complex. It is sufficient to say that it is dependent on the timing of the handling of price changes. Additional markups are handled *before* calculation of the "cost multiplier," and markdowns are handled *after*. The presentation of a complete retail statement will clarify these terms and assist understanding the statement in Figure 13–7.

multiplier says that for every retail dollar in inventory, 62.069 percent, or 62+ cents, represent cost dollars. The assumption of the retail method is that if cost and retail have this relationship in goods handled during a period, then that same relationship exists for all of the merchandise remaining in stock, that is, the ending inventory at retail. The cumulative mark-on is the complement of the cost multiplier (that is, $100.000 - 62.069 = 37.931$) and is the control figure to compare against the planned initial markup (see Chapter 14, where this planned figure is discussed). For example, let's assume that the planned initial markup is 37 percent. If our interim statement shows, as ours does, that our cumulative mark-on is 37+ percent, then management will consider that operations are effective, at least as they relate to the planned markup percentage. As will be evident in the pricing discussion in Chapter 14, the initial markup is planned so as to cover reductions (markdowns, employee discounts, and shortages) and provide a maintained markup (or gross profit or margin) at a level sufficient to cover operating expenses and to assure a target rate of profit return.

3. *Compute the retail deductions from stock.* Step 3 includes all of the retail deductions from the total retail merchandise dollars handled during the period. Sales are recorded and adjusted by customer returns to determine net sales. Markdowns are recorded as they are taken.

As an example, let's assume that during this period a group of 1,200 sport shirts retailing for $25.95 are put out for a special sale at $15.95. We would thus take a markdown of $12,000 before the sale. After the sale we want to bring the merchandise back to the regular price; an additional markup is not appropriate since we are merely cancelling an original markdown. Consequently, we put a markdown cancellation through the system for the remaining number of shirts—in this case 150 were not sold, making a cancellation of $1,500 which will reestablish the original retail price of $25.95. Employee discounts are included as deductions because employees will receive a 20 percent discount on items purchased for personal use. If a shirt retails for $19.95, the employee would pay $15.96. If the discount were not entered as a separate item in the system, the difference between the retail price and the employees' price would cause a shortage. Recording employee discounts as a separate item also gives management a good picture of employee business obtained and affords a measure of control over the use of the discount.

4. *Calculate the closing book (and/or physical) inventory at cost and retail.* The statement thus far has afforded us a figure for the dollars at retail which we had available for sale ($435,000) and what we have deducted from that amount ($312,000). Thus we are now able to compute what we have *left* ($435,000 - $312,000), or the ending *book* inventory at retail—$123,000. In this illustration we are assuming that this is a year-end statement and that we have an audited physical inventory of $120,750. Consequently, we can now determine our shortages by deducting the amount of the physical inven-

FIGURE 13–7

STATEMENT OF RETAIL METHOD OF INVENTORY COSTING METHOD

Calculations	Step	Items	Cost	Retail	Cost	Retail	Percent
	1	Beginning inventory			$ 60,000	$105,000	
		Gross purchases	$216,000	$345,000			
		Less: Returns to vendor	(9,000)	(14,000)	207,000	330,900	
		Transfers in	3,000	4,800			
		Less: Transfers out	(4,500)	(7,200)	(1,500)	(2,400)	
		Transportation charges			4,500		
		Additional markups		2,100			
		Less: Cancellations		(600)		1,500	
		Total merchandise handled			270,000	435,000	
($270,000 ÷ $435,000)	2	Cost percent/Cumulative mark-on					62.069/37.931
	3	Sales, gross		309,000			
		Less: Customer returns		(9,000)		300,000	
		Gross markdowns		12,000			
		Less: Cancellations		(1,500)		10,500	
		Employee discounts				1,500	
		Total retail deductions				312,000	
($435,000 − $312,000)	4	Closing book inventory @ retail				123,000	

Formula	Ref	Item	Value	Amount	%
		Closing physical inventory @ retail		120,750	0.75
($123,000 − $120,750)		Shortages		2,250	
($120,750 × 0.62069)		Closing physical inventory @ cost	74,949		
($270,000 − $74,949)	5	Gross cost of goods sold	195,051		
($300,000 − $195,051)	6	Maintained markup	104,949		34.9
		Less: Alteration costs	(3,000)		
		Plus: Cash discounts	6,000		
($104,949 + $3,000)		Gross margin	107,949		35.9
		Less: Operating expenses	75,000		25.0
		Net profit	32,949		10.9
	5	Gross cost of goods sold	195,051		
		Less: Cash discounts	(6,000)		
		Net cost of goods sold	189,051		
		Plus: Alteration costs	3,000		
		Total cost of goods sold	192,051		
($300,000 − $192,051)	6	Gross margin	107,949		35.9
		Less: Operating expenses	75,000		
		Net profit	32,949		10.9

tory from the book inventory ($123,000 − $120,750) = $2,250, or 0.75 percent of sales.

Let's assume that we were working with an interim statement rather than a fiscal year statement. If this were the case, we would include in our retail deductions from stock (Step 3) an *estimated* shortage figure which would give us the most nearly accurate total deductions and consequently the closing book inventory figure at retail. If we have an interim statement, then the cost multiplier is applied to the *book* inventory at retail to determine the cost value; if there is a physical retail inventory figure, as in Figure 13–7, then we use that figure for cost conversion, since the physical inventory figure is accurate.

The key to the retail method, as noted, is the reduction of the retail inventory to cost by multiplying the retail value by the cost multiplier ($120,750 × 0.62069). In our illustration we get a value of $74,949. With this figure it is now possible to go the next step.

5. *Determination of gross cost of goods sold.* Since we know the amount of the merchandise handled at cost ($270,000) and we know what we have *left* at cost ($74,949), we can determine the cost dollars which have moved out of stock ($195,051).

6. *Determination of maintained markup, gross margin, and net profit.* At this step, two procedures may be followed. Because of the emphasis given to the concept of maintained markup in Chapter 14, we prefer the first method. The gross margin and net profit figures in either case are identical; it is in reality a slightly differing accounting philosophy which is determining, and the justification of either method is neither appropriate nor valuable here. We show the two ways simply to let you see the differences between them. Gross cost of goods sold is deducted from net sales to determine maintained markup ($300,000 − $195,051 = $104,949). Alteration costs (or workroom expenses) are traditionally considered in retailing as a merchandising, nonoperating expense, and in this first method are offset by cash discounts earned (nonoperating income). The net difference between the two is added or subtracted from maintained markup to derive the gross margin ($104,949 − $3,000 + $6,000 = $107,949), from which operating expenses are deducted to calculate net profits before taxes ($107,949 − $75,000 = $32,949). The various percentages appearing on the statement are all on a sales base (with the exception of the cost percentage and the cumulative mark-on).

The second process for determining gross margin and net profits differs in that cash discounts earned are deducted from gross cost of goods sold ($195,051 − $6,000) to derive *net* cost of goods sold ($189,051). Alteration costs are added to that figure to obtain *total* cost of goods sold ($139,051 + $3,000 = $192,051). Total cost of goods sold is deducted from net sales ($300,000 − $192,051) to obtain the gross margin figure of $107,949.

Evaluation of the retail method

The determination of profits by the retail method of inventory costing is not a new system, and over the years problems have occurred with it. A major complaint has been that it is a "method of averages." This refers to the determination of the cost multiplier as the "average relationship" between all the merchandise handled at cost and retail and then the application of this average percentage to the closing inventory at retail to determine the cost figure. Such a disadvantage, more real in the past than today, can be overcome by classification merchandising or dissection accounting, that is, breaking departments into small subgroups with homogeneity in terms of margins and turnover. The new technology in point-of-sales systems affords unlimited classifications and thus allows the homogeneity necessary for implementation of the retail method, giving management a good measure of the actual effectiveness of operations.

Another disadvantage of the method has been admitted by the National Retail Merchants Association, the nation's most visible retail association, which has publicly admitted that the FIFO-based retail method overstates cost significantly. The overstatement results because the mix in the closing inventory is not actually representative of the mix in the purchases, which becomes a part of the component needed to determine the cost multiplier. It is claimed that there is likely to be an underrepresentation of lower markup goods in the ending inventory and that the cost percentage will therefore be too high.[8] As is true in the solution of the disadvantage of "averages," it is possible to take the necessary steps to improve the accuracy of the cost percentage. The method of recording purchases must be modified. Items which are not "normally" carried in stock (for example, closeouts, special purchases) must be earmarked in advance and posted to a special purchase account that will not be used in computing the cost multiplier. In this way the cost percentage will be more representative of the ending inventory and the existing disadvantage will be modified.

The retail method of inventory is not applicable to all departments within a store. For example, unless the purchases can be "retailed" at the time of receipt of the goods, the system will not work. The drapery workroom could not be on the retail method. Consequently, there are certain "cost" departments within many establishments. Such a condition does not lessen the value of the system where it is appropriate.

Finally, the retail method is easily programmed for computer systems and has proved most effective for management decisions. All accounting entries into the system can be automated, and the management reports which can be "called" are virtually limitless.

---

[8] Robert Kahn (ed.), *Retailing Today*, vol. 12, no. 1 (January 1977), p. 3.

SUMMARY

This chapter has complemented Chapter 12, and in effect the material it contains has focused on the measurement of the profitability of the retail manager's merchandise management activities. The key accounting statements (the balance sheet and especially the income statement) and ratios have been presented, but the essential concern of the chapter has been the importance, problems, and method of determining the cost of merchandise inventory. The cost value of the ending inventory, essential in determining cost of goods sold, was calculated primarily by the so-called retail method of accounting, the methodology for which was described in detail.

It should be pointed out that this chapter has focused only on merchandise accounting. Chapter 19 applies accounting methodology to the measurement of the effectiveness of operating decisions and deals with operating expenses classification, allocation, budgeting, and control.

KEY CONCEPTS

Key financial statements
   The balance sheet
   The income statement
Financial ratios
   Current ratio
   Worth to debt
   Profit on sales
   Inventory turnover
   Receivables turnover
   Profit to net worth
   Sales to working capital
FIFO
LIFO
Conservative valuation of inventory (cost or market, whichever is lower)
The retail method of accounting
   The cost multiplier
   Cumulative mark-on
   Shortage
   Overage
   Maintained markup
   Gross margin
   Net cost of goods sold
   Total cost of goods sold
   Gross cost of goods sold

DISCUSSION QUESTIONS

1. Explain the effects which a correct versus an understatement and an overstatement of the period's ending inventory will have on net profits.

2. Distinguish between the balance sheet and the income statement. Illustrate an advocated format for each.

3. Cite the most important of the financial ratios, and explain their value to retail management.

4. Why is it difficult to determine cost of ending inventories? How do (a) FIFO and (b) LIFO relate to the problem? Explain the assumptions of each method. Contrast the two methods.

5. Explain the *conservative valuation of inventory,* and discuss the rationale of accountants who support this "rule."

6. Explain in the simplest terms what the retail method of inventory costing involves. What is the relationship between "the retail method" and a retail book inventory? What are the advantages of the retail method over the cost (nonperpetual, or no book inventory) method of inventory?

7. Describe in detail the steps of the retail method. Evaluate the method.

PROBLEMS

Use the retail method of accounting. Prepare well-organized statements and determine for each of the following sets of figures:

a. Cumulative mark-on percentage.
b. Ending inventory at retail and cost.
c. Maintained markup in dollars and percent.
d. Gross margin of profit in dollars and percent.
e. Net profit in dollars and percent.

Item	Cost	Retail
1. Gross sales		$ 25,800
Inventory, June 1	$11,000	16,000
Customer returns and allowances		350
Gross markdowns		2,000
Gross additional markups		620
Transportation charges inward	550	
Merchandise returned to vendors	800	1,300
Discounts to employees		350
Gross purchases	16,400	26,310
Markdown cancellations		300
Operating expenses	7,200	
Cash discounts earned on purchases	410	
Additional markups canceled		150
Alteration and workroom net costs	325	
Estimated shortages, 0.5% of net sales		
2. Beginning inventory	20,000	35,000
Gross purchases	72,000	115,000
Purchase returns and allowances	3,000	4,700

Item	Cost	Retail
Transfers in	1,000	1,600
Transfers out	1,500	2,400
Freight in	1,500	
Additional markups		700
Additional markup cancellations		
(revision of retail downward)		200
Gross sales		110,000
Customer returns and allowances		10,000
Gross markdowns		4,500
Markdown cancellations		1,000
Employee discounts		500
Ending physical inventory		40,250
Cash discounts on purchases		2,000
Workroom costs	1,000	
Operating costs (expenses)	30,000	

3.	Additional markup cancellation		150
	Estimated shortages		0.75% of net sales
	Gross markdowns		2,150
	Workroom expenses	510	
	Sales returns and allowances		385
	Transportation charges	580	
	Beginning inventory	14,300	20,100
	Vendor returns	830	1,650
	Markdown cancellations		300
	Gross purchases	17,200	27,520
	Gross additional markups		650
	Gross sales		27,200
	Employee discounts		500
	Cash discounts		505
	Operating expenses	7,700	

PROJECTS

1. One of the exciting technological advances of the current era has been the widespread utilization of point-of-service (sale) terminals. Attempt to make a contact with a local merchant in your area who would be willing to have you sit through a training session for using these terminals (similar to the traditional "cash register training"), and after being "trained" in their use, explain the system and how the various inputs assist management in decision making. Describe what the store *is* doing, what it is *not* doing, and what the future holds for total utilization of the equipment.

2. Select at least five different general merchandise stores in your area. They should differ as to size, extent of product line, and market image. Interview the controller (or the person responsible for that function), and determine the type of merchandise accounting procedure employed by each firm (retail, direct cost, and so on). Attempt to determine whether any of the variables distinguishing the firms (age, size, product line, and so on) affect the type of accounting system utilized. If you can get qualitative evaluations of the existing systems, do so. Also, how "sophisticated" is the technology utilized by the stores to obtain the needed accounting data? What problems are apparent in the systems used in each store? Make a comparison chart.

CASES

Case 1. Miss Jennifer Goodman, a 1965 graduate of her state university with a B.S. in Accounting and a master's degree in Marketing-Retailing, opened her long-wished-for tall girl's boutique. She saved, sacrificed, and as she said recently, prayed a lot before she accumulated enough venture capital to open her shop in 1972. She had inherited some money a few years prior to the store opening, this plus her own savings enabled her to get a good line of credit at the local bank with which her prominent, physician father had dealt since he set up practice.

Jennifer had made good money in her accounting job; after all, she graduated during the beginning of the "era of the woman" and was of a minority race. She admitted that while she never wanted to be given a job because of sex or color, her timing had been awfully good. Her master's degree added that extra dimension which set her up for a most lucrative career in accounting. But that was merely a means to an end—her tall girl's boutique. She had spent many years looking desperately for fashion-right apparel and accessories for the tall figure, and the desire to serve that market was the driving force in her life.

Jennifer opened her boutique in the newest regional mall in her hometown—a Gulf Coast vacation city of some 60,000 plus an undetermined number of vacationers "in season." She was proud of herself after her several years of operations. She was comfortable in her relationships with her employees; she received favorable comments from her customers; and she was especially pleased with the word-of-mouth visitors who had heard of "Jen's Tall Look." Her $185,000 annual volume, up from a rather dismal first-year $75,000, was also encouraging. She drew a fairly modest salary and tried not to take out too much profits, but was reinvesting in fixturing, some expansion, and "saving" for that day when she might open Jen's #2.

With her accounting expertise she was her own controller. She installed a retail accounting system, had dollar control by major classifications, and had recently purchased an electronic cash register which gave her much information for decision making. Her unit control on dresses was perpetual, and in her accessories she used a nonperpetual system. She had a clerk who handled all these details, but Jen was always "in there" studying the various reports she felt she needed.

She feels that her vendor contacts and relationships are firm. Because of the transient nature of the city, most of her customers pay cash; but recently her credit sales have been increasing, and she has two major bank card plans available.

For the past two years she has had to borrow rather heavily from her bank to meet day-to-day expenses. With her growth in sales and profits, she is concerned about her need for additional working capital. Just this week, a salesman from one of the business machine companies made a presentation to her concerning a new POS terminal tying into a local data center which could handle her unit and dollar control and give her much more information than she now has. He also stressed that her retail accounting method would easily be programmed into this new system.

Analyze Jennifer Goodman's situation.

Case 2. Bobbie's Fashiontique is a small, family-operated store. The staff consists of Mr. and Mrs. Townsend (in their late 50s) and their unmarried daughter, Bobbie, for whom they started the business some years ago when Bobbie was unhappy in her job as an elementary school teacher. The Townsends had been employed by a large department store in their town for all of their working careers until opening

Bobbie's—in fact, their romance started in the stockroom of the store and in the course of time a store wedding followed! Mr. Townsend was the manager of warehouse and traffic and delivery at the department store when he left (having previously been in charge of receiving and marking), and Mrs. Townsend had been in charge of alterations and fur storage. She had at one time also been in charge of a customer adjustment department.

Consequently, the Townsend family had no real merchandising or control background, and whenever they were faced with an accounting problem, they ignored it or turned it over to the accounting firm which did their routine bookkeeping and tax returns.

Recently, realizing that their degree of management sophistication was limited, Bobbie joined the state retail association and went to a seminar on financial management. She was confused and frustrated, but decided that something had to be done. After the conference she was convinced that they didn't even know whether they were making any money. She felt that they had to start doing something to obtain more information. What impressed her most was a lecture on and discussion of operating ratios. Many of the participants had figures with them and were discussing them with much authority. Thus Bobbie wanted to focus on operating ratios when she called her accounting firm and asked that it send someone over to do a job for her.

Tom Maden, a junior member of the firm, was assigned the responsibility of working with Bobbie. Bobbie told him that she wanted him to calculate key ratios for her and to tell her what they meant. Tom took the latest balance sheet and operating statement of the Fashiontique and came up with the following figures for Bobbie's firm and similar companies:

Ratio	Bobbie's Fashiontique	Trade
Current	1.5	2.0
Net worth to debt	135 : 100	125 : 100
Inventory turnover	1.24	1.68
Receivables turnover	9.3	11.6
Sales to working capital	3.0	4.0

You are Tom Maden—report to Bobbie Townsend and interpret the data for her. Point out the strengths and weaknesses of Bobbie's Fashiontique and the areas which need particular attention.

14

THE FOUNDATIONS
OF RETAIL PRICING

*I*n the science of retailing, one fundamental factor touches all of the elements that ultimately trigger the true success of an operation: the price at which merchandise is offered to the consumer. The practitioner who is able to identify the ideal selling price has the ability to maximize sales, maintain a desired competitive position, and achieve his profitability goals. The student who recognizes the importance of those facts must build a base from which to operate. To both, knowledgeability in the field, creativity, and practical judgment are important factors.

"The Foundations of Retail Pricing" is a vital subject that provides an important background for the "how-to's" so necessary to professionalism and success!

Anne Stegner, Vice President
General Merchandise Manager
Bullocks Wilshire
Los Angeles, California

Retail pricing is a function of costs, competition, demand, and profit. Economics teaches us that profits are maximized in the purely competitive model at the point where marginal revenue equals marginal cost, as shown in Figure 14–1. This concept assumes a profit-maximizing firm which knows the demand and cost functions for the product. However, marginal revenue and marginal cost are hard to operationalize in actuality. Why? For one thing, firms often do not seek to maximize profits in the short run and may simply follow cost-plus formulas, as will be indicated later, because this is

FIGURE 14–1
THE SHORT-RUN PROFIT-MAXIMIZING POSITION OF A PURELY
COMPETITIVE FIRM

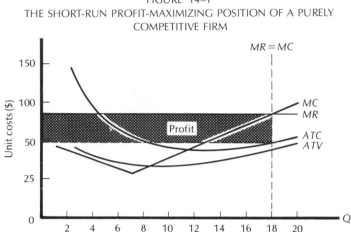

the customary practice. Also marginal analysis should be considered for each product. A different cost and revenue schedule would have to be derived for the thousands of products which may be carried by the retailer if marginal analysis is to be fully useful. Probably the most critical factor may be the absence of the necessary cost and demand schedules for conducting marginal analysis. Still, the economic concepts of marginal revenue, marginal cost, and fixed costs are useful as an overall guide in pricing decisions.[1]

From a retailing perspective, one of the major problems is that no consideration is given by the marginal cost model to nonprice variables. It is difficult to determine "true price" for a particular product or service, especially since price is at least partly a function of advertising strategies and other elements of the marketing mix. When one of these elements is changed, an entirely new demand curve may have to be estimated and a new pricing decision made.

[1] These points are based on André Gabor, "Customer-Oriented Pricing," in David Thorpe (ed.), *Research into Retailing and Distribution* (Lexington, Mass.: Lexington Books, 1974), pp. 43–44.

The price of a product or service changes whenever any of the various elements in the pricing mix are changed. If a store discontinues giving trading stamps, the real price paid by the consumer increases if the marked price of the merchandise is not decreased. Numerous other examples exist. For instance, court cases have opened the way for merchants to offer a discount for cash and possibly to include a charge for credit card use.[2] As a result, Exxon Corporation has experimented with a 5 percent discount to customers who pay cash.[3] Vehicle Protection Corporation now offers used car dealers a protection plan that guarantees major automobile components for one year or 12,000 miles. It sells the plan to dealers who build the cost into the price of a used car. The cost to the dealer is $60–$95, depending upon the make and condition of the automobile.[4] Finally, buyers of Nikon cameras receive a free, four-hour course in camera care and handling with the purchase of a camera. Nonpurchasers may attend the course for a fee of $10.[5] These types of changes complicate the comparison of price and cost structures for retail outlets.

Price policy for a retailer is simply an overall guide to pricing and consists of a set of rules which the retailer follows in making day-to-day pricing decisions. The retailer may have more than one price policy if a variety of products are sold. Pricing depends on a variety of factors, including the price elasticity of the product, the "fair price" of the product, the position of the retailer in the market relative to other retailers, consumer acceptance or rejection of particular prices, and the degree of product differentiation.

Because of the importance of price in the retailing mix, the objectives of this chapter are to:

1. Review internal and external considerations affecting price policy.
2. Review possible objectives in pricing.
3. Focus on actual price-setting practices.
4. Focus on models for price setting.
5. Focus on the meaning of product line pricing.
6. Focus on possible consumer reactions to price changes.
7. Introduce the arithmetic of retail pricing.

Price cannot be an effective sales-producing tool if it is not in harmony with the other elements of the retailing mix. A change in any element of the mix will have an impact on other elements. If the price for the product being offered is increased, must the retailer increase promotional expenditures to offset the effect of the price increase? The most obvious way in which price can be used as a sales-generating tool is through price cutting, particularly if

---

[2] James A. Hurdle, "Who Should Pay for Credit Card Use?" *Marketing News,* January 30, 1976, p. 4.

[3] "New Price Weapons for Gasoline Dealers," *Business Week,* October 4, 1976, p. 32.

[4] "Marketing Observer," *Business Week,* December 1, 1975, p. 54.

[5] "Marketing Observer," *Business Week,* February 23, 1976, p. 96.

the demand for the product is elastic. However, this approach may be disastrous for the retailer if it diminishes profit margins or if the courts view it as designed to drive the competition out of business.

FACTORS INFLUENCING PRICE SETTING

The type of good

Pricing decisions are often constrained by whether the products offered are shopping goods, convenience goods, or specialty goods. Typically major product differentiation does not exist for convenience goods, and the prices of such goods are virtually identical for all retailers. An exception includes grocery stores, which may vary the prices on convenience items, particularly as loss leaders, and, depending upon the marketing mix, may strive for a general price level at, above, or below the market price. Greater product differentiation exists for shopping goods, and the consumer is probably searching for some unique aspect of the merchandise. Thus, the retailer has more leeway in prices for this type of product. For specialty goods, prices are of limited importance, at least as compared with shopping and convenience goods. The consumer will make a major effort to acquire a particular brand.

The retailer cost structure

The cost structure of the retailer is also important. Costs are difficult to establish for the multiproduct retailer. However, every effort should be made not to price individual products below the overall cost structure of the firm. The importance of selected factors in pricing varies on a product-by-product basis, however. For example, retailers may be willing to cover only variable costs for some products which they are using as loss leaders.

The demand structure

Elasticity is a key element in demand analysis. It is defined as the ratio of the percentage response in the quantity sold to a percentage change in price or one of the other marketing mix elements, such as advertising expenditures. In general terms it measures the sensitivity in quantity demanded to a change in a demand determinant. Mathematically, elasticity may be calculated as follows:

$$\text{Elasticity} = \frac{\%\ \text{change in quantity demanded}}{\%\ \text{change in any demand determinant}}$$

Elasticity should always be calculated in percentage terms instead of absolute units to allow for comparisons of demand sensitivity for different products. There are as many types of demand elasticity as there are demand determinants.

Price elasticity.   Retailers typically think in terms of price elasticity when evaluating demand structure. Price elasticity of demand can be defined as:

$$\text{Price elasticity} = \frac{\% \text{ change in quantity demanded}}{\% \text{ change in price}}$$

The coefficient of price elasticity is nearly always negative because price and quantity are inversely related; that is, when the price falls, the quantity demanded tends to rise, and when the price rises, the demand tends to fall. Thus, retailers are most interested in the size of the coefficient. A coefficient of more than one indicates that demand is elastic, and a coefficient of less than one indicates price inelasticity.

Clearly, then, markups on highly competitive merchandise tend to be low because the demand for such items is price elastic. Thus, retail markups probably should vary inversely with price elasticity of demand if profits are to be maximized. Low markups on highly price-elastic merchandise can be offset by higher markups on items which are not highly competitive and for which prices are not as readily known by consumers. Lee Preston has offered the following generalizations about markup. These are related to the concept of elasticity:

1.   Markups should vary inversely with unit costs.
2.   Markups should vary inversely with turnover.
3.   Markups should be higher and prices lower on resellers' (private) brands than on manufacturers' brands.[6]

Based on his generalizations, markups will typically be higher on low-price items, lower on items with a high rate of turnover, and higher on private brand items.

Generic and brand influences.   Retailers must also think in terms of both generic demand for the product or service (industry-wide demand) and demand for the individual brand which the retailer is offering (brand elasticity) when considering the concept of elasticity. Gasoline is often used as an example in talking about generic and brand elasticity at the retail level.

Industry demand for gasoline is basically inelastic. As observed in recent years, even large increases in the price of gasoline do not greatly affect the quantity purchased. However, brand elasticity may be quite high. Small changes in the price for a particular brand can cause major shifts in the quantity purchased. Brand elasticity for any product is likely to exist when consumers do not perceive major differences between the products offered by various retailers. This is one reason why large retailers and manufacturers try so hard to establish brand differentiation in their products.

Cross-elasticity of demand.   A further complicating problem in pricing decisions for the retailer is the cross-elasticity of demand, especially where

---

[6] Lee Preston, *Profits, Competition, and Rules of Thumb in Retail Food Pricing* (Berkeley: University of California Institute for Business and Economic Research, 1963), p. 31.

products or outlets are close substitutes. As has been noted, "Price-value competition can also come from different distribution channels. Dollar for dollar, eating at home is less expensive than eating out, especially with gas costs. Yet fast-food sales were far less negatively affected during the recent energy crisis/economic downturn than the industry had anticipated."[7] As a result, chain food store executives are increasingly concerned about fast-food competition.

The measurement of elasticity.   We often assume that price elasticity is hard to measure for retail management. This is probably the case for the small retailer, even though experience can yield useful guidelines. However, large retailers probably know a surprising amount about the elasticity of demand for certain products or services. For example, a variety of experimental procedures can be used to determine the effects of price changes on demand. In marketing research classes these approaches are often discussed in the context of experimental designs.

Experimentation is simply an effort to measure the effects of a price change on demand under controlled conditions. Experimentation may occur in the form of laboratory experiments or in-store situations. Another method is by the use of surveys, which simply involves asking consumers their reactions to anticipated price changes. This is at best, however, a crude method of establishing whether demand is sensitive to price.

Let's look briefly at the use of a simple before-after experimental design with a control group which retailers can use to measure the reaction of demand to price changes in a product. In the research design shown in Table 14–1, the retailer selects two stores which are matched in terms of customer

TABLE 14–1

	Before/after with control	
Measurement	Test group (Store 1)	Control group (Store 2)
Measurement of sales before price change	Yes (10)	Yes (10)
Price reduction of 10 percent	Yes	No
Measurement of sales after price reduction of 10 percent	Yes (20)	Yes (15)

profiles, management policies, store size, and other features so that they are as similar as possible. Unit sales in both stores are then determined for the product of interest. Since the stores are matched, the level of sales should be the same—ten units in each outlet. The price level for the product in Store 1 is reduced by 10 percent and left unchanged in Store 2. At the end of the specified period of time, sales are measured in both stores. As noted, sales increased from 10 units to 20 units for the store in which the price was reduced. However, sales also increased from 10 units to 15 units in the store

---

[7] *Grey Matter* (New York: Grey Advertising, Inc., 1977), p. 2.

for which the price was not reduced. This five-unit increase was due to various forces beyond the control of the retailer and probably would also have occurred in Store 1 even without the reduction in price. Thus, the net effect of the price reduction was five units: $20 - 15 = 5$.

More sophisticated designs can be used to determine the effects of more than one variable on the level of retail sales. The Latin square in Figure 14–2, is one such design. With this design the retailer can determine the effects of the position of the product in the store, the time of the month, and package color (labeled A, B, or C) on sales, each independently of the other two variables. The row values distinguish the effects of time of month, if any; the column values identify differences between the various positions in the store; and compiling the like color treatments will distinguish possible color preferences. Analysis of variance is used to determine the differences.

FIGURE 14–2
LATIN SQUARE

Week (row)	Position in store (column)		
	1	2	3
1	A	B	C
2	B	C	A
3	C	A	B

These procedures, though very useful, are costly and time consuming and are typically used to determine the elasticity of prices for only the most important products.

Consumer behavior during the rapid price increases of the early 1970s indicates the practical importance of price elasticity in retail decisions. It was found that "when prices escalate sharply and suddenly, as with meat, gasoline, and more recently, coffee, people tend to think they have risen higher than reality."[8]

The market structure

Market structure is affected by the number and size of competitors and the amount of product or store differentiation, which in turn affect pricing. Eco-

---
[8] Ibid., p. 4.

nomics teaches us that in theory there are essentially four kinds of market structures—pure competition, pure monopoly, oligopoly, and monopolistic competition.

Pure competition. Pure competition in its true form probably never existed. However, some retailing markets may approach this theoretical model and provide a basis for understanding the forces which affect pricing at the retail level. Specifically, the demand for a particular item may have great elasticity between stores which means that the retailer has little control over price.

Roadside stands selling fresh fruits and vegetables probably come closest to the purely competitive model in retailing. All retailers selling a product which is perceived as homogeneous, for which brand preference is weak or nonexistent, and for which there are a large number of alternative sources of purchase, face this situation.

Market forces essentially set the price for these products. Whenever demand and supply conditions allow the retailers to earn more than a normal profit, new outlets are induced to enter. In these situations, consumers probably are receiving maximum protection from "exploitation" by business firms. Thus, this is the epitome of the so-called free market where government regulation is minimal. In the long run, products are offered at the lowest price covering fixed and variable costs. Consumers obtain the product at the lowest economically feasible price. The retailer has little discretion over price and must price "at the market" since the demand curve is horizontal, as shown in Figure 14–1.

Monopolistic competition. We know that neither products nor retail outlets are totally homogeneous in retailing because each product and outlet is differentiated in some way from competitors. This differentiation occurs through the use of such factors as advertising, brand names, and location. Thus, the monopolistically competitive market, which is the model most familiar in retailing, is characterized by many firms which sell weakly differentiated products. Monopolistic competition characterizes such outlets as shoe stores, furniture stores, food stores, and clothing stores. Each of these firms has a limited kind of monopoly based on the manipulation of the various elements of the retailing mix.

Retailers have a limited amount of influence over price in this model. The greater the success of management in differentiating the outlet, the greater the latitude it has in establishing prices. As an example of retail pricing under monopolistic competition, Louisville-based Convenient Industries of America, which operates 272 convenience stores, "sets its prices between those of the supermarket and the 7–11's."[9]

Vigorous nonprice competition is more likely to be practiced than is price competition to avoid profit erosion.[10] Because retail outlets in this market

---

[9] "Convenience Stores: $7.4 Billion Mushroom," *Business Week*, March 21, 1977, p. 62.

[10] In an extreme move to avoid price competition, retail firms may engage in the illegal practice of price-fixing. In recent years such retail giants as Saks, Bergdorf Goodman, Bonwit

model have some discretion in establishing price, the firm has a downward-sloping demand curve, as shown in Figure 14–3. Hence, if the firm raises prices, it can expect a decline in sales as some customers may switch to lower price brands or to other outlets selling the same item at a lower price. The firm can probably also sell more of an item at a lower price than at a higher price.

FIGURE 14–3

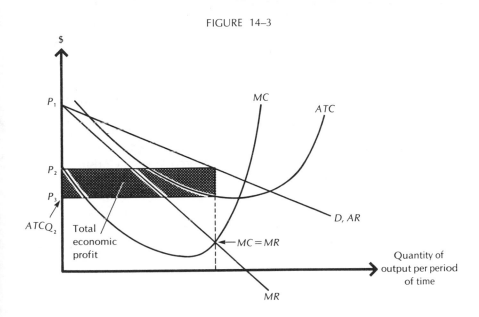

If a large number of good substitutes are available, as in the case of automobile tires, for example, the demand curve for any one firm may be highly elastic over the relevant range of prices. In the final analysis, the degree of price elasticity is a function of the number of rival competitors and of the extent to which the products or outlets offered are differentiated in the minds of customers. The less the degree of product or store differentiation, and the larger the number of competitors, the higher the price elasticity of demand for the firm's offerings.

The tendency in this model is for profits to move toward normal rates of return. However, the tendency toward long-run equilibrium can be interrupted. Clearly, some retailers may have an especially favorable location which allows them to earn economic profits. This may be the case, for example, with strategically located motels, shopping centers, restaurants,

Teller, I. Magnin, and Genesco have been charged by the FTC with price fixing ("Exec Fined $25G," *Chain Store Age*, September 1975, p. 10(a); "Saks, I. Magnin Hit on Pricing," *Chain Store Age*, June 1976, p. 4; "Price Fixing Suit Accord?" *Chain Store Age*, August 1976; and "Saks Is Sued on Price Fixing," *Chain Store Age*, March 1977, p. 18).

and similar organizations. Likewise, even in the long run some firms may exist with below-normal profits. This may be the case for the corner grocery store.

Because consumer tastes and preferences are not uniform, it is profitable, as noted earlier, for retailers selling similar products to pursue various segmentation strategies aimed at specific buyers and market segments. Each possible combination of price, product offering, and promotional expenditures yields a different demand and cost situation for the firm.

Only one of these combinations will yield maximum profit. Trial and error is typically necessary in developing this ideal combination. Thus, the competitive strategies of retail outlets in this market model will assume a variety of different forms. Some may compete on price, others primarily on the basis of product quality, and still others on the basis of heavy promotional expenditures or some other variable. Each strategy is an effort to make the demand curve facing the outlet a little less elastic. Perhaps the ultimate in an inelastic demand curve in this type of market is portrayed in the behavior of Levi Levitz, co-founder of Marshall Field, who could berate customers and still experience an almost reverent attitude toward the store: "Even the old, ultraconservative payment plan of 30 days to pay at no interest would have stirred the wrath of co-founder Levi Levitz. . . . He was notorious for chasing delinquent debtors from his office even after they had paid their bills, brandishing his cane and refusing to sell them thereafter, even for cash."[11] Few retailers today can afford the luxury of this type of behavior.

Oligopoly.   Market structure is oligopolistic whenever a small number of retailers dominate sales in an area. These firms may be small and still be oligopolistic if they are large relative to the size of the total market. Oligopolistic retailers occupy sufficiently prominent market positions to influence the decisions and actions of competitors. In these situations what one firm does affects the others. If a price change is announced, the competition is likely to make a similar change. This interdependence extends to pricing, promotional strategies, customer services, and similar aspects of competition in the differentiated oligopoly model. Indeed, competitive interaction among retailers is the key feature of oligopoly. Oligopoly is clearly demonstrated in the behavior of banks in the retail market. If one bank raises the interest rate it pays on consumer savings, the others will probably do likewise. Also, if a key department store opens on Sunday, competitors will also soon remain open. Firms which specialize in products with a rather narrow market, such as musical instruments or auto rentals, are typically part of an oligopolistic market structure. Likewise, if one or two large retailers such as Sears dominate a market area they can be considered as oligopolists, particularly if they exercise price leadership. In these situations, locally owned retail firms with comparable products are really part of the competitive fringe which must meet the prices of the dominant retailer. On the other hand, these firms also

---

[11] "Why Profits Shrink at a Grand Old Name," *Business Week*, April 11, 1977, p. 78.

have to be wary of excessive price cutting or they may face retailiation by the national retailer.

Numerous oligopolistic pricing models exist, but the kinked demand curve model shown in Figure 14–4 is one of the most common models and depicts what is likely to happen in an oligopolistic retail structure in the absence of strong price leadership by one firm.

FIGURE 14–4
THE KINKED DEMAND CURVE

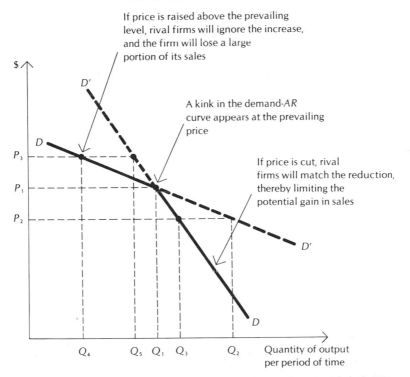

If price is raised above the prevailing level, rival firms will ignore the increase, and the firm will lose a large portion of its sales

A kink in the demand-*AR* curve appears at the prevailing price

If price is cut, rival firms will match the reduction, thereby limiting the potential gain in sales

In this model, price cuts will be matched by competitors to prevent the price-cutting firm from gaining customers, as in the case of competition among the several Ford dealerships in a large metropolitan area. However, price increases will be largely ignored because the retailers who do not raise price will gain the business lost by the firm which raises its price. Thus, each firm has a kinked demand curve for its product like the solid line *(DD)*, with the kink occurring at the prevailing price. In these situations, an independent price increase will cause a large decline in the retailer's sales volume, whereas a price cut will yield only small sales gains since it will be matched by the price cuts of competitors.

The oligopolistic models indicate that retailers will tend to refrain from independently raising prices above a going rate for fear that they will experience a substantial decline in profits, sales, and market share. They are also not likely to cut prices drastically because the price cuts will be matched by those of competitors. Thus, in an oligopolistic pricing structure all retailers will charge essentially the same prices for their products because they cannot expect to sell essentially similar products at significantly higher prices than the competition.

Where outlets or products are not strongly differentiated, the oligopolist will tend to charge comparable prices. This is true, for example, for Ford, Chevrolet, and Plymouth dealers at the retail level. It is also true for comparable brands of television sets.

Technological changes

Pricing on a learning curve, with prices dropping to lower and lower levels as new technologies permit, can prove disastrous, as demonstrated by pocket calculators. Prices for these types of products tend to be much more volatile than the prices of products which have been on the market for a longer period of time. Hand-held electronic calculators and digital watches were introduced only a few years ago. Yet their prices have been greatly reduced. Electronic calculators that sold for $200 or more were selling for $25 or less within two years. There have been similar trends in the prices of digital watches and video games. Retailers caught in this type of situation may suffer adverse consequences, particularly if they are not stocking the new-technology items. Indeed, in the case of digital watches the market shares of selected brands of conventional watches were drastically reduced and traditional retail distribution outlets suffered lost sales. Especially hard hit was the distribution of luxury watches through jewelers. The price cutting drove the prices of digital watches from $2,000 to $10 in just five years. Gruen Industries, producers of traditional luxury watches, was so hard hit that it filed for reorganization under the federal bankruptcy laws.

Supplier policies

Suppliers often recommend prices to retailers. The greater the degree of the retailer's dependence on the supplier, the more influence the supplier is likely to have in pricing decisions. However, manufacturers appear to be losing control over the prices paid by the consumer because of the pricing actions of profit-pressed retailers. As has been noted, "This trend will continue and may result in the end of pre-pricing. Ten years from now there may not even be a suggested list and no way for a manufacturer to indicate his preferred consumer price. It will be illegal to enforce a consumer price."[12]

---

[12] Grey Matter, p. 4.

Indeed, even today without a consignment-type sale, any formal enforcement of resale price is illegal in interstate commerce—which includes practically all of retailing.

PRICING STRATEGIES

Cost-oriented pricing

Typically, retailers simply add a fixed percentage to the wholesale cost of the products or services which they sell. This approach is attractive because It Is simple and easy to implement. However, it may ignore demand and market structure realities. Nevertheless, cost-oriented pricing is popular because retail management knows far more about the cost structure of the firm than it knows about demand. It perceives demand as too difficult to model.

One of the most serious drawbacks of cost-oriented approaches to pricing, in addition to their failure to take into account the differing price sensitivities of various market segments, is the price squeeze that may result when consumer demand is reduced. This occurred in the early 1970s because of the effects of simultaneous recession and inflation on consumers. If the retailer continues to raise prices under such circumstances simply to preserve desired profit margins, the result may be reduced consumer demand, particularly if prices are in the elastic section of the demand curve. When demand for a product is becoming increasingly elastic, lower margins may be necessary to maintain adequate demand. Alternatives may exist to steadily increasing prices, however. For example, by restricting price increases to replacement parts, services, and related items, the retailer may be able to hold the line on prices established for the original item.[13] The retailer may also elect to employ new sales incentives for store personnel to help meet volume and margin objectives.

Market-oriented pricing

Pricing above the market. On some occasions management may be able to price products without undue regard to reactions by consumers. This may be true when an item is regarded as a specialty product or when the outlet can be strongly differentiated from its competitors. For example, management may be able to charge an above-the-market price because it is willing to take greater than normal risks with credit terms or similar arrangements which make the consumer willing to pay a higher price than is charged for the same item by a competitor. Another differentiating feature may be locational and/or time convenience. Neighborhood mini-supermarkets often charge higher prices than do conventional supermarkets

---

[13] Joseph T. Guiltinan, "Risk-Aversive Pricing Policies: Problems and Alternatives," *Journal of Marketing*, vol. 40 (January 1976), p. 14.

because of the convenience of location. Likewise, stores that stay open on Sunday and have late evening hours may be able to charge a higher than normal price for these reasons. Finally, outlets with a highly prestigious reputation may be able to charge above-the-market prices. However, higher prices do not necessarily mean higher profits, particularly if overhead costs are higher.

Pricing at the market level.   The majority of retailers offer merchandise at prices which are roughly comparable to the prices of their competitors. A decision of this nature typically means that the outlets are not strongly differentiated in terms of location, brands carried, or whatever. Also, as we noted in talking about an oligopolistic market structure, little incentive may exist to lower or raise prices because the cuts will be followed by competitors and the increases may not be followed, which will lower demand. Firms in monopolistically competitive markets may seek to differentiate their outlets on bases other than price.

Pricing below the market.   Below-the-market prices are typically offered by retailers who have a low overhead and high volume, such as discount operations in low-cost locations. This is why discounters are not often located in shopping centers, which are high cost locations. Retailers offering below-the-market prices typically carry only the fastest-moving brands and styles of a particular line of merchandise and keep overhead low by not offering customer services offered by full-service retailers, such as delivery, credit, and product installation. Competition is almost entirely on the basis of prices.

Other dimensions in pricing

The pricing of private brands.   Major retailers often feature items which carry a private brand instead of featuring manufacturer labels. Such outlets as Sears, A&P, and Montgomery Ward feature well-known private brands. These brands are typically offered at below-the-market prices made possible because of the absence of promotion costs associated with selling manufacturer brands. Also, private brands may cost the retailer less than manufacturer brands. Greater freedom is enjoyed in pricing private brands than in pricing manufacturer brands.

As a class, private brands offer a higher proportion of good buys in terms of price-quality relationships. Almost 70 percent of the private brands in one study were underpriced relative to manufacturer brands.[14] Private brands seem to widen consumer choice by providing reasonable performance at a relatively low price.

The one-price system.   The majority of retailers have a one-price system such that each customer pays the same price for identical products. The

---

[14] John E. Swan, "Price-Product Performance and Competition between Retailer and Manufacturer Brands," *Journal of Marketing*, vol. 38 (July 1974), p. 52.

one-price policy is particularly common for convenience goods and items which are purchased frequently and at low prices. The advantages of such a policy are numerous: consumers do not expect to bargain, retail sales clerks are not under pressure to give price reductions, marking of items is easier, and the concept also makes self-service easier for the consumer.

The one-price policy may be less common for costly and infrequently purchased items. In buying such items, the consumer may expect to engage in price negotiations and comparison shopping between stores. Negotiated prices are particularly common in the sale of automobiles and many major appliances. One study found that 32 out of 37 retailers sold major consumer durables at different prices to different consumers. The typical reason for this differentiation was to allow for the bargaining strength and knowledge possessed by the consumer.[15]

The negotiated selling process can be approached in a variety of ways. If the suggested retail sales price of an item is not changed, the retailer may still allow a higher than normal trade-in for a used item, provide free delivery and installation, or provide liberal credit terms or some type of special discount. Negotiated pricing may be more costly because it often requires a larger and more highly trained sales staff than is the case for the routine order processing of inexpensive, frequently purchased items.

Numerous other forms of price discrimination may also occur. These are shown in Figure 14–5.

Psychological pricing.   Certain types of prices have long been held to have special psychological effects on consumers. Odd-even prices are those which are set just below the dollar figures, such as $1.99 instead of $2.00. One apparent reason is the belief that consumers perceive odd-ending prices as substantially lower than prices with even endings, despite the fact that the prices are only slightly lower in actual dollar terms. Most of the previous research on odd-even pricing has focused on sales effects and not on perceptual distortions or price illusions associated with odd-even pricing. Further, the perceptions are subject to a variety of confounding influences. Research by Zarrel Lambert on the effectiveness of odd pricing was inconclusive. His research suggested that illusions of lower price are associated with odd prices under some circumstances.[16]

Odd pricing often suggests the price has been established at the lowest level possible. The retailer using odd prices is probably assuming that the demand curve for the item in question is jagged, as shown in Figure 14–6. This curve indicates that sales are larger when price is expressed as an appropriate odd number than when it is expressed as an even number or as a less satisfactory odd number. Thus, consumers may actually buy less when the price is lowered from the appropriate odd number price to the next lower

---

[15] Walter J. Primeaux, "Price Variability and Price Discrimination: A Case Study," *Marquette Business Review,* Spring 1973, pp. 25–29.

[16] Zarrel V. Lambert, "Perceived Prices as Related to Odd and Even Price Findings," *Journal of Retailing,* vol. 51 (Fall 1975), p. 22.

FIGURE 14–5
TYPES OF PRICE DISCRIMINATION

Individual customer discrimination

1. *Bargain-every-time*. Each sale is an individually negotiated deal. The classic case is the purchase of new and used cars; other examples include made-to-order sales and art objects.
2. *Size-up-his-income*. Wealthier customers are charged more than less affluent customers; price is partially a function of income. Standard examples are the pricing of medical, legal, accounting, and management consulting services.
3. *Cut-the-price-if-you-must*. Departures from list price are made when buyers shop diligently for the best price; sellers grant secret concessions as a last resort.
4. *Count-the-use*. Price is based upon the level of use, even though unit costs do not vary appreciably with volume. For example, the rental fees on Xerox copying machines are based upon the number of copies made.

Group discrimination

1. *Promote-new-customers*. New customers are offered "special introductory prices" lower than those paid by established customers in the hopes of enlarging the firm's regular clientele. Record and book clubs and magazine publishers are avid practitioners of this pricing policy.
2. *Skim-the-market*. A product is introduced at a high price within reach mainly of only high-income buyers. Price is then periodically reduced, step by step, to allow steady, but gradual, penetration of broader markets. The pricing of TV sets and Polaroid cameras has followed this pattern.

Product discrimination

1. *Make-them-pay-for-the-label*. Retailers sell a relatively homogeneous commodity under different brand names, charging higher prices for the better-known, more prestigious brand names. Automobile tires, paints, articles of clothing, and food products are examples.
2. *Appeal-to-quality*. Products are offered in packages ranging from the budget variety to the super deluxe. Differences in price are more than proportional to the differences in cost. Household appliances are an obvious example. Traveling first class as compared to tourist class is another example.
3. *Get-rid-of-the-dogs*. Price concessions in the form of "special" sales are made periodically or continuously in the bargain department of the retail store, in order to reduce stocks of poorly selling items and to make room for new merchandise. The seemingly perpetual end-of-the-model sales, closeout specials, anniversary sales, and inventory reduction sales serve as good examples.
4. *Switch-them-to-off-peak-periods*. Lower prices are charged for services identical except for time of consumption in order to encourage fuller and more balanced use of capacity. Off-season rates at resorts are an example.

Source: Adapted from Arthur A. Thompson, Jr., *Economics of the Firm: Theory and Practice,* 2d ed., © 1977, pp. 437–38. Reprinted by permission of Prentice-Hall, Inc., Englewood Cliffs, New Jersey.

FIGURE 14–6
ODD PRICING

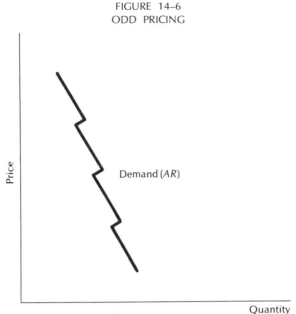

Source: Donald V. Harper, *Price Policy and Procedure* (New York:
Harcourt, Brace and World, 1966), p. 283.

even number price. This reaction by consumers is contrary to the economists'
law of demand, which assumes a smooth demand curve convex to the origin
and sloping to the right. Further, research has shown that "for product
classes where prices are relatively unstable, pricing a product at $19.95 or
$19.99 . . . might lead to greater resistance to a future price increase than if
the initial price had been $20.00.[17]

Price lining.   Retailers who practice price lining feature products or services at a limited number of prices. Merchandise offerings may be limited to
two or three price categories which reflect varying merchandise quality. For
example, neckties may be featured at $5, $10, and $15. Donald Siebert,
chairman of the board of J. C. Penney, has stated that "Penneys will be
seeking 'to match the merchandise character and flexibility of the traditional
department store,' concentrating on 'price points representing three-quarters
of the dollar volume in each line' . . . and seeking a '10 to 20 percent price
edge where possible, over department stores.' "[18]

Sherwin Williams, in seeking to broaden the market appeal of its paints,
offered paints at prices ranging from $7.99 to $11.99 per gallon and occa-

---

[17] Nonyelu Nwokoye, "An Experimental Study of the Relationship between Responses to
Price Changes and the Price Level for Shoes," in M. J. Schlinger (ed.), *Advances in Consumer
Research,* vol. 2, 1975, p. 701.

[18] "'77 Focus Is on Changing Consumer Habits and Bottom Line," *Stores,* January 1977, p.
19.

sionally promoted them at $5.99 to compete with the low end of the price range of Sears paint.[19]

Price lining makes the pricing task simpler because inventory control is easier. Lastly, problems with sales clerks are reduced because the salesclerks do not have to be familiar with as many different prices.

More recently, price lining has created problems because of rapidly rising costs. The result is that the retailer is often stuck with a rather inflexible pricing policy. Also, historical price-quality relationships which may have been established by price lining can be distorted because of rapid price changes. The breakdown of historical price-quality relationships in the mind of the consumer reduces the usefulness of statistical demand curve models based on price lines.

Research has shown that retailers have a lack of sophistication about price lining and cite cost/markups and manufacturer list prices rather than sales/profits or competition as reasons for the practice. They recognize that price lining is easy to administer but have no idea of its effects on sales or profits.[20]

Leader pricing.   A common practice by retailers is to mark down the price of selected merchandise as a promotional effort to attract additional customers. Typically leader pricing does not occur for all items. The characteristics of the best price leader are as follows:

It is well known and widely used.

It is priced low enough to attract numerous buyers.

It is not usually bought in large quantities and stored.

It enjoys a high price elasticity of demand.

It does not compete closely with other products in the retailer's assortment of merchandise.[21]

The basic idea behind leader pricing is to attract consumers into the store who will purchase merchandise in addition to the featured loss leaders.

Price adjustments

Retailers frequently raise or lower prices from the originally marked price. Price changes are usually an effort to increase sales. Some retailers, however, offer special merchandise discounts to such groups as college professors, members of trade unions, and persons 65 years of age or older. These discounts may be designed to attract a disproportionate amount of trade from a particular group or may simply be an act of social responsibility.

---

[19] "A Paintmaker Puts a Fresh Coat on its Marketing," Business Week, February 23, 1976, p. 95.

[20] Richard T. Hise and Myron Gable, "Analyzing Retailer Price-Lining Policies," in Henry Nash and Donald Robin (eds.), Proceedings: Southern Marketing Association, 1976 p. 40.

[21] Donald V. Harper, Price Policy and Procedure (New York: Harcourt, Brace and World, 1966), p. 253.

Markups. Markups are occasionally necessary to offset rapidly rising prices by the supplier. Markups on shelf merchandise are a major source of consumer dissatisfaction with retailing.

Markdowns. Virtually all retailers have occasion to use price markdowns. These should be part of a planned pricing strategy, and not as has been reported for cosmetics: "When it came time for sales in every other store department, we'd concoct some sort of price-off scheme just to stay in rhythm with the rest of the store."[22] Many markdowns are planned to occur at the end of each season of the year. For example, winter merchandise may be marked down in December or January to make room for spring merchandise. Such markdowns are typically in the form of a clearance sale. The retailer may also engage in markdowns simply to reduce inventories or to move merchandise which is selling very slowly. However, even markdowns of 40–50 percent will not guarantee large sales increases.[23]

As shown in Figure 14–7, the retailer typically has five alternatives when merchandise is not moving at the originally marked price:

1. An element of the retailing mix other than price can be changed.
2. The merchandise can be carried forward to the next selling season.
3. Additional markups can be placed on the merchandise.
4. A markdown can be taken.
5. The merchandise may be donated to a charitable organization.

Markdowns are the most frequently used method of moving merchandise.

The markdown price for merchandise is typically established on the basis of a predetermined percentage off the retail price, such as 20 percent. Thus, an item previously featured at a retail selling price of $100 would now be featured at $80. Some retailers, on the other hand, adopt a dollar markdown as opposed to a percentage markdown.

Management needs to give careful attention to markdowns so as to keep them to a minimum. For example, it may be determined that a selected number of brands require a disproportionate number of markdowns. The retailer may also decide to offer special incentives to salespersons for selling slow-moving merchandise. Finally, buying strategies may need to be altered.

Markdowns in excess of 20 percent may be viewed with suspicion by consumers, though the reaction may vary by product. For luxury items, consumers probably do not expect any appreciable markdown and may doubt product quality if the price is slashed. Seasonal, perishable, and obsolete stock are exceptions. Overall, however, excessively high markdowns may cause consumers to question a seller's integrity or fairness.[24] This finding lends strong support to the Fair Price Hypothesis mentioned in Chapter 5.

---

[22] "Management Realists in the Glamour World of Cosmetics," *Business Week*, November 29, 1976, p. 45.

[23] "Hoopla to Cure Sagging Sales," *Business Week*, July 19, 1976, p. 18.

[24] Nwokoye, "Experimental Study," p. 701.

FIGURE 14–7
REASONS FOR MARKDOWNS AND ALTERNATIVES

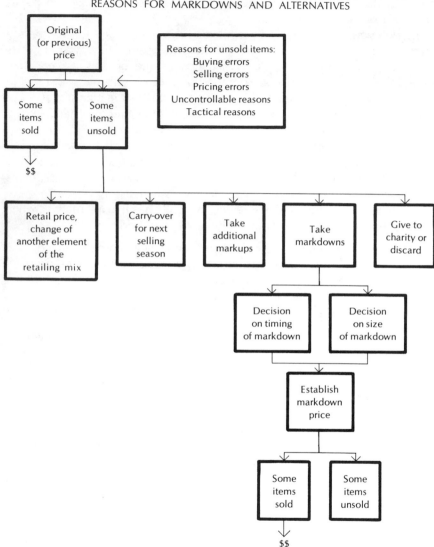

Source: *Retailing Today,* by Don L. James, Bruce J. Walker, and Michael J. Etzel, © 1975 by Harcourt Brace Jovanovich, Inc. Reproduced by permission of the publishers.

Too frequent markdowns also cause problems. As has been noted, "the public will grow to expect them, and like the boy who 'cried wolf' too often, we will lose our credibility with our customers. Specials should not be taken for granted."[25]

---

[25] "Selling Fashion," *Retail Directions,* May–June 1975, p. 25.

Organization for pricing

Pricing in the retail firm is typically decentralized. This means that prices are ordinarily not set by top management. Rather, retail prices are set at the store management level or even at the buyer level. For chain stores, prices may be established in a central buying office, but these prices are generally suggestions from which the retail store manager may deviate in order to meet local competition. If prices are set by department buyers, they are typically established as policy by higher management. Often national averages by type of merchandise are used as the basis for establishing price guidelines. Flexibility in price setting at the retail level allows management to respond more readily to price changes by competition and to operate more competitively in local markets.

Some controls on decentralized pricing are necessary, however, to avoid having stores of the same chain in a metropolitan area compete with themselves, as was the situation for W. T. Grant. Controls must also be exercised to the extent of ensuring that profitability, market share, or some other goal of the corporate organization is being met.

THE MATHEMATICS OF PRICING

This section of the chapter covers the basic material essential to understand the arithmetic of pricing. Our approach is pragmatic and does not overemphasize the act of computation. Every retailer will be faced with the types of issues discussed in this section. Admittedly, the field of retailing has been provided with "crutches" in the form of "profit flashers," "markup wheels," and the like. However, the astute student and/or practitioner of retailing management needs to understand the various relationships which are stressed here. Retail firms expect their management trainees to understand the concepts and to be able to relate the various pricing components in such a way as to solve for any unknown in a pricing problem.[26]

Concepts of retail price

The *original retail price* of an item or a group of items is the first price at which the merchandise is offered for sale. The *sales retail* is the final price for which a product or a classification of products is sold. (See Figure 14–8 for the concepts.) The difference between the sales retail and the original retail price comprises the reductions incurred before the item is sold. These reductions may be any or all of the following: markdowns, employee discounts, and shortages (or shrinkage).

---

[26] Key determinants of the *real* price paid by retailers are discounts received. The following chapter in presenting *terms of sale* covers the subject in adequate detail.

FIGURE 14–8
CONCEPTS OF RETAIL

Original retail price—$1,000 {
┌─ ─ ─ ─ ─ ─ ─ ─ ┐
│   20%, or $200,   │
├─ reductions ─ ─ ┤
│   │
└───────────────┘ } Sales retail—$800

Concepts of markup

The concept of *initial* markup (or mark-on) is the difference between the invoice cost and the original retail price, expressed in dollars. Initial markup in Figure 14–9 is $22,000 ($102,000 − $80,000). Expressed in percentage, it is related to the original retail price, $22,000/$102,000 = 21.6 percent. Initial markups is an aggregate planning concept, as was discussed in Chapters 12 and 13 on merchandise planning and accounting.

FIGURE 14–9

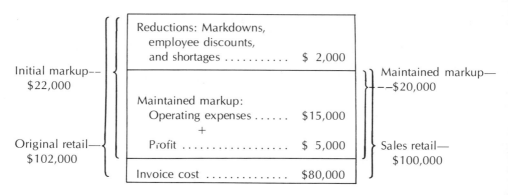

Initial markup—
$22,000

Original retail—
$102,000

Reductions: Markdowns,
    employee discounts,
    and shortages . . . . $ 2,000

Maintained markup:
    Operating expenses $15,000
                +
    Profit . . . . $ 5,000

Invoice cost $80,000

Maintained markup—
—$20,000

Sales retail—
$100,000

Maintained markup (or mark-on) is the difference between the invoice cost and sales retail—that is, $100,000 − $80,000, or $20,000. Expressed in percentage terms, the dollar amount is related to sales retail—$20,000/$100,000 = 20.0 percent. The maintained markup covers operating expenses and provides a profit return to the firm (Figure 14–9). Maintained markup differs from initial markup by the amount of the various reductions ($2,000) shown in Figure 14–7.[27] The markup data shown in Table 14–2 is useful as a handy guide to both students and retailers.

---

[27] The difference between *maintained markup* and *gross margin* is explained in Chapter 13. In some circles the terms are used interchangeably.

TABLE 14–2
MARKUP TABLE

To use this table find the desired percentage in the left-hand column. Multiply the cost of the article by the corresponding percentage in the "markup percent of cost" column. The result, added to the cost, gives the correct selling price.

Markup percent of selling price	Markup percent of cost	Markup percent of selling price	Markup percent of cost	Markup percent of selling price	Markup percent of cost
4.8	5.0	18.5	22.7	33.3	50.0
5.0	5.3	19.0	23.5	34.0	51.5
6.0	6.4	20.0	25.0	35.0	53.9
7.0	7.5	21.0	26.6	35.5	55.0
8.0	8.7	22.0	28.2	36.0	56.3
9.0	10.0	22.5	29.0	37.0	58.8
10.0	11.1	23.0	29.9	37.5	60.0
10.7	12.0	23.1	30.0	38.0	61.3
11.0	12.4	24.0	31.6	39.0	64.0
11.1	12.5	25.0	33.3	39.5	65.5
12.0	13.6	26.0	35.0	40.0	66.7
12.5	14.3	27.0	37.0	41.0	70.0
13.0	15.0	27.3	37.5	42.0	72.4
14.0	16.3	28.0	39.0	42.8	75.0
15.0	17.7	28.5	40.0	44.4	80.0
16.0	19.1	29.0	40.9	46.1	85.0
16.7	20.0	30.0	42.9	47.5	90.0
17.0	20.5	31.0	45.0	48.7	95.0
17.5	21.2	32.0	47.1	50.0	100.0
18.0	22.0				

Source: *Expenses in Retail Business,* a publication of NCR Corporation, Dayton, Ohio.

Planning the required initial markup goal

In the discussion of merchandise planning in Chapter 12 it was noted that as a part of the total merchandise plan, initial goals for margins are essential. It is also essential to plan sales and reductions.

As a means of understanding the process of initial markup planning, let's look at Figure 14–9 and work backward. Assume that management has forecast sales of a particular merchandise line at $100,000, expenses of $15,000, and a profit return of 5 percent of sales, or $5,000. Figure 14–9 shows the *results* expected in operations with these planned figures—that is, a maintained markup of $20,000, or 20 percent. Figure 14–10, on the other hand, reveals that management experience indicates that reductions such as markdowns and employee discounts are normally 2 percent of sales, or $2,000. From Figures 14–9 and 14–10 we can see that a planned initial markup of $22,000, or 21.6 percent ($22,000/$102,000), is necessary to

FIGURE 14–10

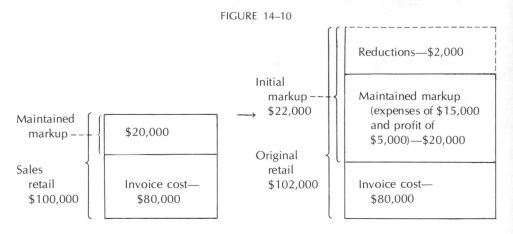

maintain a markup of $20,000, or 20 percent ($20,000/$100,000). This type of planning causes management to consider all of the elements which can affect profit.[28]

No thoughtful merchant can afford to endorse a uniform markup policy which suggests that every piece of merchandise brought into the retail store will carry an identical markup. Too many institutional and environmental factors are operating to prohibit such behavior. The planned initial markup figures do however give a "check," or planned figure, against which management can compare the cumulative mark-on (see Chapter 13 for an explanation of this control performance figure) and take necessary remedial action if the two figures do not show the proper relationship during an operating period.

Computations

Every merchandiser needs practice in computing some routine relationships among costs, initial markups, and original retail prices. We have no desire to impose formulas on you[29]—merely remember that Cost + Initial markup = Original retail price and express the equation in the following format for ease in "working the puzzles" which follow as illustrations.

---

[28] For the formula oriented, the relationships can be shown as:

$$\text{Initial markup percentage} = \frac{\text{Expenses} + \text{Profit} + \text{Reductions}}{\text{Sales retail} + \text{Reductions}}$$

Substituting from the above:

$$\text{Initial markup percentage} = \frac{15,000 + 5,000 + 2,000}{100,000 + 2,000} = \frac{22,000}{102,000} = 21.6\%$$

[29] Again, for those who feel comfortable with formula presentations, we are indicating them in the appropriate place.

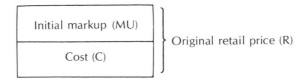

Given cost and retail.   A color TV costs the retailer $500. The original price is decided to be $800. Find the initial markup in dollars and percent computed on cost and retail bases.

The difference between R and C is $800 − $500 = $300. Based on cost, the markup would be $300 ÷ $500 = 60 percent; based on retail price, the markup is $300 ÷ $800 = 37.5 percent.[30]

Conversion of markup—Retail to cost.   In working with pricing, the buyer is often confronted with the problem of converting a markup on retail to a markup on cost. This might occur if the store utilizes cost as a base for calculations. Most large progressive firms think in terms of retail bases, but conversions are often necessary. The initial markup is 42 percent on retail. What is the markup on a cost base?

If the retail markup is 42 percent, then retail is 100 percent and cost must be 58 percent; consequently, markup as a percentage of cost is 0.42 ÷ 0.58 = 72.4 percent. In other words, 42 percent markup on retail is equivalent to 72.4 percent on cost.[31] Clearly, markup on cost will always be arithmetically larger than markup on retail since the cost base is smaller than the retail base and the markup is constant.

---

[30] Markup percentage on cost = $\dfrac{\text{\$ markup}}{\text{\$ cost}}$, and markup percentage on retail = $\dfrac{\text{\$ markup}}{\text{\$ retail}}$

[31] Markup percentage on cost = $\dfrac{\text{Markup \% on retail}}{100\% - \text{Markup \% on retail}}$

Cost to retail. The initial markup is 60 percent on cost. What is the markup on a retail base?

```
┌─────────────────────┐
│  MU/C = 60%         │ ⎫
│                     │ ⎬  R = 160%
│  MU/R = ?           │ ⎭
├─────────────────────┤
│  C = 100%           │
└─────────────────────┘
```

If the cost markup is 60 percent, then cost must be 100 percent and retail must be 160 percent; consequently, markup as a percentage of retail is $0.60 \div 1.60 = 37.5$ percent. This says that 60 percent markup on cost is equivalent to 37.5 percent markup on retail.[32]

Various relationships. For additional types of relationships which will face the merchant, the following examples are noted and the results calculated.

1. A chair costs a retailer $420. If a markup of 40 percent of retail is desired, what should the retail price be?[33]

```
┌─────────────────────┐
│  MU/R = 40%         │ ⎫
│                     │ ⎬  R = 100% and $?
├─────────────────────┤
│  C = 100 − 40 =     │
│  60% ; $420         │
└─────────────────────┘
```

If 60 percent = $420, then 100 percent = $420 ÷ 0.60$, or $700, the retail price needed to achieve the desired markup of 40 percent on retail.

2. A dryer retails for $300. The markup is 28 percent of cost. What was the cost of the dryer?[34]

```
┌─────────────────────┐
│  MU/C = 28%         │ ⎫
│                     │ ⎬  R = $300 and 128%
├─────────────────────┤
│  C = 100%           │
│      $?             │
└─────────────────────┘
```

If 128 percent = $300, then 100 percent = $300 ÷ 1.28$, or $234.37; the cost which is needed to achieve the desired markup of 28 percent on cost.

---

[32] Markup percentage on retail $= \dfrac{\text{Markup \% on cost}}{100\% + \text{Markup \% on cost}}$

[33] Whenever the retail price is to be calculated and the dollar cost and markup % on retail are known, the problem can be solved with the following:

$$\$\text{ retail} = \frac{\$\text{ cost}}{100\% - \text{Retail markup \%}}$$

[34] Whenever the cost price is to be calculated and the dollar retail and markup percentage on cost are known, the problem can be solved as follows:

$$\$\text{ cost} = \frac{\$\text{ retail}}{100\% + \text{Cost markup \%}}$$

3. A retailer prices a sport jacket so that the markup amounts to $36. This is 45 percent of retail. What are the cost and retail figures?[35]

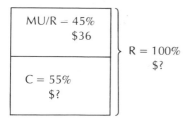

MU/R = 45%
$36

R = 100%
$?

C = 55%
$?

If 45 percent = $36, then 100 percent = $36 ÷ 0.45, or $80. If retail is $80 and markup is $36, then cost is $80 − $36 = $44.

SUMMARY

Many retail price decisions must be based on judgment. Retail pricing involves trial and error, awareness of customer needs, the behavior of competition, and the cost and profit goals of the firm. Store managers who sell thousands of items cannot spend much time on pricing any one item. Therefore, it is typical to rely on a standard markup percentage in these situations. Other retailers, however, are unwilling to routinize the pricing procedure to such an extent. This is particularly true for retailers who sell highly competitive high-priced merchandise. Also, many small retailers establish prices on the basis of what they believe their customers are willing to pay. For many retailers, pricing is basically determined by suppliers.

Overall, the most common approach to pricing is to add a predetermined percentage markup to the cost charged by the supplier. However, cost-plus pricing has major limitations, particularly because it may bear little resemblance to the elasticity of demand for the product. Greater profits may result by employing other methods of retail pricing.

Typically, the retailer has three choices in pricing. Prices may be set at the market, below the market, or above the market. For many products, the retailer has little choice other than to price a product at basically the same price as is charged by competition. Lower than market prices may be possible if the retailer is operating on a high-volume/low-markup basis. The retailer may be able to price above the market for prestigious items or for items about which consumers have little information.

Most retailers follow a single-price policy, though for infrequently purchased expensive items a negotiated pricing policy may be followed. In these circumstances, it may be difficult to determine the true price because price can be manipulated in terms of trade-in allowances, the extension of credit terms, free delivery, a free service period, or other means of changing the price without altering the originally marked price.

---

[35] Whenever the dollar markup and the retail markup percentage are known, the retail price can be determined as follows:

$$\$ \text{ retail} = \frac{\$ \text{ retail markup}}{\% \text{ retail markup}}$$

Regardless of the structure utilized in setting prices, all retailers must have a fundamental understanding of the mechanics of markups and markdowns. Such factors as markdowns can be a key variable in retail strategy development. More than a simple knowledge of the mechanics of pricing is required to achieve the greatest profit levels for the retail outlet.

KEY CONCEPTS

Factors influencing price strategy

Pricing strategies
  Cost oriented
  Market oriented
  The one-price system
  Psychological pricing
  Price lining

Price adjustments
  Markups
  Markdowns

Organization for pricing

The mathematics of pricing
  Definition
    Discounts
    Cost of goods sold
  Concepts of retail price
  Concepts of markup
  Initial markup goals

DISCUSSION QUESTIONS

1. For which of the following types of products does the retailer have the greatest flexibility in pricing: convenience goods, shopping goods, or specialty goods? Why?

2. Is it possible for the retailer to set a price at such a low level, assuming that the price is still above the cost structure for the firm, as to adversely affect demand? Justify your reasoning.

3. How are private brands typically priced relative to manufacturer brands? What are the reasons for the differentials in price?

4. In structuring a retail sale, why is an understanding of price elasticity important to the retailer?

5. What types of products do you believe are price elastic, and what types do you believe are price inelastic? Justify your reasoning.

6. Define the following terms: *customary pricing, price lining, odd pricing, psycho-*

logical pricing, cost-oriented pricing, leader pricing, above-the-market pricing, price elasticity, one-price system, and *price adjustments.*

7. Under what circumstances is a retailer likely to be able to charge above-the-market prices for merchandise? Is the retailer justified from an economic point of view in charging above-the-market prices? Is the retailer justified from a social perspective? Explain your answers.

8. If the retailer desires to avoid increasing prices during a period of rising costs, what are some of the strategies which can be employed to retain overall profit margins without necessarily increasing retail prices?

PROBLEMS

1. A retailer who used markup on cost in pricing her goods misplaced her list of retail equivalents. The cost percentages most commonly used in the store were 20 percent, 25 percent, 35 percent, 40 percent, 50 percent, 60 percent, 75 percent, and 100 percent. What retail equivalents should she have calculated for each of the cost percentages?

2. Men's hose may be purchased for $9.50 per dozen and women's hosiery for $13.50 per dozen.
   a. If the hose are marked up 70 percent on cost, and the hosiery are marked up 90 percent on cost, what retail price will be set per pair?
   b. If a markup of 45 percent on retail were applied, what prices would be set per pair?

3. An item carries a markup on retail of 37 percent. What is the equivalent markup percent on cost?

4. A retailer prices a chair so that the markup amounts to $36. This is 42 percent of retail. What are the cost and retail figures?

5. A snow suit costs a retailer $4.80. If a markup of 45 percent of retail is required, what must the retail price be?

6. A cotton blouse costs a retailer $6.60. If a markup of 30 percent on cost is desired, what will the retail price be?

7. A retailer has been pricing merchandise at 45 percent on cost. What is the equivalent markup percent of retail?

8. A markup of 38 percent retail is equivalent to what markup percent on the cost base?

9. The retail price is $92; the cost markup is 34 percent. What is the cost?

10. A retailer prices a dress so that the markup amounts to $72. This is 50 percent of retail. What are the cost and retail figures?

11. What should the initial markup percent be in a department that has the following planned figures: expenses, $12,000; profit, $3,000; sales, $45,000; markdowns, $700; stock shortages, $300?

12. An item has been marked down to $3.95 from its original price of $5. What is (a) the markdown percentage and (b) the off-retail percentage? ·

13. Department A has taken $2,100 in markdowns to date. Net sales to date are $70,000. What is the markdown percentage to date?

14. Sales of $60,000 were planned in a department in which expenses were established at $18,000; employee discounts, $600; and markdowns and shortages, $3,400. If a profit of 4 percent were desired, what initial markup would be planned?

15. An item that was originally priced at $14.00 has been marked down to $11.50. What is (a) the markdown percentage? (b) the off-retail percentage?

PROJECTS

1. Devise a questionnaire to get consumer reaction to the practice of raising the price of goods already on display. (Grocers frequently do this by putting the higher price tag directly on top of the former price.) Do consumers feel that this practice is fair or unfair? Why? Allow room for individual consumer comment on your questionnaire.

2. Devise a method for determining whether people perceive odd or even prices as being lower. This can be done, for example, by interviewing store managers or consumers or by observing behavior in a store. Visit two types of stores, such as a hardware store and a clothing store; what pricing strategy does each follow? Why?

3. Assume that you are a management trainee for a major supermarket chain. Select a market basket of products which are available in all stores and easily comparable (for example, no private brands), and compare prices (including specials) in a conventional supermarket (that is, your own), a "warehouse-type" outlet, and a convenience store (a 7–11). Keep your record over a period of time, present your data in an organized format, and draw conclusions about the pricing philosophy of the different types of food operations.

4. Health and beauty aids are carried in many different kinds of retail establishments (for example, conventional drug stores, supermarkets, discount drugstores, and department stores), and often each type of establishment promises "lower prices," better "assortments," and so on to establish a differential. Prepare a list of selected items available in each store (by comparable size), and compare and contrast the items among the various types of stores. See what you find to be the "real" strategy of the competing stores in the market. Why is the lowest priced store able to price as indicated? What are the specials? Are they similar for all stores?

5. Since meat is such an important item in the family purchasing budget, focus a project on the pricing strategy of competing food stores relative to key meat items. You will have to interview butchers to determine what kinds of meat items you should investigate to make your comparisons. Include different types of "image" stores, and see how "in fact" meat prices follow the images projected by the stores. Charts comparing the prices by type of meat item may show an interesting relationship. Watch for "specials"—try to use the "regular" prices for your comparisons. Come up with some strategy conclusions from your study.

CASES

Case 1. Del-Ray Supermarket had been enjoying a profitable operation for several years. Recently Discount Foods, a new-type grocery store, opened nearby. The new store emphasized low prices and fewer customer services. Del-Ray Supermarket immediately experienced a drastic reduction in business—a nearly 50 percent decline the first week. Del-Ray Supermarket's manager is desperate and decides to employ a loss leader strategy to regain his lost customers. He decides that he will use Discount Foods feature items for his loss leaders. Business picks up, but most of the volume is on the loss leader items, resulting in profitless sales.

What actions should be taken by Del-Ray Supermarket's manager?

Case 2. During a recent trip to Dallas, Texas, Lynn Brown went shopping in Neiman-Marcus. She saw a beautiful cut glass bowl and inquired about the price. "$500," said the salesperson. "Ridiculous," Ms. Brown replied, "I can get the same thing at home for about half that amount." "Perhaps," said the salesperson, "but *this* is Neiman-Marcus." Is the bowl worth $500? How can retailers such as Neiman-Marcus charge above the market for the bowl if this woman can indeed get it at home for $250?

15

BUYER AND
SUPPLIER
RELATIONSHIPS

The terms of sale (continued)
  Datings
    Cash datings
    Future datings
      End of month (EOM)
      Date of invoice (DOI)
      Receipt of goods (ROG)
      Advance
      Extra
    Anticipation
  Shipping costs (f.o.b.)
The need for good vendor relationships
Receiving and marking merchandise

*M*any factors determine the degree of success a retailer may enjoy. I am one of those who are convinced that supplier selection and relationships between the retailer and suppliers are of key significance. A retailer can only be as strong in his merchandise lines as his suppliers. Suppliers dealing with many retailers all over the country can provide much helpful information on improving one's operations. This is an opportunity that the alert retailer should take full advantage of.

Martin B. Seretean, Chairman of the Board
Coronet Industries, Inc.
Dalton, Georgia

Buying to meet a merchandise plan is the first requirement for satisfying customer needs, as noted in Chapter 12. Retail success depends on the effectiveness of this function. Otherwise, out-of-stock situations may be too frequent or, at the other extreme, excessive markdowns may have to be taken. Slow-moving merchandise especially presents a problem for the retailer.

Buying difficulties are compounded because buyers typically purchase merchandise for target markets which they may not fully understand. Further, they often operate under restrictions as to maintained markups set as goals by management. Thus, buying is an integral part of merchandise control.

Given the importance of the buying function to retail success, the purposes of this chapter are to acquaint students of retailing with (1) the sources of supply available to the retailer, (2) the most typical methods of contact with suppliers, (3) the importance of good supplier relationships, (4) the complexities of the terms of sale, and (5) trends in the receiving and marking of merchandise.

Typically several different vendors can provide desired merchandise to a buyer. Selecting the proper vendor is not an easy task. Often conflict may arise between the retailer and the suppliers because of the many complex decisions that must be made. Once the merchandise is agreed upon, numerous other matters, such as price, terms of sales, promotional aids, and delivery dates, must still be resolved. As noted in Chapter 8, which focuses on channel dynamics, an independent retailer may be negotiating with suppliers from a position of virtually no power. In such instances the retailer will badly need the supplier and may thus make major concessions to get desired merchandise.

Recently, a group of wholesale distributors banded together and introduced a line of privately branded, Crosley appliances for sale to retailers. Many manufacturers had discontinued making appliances, and the remaining manufacturers were selling direct to dealers. The distributors felt that complete control of the *revived* Crosley brand was essential if they were to compete with the marketing merchandisers and the big chains which had taken much of the market for white goods, such as Sears and Penneys.[1]

In other instances, the retailer, such as Rich's in Atlanta, may be so strongly a part of the metropolitan area market that suppliers will make major concessions to have the retailer feature their merchandise. Much of retailing consists of independent retailers dealing with small-scale vendors. In these circumstances, neither party is working from a dominant position and agreement on merchandise terms can readily be reached.

All of those involved in the marketing channel—that is, the manufacturer, wholesaler, the retailer, and the consumer—offer possibilities for channel conflict. The costs of conflict can be quite severe. For example, it has been noted that "Ford and Chrysler-Plymouth dealers who frequently disagree with their manufacturers do so at the cost of decreasing their return on assets and asset turnover. Minimizing conflicts with manufacturers appears to be

---

[1] "Distributors Bring Back the Crosley Appliance," *Business Week*, January 31, 1977, p. 92.

the best strategy for dealers."[2] Dealers who frequently disagree with manufacturers could possibly be "punished" by such means as unfair distribution of "hot models," slow payment on warranty work, bureaucratic red tape, which would tend to worsen dealer operating performance. Thus, it is to the benefit of all parts of the merchandising channel to strive to hold conflict to a minimum.

The basic dimensions of the buying function are: (1) formulating effective buying policies; (2) determining customer wants; (3) selecting sources of supply; (4) determining the suitability of the merchandise offered for sale; (5) negotiating the terms of sale; and (6) transferring title.[3] Depending on the size of the retail organization, a buyer may perform all of these functions or only one of them. The larger the outlet, the more specialized the job responsibility of the buyer. Let's look in some detail at the more important buying functions so that we can develop a greater appreciation for the various dimensions of merchandise procurement.

CHOOSING MERCHANDISE RESOURCES

Retailers often have a wide choice in the type of marketing channel with which they become affiliated. The establishment of good channel relationships is important because retailers have major psychological and monetary investments in these relationships. Ideally, the relationships continue over a long period of time. Further, retailers may find it difficult to move freely from one vendor to another without major inconvenience.

The primary goal of any marketing channel is to determine the place in the channel at which the necessary functions can be performed most efficiently. For example, a central buyer in New York City may be able to effectively represent several small independent retailers. Likewise, manufacturers may find that the selling function can best be performed at the retail level.

Wholesalers

Wholesalers have long been a major source of supply in retailing. They can be classified as those who take title to goods—merchant wholesalers—and those who do not take title—typically known as agents. "Probably almost half of all manufactured consumers goods go through the hands of wholesalers. They may handle as much as 90 percent of all goods in the hardware trade and nearly 70 percent of all drugstore merchandise."[4] Thus, most retailers do not buy directly from the manufacturer.

---

[2] Robert F. Lusch, "Channel Conflict: Its Impact on Retailer Operating Performance," *Journal of Retailing,* vol. 52 (Summer 1976), p. 12.

[3] Delbert J. Duncan, Charles F. Phillips, and Stanley C. Hollander, *Modern Retailing Management: Basic Concepts and Practices* (Homewood, Ill.: Richard D. Irwin, 1972), p. 236.

[4] Ibid., p. 254.

Full-service wholesalers. Full-service wholesalers serve as buying agents for many retailers. In so doing, they seek to anticipate retailer needs, purchase merchandise for resale to the retailer, and may even perform such services as storage, delivery, credit, and stocking. These services are particularly valuable to small retailers who may use this source of supply more frequently than any other source. Typically, large retailers such as A&P or Sears perform many of the wholesaler functions themselves.

Limited function wholesalers. Limited function wholesalers may simply stock fast-moving items and offer no sales assistance, credit, or delivery. However, they offer lower prices to retailers, which may be very important, particularly to small ones.

The rack jobber. The rack jobber typically functions as a wholesaler of nonfood items, especially those sold in supermarkets. A rack jobber will select the items to be displayed, deliver the merchandise, arrange display, price the merchandise, provide necessary promotional support, and guarantee a specified profit margin to the retailer. Thus, no risk is involved to the retailer other than providing shelf space. Rack jobbers provide over 40 percent of all health and beauty aids for supermarkets, as noted in Figure 15–1.

FIGURE 15–1
MAJOR SOURCES OF HEALTH AND
BEAUTY AIDS

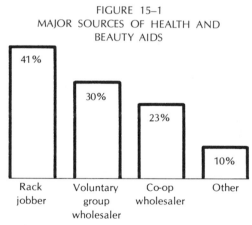

Source: *Progressive Grocer*, April 1974, p. 184.

As shown in Table 15–1, most supermarkets feature such nonfood items as small batteries, cosmetics, home supplies, and paperbacks. As shown in Table 15–2, health and beauty aids and general merchandise account for nearly 6 percent of all grocery store sales. These items are popular because they carry a gross margin of almost 40 percent, compared to 15 percent for groceries, 30 percent for produce, and 20 percent for meats.[5] Indeed, A&P is allotting 27 percent of the floor space in its new or remodeled stores to

---

[5] "Supermarkets Eye the Sunbelt," *Business Week*, September 27, 1976, p. 61.

TABLE 15–1
NONFOOD SUPERMARKET LINES

	Percent of stores carrying
Batteries	92%
Flowers and vegetable seeds	82
Fireplace logs	81
Cosmetics	73
Camera film and supplies	71
National weekly newspapers	68
Greeting cards	67
Paperbooks	61
Toys	61
Beer	56
Motor oil	56
Home sewing supplies	54
Soft goods (other than panty hose)	49
Fresh plants, flowers	46
Garden supplies	43

Source: *Progressive Grocer*, April 1976, p. 170.

TABLE 15–2
NONFOODS IN GROCERY STORES

	1975 (000s)	Percent change over 1974	Percent of nonfood sales	Percent of total store sales
Health and beauty aids	$4,135,000	+12.8	50.5%	2.9%
General merchandise	1,060,000	+11.8	49.5	2.8
Housewares, hardware	1,726,000	+10.0	21.1	1.2
Soft goods, panty hose	640,000	+12.2	7.8	0.4
Magazines, books	455,000	+10.2	5.5	0.3
School supplies, stationery	221,000	+14.4	2.7	0.2
Sewing notions/yarn	107,000	+10.6	1.3	*
Greeting cards	79,000	+23.6	0.9	*
Photo film, flash, finishing	145,000	+17.3	1.8	0.1
Pet supplies	165,000	+13.1	2.0	0.1
Continuity, seasonal, and all other	522,000	+11.5	6.4	0.4
Total all nonfoods	$8,195,000	+12.3	100.0	5.7

* Less than 0.1 percent.
Source: *Progressive Grocer*, April 1976, p. 173.

general merchandise. Experiments are now under way to sell classical records through the supermarket.[6]

Manufacturers

In some instances, merchandise may be purchased directly from the manufacturer. Here the wholesaling functions are performed at either the

[6] "Marketing Observer," *Business Week*, October 4, 1976, p. 104.

manufacturing or the retail level. Some large chains, such as Montgomery Ward and Sears, are larger than most wholesalers. Thus, they are able to purchase more cheaply by buying directly from the manufacturer.

Some retailers may purchase tailor-made merchandise from the manufacturer. This is particularly true for private label brands. The manufacturer may simply attach the retailer's brand to the merchandise or may physically differentiate it in some way. If time is particularly important, for example, in fashion merchandise, the retailer is more likely to purchase directly from the manufacturer.

Cooperative retailers

As noted in Chapter 8, independent retailers have strengthened their competitive positions relative to chain groups by forming groups of

TABLE 15–3
TYPES OF MIDDLEMEN SERVING RETAILERS

Type of middleman	Characteristics
Service (regular) wholesaler	Serves as the retailer's buying agent by assembling and collecting goods, storing goods, providing fast delivery, extending credit, and furnishing market information. These services appeal especially to small- and medium-size retailers.
Limited function wholesaler	Charges less because he provides less service, as he generally does not grant credit or offer delivery service. Offers only fast-moving items; may do business only by mail.
Rack jobber	Supplies mainly nonfood items to supermarkets. Sets up displays, maintains merchandise assortment, and receives payment only on goods actually sold; thereby guarantees a prespecified percent markup to the outlet.
Broker	Receives a commission to bring retail buyers and suppliers together; does not handle merchandise or take title to goods. Handles only a few lines—mainly grocery specialties, dry goods, fruits, vegetables, drugs, and hardware.
Commission agent	Similar to broker, except that he handles merchandise, although he does not take title to it; supplies mainly large retailers with dry goods, grocery specialties, fruits, and vegetables.
Manufacturer's agent (representative)	Renders services similar to those of a salesperson; is restricted to a limited territory and by limited authority to negotiate price and terms of sale; sells only part of client's output.
Selling agent	Similar to manufacturer's agent, except that selling agent is responsible for disposing of entire output of client.
Auctioneer	Places product on display and sells it to highest bidder. Used mainly to sell livestock, fruits, and vegetables to small restaurants, large chains, or other wholesalers.

Source: From *Retail Management: Satisfaction of Consumer Needs* by Raymond A. Marquardt, James C. Makens, and Robert G. Roe. Copyright © 1975 by The Dryden Press, A Division of Holt, Rinehart and Winston. Reprinted by permission of Holt, Rinehart and Winston.

cooperating retailers to secure greater strength in buying, merchandising and in promotion. For example, a voluntary chain may be organized by a wholesaler to allow retailers to compete more effectively against the chains. The retailers purchase all needed merchandise from the wholesaler. Because of the large amount of purchases involved, they are likely to obtain better prices than if they acted alone. The Independent Grocers' Alliance and Western Auto Stores are examples of groups of independent retailers who are affiliated with a voluntary wholesaler.

A similar arrangement exists whereby independent retailers may organize their own wholesaling facility. These retailers use common storefronts, share promotional materials, exchange market information, and so on.

Various less frequently utilized sources of supply are also available. These include brokers who receive a commission to bring suppliers and retailers together, and manufacturers' agents, who are similar to salespersons but sell part of the line of several suppliers. Other sources of supply include selling agents and auctioneers, as shown in Table 15–3. Let's now look at the various methods of buying merchandise.

MARKET CONTACT WITH VENDORS

Vendor contact

Vendor contact with the retailer may begin through catalogs and price lists which are available to all retailers. For example, catalogs may be used by resident buying offices in such places as New York to assist retailers in making purchases. Another important source of vendor contact is salespersons who call on the retailer. In such lines as groceries and drugs, merchandise turnover is rapid. Thus, salespersons may call on the retailer almost weekly. For other merchandise, such as clothing, contact may be on a seasonal basis. The salesperson can be an important source of information for the retailer.

Retailer contact

Retailers are becoming more aggressive in seeking out sources of supply. Specifically, they may want to compare the advantages of purchasing from several vendors and of discussing merchandising ideas with them. A problem, however, is that manufacturers of such goods as fashion merchandise or furniture are concentrated in a few areas. Thus, it is easier and more economical for retailers to go to the showrooms of the vendors rather than try to have the vendors' salespersons come to them.

Purchasing may be from local, regional, national, and even foreign markets. Typically only small retailers purchase merchandise from local markets, and this may include the purchase of fresh fruits and vegetables on a seasonal basis. Even large retailers, however, may acquire as much of their supply as possible in local markets. Typically, they deal with a farmers' co-op market or with a similar centralized arrangement for the sale of the products of local craftspersons.

The central market

A central market is simply a place where a large number of suppliers are concentrated. It may be a single building, such as a merchandise mart, or an area in the same general section of a city. Typically, only larger retailers and retailers of fashion goods buy in central markets. For example, New York City is still the primary central market for many types of merchandise, particularly women's wear. Chicago and High Point, North Carolina, are well known for furniture. For still other types of merchandise, Dallas, New Orleans, and Atlanta may be the central market. In these situations, retail buyers visit the displays of several different vendors at the centers. Some centers, such as the Atlanta merchandise mart, display a wide variety of merchandise. The furniture mart in Chicago displays only furniture and related products, and the apparel mart in Dallas offers only apparel. Not all central markets are permanent. Showings may be held periodically. Such showings may be seasonal, semiannual, or perhaps annual.

The frequency of the retailer's visits to central markets depends upon whether the retailer maintains a resident buying office, the volume of business handled by the retailer, and the type of merchandise which the retailer sells.

Full information is necessary before the retailer can make final merchandise selections. Thus when a new buyer first visits a central market, it is probably important to become thoroughly acquainted with the offerings of each vendor in terms of price, styles, and similar information.

The retailer now faces a decision as to the number of vendors with whom to deal. The fewer the suppliers with whom the retailer deals, the better the price and credit terms are likely to be because of volume purchases. Also, delivery may be faster, and more care may be given to the order. On the other hand by concentrating purchases with only a few suppliers, the retailer faces risks—for example, strikes by the suppliers' employees and possible supplier bankruptcy—which can be minimized by spreading purchases over a larger number of vendors. No general rule of thumb exists as to how many vendors the retailer should work with.

Resident buying offices

Resident buying offices are becoming increasingly important. The specialized market knowledge of these agencies gives the retailer access to instant expertise in the major merchandise markets. These specialists are in continuous contact with both manufacturers and retailers, and hence are able to note the movement of merchandise, expected price changes, and similar information. Buyers are powerful persons with both the retailer and the manufacturer.

If resident buying offices are independent, affiliation is voluntary on the part of both parties. The most typical arrangement is for the retailer to pay a minimum annual fee for the right to work with a resident buyer. Other types of buying offices also serve the retail markets. For example, large retailers may maintain a private buying office. An office may also be maintained by a group of several independent retailers or by an ownership group of stores. The most common types of resident buying offices are shown in Table 15–4.

TABLE 15–4
FOUR PRIMARY TYPES OF RESIDENT OFFICES

Title or type	Controlled by	Examples
Cooperatively owned—associated type	Stores that own it Stores it serves Directors are usually executives of member firms	Associated Merchandise Corp. Specialty Store Association Frederick Atkins, Inc.
Divisional resident office—syndicated type	A division of a corporation that owns a chain of dept. stores	Allied Purchasing Corp. Associated Dry Goods Corp. Gimbel's, Macy's, May Co. buying offices
Specialty—independent buying office	Completely independent relationship, sets own policies, handles both hard- and soft-line goods	Arkwright Independent Retailers Syndicate Felix Lilienthal and Co. Mutual Buying Syndicate
Company-owned buying office	Controlled by its management (buying primarily women's, men's, infants', children's wear)	Jack Braustein, Inc. S. Irene Johns, Inc. William Van Buren, Inc.

Source: Winston Borgen, *Learning Experiences in Retailing* (Pacific Palisades, Calif.: Goodyear Publishing Co., 1976), p. 156.

The primary role of resident buying offices is to provide advice and information to the retailer. These offices range from one-person operations to large organizations which may provide space, stenographic services, and similar assistance for the retailer's buying trips.

METHODS OF BUYING

Group buying

Group or cooperative buying simply involves purchasing of merchandise jointly by a number of noncompeting and nonaligned stores. By combining their orders into one large order, these stores are likely to achieve lower prices. Further, the participating buyers are able to share knowledge on markets, fashion trends, and so forth. The buying function may also be handled more quickly in this way. In spite of these advantages, buyers may resent such an arrangement as decreasing their importance to the firm.

Group buying is done primarily for staples and by middle-of-the-line retailers. Fashion merchants simply cannot participate in this type of buying because their customer needs are typically too unique. For discounters, group buying is typically done from manufacturers' stock which has already been produced. Other merchants may insist on differentiated merchandise. Locational differences and differences in customer preference may limit the effectiveness of this type of buying for some retailers.

Central buying

Central buying is most frequently practiced by store chains. As noted in Chapter 4, department stores with branches may buy centrally for both the main store and the branches. Central buying simply means that the buying of selected merchandise items for all outlets is handled by one person whose full-time job is procuring merchandise from vendors. Staples are most frequently purchased centrally.

Thus, in organizations with central buying a large part of the authority for buying may lie outside the individual retail outlet. Even in such organizations, however, store managers may still purchase some merchandise, particularly shopping goods, for the individual outlet.

To be successful, central buyers must have constant information about customer needs at the local level. Thus, good inventory control plans and systems are vital. Increasingly, the new electronic technology is able to supply this information to central buyers in a timely manner.

Buying committees

Committee buying is a version of central buying. It is an effort to achieve the economies of central buying while having more than one person share buying responsibilities. Buying committees are particularly common in organizations which are basically selling staple merchandise, such as hardware stores.

Consignment

Still another form of buying is consignment. Some suppliers will guarantee the sale of merchandise and will remove it from the retailer's shelf if it does not sell. This type of inducement is particularly strong for buyers who have no more open-to-buy or who have doubts about the marketability of the merchandise. By means of consignment, the merchandise can be displayed in the store with no risk to the retailer. Nevertheless, many merchants are hesitant to accept consignment merchandise, primarily because of the assumption that the merchandise would not be offered on consignment if it could be sold in any other way.

Leased departments

Specialized departments in a department store may be operated on a leased basis if the store management does not have the expertise to operate them. For example, in many department stores the camera shop, beauty salon, restaurant, and luggage department are on a leased basis. The operating policies of the leased department are the same as those for the store as a whole, and the arrangement is typically unknown to the consumer. By leasing, the retailer can provide highly specialized merchandise without the pitfalls that would result from inexperience in handling such merchandise. Leased departments are particularly strong in discount houses.

The lessee, however, always faces the risk that store management, after becoming familiar with the various operating dimensions of the department, may not renew the lease and may simply take over the department as part of normal store operations.

Other dimensions of buying

Other negotiations than those discussed above are typically necessary in merchandise procurement. For example, the retailer may want the exclusive right to market certain merchandise. This may be even more important than low prices, particularly for higher priced merchandise. This arrangement eliminates direct price competition from other retailers since they do not have the merchandise. Also, considerable prestige may go to an outlet which is the exclusive dealer for quality merchandise. Other matters to be negotiated may include credit, discounts, promotional assistance, and delivery schedules.

As was suggested at the beginning of this chapter, the potential for conflict in the buyer-seller relationship always exists. Small- and medium-sized retail establishments are often "used" by manufacturers who want to introduce a new product or line into a market. With a promise of "exclusivity," the local prestige retail outlet invests effort in introducing the brand into the market. This is particularly true of independent merchants with a loyal customer following.

Sometimes, however, the manufacturer reneges on his promise of exclusivity after a successful "launch" has been accomplished. In such situations, all of the retailer's investment is frustratingly negated by the vendor who offers the "exclusive" merchandise to another retailer in the same market. The vendor's position may be one of attempting to convince the offended store that the markets are really different (which they may be), but a promise has been broken and the relationship has suffered severely. Perhaps the manufacturer does not need the small retailer as much as the small retailer needs the manufacturer, but reputations can be greatly affected by such actions. The aggrieved retailer might attempt to negotiate for separate items, protected models, and the like. In addition, if negotiation does not work and the retailer is a member of a resident buying office, the unfortunate situation can be broadcast. If the buying office has market impact (which many of the larger ones have), the office might intercede to assist in working out a solution more palatable to the member store. Buying offices can become much more important in setting up sound relationships between the retailer and the vendor than they have been in the past. At least an understanding about a specific time frame for the exclusive dealership rights could be worked out in advance. If such an agreement existed, retailer-vendor relationships could be protected.

Little question exists that a compromise must be worked out in advance, or conflict will result—conflict which may lead to an irreparable break in existing relationships. Moreover, the retailer must know whether the person with whom the arrangement is made has the authority to commit for a protected market position. A "hungry" salesperson may, in the anxiety to make a sale, promise something which is impossible to grant.

In summary, the retailer must take every precaution not to be misled in the buyer-seller relationship and must be alert to the vendor's policies and use any buying office assistance which may be available to help assure a good deal.

THE TERMS OF SALE

The terms of sale (or purchase) are a crucial element in purchasing and a key determinant of the real price paid by the retailer. A retailer may be offered identical list prices by various vendors, but differing "terms of sale," for example, different discounts and different provisions as to who will be responsible for paying transportation costs. An understanding of the various components of the purchase terms is necessary if a person is to negotiate the best price for merchandise.

Discounts

Trade. A trade discount is a reduction of the seller's list price and is granted to either a wholesaler or a retailer who performs functions which are normally the responsibility of the seller. Trade discounts are common in retailing. Vendors (typically manufacturers) normally offer larger trade discounts to wholesalers than to retailers. Large retail groups may also be granted discounts larger than those granted small retailers.[7]

Illustration. A trade discount may be offered as a single percentage off list price or as a series of percentages in determining the net or real price to be

---

[7] Trade discounts given to middlemen who perform wholesale functions are called "functional" discounts. In the past, certain court cases have declared functional discounts as discriminatory under interpretation of the Robinson-Patman Act.

paid by the retailer. Let's assume a list price on a sport shirt of $14.95, with a trade discount of 40 percent. The retailer will thus pay $8.97 for the shirt ($14.95 − $5.98); the $5.98 ($14.95 × 0.40) is the trade discount. The same buyer might be offered an identical sport shirt from another manufacturer at a list price of $14.95 less 30 percent, 10 percent, and 5 percent. The 30–10–5 was initially introduced as a way of lowering vendors' prices without changing their price schedule. With the new technology, prices can be easily changed and the 30–10–5 is now mainly tradition. However, the net price in this case would be computed as follows:

$$
\begin{array}{rl}
\text{List price} = \$14.95 & \\
- \quad 4.48 & (\$14.95 \times 0.30) \\
\hline
= \quad 10.47 & \\
- \quad 1.05 & (\$10.47 \times 0.10) \\
\hline
= \quad 9.42 & \\
- \quad 0.47 & (\$9.42 \times 0.05) \\
\hline
\text{Net price} = \$\;9.95 &
\end{array}
$$

Quantity.   A *quantity discount* is a reduction in the cost of items offered for sale, based on the size of the order. The economic justification for quantity discounts is that large orders result in lower unit costs for the seller. Such discounts may be noncumulative (the reduction is based on one order) or cumulative (the reduction is computed over purchases for a specified period of time). Quantity discounts encourage the retailer to concentrate purchases with a particular vendor. Although the Robinson-Patman Act does not mention quantity discounts, they may be subject to cost justification if the Federal Trade Commission believes that a certain quantity discount schedule is discriminatory. (See Chapter 9 for a more detailed discussion of the Robinson-Patman Act.)

Seasonal.   A *seasonal discount* is a special discount which is given by vendors to retailers who place orders for seasonal merchandise in advance of the normal buying period. Advantages exist for both the seller and the retailer in this arrangement. From the retail management point of view, it is important that the costs incurred by early purchase (for example, storage, cost of capital, and risks) be more than offset by the advantages of the discount offered. Manufacturers offer the special discount to smooth out production schedules and reduce the costs which the retailer assumes. Within our sport shirt classification, a seasonal discount might be offered to retailers who agree to take delivery on Christmas gift shirts in late spring or early summer instead of the more usual late summer or early fall.

In terms of legality, seasonal discounts are admissible under Robinson-Patman Act interpretations as long as comparable buyers are offered the same discount.

Promotional allowance.   Vendors offer discounts to retailers to compensate them for money spent in advertising particular items or for preferred window and interior display space for the vendors' products.

Promotional discounts are given to the retailer because the promotion function has been shifted away from the manufacturer. The Robinson-Patman Act specifically stipulates that promotional allowances must be given to all buyers on proportionately equal terms.

Cash.   When credit terms are extended by sellers to retailers, a premium is often granted by the vendor for cash payment prior to the time that the entire bill must be paid. The three components of the cash discount are: (1) a specified percentage discount; (2) a period in which the discount may be taken; and (3) the net credit period, which indicates when the full amount of the invoice is due.

Illustration.   Assume that in the above example of a trade discount the cash discount is stated (in addition to the trade discount) as 2/10, n/30. This means that the retailer must pay the invoice within 10 days to take advantage of the discount of 2 percent and that the full amount is due in 30 days. The 2 percent cash discount represents an annual rate of 36 percent. Let's look at the structure of this discount more closely. The full invoice payment is due in 30 days; since the 2 percent cash discount can be taken if the invoice is paid within 10 days, the discount is allowed for 20 days prepayment of the bill. Since there are 18 20-day periods in the year of 360 days, this comes to 36% annually (18 × 2 percent).

Returning to the $9.95 net bill for the sport shirt, assume that the invoice is dated May 22. The retailer has ten days to take the discount. Full payment is due June 1 (nine days in May and one in June). If the invoice is paid within this time, the retailer will remit $9.75 instead of $9.95 ($9.95 × 0.02 = $0.20). If the retailer does not discount the invoice, then the bill must be paid in full by June 21.

Datings

Cash datings.   The agreement between the vendor and the retailer as to the time the discount date will begin is known as dating. Technically, if the terms call for immediate payment, the process is known as cash dating and includes COD (cash on delivery) or CWO (cash with order). Cash datings do not involve discounts and consequently do not present any problem here.

Future datings.   The focus of this section is "future datings," which include end of month, date of invoice, receipt of goods, advance dating, extra dating, and anticipation.

End of month (EOM).   If an invoice carries EOM dating, the cash and net discount periods begin on the first day of the following month rather than on the invoice date. To allow for goods shipped late in the month, an invoice dated after the 25th of the month may be considered as having been dated on the 1st of the following month. Thus, on a 2/10, n/30, EOM billing dated May 26 the ten-day discount period begins on July 1, not June 1. As a result, dating is further extended.

Illustration.   Let's assume that the terms in the above illustration now read "2/10, n/30, EOM." If the $9.95 invoice were dated May 22, the retailer would have until June 10 to pay the invoice and take the 2 percent discount (that is, pay $9.75). If, on the other hand, the invoice were dated May 26 (with the same EOM terms), then the retailer would have until July 10 to take the 2 percent discount.

Date of invoice (DOI). Date of invoice (DOI), or ordinary dating, is self-explanatory. Prepayments begin with the invoice date, and both the cash discount and the net amount are due within the specified number of days from the invoice date. The DOI method is not particularly favorable to the retailer because the vendor has some discretion in setting the date. If the vendor is slow in shipping the merchandise, payment may actually be due before the merchandise arrives.

Receipt of goods (ROG). Certain vendors are more distant from their customers than are their competitors. Rather than be at a competitive disadvantage with ordinary datings, they may offer receipt of goods (ROG) datings. These indicate that the time allowed for discounts and for payment of the net amount of the invoice begins with the date that the goods are received at the buyer's place of business.

Advance. When terms allow advance dating, the invoice is postdated to allow for shipment of the merchandise. As a result, the retailer has additional time in which to make payment and take cash discounts.

Extra. The effect of extra datings is similar to that of advance datings, but the mechanics are different. Extra datings allow the retailer extra time to take the cash discount. An example might be 2/10—60 extra, n/90, which means that the buyer has 70 days to take the cash discount and that the net amount is due in 90 days.

Illustration. Returning to our example, if the invoice were dated May 22 with ordinary dating, the invoice would be due (assuming 2/10, n/30) on June 1. However, with 2/10—60 extra, n/90, the retailer could take the 2 percent cash discount through August 1 (10-day discount period through June 1, 29 additional days in June, and 31 days in July).

Anticipation. Anticipation is a discount offered in addition to the cash discount if an invoice is paid prior to the expiration of the cash discount period. Usually the discount is at the rate of 6 percent per annum. Anticipation is most common with extra or advance datings to those retailers who are able to pay the invoice in advance of the expiration of the discount period.

Illustration. In the prior example of extra datings, assume that the retailer pays the invoice on June 1, or 60 days prior to the expiration of the cash discount period. The 2 percent discount on the $9.95 will bring the cost to $9.75. The anticipation at 6 percent will allow the retailer to deduct the following additional discount (or anticipation):

$$\$9.75 \times \frac{6}{100} \times \frac{60}{360} = \$0.10, \text{ or a net bill of } \$9.65.$$

This may seem like a small amount. However, if we are ordering 1,000 shirts, then $0.10 per shirt would mean an additional discount of $100 off the total price.

Shipping costs (f.o.b.).   The final part of the terms of sale relates to who will bear the responsibility for shipping costs. The most favorable terms for the retailer are f.o.b. destination. In this arrangement, the seller pays the freight to the destination. Title does not pass until the merchandise reaches its destination. A more common shipping term is f.o.b. origin, in which the vendor delivers the merchandise to the carrier and title passes to the retailer at that point. The retailer thus pays for the freight and makes any adjustment claim necessary for goods damaged in shipment.

Small retailers typically do not have the power to bargain with a vendor over the nature of the discount or the transportation schedule. On the other hand, large retailers may be able to obtain price concessions from the supplier by bargaining on discounts even though the list price of the merchandise does not change.

THE NEED FOR GOOD VENDOR RELATIONSHIPS

Good relationships are important to both the supplier and the retailer. The experiences of many retailers in periods of shortages and allocations such as we have undergone in the 1970s underscore the advantages of building strong and continuing vendor relationships. Further, strong advantages can accrue to the retail buyer who is given the opportunity by suppliers to participate in purchasing closeouts, special job lots, and similar arrangements, all of which can result in lower prices. The retailer who tries to unduly abuse suppliers in terms of special concessions, delivery terms, and so forth is not likely to be let in on such special situations.

Order cancellations and returns are a continuing problem to the retailer and good relationships with the supplier may be strained if the retailer abuses these privileges. On many occasions it may be desirable to return merchandise for legitimate reasons. However, management should not seek to return merchandise simply because it is left unsold at the end of the season or is slow moving. If such unjustified actions are taken, the goodwill of the supplier is likely to be lost.

The retail buyer must consider numerous factors in deciding from whom to purchase stock. The buyer is likely to have many sources of supply which can provide exactly the products wanted. What other criteria are utilized in making the decision? Profitability is one criterion. The object is for the retailer to make as large a gross margin as possible. Not all vendors offer equally profitable merchandise even though the retail prices of the merchandise may be the same. Other factors which must be considered are the size and nature of the discounts offered, the nature of the selling terms, vendor credit policy, and even delivery charges. If one vendor is physically closer to a retailer than another, lower freight charges may indicate that merchandise should be purchased from the closer vendor.

The vendor's reputation is an important consideration. Is the firm prompt in handling complaints? Is its merchandise stable in quality? Is delivery rapid and on schedule? Does the outlet have an overall reputation for good service?

The reputation of the brand purchased is also important. Some vendors, particularly manufacturers, will spend large amounts of money in promoting and winning consumer acceptance of their brand. The brands of such manufacturers are thus the easiest to sell. On the other hand, the gross margin offered on these brands is likely to be less.

Vendors offer assistance in sales training or supply promotional aids. In the final analysis, however, the selection of a vendor may boil down to such subjective criteria as the personality of the vendor's staff.

RECEIVING AND MARKING MERCHANDISE

After the retailer has purchased merchandise from the supplier, the merchandise must be moved to the retailer. Upon arrival, it must be examined to make sure that it is of the quality and in the quantity ordered by the buyer. Further, the goods must be marked, prepared for sale, and displayed in the store selling area. Tight control must be maintained at all points to avoid pilferage and damage. Finally, if the merchandise does not sell, arrangements must be made to dispose of it by returning it to the vendor, selling it through other retail outlets, or donating it to charity.

Receiving and related activities are typically centralized in a place which has low sales value—for example, an upper floor level. Receiving, checking, and marking are usually centralized in order to ensure proper merchandise control and the handling of the merchandise by personnel who specialize in checking and marking, and to avoid having salespersons perform these activities since they generally resent this.

Numerous advances are occurring in marking technology. As indicated in Chapter 9, government regulations are altering various price markings. One of the better-known voluntary programs, which reflects a modification of typical management practice, is marking the merchandise with the last date that it can be purchased without loss of freshness.

In an effort to reduce expenses and speed up the movement of merchandise to the sales floor, large retailers have been trying to get vendors to mark merchandise prior to shipment to them. Receiving and marking costs per $1,000,000 in merchandise are typically around $11,000 if the merchandise is marked down to the SKU level at the retailer's warehouse. Over $10,000 of this amount could be eliminated if the merchandise were source-marked and sent directly to the branches.[8] Staples are most likely to be source-marked, although other merchandise, such as men's clothing and even greeting cards, may be source-marked.

As discussed in Chapter 11, the universal product code (UPC) is a major advance in the marking of merchandise, in inventory control, and in the

---

[8] "Point of Sale Recording Systems Benefit Both Retailers, Garment Manufacturers," *Marketing News*, May 23, 1975, p. 12.

control of employee errors. Merchandise premarked with the UPC, which can be printed on price tickets and other types of retail documents, allows this code to be read by retailers, vendors, and others. Premarked merchandise identifies the manufacturer as well as the style, size, and color of merchandise, all of which speeds up the retailer's receiving and marking functions.

Automated retail systems are available which can handle such tasks as the marking, checkout, and recording of data. The NCR–280 is one such system. With this equipment, the merchandise is marked by color bar–coded tags which are read by wand at the retail checkout. The entire system from marking to checkout is electronically controlled. For example, the NCR–747 tag printer virtually eliminates repricing costs resulting from human errors. Price changes can easily be handled by the use of color bar–coded overlays which can be printed by the tag printer. Further, the self-checking features of the various wand-reading systems can ensure almost complete accuracy at the checkout counter. These features, coupled with the inventory replenishment models available for some systems, greatly reduce out-of-stock conditions and lost sales.

Wholesalers are also offering a variety of electronic systems to assist retailers with merchandise management. For example, in food retailing, the information most frequently supplied by wholesalers offering customer data processing services is case label marking, followed, in turn, by withdrawal information, gross margin data by item, product movement data, accounting services, and space management systems, as shown in Table 15–5.

TABLE 15–5
FIRMS OFFERING DATA PROCESSING CUSTOMER SERVICES
(percent)

	Case label markings	With-drawal printout	Margin data by item	Product movement data	Account-ing services	Space management systems
Voluntary	82	82	76	66	62	34
Cooperative	88	84	70	73	57	30
Unaffiliated	11	14	14	16	11	2
Total	57	56	51	46	39	19

Source: *Progressive Grocer*, April 1976, p. 155.

SUMMARY

The success of a retail operation depends to a large extent upon the effectiveness of its merchandise buying. Buyers in turn are constrained by the objectives of the store, including objectives for gross margins, customer service, and even store image.

Buying for a large retailer is typically handled by a person who specializes in this function. The buyer keeps up with the latest trends in fashion, knows

the reputation of various suppliers, and has up-to-date information on consumer needs and wishes. Smaller retailers may buy cooperatively through a
voluntary wholesaler or in the case of staples and other frequently purchased
items, from a salesperson who makes regular calls.

Merchandise may be purchased at central buying marts. Such marts
either specialize in certain items, such as furniture, or handle a wider range
of products. Typically, a retail buyer will deal with a central buying office. It
may be an independent office with which the retailer maintains a continuing
affiliation by paying a minimum monthly fee or a private buying office
maintained by a large retailer. A group buying office may be maintained by
several noncompeting retailers

Not all buying by large retailers is handled by a single buyer. Some
organizations, for example, may allow individual store managers to
negotiate for at least a part of their merchandise. Buying may also be handled by a committee.

Typically, the retailer takes title to the merchandise purchased and assumes all of the risks that go with taking title. Occasionally, however, high-
risk new merchandise may be placed in outlets on a consignment basis,
whereby the title remains with the vendor.

Selecting proper sources of supply is of extreme importance because
changing suppliers can be costly and time consuming. A variety of considerations other than price may enter into the retailer's decisions as to choice of
supplier. Among these considerations are the reputation of the supplier, price
concessions in the form of discounts, credit terms, and delivery terms. The
relative proximity of one supplier as compared to another may be an important consideration. Good vendor relationships are particularly important in
periods of materials shortages. These types of problems suggest the advantages of vertical integration for the retailer.

KEY CONCEPTS

Merchandise resources
   Full-service wholesalers
   Limited function wholesalers
   The rack jobber
   The wholesaler-sponsored voluntary chain
   The retailer-owned cooperative warehouse

Central markets

Resident buying offices

Methods of buying
   Group buying
   Central buying
   Buying committees
   Consignment

Leased departments
The terms of sale
  Discounts
    The trade discount
    The quantity discount
    The seasonal discount
    The promotional allowance
    The cash discount
  Datings
    EOM (end of month)
    DOI (date of invoice)
    ROG (receipt of goods)
    Advance dating
  Anticipation
  F.o.b. (destination and origin)

DISCUSSION QUESTIONS

1. What are the various channel relationships which the retailer can establish in terms of merchandise procurement?

2. Is it to the retailer's advantage to consider the use of a rack jobber for certain kinds of merchandise? Why or why not?

3. What are the legal constraints, if any, which limit the retailer from negotiating lower prices on merchandise?

4. In your opinion, should a manufacturer be allowed to sell directly to the retailer as well as to wholesalers? Why or why not?

5. Why would a retailer choose to purchase merchandise through a cash-and-carry wholesaler as opposed to a full-service wholesaler?

6. What is the difference between trade discounts and quantity discounts?

7. What are the various ways in which a retailer can legally obtain price advantages for the retail outlet?

8. What are the various ways in which a wholesaler can assist a small retailer?

9. What is the function of the wholesaler in a voluntary cooperative chain?

10. Why is such merchandise as fashion goods typically purchased directly from the manufacturer?

11. How does group buying differ from central buying?

12. What are the main forms of buying systems which are usually available to retailers?

13. What factors are most likely to influence the buying policies of a retail buyer?

14. What are likely to be the benefits of the emerging electronic technology in terms of the marking and checkout of merchandise?

PROBLEMS

1. A manufacturer of mattresses in Connecticut offers terms of 2/30, n/60. A furniture store places an order for six mattresses at $38 each and receives an invoice dated August 7. The invoice is paid October 6. Failure to obtain the discount is equivalent to paying what annual rate of interest? (Use 360 days as a year.)

2. Willmette Mills, Inc., a textile manufacturing firm in New England, sells on terms of 3/10, 2/70, n/90, ROG, no anticipation allowed. A dry goods store in Denver, Colorado, received an invoice dated September 8 for ten dozen, 81-inch × 108-inch plain hem sheets at $49.08 per dozen. The merchandise arrived on September 18, and the invoice was paid on September 28. What was the net cost per sheet to the store?

3. A Wisconsin manufacturer of kitchen utensils quotes terms of 2/10, n/30. The company grants chain store trade discounts of 25, 20, and 10 percent. The list price of a five-quart stainless steel mixing bowl is $48 per dozen. A chain of general stores receives an invoice dated November 19 for five dozen of these bowls. The invoice is paid November 20. What is (a) the net cost to the chain per bowl? (b) the amount of the cash discount the chain receives?

4. A manufacturer of men's shirts, pajamas, and sportswear offers terms of 3/10 EOM or 2/10—60 extra. Stores may choose either set of terms. Anticipation is allowed at the rate of 6 percent with either set of terms. An invoice for a billed amount of $482.29 is dated October 26 and is to be paid on November 5. Which set of terms should be chosen? Show why.

PROJECTS

1. To clarify the relationships between the buyer and the supplier, the text approaches the subject from the retail point of view. It may be valuable to approach the subject from the other point of view. Make contacts with local suppliers (wholesalers, agents, or local manufacturers who sell to retailers), and see what they attempt to do to strengthen their relationships with their customers. What problems do they incur in these relationships? What efforts do they make to "improve" the relationships?

2. Select a product line in which you are particularly interested. Spot merchants in your area who handle this line. Set up interviews after you have devised a questionnaire which is to determine how important the merchants believe relationships with suppliers are and administer the questionnaires to the managers of the stores. Attempt to find out how these managers implement their "philosophy" of relationships with vendors. If you can get measurements of the "success" of the various stores, see whether you can attribute some of that success to the "programs" for vendor relationships which you discover. This will be a difficult project, but attempting to carry it out will be a good experience, regardless of the outcome.

3. In interviews with retailers with whom you can establish good rapport, attempt to find out: (1) what special problems have been encountered with vendors, (2) what kinds of special "concessions" are offered to the retailers (give your reac-

tions to these concessions); (3) whether any particular plans have been effective in improving (or continuing) good relations with vendors; (4) what company policies exist relative to relationships with vendors; (5) why vendors are "dropped."

CASES

Case 1.   Judy Bennett was 40 years old and frustrated about her future. She had raised four children who were either in junior high school, high school, or college and didn't need her as they used to. Her family store was located in the central business district, and she had grown up in the business—working there as a girl, working part-time with her husband who took over the managership when they were married. Now merely selling, especially on a part-time basis, was not enough for her. She had some ideas of her own about what would "fulfill" her aspirations—and incidentally add to her income. The family store was doing well, and her husband agreed to help her set up a "fashion-right" separates shop adjacent to the local university campus right in the heart of the women's dormitory area. He made it clear that only a certain amount of capital would be supplied and that she would either "make it or get out"—the venture capital was limited, but because of the successful family business, her "borrowing power" was substantial.

The new store—Judy's Place—carried separates exclusively. It prospered from the start. Judy established a "personality" store which was all hers. She used part-time student salespersons, a part-time bookkeeper, and one full-time salesperson. That was ten years ago. The building next door to her original site became available, and because she had been so successful in the first space, she leased the additional space, doubling her square footage.

Over the years Judy's product line expanded. First she added handbags and jewelry. The business was booming, but fashions were changing so rapidly that Judy felt uncertain of her abilities to keep the correct fashions in stock, and if she had a "winner" the deliveries were terrible. One of Judy's major suppliers offered to "program-merchandise" her line so that she would only have to sit back and rake in the profits. The manufacturer's "name" was good in the market, and Judy believed that the arrangement would be advantageous to her. Consequently she turned over much of her "buying" and promotion to the vendor.

Six months after making this agreement with the major resource, she was becoming disenchanted with it. She felt that she was being overstocked and that wrong "numbers" were being shipped in without her approval. Deliveries were not up to her expectations. The final blow came when a department store opened in a regional mall within two miles of Judy's Place and its major line was her "exclusive" programmed line. Judy was distraught!

Advise Judy, and analyze the situation faced by the small retailer in such situations. What, if anything, could the supplier have done? Were supplier-retailer relationships a problem?

Case 2.   The Lyon's Den had been a winner ever since Jane and Jim Lyon opened their gift shop in an old renovated home and moved in over it. The business was started in 1950, and over the years it had become "the" place for gifts and eventually decorating services in a city of some 70,000 and a trading area at least twice that size. Jane said on occasion that the Lyons had made it fashionable "to live over the store."

Their apartment was a virtual showcase for the many lines of fine silver, china, crystal, and decorator furniture items which were carried in the shop. The Lyons made no pretense of *not* using their home to display their wares—they felt that such items in use were virtually presold.

Over the years their lines expanded. To the traditional gift lines they added cosmetics and linens—nothing carried in the shop was carried anywhere else in the trade area. Jane and Jim felt that "exclusivity" was a major differential advantage for the Lyon's Den.

Several years ago, Jane, who does the bulk of the buying while Jim is the decorator and "money man," felt that she had really secured a market *first* for the area. She was able to secure the finest and most prestigious line of stainless Hensen. The name was not known in the market, but the quality was unsurpassed. Jane knew that, given an exclusive, she could develop a "demand" for the line that would make her a leading outlet for the merchandise. She had done this before, and she knew merchandise and was a merchant with foresight and an entrepreneur who liked a challenge. The salesperson, whom she met at a regional trade show, assured her of market protection, and thus she set out to launch the new line.

She ran ads and invited "special" customers to attend a reception to "meet the manufacturer." The market had probably never had such a dramatic introduction, and perhaps it never would again. After a year and a half, the line was one of the most profitable in the shop and brides were convinced that without Hensen from the Lyon's Den marriage was out of the question. Jane had done what she set out to do—"created" a market demand for the line and brought in new customers through the line.

Just this morning Jane got a phone call from the New York office of Hensen's. The national sales manager was on the phone with some distressing news for the Lyons. Lucille's Table Top, a new market entrant carrying medium- to high-priced table accessories, had just been into the New York showroom and had bought the Hensen line. The sales manager felt that since Lucille's was in a shopping center some distance from the Lyon's Den, the competition would be negligible. In addition, the sales manager said that company policy was actually not to give exclusives in a market. The salesperson who originally opened the Lyons account had not been aware of the policy.

Role-play the situation. Become Jane (or Jim), and respond to the situation. Then "move out" and analyze the various relationships and rationales which were obviously involved.

16

COMMUNICATION WITH THE CONSUMER

Personal selling
  Self-service or full service?
  When salespersons are needed
  Increasing sales force productivity
Types of retail selling
  Transaction processing
  Routine selling
  Creative selling
  Helping people to buy
Ethical and legal dimensions of advertising

*T*hinking retailers have long since learned that a 100 percent downtown location is no longer an assurance of success. In fact, a common characteristic of recently and currently troubled retail enterprises is that of inadequate positioning—ranging in scale from a complete void to undistinctness to, in at least one instance, contradictory. Today, major national, regional, and local retailers are in varying stages of researching, evaluating, and formulating their positions on a store-for-store basis.

If not the foundation, then certainly the framework of a successful retail business is its ability to identify and understand the needs and motivations of existing and prospective customers and to develop appropriate marketing policies and strategies. Unless and until these policies and strategies are communicated to the consumer, they will remain academic.

From the basic function of Market Research to the crucial importance of Sales Training, the ensuing chapter comes to laudable and practical grips with the "why" and "how to" of these processes.

James Robertson, Director
Advertising and Promotion
Monsanto Agricultural Products Company
St. Louis, Missouri

Promotion must grow out of a firm's total merchandising process. If an outlet's promotional efforts are not in harmony with decisions on pricing and other elements, a confusing and distorted image of the outlet will result. This is likely to have an adverse effect on profits. Thus the purposes of this chapter are to introduce:

The concept of the promotion mix.

Possible promotion objectives.

The essentials of a promotion plan.

Key promotion decisions.

The elements of a successful promotional strategy.

The concept of media mix.

The place of personal sales skills in promotional plans.

A proper communications strategy can only be developed in the context of the firm's objectives and of its marketing strategies. These include target segments to be served. As has been noted throughout this text, mass markets do not exist. Retailers must focus on the narrowly defined target markets most likely to respond to a particular appeal. Thus advertising should seek to tap the buying motivation of the specific market groups to which promotion is directed.

A variety of choices are available in developing such communications programs. These choices include advertising, sales promotion, resellers' promotion activity, personal selling, public relations, and publicity.

The key to all retail promotions is information. Shoppers with much information are likely to take higher degrees of risk.[1] For so-called search goods, such as clothing, whose product qualities can be checked prior to purchase, direct information on product quality and characteristics should be provided because the consumer can easily check that information before purchase. However, for "experience goods" which have to be purchased before claims can be checked, such as soft drinks, it is more difficult to convey information on quality and product characteristics.[2]

Research continues to emphasize the importance of information in retail advertising. As has been noted, "The retail advertiser would be well advised to provide the consumer with information which would permit her to make a reasoned assessment of the purchase offer."[3]

---

[1] "Working Women, Consumer Movement Spur Growth of Direct Marketing," *Marketing News*, December 5, 1975, p. 12.

[2] "A New View of Advertising's Economic Impact," *Business Week*, December 22, 1975, p. 49.

[3] James G. Barnes, "Factors Influencing Consumer Reaction to Retail Newspaper 'Sale' Advertising," in Edward M. Mazze (ed.), *Marketing in Turbulent Times and Marketing: The Challenges and Opportunities* (Chicago: American Marketing Association, 1975), p. 477.

PURPOSES OF COMMUNICATION

The primary objectives in retail communications are to sell more merchandise by keeping existing customers happy and returning to the store and by attracting additional customers. However, retail advertising may be expected to perform any or all of the specific tasks shown in Figure 16–1.

Remember, however, that the most effective advertising program in the world cannot overcome inferior products, cannot change a reputation overnight, and cannot make a store better than its location. The key to helping the consumer to develop an awareness and appreciation of the firm and its products and services is to alter the mental state of the consumer by stimulating the seeking of information. To do this, the retailer must be able to predict the response of market segments to particular messages or media. Communications theory provides insights into the kinds of information presentations which will cause desired responses.

THE COMMUNICATIONS STRATEGY

As revealed in Figure 16–2, the major elements of a successful communications strategy for the retailer include:

1. Definition of the communications task.
2. The identification of the communications alternatives.
3. Identification of key uncertainties in predicting consumer response.
4. Gathering appropriate data to evaluate alternatives.
5. Synthesizing campaign elements.

The key in any communication is an awareness of audience predisposition toward the product, the outlet, and the overall store or merchandise image. This information will determine the structure of communications by the retailer. As stated by Marvin Rothenberg, marketing services director for Westinghouse Broadcasting Company, "Stores have to segment their messages as well as merchandise assortments. . . . It all goes back to knowing precisely who your customer is and understanding the lifestyle."[4]

POSSIBLE PROMOTION OBJECTIVES

In developing a campaign which uses all of the elements of promotion, the desired response from the consumer must be identified. Let's look at some of the broad objectives of retail promotion programs and at the results achieved by these programs.

---

[4] "Department Stores Redefine Their Role," *Business Week*, December 13, 1976, p. 48.

FIGURE 16-1
ILLUSTRATIONS OF THE TASKS TO BE ACCOMPLISHED BY RETAIL ADVERTISING

Increase the variety and volume of merchandise and services sold to present customers.

Step up traffic in dull periods.

Clear leftover merchandise at the end of a selling season.

Develop weak departments into strong ones, and create an awareness of new departments (or of services that may not have been offered in the past).

Turn special opportunities such as manufacturers' cooperative advertising offers or townwide promotional events into sources of sales for the store.

Attract new customers from among newcomers to the community, those dissatisfied with other stores, and those interested in new products, new fashions, and bargains.

Penetrate or create new markets for the store's goods and services.

Hold on to present customers when competitors make overtures to them, and win over other stores' customers.

Build the store's reputation.

Introduce a new product.

Increase the sales of a product by suggesting new uses for it.

Build goodwill by providing a public service.

Directly support the store's personal selling program.

Reach customers who seldom or never come in person to the store.

Acquire a list of prospects for salespersons to call on.

Increase shopper traffic (and hence sales) in the district or shopping center as a whole.

Increase consumer awareness of the assortment, quality, fashion, or low price of merchandise with a particular appeal for specific market segments.

Encourage more people to become charge account customers of the store or to use bank credit cards.

Make people more aware of conveniences offered by the store, including free or inexpensive parking, delivery service, and evening, weekend, or holiday shopping hours.

Build consumer confidence by explaining how to select, use, and care for certain types of merchandise.

Identify the store with specific nationally advertised brands.

Produce telephone and mail orders.

Contribute to the store's overall public relations effort.

Explain store policies, including "negative" ones that will have less adverse effect on the public if they are fully understood.

Reach the public quickly with messages of an emergency nature.

Source: William Haight, *Retail Advertising; Management and Technique,* Copyright © 1976, Silver Burdett Company (General Learning Press), pp. 139–40. Reprinted by permission.

FIGURE 16–2
COMMUNICATIONS STRATEGY

I.   Define the communication task
    A.   What are the problems to be solved?
    B.   What are the opportunities?
    C.   What are our objectives? What response is desired from what audience?
II. Identify the communications alternatives. What tasks should be assigned to:
    A.   Advertising?
    B.   Personal selling?
    C.   Packaging and branding?
    D.   Sales promotion and display?
    E.   Public relations and publicity?
III. Identify key uncertainties in predicting response
    A.   The characteristics of potential customers
        1.   Demographics—age, income, location, and so on
        2.   Predispositions—awareness, attitudes, habits
    B.   The influence of informal communications
        1.   Group influences
        2.   Cultural influences
    C.   The influence of formal communications
        1.   The relative influence of elements in II.A (as above) compared with the expected strategy of competitors
        2.   The influence of specific vehicles, especially:
            a.   Advertising media
            b.   Salespersons
IV. Gather data to evaluate the alternatives
    A.   Data about markets (as in III.A above)
    B.   Data about media
        1.   Circulation
        2.   Readership
        3.   Impact (qualitative)
    C.   Data about messages
        1.   Pretesting
            a.   In the laboratory
            b.   In the field
        2.   Posttesting
V.   Synthesize the campaign elements
    A.   Combine markets, messages, and media
    B.   Subject the communications strategy to continual evaluation and control (the cycle goes back to A)

Source: Adapted from Frederick E. Webster, Jr., *Marketing Communication: Modern Promotional Strategy*. Copyright © 1971, The Ronald Press Company, New York.

Additional buyers

New customers can be attracted in various ways. Consumers may shift from one brand of merchandise to another or may be induced to try a new outlet as a result of astute advertising by the retailer. Consider the case of the boom in houseplant sales. Growers, wholesalers, and retailers have benefited since plants have become almost a necessity in homes, offices, hotels, and restaurants. Sales of houseplants are more than $2 billion annually.[5] In addition, the market has expanded to include do-it-yourself greenhouses, plant rental services, and interior landscaping. Plant parties similar to those which have long been held to sell such products as Tupperware have sprung up.

Imaginative in-store point-of-sale promotions may expand sales by attracting new buyers for the product. One experiment showed that point-of-sale promotion was twice as effective as a price reduction in stimulating sales of instant coffee.[6] As has also been noted, "Revlon, Avon, Lauder and other industry leaders are . . . sharpening their advertising impact by coordinating TV ads with print ads, point-of-sale promotions and direct mail pieces."[7]

Various unique in-store promotional services can be used. For example, Hewlett Packard Company tested a WATS-line telephone service for informing potential customers about its hand-held calculators. Customers with questions about the calculators were encouraged to call company headquarters and talk with a calculator specialist. The company had been losing sales because retail store clerks were often unable to explain the technical points of calculators. Most retailers would probably be willing to pay a small fee to have this kind of service as an aid in expanding the sales of a high-cost item.[8]

Consider also Campbell Soup Company's "labels for education" program. Campbell offers a number of teaching aids in return for soup labels. Participating schools sent in more than 92 million labels for merchandise which was valued at more than $1 million. The pressure by children to bring these labels to school has clearly expanded the market for Campbell Soup products.[9] The alert retailers who tied into this nationwide program probably experienced an increase in both profits and customer goodwill. However, this type of activity must be evaluated in terms of the consumerist issues discussed in Chapter 10. At least one article has criticized using children to further manufacturers' goals under the guise of helping the schools.

Reminder promotions

Effective seasonal promotional efforts can increase the sales of selected products. Such efforts have been especially successful in getting consumers to stock large amounts of products prior to seasonal increases in sales,

[5] "Growing Trend: The Indoor Plant Craze," Ladies' Home Journal, September 1975, p. 70.

[6] Arch G. Woodside and Harold L. Waddle, "Sales Effects of In-Store Advertising," Journal of Advertising Research, vol. 15 (June 1975), p. 32.

[7] "Management Realists in the Glamour World of Cosmetics," Business Week, November 29, 1976, p. 45.

[8] "Marketing Observer," Business Week, October 27, 1975, p. 122.

[9] Ibid.

anticipated product shortages, and anticipated price increases. For example, sales of antifreeze can often be successfully promoted during the months of June and July by reminding consumers to purchase these products while supplies are strong.

Customers can also be held through reminder promotion programs. For example, such retailers as Sears have been remarkably successful in selling consumer durables because of the nationwide product service guarantees and warranties which they feature.

Market expansion

One of the more notable expansions of product sales has been that of citizens band (CB) radios. For many years such radios were used primarily by commercial truck drivers. However, as a result of astute retail promotion and changes in environmental conditions, such as the public response to the 55-miles-per-hour speed limit, CB radios have become a recreational item for many consumers, even though many of the radios sell for over $100. Thus the product is now being promoted to both commercial and retail markets.[10]

Consumer conversion

Price battles break out occasionally as campaigns are launched to get consumers to switch brands or stores. Such campaigns depend heavily on retail advertising. For example, the big three auto rental agencies occasionally wage fierce price battles when the smaller outlets endeavor to undercut their prices. Occasional price wars between the major oil companies and the independents still occur as the independents battle for additional customers. The FTC has even had to investigate a supermarket price war between competing supermarket chains in San Antonio, Texas.[11] However, it is hoped that customer conversions can occur without such drastic measures as these, which greatly affect profits.

Image development

Promotion can be used over a period to enhance and/or change an image. Image maintenance is a problem for many retailers. A common problem for even the largest retailers is failing to identify a particular market niche and consistently promoting to it. For example, it has been observed that Sears may be losing its appeal to low-income consumers by promoting high-priced items. "More and more for Sears, it comes down to the ultimate question of identity in figuring out just what it wants to be to its customers."[12] This problem plagued W. T. Grant to such an extent that it ultimately

[10] "Industry Grants Get a Handle on CB," *Business Week*, June 21, 1976, p. 93.

[11] "FTC Probes Texas Price War," *Chain Store Age Executive*, August 1976, p. 4.

[12] "Sears' Identity Crisis," *Business Week*, December 8, 1975, p. 53.

went bankrupt. Also, the image problems of the giant A&P chain have caused several drastic realignments in its promotion strategies as it shifted to its Price and Pride campaign to reestablish a clear image for itself.

Market positioning

A merchant may use communications strategies to reposition a store in the minds of consumers so as to broaden the customer base. It has been noted:

For increasingly, the smart retailer is recognizing that he must communicate his "positioning" with consumers through *every single one of his contacts with them.* *Employee attitudes, service policies, and store decor* are just as vital to the totality of *people's perception of a retailer's stance* as the more obvious aspects like merchandise, pricing and advertising. . . . Older "class" stores once targeted at the carriage trade, in particular, are finding they must *completely reeducate personnel* to meet changing needs of new customers.[13]

Probably one of the best-known instances of a lack of proper positioning is the world-renowned Abercrombie and Fitch, a seller of sporting goods to the "carriage trade" for more than 80 years. In 1976, the company went to federal bankruptcy court to try and hold off creditors in a last desperate effort to reorganize. Let's look at the reason for its near demise:

As participant sports became more and more popular in the U.S. in the 1950's and 1960's, Abercrombie opened branches in San Francisco; Troy, Michigan, and Colorado Springs, and it began dealing more in fashion. Other high-priced stores— notably Tiffany—successfully made the difficult transition to a broader market by combining friendliness with lower-priced items, but A&F did not move far or fast enough. As recently as the mid-1960's, complains a New York advertising man, A&F was run "like a stuffy club"—still catering to wealthy Midwestern physicians who take four weeks off to shoot game in Wyoming. Young, affluent skiers, backpackers and tennis players came into A&F to admire its tony, well-stocked departments but they bought their gear at cheaper places, such as Korvette's, Two Guys Stores and other discount operations catering to the outdoors set. None of those were around, of course, when Theodore Roosevelt went on safari.[14]

REQUIREMENTS FOR GOOD PROMOTION PLANS

What are the requirements for good promotion plans? Such plans are: (1) appropriate, (2) feasible, (3) comprehensive, (4) management-specific, (5) time-specific, (6) dollar-specific, and (7) reviewed regularly.[15] The key word

---

[13] *Grey Matter*, vol. 45, no. 6 (New York: Grey Advertising, 1975), p. 7.

[14] "Abercrombie's Misfire," *Time*, August 23, 1976. Reprinted by permission from *Time*, The Weekly Newsmagazine; Copyright Time Inc. 1976.

[15] Rollie Tillman and C. A. Kirkpatrick, *Promotion: Persuasive Communication in Marketing* (Homewood, Ill.: Richard D. Irwin, 1968), p. 385.

here is *planning*. Communications plans must be carefully developed in advance of their implementation if maximum gains are to be obtained. Goals must be defined, the means of accomplishing them must be agreed upon, and the necessary funds must be earmarked. This allows better coordination of advertising with public relations and with window displays and similar types of information. For the small retailer, advance planning is particularly essential because of the myriad of activities in which a one-person store gets involved. The small retailer, unlike the larger outlets, cannot shift the responsibility for advance planning to a specialist.

FACTORS IN MEDIA SELECTION DECISIONS

What determines media selection decisions? As noted in Figure 16–2, the first problem in reaching prospective consumers is to identify them. The retailer's job is easier when prospective consumers can be defined demographically because published information on audiences is typically reported in demographic terms.

The retailer must determine the frequency with which the audience should be exposed to promotional efforts and must also decide whether that frequency should remain constant over time.

The nature of the message will also affect promotional strategy. A complex message delivered over television or radio will require repetition. However, complexity is not likely to be a problem with print media, since people can study an advertisement at their leisure.

Typically the longer the time between purchases of a product, the more appropriate it will be for the retailer to "pulse" advertising. Conversely, high-frequency promotion will work better for products which are purchased on impulse. Products with a high degree of brand loyalty will probably require a lower frequency of exposure.

For the larger metropolitan areas, geographic coverage is an important problem. The retailer wants to reach as many prospects as possible. To reach the desired markets, it may be necessary to use several radio stations and/or television stations because, particularly for radio, each station is likely to have a different audience profile.

The following factors have a major impact on the attention value of a medium:

Audience involvement with editorial (or program) material and advertising content.

The ability to provide a specialized audience with group identification.

The ability to offer the advertiser a monopoly over communication on the subject.

The quality of advertising reproduction.

The time of message delivery.[16]

---

[16] Kenneth A. Longman, *Advertising* (New York: Harcourt Brace Jovanovich, 1971), p. 351.

Numerous other factors also affect the choice of media for promotional campaigns. These include the objectives of the promotion, the available budget, competitive promotional campaigns, and the cost of various media.

THE CHOICE OF MEDIA

A variety of media can be used as part of a communications strategy. Let's look briefly at the major ones before we take up retailer uses of various media combinations, and the communications alternatives which can be assigned to each.

Newspapers

Newspapers offer a number of advantages. They are sold in a carefully defined trading area and place a major stress on events of local interest. Further, they provide flexibility and immediacy in the placing of advertisements because of the closeness of their deadlines.

Newspapers also assist small retailers in placing ads by helping them to plan advertising programs and to prepare advertisements. Some of the larger newspapers also conduct studies of buying habits and product usage.

A quick sales response is more likely to result from newspaper advertising than from other kinds of promotion. However, newspapers present such problems as wasted circulation, poor reproduction quality, and competition with other ads. Particularly in small communities, the daily newspaper is perceived "as the primary source of local news and it's relied on by its readers for information concerning where to shop."[17] Branding and price discounting are the most significant keys to newspaper advertising success.[18] Newspaper advertising constitutes the bulk of retail promotion. Indeed, it accounts for 70 percent or more of the ad budgets of such retailers as I. Magnin, J. L. Hudson, Garfinckels, J. C. Penney, and Bloomingdale's.[19]

Magazines

Suppliers can often induce local retailers to make use of national magazine advertising through local tie-ins. The retailer may use window displays, point-of-purchase displays, or other forms of local promotion to point out that a product sold in an outlet is advertised in a national magazine.

Many magazines now feature regional or metropolitan editions whereby retailers may buy only that part of the audience within the trading area of the retail outlet. Despite cost per thousand increases of 25 percent by 1980,

---

[17] Ernest F. Larken and Gerald L. Grotta, "Consumer Attitudes toward and Use of Advertising Content in a Small Daily Newspaper," *Journal of Advertising,* vol. 15 (Winter 1976), p. 31.

[18] "Counting on Perception of Product Price and Quality in Newspaper Advertising," in Howard C. Schneider (ed.), *1976 American Institute for Decision Sciences Proceedings,* p. 585.

[19] "Feature of the Month: Media," *Stores,* November 1976, pp. 19–20.

increased use of magazines will occur. A major drawback to the use of magazines, however, may be the lack of an audience psychological profile against which management can match the psychographics of its prime customers.[20] Life-styles are increasingly the key to the selection of magazines which serve narrow market segments.

Television

Until recently, television has not been heavily used in retailing, particularly at the local level. Local retailers still use TV and radio primarily to supplement newspaper advertising. Television has become more attractive, however, because newspaper advertising rates have increased and because the growth of suburban retail branches has caused too much splintering of the advertiser's dollar.

Increasingly, sophisticated retailers are finding effective and cost-efficient ways of integrating television into their media programs. This is especially true for store openings and major sales events. For example, Bon Marche (Seattle) and Burdines (Miami) are the largest TV advertisers in their respective markets,[21] and Sears is the top local TV advertiser among retailers, investing $21.6 million for local TV advertising in 1975. In addition, Sears spent almost $47 million on network television in 1975.[22] Other heavy users of local TV include Montgomery Ward, May Department Stores, and the Kresge Company, as shown in Table 16–1. The main reason many stores have held back from using television is force of habit.

Direct retailers are now also looking at TV as a key medium. In 1969, $22 million was spent on direct-response TV advertising. In 1975 the amount was estimated at more than $280 million, and it is forecast to pass $500 million by 1980.[23] The products typically sold in this way have been records and tapes, but increasingly insurance, books, and magazine subscriptions are being sold through direct-response TV ads. Soon we will also see increasing numbers of retailers promoting merchandise via direct-response selling on TV and radio.[24]

The primary stumbling block for retailers who desire television advertising is still its cost. The production of TV ads is expensive, as is the purchase of TV time. TV time costs $30–40 for 30 seconds even in small communities. Purchasing TV time is simpler than purchasing radio time because there are fewer stations. However, it is not possible to be as selective in demographic terms. TV rate increases from 1977–80 will be much slower than those experienced in 1976 because of the presidential election.[25] An effort is being

[20] *Grey Matter*, vol. 47, no. 4 (New York: Grey Advertising, 1976), p. 3.

[21] Ibid.

[22] "Sears Top Retail User," p. 15.

[23] Eric Levin, "Act Now," *TV Guide*, December 13, 1975, p. 14.

[24] *Grey Matter*, vol. 45, no. 6, p. 6.

[25] *Grey Matter*, vol. 47, no. 4, p. 4.

TABLE 16–1
INVESTMENTS IN LOCAL TELEVISION BY DEPARTMENT STORES
AND DISCOUNT DEPARTMENT STORES

Company	January–June 1976	January–June 1975	Percent change
Sears, Roebuck and Co.	$10,373,800	$10,121,100	+ 2
Mobil Oil Co. (Montgomery Ward & Co., Jefferson Stores)	9,636,300	7,254,800	+ 33
May Department Stores Co.	4,804,500	3,943,200	+ 22
Kresge Company (K mart)	4,559,900	3,203,800	+ 42
Federated Department Stores, Inc.	4,552,700	2,683,700	+ 70
J. C. Penney Co., Inc.	4,040,200	3,620,100	+ 12
Vornado Inc. (Two Guys)	3,940,200	1,076,800	+266
Allied Stores Corp.	3,786,900	2,377,500	+ 59
F. W. Woolworth Co.	3,135,500	3,298,000	− 5
R. H. Macy & Co., Inc.	2,133,700	1,802,300	+ 12
Dayton-Hudson Corp.	1,914,900	743,000	+158
Associated Dry Goods Corp.	1,843,700	1,168,900	+ 58
British-American Tobacco Co. Ltd. (Gimbels)	1,668,800	1,214,500	+ 37
Arlen Realty & Development Corp. (Korvettes)	1,521,500	1,437,800	+ 6
Rich's, Inc.	1,030,500	547,800	+ 88
Total for the top 15	$58,943,100	$44,493,300	+ 32

Data: Television Bureau of Advertising, based on Broadcast Advertisers Reports (BAR) figures.
Source: *Chain Store Age*, November 1976, p. 34.

made to overcome the cost barrier through the use of modular commercials which are produced by national manufacturers for retail use. Such commercials make it possible for a store name to be inserted within the ad itself instead of as a trailer at the end of the ad.

Radio

Radio has long been a popular medium with retailers, and it is increasing in popularity. Radio stations are beginning to push for a larger share of the 3 billion co-op dollars made available annually to retailers by 2,000 companies.[26] Radio permits greater selectivity of audiences by program, station, and time of day than is available by newspaper. It is also more timely and can provide a more immediate response than any of the other media. Radio is typically purchased in spots of 10 to 60 seconds each. A careful selection of stations with demographic profiles similar to the target market of the retailer is essential. Radio is by nature a medium requiring high frequency of use.

Outdoor advertising

Almost all Americans commute to work daily and also travel for business and pleasure. Thus, a position medium such as outdoor advertising may be

[26] Ibid., p. 7.

of great use to the retailer. The suburban movement of population and the growth of suburban shopping centers have contributed to the opportunities for the use of this medium.

Outdoor advertising messages must be brief. Consequently, outdoor advertising is particularly useful for reminder purposes. It is also a useful information source when it is placed on major highways leading into an area to inform travelers of available facilities. Thus, large local users of outdoor advertising include restaurants, souvenir shops, resorts, and motels.

A twist in outdoor advertising is the use of the so-called beetle-boards—Volkswagens painted with advertising. Levi Strauss has used these beetle-boards to promote its lines of shoes.[27]

Direct advertising

Direct advertising, one of the oldest advertising methods used by retailers, is a strong supplemental medium. Through direct advertising, potential consumers may be reached in a short period of time with a personal appeal which is hidden from competitors. Thus, retailers guard their customer lists very carefully. This is one of the major problems in getting mass retailers to abandon their credit cards in favor of BankAmericard or Master Charge. If they did this, they would no longer be able to promote effectively to their own customers via direct mail.[28]

However, direct mail promotion is a high-cost medium. Moreover, if the mailing list is not carefully prepared, the results may be poor. Finally, direct mail promotion by the retailer always runs the risk of being regarded as junk mail and discarded. Too often, direct mail is still relegated to the seasonal, holiday, and special sale categories.

Catalogs

Along with the growth of direct advertising, the use of catalogs has increased in popularity. Catalogs are not only a source of purchase information, but may also stimulate the desire for merchandise.

Special issue catalogs are very popular. For example, B. Altman sends out over 1½ million catalogs to charge customers and through inserts in local newspapers. Abraham and Strauss, which circulates over 2 million catalogs, gets a yield of $10 for every dollar spent. Shillitos spent over $125,000 for a men's wear book and a home accessories book in 1975 with the expectation of a return of four to six times the cost of the books.

Catalogs can be used to test other areas of the country for expansion. For example, Bloomingdale's circulated over 2.5 million of its 100-page catalogs to charge customers in Washington, D.C., where it was opening two

[27] "Now Levi Puts Its Brand on Shoes," *Business Week,* November 10, 1975, p. 124.

[28] Morris L. Mayer and Joseph Barry Mason, "The Status of Point-of-Sale Systems in Department and Apparel Stores-1975," paper presented at the annual meeting of the National Retail Merchants Association, New York City, January 12, 1976.

new stores. It also circulated catalogs in Chicago to test the response to catalog buying. Thus, catalogs can allow retail outlets to gain business well beyond their trading areas and to step up traffic with new customers.[29] For example, L. L. Bean sends out 2 million catalogs quarterly to keep up its mail-order business.[30] Some retailers are beginning to experiment with selling catalogs instead of giving them away.

Let us now look at the overall trends in the use of these media by retailers.

General media trends in retailing promotions

Even though newspapers continue to be the primary advertising medium for retailers, television retail advertising dollars increased 131 percent from 1971 to 1975—to a total of more than $447 million, whereas newspaper expenditures by retailers increased only 39 percent during the same period.[31] As has been noted, "The fastest growing segment of the broadcast business is that of retail advertising."[32] Indeed, in 1975 retailers increased their TV and radio budgets by 55 percent and 50 percent, respectively, compared to 40 percent for their newspaper budgets.[33]

Part of this growth in TV and radio retail advertising has been due to the tremendous rise in newspaper rates—14–15 percent a year for the last two or three years. Thus, television has become more cost competitive. In addition, television has become more aware of and responsive to the needs of retailers to change their advertising on a constant basis. Finally, television now reaches more homes than do newspapers.

Still, television commercials are primarily image building and not price oriented. As Malcolm Anderson, advertising vice president for A&P, has noted, "The multi-media Price and Pride campaign . . . was used successfully to 'resell' our overall image to the consumer. Image ads are not created to sell products immediately but to influence future sales. It's investment advertising, which also influences a company internally, energizing your own people, which will in turn generate future sales."[34]

As testimony of the increasing popularity of television among retailers, Federated Department Stores, the May Company, and S. S. Kresge were in the top 100 combined network and spot TV investors in 1975.[35]

Supermarkets make especially heavy use of newspapers, the number one medium used by retailers. Comparison shopping for foods across several supermarket ads in the same paper is quite common. Further, newspapers

---

[29] "Retailing: A More Confident Countdown," Business Week, December 8, 1975, p. 23.

[30] "The Call of the Wilderness," Time, November 29, 1976, p. 52.

[31] "TV Fights Papers for Retailers' Ads," Chain Store Age Executive, July 1976, p. 13.

[32] Marvin J. Rothenberg, "Retail Research Strategies for the 1970's," in Edward M. Mazze (ed.), 1975 Combined Proceedings (Chicago: American Marketing Association, 1975), p. 406.

[33] "Department Stores Redefine Their Role," Business Week, December 13, 1976, p. 47.

[34] Ibid., p. 14.

[35] "Three Major Retailers Join Television's Top 100 List," Editor & Publisher, May 29, 1976, p. 26.

are adding innovations to combat television. For example, they are targeting their local issues and providing detailed demographics on the various segments. Thus, in some instances retailers can now confine their advertising to that portion of the total circulation in which they have an interest.

Preprinted newspaper inserts have become increasingly popular. These inserts allow retailers to get a large number of items in a single ad at a low price. For example, Foley's, Federated Department Stores' Houston Division, is using "many more inserts . . . as there are economies in big print runs. We've tripled our number of catalogs and insert them over a number of weeks, changing the cover and maybe the third page so when the reader sees the catalog it looks like a new book."[36]

Newspaper inserts are also becoming increasingly popular because of the rise in postal rates, which has made it uneconomical to use direct mail in many types of circulation. Also control over day of delivery is now difficult if the postal service is used.

The use of direct mail is gaining in popularity with retailers whose POS systems enable them to pinpoint customers who are particularly good prospects for particular items of merchandise. Through the use of their POS systems, Foley's and Jordan Marsh are carefully targeting direct mail by sending shirt catalogs to customers who purchased shirts at the store in the previous six months. These mailings go only to charge customers, but the success rate is high.

"Radio is also growing in retail usage; retail dollars have reportedly doubled in the past five years. Many retailers, such as J. L. Hudson, the Detroit-based department store chain, find it especially useful for reaching teenagers."[37] Radio is particularly useful in reaching ethnic markets and in targeting audiences—such as working women during the time they are driving to and from their jobs.

Regardless of the popularity of certain media with retailers, no one mix is best for all merchants. The astute retailer strives to obtain the particular strengths of each medium in seeking the maximum return on advertising dollars.

Finally, the development of in-house advertising production facilities is becoming increasingly popular. More and more large retailers are developing their own radio commercials and buying their own time. In addition, co-op advertising is on the increase in many segments of retailing.

Let us now look specifically at the retail media mixes of selected retailers.

SELECTED RETAIL MEDIA MIXES

Sears. Sears local market media mix consists of 82 percent in newspapers, 9–10 percent in radio and TV, and the rest in direct mail, circulars, and local sales promotion.[38]

---

[36] "TV Fights Papers," pp. 14–15.

[37] Ibid., p. 15.

[38] "Sears Switches Print Format," *Chain Store Age Executive*, July 1976, p. 16.

Sears buys radio, TV, and newspaper ad space locally. Local outlets are encouraged to use full-page newspaper ads to obtain cost economies because larger discounts are granted on full-page ads. In response to rapidly rising newspaper costs, Sears is also giving increasing emphasis to local radio because of its cost effectiveness, immediacy, and limited production costs.

Sears uses national ads primarily to introduce new products and to increase the market share for certain product lines. Sears TV commercials are produced by outside agencies.

When Sears decides to run a coordinated nationwide promotion, network TV is used to introduce the promotion. This is followed by the use of local newspapers, radio, and perhaps television.

Walgreens. All chain-wide ads for Walgreens are produced and scheduled centrally. Overall, 82 percent of its ads are in newspapers and 18 percent in broadcasting. However, only 7 percent of its ads were in broadcasting in 1971.[39]

In the Chicago area, Walgreens places strong emphasis on ethnic advertising, especially for such products as cosmetics, and makes use of black-oriented newspapers. Spanish-speaking radio commercials are used heavily in the Florida markets.

Walgreens is beginning to experiment with TV as a means of meeting direct sales goals rather than as a vehicle for institutional advertising. It is now beginning to use television to announce opening sales, new store locations, and occasionally even to advertise items and prices.

Direct mail is not a major part of the Walgreen promotion plan because it has not been found to be highly cost effective.

Penneys. Penneys still concentrates primarily on printed ads and makes heavy use of inserts. It is now beginning to experiment with newspaper advertising other than inserts. Most of its advertising dollars are spent in local markets where the responsibility for the media mix resides with the local market managers. Penneys recently upped its local TV expenditures by 23 percent while reducing national TV expenditures.[40]

No institutional advertising is done by Penneys. The firm's belief seems to be that the merchandise offered provides a sufficient image for the chain.

Abraham and Straus. Newspapers are the primary advertising vehicle of Abraham and Straus, though the use of direct mail and broadcasting is increasing in importance.[41] Only in the early 1970s did A&S begin to experiment with TV. However, with the reduction in the cost differential between TV and newspaper advertising, TV is getting increasing play.

The production of commercials is done internally, but time is bought through an advertising agency. A&S features both price and item ads on TV but does not use TV institutional ads. A&S institutional advertising is primarily local, with a focus on the community involvement of store personnel.

---

[39] "Walgreen Ups TV Ads and Colorprint," *Chain Store Age Executive*, July 1976, p. 17.

[40] "Sears Top Retail User," p. 15.

[41] "More Direct Mail, Broadcast for A&S," *Chain Store Age Executive*, July 1976, p. 18.

Color has become increasingly important in A&S advertising. "The importance of color partly accounts for direct mail taking the No. 2 position in the chain's ad budget, plus the fact that 'catalogs have long shelf value.' . . . A&S uses the same catalog for newspaper insertion as is sent to charge account customers and has stopped up the frequency to 10–12 times per year."[42]

Jewel supermarkets. Jewel supermarkets used more radio and TV between 1971 and 1976. In 1976 their budget was "50% print—ROP (Run of Paper) and inserts—and 50% broadcast, which is 80% TV and 20% radio."[43]

Jewel takes advantage of whatever co-op advertising is available, but such advertising is not a major part of its budget. It advertises regularly in Spanish language and black-oriented newspapers. Further, Jewel utilizes foreign language TV commercials. It maintains an in-house ad agency to produce its commercials. Direct mail is not an important part of the Jewel advertising program.

Tempo-Buckeye Mart. Tempo-Buckeye Mart is the 56-store discount division of Gamble Skogmo. Tempo-Buckeye phased out its broadcast advertising during 1975 and went heavily into preprints—placing approximately 50 percent more preprint newspaper inserts than it had placed previously. Earlier the chain had tested television spot ads in several markets, but it found that customer impact was greatest with preprint inserts distributed with newspapers. The chain felt that the consumer was more likely to read a preprint than ROP ads placed throughout the newspaper.

The chain has centralized its advertising program in the belief that uniform preprint circulars have a greater impact than do locally produced materials. However, the individual stores still may develop their own ads for some local events.[44]

Western Motels. Western Motels is the parent of Best Western Motels. Its advertising budget of approximately $2 million is spent primarily on print and outdoor advertising. The company is no longer investing ad dollars in television. It has found that its customers are heavy readers of magazines and that over half of its customers travel by car. Thus, it believes that a combination of billboards, magazines, and newspaper ads is the most effective way of reaching its market.[45]

The above examples indicate the diversity of the media mixes available to retailers. Each mix is unique to the retailer and the target market. Nevertheless, the key appears to be balance and a carefully reasoned out plan within the framework of agreed-upon objectives. The following is the essence of a model plan for department store advertising, but the plan can be adapted to suit the needs of almost any merchant.

[42] Ibid., p. 19.

[43] "Jewel's Ads: Half Broadcast, Half Print," *Chain Store Age Executive*, July 1976, p. 19.

[44] John Consoli, "Retailer Hikes Preprints, Phases Out Broadcast Ads," *Editor & Publisher*, May 1, 1976, p. 48.

[45] "Motel Chain Drops TV, Hikes Print, Outdoor," *Editor & Publisher*, May 1, 1976, p. 48.

If we take the basic objectives of department store advertising:

To create an umbrella that communicates the total character of the store.

To establish consumer acceptance for individual classifications of the store's merchandise

To stimulate and maintain a constant flow of shopping traffic

To sell merchandise directly

And combine these objectives with an understanding of management's merchandising goals and store character objectives and the basic source material, a framework can be created . . . that can be structured and directed toward the determination of:

What to advertise . . . . merchandise
When to advertise . . . . timing
Where to say it . . . . media
How to say it . . . . technique
Whom to reach . . . . audience
How to provide balance . . . . planning.[46]

MEDIA SELECTION

Most retailers simply cannot afford constant exposure in all advertising media. Thus, decisions must be made as to the most suitable media. Historically, retailers have relied principally on newspaper advertising. This remains the case even though they are making increasing use of radio and television.

Cost per thousand

The cost per thousand (CPM) formula is often used to measure the comparative efficiency of two or more media. This formula simply involves dividing the total cost of a given ad by the number of households or persons reached by a medium and then moving the decimal point three places to the left to give the cost of reaching one thousand homes with the ad. Let's look at an example. If a newspaper has a circulation of 25,000 and the cost of a full-page ad is $500, the CPM is calculated as follows:

$$\frac{\text{Cost in dollars}}{\text{Circulation in thousands}} = \frac{\$500}{25,000} = \$20$$

The CPM formula is used primarily to compare two or more media of the same type. Cross-media comparisons are not very useful because of the major differences in the types of media.

The effective use of the cost-per-thousand criterion requires specific information on demographics about the audiences reached by the various

[46] Marvin J. Rothenberg, "Retail Research Strategies for the 1970's," in Edward M. Mazze (ed.), 1975 Combined Proceedings p. 409, published by the American Marketing Association.

media. Sources of such information include the Standard Rate and Data Service, which publishes information on rates for newspapers, radio, magazines, television, and other media. The retailer may also wish to use data developed by the Radio Advertising Bureau or Pulse Audience Listenership Data. The Nielsen Station Index provides viewer profiles for television stations.

You will probably only be able to determine the optimum combination of media by engaging in research to determine which media are attracting the most customers to the outlet. Research among NRMA members on the measurement of advertising results revealed that 94 percent based such measurements on sales increases, 41 percent on traffic, and 38 percent on image.[47]

How much to spend for advertising

This question is always a crucial one in retail planning. Retail ad budgets are most typically allocated on the basis of the contribution of a particular department or merchandise line to sales or profit. These contributions fluctuate from month to month and from season to season. Thus, the proportion of ad funds for various merchandise lines and departments should vary accordingly on a monthly or seasonal basis. Barbecue supplies will be more heavily advertised in June and July than in January.

The basis of advertising allocations. Decisions must be made as to whether advertising will be allocated on the basis of sales, of contribution to profit, of the traffic-drawing ability of various kinds of merchandise, or of the growth potential of certain departments. Particularly for small stores, advertising will probably be allocated in proportion to the projected sales volume of the various merchandise departments.

A realistic basis for allocating advertising is to look at differences in the profit percentages among the various merchandise lines or departments featured by the store. One department may have a 40 percent gross profit while another has only a 25 percent gross profit. Obviously sales of the item with the larger gross profit are worth more to the retailer than sales of the item with the smaller gross profit.

On the other hand, is drawing traffic important? Perhaps a department with a low profitability or low merchandise turnover may be instrumental in drawing large numbers of customers to the outlet, thus enabling other departments to make sales. Such a department would be heavily promoted.

But the retailer must be alert to the growth potential of certain merchandise departments. This is particularly true during periods in which there are rapid shifts in the economy. No formula exists for the allocation of advertising dollars. Such decisions must be the result of informed judgment arrived at after considering factors like those outlined above.

---

[47] "Advertising: Sell the Store, Not Only the Item," *Stores*, February 1977, p. 40.

The evaluation of advertising effectiveness.   Unless a person is exposed to an ad relatively often and within a short time interval, the ad begins to be forgotten almost immediately. Just how many exposures are enough? The few studies which have been conducted indicate that three exposures are probably enough, depending on the circumstances. One researcher has indicated that the first exposure elicits attention or curiosity, that the second elicits recognition, and that the third is a reminder of the need to take action.[48]

Media research by larger retailers may also be in order to allocate advertising among various media. Among media models, linear programming has enjoyed some popularity. Criticisms of its use have included the insensitivity of the computer approach and questions of data quality and of data comparability across various media.

Numerous approaches to measuring advertising effectiveness are possible. For example, telephone surveys may be conducted of unaided recall of television or radio commercials by simply asking respondents, "What was the product advertised on the last commercial on channel _____?" Often posttesting of advertising effectiveness is done by management or outsiders. For example, retailers may compare advertisements which generated a high response to those which generated a low response. Future ads can then incorporate the features which appear to be the most directly related to sales.

More sophisticated approaches are sometimes used in measuring the results of advertising if budgets are sufficiently large. For example, retailers can take advantage of the split-run testing offered by some newspapers. These newspapers will allow advertisers to run two ads which are the same in size and have the same position in the newspaper but feature different copy themes. Half of the newspapers feature one ad, and the other half feature the alternative version. The relative effectiveness of the two versions can then be determined. The ad which generates the most response, perhaps to a coupon cents-off offer, is judged to be the most effective.

Questionnaires can also be used to elicit information on advertising effectiveness. These can be completed by store personnel, mailed to customers' homes, or administered over the telephone. Another approach has been to use focused group interviews to obtain responses to copy themes, color formats, or other advertising features. Typically, advisory boards of one sort or another are used in focused group sessions. These boards are shown ads and are asked which ones they like or dislike. They may even be shown ads which have not yet run and be asked to comment upon them.

Coupons are also a time-honored way of measuring advertising effective-

---

[48] Herbert E. Krugman, "Why Three Exposures May be Enough," *Journal of Advertising Research,* vol. 12, no. 6 (1972), pp. 11–15; see also Robert Grass and Wallace H. Wallace, "Satiation Effects of TV Commercials," *Journal of Advertising Research,* vol. 9, no. 3 (1969), pp. 3–9; and Krugman, "The Effect of Scheduling on Advertising Productivity," *A.N.A. Advertising Research Workshop,* February 1974.

ness, especially in the food industry. Retailers simply count the number of cents-off coupons turned in to them. The universal product code allows retailers to obtain detailed information on inventory movement at the point of sale and will be a great boost to advertising research efforts.

Evaluation of the effectiveness of institutional image-creating ads is difficult when compared to testing responses to a particular cents-off ad for a product. Institutional or attitude-changing ads can best be evaluated by professional research firms.

The methods of evaluating advertising effectiveness discussed in this chapter simply highlight the numerous ways in which the retailer may seek to measure the effectiveness of advertising and to make media allocations. The details of the specific techniques mentioned are beyond the scope of this books. You will cover them either in an undergraduate marketing research course or in an advertising or promotion management course.

The timing of ads.   The calendar month is the most typically used planning method for the allocation of advertising funds. The year may be viewed simply as four seasons of three months each or perhaps as two semiannual periods. In any case, it is necessary to determine the proportion of annual sales realized each month during the past year. If a particular month generated 15 percent of sales last year, 15 percent of advertising would be allocated for that month this year. However, simply using last year's data may present problems. For example, the calendar is not the same for any two successive years. Adjustment must be made for official holidays which vary in length and fall on different days. Also, some months have more Fridays and Saturdays than do others. When a 31-day month has five Friday–Saturday shopping periods, that month certainly should receive more money than the month with only four such combinations. Further, it is necessary to consider local paydays in adjusting advertising budgets. Finally, because of the increasing popularity of Sunday shopping, five-Sunday months call for a larger share of advertising dollars.

External forces.   In addition to the advertising budget which is developed and paid for by the retailer, other types of advertising must be recognized as affecting promotion plans. These include cooperative advertising and other dealer-support measures. All such efforts must be integrated with the local advertising plan. Co-op ads account for approximately 25 percent of all retail advertising. The local retailer using co-op ads is part of an integrated campaign which is being run nationally by the supplier. The use of such ads usually allows a store to sell more merchandise with only a limited increase in its own advertising costs. This is because the retailer typically obtains a lower per unit ad rate from the media. In addition, co-op advertising provides small retailers with professional ads developed by national advertising agencies. This ensures more professionalism in the advertising of the small store and can greatly help its prestige. Further, it may also be possible to tie co-op ads into window interior displays and other types of sales-promoting activities. However, the co-op advertising program must not draw away too much of the advertising budget, thereby leaving inadequate funds for local institutional promotions.

Co-op advertising and couponing are on the increase as part of retailer advertising budgets. Still, more than $1 billion in budgeted co-op funds are unspent each year. Nationally over 92 percent of manufacturers offer co-op advertising programs for retailers. A national survey has indicated that manufacturers expect to expand co-op ad budgets an average of 48 percent by 1981.[49]

Manufacturers also offer a large number of other inducements to both consumers and retailers in efforts to move additional merchandise. As noted in Table 16–2, the billback is the most frequently used promotion offered by

TABLE 16–2
MANUFACTURER TRADE PROMOTIONS MOST FREQUENTLY OFFERED TO RETAILERS

Promotion type	Combination frequency	Percent	Type frequency	Percent
Billback	481	48.5	680	54.8
Off-invoice	234	23.6	343	27.7
In-ad coupon + billback	123	12.4		
Off-invoice + billback	61	6.1		
In-ad coupon + off-invoice	32	3.2		
In-ad coupon	30	3.0	197	15.9
Off-invoice + billback + in-ad coupon	11	1.1		
Free goods	9	0.9	20	1.6
Other	11	1.1		
	992	100.0	1,240	100.0

Source: Michel Chevalier and Ronald C. Curhan, "Retail Promotions as a Function of Trade Promotions: A Descriptive Analysis," *Sloan Management Review*, Fall 1976, p. 22.

the manufacturers to the retailer. This is followed by the off-invoice and the in-ad coupon. Billback allowances are simply amounts that are paid retroactively for all purchases within a given period. Off-invoice allowances are direct reductions of invoice amounts. For example, the retailer may be allowed to deduct 10 percent of the invoice cost for an off-invoice promotion.

Retailers typically do not pass the cost savings given to them by manufacturers to the consumer. Discounts at the retail level are usually only a fraction of the allowances received. Thus, trade promotions are typically quite profitable to the retailer. As has been noted, "It would seem that allowances must be greater than 10 percent if there is to be any likelihood that they will result in retail price cuts. Trade incentives must allow retailers to increase percentage margins for promoted products and consumer coupon offers must be 'sweetened' by additional allowance monies."[50]

[49] *Marketing News,* June 18, 1976, p. 2; and Edward H. Zimmerman, "Make Your Co-op Advertising Pay Off," *Product Marketing,* February 1977, pp. 17–21.

[50] Michel Chevalier and Ronald C. Curhan, "Retail Promotions as a Function of Trade Promotions: A Descriptive Analysis," *Sloan Management Review,* Fall 1976, p. 32.

PERSONAL SELLING

The earliest impressions that a customer gets from a retail outlet are from contact with sales personnel, as noted in the influence of formal communications section of Figure 16–2. Thus, management must establish a positive image through salespersons. The development of an effective sales force is one of the most difficult and challenging promotional tasks. The difficulty is compounded because retail selling is typically characterized by low wages and low occupational status and hence does not attract high-quality sales personnel.

Self-service or full service?

The key to a successful sales force is the interaction among the merchandise, the customer, and the salesperson. However, merchandise may be sold on a self-service basis for at least a limited number of product categories. Another alternative is to maintain a fully staffed store. The third possibility is a combination of self-service and full staffing. Consumers have demonstrated that for certain types of products they are willing to serve themselves. This is true of supermarkets and gasoline stations. Customers assume such burdens as a way of avoiding higher costs.

When salespersons are needed

A salesperson is essential when customers have little knowledge about product features. Second, salespersons are necessary when negotiation over price is expected, as is often the case when an automobile is purchased. Lastly, the sale of a technically complex product may require the presence of a salesperson.

Above all, retail selling must be regarded as a communications function and as a part of the total communications mix. If, for example, the communications mix of the retail outlet does not connote an atmosphere of high volume and low markup, efforts to employ self-service in moving merchandise are not likely to be successful.

In spite of traditional low wages, the cost of retail selling is high. As shown in Table 16–3, selling cost as a percentage of sales ranges from a low of 5 percent to a high of almost 10 percent for some retail merchandise categories. For department stores, selling expenses are almost 25 percent of total store expenses. Thus, salespersons represent a costly service. The cost can only be offset by increasing the productivity per worker.[51]

A properly trained and effective sales force can be a major differentiating store feature. Competing firms can duplicate price cuts and promotion, but it is more difficult to develop a quality sales force.

---

[51] See Richard Furash, "Salesforce Schedules Simplified," *Stores,* June 1975, p. 5.

TABLE 16–3
COMPARISON OF SELLING COSTS AND TOTAL EXPENSES OF RETAIL FIRMS

	Selling costs as a percentage of sales	Total expense as a percentage of sales	Selling costs as a percentage of total expense
Department and specialty stores	7.73%	31.76%	24.3%
Furniture stores	7.21	36.41	19.8
Gift and novelty shops	9.79	26.74	36.6
Jewelry stores	9.8	38.5	25.5
Appliance and radio-TV dealers	5.0	28.3	17.7
Men's wear stores	9.7	25.1	27.6

Data: National Retail Merchants Association; National Home Furnishings Association; Accounting Corporation of America (wages excluding proprietor's wages); Retail Jewelers of America, Inc. (sales volume over $500,000); National Appliances and Radio-TV Dealers Association (sales volume over $500,000); and Menswear Retailers of America.

Source: David J. Rachman, *Retail Strategy and Structure*, 2d ed., p. 263. Copyright 1975. Reprinted by permission of Prentice-Hall, Inc., Englewood Cliffs, New Jersey.

Increasing sales force productivity

Good management in the sales area simply means planning for productivity. As has been noted, "With selling expenses typically ranging around 8% of sales and assuming pre-tax profits of 4%, a 10% increase or decrease in the selling expense ratio can have an impact on pre-tax profits of as much as 20%! It generally is the most flexible payroll expense item in a store, particularly in the short-run."[52]

The level of selling expense necessarily varies from store to store because of differences in the merchandise mix, store location, wage rates, store hours, and other variables. It may even vary from department to department because of differences in merchandise and customer service needs. Nevertheless, some generalizations are possible. For example, Ray Killian of Belk stores told an NRMA store manager seminar that "if you have people on your payroll who are selling less than $62,000, you are losing money on them."[53] Killian's calculations were based on a minimum wage of $2.30 an hour. This wage is likely to increase to $3.00 an hour in the near future so that sales force productivity will be even more critical. Killian further points out that at Dayton-Hudson, which ranks number one in people productivity, sales generation per employee on the payroll, including office staff, is $60,000 per year. The figure for Mercantile Stores is $50,000 per employee; for Kresge, $47,000; for Federated Department Stores, $45,000; and for J. C. Penney, $43,000.

What are the controllable productivity opportunities in retail sales? The key is better salesperson scheduling in balancing customer service requirements and acceptable expense levels. The typical activity of salespersons is

[52] Steven P. Cron, "Control of Retail Selling Costs," *Retail Control,* August 1976, p. 60.
[53] "Upping People Productivity," *Stores,* December 1976, p. 33.

as follows: 35 percent selling, 25 sales-supporting, 20 percent delay-idle, and 20 percent out of the area.[54] The percentage of selling time can clearly be increased. A major continuing difficulty is overscheduling of employees and the lack of accurate forecasts of the number of salespersons needed. Retail management needs to consider scheduling "less overtime, more part-time; avoid peak 'offs' such as lunchtime; and perhaps even split schedules."[55]

Other opportunities for productivity increases include:

1. Evaluating the physical work area to which sales employees are assigned, and perhaps expanding it.
2. Modifying the work flow and systems efficiencies. For example, should the level of service for some store departments, such as sewing notions or greeting cards, be less than one sales employee per department?
3. Focusing on store hours. Perhaps low-volume hours can be eliminated by later openings and an extension of the evening high-productivity periods.

TYPES OF RETAIL SELLING

Transaction processing

Several types of personal selling occur in the retail outlet, and the kinds of personnel required for each type are different.[56] The easiest selling task is transaction processing. Here retail employees simply function as checkout clerks or cashiers and engage in little personal selling. A typical example is the checkout clerk in a supermarket.

Routine selling

Routine selling requires a slightly larger amount of sophistication and a more organized approach to the sales task. It involves the sale of nontechnical merchandise, such as clothing. The salesperson makes contact with the shopper prior to the shopper's decision to buy.

Creative selling

Creative selling requires more skill on the part of retail salespeople. The salesperson needs complete information about product lines and their probable uses, an understanding of technical terms, and a good personality. Often such salespersons are referred to as sales consultants. They may, for example,

---

[54] Cron, "Control of Retail Selling Costs," p. 62.

[55] "Upping People Productivity," p. 33.

[56] Don L. James, Bruce J. Walker, and Michael J. Etzel, *Retailing Today* (New York: Harcourt Brace Jovanovich, 1975), p. 352.

work as interior design specialists in a furniture store. Proper suggestive selling can increase retail sales by as much as 10 percent.[57]

Not all selling at the retail level occurs on a personal basis. Retail sales may also be transacted by telephone. Sears, Roebuck regularly uses this approach. Small specialty shops often maintain a list of preferred customers whom they call after the receipt of a shipment of merchandise which they think will be of interest to these customers.

Helping people to buy

The reasons for shopping and buying by consumers were outlined in Chapter 5. However, it might be well to review these reasons as we identify the requirements for a successful salesperson. Salespersons must understand more than merchandise styles, sizes, prices and quality. The key to increased sales at the retail level is understanding the motives that cause an individual to buy. These motives may be rational or emotional, as shown in Table 16–4. They are

TABLE 16–4
BUYING MOTIVES

Rational considerations	Emotional considerations
Cost	Ease and convenience
Durability	Safety and protection
Depreciation	Play and relaxation
Efficiency	Pride and prestige
Economy	Love and affection
Degree of labor necessary	Sex and romance
Saving of time and space	Adventure and excitement
Length of usage	Aesthetic pleasure
Profit and thrift	Urge to create

Source: *Learning Experiences in Retailing* by C. Winston Borgen, p. 271. Copyright © by Goodyear Publishing Co. Reprinted by permission.

the motives which retail salespeople seek to tap in serving the needs and wants of customers.

Beyond motives for buying, what does the retail salesperson need to know about the customer? Table 16–5 outlines the characteristics of 12 types of customers whom retail salespersons are likely to encounter and the responses by which the salespersons are likely to generate additional sales.[58]

The key dimensions of the sales management function in retailing are covered in Chapter 20. These dimensions include the recruitment, training,

---

[57] Edith Gumm, "Suggestive Selling," *Stores*, March 1975, p. 27.

[58] Persons interested in more information on the basic selling steps, including prospecting, planning the sale, the approach, presentation, closing the sale, and follow-up, should consult a personal sales text. A typical text is W. J. E. Crissy, William H. Cunningham, and Isabella C. M. Cunningham, *Selling: The Personal Force in Marketing* (New York: John Wiley and Sons, 1977).

TABLE 16–5
RECOGNIZING CUSTOMERS OF ALL TYPES

Basic types of customer	Basic characteristic	Secondary characteristics	Other characteristics	What salesperson should say or do
Arguer	Takes issue with each statement of salesperson	Disbelieves claims, tries to catch salesperson in error	Cautious, slow to decide	Demonstrate Show product knowledge Use "Yes, but . . ."
Chip on shoulder	Definitely in a bad mood	Indignation Angry at slight provocation	Acts as if being deliberately baited	Avoid argument Stick to basic facts Show good assortment
Decisive	Knows what is wanted	Customer confident choice is right	Not interested in another opinion —respects salesperson's brevity	Win sale—not argument Sell self Tactfully inject opinion
Doubting Thomas	Doesn't trust sales talk	Hates to be managed	Arrives at decision cautiously	Back up to merchandise statements by manufacturers' tags, labels Demonstrate merchandise Let customer handle merchandise
Fact-finder	Interested in factual information— detailed	Alert to salesperson's errors in description	Looks for actual tags and labels	Emphasize label and manufacturers' facts Volunteer care information
Hesitant	Ill at ease— sensitive	Shopping at unaccustomed price range	Unsure of own judgment	Make customer comfortable Use friendliness and respect
Impulsive	Quick to decide or select	Impatience	Liable to break off sale abruptly	Close rapidly Avoid oversell, overtalk Note key points
Look around	Little ability to make own decisions	Anxious—fearful of making a mistake	Wants salesperson's aid in decision—wants adviser—wants to do "right thing"	Emphasize merits of product and service, "zeroing" in on customer-expressed need and doubts
Procrastinator	I'll wait 'til tomorrow	Lacks confidence in own judgment	Insecure	Reinforce customer's judgments
Silent	Not talking—but thinking!	Appears indifferent but truly listening	Appears nonchalant	Ask direct questions— straightforward approach Watch for "buying" signals
Think it over	Refers to need to consult someone else	Looking for another adviser	Not sure of own uncertainty	Get agreement on small points "Draw out" opinions Use points agreed upon for close

selection, motivation, and control of sales personnel. The importance of the salesperson as a key element in the communications program of the retail outlet cannot be overemphasized.

ETHICAL AND LEGAL DIMENSIONS OF ADVERTISING

No thoughtful retailer wants to sponsor advertising that is false or deceptive. Still, retailers are likely to continue to come under attack for the way they advertise. As was noted in Chapter 9, a variety of laws at the local, state, and national level regulate retail advertising. Thus, even the smallest retailer is well advised to adhere to a philosophy of ethical advertising. The Federal Trade Commission is increasingly issuing guidelines, rulings, and consent agreements toward this end.

Many of the rules and regulations designed to protect consumers are issued and policed by the FTC. During the 1970s, the FTC began focusing more attention on both large and small retail businesses. Among the key issues is the question of substantiation. Retail advertisers must have written proof of any product claims made in their ads. The FTC has even gone so far as to direct advertisers to sponsor advertising to correct wrong impressions given by unsubstantiated advertising claims.

Bait and switch advertising and ads for unavailable merchandise have also been major problems. It is illegal to advertise merchandise which is not actually available in reasonable quantities in the store. Unavailability is a particularly difficult problem for supermarkets, which may stock several thousand different items.[59] During the past several years, charges have been brought against virtually all of the major supermarkets because of alleged violations of the FTC trade rule on mispricing and unavailability.

Other regulations have to do with the credit terms and truth in lending. For example, if such phrases as *no down payment* are used in an ad, the retailer must also provide all other information on the credit programs involved. When guarantees and warranties are mentioned in ads, the ads must provide full details about the warranty and state where a copy of the warranty can be found.

In the face of these kinds of regulations and consumer pressures, retailers are trying to upgrade the quality and content of their advertising. For example, Sears has announced that it is removing most of the puffery and adjectives from its general merchandise catalog. The major reason for the rewrite is that Sears believes that otherwise shoppers will become increasingly hostile to advertising claims in general.[60] Still, difficulties continue to exist since some retailers apparently do not adhere to strong ethics in advertising. For example, "Miami-based Levitz Furniture has entered into a consent

[59] J. Barry Mason and J. B. Wilkinson, "An Analysis of Mispricing and Unavailability in Supermarkets," *Journal of Business of the University of Chicago,* April 1976 p. 219–25.

[60] Sears and Puffery," *Wall Street Journal,* November 18, 1975, p. 15.

agreement with the Federal Trade Commission, prohibiting it from making false and misleading representations concerning price savings, comparable value, warranties, and furniture composition."[61]

SUMMARY

Establishing an appropriate communications plan for retailing requires much thought and analysis. A good communications program can help to sell merchandise and to create acceptance of the store and its services. However, communications is no cure-all that can overcome the problems of inferior products, bad locations, and other basic defects of the marketing plan.

Astute retail managers will strive to determine the most profitable level of advertising expenditures and will ideally budget advertising as long as marginal sales beyond the cost of the advertising can be obtained. Many factors must be considered in planning the communications program, including the location of the store, the nature of the trading area, the media available, supplier cooperation in paying advertising costs, the existing competition, and even the state of the economy.

Advertising expenditures can be appropriated on the basis of the sales or the traffic-building potential of the various departments, on profitability, or in terms of the growth potential of a particular department.

The choice of the most appropriate medium is not easy. Traditionally newspapers have been the primary medium in retailing. Today, a multimedia approach including the use of radio and television is becoming popular. In any case, key questions in deciding upon a communications mix include the coverage of the audience, the frequency with which the advertising is to occur, and the extent to which consumers recall having read, viewed, or heard the message.

Not to be overlooked is the role of sales personnel in the communications process. Creative selling can do much to increase the overall profitability of a retail outlet. Far too often the role of competent salespersons is overlooked.

KEY CONCEPTS

The concept of integrated communications

Principles of mass communication

Advertising and promotion objectives
  Image development
  Increased sales
  Maintain or improve market share
  Brand recognition

---

[61] "FTC Hits Levitz," *Chain Store Age Executive*, August 1976.

The promotion plan—fundamental considerations
    Relation of promotion to the other strategy variables
    Desired image
    Store location (isolated, CBD, shopping center)
    Existing support at the corporate level
    Target markets
    Advertising content (product, brand, or company)
    Type of appeal
    Intended effect
Key advertising decisions
    The amount of money to be spent
    The content of the message
    The choice of media
    The timing of the advertising
    Advertising effectiveness measures
Advertising strategy
    Types of media
    Media mix
Personal sales
    Sales force productivity
    Types of retail selling
Ethics in promotion

DISCUSSION QUESTIONS

1. Is it possible to increase advertising expenses as a percentage of sales and yet also increase the profitability of the firm?

2. What are the key elements in an appropriate communications plan?

3. Why is it important to plan advertising well in advance of the time at which it is actually to reach the public?

4. What is the role of institutional advertising for the typical retailer?

5. What are the various factors to be considered in deciding how much of the communications budget is to be allocated to the various departments within a retail outlet?

6. Why should a retailer consider the use of co-op advertising funds? What are the best ways of determining which suppliers offer co-op advertising to the retailer?

7. Describe the strengths of the following media: newspapers, radio, television, direct mail, preprinted inserts.

8. What are the limitations of the CPM formula?

9. Why do you believe that retailers continue to use more advertising in newspapers than in any other media type?

10. Why should a retail outlet consider a multimedia mix?

11. Briefly evaluate the media mixes of the various retailers discussed in the text,

and discuss the reasoning which is probably behind the choices of the various alternatives.

12. Under what circumstances is the presence of sales personnel most essential?

13. Why is sales force productivity so important? How may it be increased?

PROJECTS

1. Imagine that you work for the promotion division of a department store and have been told that you are to prepare a campaign for a new product. Select your own "new product," plan the campaign, select the media, and prepare the message.

2. Choose any currently popular product. Determine the number of ways in which it is advertised. What are the differences and similarities among the methods?

3. Assume the role of a "professional shopper" (with store approval) and work out a shopping report for management. Actually compare the degree of expertise in several competing stores on variables which management believes to be most important in "making a good salesperson." You will report to management the result of its particular store, but do not report the results of your investigations in the other stores. But, for your project, compare the stores and rank them in order of effective presentations on the basis of criteria which you can discover from the literature.

4. Make contacts with dealers in a specific product line (for example, automobiles) which have definite differences in product image, price, quality, and so on. Through interviews with the dealership managers, attempt to determine the allocation of the advertising (promotional) budget among the various media. Compare and contrast the dealerships in the group. If actual dollars of promotional expenditures are not available, then utilize percentage allocations. In addition, collect national and local ads for the same dealerships/brands, and evaluate the differences and the similarities noted.

5. If possible, try to get the cooperation of a local merchant to test the effectiveness of a particular promotion in which he/she is interested. Try to work out a "control" situation to test the promotion of interest to the merchant. This project will be possible only if a close relationship is established with the merchant, but it can be very interesting and helpful if it is carefully worked out. Imagination is essential to work out a good project here.

6. Select several local automobile dealerships who seem to you to project differing public images. Interview the management of each to determine its particular image perceptions of itself and perhaps of its competition. Prepare a portfolio of ads of each dealership and also of the national ads of that same dealership's make of auto. Compare the images which seem to be projected by the local versus the national promotions. Attempt to reach certain strategy conclusions from your investigation.

7. Identify the main audiences of a selected retail establishment by interviewing in depth the management of that firm. After your investigation, establish a working copy platform that can be carried on within the major types of advertising media which are available in the particular market area (for example, radio, newspaper,

television, and outdoor). Then develop a main selling point that will appeal to the identified audience and can be carried throughout the campaign.

CASES

Case 1. A new regional mall promoted itself as a fashion mall. One of the anchor stores, Sutherlands, promoted itself as a fashion department store. The Sutherlands mall location was actually a branch. The original store was 200 miles away. Both the mall and Sutherlands were successful in developing the fashion image. While visiting, Sue Jackson, who was used to shopping in the original Sutherlands, remarked to her friend Gail Miller, "I can't believe I'm in the same store. At home Sutherlands is just another department store. Here they're 'fashion.'"

What has Sutherlands done? How did it do it?

Case 2. During and after World War II, Charles Brady, Sr., operated a neighborhood grocery store serving the old central city market. During and after the war, goods, especially gift items, were in short supply. Charles, Sr., realized this and decided to package fruit and sell it as gifts. His current suppliers provided him with good fruit, and he hired high school girls to package and wrap it. Then he added cheeses to his gift packages. He found himself less and less in the grocery business and more and more in the gift business. Eventually he started carrying fine china, crystal, and imported objects of art, still within a grocery store atmosphere. At present there are no groceries and most of Brady's advertising budget is devoted to the national market in magazines with nationwide circulation. The rest of his advertising budget is spent on spot radio ads. He resorts to the newspaper only at Christmas time.

Did Charles Brady, Sr., communicate with his customers? How was his image established?

Case 3. Mrs. Gardner, the manager of Phoebe's ready-to-wear, which caters mainly to college girls, was experiencing difficulty in keeping college girls as salesclerks. They seemed to have little commitment to the job, and she felt that it was a waste of time to give them much training since they would leave almost as soon as she had trained them. On the other hand, the college girl clerks seemed to relate to college girl customers much better than did older but better-trained salesclerks. At present, Mrs. Gardner pays only the minimum wage and no commissions on sales.

What advice would you give Mrs. Gardner?

17

FACTORS AFFECTING RETAIL LOCATION

*T*o those in the real estate industry, "the three most important factors in real estate are location, location, location." And if location is important to the developer, it is only so because it is crucial to the developer's success in finding tenants.

Of all the major expenses involved in being a retailer, lease costs are the smallest—certainly less than inventory or personnel. Working with the concept that there is a pot for every lid or, more on point, a market for every product, being where that market is located is crucial. The very best location you can buy is the very best bargain you can find. Unless you are selling to customers door-to-door, it behooves you to be the first door the customers come to when buying. A thorough analysis of whom you are trying to reach and who, in fact, will reach you is essential.

Louis Vigoda, President
Hera Investment and Management
Denver, Colorado

Population shifts, consumer mobility, and increases in discretionary income affect consumer shopping habits. Consumer shopping habits, in turn, affect retail locational decisions. Locational decisions are among the most important decisions a retailer will make. Indeed, site selection is likely to occur only once in the lifetime of a retail institution. Careful consideration must be given to location in relation to the other elements of the retailing mix.

Thus, the purposes of this chapter are to acquaint the student of retailing with:

1. The interrelationships which exist among cities and how these interrelationships affect the choice of retail locations.
2. The evolution of land use patterns within an urban area, and how these patterns affect retail locations.
3. The specific elements of retail structure within a metropolitan area, and the changes which are occurring within these elements.
4. The techniques which are available to aid in estimating the trading area for a proposed outlet and in determining its economic potential.
5. The key factors in the retail site selection process.

REGIONAL DEVELOPMENT (CENTRAL PLACE THEORY)

The nature of regional development plays a major role in the structure of an urban area, and this affects the nature of the sites available for retail expansion. The theories explaining regional development and the arrangement of cities are many. However, the majority of these have their roots in central place theory, which was developed by Walter Christaller in 1933 and reflects the interlocking systems nature of consumer shopping behavior. A central place is a center of trade, or a cluster of retail institutions located at the center of minimum aggregate travel for the consumer. It is a source of goods and services for an area larger than itself. Essentially, then, central place theory says that the location, size, nature, and spacing of communities is based on the specialized nature of the available retailing facilities and the shopping behavior of consumers.[1] This theory provides much of the basis for the geography of retail location.

Central place systems consist of a series of progressively larger communities which exist in the form of a hierarchy.[2] Each city performs a particular group of retail functions, ranging from the most basic for the hamlet to the most highly specialized in the largest metropolitan areas. The larger the center, the greater the specialization which is possible. Each larger central place

[1] Joseph Barry Mason, "Threshold Analysis as a Tool in Economic Potential Studies and Retail Site Location: An Illustrative Application," *The Southern Journal of Business,* vol. 7 (August 1972), p. 43.

[2] Brian Berry and William Garrison, "The Functional Bases of the Central Place Hierarchy," *Economic Geography,* vol. 34 (April 1958), pp. 146–49.

supports, in addition to its own more specialized retail functions the same functions as those supported by the smaller central places.

A variety of factors determine what goods will be offered at each central place. These include:

The price of the good at one central place relative to its price at another central place.

The number of inhabitants concentrated at the central place.

The density and distribution of population.

The income and social structure of the population.

The proximity of other central places.

Each central place has a unique trading area. However, some generalizations about the ability of different-sized cities to support certain types of retail activities are possible.

Three separate studies have agreed that the following 9 functions will be found within the first 20 functions to appear in a community. In order of appearance, these are:

1. Gasoline service station.
2. Grocery store.
3. Restaurant.
4. Physician.
5. Insurance agency.
6. Beauty salon.
7. Real estate agency.
8. Auto parts dealer.
9. Furniture store.

Two out of the three studies also agreed that 5 additional central functions would be among the first 20 to appear in a community. These are:

10. Automobile dealer.
11. Lawyer.
12. Hay, grain, and feed store.
13. Women's ready-to-wear.
14. Dry cleaner.

Thus, two out of the three studies concur on the first 14 out of 20 functions that can be supported in a community. More important, we are able to determine the order in which these functions are likely to appear.[3] The number of functions which can be supported has a strong relationshp to the population of the trading area, as shown in Figure 17–1.

What does all of this mean for students of retailing? It means that the more highly specialized the particular product or service being offered, the larger

---

[3] Berry and Garrison, "Functional Bases of the Central Place Hierarchy"; J. Hurlebaus and R. Fulton, "Community Size and the Number of Businesses and Services," *Tennessee Survey of Business*, vol. 3, (1968); and Mason, "Threshold Analysis," p. 33.

FIGURE 17–1
RELATIONSHIPS OF POPULATION TO NUMBER OF ACTIVITIES*

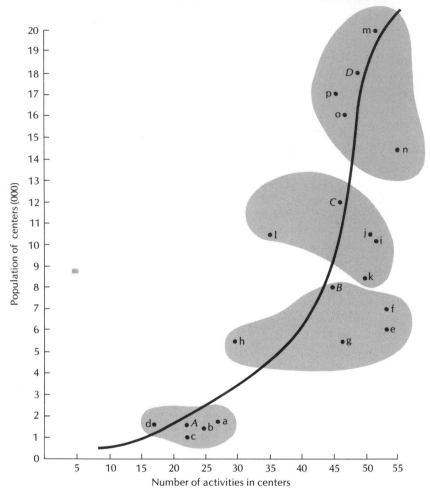

* Each small case letter represents one of the 16 communities included in the research.
Source: Joseph Barry Mason, "Threshold Analysis as a Tool in Economic Potential Studies
and Retail Site Location: An Illustrative Application," *Southern Journal of Business*, vol. 7
(August 1972), p. 51.

the community must be before the service can be supported. Clearly, the
population and income requirements to support a gasoline service station are
less than the requirements for a gourmet food shop. It also means that general
rules have been developed which can tell retailers the size and types of
businesses which communities of various sizes can support. Thus this approach can serve as an initial screening device in deciding whether to further
investigate the possibilities for location within a particular region or urban
area.

THE METROPOLITAN ECONOMY

After it has been determined that a metropolitan area can support a particular type of retailing establishment, what theories of development are available to help in deciding where to locate within the area? Specialized land use patterns emerge as retailers and other land users bid for the sites most favorable to their activities. The function which stands to make the most profit from a location can afford to pay the highest rent. The result of this competitive bidding is a land use pattern which is most capable of supporting the specialized activities of urban life. Several models have been developed to describe the spatial patterns which emerge as a result of this process. These models state that land use tends to be distributed in concentric zones, as sectors, or as multiple nuclei. All of these distributions supposedly contribute to the aggregate convenience of the citizens of the area by allowing them to conduct as many activities as possible with a minimum of movement.

Concentric zone theory

Concentric zone theory states that a city will assume the form of five concentric urban zones, as shown in Figure 17–2. These are as follows:

1. The central business district.
2. The zone in transition.
3. The zone of working persons' homes.
4. The zone of better residences.
5. The commuters' zone.

Growth is accomplished by the expansion of each zone into the next zone. As the residential areas move farther outward, new retail facilities, such as shopping centers, emerge to serve these areas. Thus, the existing shopping facilities closer to the central business district are likely to decrease in quality and importance because fewer people will now travel to shop at them.

Sector theory

Sector theory is also shown in Figure 17–2. It is primarily concerned with residential areas, but it considers commercial areas in relation to residential development. The theory states that land uses are arranged in wedges which radiate outward from the city along major transportation routes and that rent patterns cause these shapes. The high-rent residential area is located in one section of the city, and a gradient of lower rents extends from this area in all directions. High-grade neighborhoods always move away from the city. The high-rent area is the most important since it pulls the city in the same direction. Sector theory states that high-rent areas first emerge close to the retail

FIGURE 17–2
THE NATURE OF CITIES

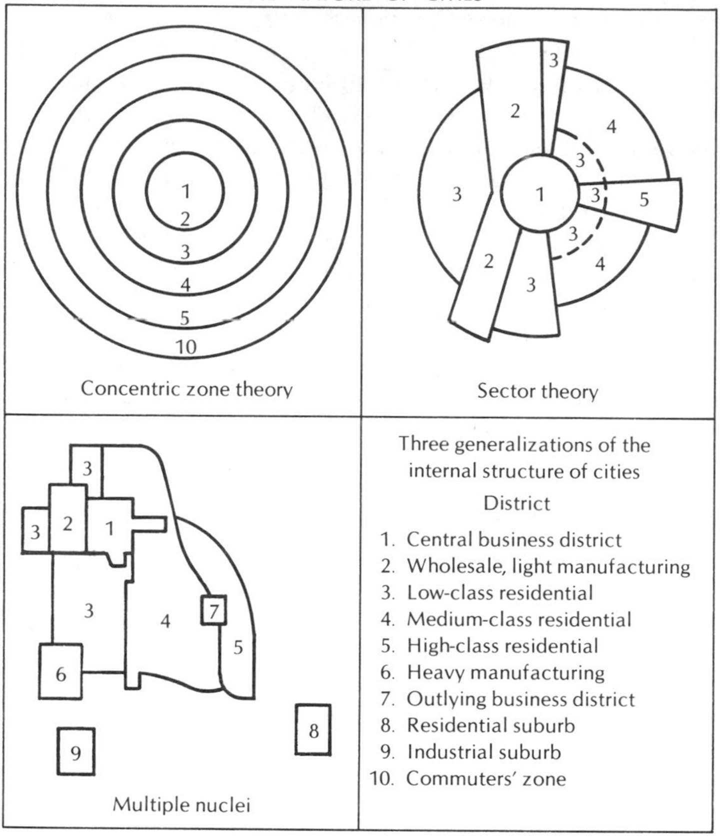

Concentric zone theory

Sector theory

Multiple nuclei

Three generalizations of the
internal structure of cities

District

1. Central business district
2. Wholesale, light manufacturing
3. Low-class residential
4. Medium-class residential
5. High-class residential
6. Heavy manufacturing
7. Outlying business district
8. Residential suburb
9. Industrial suburb
10. Commuters' zone

Generalizations of the internal structure of cities. The concentric zone theory is a generalization for all cities. The arrangement of the sectors in the sector theory varies from city to city. The diagram for multiple nuclei represents one possible pattern among innumerable variations.

and office center and at the point which is farthest removed from the industrial and warehouse area. The most complete and sophisticated retail structures are thus most likely to follow the high-rent areas away from the city.

The multiple nuclei concept

R. D. McKenzie developed the multiple nuclei concept after observing that a city develops a series of land use patterns and that similar activities tend to group together. These nuclei include suburban shopping centers, the central business district, bedroom communities, and industry. McKenzie states that such nuclei are descriptive of the general pattern of city development. Four factors explain the development of the separate nuclei.[4] These are:

1. The interdependence of some urban activities, accompanied by a mutual need for a close physical relationship. Thus, the retail district initially emerged at the point of greatest shopper accessibility. The same is true of the regional shopping centers of today.

2. A natural clustering tendency of some activities. For example, the emergence of specialized retail districts, such as automobile rows, allows a greater concentration of shoppers and the possibility of comparison shopping.

3. The mutually detrimental character of some unlike activities. For example, the high concentration of traffic in retail centers is not compatible with the needs of wholesaling establishments for loading and unloading trucks.

4. High rents or land costs which assert an attracting or repelling force on certain uses of land. Low-class housing cannot afford the high cost of hilly terrain with good views. Retail discount centers, catalog-showrooms, and similar retail facilities cannot afford the high-rent costs which are paid in shopping centers or similar locations.

No city conforms exactly to these theories, but each theory provides a useful predictive guide to the likely growth expansion of the communities in which the retailer may be interested. For example, the central business district is now the general retailing center primarily for the area closely surrounding it, the specialty seller for the city, and the office center for the metropolitan region.

THE RETAILING STRUCTURE

On a more specific level, the retail structure may be viewed in a variety of different ways. Table 17–1 provides a typical portrait of retailing structure in a metropolitan area and the features which define each segment of the total structure. The structure of a community increases in complexity with city size. At the metropolitan area level, for example, we encounter a series of commercial centers ranging from the densely used central business district to isolated clusters of stores. Let's briefly look at these various centers.

The central business district (CBD)

The central business district (CBD) contains the real estate of highest value, the largest number of retail stores, and the most office buildings. It is characterized by commercial intensity and is the area in which front-foot

---

[4] Chauncy D. Harris and Edward L. Ullman, "The Nature of Cities," *Annals of the American Academy of Political and Social Sciences*, November 1945.

TABLE 17–1

THE RETAIL STRUCTURE OF THE METROPOLITAN ECONOMY

Retail element	General character	Source of customers	Store types	Parking	Traffic	Goods sold
1. Central business district A. Inner core B. Inner belt C. Outer belt	Inner core and belt solidly commercial. The business and recreational heart of the metropolitan economy. Residents fill in back streets. Typically, residential areas are blighted.	Come from all parts of city and tributary area. Sites are most accessible to most consumers. Intra-city transportation converges in this element.	Largest in floor space and volume. Multi-story department store is symbolic. Home of leading specialty shops. Outer belt activity less intense. These stores do smaller volume per unit.	Totally inadequate in inner core and belt. Trend to provide public lots and commercial parking lots to supplement limited curb parking in inner belt and outer belt.	Extremely heavy. Congested during peak periods.	Shopping and specialty goods emphasis. Area is center of apparel, home furnishings, other department store lines. Service and other commercial activities found in belts.
2. Main business thoroughfares (string streets)	Mixed zone of retail and light industrial enterprises and working-class homes. Featured by long series of miscellaneous stores.	Basically trade is transient, consisting of commuters, suburbanites, and inter-city automotive traffic. Some patronage also from neighborhood residents.	Concentration of larger food stores, automobile dealers, supply houses, and service and convenience goods stores.	Usually dependent on curb parking. Inadequate during most periods.	Streets are main traffic arteries. Usually heavy, but particularly so during commuting peaks.	Essentially business streets. Stores are widely spaced over length of artery.
3. Secondary commercial sub-districts (unplanned) A. Neighborhood. B. Community or district C. Suburban or outer	More residential than first two elements. Owner-occupied residences increase with distance from general business districts. The subdistricts tend to appear, islandlike, along string streets.	Come basically from A, B, or C trade areas. The districts developed as the city grew at focal points of intracity transportation. Dependent on traffic brought by public carriers.	Unplanned competition featuring convenience and shopping goods. B and C tend to be miniatures of central business districts.	Mostly curb, plus some off-street parking provided by individual merchants.	Since stores typically clustered at key intersections and transfer points of public carriers, this traffic is heavy.	Convenience goods featured in A. Increasing shopping goods emphasis in B and C.

3a. Controlled secondary subcenters a. Neighborhood b. Community or district c. Suburban or outer	Waste area and marginal stores at a minimum. Found near more prosperous residential areas. Unified architecturally. Most built after World War II. New, fresh appearance compared to 3.	Greater dependence on automotive traffic. Parking provided, so customers drawn from greater distances than in case of unplanned centers. Generally found in suburban districts.	Balanced collection of supplementary stores possessing aesthetic appeal. Centers stress convenience and service, not price appeals.	Provided on a cooperative basis within the center. Parking and other facilities related in size to surrounding trade area.	Parking for private automobiles key consideration. Even so, in peak periods automotive traffic heavy.	Attempt made to present an integrated retail organism to customers coming from a, b, or c distances; a stresses convenience goods; b and c feature shopping and specialty merchandise.
4. Neighborhood business streets	Residential, with commercial usage distinctly secondary.	Neighborhood is primary source. Most customers come from within walking distance or five-minute driving distance.	Usually rows of convenience goods outlets found in center of neighborhood community.	Mostly curb. Due to convenience goods nature of most items sold, parking turnover is rapid.	Heavy during peak hours. Otherwise not a handicap to trade.	Emphasis on food and drugs. Grocery store-drug combination frequent. Service stores common.
5. Small clusters and scattered individual stores	More thinly populated residential areas. Neighborhoods served tend to be middle class.	Come from homes not within easy reach of larger elements in structure. Many walk to stores.	Smallest outlets in structure. Many are marginal. This classification dominated by food and general stores.	Curb and small-lot parking usually adequate.	Usually not a problem. The lack of traffic congestion, plus the availability of parking, represents an appeal of this element to customers beyond their normal range.	Usually supplementary and not directly competitive.
6. Controlled regional shopping centers	Overall unity obvious at a glance. Landscaped frequently. Off-street parking. Harmonious effect is objective. May be equipped to serve as area's civic and cultural center.	Draw from families within 30 minute driving range. Customers typically come from a number of suburban communities. Pull varies with effectiveness of central business district retailers and competing centers.	Attempt made to duplicate shopping facilities of central business district with minimum of overlapping. "One-stop shopping in the suburbs."	Usually best facilities in metropolitan area. Adequate for all but occasional peak periods.	Problem usually under control as a result of coordinated planning.	One or two department store branches and satellite stores offer widest range of merchandise and services outside central business district.

Source: Eugene Kelley, *Locating Controlled Regional Shopping Centers* (Saugatuck, Conn.: Eno Foundation, 1956), pp. 66–67.

land values are highest. The CBD has the maximum pedestrian concentration and often the greatest vehicular congestion. Land uses are the most intense in the CBD because of its good accessibility to customers and the resulting large number of high-rise buildings.

In recent years retail sales in the CBD have been declining and have generally shifted to suburban areas. The reasons for this shift include inadequate public transportation, the continuing physical decay of the downtown area, and the movement of higher income families to outlying areas. The new retail facilities have thus followed these families outward. Also, CBD stores typically do not have the common hours of operation or the area-wide promotions which characterize the shopping centers. Shopping centers now compete as a unit, whereas the unit of competition in the CBD is the individual store.

From a locational perspective, the retailer needs to determine whether to build downtown, to rehabilitate an existing downtown outlet, or to follow the trend to the suburbs. Some efforts to revitalize downtown retailing have been successful. The downtown mall has been one such success. Research indicates that shoppers go downtown more frequently after the development of a downtown mall which offers many of the features of a suburban shopping center.[5] Overall, these malls appear to be having a favorable impact on the economic, social, and cultural life of downtown areas. In one nationwide survey of 23 downtown malls, 35 percent reported increased rates of property improvement, 54 percent an increase in the use of adjacent retail space, 55 percent a reduction in store vacancies, and 79 percent an increase in the number of both old and young people shopping in the downtown area. Annual retail sales were also up.[6]

Novel methods are often employed to attract customers to the CBD. For example, downtown merchants in Colorado Springs, Colorado, entered into an agreement with the Eagle Stamp Company that only CBD merchants could give Eagle Stamps. The merchants reported an increase in sales after they began using the stamps to counter the loss of customers to suburban shopping centers.[7] Other special features, such as "moonlight madness" sales, are common.

The following trends are likely to help downtown development in the future:

Suburban development opportunities are often increasingly limited because most of the best sites are already developed, because major highway building which creates sites is slowing down, and because suburban land costs and taxes are higher.

Environmental regulations may add uncertainty to plans for suburban centers.

[5] "Downtown Mall Report Available," *Chain Store Age*, July 1975, p. 6.

[6] ". . . Survey Rates Them Favorable," *Chain Store Age*, July 1975, p. 6.

[7] "Marketing Observer," *Business Week*, November 10, 1975, p. 124.

Transportation improvements—in street systems, links to highways, and mass transit—are downtown oriented.

There is often better land use downtown, and increased market potential in connection with housing, population, spending power, and daytime jobs.[8]

Non-CBD locations

Realistically, the various non-CBD locations are often the best opportunities for many retailers. These locations include neighborhood locations for isolated outlets, string street locations along major thoroughfares, and the various types of shopping centers described in Table 17–1. Depending on the type of outlet, all of these locations offer profit opportunities.

Retail areas often develop along a major highway leading away from the outlying major business district. Such a highway provides a large amount of space for the convenience goods stores which are located along it. These are typically known as string streets and are characterized by a heavy density of vehicular traffic. All of us are familiar with the service stations, accessory shops, automobile dealerships, and low-priced restaurants along these thoroughfares.

A shopping center is considered as a total business sytem which is built after an evaluation of the area and the needs of the people. Typically, the land on which the center is located is owned by a single person or an organization. The person or organization also typically owns the buildings within the center and leases them to the different retailers. The owner can exercise some control over the types of retail establishments in the center, architectural plans, parking, and similar matters. Efforts are made to balance the array of goods and services offered so that a shopper can typically make one stop and satisfy all of his or her needs at that one center. Shopping centers can be classified in various ways, based primarily upon size. The basic types are depicted in Tables 17–2 and 17–3.

The *neighborhood shopping center,* which is the smallest shopping center, typically has at least one supermarket, a drugstore, a hardware store, and perhaps a few other convenience shops located on a site of 5–20 acres. Only

TABLE 17–2
CHARACTERISTICS OF PLANNED SHOPPING CENTERS

Type	Trade area population	Ground area (acres)	Floor area (square feet)	Major tenant
Regional	Over 250,000	40	500,000	Department store
Community	30,000–90,000	20–40	150,000– 300,000	Junior department store or variety store
Neighborhood	20,000	5–20	50,000	Supermarket or superdrug

---

[8] "Downtown Stores Not Like Suburban Malls," *Chain Store Age,* January 1975, p. 5.

TABLE 17–3
INDICATORS OF TYPES AND SIZES OF SHOPPING CENTERS

	Neighborhood	Community	Regional
Average gross floor area	40,000 sq ft	150,000 sq ft	400,000 sq ft
Range in gross floor area	30,000–75,000 sq ft	100,000–300,000 sq ft	400,000 to over 1,000,000 sq ft
Coverage of minimum site area	4 acres	10 acres	40 acres
Minimum support	1,000 families: 7,000–20,000 people	5,000 families: 20,000–100,000 people	70,000–300,000 families: 250,000 or more people
Leading tenant	Supermarket or drugstore	Variety or junior department store	One or two department stores

Walter D. Stoll, "Characteristics of Shopping Centers," *Traffic Quarterly*, April 1967, p. 161.

limited parking is needed, and the center may serve up to 3,000–4,000 people. Larger neighborhood centers may also feature a variety of stores but typically these centers will serve a minimum of 5,000 families, or 15,000 persons.

The *community center* serves a minimum of 20,000–100,000 persons. In addition to the outlets featured by the neighborhood center, it usually contains a large variety store or a junior department store. Other specialty shops, such as florist or gift shops, may also be available. The community center is characterized by a greater depth of merchandise than is available in the neighborhood center. Trade may be drawn from a distance of one to three miles.

Regional shopping centers have cut into the trade of both community and neighborhood centers. A trading area of at least 250,000 people is necessary to support a regional center. These persons typically reside within 30 minutes' driving time of the center. The center contains the branch of at least one major department store, but often of two or more, as well as an array of convenience, variety, and specialty outlets. A minimum of 50 stores are in the center, including home furnishings, household equipment, and similar outlets. Thus the regional center offers all of the services of the central business district in addition to ease of access and parking. However, the department stores in the regional shopping centers do not usually offer the depth of stock which is found in the main store in the central business district.

An emerging trend is the so-called *mini-mall*. This is an enclosed mall which ranges from 150,000 to 300,000 square feet in size and offers the features of a regional mall but is designed to fill in the locational gaps formerly bypassed by the giant regional centers. Many mini-malls are closer to the downtown area than are the giant regionals.[9]

---

[9] John H. Fulweiler, *Profitable Energy Management for Retailers and Shopping Centers* (New York: Chain Store Age, 1975), p. 159.

Customer traffic and location

The decision of whether to locate in a shopping center or in a more isolated location depends upon the type of shopper traffic which comprises the majority of a store's customers. Richard Nelson has classified customer traffic as generative, shared, and suscipient.[10]

Generative business is that which is generated by a retail outlet through heavy advertising or various other methods, such as superior merchandise. A firm which generates all of its own business has to be in the most accessible location possible, assuming that the costs are not too high.

Shared business is the business which a retail store obtains largely because of the traffic-generating power of its neighbors. Thus, consumers may shop at the store even though they are in the vicinity primarily to patronize another outlet. For example, a magazine shop in a heavily congested central business area depends primarily on shared business. Likewise, many of the outlets in a major shopping center owe their existence to the traffic-drawing ability of the anchor tenants.

Suscipient business occurs when people shop in an outlet even though their purpose in being near the store is other than buying. For example, the retail outlets in an airport depend entirely on suscipient business. They engage in no advertising and generate no business on their own. Rather, they are a service to travelers. Some central business district stores and some shopping center stores also exist in this manner.

Almost all firms probably depend to at least a limited extent on all three types of business. However, generative outlets have more options in location than do firms depending largely on shared or suscipient business. The locational decisions of the latter are largely dictated by the major traffic generators, such as department stores or discount houses.

Other locational considerations

What additional forces are at work in the urban area which will shape retail location decisions? On the one hand, we are continuing to see commodity specialization—for example, gourmet food shops and bath shops—and on the other hand, we see increasing locational specialization, which is characterized by fewer but larger outlets serving larger areas. The major regional shopping centers have emerged as the mass sellers for the suburbs, whereas the CBD has become the shopping center for white-collar office employees.

The trend has been toward increasing scale in retailing. The reasons include greater mobility, improved transportation facilities, and similar developments which exert pressure for fewer but larger retail centers and the elimination of centers of the lowest type. However, the increasing cost of fuel and the conservation ethic make it uncertain whether this trend will continue.

---

[10]Richard Nelson, *The Selection of Retail Locations* (New York: F. W. Dodge Corporation, 1958), pp. 51–56, 65–68.

Overall, our notions about retailing competition have shifted to the level of mass centers as opposed to the traditional concept of competition between small, isolated establishments. Now competition is between shopping centers, not individual stores.

Population shifts and shifts in income patterns have been speeding the decline of older retailing areas. These older areas have moved through their life cycle and declined in importance rather rapidly. The large centers do, however, provide opportunities for smaller but highly sophisticated specialty retailers to serve markets which cannot be served effectively by mass merchandise retailers.

TRADING AREA ANALYSIS

The previous discussion in this chapter provides a theoretical perspective for pragmatic decisions relating to the selection of a city in which to locate, of an area within that city, and then of a specific site. (In practice, however, a specific site may become available to a potential retailer, and in that case the consideration of a community or an area becomes academic. Or a space in a shopping center may become available, and the retailer must then consider the site and the area rather than the city.) In this section, we present the process which might be followed by a merchant in deciding whether to select a particular location. The large, progressive chain organizations have sophisticated models for making locational decisions and can computerize the data for decision making. For the myriads of prospective small retailers, however, the following discussion focuses attention on key variables to investigate.

The area from which the bulk of an organization's customers are drawn is called its "trading area." A convenience store may find that approximately 80 percent of its customers live within a one-mile radius, whereas a major department store may draw the bulk of its patronage from an area encompassing many miles. Trading areas are irregular in shape, overlap, and differ for individual stores within a shopping complex. Consequently, a great deal of judgment is required to determine the actual trading area of an outlet.

Trading area delineation

Specifying the shape and structure of retail market areas is a potentially useful way of summarizing the number and characteristics of potential customers. The shape of market areas is typically specified by central place theory, as discussed earlier. The retailer's primary source of ideas about the structure of market areas is the gravity model.[11] The gravity model states that

---

[11] Peter L. Simmons, "The Shape of Suburban Retail Market Areas: Implications from a Literature Review," *Journal of Retailing*, vol. 49 (Winter 1973–74), p. 69; also Joseph Barry Mason and Charles Thomas Moore, "An Empirical Reappraisal of Behavioristic Assumptions in Trading Area Studies," *Journal of Retailing*, vol. 46 (Winter 1970–71), pp. 31–37.

the volume of purchases by consumers and the frequency of trips to an outlet are a function of the size of the store and of the distance between the store and the origin of the shopping trip. In the 1920s, a formula was developed to delimit retail trading areas between two communities. This formula, known as the Law of Retail Gravitation, was developed by William J. Reilly. The most frequently used version of the formula is as follows:

$$\text{Breaking point, miles from B} = \frac{\text{Miles between A and B}}{1 + \sqrt{\dfrac{\text{Population of A}}{\text{Population of B}}}}$$

Reilly's formula allows the retailer to determine the geographic area from which the bulk of customers can be attracted. However, the formula is useful primarily in defining customer drawing power between two communities. It is not useful on an intraurban basis, such as defining the trading area for two shopping centers.

Probability models. David Huff has attempted to bridge the gap between statistical formulations of shopper behavior and the underlying behavioral bases used in defining trading areas. Huff developed an intraurban model based on the assumptions that consumers:

1. Isolate a subset of "alternative shopping center choices" from a much larger set consisting of all possible alternatives.
2. Calculate a positive measure of utility for each of these perceived alternatives.
3. Distribute their retail patronage spatially in a probabilistic fashion.[12]

A formal expression of Huff's model is:

$$P_{ij} = \frac{\dfrac{S_j}{T_{ij}\lambda}}{\displaystyle\sum_{j=1}^{n} \dfrac{S_j}{T_{ij}\lambda}}$$

where

P_{ij} = the probability that a consumer at a given point of origin i will travel to a particular shopping center j;

S_j = the size of a shopping center j;

T_{ij} = the travel time involved in getting from a consumer's travel base i to a given shopping center j; and

λ = a parameter which is to be estimated empirically to reflect the effect of travel time on various kinds of shopping trips.

The expected number of consumers at a given place of origin i who shop

---

[12] David Huff, "A Probabilistic Analysis of Consumer Spatial Behavior," in William S. Decker (ed.), *Emerging Concepts in Marketing,* proceedings of the winter conference of the American Marketing Association, December 27–29, 1972, pp. 443–61.

at a particular shopping center j is equal to the number of consumers at i multiplied by the probability that a consumer at i will select j for shopping. That is,

$$E_{ij} = P_{ij}C_i$$

where

E_{ij} = the expected number of consumers at i who are likely to travel to shopping center j; and
C_i = the number of consumers at i.

The result is a trading area expressed as a series of probability contours, as shown in Figure 17–3. The model may be applied to analyses of retail

FIGURE 17–3
A RETAIL TRADING AREA PORTRAYED IN TERMS OF
PROBABILITY CONTOURS

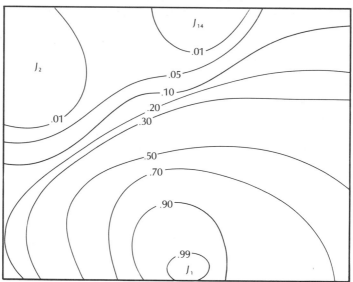

Source: David L. Huff, *Determination of Intra-Urban Retail Trade Areas* (Los Angeles: University of California, Real Estate Research Program, 1962).

locations for individual outlets as well as to analyses of shopping centers. Also, stores of different sizes can be considered at each potential location, and the sales volume and profitability of each compared and analyzed.

The numerator of the model uses the square footage of retail selling space as a measure of attraction. The denominator is travel time from the place of residence to the retail outlet. A series of distance exponents are applied which vary with the type of merchandise. This is done because consumers spend varying amounts of time in search, depending on the type of merchandise.

Huff's primary contribution is the development of the probabilistic notion of consumer behavior, namely, that patronage declines with distance and is also a function of competing outlets. Realistically, a different profile shape probably exists for each type of merchandise in each retail store. Further, market area profiles probably vary through time. Nevertheless, Huff's model provides a more realistic portrait of shopper behavior than do the behavioral assumptions underlying Reilly's Law.[13] Reilly assumed that most customers would come from within the defined area and did not recognize that patronage declines with distance. Neither model adequately reflects the importance of image and other factors in affecting consumer patronage decisions. Limited research has shown that the addition of an image measure significantly affects the ability of the Huff model to explain variations in retail patronage.[14]

Other techniques.[15] A variety of other techniques can be used in trading area analysis. Some, such as license plate analysis or check clearance data can only be used to analyze the trading area of existing outlets, whereas others can be used in determining the economic potential for a new outlet.

One of the more common methods is that of automobile license plate analysis. The retailer determines the origin of the vehicles in the parking lot of the store. By plotting these locations on a map, the retailer is able to determine the general nature of the trading area for the outlet.

Check clearance data can be used to determine the distribution of out-of-town checks which the retailer receives. This technique assumes that the geographic distribution of cash customers and charge customers is basically the same. The technique is useful primarily in determining the percentage of trade which is being attracted from surrounding communities. The technique is likely to give a distorted picture of the trading areas of outlets which have a large percentage of rural customers who bank a sizable distance from their homes.

Analysis of newspaper circulation is probably the simplest and least expensive technique for developing trading area information. The retailer plots the location of a sample of newspaper subscribers. This technique assumes that subscribers will shop at stores in the community in which the paper is published.

Credit records can also be analyzed to delineate trading areas. A sample of charge accounts is selected, and customer addresses are plotted on a map. This technique can be used only by retailers who maintain their own credit records. If the credit records for all retail merchants are maintained at a

---

[13] Joseph Barry Mason, "Retail Market Area Shape and Structure: Problems and Prospects," in Mary Jane Schlinger (ed.) *Advances in Consumer Research*, vol. 2 (Chicago: Association for Consumer Research, 1975).

[14] Thomas J. Stanley and Murphy A. Sewell, "Image Inputs to a Probabilistic Model: Predicting Retail Potential," *Journal of Marketing*, vol. 40 (July 1976), pp. 48–53.

[15] For more information on the strategy implications of these various techniques, see Bert Rosenbloom, "The Trade Area Mix and Retailing Mix: A Retail Strategy Matrix," *Journal of Marketing*, vol. 40 (October 1976), pp. 58–65.

central credit bureau, a sample of these records may be plotted and a trading area derived for the entire city. The retailer can then assume that the distribution of store customers approximates the spatial distribution of the addresses of the sample of credit customers.

Probably the best way to determine a trading area and also to develop insights into customer behavior is to conduct or sponsor a customer survey. The survey can be in the form of a mailed questionnaire, telephone interviews, or personal interviews. Personal interviews may be conducted at the store. A sample can also be chosen from customer records and called on the phone or mailed a questionnaire. It may also be possible to participate in a survey sponsored by the Chamber of Commerce or a similar organization. The survey technique is used not only to define a trading area but to develop data on store images and reasons for patronage decisions.

Regardless of the technique utilized, the delineation of the trading area is the first step in adjusting the retail mix to an outlet's probable customers of the area and in estimating an outlet's probable economic potential.

Investigation of all the retail environments

It is important to take into account all of the relevant external environmental conditions that affect locational decisions. Careful investigation should be made of economic conditions, competition, and the positive and/or negative climate that bears on legal, social, and technological issues.

The business which can be done in the trading area

Management must get accurate estimates of the amount of business which can be done in the specific line of goods in question. If the line is children's clothes, the best data available on family expenditures for children's wear (Bureau of Labor Statistics expenditure data) should be applied to the number of families determined to be in the defined trading area to determine how many dollars of children's business *could* be available in the trading area.

How much business the new firm can expect

Next, competition within the area should be plotted and estimates of the sales volume of each competitor should be developed. Some insights into sales volume can be obtained by using such indicators as number of checkouts, number of employees, and square footage.

The concept of store saturation may be helpful here. Saturation measurements are typically also used in larger areas to help retailers choose among possibilities for the location of new outlets. The idea is that if the defined area has a low level of retail saturation, the likelihood of success is higher than would otherwise be the case. Numerous saturation measures have been used. The formal relationships are shown below:[16]

$$IRS_1 = \frac{C_1 \times RE_1}{RF_1}$$

where

IRS_1 = Index of retail saturation for area one
 C_1 = Number of consumers in area one
RE_1 = Retail expenditures per consumer in area one
RF_1 = Retail facilities in area one

The data utilized in the formula are readily available to the retailer. Census data, for example, can be used to determine the number of customers within a defined trading area. Bureau of Labor Statistics expenditure data can be used to develop retail expenditure information per consumer by product type. The number of facilities within the trading area can be determined by actual observation. Consider the following example in analyzing supermarket potential in Market A.

The 100,000 consumers in Market A spend an average of $5.50 per week in food stores. The 15 supermarkets serving market A have a total of 144,000 square feet of selling area.

$$IRS = \frac{100,000 \times \$5.50}{144,000 \text{ sq ft}} = \frac{\$550,000}{144,000 \text{ sq ft}} = \$3.82/\text{sq ft}$$

The $3.82 per square foot of selling area measured against the dollars per square feet necessary to break even would provide the measure of saturation in Market A. The $3.82 figure would also be useful in evaluating relative opportunity in different market areas.

If it is assumed that enough potential is available in the market to reduce the risks of investment sufficiently, then management may decide to go ahead with the venture.

The foregoing location analysis is a valuable process to ensure consideration of the relevant factors involved in making a locational decision. It should not be considered, however, to provide a real market potential in actual dollars.

SITE EVALUATION

In addition to taking into account factors which will help determine the general area in which the outlet will be located, the retailer also needs to give careful consideration to the specific site of the outlet. A poor site even in a desirable area of a community will have an adverse effect on profitability.

[16] Bernard LaLonde, "The Logistics of Retail Location," in William D. Stevens (ed.), *1961 Fall American Marketing Association Proceedings*, p. 572.

Features of importance

Site evaluation requires the consideration of many factors, including accessibility to automobile traffic, to pedestrian traffic, and in some instances, to public transportation. Other factors of importance include the existence of a buffer area if undesirable features such as noise are present, possibilities for expansion, the adequacy of parking facilities, and the physical characteristics of the land. Utilities and zoning are also important. Certain specialized locations, such as those at interchanges along the Interstate Highway System, require consideration of such unique site problems as ingress and egress.[17]

Table 17–4 depicts a profit-loss table for the retailer to use in evaluating possible sites and in determining the funds available for the use of a specific site. If the retailer owns the building, such costs as rent are nonexistent. On the other hand, the retailer may elect not to tie up working capital in a building but instead to maximize cash flow by renting. Also, location in a shopping center is likely to require higher rent. Thus, proportionately less money is available for such expenditures as advertising. In choosing a shopping center location, the retailer is in effect stating that location utility is superior to promotion in the retailing mix for a given outlet.

Site evaluation in a shopping center

Until recently, the shopping center developer and the anchor tenants were able to impose such a large number of tenant restrictions that small independent stores were almost totally at the mercy of major department stores if they desired to locate in a shopping center. However, the Federal Trade Commission has held that it is an unlawful restraint of trade for shopping center developers or anchor tenants to include limitations on the merchandise lines, advertising policy, hours and days of business, expansion, and merchant association membership of smaller stores.[18] Still, the relatively new independent retail firm without a record of success is likely to be at a disadvantage in seeking access to a shopping center. Such a firm is perceived as representing a potential rent-loss hazard to the developer.[19]

Rental agreements

Rental agreements are also important in determining the site which the retailer can afford. Rents may be negotiated on a flat dollar basis or on a

---

[17] Joseph Barry Mason and Charles Thomas Moore, "Commercial Site Selection at Interstate Interchanges," *Traffic Quarterly*, vol. 27 (January 1973); also Joseph Barry Mason and Charles Thomas Moore, "Interchange Location Practices by Developers of Major Retail Centers," *Land Economics*, vol. 48 (May 1972).

[18] Joseph Barry Mason, "Power and Channel Conflicts in Shopping Center Development," *Journal of Marketing*, vol. 39 (April 1975).

[19] William N. Kinnard, Jr., and Stephen D. Messner, "Obtaining Competitive Locations for Small Retailers in Shopping Centers," *Journal of Small Business Management*, vol. 10 (January 1972), p. 23.

TABLE 17-4
PROFIT PORTRAYAL FOR A PROPOSED RETAIL OUTLET

	1976		1977		1978	
Estimated sales		$488,000		$600,000		$700,000
Cost of goods sold		268,000		285,000		370,000
Gross margin		220,000		315,000		330,000
Expenses						
Salaries and benefits		65,000		94,000		113,000
Net occupancy expense		33,400		35,200		37,200
Rent	$ 5,200		$ 5,200		$ 5,200	
Depreciation						
Repairs						
Maintenance (including building and staff salaries)	3,600		4,000		4,500	
Insurance	2,000		2,000		2,000	
Taxes on real estate	17,000		17,000		17,000	
Utilities (heat, light, power, and so on)	3,600		4,000		4,500	
Other occupancy costs	2,000		2,000		2,000	
Other operating expenses						
Advertising		6,000		8,000		10,000
Telephone		3,000		3,600		5,000
Legal		500		500		500
Postage		3,000		3,000		3,000
Computer service		9,000		12,000		15,000
Miscellaneous		33,000		30,000		30,000
Net organizing expense		8,000				
Total estimated expenditure		$169,000		$195,900		$213,700
Estimated profit (loss)		$ 51,000		$119,100		$116,300

percentage of sales. Typically the more successful the record of a store in drawing traffic to a location, the lower the percentage of rent which the store is likely to pay. Research has generated the following weak generalizations about rental rates:

As the gross leasable area increases, the rent percentage decreases.

As the sales per square foot increase, the rent percentage decreases.

As the profit margin increases, the rent percentage increases.

As the size of the shopping center increases, the rent percentage increases.[20]

TABLE 17–5

TENANTS MOST FREQUENTLY FOUND IN REGIONAL SHOPPING CENTERS

Tenant classification	Rank	Median GLA*	Median sales volume per square root of GLA	Median total rent per square root of GLA
Food and food service				
Candy, nuts	9	800	$ 86.83	$9.38
Restaurant without liquor	12	2,760	80.59	5.30
Fast-food/carryout	17	1,057	113.49	9.59
General merchandise				
Department store	14	122,621	61.41	1.44
Variety store	18	27,750	36.74	2.09
Clothing and shoes				
Ladies' specialty	6	1,749	81.00	5.87
Ladies' ready-to-wear	1	4,005	85.76	4.83
Men's wear	2	3,276	96.66	4.83
Family wear	11	8,883	78.29	4.35
Family shoe	3	8,840	67.75	4.63
Ladies' shoe	7	4,000	67.46	5.03
Men's and boys' shoe	20	1,500	107.87	7.17
Dry goods				
Yard goods	13	4,132	58.52	4.00
Other retail				
Books and stationery	8	2,786	79.23	5.51
Drugs	19	10,116	79.83	2.95
Jewelry	5	2,079	141.21	7.65
Cards and gifts	4	1,959	70.97	6.38
Financial				
Banks	15	3,600	—	4.45
Offices				
Medical and dental	16	720	—	6.00
Services				
Beauty shop	10	1,422	61.38	4.94

* GLA = gross leasable area.

Source: *Dollars and Cents of Shopping Centers: 1975.* ULI—the Urban Land Institute, 1200 18th Street, N.W., Washington, D.C. Excerpts from a triennial report on data representative of 1974 reporting information and therefore not reflective of current information.

---

[20] Robert L. Fitts and Bixby Cooper, "An Empirical Examination of Retail Rental Costs," in Barnett Greenberg (ed.), *Southern Marketing Association: Proceedings,* 1974, p. 185; also Robert L. Fitts, "Basic Procedures and Considerations for Resolving Site Selection–Tenant Mix Problems," *Alabama Retail Trade,* June 30, 1973.

TABLE 17–6
HIGH-SALES-VOLUME TENANTS IN
REGIONAL SHOPPING CENTERS

Tenant classification	Median sales volume per square foot of GLA
Watch repair	$185.40
Camera	165.30
Key shop	163.89
Costume jewelry	146.86
Jewelry	141.21
Tobacco	138.22
Meat, poultry, fish	131.21
Records and tapes	122.97
Musical instruments	121.68
Radio, TV, hi-fi	120.22

Source: *Dollars and Cents of Shopping Centers: 1975.* ULI—the Urban Land Institute, 1200 18th Street, N.W., Washington, D.C. Excerpts from a triennial report on data representative of 1974 reporting information and therefore not reflective of current information.

TABLE 17–7
HIGH-TOTAL-RENT TENANTS IN REGIONAL
SHOPPING CENTERS

Tenant classification	Median total rent per square foot of GLA
Key shop	$26.00
Watch repair	11.91
Hosiery	11.56
Costume jewelry	10.04
Photographer	10.00
Fast-food/carryout	9.59
Tobacco	9.44
Candy, nuts	9.38
Camera	9.34
Millinery	8.57

Source: *Dollars and Cents of Shopping Centers: 1975.* ULI—the Urban Land Institute, 1200 18th Street, N.W., Washington, D.C. Excerpts from a triennial report on data representative of 1974 reporting information and therefore not reflective of current information.

TABLE 17–8
LOW-SALES-VOLUME TENANTS IN REGIONAL
SHOPPING CENTERS

Tenant classification	Median sales volume per square foot of GLA
Bowling alley	$12.48
Car wash	19.90
Cinema	27.59
Laundry	28.75
Cleaners and dyers	30.39
Figure salon	31.46
Variety store	36.74
Automotive (TB&A)*	38.67
Furniture	43.88
Paint and wallpaper	46.30

* TB&A-tires, batteries, and accessories.

Source: *Dollars and Cents of Shopping Centers: 1975.* ULI—the Urban Land Institute, 1200 18th Street, N.W., Washington, D.C. Excerpts from a triennial report on data representative of 1974 reporting information and therefore not reflective of current information.

TABLE 17–9
LOW-TOTAL-RENT TENANTS IN REGIONAL
SHOPPING CENTERS

Tenant classification	Median total rent per square foot of GLA
Warehouse or storage	$1.05
Department store	1.44
Bowling alley	1.47
Catalog store	1.49
Department store—discount	1.53
Automotive (TB&A)	1.90
Supermarket	1.92
Post office	2.00
Variety store	2.09
Car wash	2.22

Source: *Dollars and Cents of Shopping Centers: 1975.* ULI—the Urban Land Institute, 1200 18th Street, N.W., Washington, D.C. Excerpts from a triennial report on data representative of 1974 reporting information and therefore not reflective of current information.

Examples of rent averages for selected types of retail outlets are shown in Tables 17–5 through 17–9.

SUMMARY

Location is a crucial element of the retailing mix, and it must be considered in relation to the pricing, promotion, and other policies of the retailer.

The shopping behavior of consumers and the information sources they rely on in shopping are also important determinants of retail location. To the extent that consumers are less inclined to physically search for most types of merchandise, location may be more important than ever. An understanding of retail location must begin with a consideration of the relationships among cities and of the factors which influence the evolution of land use patterns within an urban area.

The forces which influence retail location are dynamic and interacting. These forces have led, for example, to the decline of the CBD as the most desirable retail location for many types of outlets. Conversely, suburban locations have increased in popularity. However, with the increased price of gasoline and other factors of transportation, central locations such as the CBD will perhaps become increasingly popular with consumers. Despite this possibility, many retailers appear to be willing to pay a premium in high rental costs to locate in a shopping center which allows close proximity to other retail outlets. These retailers recognize that consumers try to minimize the cost of shopping by conducting as many transactions as possible at a single location.

KEY CONCEPTS

Central place theory	The retailing structure
Threshold analysis	The Law of Retail Gravitation
Concentric zone theory	Probability models
Sector theory	Index of retail saturation
Multiple nuclei theory	Site evaluation

DISCUSSION QUESTIONS

1. What factors have led to the decline of the CBD as a desirable location for many retail outlets? What can be done to overcome these increasing disadvantages?

2. What factors have caused suburban shopping center locations to be increasingly popular with consumers? What are the probable effects of the increasing price of gasoline and the increasingly higher price of all types of transportation on consumer patronage of retail outlets?

3. Apply Reilly's Law to delineate the trading area between the community in which you reside and the surrounding communities. In your opinion, does the technique provide a realistic division of retail trade? What are the shortcomings of Reilly's Law? What additional information would you need to determine whether the delineated area has sufficient economic potential to support a specified type of retail outlet?

4. Is the model of retail trading areas developed by David Huff more realistic than Reilly's Law? Why or why not?

5. What factors do you consider to be of primary importance in selecting a site for a fast-food outlet? How do these factors contrast, if at all, with your perception of the key factors for the location of an outlet selling stereo components?

6. Discuss the factors which can justify the payment of a higher rent for location in a shopping center than for location in a non–shopping center. Why is an outlet such as K Mart typically not located in a shopping center?

PROJECTS

1. Select a medium to large mall. Make a license plate survey of the cars on the lot (noting only the county and state symbols on the license plates) at three different times of the day: midmorning, midafternoon, and evening. Make an analysis of your findings, including such things as a percentage analysis of in-county, other-county, neighboring-county, out-of-state-county, etc., license plates, and do a map plotting. Compare and contrast the results of your finding for the three times of day.

2. Devise a questionnaire to obtain the following information:

    a. Shopping center frequented most.
    b. Distance traveled to the shopping center.
    c. Number of visits per week/month.
    d. Items usually purchased at the shopping center.
    e. Factors most liked about the shopping center.
    f. Dominant reason for shopping there.
    g. Opinion about the prices of merchandise.
    h. Opinion about the quality of merchandise.
    i. Opinion about the selection of merchandise.
    j. Opinion about salespeople.
    k. Opinion about the convenience of location (open-end question).
    l. Amount spent here on the average per week/month.

    Expand this questionnaire to obtain similar information about the shopping center frequented second most.

    Using the data obtained from your questionnaire, do an analysis to isolate the factors which determine the choice of shopping centers. Which factors are the most important? Which are the least important? Are greater dollar amounts spent at the shopping center visited most frequently? What meaning does this have for the retailer? What are the similarities and differences in the reasons given for the shopping center visited most and the one visited second most?

3. A topic of interest in many cities is the future of the central business district (CBD). If you are in a city which has gone through a downtown revitalization program, arrange to have interviews with the public servants (and volunteers) who were responsible for getting the program "going." Describe the program; indicate the perceptions of success; and indicate future directions. If you are not fortunate enough to be in such a situation, search the current literature for examples of cities which have done downtown revitalization jobs. Contact the chambers of commerce for information, and indicate some of the efforts that have been made along these lines. There are many such cities to discover in our country.

4.   Prepare a location and site analysis for a good quality cafeteria (other types of service retailer or tangible goods establishments may be used) for your local community based on the information in the text. You must assume the strategy of the firm in terms of locational demands (for example, transient, string street, or defined trading area). Assume that the cafeteria is a regional chain with excellent regional recognition and acceptance but that it is not in your community. Prices are higher than those of "fast-food" outlets but lower than those of "service restaurants" dispensing food of comparable quality.

CASES

Case 1.   The Mayfair Department Store, located in a city of about 1 million people, added 300,000 square feet to its existing facility.

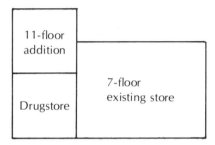

The expansion was to the firm's dominant downtown location. To gain access to the expansion property, Mayfair had to agree to lease part of the first-floor addition to an existing drugstore outlet of a regional chain. The other part of the main floor was thus available for lease to another retail outlet. The size of the remaining space was approximately 40 feet frontage by 75 feet depth. The space available is obviously the 100 percent location for shopping goods in the city. Speculate as to who should be interested in the available site. Consider such factors as rent-paying capacity and the advertising expenditures necessary in a 100 percent location. Support any conclusions you reach with facts and figures if possible (see NRMA operation data, for example).

Case 2.   Gorman's, a local department store in a medium-sized city, operates a number of branches. The first, opened in 1960 with a 25-year lease, is the smallest branch. It is a part of a strip of high-fashion stores located in the highest income area of the city. Within five minutes' driving time is the largest Gorman's. It is located in a fashion mall opened in 1975 with a long-term lease. Ten minutes' driving time in the other direction from the smallest store is another Gorman's branch. This store is also located in a mall, but it was opened in 1965 with a long-term lease. The area surrounding this mall is a blue-collar neighborhood.

Why does Gorman's have stores so close together? Aren't they competing with themselves? What do you predict will happen to these three branches over the next ten years?

18

OPERATING DECISIONS

Services offered (continued)
    Complaint policies
        Centralized or decentralized handling
        The abuse of complaint policies
Shoplifting and pilferage
Product recalls
Cost effectiveness of services offered
Operating policies and productivity

The following chapter, "Operating Decisions," contains concise descriptions of fine-tuned current strategies and data being utilized by successful retailers in their decision making.

Knowledge of its contents will not only ease the transition from student to retailer, but will be beneficial to the small retailer who has limited resources at his disposal.

Bob Wilhelmi, Vice President
Operations and Construction
Lipmans
Portland, Oregon

Operating policies reflect the basic management philosophy of the firm and project its image. Consequently, an analysis of alternatives in operating policies is crucial in ensuring a profitable operation. Thus, the objectives of this chapter are: (1) to present the alternatives possible in store design and layout because decisions on each alternative affect operating policies; (2) to focus on the alternatives available in consumer credit policies; (3) to discuss the various services which are typically offered to consumers; and (4) to discuss the cost effectiveness of operating policies.

DESIGN OBJECTIVES

Consumer behavior and retail store space

Consumers respond to more than a tangible product or service. Thus, retailers cannot neglect the psychological effects of their outlets on consumer purchasing behavior. These effects are the so-called silent language of communication. As has been pointed out,

A subtle dimension of in-store customer shopping behavior is the environment of the space itself. Retail space, i.e., the proximate environment that surrounds the retail shopper, is never neutral. The retail store is a bundle of cues, messages, and suggestions which communicate to shoppers. Retail store designers, planners, and merchandisers shape space, but that space in turn affects and shapes customer behavior. The retail store . . . does create moods, activate intentions, and generally affect customer reactions.[1]

Thus, we can shape behavior by modifying consumer demand, buying habits, and store patronage through store design. Too often we think only in terms of costs when discussing store layout. Economics and engineering are important, but we need to look beyond such measures as sales and cost per square foot.

Planning for space should be an extension of overall merchandising strategy. We must appreciate the significance and importance of space utilization, color, lighting, and store design as part of an overall strategy.

How retail space affects behavior

The following propositions have been offered about the influence of store space on consumer shopping behavior:

1. Space is an important modifier and shaper of behavior.
2. The retail store as a proximate environment affects behavior by a psychology of stimulation.
3. The retail store, like other aesthetic surroundings, affects customers' perceptions, attitudes, and images.

[1] Rom J. Markin, Charles M. Lillis, and Chem L. Narayana, "Social-Psychological Significance of Store Space," *Journal of Retailing*, vol. 52 (Spring 1976), p. 43.

4. Space utilization and store design can be deliberately programmed to create desired customer reactions.[2]

Let us briefly look at the authors' key points about each of these propositions.

The notion of territoriality is implicitly understood by retail store management, where management believes it profits by giving customers individual areas, i.e., private dressing rooms, boutique or cluster shops, fashion salons, bargain basements, or other specially contrived design and space features. There is a relationship between status and space. Invariably higher status people have more and better space as well as greater freedom to move about.[3]

Retail space creates expectations through stimulation. For example, if a retailer wants to capitalize on high turnover, he will probably use high illumination and not worry too much about using sound deadening materials. On the other hand, if he wants customers to linger or browse, he uses dim lighting and sound-proofing surfaces such as carpeting, drapes, and padded or acoustical ceilings. . . . Retail stores thus become systems of communication whose primary purpose is to provide cues toward which energy can be expended. . . . what is expended is energy and what is purchased is reward, pleasure, satisfaction, and excitement. Thus, retail store designers can evoke desired expectations through the implementation of a psychology of stimulation.[4]

Through effective design and space utilization, customer behavior can often be affected by changing or by modifying attitudes and images. Via design features, attitudes and images are created; that is, store personalities are created and shaped, and these personalities—friendly, upper high class, aloof, high quality, low priced, convenient, warm, inviting, cool, haughty, etc.—are in turn meant to affect customer attitudes and images and hence to shape behavior.[5]

Space communicates and, to the extent that it communicates in a rewarding manner, SELLS! Aside from moving merchandise, space sells corporate or company image; it creates mood, and it activates latent intentions through the acceleration of impulse purchasing via suggestion and reminder buying. . . . The retail store can be programmed or designed to reinforce customer behavior. It does so by dispensing rewards and by reinforcing customers who have entered the store, shopped, and purchased.[6]

In commenting on the importance of design as a tool in retail planning, Philip Kotler suggests that the following questions must be asked before developing a proper store design:

1. Who is the target audience?
2. What is the target audience seeking from the buying experience?
3. What atmospheric variables can fortify the beliefs and the emotional reactions that the buyers are seeking?

---

[2] Ibid., p. 45.

[3] Ibid., pp. 46–47

[4] Ibid., p. 49.

[5] Ibid., p. 51.

[6] Ibid., p. 52.

4. Will the resulting atmosphere compete effectively with competitors' atmospheres?[7]

Effects of crowding

The effect of crowding on shopper behavior in retail outlets is still largely unexplored, but some limited generalizations are possible about this aspect of retail store layout. For example, crowding may lead to information overload, confusion, and frustrated goal seeking. The retailer faces a dilemma. The desire is to attract as many customers as possible in order to maximize profits. However, excessive crowding may adversely affect shopper behavior and sales.[8] Thus, how does one increase density without driving customers away from the store? Figure 18–1 shows a model of buyer behavior under conditions of crowding and the strategies which are followed by shoppers. The possible outcomes of shopper reactions to crowding are also shown. Crowding is a relative concept, depending on a person's background. A rural shopper may feel quite crowded in an outlet which is perceived as relatively vacant by a major metropolitan shopper.

What are the results of crowding in the store? As noted in Figure 18–1, less time is allocated to each product decision. Also, less time may be spent in evaluating in-store advertising, in using unit pricing, in making impulse purchases, or in making purchases which can be delayed. The absence of crowding encourages a comparison of product offerings and exploratory shopping. After evaluating the effects of crowding on grocery shopping behavior, one study concluded that "an opportunity may exist for increasing the average sales volume per store by decreasing the level of perceived crowding, without actually decreasing the physical density of shoppers."[9] The authors suggest the manipulation of architectural features while holding the room area constant. They stated that a reduction in perceived crowding would lead to greater store loyalty and a higher level of average purchases.

The question of whether crowding is a problem or an opportunity for the retailer is clearly an area in which further research is needed. At least one retailer apparently views crowding as beneficial. As Stuart Orton, president, Foleys, Houston, has noted, "Crowded, busy stores—stores that are crying to be expanded—are more interesting to the customer and more profitable to us."[10] Crowding does not in fact always lead to greater interest and profit, and we repeat that research efforts must be made to get more insight into this matter. If crowded stores "are crying to be expanded," perhaps such expan-

---

[7] Philip Kotler, "Atmospherics as a Marketing Tool," *Journal of Retailing*, vol. 49 (Winter 1973–74), p. 48.

[8] Gilbert R. Harrell and Michael D. Hutt, "Crowding in Retail Stores, *MSU Business Topics*, Winter 1976, p. 33.

[9] Phillip B. Niffenegger and Phillip B. Anderson, "Store Satisfaction and Crowding: An Exploratory Study of Grocery Shoppers," in Henry Nash and Donald Robin (eds.), *Proceedings: Southern Marketing Association, 1976*, p. 88.

[10] Presentation to New York Society of Security Analysts, November 21, 1974, p. 13.

FIGURE 18–1
BUYER BEHAVIOR UNDER CONDITIONS OF CROWDING

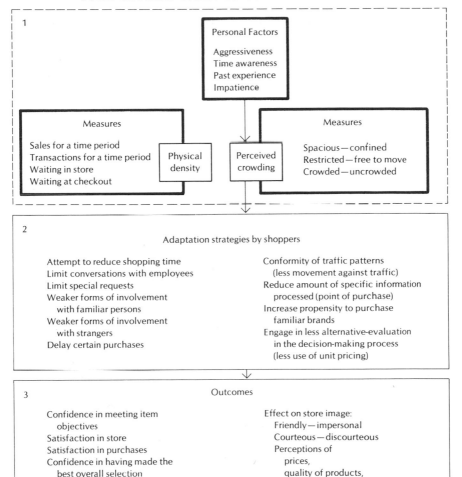

Source: Gilbert R. Harrell and Michael D. Hutt, "Crowding in Retail Stores, *MSU Business Topics,* Winter 1976, p. 35. Reprinted by permission of the publisher, Division of Research, Graduate School of Business Administration, Michigan State University.

sion would be more conducive to shopping and shopper interest, and could increase total profitability, if not profitability per square foot.

THE BASICS OF DESIGN

Let's look for a moment at how some retail outlets use the basics of design to modify consumer behavior or to create desired images. Specific store examples are cited.

Interior lighting

Retailers today use flexible lighting, that is, a combination of fluorescent lights or more basic lighting and incandescent lights to provide emphasis. Colored lights and movable lights are also becoming increasingly important. However, when lighting is used for special effects, expert planning is needed.

As has been noted for one store, "Other touches which add to the fashion image are use of HID lighting to add 'sparkle' to the merchandise and imaginative fixturing. Men's packaged shirts, for example, are displayed on smoked plexiglass L-shaped fixtures and suspended from the ceiling by chains."[11]

For still another store, four types of light are used—natural, from the skylight (providing about 8 percent of the store's light); fluorescent; incandescent; and quartz. Quartz light is used for accent light throughout the store because it "gives a good crisp light and the best color rendition."[12]

Store equipment

Store equipment is a broad term which includes all of the physical objects in the store, such as counters, elevators, escalators, signs, and area dividers. Each of these objects has major effects on the operations of the store.

For example, in a multilevel store an important design question is where to place escalators or elevators to best serve people and yet effectively sell merchandise. Considerations include the number of people to be moved, the distance they are going to travel, and the capacity of the equipment. Lord & Taylor used the escalator arrangement in one of its stores in such a way as to lead customers through its multilevel outlet. As noted:

The street level has a 23-foot-high ceiling, accentuated by a horseshoe-shaped mezzanine and polished stainless steel columns, also 23 feet high. The mezzanine is horseshoe-shaped because a circle has been cut out of it surrounding the escalator. This and curves in the wall are softening effects which help lead the customers back and up.[13]

Counters and display cases

Many different types of display cases and counters can be used, and all of these serve to create a mood in the outlet. Consider the case of an exclusive men's shoe store:

The store lacks the usual white enamel display tables and metal racks, typical of many contemporary shoe stores. Merchandise is displayed on antique reproduction furniture and hand-painted oriental cabinets. . . . straight back armchairs are replaced by a couch and French Provincial living room chairs. Handbags dangle from

---

[11] "The New Look at Caldor," *Chain Store Age Executive*, March 1976, p. 25.

[12] "Mirrors, Light Mark Store," *Chain Store Age Executive*, April 1976, p. 21.

[13] "Lord & Taylor: Odd Layout," *Chain Store Age Executive*, February 1976, p. 29.

wooden coat trees and are also displayed on cabinets. The manager works on a Louis XIV desk and chair; the cash register is hidden in the back of the store.[14]

Contrast these features to those of low-margin/high-turnover discount houses. What image do these outlets project through the gondola fixtures and counters which they utilize?

Signs

Large signs with fancy artwork are now being used to attract and inform customers. The tendency to group highly specialized merchandise within a given department—for example, men's sportswear within the clothing department—makes signing important. For one store, "signing which runs diagonally across the aisle identifies each shop; visually, because of the unity of color and same carpeting used throughout, they look like one entity . . . and the diagonal signing . . . lends motion to the eye."[15]

Store dividers

The key in retail design today is flexibility to improve customer service, increase store and employee productivity, and reduce operating costs.[16] Thus, there has been a shift from permanent interior walls to movable area dividers, even though controversy continues to exist as to whether flexibility is the appropriate design for all stores. Movable features may be incompatible with the desired image of some stores, particularly those merchandising high fashion. In any case, the current objectives are space flow, flexibility, and density. Store flexibility has at least three dimensions in which store dividers are involved. "The first priority is flexibility as related to merchandise requirements, an ability to utilize fixturing to change merchandise categories within a given space. The second priority is the ability to change the look easily, the decorative aspect. The third priority is flexibility in changing store spaces—most everyone starts with No. 3."[17]

Other questions which must be considered include the degree of flexibility, the cost of flexibility, and the type of image to be projected through the use of flexible interiors.

STORE LAYOUT

The purposes of store layout are to provide for customer movement and to present merchandise or services attractively. Layout and interior design should complement each other. The three most typical store layout types are

[14] "Is This Ritzy Living Room Really a Shoe Store," Chain Store Age Executive, April 1976, p. 28.

[15] "Mirrors, Light Mark Store," p. 21.

[16] "Penney's Flexible Fixtures," Chain Store Age Executive, September 1976, p. 50.

[17] "Flexibility: What's Needed?" Chain Store Age Executive, March 1976, p. 22.

the grid, the free flow, and the boutique. Other possibilities exist which are really variations of these types. Let's briefly look at these layout alternatives.

Grid

The most traditional retail layout is the grid, which is shown in Figure 18–2. The grid is designed primarily for retailing efficiency as opposed to customer convenience. The layout actually serves as a barrier to free movement. Customer flow becomes a function of the aisles as opposed to customer desire for merchandise. The grid layout, however, maximizes selling space and simplifies security. As noted in Figure 18–2, 80–90 percent of all customers shopping in a supermarket utilizing a grid layout pass the produce, meat, and dairy counters, whereas a smaller proportion of shoppers pass other displays. This is because the grid layout in a supermarket forces customers to the sides and the back of the store.

In department and specialty stores, the grid arrangement is more likely to force customer traffic down the main aisles. The result is that shoppers are more likely to ignore merchandise along the walls. If the grid display is used in department and specialty stores, highly sought merchandise should be placed along the walls instead of the main part of the store so that customer traffic will be drawn to these normally slow-moving areas. This layout type is typically found on the main floors of multilevel department and specialty stores and mass merchandising firms. Figures 18–3 and 18–4 are the layouts for a typical department store of a national chain and show the most common arrangements for the first and second floors. These layouts contain elements of the grid, free-flow, and boutique arrangements. Note, for example, such notations as social expression shop, contemporary fashions, and conservative fashions.

Free flow

The free-flow design is designed primarily for customer convenience and maximum customer exposure to merchandise. It lets customers move in virtually any direction in a relaxed atmosphere. Browsing and impulse purchasing are encouraged by this type of arrangement. However, the use of space is less efficient than that of the grid.

Boutique

The boutique arrangement has become increasingly popular in department stores. This arrangement brings together complete offerings in one department as opposed to having separate departments for, say, shoes, suits, and similar merchandise. For example, a tennis boutique in a department store will feature rackets, balls, shoes, and warm-up suits. Thus the boutique arrangement allows shoppers with a particular interest or life-style to shop in one location for a complete assortment of related merchandise.

FIGURE 18–2
THE GRID LAYOUT

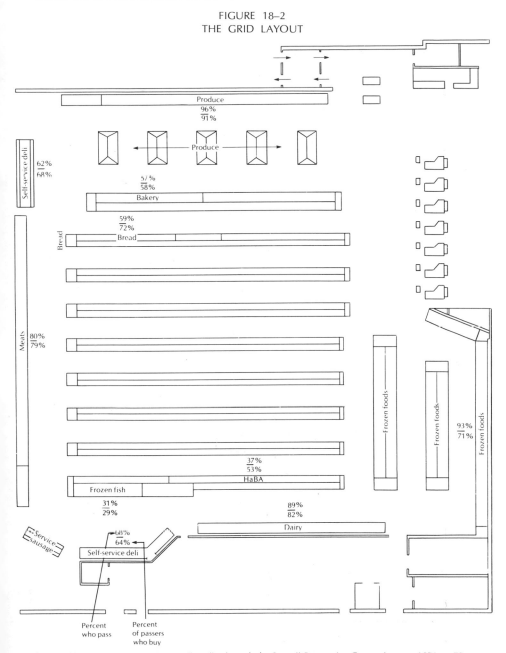

Source: "How Major Departments Pull Traffic through the Store," *Progressive Grocer*, January 1976, p. 72.

FIGURE 18–3

FIRST-FLOOR LAYOUT FOR A TYPICAL DEPARTMENT STORE OF A LARGE NATIONAL CHAIN

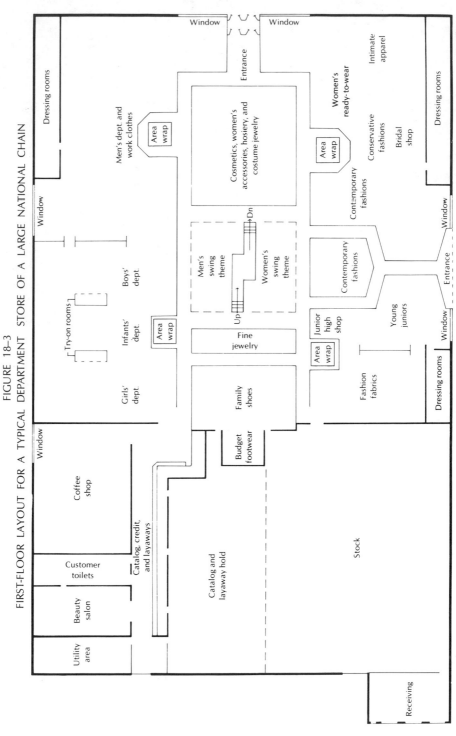

FIGURE 18–4

SECOND-FLOOR LAYOUT FOR A TYPICAL DEPARTMENT STORE OF A LARGE NATIONAL CHAIN

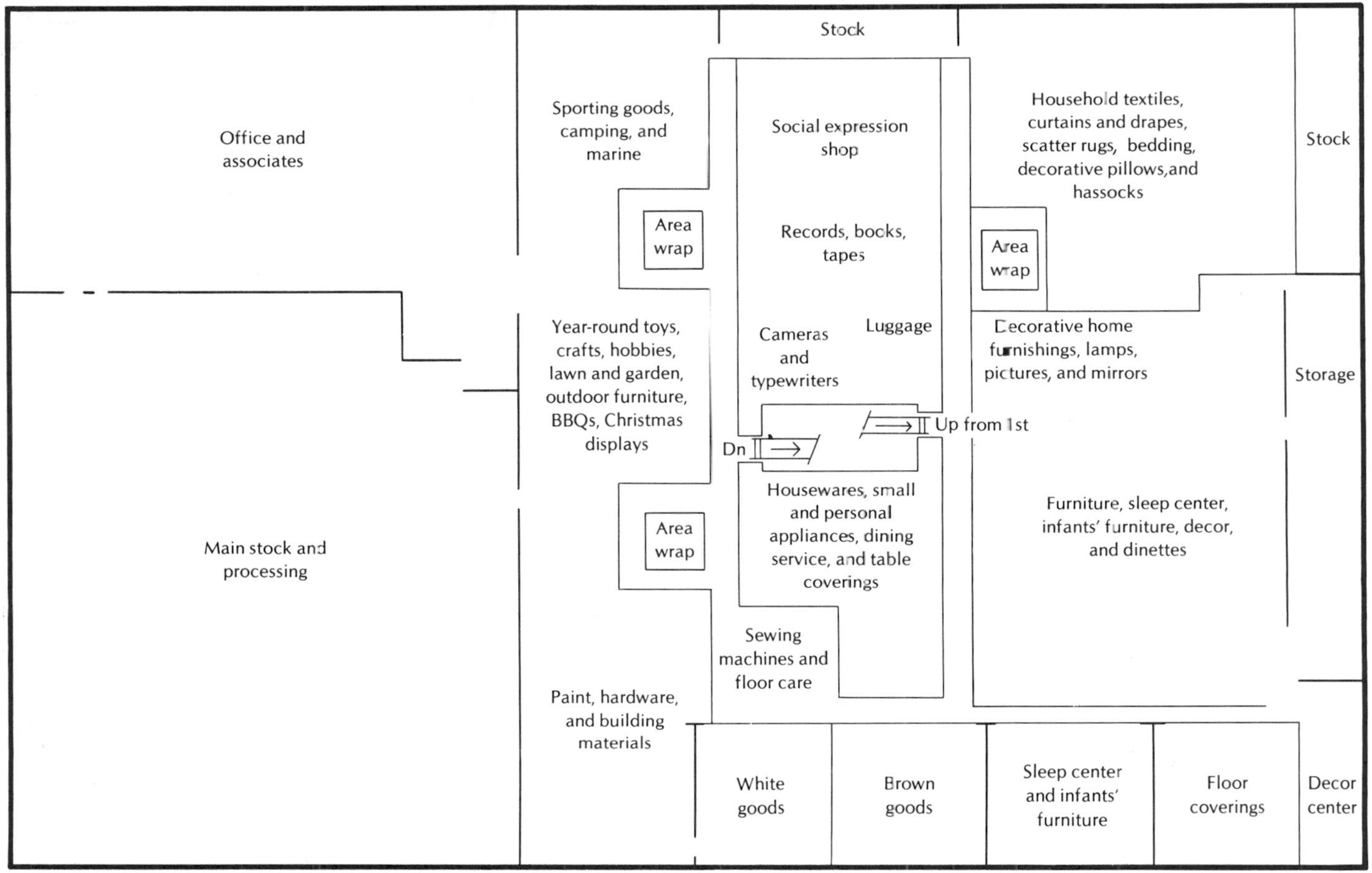

Second floor

Other considerations

As a rule of thumb, items which require comparison and physical handling should be separated from items which are purchased largely on impulse so that these two types of purchases do not interfere with each other. Purchasers of shopping goods may want to give undivided attention to the merchandise.

Finally, for multilevel outlets it is probably wise to display a limited number of items from each floor on the main floor, perhaps in window displays, to attract the attention of the customer. This encourages shoppers to seek the more complete selections available elsewhere in the outlet. In doing so, they are likely to pass an extensive array of other merchandise, increasing the likelihood of some type of unplanned purchase.

In summary, creativity in store layout is not prohibitively expensive. The advantages of developing a unique identity for the outlet outweigh the possible extra effort and additional expense. A focus on design should include an evaluation of both selling and nonselling areas, traffic flows, and desired traffic patterns. Lighting should highlight the merchandise instead of calling attention to itself. Traffic patterns should be designed to encourage customer browsing and purchasing.

THE ALLOCATION OF SPACE

Even after a basic layout has been selected, decisions must be made on the allocation of space between selling and nonselling areas and the amount of space to be given to specific items in the sales area. Design at this point becomes particularly important. Typically sales space occupies two thirds of the total space available in the outlet, as shown in Table 18–1, but the proportion tends to be somewhat smaller for specialty stores (see Table 18–2). Typically, the larger the store the greater the percentage of nonselling (or sales-supporting) space.

TABLE 18–1
SELECTED OPERATING DATA FOR DEPARTMENT STORES WITH
SALES OF OVER $50 MILLION, 1973

Space data	Typical figures	Middle range	Goal figures
Sales per square foot of selling space (dollars)	90.40	77.75–106.71	112.48
Sales per square foot of total space (dollars)	57.43	49.72– 67.71	75.81
Selling space percentage of total space	65.06	58.84– 72.04	67.37

Source: Jay Scher, *Financial and Operating Results of Department and Specialty Stores,* (New York: National Retail Merchants Association, 1974), p. 53.

TABLE 18–2
SELECTED OPERATING DATA FOR DEPARTMENT STORES WITH
SALES OF OVER $5 MILLION, 1973

Space data	Typical figures	Middle range	Goal figures
Sales per square foot of selling space (dollars)	170.39	59.98–276.26	200.20
Sales per square foot of total space (dollars)	89.20	42.25–138.30	111.68
Selling space percentage of total space	58.64	38.98– 95.07	55.37

Source: Jay Scher, *Financial and Operating Results of Department and Specialty Stores* (New York: National Retail Merchants Association, 1974), p. 71.

Nonselling space is as important as selling space because of the importance of areas for merchandise marking and storage. The amount of nonselling space varies greatly by type of merchandise outlet. For example, jewelry stores may have virtually no nonselling space, whereas such outlets as home improvement centers may have more space for warehousing and storage than for actual selling.

The amount of selling space which is allocated to each product line has a major impact on store profitability. A variety of methods can be used in space allocation. Probably the most commonly used information is industry average figures for various types of merchandise. The National Retail Merchants Association provides information on merchandising and operating results by product line. The Urban Land Institute publication *Dollars and Cents of Shopping Centers* also provides useful information.

As noted in Table 18–3, the sales per square foot of gross leasable area varies widely by merchandise line. A careful evaluation of this information can help the retailer establish standards of operation. However, industry averages can only serve as guidelines because each outlet is unique.

The sales productivity method

The allocation of space can also be made on the basis of the sales productivity of various product lines. For example, let us look at the unisex/jean shop for which data are provided in Table 18–3. The average annual national sales are $105,600 (1,600 square feet of gross leasable area × $66 of sales per square foot). Let's assume that the sales of knit tops in the outlet are $60 per square foot, based on known industry averages by product line. From prior experience the retailer knows that approximately 10 percent of total sales can be generated from the sale of these knit tops. Let's look then at the amount of space which should be allocated to the knit tops in relation to the total amount of space available in the store. As indicated below, 160 square feet of gross leasable area should be allocated to the knit tops. These deci-

TABLE 18–3

OPERATING CHARACTERISTICS FOR SELECTED TYPES OF OUTLETS LOCATED IN COMMUNITY SHOPPING CENTERS, 1975

Tenant classification	No. in sample	GLA in square foot,* Median Lower decile—Upper decile		Sales per square foot (dollars) Median Top 10 percent—Top 2 percent		Rate of percentage rent Median Lower decile—Upper decile		Total rent per square foot (dollars) Median Top 10 percent—Top 2 percent		Common area charge per square foot (dollars) Median Top 10 percent—Top 2 percent	
Unisex/ jean shop 67	21	1,600	865—2,500	66.12	140.39—194.73	5.00	3.00—6.00	3.11	9.41—10.89	0.21	0.43—0.88
National chain	6	2,300	1,545—3,067	52.81	156.86—207.41	5.00	3.00—5.00	3.06	6.91—10.64	0.20	0.20—0.20
Local chain	8	1,256	850—2,420	60.00	104.54—133.64	5.50	3.00—6.00	3.05	7.34—8.24	0.23	0.56—0.91
Independent	7	1,300	820—1,960	116.42	139.22—139.88	5.00	5.00—6.50	4.15	9.65—9.88	0.26	0.43—0.58
Yard goods 71	113	3,767	1,458—9,710	43.19	66.94—89.56	5.00	3.50—6.00	3.03	4.35—5.56	0.15	0.46—0.87
National chain	51	4,264	2,515—12,000	44.03	68.06—90.43	4.00	3.00—5.00	2.83	4.00—5.50	0.12	0.31—0.72
Local chain	23	4,096	1,357—8,550	41.08	62.16—70.10	5.00	4.00—6.00	3.29	4.00—4.94	0.18	0.64—1.00
Independent	39	2,450	698—4,866	42.02	66.38—90.17	5.00	4.50—6.00	3.25	4.86—5.52	0.16	0.38—0.84
Curtains and drapes 72	16	2,400	492—3,860	54.79	70.36—79.09	5.50	3.20—7.80	3.02	4.33—7.35	0.12	0.21—0.30
National chain	1										
Local chain	3										
Independent	12	1,902	484—3,552	45.95	64.11—78.73	5.50	5.00—8.20	2.79	3.98—4.38	0.12	0.24—0.30

Imports 75	28	1,640 / 496—9,444	33.68 / 53.12—87.39	6.00 / 5.00—8.00	3.50 / 5.26—9.50	0.18 / 0.71—0.89
National chain	6	7,872 / 1,600—11,900	38.14 / 50.22—52.16	5.00 / 4.00—7.00	3.14 / 3.49—3.62	0.16 / 0.47—0.65
Local chain	7	1,090 / 400—2,552	35.57 / 64.95—87.05	8.00 / 5.64—8.00		
Independent	15	1,280 / 420—2,796	31.73 / 50.62—73.82	6.00 / 5.10—7.90	3.58 / 6.40—10.27	0.21 / 0.64—0.92
Luggage, leather goods 76	10	1,104 / 192—2,412	52.34 / 336.05—585.35	6.00 / 6.00—7.20	5.03 / 25.00—37.93	0.35 / 0.74—0.95
National chain	1					
Local chain	3					
Independent	6	904 / 50—1,200	56.58 / 417.87—601.71	6.00 / 6.00—6.00	4.75 / 19.76—36.88	0.41 / 0.70—0.94
Furniture 81	46	7,764 / 1,670—23,694	43.61 / 93.98—108.95	4.50 / 2.80—6.00	2.30 / 5.30—7.84	0.16 / 0.74—1.05
National chain	7	13,260 / 7,443—24,753	34.83 / 67.87—99.39	4.00 / 1.00—4.50	1.90 / 3.62—5.24	
Local chain	15	13,000 / 2,372—23,375	51.59 / 92.15—103.63	4.50 / 3.60—5.40	2.40 / 5.28—6.04	0.23 / 0.62—0.72
Independent	24	4,950 / 1,080—16,850	48.03 / 88.89—104.99	5.00 / 2.40—6.00	2.30 / 4.49—13.34	0.15 / 0.75—1.04
Appliances 83	33	3,458 / 1,113—9,333	62.24 / 145.46—202.93	3.00 / 2.50—6.00	2.75 / 4.83—5.69	0.12 / 0.33—0.78
National chain	6	6,954 / 1,380—8,633	41.01 / 48.73—51.91	3.00 / 3.00—4.20	2.47 / 4.30—5.56	0.07 / 0.10—0.12
Local chain	8	3,429 / 1,275—18,800	88.91 / 193.79—215.12	2.50 / 1.00—4.20	2.43 / 3.82—4.83	0.12 / 0.39—0.65
Independent	19	3,402 / 790—5,110	63.54 / 110.10—148.40	3.05 / 2.60—6.80	2.76 / 4.35—5.47	0.14 / 0.33—0.72

* Gross leasable area in square feet.

Source: Dollars and Cents of Shopping Centers: 1975, ULI—the Urban Land Institute, 1200 18th Street, N.W., Washington, D.C. 20036. Excerpts from a triennial report on data representative of 1974 reporting information and therefore not reflective of current information.

sions are unique to each outlet, depending upon the characteristics of the outlet and the area in which it is located.

$105,600 (total expected sales) × 10% (share of sales from knit tops)
= $10,560 (expected knit top sales)

$$\frac{\$10,560 \text{ (expected knit top sales)}}{\$66 \text{ (average sales per sq ft)}} = \begin{array}{l} 160 \text{ sq ft to be allocated} \\ \text{to the sale of knit tops} \end{array}$$

The buildup method

The above method offers ease of calculation when appropriate data are available. However, the merchant may plan space needed for a department or a store and then find that the available space is too small or too large. In such instances, a checklist approach to space determination can also be used.[18] Stores using this method must have a formal system of stock planning and control (see Chapter 12) and a model or basic stock.

For illustrative purposes, let's work with a ladies' blouse department. The buildup step method would proceed as follows:

1. *What is the ideal stock balance necessary to achieve expected sales volume?* The merchant, based on past experience, may believe that sales of $30,000 per year are obtainable. Trade sources indicate that in the price line planned, three turns per year is realistic. Within the price-line[19] structure, the average price of the blouses is $15. Given these assumptions, approximately 666 blouses will be needed as a normal offering during each turnover period ($30,000 ÷ 3 = $10,000 in merchandise; $10,000 ÷ $15 = 666 blouses). *Normally* 666 blouses must be in stock. However, the merchandise planner may vary from this number during high- and low-sales-volume months. Thus, planning under this method ties merchandise needs to actual seasonal variations rather than yearly averages. For example, Mother's Day might be the yearly peak sales period and should be considered in layout arrangements.

2. *How many blouses should be kept on display, and how many should be kept in reserve stock?* How many of the 666 blouses should actually be displayed? Ideally, 100 percent should be on display, as goods do not sell if they are not seen. Since this is not realistic and the decision is judgmental, let's assume that two thirds of the stock will be on display and one third in reserve. Thus, approximately 444 blouses will be displayed.

3. *What is the best method of displaying the merchandise?* This decision depends on the merchandise display equipment available and the affordable opportunities for display. Let's assume that we will hang the two less expensive blouses on circular steel racks which have a glass top for display purposes. The most expensive blouses will be displayed in glass cases which

---

[18] This approach was originally developed by William R. Davidson of Ohio State University.

[19] Price line is the policy of predetermining price points at which merchandise will be offered for sale, for example, $10.95, 14.95, and 19.95 in the hypothetical blouse department.

can be accessorized with jewelry, scarves, and other small items. Reserve stock will be stored in drawers beneath the display cases. Only one of a style will be displayed.

4. *How many display racks and cases are necessary to display the items?* The physical size and capacity of the fixtures must be determined to answer this question. Scale models of fixtures are often placed on floor plans to assist in the layout process.

5. *What is the best way to handle the reserve stock?* We have already determined that the reserve stock for the expensive blouses will be maintained under the display cases. For the remaining items, space can be allocated in special storage fixtures on the selling floor or in a remote stock area which is as close to the selling area as possible.

6. *What service requirements are necessary for the department?* In the blouse department, fitting rooms and a point-of-sale register will be needed. Likewise, depending on the nature of the operation, space for wrapping will be critical. Finally, all departments require aisles.

7. *What are the total space requirements?* The total space needs can be determined by a summation of 4, 5, and 6.

Gross margin influences

Gross margins influence the allocation of the amount and type of floor space. For example, large, bulky items such as furniture require much floor space. Thus, these items may be placed in less desirable areas, such as an upper floor. In any case, the markup on furniture is likely to be quite high because of the large amount of floor space involved as well as the infrequency of purchase. Markups on furniture in conventional outlets may be as high as 100 percent to cover costs and allow for a normal profit.

Unquestionably, the use and allocation of space will become increasingly important as retailers strive to obtain greater productivity from existing space without adding to the cost structure of the firm. As was noted for J. C. Penney:

A denser and more concentrated use of display space can raise overall selling floor capacity 10% to 40% and reduce merchandise handling and storage costs 50% or more while creating merchandising excitement. . . . Carter Hawley Hale Stores, Inc. President Philip M. Hawley predicts that fully half of the industry's future growth will come from this type of "internal expansion."[20]

Let's look now at the various operating policies which can be used by the retailer. The policies followed should be in harmony with the image created in the layout and design of the outlet.

---

[20] "J. C. Penney: Getting More from the Same Space," *Business Week*, August 19, 1975, pp. 80–82.

SERVICES OFFERED

Table 18–4 shows the services which are typically offered in retail outlets. Few stores offer all of these services, but let's look at the more common ones.

TABLE 18–4
TYPICAL RETAIL SERVICES

Prepurchase services
1. Accepting telephone orders
2. Accepting mail orders (or purchases)
3. Advertising
4. Window display
5. Interior display
6. Fitting rooms
7. Shopping hours
8. Fashion shows
9. Trade-ins

Postpurchase services
1. Delivery
2. Regular wrapping (or bagging)
3. Gift wrapping
4. Adjustments
5. Returns
6. Alterations
7. Tailoring
8. Installations
9. Engraving
10. COD delivery

Ancillary services
1. Check cashing
2. General information
3. Free parking
4. Restaurants
5. Repairs
6. Interior decorating
7. Credit
8. Rest rooms
9. Baby attendant service

Source: Carl M. Larson, John S. Wright, and Robert E. Weigand, *Basic Retailing*, p. 364. Copyright 1976. Reprinted by permission of Prentice Hall, Inc., Englewood Cliffs, New Jersey.

Services are a major element of competition. They are a nonprice way in which firms can be differentiated. Nonprice competition is more difficult to duplicate than price competition. In nonprice competition, we try to change the demand curve without changing prices.

Credit

Credit is probably one of the most important services which a retailer can offer. Over 80 percent of all citizens now possess some type of credit card, and more than 50 percent of these have a Wards, Sears, or Penney's card. Women are more likely than men to have a department store charge card.[21]

Credit is a strategy used to increase sales by stimulating installment buying. Credit may also stimulate impulse buying. In addition, credit buyers appear to be less price conscious than persons paying cash.[22]

Consumer credit has grown at an astounding rate. Consumer installment credit increased from almost $71 billion in 1965 to almost $167 billion in

---

[21] Douglass Hawes, Roger Blackwell, and Wayne Talarzyk, "Consumers' Use of Credit: Results of a Nationwide Study," paper presented at the annual meeting of the Southwestern Marketing Association, San Antonio, Texas, March 18, 1976, p. 4.

[22] H. Lee Mathews and John W. Slocum, Jr., "Social Class and Commercial Bank Credit Card Usage," *Journal of Marketing*, vol. 33 (January 1969), p. 77.

TABLE 18–5
INSTALLMENT CREDIT EXTENSIONS AND REPAYMENTS
(in $ millions)

Holder and type of credit	1973	1974	1975
Total	164,527	166,170	166,833
By holder			
Commercial banks	72,216	72,602	73,186
Finance companies	43,221	41,809	39,543
Credit unions	21,143	22,403	24,151
Retailers	25,440	27,034	27,369
Others	2,507	2,322	2,584
By type of credit			
Automobile, total	46,406	43,431	46,530
Commercial banks	29,368	26,407	26,693
Purchase	17,497	15,575	14,758
Direct	11,871	10,831	11,936
Finance companies	9,685	8,851	9,651
Credit unions	7,009	7,788	9,702
Others	424	385	484
Mobile homes			
Commercial banks	4,437	3,486	2,349
Finance companies	1,673	1,627	1,018
Home improvements, total	4,828	4,854	4,333
Commercial banks	2,489	2,790	2,515
Revolving credit			
Bank credit cards	13,862	17,098	19,567
Bank check credit	3,373	4,228	4,214
All other, total	89,864	91,455	88,818
Commercial banks, total	18,683	18,602	17,844
Personal loans	12,927	13,177	12,623
Finance companies, total	31,032	30,764	28,654
Personal loans	18,915	18,827	18,406
Credit unions	13,768	14,228	13,992
Retailers	25,440	27,034	27,369
Others	941	827	959

Source: *Federal Reserve Bulletin,* April 1976, p. A47.

1975.[23] As shown in Table 18–5, automobile credit accounts for more consumer installment credit than does any other source.

Types of credit.   The shopper generally may use either store charge accounts or bank credit cards. Store charge accounts typically must be paid within 30 days after the purchase. Other plans include an installment payment arrangement and revolving credit accounts which require an interest charge payment on remaining balances. Often, except for small stores, such installment credit is handled by a store charge card, as is the case for Sears and Ward outlets.

The use of bank credit cards has grown rapidly since 1960 and has cut into the popularity of the department store cards. About 37 million people have Master Charge cards, and about 31 million have BankAmericards.

[23] *Federal Reserve Bulletin,* April 1976, A47, and February 1975, A47.

About 1.7 million merchants throughout the world honor Master Charge, and about 1.8 million accept BankAmericard (Visa).[24]

The cost of credit.   Bad-debt losses are substantial for retailers maintaining their own credit plans. In addition, the cost of maintaining credit is high. Thus, many stores will offer customers revolving accounts to which they automatically add an interest charge when a customer does not pay the full account within 30 days. The interest charge is usually 1 ½ percent per month, or 18 percent annually, on the unpaid balance.

Banks typically charge retailers using bank credit cards 4–6 percent of sales for the use of the service. Some retailers now offer customers a discount for paying cash which is equal to the 4–6 percent fee charged by the banks. Some banks are considering whether to charge customers who pay the entire amount due on their bank charge card within 30 days after receipt of the bill. Banks lose money on customers who pay their bills within the prescribed period and thus avoid the 18 percent interest charge. Thus, banks face the same problem as retailers—namely, whether to offer a service at a loss in order to maintain customer goodwill.

Michael Etzel conducted 15 in-depth case analyses of the retail credit operations of small ready-to-wear establishments. All of the outlets offered bank credit cards as part of their consumer credit program. Etzel analyzed the cost of each of the retail credit alternatives. His findings are shown in Table 18–6. As can be observed, generalizations about the cost of the various

TABLE 18–6
THE COST OF CREDIT

Store	Type of internal credit	Internal credit sales	Direct cost of internal credit sales as a percentage of internal credit sales	Bank credit card sales	Direct cost of bank credit card sales as a percentage of bank credit card sales
A	30–60–90-day single payment and installment	$ 24,151	8.02%	$ 5,927	5.43%
B1, B2, B3	30–60–90-day single payment and installment	40,301	5.89	17,249	5.44
C	30-day single payment	17,898	2.77	3,055	5.34
D	None	—	—	4,045	5.36
E	None	—	—	2,021	5.38
F1, F2	30-day single payment	118,989	3.84	10,167	5.26
G1, G2	Factored	121,543	6.26	18,387	5.42
H	30–60–90-day single payment and installment	75,456	4.73	22,215	5.46
I1, I2	Factored	19,327	11.08	16,982	5.80
J	Factored	5,619	12.55	11,449	5.54

Source: Michael J. Etzel, "How Much Does Credit Cost the Small Merchant?" *Journal of Retailing*, vol. 47 (July 1971), p. 71.

---

[24] William Flanagan, "Playing Your Credit Cards Right," *New York*, June 7, 1976, p. 90.

credit alternatives are risky. The internally financed plans and the factored plans vary in cost. (Factoring occurs when the retail merchant sells accounts receivable at a discount to a financial establishment. The merchant receives payment for the accounts, and the consumer then makes payments to the financial institution.) It is not possible to state categorically that one form of credit is less expensive to the retailer than another.

Consumer preferences for credit plans. Major differences exist in consumer perceptions of the alternative credit plans available. Research has revealed significant differences in consumer perceptions of such factors as cost, merchant performance, convenience, personal service, and the prestige associated with the use of a credit card.[25]

The monthly finance charges of a department store are perceived to be the most expensive method of credit, whereas the independent retailer is perceived as offering the least expensive method. Bank credit card plans are seen as the most efficient and convenient in billing. The independent retailer is perceived as offering the greatest amount of personal attention. Thus, a credit arrangement with the independent retailer is looked upon as the most prestigious type. These various dimensions of consumer perception suggest a series of strategy alternatives which can be followed by the retailer in increasing the volume of credit sales.

The management of internal credit. Virtually all retailers issuing any type of credit use a formal application which provides sufficient personal information to allow an evaluation of the applicant's creditworthiness. One commonly used method is point-scoring. This method allocates points to various types of information on an application. The points are determined through an evaluation of information obtained from former accounts which were both good and bad.

Another possible aid is the use of the local credit bureau. Credit bureaus typically charge an annual fee as well as a small per request fee. They can provide a retailer with a summarized history of the credit of an applicant.

Keys to credit management are good records and proper billing and collecting procedures. Bad debts are a threat to any credit program. However, the absence of bad debts is also a sign for concern because it may mean that credit policies are overly restrictive. The result is that sales are being lost unnecessarily. Industry averages on bad-debt losses are available for use in planning. For example, industry averages indicate that bad-debt losses for department stores and specialty stores should be less than 1 percent.[26]

A well-managed collection program is also necessary. The retailer should have several routine letters which are sent to customers with overdue accounts in an effort to have them pay. If this method fails, the retailer may turn the accounts over to a collection agency. The agencies typically work on a

[25] Michael Etzel and James Donnelly, "Consumer Perceptions of Alternative Credit Plans," *Journal of Retailing,* vol. 48 (Summer 1972).

[26] J. Scher, *Financial and Operating Results of Department and Specialty Stores in 1973* (New York: National Retail Merchants Association, 1974).

contingency fee based on a percentage of the total amount of funds collected.

Credit as a loss operation. Credit costs money and is typically a loss operation for even the most efficient system. Indeed, credit costs exceed revenues by a considerable amount. For example, a study of 17 stores of varying sizes, types, locations, and methods of finance charge computation found that the loss on credit services "was 2.2% of credit sales, based on an 8% cost of capital. Using the actual cost of capital (11%) for these stores, the average loss was 3.7% of credit sales and the maximum loss 8.0%."[27]

In spite of probable operating losses there are sound reasons for continuing credit operations. The credit department must make sure that these reasons—increased sales and earnings—are recognized by senior management. Indeed, major retailers such as Sears and Penneys typically have several million dollars worth of consumer credit outstanding at any given time, as shown in Table 18–7.

TABLE 18–7
COMPARISON OF CUSTOMER ACCOUNTS RECEIVABLE
FOR SELECTED RETAILERS

Company	Customer accounts receivable (000), 1974*
Sears, Roebuck and Co.	$4,979,355
J. C. Penney Co., Inc.	1,636,560
Federated Department Stores, Inc.	551,260
The May Department Stores Co.	406,664
R. H. Macy & Co., Inc.†	311,754
Carter Hawley Hale Stores, Inc.	265,832
Dayton Hudson Corp.	220,210
Marshall Field & Co.	85,775
City Stores Co.	81,232

* Fiscal year ended January 31, 1975.
† Figures reported for fiscal year 1974, ended July 31, 1974.
Source: Adapted from Harvey Berenson, "Profit through Retail Credit," *Stores*, October 1975, p. 35.

Poor credit management has been the downfall of more than one retailer. Consider the case of the now bankrupt W. T. Grant Company: "We gave credit to every deadbeat who breathed. . . . The stores were told to push credit and had certain quotas to fill. Up until 1974, we really had 1200 credit offices. . . . On top of that, Grant was unusually generous in its terms. Until 1975 it allowed 36 months to pay, with a minimum charge of $1 per month."[28]

[27] G. Robert Myers and David V. Burchfield, "Sustaining In-house Credit," *Stores*, February 1976, p. 6.
[28] "Investigating the Collapse of W. T. Grant," *Business Week*, July 19, 1976, p. 61.

Trends in credit. Credit sales from credit cards now account for 50–60 percent of all department store and general merchandise sales. As noted by the general credit manager for Carson Pirie Scott, Chicago, "We're trying to get more credit customers and promote to them by direct mail. They become a captive audience."[29]

Department stores are making increasing use of bank cards. In 1977, 23 out of every 100 department stores accepted the cards, compared to 10 in 1975.[30] The supermarkets continue to resist the cards, at least in part because their 1 percent profit margin makes it hard to afford the discount they would have to pay on the bank cards.

A growing number of retailers are placing their charge programs with outsiders who purchase the receivables for cash and run the entire credit operation. The retailers who are following this route include Korvettes, Zayre, Caldor, Levitz, Bond's Lerner Shops, Singer Sewing Centers, and Roos-Atkins.[31] This approach simplifies the problems of the credit function for management.

Delivery

Delivery is a significant item of expense for many outlets, particularly department stores, which must deliver big-ticket items such as furniture and household appliances. Retailers are often pressured not to charge extra for delivery service. That service, however, must then be added into the overall cost structure of the firm. Thus, cash-and-carry customers pay for the delivery service even if they do not use it. The cost of delivery has increased rapidly because of increasing fuel and labor costs. Also, suburban deliveries have become increasingly expensive. Delivery systems can be store owned or independently owned, or can involve the use of parcel post. Some retailers, particularly small ones, operate their own delivery service. Most of us are familiar with the delivery service of the corner drugstore—often a person in a worn-out compact automobile who shows up as needed. Typically, the retailer will either lease an automobile for such purposes or pay an employee a mileage allowance to use his or her automobile.

Large retailers have better organized and more formal systems. Some prestige possibilities exist for having a fleet of trucks owned by the retailer. An owned fleet also has the advantage of flexibility in delivery. However, the cost of initiating such a system is great. A possible alternative is the use of independent services such as United Parcel, which can deliver parcels intramarket as well as all over the United States.

A third possibility is to use parcel post and service express. Retailers use these services in addition to independent delivery services, particularly for

---

[29] "The Big Push for Credit," *Chain Store Age,* January 1977, p. 23.

[30] Ibid., p. 25.

[31] "Chains Going to Outside Plans," *Chain Store Age,* January 1977, p. 27.

small packages, for customers who may live some distance from the outlet. This is particularly true for mail-order retailers.

Extended shopping hours

A major service which is being offered increasingly to consumers is longer shopping hours. This service is especially common in suburban areas, where stores may be open late each night of the week and may even be open on Sunday. Sunday and evening hours are less frequent in the central business districts.

Some retailers are enthusiastic about late evening and Sunday hours. A retailer has high fixed costs in buildings and equipment. The extra sales volume generated by additional store hours spreads the fixed costs over more units of sales. However, a careful analysis is in order to determine whether the cost of the additional store hours is more than covered by an increase in profitable volume.

Often, shopping centers have a uniform hours policy by which all outlets must abide. This can cause problems for some outlets, particularly small ones, which can perhaps operate most effectively if they open at noon and close at six, but which must abide by the hours within the center. Still other stores would like to remain open in the evenings or on Sundays only during major store volume periods, such as the Christmas holidays.

The effects of the increasing price of energy on store hours have not yet been determined. Whatever these prove to be, however, increasing numbers of working wives are likely to demand that retail outlets remain open in the evening and on Sundays to serve shoppers who are unable to shop during normal store hours. Some retailers remain closed on Sunday to avoid further aggravating already complicated personnel scheduling. However, the legal restrictions against Sunday openings are continuing to disappear.

Check cashing

Virtually all types of retail outlets cash checks for consumers. Because of the volume of checks, a standardized policy must be established to which all employees adhere. Most typical policies, in order of ascending rigor, are as follows:

1. Purchase by personal check permitted only when the check is imprinted with the customer's name, address, and telephone number.
2. Check accepted only when it is imprinted with the customer's name, address, and telephone number and is supported by two other forms of identification.
3. Submission of "check-cashing card" which reflects name of the customer, address, former address, name of employer, length of employment, name of spouse's employer, and the customer's telephone number.

4. The customer presenting the check is photographed along with the check and at least one other form of identification.
5. The customer presenting the check is fingerprinted.[32]

The majority of shoppers have no objection to a store policy requiring a preprinted check for identification. Customer reaction becomes increasingly unfavorable as one moves from policy 1 to policy 5. For example, research on check-cashing policies showed that three fourths of the respondents objected to having their photograph taken before cashing a check. Almost nine out of ten objected to being fingerprinted.

Retailers simply must have a policy on this matter and must carefully enforce it to avoid increasing losses. The average amount of a returned check is in the range of $25–$35.[33] Losses of this magnitude severely affect profitability.

Retailers can detect patterns of possible bad checks by the type of merchandise purchased, by shoppers' random selection of merchandise, and by lack of shopper concern about prices. These types of behavior may be tip-offs to exercise extra caution when accepting a check. A careful evaluation of bad-check patterns at the individual store level may yield valuable guidelines for the retailer.

Complaint policies

Retailers have varying policies with regard to consumer complaints even though merchandise return privileges are offered as a service by many stores. Some retailers may feel that the customer should be satisfied at any price. Virtually all retailers, though not guaranteeing customer satisfaction, do endeavor to be fair to the customer. Customer complaints can include complaints about the product, poor installation, problems with delivery, damaged merchandise, errors in billing, and so forth.

Centralized or decentralized handling. Complaints typically can be handled on either a centralized or a decentralized basis. Stores with a centralized complaint policy deal with all complaints, regardless of the department, at a central level in the store. This allows them to maintain a standardized complaint and adjustment policy which is uniformly administered. In a decentralized approach, complaints are handled on the sales floor by the person who sold the merchandise to the customer. Greater personal attention occurs in this process, and those who use it hope that in this way the relationship between the customer and the store employee will be reestablished.[34]

---

[32] Charles W. Golden and R. Gene McCloud, "Effects of Check Cashing Policy," *Stores*, February 1976, p. 16.

[33] "Returned Checks—What Can Be Done?" *Stores*, May 1976, p. 19.

[34] Larry J. Rosenberg, "Retailers' Responses to Consumerism," *Business Horizons*, October 1975, p. 40.

Generally, retailers prefer not to give cash refunds. They prefer to encourage the customer to exchange the merchandise or to accept a slip (a "due bill") for a purchase at a comparable price during the next several months. Either of these latter policies is likely to keep the customer coming back to the store. Some retailers do feel, however, that customers should be given cash because they are more likely to be satisfied if they are given an immediate refund.

The abuse of complaint policies.   Retailers must guard against fraud or general abuse of complaint policies. Table 18–8 presents the results of an

TABLE 18–8
CONSUMER COMPLAINTS

Judgment of consumer complaint	Number of obser- vations (N = 134)	Percent of total	Evidence of consumer intent to deceive?	Consumer given remedy desired?
Routine complaints about product return	104	77.6	No	Yes
High expectations about product	14	10.4	No	Yes
Suspected fraud	6	4.4	Yes*	Not†
Provable fraud	10	7.6	Yes	No

* The consumer's statements are doubted, but concrete evidence of fraud is missing.
† The consumer was usually given a remedy, but it was not necessarily the one wanted.
Source: Noel B. Zabriskie, "Fraud by Consumers," *Journal of Retailing*, vol. 48 (Winter 1972–73), p. 25.

analysis of consumer complaints brought to the customer service department of a major retail outlet. Approximately three fourths of the complaints were of a routine nature. More than 10 percent reflected unrealistically high expectations about the product, and 12 percent reflected suspected or provable fraud. Several signs indicate possible fraud in returns or consumer complaints. These include missing sales receipts and the presence of tags which are normally removed when merchandise is sold.

SHOPLIFTING AND PILFERAGE

On a less positive note, management should establish and publicize the policies of the store on shoplifting. Similar steps should be taken on internal pilferage to keep dishonest employees from stealing. Business thefts now add from 5–15 percent to the cost of consumer products. More employees lose jobs each year because of shortages than for any other reason.[35]

---

[35] R. Dean Lewis, "Internal Security Systems for Retailers and the Polygraph," in Henry W. Nash and Donald P. Robin, (eds.), *Proceedings: Southern Marketing Association*, 1975, p. 198; also Joseph F. Hair, Jr., et al., "Employee Theft: Views From Two Sides," *Business Horizons*, December 1976.

One author has noted that "shoplifting in the United States increased by 221% in the 1960's. Estimates of the amount of shoplifting vary from 15–33% of stock shortages, which are valued from .7–1.7 billion dollars a year." The ratio of shoplifters among customers ranges from 1 in 8 to 1 in 20.[36] Most shoplifting occurs between 2:00 and 6:00 P.M. on Thursdays, Fridays, and Saturdays. In addition to food products, items frequently subject to shoplifting include main floor merchandise, such as jewelry, billfolds, purses, and cosmetics.

Typically only about 7 percent of shoplifting occurs in the evening.[37] Also, "thefts usually occur in a pattern of about 41% of merchandise, 29% cash, and 16% under-rings. Sixty-three percent of all thefts take place at point-of-sale."[38] However, we do not know the types of theft which are most likely to occur at the point of sale.

A variety of steps can be taken to control shoplifting and internal pilferage. These steps include test-shopping of sales personnel, analysis of departmental merchandise returns, and surveillance of the main store areas. However, caution must be observed to make sure that none of the tests or policies constitute entrapment, which is illegal.

Consumers are generally unwilling to report observed fraudulent behavior. Thus, increased reliance on internal security systems seems inevitable. Public embarrassment may also be an effective deterrent to fraudulent behavior.[39]

Security experts estimate that 30 percent of store employees will make a strong effort to steal, that 30 percent will never steal, and that 40 percent can go either way.[40] These experts suggest such steps as regular internal audits, surprise outside audits, and tight controls over petty cash, accounts receivables, payroll, and inventory.

If any doubt exists as to whether a crime was committed, it is better to let the person go, for a false arrest could cost a store up to $100,000. Some managements have established minimal amounts on which a shoplifter is ignored. Is a 29-cent pen worth a chance of false arrest? Probably not. The tale is told of "one woman who was falsely accused and then invited to select anything in the store, without charge, as an apology. She chose a grand piano for her home!"[41]

[36] Amin El-Dirghami, "Shoplifting among Students," *Journal of Retailing*, vol. 50 (Fall 1974), p. 33.

[37] Michael D. Geurts, Roman R. Andres, and James Reinmuth, "Research in Shoplifting and Other Deviant Customer Behavior Using the Randomized Response Research Design," *Journal of Retailing*, vol. 51 (Winter 1975–76), p. 46.

[38] "Preventing Internal Theft," *Stores*, May 1975, p. 27.

[39] Robert E. Wilkes and Glen Riechen, "Retail Level Fraud by Consumers: An Empirical Study," in Henry R. Nash and Donald Robin (eds.), *Proceedings: Southern Marketing Association*, 1976, p. 275.

[40] "Employee Theft: A Billion Dollar Business," *Hardware Retailer*, November 1976, p. 126.

[41] "Shoplifters' Habitat," *Department Store Economist*, September 1975, p. 14.

PRODUCT RECALLS

Reputable retail outlets have traditionally encouraged consumers to return defective products, often with a "no questions asked" policy. This privilege has on occasion been abused. In recent years, the manufacturer has come between the retailer and the consumer in the matter of product recalls. As noted in connection with a recall of Corning percolators, "Corning is asking consumers to return pots directly to a Corning factory for replacement, rather than to a retailer, because retailers deal with hundreds of different products and the company felt it could please its customers better by handling the pots themselves."[42] If retailers are to continue to strive for customer goodwill under these circumstances, better lines of communication need to be opened with manufacturers so that both the manufacturer and the retailer can work together in an effective manner to control recalls. Otherwise, the manufacturer-initiated policy of product recalls may contribute to increasing isolation of the retailer from the consumer.

Many retailers, however, are not prepared to cope with either their role or their responsibilities in a product recall situation. They need more specific written guidelines from the manufacturer to help them handle recalls more effectively and to avoid disruption in normal store operations. The quantity and quality of the information made available by manufacturers are often inadequate for the retailer. Also, the failure of manufacturers to reimburse retailers for out-of-pocket expense incurred in product recalls may be a source of tension between these two channel members. Product recalls typically, however, do not have an effect on the overall sales of retailers.[43]

One of the largest product recalls at the retail level in recent years was that of sleepwear for children which contained the fire-retardant chemical TRIS. The ban was issued on April 8, 1977. Over 20 million garments were involved. Retailers were required to buy back all of the unwashed garments. The recalls occurred because of studies by the Environmental Protection Agency and the Environmental Defense Fund which linked certain chemicals used as fire retardants on garments to cancer. Further investigations into the chemical content of clothing—for example, polyvinyl chloride (PVC) fibers—are likely to occur under the umbrella of the Toxic Substance Control Act. Clothing is now 5th in the priorities of product categories for which standards are to be established by the Consumer Product Safety Commission—up from 23d place in 1975.[44] However, in June 1977 a U.S. district court judge ruled that the data behind the complaint were "unverified, uninterpreted, and uncertain." As a result he nullified the Federal

---

[42] "How to Turn a Recall into a Sales Pitch," *Business Week,* August 30, 1976, p. 21.

[43] Mary C. Harrison and M. Bixby Cooper, "An Analysis of Retailer Participation in Product Recalls," in Henry W. Nash and Donald P. Robins (eds.), *Proceedings: Southern Marketing Association,* 1976, p. 91.

[44] Patricia Chapman, "After TRIS, Now What and from Where?" *Stores,* June 1977, pp. 47–52.

Consumer Products Safety Commission's ban on the fire-retardant chemical. At present, the outcome of the entire matter is uncertain at best.

THE COST EFFECTIVENESS OF SERVICES OFFERED

All services offered by the retailer cost money. The costs may be in the form of additional employees who are needed to offer the service. Such costs must be balanced against additional revenue, since the retailer offers services in an effort to extend the demand curve to the right, in economics terms.

Services are not proportional in cost to sales. Therefore, management cannot precisely determine the impact of each service on sales. Further, if certain valued services are offered by competitors, the retailer must also offer the services in order to retain customers.

Table 18–9 depicts the costs of four typical department store services. These costs range from a low of 0.25% for customer services to a high of 1.42% for credit and collection.

TABLE 18–9
TYPICAL COST OF SELECTED SERVICES FOR A
DEPARTMENT STORE WITH SALES OF OVER $50 MILLION
(percent of total company sales)

Service	Typical figure	Middle range
Credit and collection	1.42	1.05–1.91
Customer services	0.25	0.16–0.36
Wrapping and packing	0.54	0.46–0.65
Delivery	0.66	0.49–0.82

Source: Jay Scher, *Financial and Operating Ratios of Department and Specialty Stores* (New York: National Retail Merchants Associations, 1975), p. 53.

Many factors must be considered in deciding whether to offer or discontinue a service or whether to charge for a service, such as a merchandise return which is not the fault of the retailer.

Some services may not be performed by the retailer and yet still be performed satisfactorily for the consumer. They can be performed either by consumers or by wholesalers or other specialized market agencies. For example, many supermarkets now have consumers bag their own groceries and carry them to their automobiles in return for lower prices. The consumer may also perform delivery—for example, of merchandise purchased at a liquidation sale or at a warehouse furniture outlet or a similar type of operation. In a limited number of instances, the retailer may sell items which are shipped directly by the manufacturer.

Other possibilities exist. For example, the camera outlets in a community may share in the services of a single repair shop. Gasoline service stations may send automobiles to specialty repair shops for sophisticated repairs, such as repairs of transmission or air-conditioning systems. This arrangement is the opposite of vertical integration, in which a variety of activities are performed by a single integrated system. However, it does reflect the specialization and division of labor which Adam Smith taught us about 200 years ago.

Management should periodically review whether it wishes to continue offering a particular service. Customer attitudes may change, and the retailer who chooses to eliminate a service as a result of such changes may get a "jump" on competition. Let us consider the practice of offering trading stamps. Historically many retail businesses, particularly supermarkets and gasoline service stations, offered trading stamps as almost a competitive necessity. In the 1970s many of these businesses eliminated the expense of stamps and were thus able to offer reduced prices to customers.

In periodically reviewing the service assortment provided to customers, the retailer must try to estimate the effect of discontinuing a service on total store demand and to balance the loss in demand against the anticipated reduction in cost. For example, deciding to drop delivery service might affect only furniture, appliances, and other bulky items. However, if dropping delivery service drastically reduced sales in these categories management would elect to continue delivery.

OPERATING POLICIES AND PRODUCTIVITY

Productivity is becoming increasingly important in retailing. All operating policies should be continuously reviewed in an effort to increase productivity. Possible sources of productivity increases are covered in the chapter on human resources management (Chapter 20) and in numerous other places throughout the text.

From an operating policy perspective, however, what are some ways in which productivity can be increased?

1. The use of part-time help to smooth out the pattern of coverage by hours yields good results.
2. Improving the relationship between management and labor will allow the substitution of technology for labor and enable management to negotiate agreements designed to benefit employees and improve productivity.
3. The substitution of leased departments as alternatives for weak departments should be considered, especially if a department is considered necessary for the image of the store.
4. Productivity can be increased by going to smaller stores and making them more compact by using less space for stockroom and administrative purposes.
5. Better use of space and flexible fixture systems will yield good results.
6. Consideration should be given to increasing productivity by selling outside the shop through catalogs, direct mail, radio, TV, newspapers, and telephone service. Visual merchandising through the use of video cassettes also offers excellent opportunities.

Gamble-Skogmo increased its sales per square foot by 20 percent as a result of fixture changes without substantively remaking its merchandise mix.[45] As noted by a Dayton Hudson senior vice president, "Mistakes made in store planning are a permanent markdown."[46]

SUMMARY

Many features of the retail store affect consumer perception and patronage. These features include store layout and interior design and credit and other supplementary services. Increasingly, retailers are recognizing the influence of store layout and design on the shopping behavior of consumers. Retailers can shape customer behavior and demand by manipulating various layout and design features. The most typical layouts are the grid, the free-flow arrangement, and the boutique.

The retailer faces a variety of choices in deciding whether to offer credit, which is a major consumer service. The retailer can extend in-store credit, use a bank card, offer a card unique to the outlet, or provide any combination of these services. In addition, the retailer may have a cash-and-carry policy. Consumer pressure for the use of bank credit cards in department stores is increasing, though many retailers do not give much attention to bank credit cards in their merchandise mix. Virtually all types of credit are offered by the retailer at a loss. However, credit is often a competitive necessity.

The retailer can offer a variety of other services. These include manipulation of the hours of business, delivery, baby sitting, interior design counseling, appliance installation, and an almost endless variety of other services. However, careful efforts should be made to balance anticipated revenues against the probable costs of such services. In addition, the retailer should be aware of the possible effect on demand of eliminating a particular service or of deciding to charge for a service.

KEY CONCEPTS

Space and consumer behavior	Delivery
Basics of design	Extended hours
Types of store layouts	Complaint policies
Space allocation	Product recall
Sales productivity analysis	Shoplifting and pilferage
Credit management	

---

[45] "How Gamble-Skogmo Increases Space Productivity," *Chain Store Age Executive*, March 1977, p. 49.

[46] "Store Planning Must Become Long Range," *Chain Store Age Executive*, March 1977, p. 46.

DISCUSSION QUESTIONS

1. Briefly discuss what we know about the influence of design and layout on consumer behavior.

2. What are the typical types of store layout? What are the advantages and disadvantages of each?

3. What variables can be manipulated in store layout to create different store images and different customer movement patterns?

4. Why are major department stores reluctant to accept bank credit cards? Why is the small retailer almost forced to accept bank credit cards?

5. Is credit normally a moneymaking device for the retailer? Why or why not?

6. What are some key factors which the retailer must consider in deciding whether to offer or discontinue a particular service?

7. Do you think that the retailer should charge customers who use such services as telephone shopping and delivery?

8. What are the effects on retail operating policies of the longer hours of many retail outlets?

9. What retail merchandise policies have allowed discounters to eliminate most store services and yet generate a high volume of store sales?

PROJECTS

1. Visit a single department (men's shirts, cosmetics) in at least three retail outlets. Identify:
   a. The type of outlet.
   b. The layout.
   c. The location of the department within the store.
   d. The physical characteristics of the department—lighting, displays, storage, and so on.
   Submit a sketch of each department along with this information.

2. Survey four department stores in your area and determine what services they provide. Do they charge for the services? If so, how much? Interview several shoppers in each store. Do they know what services are provided and how these services are provided? How important are services in attracting these customers to the store? (Devise a questionnaire to use on your interviews.)

3. Devise a research plan to investigate selected retail firms in your area to see what has happened in the sphere of retail services (charged for, free, paid for in part) in the era of inflation. If nothing tangible has been done, see whether you can find out what opinions are being expressed about the issue. For example, what is being done in the areas of gift wrapping, alterations, delivery, and so on?

4. Shoplifting is a major problem in all types of retail stores. Interview as many retailers in your area as possible to determine: (a) the extent of the problem as they perceive it; (b) the efforts that are being made to reduce shoplifting; (c) the

effectiveness of these efforts; *(d)* consumer reactions (for example, to electronic systems, convex mirrors, uniformed guards, or observation booths). Check with local merchant groups to see what concerted efforts are being made to solve the problem.

5. Select two competing (but different) types of retail establishments (for example, a department store and a promotional discount department store) and compare, and contrast them in terms of store layout, interior and window display, credit authorization, services offered, and other operating policies which you may determine could be interesting to investigate. Make up a summary chart of your comparisons, and then write up a narrative suggesting the operating strategies of the two establishments as evidenced by the policies described by you.

6. *Atmospherics* is a very "in" word in retailing. Select three different types of stores (for example, a conventional department store, a promotional department store, and a corporate chain department store), and carefully observe their displays, appearance, fixturing, and so on—all the elements that make up the atmosphere of the individual stores. Choose a certain department to study within the stores (for example, junior sportswear), and use this as your laboratory. Take pictures (with permission) to illustrate your positions. See how the atmospherics differ among the stores and how these differences relate to image projection and market segmentation.

7. Layout, fixturing, and color can affect the way a customer progresses through a store. Make arrangements with a local supermarket manager (or the manager of another type of store) to allow you to "track" customers throughout their shopping trip in the store. You will see patterns evolve—where purchasing takes place, where stopping occurs, where "backtracking" is evident, "dead" spaces, the most effective shelf displays in terms of customer attention, and so on. After a number of "trackings," the patterns should be plotted and certain findings should be evident. You can include a personal interview with the customer at the end of the "tracking" to get certain demographic information and information on shopping patterns in the area. This can be a useful experience to you and to the store management.

CASES

Case 1.   Robert Talbot owns and operates a ladies' ready-to-wear store, Talbot's, in the downtown business district. He is in the process of opening a branch of approximately 3,500 square feet in the new suburban mall. He has had no experience in opening branches. Sales are budgeted at $175,000 for the new store. He has asked the buyer of jewelry how much space she will need for her department, assuming that he wants 5 percent of budgeted sales from that department.

How much space does she need? How did you determine it? Why did you use that particular method?

Case 2.   Smith and Son has merchandise arranged in a grid pattern which allows customers to move quickly through the store. The store is located on a New York City street with many office buildings. The store has an opening to the street and a second opening from the subway. Each day many people go through the store on their way to and from the subway. A few stop to look at the merchandise, but sales from this walk-through traffic are very low.

In an effort to increase sales from the walk-through traffic, the management has decided to change the layout of the store.

What method of arrangement would you recommend that it use? Why?

19

ACCOUNTING FOR OPERATING EFFECTIVENESS

*R*etailing has traditionally been a highly competitive business, as evidenced by the industry's low net profit. Additional operating costs are often completely or partially absorbed rather than passed through in the form of higher retail prices.

This situation has created an awareness of the need for planning, controlling, and evaluating operating expenses. This chapter, "Accounting for Operating Effectiveness," provides the necessary guidelines for accumulating expense data by area of responsibility so as to permit retail management to effectively evaluate performance and to handle the decision-making process on a timely basis.

Since many operating expenses bear a direct relationship to sales, the proper accumulation and analysis of such data make possible the preparation of the long- and short-term plans so essential to the growth and profitability of a retail business.

Jay Scher, Vice President
Financial Executives Division
National Retail Merchants Association
New York

The previous chapter presented the operating decisions which retailing management must make in order to gain a differential advantage in the marketplace. As suggested in the last section of Chapter 18, whatever operating alternatives are chosen, accountability for the effectiveness of the choice is essential. This chapter continues that focus. Its objectives are: (1) to present the traditional methods for classifying expenses; (2) to explore the issues in expense allocation; and (3) to discuss expense budgeting and controls applicable to all kinds of retail enterprises.

EXPENSE CLASSIFICATION

The purpose of expense analysis is to evaluate the effectiveness of the management function associated with an expense. Classification is thus necessary for expense analysis and control. Expense control does not necessarily mean reduction of expenses; rather, it means effective results from expense investment.

Ideally, the retailing industry should adopt a uniform method of expense classification, but this is not likely to occur because philosophies differ, organizations are diverse in size, and varied types of merchandise are offered. However, the major trade associations have made efforts at standardization, which provide assistance in the evaluation of performance effectiveness. Examples of such standards are included in the subsequent discussion.

The three major expense classifications are: (1) natural, (2) functional, and (3) expense center. The best-known expense classification system is presented in the *Retail Accounting Manual* of the Controllers Congress, National Retail Merchants Association. This trade association representing department and specialty stores promotes two of the three major expense classification methods.

Natural

The "natural" classification of expenses follows an arrangement that one might use after taking a basic accounting course. Figure 19–1 illustrates a natural expense classification in a situation where management is in continuous contact with all operations and there are relatively few transactions.

This system is most appropriate for small retail stores.[1] It gives the management of such operations sufficient detail for decisions. Figure 19–2 gives the natural expense division suggested by the NRMA. Figure 19–3 illustrates the Super Market Institute's adaptation of a natural classification for its membership. Finally, Figure 19–4 illustrates the Menswear Retailers of America adaptation of a natural division which it promotes for operators of men's stores. All four systems are similar.

---

[1] For purposes of this discussion, a *small* store is one with sales under $500,000; *medium-sized,* $500,000 to $5,000,000; and *large,* over $5,000,000.

FIGURE 19–1
ILLUSTRATIVE INCOME STATEMENT SHOWING NATURAL
EXPENSE CLASSIFICATION

Gross sales	$334,098	
Less: Customer returns	6,550	
Net sales		$327,548
Cost of merchandise sold		202,610
Gross margin		124,938
Operating expenses		
Selling		
Salaries	$40,088	
Promotion	6,920	
Depreciation selling equipment	2,200	
Insurance expense—selling	1,160	
Store supplies	840	
Miscellaneous selling expense	460	
Total selling expenses	51,668	
General		
Salaries	12,064	
Taxes	3,620	
Depreciation—building	3,000	
Depreciation—office equipment	980	
Insurance expense—general	400	
Office supplies	660	
Miscellaneous general expense	620	
Total general expenses	$21,344	
Total operating expenses		73,012
Operating income		$ 51,926

Functional

At one time the NRMA promoted a functional expense classification. This type of classification system identifies the *purpose* of an expense, whereas the *natural* system focuses on the *nature* of the expense. The major functions promoted by the NRMA (actually in the era when it was known as the National Retail Dry Goods Association) were: (1) administration, (2) occupancy, (3) publicity, (4) buying, and (5) selling.

The medium-sized store in particular can benefit from a combination of the natural and functional systems. Figure 19–5 illustrates a typical presentation of such a system with subfunctions and a somewhat different group of natural expenses than that displayed in Figure 19–2. For the medium-sized store, this approach is as applicable today as it was when it was first formulated. Still a common approach to expense classification and analysis, it allows a merchant to achieve greater precision in determining the nature of expenses and in locating problem areas.

As an example, assume that the payroll total has risen unexpectedly for a particular period. The classification illustrated in Figure 19–5 would allow a

FIGURE 19–2
ILLUSTRATIVE NATURAL EXPENSE DIVISION FOR USE BY MEMBERS
OF THE NATIONAL RETAIL MERCHANTS ASSOCIATION
(percent of total company sales)

	Typical figures	Middle range	Goal figures	Your company's figures
Payroll (01) Advertising (03) Taxes (04) Supplies (06) Services purchased (07) Unclassified (08) Travel (09) Communications (10) Pensions (11) Insurance (12) Depreciation (13) Professional services (14) Donations (15) Bad debts (16) Equipment costs (17) Real property rentals (20)				

Source: Excerpted from *Financial and Operating Results of Department and Specialty Stores*, Controllers Congress, National Retail Merchants Association.

more accurate pinpointing of the functional area within which the trouble is occurring. Thus, corrective action could be taken with more certainty.

Large stores do not typically use a functional classification system because major responsibilities in a large store may not correspond with the functions designated. Expense center accounting is more common in large stores.

Expense center accounting

Expense center accounting is a development of the mid-1950s. Figure 19–6 indicates the recommended NRMA expense centers and the suggested numbering system. The appropriate natural expenses become a part of the expense center approach to classification. The specific natural expenses relating to the expense centers are indicated in Figure 19–2.

The promotion of expense center accounting by the NRMA provides an available data base which is an invaluable source of expense planning, analysis, and control information for managements which utilize the NRMA format. The NRMA publishes both ranges and typical expenses for many different expense categories.

FIGURE 19–3
ILLUSTRATIVE NATURAL EXPENSE CLASSIFICATION FOR
USE BY MEMBERS OF THE SUPER MARKET INSTITUTE

Description

Sales trend
    1. This quarter versus same quarter last year (all stores)
    2. This quarter versus same quarter last year (identical stores)
    3. This quarter versus last quarter (all stores)
    4. This quarter versus last quarter (identical stores)
Gross profit and store door margin
    6e. Gross profit
        6e–1. With warehouse
        6e–2. Without warehouse
    7. Warehouse delivery and headquarters costs
        7a. Warehouse (own)
        7b. Delivery (own)
        7c. Headquarters
    8. Store Door margin
Store expenses
    9. Store labor expense
        9a. Regular
        9b. Fringe
    10. Advertising and promotion expense, excluding stamps
    11. Trading stamp expense (regular)
    12. Store supply expense
    13. Store occupancy expense
        13a. Rent and real estate
        13b. Utilities
    14. Equipment depreciation or rental costs
    15. Maintenance and repairs
    16. All other store expenses
    17. Total store expenses
Profit before income taxes
    18. Operating profit/loss
Store labor control
    19. Sales per man-hour
    20. Average hourly labor cost
Operating and merchandising ratios
    21. Weekly sales per square foot (selling area)
    22. Average sale per customer transaction
    23. Average grocery inventory turns (store)
    30. Average grocery inventory turns (warehouse)
    31. Warehouse level of service
Grocery retail reductions
    24. Grocery markdowns, at retail
    25. Grocery inventory shortage, at retail
Owners' salaries
    32. Owners' salaries

Source: Excerpted from *Operations Review—Comparison of Merchandising and Operating Results,* Super Market Institute.

THE ALLOCATION OF EXPENSES

Some expenses can easily be allocated to departments (for example, to
such selling departments as men's furnishings or to such large classifications
as sport shirts), branch stores, and the like. These are called *direct* expenses

FIGURE 19–4

ILLUSTRATIVE NATURAL EXPENSE CLASSIFICATION FOR USE BY MEMBERS
OF THE MENSWEAR RETAILERS OF AMERICA

*Expense
division
no.**

9.	01	Payroll (total)
		a. Payroll of owners and officers
		b. Selling payroll
		c. Nonselling payroll
		d. Sick leave, holiday, military leave and severance pay
10.	03	Advertising
11.	04	Taxes (total)
		a. All state and local taxes with the exception of payroll taxes and federal income taxes
		b. Social Security and unemployment taxes
12.	06	Supplies
13.	07	Services purchased
14.	08	Unclassified
15.	09	Traveling
16.	10	Communications
17.	11	Pensions
18.	12	Insurance (total)
		a. Workmen's compensation insurance, sickness, accident, group medical, group hospital and life insurance premiums
		b. All other insurance premiums
19.	13	Depreciation (total)
		a. Depreciation on owned fixtures and equipment
		b. Depreciation on building or leasehold improvements
20.	14	Professional services
21.	15	Donations
22.	16	Bad debts
23.	17	Equipment costs
24.	20	Real property rentals
25.		Total Expenses

* Expense division numbers and definitions are in accordance with the merchandising and accounting manual of the MRA Financial and Operations Group.

Source: Excerpted from *Annual Business Survey, Men's Store Operating Experiences,* Menswear Retailers of America.

because they can be assigned to a specific area. They are also called *controllable* because they are under the direct control of a particular department. If the department were discontinued, the expenses would be discontinued. If the sport shirt classification were eliminated from a store, then salaries of salespersons working entirely within the classification would be eliminated, as would supplies used by the employees and the specific promotional costs of the classification.

Direct expenses cause less of an allocation problem than do *indirect* (or *uncontrollable*) expenses, which are costs that would exist even if a particular department were eliminated. Such costs include rent, heat, light, and administrative salaries.

The allocation of expenses to various departments within a store is critical because the various classifications, though important as managerial informa-

FIGURE 19-5

ILLUSTRATION OF NATURAL DIVISIONS OF EXPENSE BY FUNCTIONS FOR USE BY A MEDIUM-SIZED STORE

Functions	Natural expense divisions														
	Pay-roll	Rent-als	Ad-ver-tis-ing	Taxes	In-ter-est	Sup-plies	Ser-vice pur-chased	Un-clas-si-fied	Trav-eling	Com-muni-ca-tions	Re-pairs	In-sur-ance	De-pre-cia-tion	Profes-sional ser-vices	Total
Administrative function															
Occupancy function Operating and housekeeping															
Fixed plant and equipment costs															
Light, heat, and power															
Publicity function Advertising															
Display															
Buying function Merchandise management and buying and outside buying offices															
Receiving and marking															
Selling function Compensation of salespersons															
General selling															
Delivery															
Total															

Source: Adapted from Figure 52., John W. Wingate and Elmer O. Schaller, *Techniques in Retailing Merchandising*, © 1950, p. 462. Reprinted by permission of Prentice-Hall, Inc., Englewood Cliffs, New Jersey.

FIGURE 19–6
ILLUSTRATIVE EXPENSES BY EXPENSE CENTER FOR USE BY MEMBERS OF THE
NATIONAL RETAIL MERCHANTS ASSOCIATION
(percent of total company sales)

110 Management
    Payroll
    Taxes
    Insurance
    Professional services
    All other
    Total
120 Property and equipment
    Taxes
    Insurance
    Depreciation
    Equipment costs
    Real property rentals
    Expense transfers and other credits
    Total
210 Accounting and data processing
    Payroll
    Services purchased
    Equipment costs
    All other
    Total
310 Accounts receivable
    Payroll
    Postage
    Equipment costs
    All other
    Total
320 Credit and collections
    Payroll
    Services purchased
    Bad debts
    Equipment costs
    All other
    Total
410 Sales promotion
    Payroll
    Advertising
    Supplies
    All other
    Total
510 Services and operations
    Payroll
    All other
    Total
550 Telephone and other utilities
    Payroll
    Communications
    All other
    Total
570 Cleaning
    Payroll
    All other
    Total

580 Maintenance and repairs
    Payroll
    Supplies
    Services purchased
    Expense transfers and other credits
    All other
    Total
610 Personnel
    Payroll
    All other
    Total
630 Supplementary benefits
    Payroll
    Taxes
    Pensions
    Insurance
    All other
    Total
720 Maintenance of reserve stock
    Payroll
    All other
    Total
740 Receiving and marking
    Payroll
    Equipment costs
    All other
    Total
750 Shuttle service
    Payroll
    Equipment costs
    All other
    Total
810 Selling Supervision
    Payroll
    All other
    Total
820 Direct selling
    Payroll
    Supplies
    All other
    Total
830 Customer services
    Payroll
    All other
    Total
860 Wrapping
    Payroll
    Supplies
    All other
    Total

FIGURE 19–6 (continued)

880 Delivery Payroll Services purchased Equipment costs Expense transfers and other credits All other Total	920 Buying Payroll Travel All other Total
910 Merchandising Payroll Services purchased All other Total	930 Merchandise control Payroll All other Total Gross operating expense Less: Accounts receivable handling charges Net operating expense

Source: Excerpted from *Financial and Operating Results of Department and Specialty Stores*, Controllers Congress, National Retail Merchants Association.

tion, do not reveal the profitability of a specific operating division of a company. Determination of profitability is the problem of expense allocation.

Why, with the emphasis placed on the determination of gross margin (see Chapters 13 and 14), isn't gross margin an adequate measure of operating effectiveness for a department or a store? The reason is that departments with identical sales and margins may have different operating costs. (For example, the sport shirt department may home-deliver very few shirts and sell few shirts on credit. On the other hand, the furniture department may deliver virtually all of the items it sells and may make most of its sales on credit.) For this reason, as many expenses as possible should be charged to a specific department.

The two methods utilized by large stores for expense allocation are (1) the contribution plan and (2) the net profit plan.

The contribution plan

Under the contribution plan, departments are assigned only those expenses that can be charged directly to them, that is, controllable expenses. Under this plan, the department is evaluated on the basis of its contribution to storewide profits rather than on the basis of its own profit. Indirect or uncontrollable expenses are not deducted; the contribution margin derived in this plan goes toward covering total store overhead costs, such as heat and light, maintenance, and rent.

The net profit plan

Under the net profit plan all expenses, both direct and indirect, are charged to selling departments. In effect, each department is viewed as a separate business to be evaluated on its profit showing. Persons who support the net profit plan believe that it makes the department manager more cost conscious and that it provides a better method of evaluating the value of each department. The philosophic differences between the two plans are somewhat technical, and the interested student with a flair for accounting may be interested in investigating them.[2] In any case, under the net profit plan the manager is evaluated on profit performance which reflects expenses over which he or she has no control. In addition, the arbitrary mechanisms for allocating indirect expenses can cause great frustrations for the department manager.

The contribution/net profit combination

Some stores combine the two systems to obtain the strengths of each. In the contribution/net profit combination plan, another category of expenses is typically established—semidirect expenses. These expenses are allocated equitably. An example of a semidirect expense would be accounts payable, which could be allocated on the basis of the number of invoices charged to specific departments. Figure 19–7 compares the contribution, net profit, and combination plans of expense allocation as these relate to profits.

EXPENSE BUDGETING AND CONTROL

An appropriate analogy to expense management (budgeting and control following classification and allocation decisions) is merchandise management (see Chapter 12). Just as the retailer is obligated to plan for merchandise needed, management must also plan for expenditures which facilitate effective merchandising. Expenses must be forecast for a specific period as in the merchandise budget. The principal connection between the merchandise and the expense budgets is that both are based on planned sales. The expense budget period coincides with the planning cycle of the merchandise budget. Let's think in terms of a six-month period for illustrative purposes.

Realistically, small stores seldom have even informal expense budgets, just as they seldom have formal merchandise plans. To the "uninformed" and unsophisticated small retailer, expense management simply means "cut expenses" to increase profits.

In addition, the managements of small- and medium-sized outlets often do not support the idea of budgeting expenses. They feel that it is too time consuming, that it breeds inflexibility,[3] that it costs more than it is worth. This

---

[2] For a more detailed discussion of the two plans, see William R. Davidson, Alton F. Doody, and Daniel J. Sweeney, Retailing Management, 4th ed. (New York: Ronald Press, 1975), pp. 616–28.

[3] Such a position is analogous to that of the merchandise planner who believes that planning markdowns in a merchandise budget breeds inflexibility or perhaps excessive marking down because a certain amount of markdown is built into the budget. Such thinking reflects a misunderstanding of the purpose of budgeting. A budget is a guide to behavior, and expert opinion must be employed to have an effective plan. Flexibility is an essential ingredient of a good budget.

FIGURE 19–7
ILLUSTRATION OF THREE EXPENSE ALLOCATION PLANS

Contribution plan

Net sales		$200,000
Cost of sales		130,000
Gross margin		$ 70,000
Direct expenses		
Promotion	$ 1,600	
Selling	17,000	
Stock maintenance	8,000	
Selling supervision	500	
Miscellaneous	1,000	
Total direct expenses		28,100
Contribution to overhead (or controllable margin)		$ 41,900

Net profit plan

Net sales	$200,000
Cost of sales	130,000
Gross margin	$ 70,000
Less direct and indirect expenses	66,000
Net profit before taxes	$ 4,000

Contribution/net profit combination plan

Net sales	$200,000
Cost of sales	130,000
Gross margin	$ 70,000
Less direct expenses	25,000
Contribution	$ 45,000
Less semidirect expenses	3,100
Contribution after semidirect expenses	$ 41,900
Less indirect expenses	37,900
Net profit before taxes	$ 4,000

point of view is exemplified by the merchant who guards expenses so carefully that he attempts to "save" money by cutting back on essential promotional activities.

Despite such objections, merchants, regardless of size, are capable of utilizing trade associations, buying offices, vendors, noncompeting retailers, trade papers, and informed accountants to assist in gaining data on which to base even the most routine expense information for planning purposes. The "reasons" for not planning expenses appear to be excuses rather than realistic impediments.

The expense-budgeting process

As was noted in Chapter 12, the major purpose of merchandise management is to maintain a healthy balance between investments in inventories and planned sales. The major purpose of expense management is to balance planned expenses with planned income. Income, or maintained markup, must cover operating expenses and profit. Thus, the need for the planning and control of expenses as they relate to profit is obvious.[4]

In larger stores, the controller (vice president, control division) is responsible for the budget process. As in the preparation of the merchandise budget, expense planning begins with the departmental level of management, as shown in Figure 19–8. The buyers (or department managers) each present a plan to the divisional merchandise manager, who combines the departmental budgets and presents a unified budget to the general merchandise manager or perhaps directly to the controller. Adjustments to the budget are made at each level. This process allows input from those who must live within the constraints of the plan. Such an approach is sounder than one in which top management takes a total expense amount (for example, a certain percentage of total sales) and allocates it to the operating departments. The latter approach may allow inequity in the allocation of expenses among departments. Undoubtedly the financial vice president has a "figure" in mind for the total expense budget. One reason for adjustments would be a sharp discrepancy between the totaled individual budgets and the controller's "projected" company target.

The expense budget is just a plan. Periodic reviews of expenses are necessary to see whether the budget is truly effective. The use of periodic reports summarizing actual expense commitments as compared to planned expenditures is a sound approach. Discrepancies can be noted and action taken. Such periodic reports can be as formalized as the open-to-buy reports

---

[4] Graphically, to review, the relationships are as follows:

Sales—$100,000	Operating expenses .... $15,000 + Profits 5,000	Maintained markup
	Invoice Cost $80,000	

FIGURE 19-8
THE EXPENSE BUDGETING PROCESS

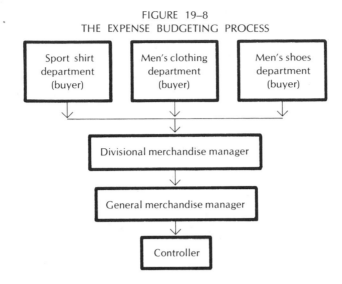

which are used to control planned purchases. The periodic report is an "open-to-spend" report that can be compared directly with the merchandise control report. Figure 19–9 indicates how a budget form for operating expenses might be set up for both planning and control purposes.

Break-even analysis

A useful concept for the analysis, planning, and control of expenses is the break-even analysis. Management has profit goals; expenses affect profit performance; expenses are either variable or fixed, and the combination of these expenses impacts on management decisions. Break-even analysis

FIGURE 19-9
ILLUSTRATION OF OPEN-TO-SPEND REPORT BASED ON EXPENSE BUDGET FOR FALL
SEASON FOR SPORT SHIRT CLASSIFICATION*

		January	February		Total
Expenses (natural) Payroll†					
	Plan	$1,200			
	Committed	600			
	Open-to-spend	600			
	Actual at end of month	‡			
Communications					
Total					$15,000

* As of January 15.
† Other expenses handled similarly.
‡ Actual put in at end of month.

FIGURE 19–10
ILLUSTRATION OF EXPENSE-VOLUME-PROFIT RELATIONSHIPS

	Fixed expenses high				Fixed expenses low			
	Lower volume		Higher volume		Lower volume		Higher volume	
Sales	$200,000	(100%)	$204,000	(100%)	$200,000	(100%)	$204,000	(100%)
Cost of sales	130,000	(65%)	132,000	(65%)	130,000	(65%)	132,600	(65%)
Gross margin	$ 70,000	(35%)	$ 71,400	(35%)	$ 70,000	(35%)	$ 71,400	(35%)
Variable costs	$34,000		$32,872		$56,000		$56,500	
Fixed costs	32,000		32,000		10,000		10,000	
	66,000	(33%)	64,872	(31.8%)	66,000	(33%)	66,500	(32.6%)
Net profit	$ 4,000	(2%)	$ 6,528	(3.2%)	$ 4,000	(2%)	$ 4,900	(2.4%)

Source: Adapted from Karen R. Gillespie and Joseph C. Hecht, *Retail Business Management*, 2d ed (New York: Gregg/McGraw-Hill, 1977), pp. 408–9. Used with permission.

provides a tool for analyzing expense-volume-profit relationships and serves to predict the impact on profits of a change in (1) selling prices, (2) the quantity expected to be sold, (3) variable costs (or expenses), and (4) fixed expenses.

Fixed expenses do not vary with the volume of business. For example, heat, light, and rent expenses remain the same, regardless of the volume of sales. *Variable* expenses change as sales increase. Examples are salespeople's salaries, delivery expenses, receiving costs, and others. Figure 19–10 illustrates the relationships between fixed and variable expenses, volume, and profits. If the fixed expenses in a particular department are high and the volume of business increases, then total expenses as a percentage of sales will decrease, thus increasing net profits. On the other hand, if fixed expenses are low, an increase in business volume will cause a much smaller change in profit performance (that is, in Figure 19–10 the change was from 2 percent to 3.2 percent with high fixed expenses, and from 2 percent to 2.4 percent with low fixed expenses).

Utilizing the "lower volume, fixed expenses high" portion of Figure 19–10, we can simulate a break-even chart to illustrate the application of this

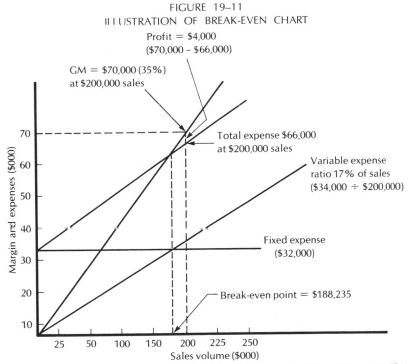

FIGURE 19–11
ILLUSTRATION OF BREAK-EVEN CHART
Profit = $4,000
($70,000 - $66,000)

GM = $70,000 (35%)
at $200,000 sales

Total expense $66,000
at $200,000 sales

Variable expense
ratio 17% of sales
($34,000 ÷ $200,000)

Fixed expense
($32,000)

Break-even point = $188,235

Margin and expenses ($000)

Sales volume ($000)

Note: *Marginal income ratio* = Gross margin − Variable expense ratio (0.35 − 0.17 = 0.18). This is the percentage of sales volume available (after allowing for variable expenses) for covering fixed expenses. Therefore, the break-even point is

$$\frac{\$32{,}000 \text{ fixed expense}}{0.17 \text{ marginal income revenue}} = \$188{,}235$$

managerial decision tool. At a volume of $188,235, the marginal income ratio is 18 percent. Any amount above this sales volume will add to the profit column. Below this point, the company suffers losses. (See Figure 19–11.)

Break-even analysis anticipates probable future performance by simulating in advance the impact on profits of a change in one or more of the decision variables. Through such analysis, a number of questions can be answered. . . . What will be the profit or loss at a given sales volume? What additional sales volume will be required to cover the additional fixed costs arising from a store modernization program? What sales volume is needed to cover additional variable costs resulting from a change in salesman's compensation rates? How will a given reduction in gross margin change the break-even point?[5]

SUMMARY

This chapter completes the planning aspects of retailing management. The student is encouraged to relate the discussion not only to the preceding chapter on operating decisions but also to merchandise management.

Expenses can be classified by natural division, functionally, or by expense centers. Further, they can be viewed as direct (controllable), indirect (uncontrollable), and semidirect. Contribution and net profit plans or a combination of the two are the primary bases for expense allocation.

KEY CONCEPTS

Expense classification
  Natural
  Functional
  Expense center
Allocation of expenses
  Direct expenses (controllable expenses)
  Indirect expenses (uncontrollable expenses)
  Expense allocation methods
    The contribution plan
    The net profit plan
    The contribution/net profit combination
The expense budgeting process
  Open-to-spend
Fixed expenses
Variable expenses
Break-even analysis

---

[5] William R. Davidson, Alton F. Doody, and Daniel J. Sweeney, *Retailing Management,* 4th ed. Copyright © 1975 The Ronald Press Company, New York.

DISCUSSION QUESTIONS

1. What purpose does the analysis of expenses serve? What is the relationship between expense classification and expense analysis?

2. Do you believe that the retailing industry as a whole will support a uniform method of expense classification in the near future? Why or why not?

3. Explain and critically evaluate the three major systems for classifying operating expenses in retailing.

4. Distinguish among direct, indirect, and semidirect expenses. How do these affect the allocation of expenses within a retailing organization?

5. Distinguish between the contribution and the net profit plans of expense allocation. Evaluate them, state which you prefer, and explain why.

6. Relate the functions of merchandise and expense management. Within a firm, are the same people involved in both types of management?

7. Illustrate how initial markup planning and expense planning are closely related.

8. Describe the expense budgeting process. Evaluate it.

9. Explain the value of and the technique employed in break-even analysis.

10. Relate "open-to-spend" and "open-to-buy." Do you think that the former is a valuable tool? Explain.

PROJECTS

1. Try to get a cooperative retailer to let you go over the accounting statements for a number of years. From such data, attempt to gain insights into particular pluses and minuses in the business. Compute key ratios, trends in certain accounts, and the impact of certain key components (for example, turnover, margin) on ROI. To get such cooperation, you must promise confidentiality and also share your findings with the merchant. It is a valuable experience but a difficult arrangement to work out. A "family" member is most acceptable to such ideas.

2. Investigate several different companies and determine the method each employs in expense allocation. Select a major general merchandise chain, a general merchandise department store, and perhaps a locally owned family clothing operation. Compare the methods among the stores, and then relate the allocation systems to those discussed in the text.

3. Make a contact with a local retailer with whom you feel you can work. If you can establish such a relationship, allow the retailer to have you work out an expense budget based on the kind of classification the retailer is currently using. A retailer who has no formalized plan may allow you to use his or her available information, and you can set up a simple system which the merchant can actually use in the future. This can be a most satisfying experience for the student and the retailer.

CASES

Case 1. Mickey Lee received his master's degree from an outstanding graduate school of business and received several good offers to join the training programs of large retail firms at salaries greater than Mickey had expected some years previously. Mickey almost accepted one of the offers as it was so good financially and he had a very carefully worked out career path and knew where he should be in 3, 5, 10, and 20 years. It was clean; it was clear; it was also a little too "pat" for Mickey.

In 1946, after World War II, Mickey's father opened a "traditional" men's store in a downtown site whose owner had decided to retire and move away. Mr. Lee did not "buy" the existing store but started "from scratch" with a new name (rather unimaginatively called "Lee's"), a new stock of merchandise, new fixtures—in fact, he only leased "space."

Over the years Lee's prospered. During the postwar suburban movement Lee's moved into the developing centers which projected the "quality" image Mickey's father demanded for his stores. The downtown location is still doing a good job as the Downtown Merchants Association has developed a successful "downtown mall" and traffic has held up fairly well. The metropolitan area has doubled since the war, and Mr. Lee now has two branches plus his downtown store and a regional mall has approached him to come in as "the" men's store. The two outlying stores are being managed by recent college graduates who have worked out satisfactorily, but Mr. Lee finds himself constantly in and out of the branches, and since he is managing the downtown store himself he is strapped for time at the moment. He doubts whether he can accept the new lease unless Mickey comes home and joins the team. Mickey has worked at Lee's since he could reach the displays and has always loved retailing—in fact, that's why the offers of the retail firms interested him. He wanted to work for a large company, get experience, and then perhaps (if things worked out that way) come home to dad.

Mr. Lee encouraged Mickey to do what appeared best for Mickey. In fact, he encouraged the "outside experience"—but deep down he wanted Mickey to say, "Dad, I'm coming home. You can teach me as much as any large firm and now we can take that new lease." Mr. Lee got his wish—Mickey, a "born entrepreneur," decided to return.

Lee's has a fairly sophisticated unit and dollar control system, but recently Mr. Lee has been concerned about his expenses being "out of line." The young managers need some controls, he believes. Thus Mickey's first "training job" (he'll take over the new store if things work out as planned) was to set up an "open-to-spend" for expenses for each store. Mickey went to work immediately, pouring over operating statements and trying to see where to start.

The following information is available for the entire company: sales—$1 million, with 50 percent in the downtown store and 25 percent each for the two branches. Expenses have not been broken down *by* store, but are as follows for the three stores: payroll—22.5 percent; advertising—3.7 percent; taxes—2.3 percent; supplies—2.8 percent; services purchased—1.3 percent; traveling—0.8 percent; pensions—2.4 percent; insurance—1.7 percent; depreciation—1.4 percent; professional services—0.5 percent; donations—0.2 percent; bad debts—0.5 percent; equipment costs—0.6 percent; real property rentals—4.0 percent; miscellaneous—1.2 percent.

Mickey also found that the operating profit for the company had been 4.2 percent of sales for the past year, that it had been maintained at about that level for some years, and that with other income and expenses, the net profit before taxes was about 4.4 percent. The gross margin had run at about 40.8 percent for the last few years.

The distribution of sales by months for the company had been: January, 8.9 percent; February 5.4 percent; March, 5.8 percent; April, 6.5 percent; May, 7.9 percent; June, 7.7 percent; July, 7.4 percent; August, 6.7 percent; September, 7.2 percent; October, 8.2 percent; November, 9.6 percent; and December, 17.5 percent.

Assume that you are Mickey. Work out an open-to-spend plan, by month, for each store for the next year based on the information you have on hand. Make any necessary assumptions.

Case 2. Mickey Lee (see Case 1 above) has been with his dad for several years. The new regional shopping center store has been open two years; Mickey is managing that store and is also assisting his father in "strategic" planning for the company. They are contemplating another branch in another trading area when the cost of capital is a bit more encouraging.

Because of Mickey's entrepreneurial spirit, and also because he knows that in the short run "plus" business will have to come from the existing stores, he has given serious thought to adding women's sportswear to the downtown store. A small adjacent shop is going out of business—it is a guild jewelry store whose young management confused the market by attempting to "trade down" and must now "call it a day." The space is sufficient for a decent assortment of junior and missy sportswear—no dresses as such; no shoes; just the "latest" in sports apparel and some fashion jewelry and handbags. Mrs. Lee has always wanted to "get involved," and with all of Mickey's sisters married she believes that she could run the new department.

Mickey is anxious to see whether the new venture can be profitable. He estimates that they should be able to do about $70 per square foot (the store is 50 × 100 feet), that total expenses will run about 35 percent, and that fixed expenses will be about $25,000. Mickey believes that they should aim for a net profit before income taxes of about 4 percent and a gross margin of approximately 38 percent.

You are Mickey. What are you willing to do with the information you now have?

20

HUMAN RESOURCES MANAGEMENT IN RETAILING

*R*etailing is fundamentally a "people business." Contributions that are made both by associates working directly in sales with customers and by those who work behind the scenes in sales-supporting departments greatly affect the growth and profit of the store. The management of retailing must be more concerned not only with the initial training of associates but with the training of supervisors to become better teachers for developing people to their maximum potential.

There is a further need to make jobs more interesting through enrichment; to create more professionalism in those associates who meet the public; and to develop pacesetters whose example will motivate others to perform and achieve to their maximum abilities. Yes, retailing is a people business, and growth will come easier through maximizing people's potential.

Fred J. Koch, Vice President of Personnel
and Organizational Development
Goldsmith's
Memphis, Tennessee

The manner in which we manage our human resources will ultimately determine the extent to which we achieve our objectives. . . . Human resource costs . . . in a typical store—that is, payroll, employee benefits, and personnel support services— represent approximately 70 percent of every expense dollar.[1]

Retailing has always been confronted with personnel problems. The wages of its lower management personnel and its salespersons are typically lower than those of comparable employees in most other industries. It usually provides only limited training. Each of us can probably recall instances in which we walked out of a store and never returned because of the rudeness or indifference of salespersons. Indeed, inadequately trained salespersons may lead to as many lost sales as the unavailability of merchandise.

Fortunately, top management is beginning to recognize the importance of human resources management and to acknowledge that personnel are likely to be a company's greatest weakness.[2] The traditional subordinate status of the personnel function has led to many of the problems in retailing, including poor salary administration techniques, limited and ineffective training programs for buyers and salespersons, the hiring of unsuitable persons, and government affirmative action programs. Moreover, in an era of inflation, personnel costs rise rapidly. Yet competitive pressures may keep retailers from raising prices.

Compounding the personnel problem is the poor reputation of retailing as a career path. In addition, low starting salaries, long working hours, and intense contact with a variety of different persons who enter the store are viewed as drawbacks.

Because of the increasing importance of human resources management in retailing, this chapter provides the student with current thinking about the various problems in this area. The objectives are to provide an overview of (1) the essentials of human resources planning and development; (2) the recruiting, selection, and training of personnel; (3) employee evaluation; (4) the compensation of employees; (5) union-management relations; and (6) motivation techniques.

THE DEVELOPMENT OF HUMAN RESOURCES

The remainder of this chapter focuses upon ways of making the personnel function an integral part of retailing. "For whatever the reasons, the personnel department in the typical store seems subdued—seems to have been relegated to confinement within rather narrow strictures. . . . personnel

---

[1] Ray A Lillian, vice president personnel and public relations, Belk Store Services, Charlotte, North Carolina, quoted in "Return on Inventory Investment Is Vital," *Stores,* February 1977, p. 35.

[2] "The Discounter Psyches Himself," *Department Store Economist,* July–August 1975, p. 25.

management appears categorized not only by a notable lack of enthusiasm or vitality but also by a deplorable absence of imagination."[3]

The following reasons have been offered for these conclusions:

(1) a simplistic approach to recruiting entry-level sales personnel that relies rather heavily on "walk-in" or "write-ins"—or on recommendations from their employees. . . .

(2) little or nothing is stipulated in the way of education background or prior working experience for most new sales applicants;

(3) inadequate interviewing; despite the fact that the personnel interview is the single most important tool in the selection process, it would seem that a typical interview of between 10 and 20 minutes duration may not permit enough probing for the interviewer to make a valid and lucid judgment. . . .

(4) little use of standardized tests. Although a number of standardized tests are available to assist the personnel department in selecting people, it appears that they are seldom used in the average department store—at least for entry-level sales applicants;

(5) over-emphasis on "on-the-job training." Although many stores do conduct formal classroom training, their programs, upon analysis, appear to reflect two interesting attitudes on the part of management: (1) to keep such training down to a minimum (in order to get the new sales people on the selling floor as soon as possible); and (2) to accent systems and techniques rather than salesmanship—a rather peculiar rerouting of priorities. . . .

(6) little use of incentive pay. . . . Moreover, some ⅔ of the stores reported a beginning hourly rate of between $2 and $2.25.[4]

HUMAN RESOURCES PLANNING

Can management develop human resources to achieve agreed-upon organizational goals? Human resources planning is the matching of management needs with human resources.

Employment planning occurs in all organizations, even though the planning may be informal in small stores. This planning provides the necessary framework and information for such personnel functions as recruiting, selection, and training.

The costs of improper selection

The costs of employee selection errors include: (1) the costs associated with hiring a person who does not perform satisfactorily (these include record-keeping costs, loss of customers, loss of goodwill, termination costs, and even lawsuits); (2) the costs associated with rejecting a person who

---

[3] Irving Bursteiner, "Current Personnel Practices in Department Stores," *Journal of Retailing,* vol. 51 (Winter 1975–76), p. 14 and 86.

[4] Ibid., p. 14.

would have made a successful employee (these include the costs of assessing additional applicants for the position).[5]

Forecasting human resources needs

Formal employment planning occurs in virtually all large retailing organizations today. The demand for retail employees depends upon the demand for the retailer's products and services. Thus, one way to determine personnel needs is to forecast the likely demand for an outlet's products and services over a specified period of time. Plans for expansion or perhaps plans to close a particular branch also provide a viable basis for employment planning. The personnel office needs to know what plans exist for opening or closing branches during the next one, two, or five years. This can help in both scheduling and training employees. At the store level, the types of forecasts necessary include an analysis of peak traffic hours so that less coverage can be arranged during off-hours. Part-time people play a particularly important role in such instances.

From a long-range perspective, the policy of having workers retire at age 65 must be reevaluated. Extrapolations into the 1980s indicate that the work force of the United States will be leveling off. Thus, management and labor shortages may cause companies to abandon mandatory retirement rules and induce older employees to remain. Furthermore, age discrimination violates the provisions of the Fair Labor Standards Act.

Job design and analysis

Employment planning and employee morale are enhanced by the development of job designs and/or descriptions. Job designs simply specify the methods and content of jobs. These are typically prepared at a level other than the personnel office, but generally are under the overall direction of the chief personnel officer.

Beyond job design, which is somewhat engineering-management oriented, job analysis is important in determining the tasks which the job will comprise. This requires an analysis of the skills, abilities, and responsibilities of the employee. Job descriptions or specifications are developed from job analysis.

Because of increased social awareness and government pressures, special human resources planning problems confront the personnel administrator. These include problems related to hiring the handicapped, women, minorities, veterans, and senior citizens.[6]

---

[5] Jan P. Muczyk, T. H. Matthiess, and Myron Gable, "Predicting Success of Store Managers," *Journal of Retailing,* vol. 50 (Summer, 1974), p. 48; also Matthiess, Muczyk, Gable, "A Longitudinal Validation of a Forced Choice Personality Test and Discriminant Analysis for Predicting Success of Store Managers," *Journal of Retailing,* vol. 53 (Spring 1977) pp. 3–16.

[6] Richard C. Sizemore, "Rules Shop Rite Discriminated against Female Employees," *Supermarket News,* May 9, 1977, p. 46.

RECRUITING, SELECTING, AND TRAINING EMPLOYEES

Recruiting

Recruiting is often not well established or well developed. More attention needs to be given to matching job needs with the interests and skills of the prospective employee. The recruiting·process has become increasingly complicated because of federal and state legislation requiring that various groups, such as women and minorities, be properly represented in the work force.

Legal requirements. The Age Discrimination and Employment Act of 1967 prohibits discrimination in the hiring of persons between the ages of 40 and 65. Thus, employees cannot be retired or terminated solely because of age until they are 65 years of age.[7] Older employees are often made to feel that they are inferior because they supposedly lack the energy, motivation, and dexterity which are found in younger people. They are often denied job opportunities simply because of age. However, if older persons remain employed, they are likely to be vested in pension systems and their wages will be higher than those of young persons. Currently, groups which represent the rights of elderly employees are attempting to eliminate company rules which force workers to retire at age 65.[8]

Title 7 of the Civil Rights Act of 1964 prohibits discrimination in hiring on the basis of race, national origin, sex, or religion. Particular attention has been given to the hiring of minority employees. At this writing, the courts have held that the percentage of minority employees working for a retail store should approximate that minority's percentage in the population of the community in which the store is located. If major differentials occur, the Equal Employment Opportunity Commission (EEOC) may conduct an investigation of the outlet. Large outlets are also required to prepare affirmative action plans showing how they plan to implement the EEOC regulations. Many states have antidiscrimination requirements similar to those of the federal government.

Court cases have indicated that these requirements will be fully enforced. The possible complications are reflected in an EEOC suit filed against the Houston-based Sakowitz department store:

A suit filed by the Equal Employment Opportunity Commission charges Sakowitz with discrimination against Blacks. The action contends that since 1965, through a variety of illegal methods, the Houston-based chain has not given Blacks equal employment opportunities. The areas of hiring, firing, layoffs, promotions and segregated job classification and placement were cited by the Commission.[9]

---

[7] "Forced Retirement," *Business Week*, December 6, 1976, p. 78.

[8] "Useful past 65," *Business Week*, March 8, 1976, p. 98.

[9] "EEOC Charges Sakowitz Bias," *Chain Store Age*, January 1976, p. 11.

The issue of discrimination in hiring has been even further complicated for management because the U.S. Supreme Court has held that a white male passed over for a less qualified black or a woman has the right to sue.[10]

Recruiting from within.   The practices of the firm also dictate the extent to which recruiting occurs. For example, some firms follow a policy of promoting from within. Thus, the only outside hiring may be for entry-level positions. This approach often assures higher employee morale and lower turnover. It also reduces training costs and gives the employer a longer period of time to evaluate candidates before deciding whether they are entitled to a promotion. The usual way of keeping records on promotable employees is through the use of a skills inventory coupled with performance appraisals, which the personnel office keeps on each employee in the organization.

Senior-level executives are not typically promoted from within the firm, however, particularly in large retail establishments. "Everyone wants a young 40-ish tiger from Allied Stores, Carter Hawley Hale, and especially Federated Department Stores, which has become the Procter and Gamble of retailing."[11]

Sources of applicants.   The typical source of employees for entry-level positions is the "walk-in" applicant. Other possible sources are state employment services, former employees, private employment services, trade schools, ads in newspapers and other media, and unions. Entry-level white-collar employees are recruited on college campuses. The advertising for job applicants must meet all the affirmative action requirements of the state and federal governments.

Selection

A variety of selection methods are available. These include personal interviews, tests, and recommendations. The personnel office must develop an objective approach which allows the best matching of persons and positions. The most satisfactory approach to this problem is to develop performance criteria. This involves identifying the characteristics of persons who perform a particular job in a superior manner. These characteristics are then sought in potential new employees. Ideally a limited number of characteristics can be isolated. Executives can then use the performance criteria to predict which applicants will perform satisfactorily. The predictors may include intelligence scores, tests of manual dexterity, formal education, and related job experience.

One potential problem facing the personnel manager is bias against some applicants because of the measures being used. Federal, state, and local governments are seeking to determine whether traditionally used selection

---

[10] "A Job-Bias Ruling in Favor of White Males," *Business Week,* July 12, 1976, p. 30.

[11] "In and out of Retailing's Revolving Door," *Business Week,* October 4, 1976, p. 58.

tools can lead to bias in hiring. Companies can continue to use various employment tests if it can be shown that the tests are valid and reliable in predicting job success. This requires the use of statistical techniques, including coefficients of correlation and other measures. Tests may be biased against minorities because of the inability of minority applicants to read or write well or because the tests are not geared to the cultural backgrounds of minorities. For example, in a federal lawsuit against Bullock's department stores, the EEOC contends that Bullock's "uses pre-employment testing procedures that result in rejection of a disproportionate number of minority applicants."[12]

The need to avoid any type of bias was pointed out in the *Duke Power Company* case. Chief Justice Burger stated:

What is required by Congress is the removal of artificial, arbitrary, and unnecessary barriers to employment when the barriers operate invidiously to discriminate on the basis of racial or other impermissible classifications. . . . Far from disparaging job qualifications as such, Congress has made such qualifications the controlling factor, so that race, religion, nationality, and sex become irrelevant.[13]

The burden of proof rests with the employer. The employer must be able to prove that the procedure utilized is capable of predicting job performance. Arbitrary job descriptions which specify age, sex, minimum educational levels, and similar requirements are open to challenge. Also, employers cannot legally advertise under separate male and female classifications or discriminate between married and unmarried persons.

The personnel department typically interviews and tests all job applicants, particularly for entry-level positions. Each applicant then sees and talks with the person who will function as an immediate supervisor. The supervisor is not permitted to ask questions about such matters as the person's age, marital status, number of children at home, religion, and creed.

Training

Training refers to any effort to increase the skill effectiveness of employees. As shown in Table 20–1, it is the largest personnel problem facing retailers. Every employee needs a minimum of training. In addition, a basic orientation to job expectations and work requirements is necessary. Special hiring and training programs should be designed to increase the percentage of women and minorities in the work force. Programs for women may take less tailoring than those for minorities. However, both groups face motivational and social adjustment problems which have to be addressed.

---

[12] "Bullock's Faces Bias Charge," *Chain Store Age*, May 1975, p. 8.

[13] Carl F. Goodman, "What Is the Real Meaning of Equal Employment Opportunity?" in *Judicial Mandates for Affirmative Action* (Washington, D.C.: National Civil Service League, 1973), pp. 13–14.

TABLE 20–1
WHAT IS THE BIGGEST PROBLEM YOUR COMPANY
IS FACED WITH IN PERSONNEL?

Problem	Percent mentioning
Lack of training	33%
Government and union requirements	19
Unmotivated personnel	15
Recruitment	11
Turnover	4
No problems	7
No answer	11

Source: "The Discounter Psyches Himself," *Department Store Economist,* July–August 1975, p. 25.

Problems with retail salespersons are a major cause of the growth in consumerism. Too often salespersons today are discourteous or unresponsive and have no product knowledge. "Large organizations are often characterized by a lessened sense of employee responsibility. Retailing employees may feel alienated in a complex organization, which may be compounded by union allegiance separate from the organization."[14] Training programs should stress that the firm is in business to serve the customer and to lessen the problems of shopping. Product knowledge should be provided, and positive attitudes toward customers should be developed.

New employees need to be assured that their opportunities for success are not limited. They also need to know the supervisors and to become familiar with the work environment. During the initial orientation and training, information should be provided on compensation and benefits, personnel practices, and the products and services offered by the outlet. It is desirable to provide some of this information prior to actual employment. The benefits of training can include increased worker productivity, greater customer satisfaction, and improved employee morale.

A far too typical attitude toward training was reported by the chairman and chief executive officer of Gimbel Brothers:

When I asked the personnel director in one of the stores how his executive development worked, he prided himself on the fact that it didn't cost the company a thing. "When we need an assistant buyer," he told me, "we hire someone right off the street, give them a do-it-yourself training book, and that's how they get trained."[15]

One of the problems leading to the collapse of W. T. Grant was an overexpansion which did not include enough training. "The expansion program placed a great strain on the physical and human capabilities of the

---

[14] Larry J. Rosenberg, "Retailers Responses to Consumerism," *Business Horizons,* October 1975, p. 39.

[15] "Kramer's Campaign to Rebuild Gimbel," *Business Week,* March 29, 1976, p. 34.

company. . . . our training program could not keep up with the explosion of stores. . . . thus it did not take long for the mediocrity to show."[16]

Formal training is characterized by the allocation of specific blocks of time for employee instruction in job-related skills and attitudes. Formal training programs are typically offered through the personnel department. Ideally, persons specializing in employee training are utilized because the success of formal training depends largely on the ability of the instructor. "In retailing, the future of productivity lies in training."[17]

The most common forms of training for new employees are on-the-job and off-the-job training. The most common method utilized in retailing is on-the-job training. The experienced employee is placed in a work environment and is instructed by a supervisor or an experienced employee. This is a relatively inexpensive process. However, allowances should be made to ensure that employees are satisfied, that equipment is not damaged, and that instruction is provided by qualified personnel.

Off-the-job training consists of training in specialized classrooms which are separate from the work environment. The choice of methods is dictated by costs, the skills of the instructor, and the efficacy of the various materials in facilitating learning. Training aids range from cases and chalkboards to movies, slides, and closed-circuit TV. Programmed instruction is also popular. The most frequently used methods are lectures and conferences. If the trainer is skilled in communication and experienced in his or her specialty, these methods can be cost effective.

EMPLOYEE EVALUATION

Employees are evaluated as a basis for wage and salary recommendations, promotions, and transfers; to correct deficiencies in work habits; and to reinforce positive work habits.

Formal performance evaluation is accomplished through the use of instruments which reflect the criteria upon which the evaluation of employees is based. Large retailing organizations use formal systems which are designed to make evaluations as objective as possible. Evaluations are made often (usually semiannually or annually) in informal organizations. If a union is involved, criteria should be developed in conjunction with the union, or the union should be given the opportunity to participate in the decision.

For entry-level employees, evaluation typically occurs twice a year. For higher level employees, annual evaluations are typical. The immediate supervisor usually conducts the performance evaluation. Occasionally, a person is rated by all supervisors with whom contact occurs on a regular basis.

---

[16] "Investigating the Collapse of W. T. Grant," *Business Week,* July 19, 1976, pp. 60–61.

[17] "Motivated Sales People: Key to Independents' Productivity," *Stores,* March 1975, p. 7.

A variety of techniques exist for employee evaluation. These include ranking scales and checklists. The newest approach to performance appraisal is called management by objectives (MBO). This provides for the creation of goals and a self-appraisal by the employee, which are discussed with the immediate supervisor. Figure 20–1 shows part of a performance evaluation rating format typical of that used by many large retailers.

Careful attention must be given to the standards utilized in employee evaluation. Supervisors must evaluate all employees on the same basis. The subjectivity implied in such words as *adequate* and *satisfactory* may cause distortions in evaluations by different supervisors. Another problem is that supervisors may rate all employees within a narrow range. Distortion may also occur because of racial differences between supervisors and employees. Moreover, a supervisor who has recently experienced dissatisfaction with an employee may evaluate that employee unfavorably even though the employee's overall performance has been satisfactory.

Whatever the methods of evaluation, management should provide evaluation interviews for employees and communicate the results of the evaluation. Both the supervisor and the employee should sign and/or witness the evaluation form. Employees who disagree with the evaluation should be given the opportunity to write an explanatory statement for the personnel record.

EMPLOYEE COMPENSATION

Compensation is the way in which employees are rewarded for their labor. Methods of compensation vary widely. Levels of compensation depend upon market conditions, union requirements, and economic conditions. The federal and state governments play an increasingly important role in compensation through legislation and wage controls. The most recent U.S. experience with wage controls occurred during the early 1970s.

The most familiar wage guideline is the minimum wage which must be paid to employees engaged in commerce. Few exceptions exist to this requirement. The minimum wage was raised to $2.30 per hour in 1976. Companies who do not pay the minimum wage to employees are subject to prosecution. For example, in 1975 the Winn-Dixie supermarkets were ordered by a federal judge to pay workers $1 million for minimum and overtime wage violations.[18] It has been proposed that the federal minimum wage be indexed at 60 percent of the wage earned by the average manufacturing production worker. Some persons contend that enactment of this proposal would sound the "death knell for many convenience food stores."[19]

All persons who perform the same job and have comparable backgrounds, abilities, and seniority must receive equal rates of pay, regardless of

---

[18] "Back Pay Owed, Winn-Dixie Told," *Chain Store Age*, August 1975, p. 12.

[19] "Minimum Pay Raise Seen Bantam Bane," *Supermarket News*, March 21, 1977, p. 1.

FIGURE 20–1
TYPICAL APPRAISAL RATING FORM

Name: _____

Date hired: _____

Job number: _____

Starting date of present job: _____

	Un-satis-factory	Fair	Good	Very good	Ex-cep-tional	Cur-rent rating
1. Job knowledge: use of practical knowledge and know-how related to present job	1	2	3	4	5	3
2. Judgment: ability to use facts and apply sound judgment	1	2	3	4	5	4
3. Attitude: enthusiasm shown for job; loyalty to company and superiors; ability to accept criticism and changes in company policy	1	2	3	4	5	3
4. Dependability: reliability in carrying out orders with efficiency	1	2	3	4	5	4
5. Creativity: ability to show imagination in job and offer suggestions for improvement	1	2	3	4	5	2
6. Association with fellow workers: ability to get along with others	1	2	3	4	5	2
7. Quality of work produced	1	2	3	4	5	4
8. Attentiveness: willingness to earn new skills or new methods	1	2	3	4	5	4
9. Honesty and integrity	1	2	3	4	5	3
10. Leadership: ability to work through others and motivate fellow workers	1	2	3	4	5	1
11. Self-confidence and self-motivation	1	2	3	4	5	2
12. Analytic ability: ability to analyze problems	1	2	3	4	5	1
13. Emotional maturity: emotional stability	1	2	3	4	5	3
14. Use of safety practices	1	2	3	4	5	5

Total points 41

Evaluated by: _____

Source: Robert W. Eckles et al., *Essentials of Management for First-line Supervision* (New York: John Wiley and Sons, 1974).

age, ethnic background, or sex. Personnel officers need to be thoroughly knowledgeable about the provisions of the Fair Labor Standards Act of 1937, which has been amended several times, most recently in 1976. The main provisions of this legislation concern minimum pay, payment for overtime in excess of 40 hours during a given week, child labor, and equal rights.

Job evaluation

How does an employer decide how much to pay for the performance of different jobs? The decision-making process begins with job evaluation. Effectiveness measures are difficult to apply. Thus, job evaluation often includes an analysis of the know-how involved in a job, the extent of problem solving, and accountability.[20]

The purpose of job evaluation is to pay employees an equitable wage. If employees are paid an equitable wage and provided with realistic benefits, their productivity and their morale should be higher, and their turnover lower. Employees should perceive their wages and benefits as equitable in terms of their inputs.

Wage structures must be developed to provide guidelines for compensation. The usual approach is to develop wage patterns through the use of wage surveys. They are designed to help the organization determine whether its wages are on a par with those paid for comparable jobs in other organizations in the area. Data on wages may be shared by firms; trade data may be used as a basis for comparison; or private organizations may provide information on wage rates.

Methods of compensation

When all of the above matters have been determined, the retailer decides how compensation is to be paid. A straight salary which is paid for work performed during a specified number of hours is the most common method. This method is particularly useful when productivity is difficult to measure.

Commissions may be paid in place of straight salaries to employees who are compensated on the basis of productivity, such as salespersons. More often, such employees are paid a combination of salary and commission. This modification avoids unnecessarily aggressive selling, which may cause customer dissatisfaction. The payment of straight commission also runs the risk of having salespersons ignore people who appear less likely to make a purchase.

A variation of the salary-commission plan is the bonus system, whereby employees are paid a bonus or commission for all sales above a quota previously agreed upon. Table 20–2 provides an overview of the more

---

[20] Harold D. Janes, "Issues in Job Evaluation: The Union View," *Personnel Journal*, September 1972.

TABLE 20–2
FOUR COMMON RETAIL COMPENSATION PLANS—SALES AND
SALES-SUPPORTING PERSONNEL

Types	Basic formula	Common positions covered by plan	Primary advantages	Primary disadvantages
Straight salary	Paid for stipulated pay period	Office employees and nontechnical sales areas	Easily understood and easy to calculate and administer	Lack of incentive
Salary plus commission	Base salary plus small additional percentage	Areas of goods where special effort might get plus sales (draperies, garden shop, etc.)	Incentive to sell more	Somewhat complicated in dealing with small amounts
Quotas	Different dollar levels of goals established at which varying percentages of sales are paid	Selected big-ticket departments or departments in which money incentives usually produce extra effort (furniture, shoes, carpeting, etc.)	Establishes a "target" for employees needing an incentive and can result in sales of more high-markup merchandise	Can become complicated to administer—especially difficult to substantiate factors used in establishing quotas
Straight commission	This is truly the incentive plan. Compensation based on percentage of sales—percentage usually goes up on price lines within a specific line of goods to encourage selling volume-profitable items	Women's coats, men's suits, furniture, carpeting, outside drapery sales, major appliances, building supplies, etc.	From employer point of view, sales performance directly tied to sales results. From employee point of view, easy to understand and a true incentive: compensated directly for efforts made	Salesperson often doesn't take care of "small-ticket" customer and uses high pressure to close sales

Source: *Learning Experiences in Retailing* by C. Winston Borgen, p. 124. Copyright © Goodyear Publishing Company, 1976. Reprinted by permission.

common ways of compensating persons in sales and sales-supporting positions.

Indirect compensation

In addition to salaries and wages, employees receive indirect compensation, which is a form of tax-free income. This may be equal to 25 percent or more of employee salaries. William Glueck has identified the following common types of indirect compensation: (1) legally required benefits which meet financial emergencies and difficulties for employees: Social Security, unemployment, and compensation payments, and worker's compensation (for accidents); (2) pension and retirement programs; (3) pay for time not worked: vacation, holidays, leave; (4) insurance: life, health, and accident.[21] In retailing, indirect compensation may also include merchandise discounts as well as spiffs, or push money, for selling discontinued merchandise, special brand names, or whatever.

For management personnel in retailing, the typical compensation plan is salary plus a percentage of the sales or profits. Some plans include stock options or guaranteed deferred retirement income.

UNION-MANAGEMENT RELATIONS

Unionized employees are becoming increasingly important in retailing. The subject of unions is beyond the scope of this chapter. Entire courses are taught on it. However, we need to understand the problems and opportunities created by unions. Unions strive to achieve a variety of goals for employees, including employment protection, safer working conditions, higher wages, and more formalized rules and procedures in such areas as promotion, salary increases, and dismissal.

The Wagner and Taft-Hartley Acts

Retailers face a variety of laws in dealing with unions. The most important of these is the National Labor Relations Act (the Wagner Act), as amended by the Labor-Management Relations Act of 1947 (the Taft-Hartley Act).

Union contracts are typically negotiated every year or two. Both workers and management then agree to abide by the terms of the contract until the next bargaining period. However, difficulties often occur during the interim period. The union then represents the employees to management in efforts to resolve differences in contract interpretation and also in handling employee complaints and grievances.

Grievance procedures

Employee grievance procedures should be established even in the absence of unions. These procedures are simply a formalized process for handling complaints. If a firm is unionized, grievance procedures and channels are, or should be, established through contract negotiations.

The advantage of grievance procedures is that they can expedite the settlement of small problems. A typical grievance procedure begins with an employee indicating a grievance to an immediate supervisor either orally or

[21] William F. Glueck, *Personnel: A Diagnostic Approach* (Dallas: Business Publications Inc., 1974), p. 451.

in writing. The supervisor makes an attempt to resolve the grievance. If the grievance cannot be solved at that level, it is then appealed progressively up the hierarchy. With union involvement, the final step is arbitration of the grievance before an independent board—usually the Federal Mediation and Conciliation Service (FMCS) or the American Arbitration Association (AAA).

Disciplinary actions

Disciplinary actions are an important component of the human resources function. The most common disciplinary problem in retailing is employee theft. One analysis determined that 50 percent of the employees admitted taking things from their employer.[22] Alcoholism and drugs have been increasingly frequent problems. One key in dealing with employees is to communicate policies and work rules and to make certain employees understand that the work rules are related to job effectiveness.

Increasingly, the question is being asked whether an employer can terminate a person who refuses to work on the Sabbath. For example, "a former employee has charged Korvettes with firing him for his refusal to work Sundays."[23] Civil rights laws state that this is not legal unless the refusal creates "undue hardship" for the company. However, "undue hardship" is a vague term. Employees who do not want to work on Saturday for religious reasons include Orthodox Jews and Seventh-Day Adventists. The following guidelines have been suggested in helping to determine whether a personnel manager can terminate an employee who will not work on the Sabbath:

Can you fire an employee who won't work on the Sabbath?

Yes, if . . .   No other employee has the skills to substitute for him. The job requires availability around the clock. The extra costs involved would hurt competitively. Employee discontent reaches "chaotic" proportions. His absence makes it unsafe for others.

No, if . . .   His absence is merely an inconvenience. A replacement would demand premium wages. Other employees would merely be resentful. Others would want the same time off privilege. Union provisions require the assignment.[24]

A formal procedure for discipline is necessary. This may begin with an oral reprimand, which may be followed by a written reprimand and then by a disciplinary suspension without pay. Management should keep a written record of these occurrences in employee personnel files. Steps must be taken to ensure that the employees' rights are protected at all times and that they

---

[22] Ronald L. Tatham, "Employee Views on Theft in Retailing," *Journal of Retailing*, Vol. 50 (Fall 1974), p. 53.

[23] "Korvettes Denies Religious Firing," *Chain Store Age*, March 1977, p. 22.

[24] Reprinted from "The Employer's New Worry: Saturday Work," *Business Week*, March 15, 1976, by special permission. © Copyright 1976 by McGraw-Hill, Inc.

receive copies of all relevant communications and are aware of their meaning.

MOTIVATION

"A human resources approach is one that emphasizes the maturation and development of people. The most powerful tool in the process is the selective reinforcement of successful behavior with immediate rewards."[25] Poor morale is characterized by increased turnover, excessive absenteeism, high grievance rates, and poor job performance. Research by Jacob Siegel and Dennis Slevin, for example, has revealed that "both buyers and department managers experience a relatively high degree of need dissatisfaction relative to other occupational groups. It appears from these data that these groups of retail personnel are receiving far less from their job than they feel that they should."[26]

Other researchers have also commented on the pressures, frictions, and conflicts facing retailing personnel. The high-pressure environment of the retail department store buyer is particularly evident because of friction as buyers battle for better positions on the floor, increased advertising allocations, and increased open-to-buy allowances.[27] Research has stressed the need for maximum discretion for retail store buyers.[28]

Managers of branches are better able to fulfill their esteem and self-fulfillment needs than are those in the main office. Perhaps it is because these managers have more autonomy and more discretion in decision making and thus achieve more self-fulfillment.[29]

The work-related behavior of employees is influenced by their attitudes toward work and life. Management must cope with these attitudes to the extent that they impinge on employee productivity. The following generalizations have been provided about the relationship between personal characteristics and job satisfaction:

1. *Age.* Job satisfaction is high when the person first starts work; it declines and stays low until the late 20s, begins to rise in the early 30s, and goes up until almost the end of the work career.
2. *Sex.* Women tend to be slightly less satisfied than men, but this is probably because of the lack of significant opportunities for them in the work place.
3. *Skill utilization.* The more the worker perceives he is using his skills or is actually using them, the more satisfied he is. . . .

---

[25] "Human Resources Management and Retailing," *Retail Control,* April–May 1976, p. 4.

[26] Jacob P. Siegel and Dennis Slevin, "Need Satisfaction and Performance of Department Store Buyers and Department Managers: Implications for Management," *Journal of Retailing,* vol. 50 (Spring 1974), p. 89.

[27] J. Liff, "Purchasing Policies for Seasonal Style Goods: A Case Study and Analysis," unpublished dissertation, Yale University, 1969.

[28] Claude R. Martin, Jr., "The Contribution of the Professional Buyer to a Store's Success or Failure," *Journal of Retailing,* vol. 49 (Spring 1973), p. 80.

[29] Reid A. Harvey and Robert D. Smith, "Need Satisfaction and Retail Management: An Empirical Study," *Journal of Retailing,* vol. 48 (Fall 1972), p. 91.

4. *Job characteristics.* The more specialized or smaller the job, the less satisfied the job holder is. The more equitably the employee feels he is paid compared to those he works with, the more satisfied he is. The higher the level in the organization, the more satisfied the person is.[30]

Increased motivation leads to better job performance. Recognition for a job well done is a key in motivation. For example, Maison Blanche instituted a program based on employee needs for recognition. Its incentive programs are divided into three categories: awards, motivational programs, and contests. Awards consist of cash or trips which are given for a variety of reasons, such as length of service and detection of sales check errors. Motivational programs include merchandise certificates on special occasions and for ideas. Contests are staged for salespersons who compete to exceed overall quotas developed for them.[31]

Robert Fulmer has combined the basic theories of Abraham Maslow with the thinking of Frederick Herzberg, as shown in Figure 20–2. Herzberg be-

FIGURE 20–2
COMPARISON OF THE MASLOW AND HERZBERG MODELS

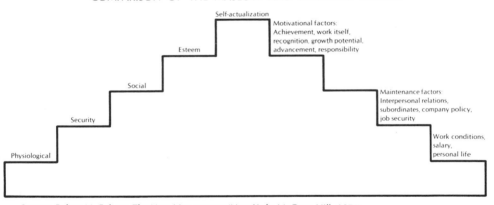

Source: Robert M. Fulmer, *The New Management* (New York: McGraw-Hill, 1974).

lieves that the first factors involved in any job situation are maintenance characteristics, such as compensation and working conditions. Only after these characteristics are present can the worker begin to feel motivation. The following dimensions of satisfied and dissatisfied workers have been identified:

1. What motivates employees to work effectively?
   A challenging job that allows a feeling of achievement, responsibility, growth, advancement, enjoyment of the work itself, and earned recognition.

---

[30] John M. Ivancevich and James H. Donnelly, "Job Satisfaction Research: A Manageable Guide for Practitioners," Reprinted with permission of *The Personnel Journal*, © copyright March 1968; see also Leslie Kanuk, "Leadership Effectiveness of Department Managers in a Department Store Chain: A Contingency Approach," *Journal of Retailing*, vol. 52 (Spring 1976), pp. 9–16.

[31] "Motivated Sales People," p. 7.

2. What dissatisfies workers?

    Mostly factors peripheral to the job—poorly conceived work rules, poor light-ing, regimented coffee breaks, inconsistency in awarding job titles, overemphasis (or underemphasis) on seniority rights, inadequate raises or fringe benefits, and the like.

3. When do workers become dissatisfied?

    When opportunities for meaningful achievement are eliminated, they are sensitized to their environment and begin to find fault.[32]

SUMMARY

The personnel function is a key to profitable retail operations. Labor costs constitute the largest single category of expenses. Yet the reputation of retail-ing is still one of paying low wages, employing primarily part-time workers, and having poor working hours. Increasing numbers of stores have tried to go to self-service to avoid these people problems.

Nevertheless, management must still grapple with the problems of recruit-ing, selecting, training, motivating, compensating, and promoting employees. A professional personnel manager is necessary to cope with these prob-lems. This is particularly true because of the increasing stress on affirmative action programs. Major problems have also emerged in the use of traditional employee screening devices, such as testing.

Motivation remains a key problem. Money alone is not sufficient motiva-tion, particularly given the wages which many retail employees earn today. Employees must be given the opportunity to realize higher level needs. This may mean giving them more responsibility in the execution of jobs. These types of problems also require placing greater stress upon training em-ployees to keep them up-to-date with the latest technology and to have them feel that they are a viable part of the organization.

KEY CONCEPTS

The development of human resources
  Human resources planning
    Job designs
    Problems of improper selection
  Recruiting, selecting, and training
    Legal problems
    Types of recruiting
    Performance criteria
  Employee evaluations

---

[32] M. Scott Myers, "Who Are the Motivated Workers?" *Harvard Business Review,* February 1964, p. 73, copyright © 1963 by the President and Fellows of Harvard College; all rights reserved.

Employee compensation
  Wage structures
  Methods of compensation
Union-management relations
  Legal dimensions
  Grievance procedures
Motivation

DISCUSSION QUESTIONS

1. What are the key federal and state regulations which affect the personnel recruitment, training, and compensation process? What are the likely effects on the retailer of these regulations?

2. Explain why the most severe problems of retailing continue to be people problems as opposed to technical problems.

3. What are the desirable characteristics of a supervisor?

4. Discuss the various methods of compensating employees. Which is likely to be the most effective for a retail salesperson? an accountant? a department buyer?

5. What do you perceive as the keys to increased productivity among retail employees?

6. Assume that you are the owner of a small retail organization and that rumors are circulating that efforts will be made to unionize your outlet. What steps can you take to deal with this problem? Discuss the likely long-run effects of the alternative courses of action which are available to you.

7. What do you perceive to be some of the special needs in retail employment of minorities, women, and the aged? What can be done to make these people feel that they are a valued part of the retail organization?

8. What are the likely effects on the personnel function of the trend toward increased Sunday openings and longer daily hours for retailers, including outlets that are open 24 hours each day?

9. Assume that you are the manager of a men's clothing outlet located close to a major university campus. What do you perceive as the basic elements of a training program for the outlet? How are the dimensions of your planned training program likely to differ from the type of training which might be offered to new employees who have recently been hired by Sears, Roebuck?

PROJECTS

1. Devise a format, and interview at least five people who have worked in the retailing industry in some capacity. Your objective in the interview is to determine the individual's honest views on wages, working conditions, superior-subordinate relationships, and so on. Prepare a report for class discussion on what you have discovered.

2. Secure an employee evaluation form from a local business. What types of specific criteria are used, and for what purposes? Do you think that the criteria are valid? Can you suggest others?

3. Select several retail companies (differing in organizational arrangement, number of stores, sales volume, and product line), and make an appointment with the executive responsible for the personnel functions in each store. Describe the employment process of each store (include selection, training, and benefits, including compensation) and draw comparisons among them. See whether you can explain the differences in the apparent effectiveness of the programs. See whether you can get the executives you visit to discuss affirmative action.

4. Arrange through your college or university placement office to spend a few minutes with all the recruiters coming to campus to interview people for retailing companies. Structure a questionnaire to administer to each recruiter to find out what he (she) is looking for in a student; how the campus interview enters into the selection process; what kinds of questions are asked of the interviewee; what the recruiter expects the interviewee to know about the company; what variables are considered in evaluating the student; and what subsequent steps are taken in the employment process.

CASES

Case 1. Sally Bright has just received her MBA degree and wants to enter the junior executive program with Austin's Department Stores, a large department store chain. Sally has heard that Austin's is interested in hiring women for this program in the immediate future, so she arranges an interview.

During her interview, Sally learns that the main reason Austin's has for hiring women into its Junior Executive Program is to comply with federal equal opportunity requirements. Sally resents this, but takes the job with Austin's anyway, as the opportunities look promising.

After she has worked at Austin's for a while, Sally meets Jim Sharp, who also has an MBA and is also in the Junior Executive Program. Sally learns that Jim is making $100 more per month from Austin's than she is, yet they both were hired at about the same time. Sally is furious about this. She had thought that discrimination in pay because of sex was a thing of the past. She announces that she is going to confront the personnel manager about this.

If you were the personnel manager, how would you handle Sally's case?

Case 2. Louise Fischer accepted a job with The Vanity, a major department store in a medium-sized Southern town. She is a high school graduate and has decided that she does not want to go to college. On the first Monday she reported to work she was introduced to the other people in housewares, her department, shown how to operate the POS terminal, and made aware of store guidelines concerning employee behavior. On Tuesday, Ms. Smith, the head clerk, was to help her get adjusted. Tuesday turned out to be a disaster. There had been an ad in Monday night's paper for a sale in housewares, and customers were waiting for the doors to open. The first transaction was a charge sale, but the woman did not have her card. The customer was in a hurry to get to work and was asking technical questions about the coffee pot she had selected. Louise explained that the head clerk was sick and that she had just started, but the woman began to get aggravated. In addition to this, the department manager was in a staff meeting. Louise forgot how to use the terminal, and amid all the bustle she went to the personnel office and quit.

Do you think a situation of this kind is common? What steps could be taken to avoid such situations?

PART SIX

RETAILING TOMORROW

In this final part of *Modern Retailing* the focus is on the dynamics of retailing as a potential career opportunity and upon the future as the forecast changes might affect the career opportunities as well as the institutions and strategies of management.

This part should perhaps be read in a very personal way by the student. The subject of this text has already been thoroughly covered and your points of view may have been strengthened or perhaps changed, by what you have read thus far. How you react to the final two chapters will be determined in large measure by how you were affected by the earlier text materials. We see opportunity, dynamics, management challenge, and perhaps most of all, un certainty. The real entrepreneur accepts all this and responds in the free enter- prise spirit. "Retailing Tomorrow" is for the imaginative, courageous, and ambitious person of *today*. Consider this well.

21

CAREERS IN RETAILING

The field of retailing has grown at an astonishing rate, expanding in every direction, utilizing the most advanced technologies, leadership techniques, and communications methods. Retailers are looked to by all as innovators—visionaries—the new captains of industry. Yet, paradoxically, they have consistently failed in what should have been their simplest task, that of informing the student and the academic community that a career in retailing is rewarding, exciting, challenging, and very important—available.

For too long we have allowed the beginner to perceive of our industry as the "last-resort career," demanding much and returning little. If we are to grow, we can only do so with the finest, the most vital, and the most enthusiastic men and women of all disciplines. It is now time for the retail industry to unveil its best-kept "trade secret," that it can offer more people better jobs and faster rewards than any other industry in this country. Retailing not only provides "equal opportunity" in its fullest sense—but better opportunities.

Howard P. Korchin
Vice President, Personnel
Robert Hall Clothes
New York

If . . . you can see using hard rock to sell bell bottoms and special inlaid writing desks to sell engraved stationery, and like the idea of running your own enterprise on our money and can make an executive decision on asparagus or architecture, snow tires, or see-through fashions, and can join in on a conference call with San Francisco and Paris, France, and like the idea of being located in the South, check out Burdines![1]

In Kresge, the entire growth pattern is geared to the continual recruiting and training of young people. We believe this program is our strongest asset. We fully expect to increase the management training program to keep pace with our continual expansion program of 70–75 new K marts each year. . . . Young people and good personnel training programs gearing them for rapid advancement are the keys to Kresge's past success and our exciting and fast growing years ahead.[2]

You know that J. C. Penney is big, diversified, and steadily growing every day. What you may not know is how little time it really takes to accept responsibility in the J. C. Penney organization. Thousands of capable young men and women have proved the worth of our extensive on-the-job and in-classroom training programs by succeeding in the exciting world of retail merchandising. We offer great futures in store management, merchandise buying, catalog operations, systems and data processing, auditing, accounting, and many other stimulating career paths.[3]

Career development and career education are natural aspects of human development. Career development consists of more than simply training for a specific job. Admittedly, training for vocational or occupational skills is necessary. However, if persons do not push forward to develop the totality of their human resources skills, progress in retailing, as in other management positions, is likely to be limited. Thus, the material presented in this chapter is designed to serve both as a guide to college students in their own development as human beings and as a framework within which to discuss the potential career patterns of persons who are considering careers in retailing.

The very fabric of a nation is reflected in its retail institutions—in the merchandise they sell, their prices, their advertising, and so forth. Retailing probably offers more variety than does any other career opportunity. You can select a store to match your personality—all the way from the most swinging "with-it" establishment to the ultraconservative and fashion-conscious firm. Consider, for example, the vast differences in the personnel, merchandise, and personality of such stores as Sears Roebuck, K-Mart, and Saks. Whether you are motivated by money, the possibilities for rapid advancement, or a pleasant environment, retailing may be for you.

Total employment in retailing exceeds 13 million persons.[4] **Thus, retailing** employs more persons than manufacturing, insurance, real estate, construction, or many other fields. The opportunities are so diverse as to be almost

---

[1] Company brochure.

[2] Company brochure.

[3] Company brochure.

[4] *Employment and Earnings,* May 1976, p. 55.

beyond one's imagination. Retail establishments are located all the way from the smallest rural village to the most sophisticated metropolitan area. The opportunity exists to fulfill almost every kind of ability, ambition, and desire. Further, employment in retailing and wholesaling is forecast to increase by 26 percent between 1972 and 1985.[5]

Given the employment possibilities in retailing, the objectives of this chapter are:

1. To examine the characteristics which best describe a career in retailing management.
2. To examine the diverse types of employment opportunities.
3. To familiarize students with typical training programs in retailing.
4. To present the advantages and disadvantages of owning your own business.

Let's look at some of the employment aspects of this exciting career path.

CHARACTERISTICS OF CAREERS IN RETAILING

Security

To many persons, security in a job is important. Retailing offers a high degree of job security. Even during periods such as the major recession of the early 1970s, retailing suffers far less in employment declines than does manufacturing or wholesaling. The reason is that persons must continue to buy merchandise, regardless of the state of the economy. Merchandise offered at reasonable prices will always be in demand. Thus, steady employment in retailing is likely, regardless of the economic condition of the nation.

Decentralized job opportunities

All persons, regardless of where they live, must purchase merchandise on a regular basis in order to maintain an adequate standard of living. Thus, the possibility of becoming successful in retailing exists even if a person does not want to move far from home. Surely a satisfactory employment opportunity can be found in the 2 million retail stores located in the United States. For persons wishing to move frequently, the opportunity for employment in retailing will be present wherever they decide to go.

The diversity of retail institutions

The U.S. Census of Business lists more than 80 different types of retail firms, ranging from drugstores to camera shops. Further opportunities exist in service establishments or in nonstore retailing, such as catalog merchandis-

---

[5] U.S. Department of Labor: *Occupational Outlook Handbook* (Washington, D.C.: U.S. Government Printing Office, 1974), p. 17.

ing. Each of these retail career opportunities requires different types of skills and abilities. Table 21–1 shows a limited number of the types of retailing opportunities available.

The largest number of job opportunities are in eating and drinking establishments. This is probably because of the rapid boom in franchising. Gen-

TABLE 21–1
NUMBER OF EMPLOYEES BY TYPE OF RETAIL FIRM,
DECEMBER 1976

Type of establishment	Number of employees (000s)
Retail trade, total	13,106.0
General merchandise	2,620.1
Department stores	1,772.1
Mail-order houses	146.1
Variety stores	316.8
Food stores	1,975.8
Grocery, meat, and vegetable stores	1,792.9
Apparel and accessory stores	812.0
Men's and boys' clothing and furnishings	140.8
Women's ready-to-wear stores	303.2
Family clothing stores	129.2
Shoe stores	164.2
Furniture and home furnishings stores	523.2
Furniture and home furnishings	319.0
Eating and drinking places	3,352.1
Other retail trade	3,823.0
Building materials and farm equipment	616.5
Automotive dealers and service stations	1,705.2
Motor vehicle dealers	769.2
Other automotive and accessory dealers	318.4
Gasoline service stations	617.6
Miscellaneous retail stores	1,501.3
Drugstores and proprietary stores	477.4
Book and stationery stores	79.5
Farm and garden supply stores	130.8
Fuel and ice dealers	97.9

Source: *Employment and Earnings*, January 1977, pp. 75–76.

eral merchandise retailing, particularly department stores, ranks second. Other major employers are food stores and automobile dealers, service stations, and other automobile-related businesses.

Opportunities for advancement

Because of the large number of retail establishments in the United States, many executive positions exist. Retailing is continuing to expand, and positions in management are being created on a basis proportionate to this expansion.

Retailing has long presented a lucrative career opportunity for women. Approximately 47 percent of all retail employees are women, as shown in

TABLE 21–2
NUMBER AND PERCENT OF WOMEN EMPLOYEES BY
TYPE OF RETAILING, JANUARY 1976

Type of employment	Number (000s)	Percent of total employment
Retail trade, total	6,075.0	47
General merchandise	1,712.9	68
Department stores	1,186.0	70
Mail-order houses	77.7	64
Variety stores	218.4	70
Food stores	775.2	40
Grocery, meat, and vegetable stores	662.7	37
Apparel and accessory stores	540.3	67
Men's and boys' clothing and furnishings	62.8	44
Women's ready-to-wear stores	266.0	88
Family clothing stores	88.9	71
Shoe stores	62.9	38
Furniture and home furnishings stores	160.4	30
Furniture and home furnishings	104.8	33
Eating and drinking places	1,820.9	57
Other retail trade	1,064.9	28
Building materials and farm equipment	115.3	20
Automotive dealers and service stations	249.0	15
Motor vehicle dealers	96.1	13
Other automotive and accessory dealers	51.4	16
Miscellaneous retail stores	700.6	47
Drugstores and proprietary stores	296.8	61
Book and stationery stores	38.5	49
Farm and garden supply stores	29.5	22
Fuel and ice dealers	20.2	19

Source: *Employment and Earnings,* May 1977, p. 63.

Table 21–2. The percentage of women employed in various types of retail trade varies widely. It ranges from a high of 88 percent in women's ready-to-wear stores to a low of 13 percent among motor vehicle dealers. Probably more women are employed in retailing than in any other sector of the economy.

Promotional opportunities are available for women in retailing. Department stores, for example, may give preference to women as buyers, particularly in high-fashion specialty stores. Women also occupy a sizeable number of executive positions in retailing. However, on the whole, retailing opportunities above the position of buyer still remain somewhat limited for women.

Salaries in retailing

As Table 21–3 shows, average weekly earnings are lower in retailing than in other major categories of employment. The data in this table are for nonsupervisory persons and exclude the salaries of persons in executive and

TABLE 21–3
AVERAGE WEEKLY EARNINGS OF NONSUPERVISORY WORKERS
BY TYPE OF INDUSTRY, MARCH 1977

Type of employment	Average weekly earnings
Mining	$294.50
Contract construction	288.51
Manufacturing	220.80
Transportation and public utilities	271.20
Finance, insurance, and real estate	165.07
Services	153.38
Retail trade, total	118.06
Retail general merchandise	111.23
Department stores	115.53
Mail-order houses	147.03
Variety stores	82.37
Food stores	145.96
Grocery, meat, and vegetable stores	150.55
Apparel and accessory stores	96.94
Men's and boys' clothing and furnishings	121.66
Women's ready-to-wear stores	83.42
Family clothing stores	100.26
Shoe stores	97.92
Furniture and home furnishings stores	151.43
Furniture and home furnishings	156.52
Eating and drinking places	77.81
Other retail trade	147.33
Building materials and farm equipment	166.66
Motor vehicle dealers	198.97
Other automotive and accessory dealers	166.83
Drugstores and proprietary stores	106.70
Book and stationery stores	124.86
Fuel and ice dealers	186.12

Source: *Employment and Earnings,* May 1977, pp. 82–94.

management positions. Beginning salaries for nonsupervisory positions in retailing are often at the minimum hourly rate established by the federal government.

The salaries of college graduates who enter retail trainee programs are also somewhat low. However, advancement can be rapid, and within five to ten years salaries earned in retailing are equal to or higher than those paid by other industries. College graduates entering training programs can expect their starting salary to increase more than three times by the end of ten years. Typical starting salaries for college graduates entering retail trainee programs are from $600–$800 per month, with an average of $6,500–$9,500 per year.

Few people achieve top executive positions in retailing simply because not many of these positions are available. However, salaries at the top are very high. For example, in 1976 the Federated Department Stores chairman of the board received a salary of $450,000; the Sears chairman, $423,000;

the J. C. Penney chairman, $352,000.[6] These figures exclude fringe benefits, such as pension plans, profit sharing, and insurance. Board chairmen of department stores with annual sales of between $5 million and $50 million received a median salary of $67,000 in 1975. In other executive positions in retailing, salaries ranged from a median of $39,000 for a merchandise manager to a median of $15,000 for a top security executive.[7] For highly specialized persons, such as those who are known for salvaging ailing companies, salaries as high as $1,000 per day may be paid for several months while a company's problems are being resolved.[8]

Even though few top-level executive positions are available in retailing, experience at all levels of retailing management prepares potential entrepreneurs for self-employment and store ownership, which can be very lucrative. Business ownership is discussed in some detail in the final section of this chapter.

Nonmonetary rewards

A person's abilities and efforts—or their absence—are quickly recognized in retailing. The position of store manager appeals to persons with the ability to organize and direct the activities of others. As store manager, you can set your own sales and profit goals, as well as control expenses, compensate employees, and perform other vital management functions. In effect, you have the opportunity to manage your own business with someone else's money. In addition, a management career in retailing offers the opportunity to work with ideas in seeking to create ways of increasing sales and profit through the imaginative use of the variables of the retailing management mix.

The diversity of job skills

When retailing is mentioned, most persons think primarily in terms of selling or perhaps of working as a cashier. Yet, these positions make up only a small proportion of the total number of retail job opportunities. Consider, for example, the need for fashion experts, accountants, specialists in advertising, personnel specialists, market researchers, and lawyers. We can go even farther and think in terms of public relations, restaurant operations, engineering, data processing, real estate analysts, and physical distribution specialists. Thus, you should not think only of the persons with whom you typically come in contact when making purchases; rather, you must try to visualize the complex organization behind most retail outlets. Figure 21–1

---

[6] "Executive Compensation," Business Week, May 23, 1977, pp. 62–63.

[7] "Department Stores' Executives Increased Compensation in '75," Wall Street Journal, March 11, 1976.

[8] "Abercrombie's Misfire," Time, August 23, 1976, p. 55.

FIGURE 21–1

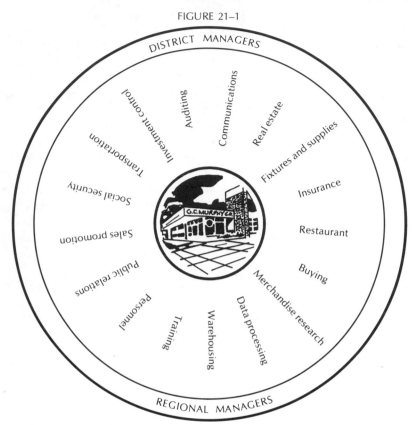

Source: G. C. Murphy Company brochure.

shows some of the myriad job opportunities which are available in a typical large retailing organization.

Working conditions

Working conditions in retailing are comparable to those in most other areas of employment. The typical workweek is 40 hours, but some overtime may exist at peak periods. Work in the evenings and on weekends is common. These hours are also common in manufacturing with its shift work, in medicine, and law, and in various public service occupations, such as utilities and protective services.

Retailing offers basically the same fringe benefits package as do other sectors of employment, including vacations, sick leave, college tuition programs, group life insurance, and merchandise discounts. Many retail companies have stock purchase plans which provide excellent retirement opportunities. Sears has been a pioneer in this respect. Working conditions in retailing will continue to improve during the coming years.

Typical employment categories

Despite the diversity of employment in retailing and despite the job opportunities which are typically not thought of as being in retailing, five areas of employment are probably common to all retail establishments, as was noted in Chapter 4.

Merchandising is one of the most important areas of employment. It encompasses the buying and selling of merchandise. Trainees typically start out in this area because it is the heart of the store and offers the greatest opportunity for advancement. Buyers work with suppliers in selecting merchandise for their outlet, work with advertising and display in the promotion of the merchandise, and may travel worldwide in seeking the latest fashions. The next position up from buyer is that of merchandise manager, which typically includes the supervision of several buyers of related types of merchandise. Exposure to selling occurs in the rotation of the trainee through the various departments in the outlet.

Operations management is really the sales support component of management. It includes general store management, warehousing, receiving, delivery, maintenance, security, and customer service. Some of this work may be done in a distribution center or a service building and not in the retail outlet.

The *sales promotion* function is closely related to merchandising. Job responsibilities in this area include advertising, display, public relations, and fashion coordination. Persons seeking careers in sales promotion must have a flair for originality and creativity in developing unusual merchandise displays and in keeping the store's name constantly before the public. For example, creative writing skills and artwork are highly desirable. Preferred job opportunities may include those of a copywriter, a decorator, or perhaps an art director.

Persons working in the *control* area of retail management are responsible for the management of the company assets. Persons with skills in statistics, accounting, and data processing and analysis are likely to be particularly at home in this area. Such functions as credit, accounts payable and receivable, auditing, and data processing are needed in this aspect of store management.

Individuals in *personnel training* are responsible for the recruitment, selection, placement, and termination of employees. They also administer the employee benefit and incentive programs, may engage in trade union negotiations, and handle training programs for both salespersons and executives. The success of all aspects of the retail firm depends upon the comprehensiveness and high quality of its training programs.

STUDENT PERCEPTIONS OF RETAILING

Professor Barbara Coe of New York University conducted a survey among over 2,100 junior and senior college students from 41 colleges and universities in the United States. The focus of the survey was student attitudes to and perceptions of retailing as a career.

Social status

The students' perceptions indicate that retailing does not have a high image as a type of business with which to begin a career. As shown in Table 21–4, retailing ranks with government and insurance as among the least

TABLE 21–4
STUDENT PERCEPTIONS OF THE SOCIAL STATUS OF RETAILING*

Type of firm	Least desirable working conditions	Lowest starting salaries	Least long-term earnings opportunities	General public opinion: Least desirable	Friends' opinion: Least desirable	Social prestige: Least desirable	Family opinion: Least desirable
Retail	2	1	2	2	3	2	3
Consumer products	9	9	9	9	9	9	9
Industrial products	1	8	8	4	4	4	6
Government.....	3	3	1	3	1	1	2
Insurance	4	4	4	1	2	3	1
Brokerage	5	6	6	5	6	6	5
Bank	6	2	3	8	5	7	7
Advertising agency	7	7	7	6	8	7	8
Airline	8	5	5	7	7	5	4

* The lowest rating is 1; the highest, 9.
Source: Used with permission. Barbara Coe, "A Survey: Attitudes of Select Business Students toward Retailing as a Career Field," New York University, 1975.

desirable employment opportunities. Among the nine types of employment possibilities surveyed, retailing was perceived to offer the lowest starting salaries. It was also perceived to be either second or third lowest in the following categories: working conditions, long-term earnings possibilities, general public opinion, the view of friends, social prestige, and the opinion of one's family.

Job opportunities

However, as noted in Table 21–5, students ranked retailing as offering the most rapid advancement and the largest number of available job opportunities, and as second highest in career goal satisfaction. Retailing was ranked third in opportunities for service to the community.

TABLE 21-5
STUDENT PERCEPTIONS OF JOB OPPORTUNITIES IN RETAILING

Type of firm	Advancement: Most rapid	Present job opportunities: Most	Present job opportunities: Best	Career goal satisfaction: Highest	Service to community: Most effective
Retail	1	1	5	2	3
Government.....	7	3	4	6	1
Insurance	6	4	7	9	6
Industrial products	4	5	2	4	7
Brokerage	8	9	8	8	8
Bank	5	7	6	5	2
Advertising agency	3	6	3	1	5
Airline	9	8	9	7	9
Consumer products	2	2	1	3	4

Source: Used with permission. Barbara Coe, "A Survey: Attitudes of Select Business Students toward Retailing as a Career Field," New York University, 1975.

Students choosing a career are motivated primarily by money and management responsibility, as shown in Table 21-6. Indeed, out of all the students surveyed, only 15 ranked social status as the most important in deciding on career objectives and only 68 mentioned contribution to society.

TABLE 21-6
RANK ORDERING OF FACTORS INFLUENCING
STUDENT OCCUPATIONAL CHOICES
IN CAREER PLANNING

Basis	Ranking
Money	1
Management responsibility	2
Rapid progress........................	3
Contribution to society	4
Social status.........................	5

Source: Used with permission. Barbara Coe, "A Survey: Attitudes of Select Business Students toward Retailing as a Career Field," New York University, 1975.

Bases of career choice

Based on the above information, it is not possible to determine the social status of retailing. A person who is asked to state his or her occupation is not likely to reply "I work in retailing." For example, if the person were employed with Sears, Roebuck, the reply might be, "I am an accountant," "I am an attorney," "I am a real estate appraiser," "I am a department manager," and so forth. Jobs of this type are likely to receive a higher social status rating from the general public.

TRAINING PROGRAMS IN RETAILING

Let's now look at the typical structure of junior executive training programs in department stores and chain stores and the likely levels of progression which can be expected for students in these programs. These are examples only, but they are typical of what the young college graduate may encounter when beginning a career in retailing.

Let's look first at the opportunities in department stores.

Department stores

Burdine's. Burdine's is an affiliate of Federated Department Stores and has home offices in Miami, Florida. It operates 12 stores. Figure 21–2 and 21–3 illustrate the Burdine's junior executive training program for store managers and the various other possibilities in sales-supporting careers. The program, as is true for most department stores, is basically an on-the-job

FIGURE 21–2
PATHWAYS TO MERCHANDISING AND STORE
MANAGEMENT*

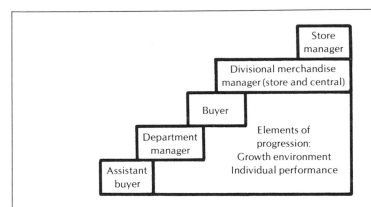

Assistant buyer: Step one. Work in a buying office. Learn what and how to buy, merchandise planning and presentation. Discover how to run a business . . . with our money!

Department manager: Progress! You have major responsibilities for running a business in one of our branch stores. Now you apply what you've learned and get quick results!

Buyer: You made it! You're totally responsible for a multi-million-dollar business. Now you may travel to Europe, New York, California . . . wherever you can buy goods to make us grow.

Beyond buyer: Keep going . . . and growing! Be promoted to divisional merchandise manager, to store manager, and beyond. Demonstrate top ability, and the future with us is virtually limitless!

* Similar positions and growth opportunities exist in Finance, Operations, and Personnel Management.

FIGURE 21-3

In <u>Control</u> areas a trainee will move through the diversified areas of sales audit, accounts payable, internal audit, credit, and accounting.

Trainees in <u>Operations</u> gain experience through assignments in warehousing, receiving and marking, distribution, and operations.

The accent is on people in <u>Personnel</u>. The opportunities exist in store personnel management, employment, and training.

<u>Sales Promotion</u> means creating an image of our stores, our merchandise, and our services, and then communicating this image to our customers and potential customers. Such communication is accomplished through media advertising, displays, public relations, fashion shows, and special events.

Source: Company brochure.

training experience. The trainee is given as much responsibility as possible in the early stages of the program. During the training period, classes are held and the trainees are familiarized with the philosophies and operating policies of the company. As shown in Figure 21–2, the typical progression through the company is assistant buyer, department manager, and buyer. More advanced positions than that of buyer are also available.

Rich's. The history of Rich's, now a Federated affiliate, is closely tied to the history of Atlanta and the Southeast. About a dozen Rich's stores are located throughout the Southeast. In addition, Rich's operates the Rich Way chain of discount stores, Rich's Bake Shops, and Rich's II boutiques. Rich's has over 200 selling departments and almost 400 nonselling positions, ranging from advertising to data processing. Sales exceed $300 million a year, and the organization employs over 12,000 men and women.

As noted in Figure 21–4, the Rich's progression sequence typically begins with the head of sales position. From this position, one can follow the sales manager route, which leads to the position of store manager, or else move through the positions assistant buyer and buyer to become a divisional merchandise manager.

FIGURE 21–4
MERCHANDISING STORE MANAGEMENT

Rich's executives are characterized by their talent, ability, drive, and zest for the fast-paced competitive atmosphere of retailing. These attributes are more important at Rich's than specific degree requirements because the scope of opportunity here covers so many fields of interest.

It is important to understand that, while retail operations are basically categorized as either merchandising or sales management, Rich's executives are not limited to emphasis in one category or the other. On the contrary, Rich's believes that executive potential is maximized by liberal experience in both areas, the pace and sequence of progress being frequently evaluated on an individual basis.

Rich's places management candidates in responsible positions at competitive salaries immediately and complements this invaluable experience with advanced classroom seminars.

The sequence of positions illustrated may be generally described as follows:

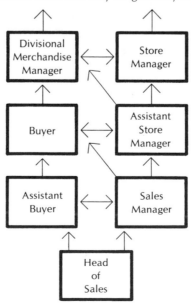

FIGURE 21–4 (continued)

Head of sales: Retailing at its primary level, including supervising department salespeople, implementing buyers' merchandising directives, and maintaining the department's inviting, attractive appearance.

Sales manager: Works with department buyer and store management to effect the best flow of merchandise; supervises heads of sales.

Assistant store manager: Works closely with the store manager in all phases of store operations.

Store manager: Charged with full responsibility for the smooth and profitable operation of a Rich's store, from the location, appearance, and staff of each department, to storewide events and customer relations.

Assistant buyer: The understudy, practicing the challenging, mercurial craft of acquiring merchandise customers will want and seeing that it sells. Under a buyer's guidance, assistants learn the processes of planning, selection, and purchase, sales promotion, and branch distribution, and develop the insight and sense of timing that make a good buyer.

Buyer: The pivotal position in retailing, dominated by astute, perceptive, quick-thinking individuals. At this level the retail process achieves critical focus as each buyer assumes full control over a department.

Divisional merchandise manager: All buyers within a division report to a DMM who supervises overall divisional planning and operation, including financial and budgetary considerations.

Source: Company brochure.

Overview. The training programs in most department stores involve rotation among the various departments until the trainee is familiar with all store operations. In the smaller stores, promotion depends upon the openings which become available. Thus, upward progression may be rather slow and somewhat limited.

In a larger store, the maximum period which a trainee is likely to remain in a store is two to three years. Progression beyond the training program is likely to involve transfer to smaller branch stores and gradually back to larger stores for various executive-level positions.

The progression through a retailing organization depends at least in part on the organizational structure. For example, in a highly centralized structure more executive-level opportunities will exist in the corporate or division headquarters. However, in a more decentralized operation, where most of the necessary functions are decentralized to the local level, additional opportunities may exist in the branch stores.

Chain stores

Let's now look at examples of the executive development programs and progression routes typical of chain stores. They are not very different from those of department stores. One difference is that the chains are likely to have more store opportunities available than do the department stores because of the larger number of outlets in chains.

Woolco and Woolworth.   The F. W. Woolworth Company operates over 2,000 stores under the Woolworth and Woolco names. As such, it is one of the largest retail organizations in the nation. Indeed, its multi-million-dollar sales place it in the top 100 corporations in annual sales.

Woolworth and Woolco try to open up to 50 new stores a year, which means literally hundreds of potential jobs in management. Large numbers of jobs thus also exist in such diverse areas as advertising, accounting, public relations, transportation, warehousing, and restaurant management.

The Woolworth and Woolco training programs consist of three one-year training sequences. The first sequence consists of basic on-the-job training in a variety of sales-supporting activities; the second consists of supervisory training; and the third consists of specialized training which prepares you either for general management positions or for more specialized functions in the structure of the company.

Kresge—K mart.   The S. S. Kresge Company is also one of the larger retailers in the United States. Major retail innovations apart from the traditional Kresge variety stores are the K marts, the largest discount operation in the country. The K marts offer a broad array of merchandise with discount pricing and central service checkout. The goal of the Kresge company has been to open one K mart per week.

To meet the ever-changing general merchandising needs, Kresge's management training program offers the latest techniques and innovations.[9] Kresge's offers a clearly defined, challenging career inviting the full use of trainees' abilities—a career leading to personal satisfaction and continued growth. The company's low managerial turnover is attributed largely to its thorough training program. The Kresge philosophy is that success is experienced by the people who know their responsibilities and how to expedite them effectively. The Kresge management believes that successful people usually stay where their chances for advancement are a known factor; thus, Kresge's promotes its employees from within. The president of the company started as a stockroom trainee.

The training at Kresge's involves learning:

Proper procedure for receiving and checking merchandise.

Correct methods for pricing, classifying, and storing.

How to fill out claim forms.

Proper methods of checking and closing out invoices.

The importance and measures of guarding against waste wherever possible.

The mechanics of purchasing merchandise.

---

[9] Information in this section is from the recruiting brochure *A Career With K mart.*

Service supervision and customer relations.

The purposes and uses of sales promotion bulletins.

How to make counter changes and maintain an attractive store.

Kresge's has a four-month orientation program which is the real test of trainees' potential—in reality a probationary period. Every six months a progress report is prepared and discussed with each trainee. Copies are sent to headquarters.

After a trainee's ability is proved in the orientation program, the trainee is ready for the first promotion—assistant manager. This promotion, like each promotion that follows, is usually to another store. This broadens training under different managers and in stores doing various volumes of business. The assistant manager has charge of a definite store area and of a specified group of departments. These are rotated approximately each six months during the training period.

After a number of promotions, the responsibilities of an assistant manager are almost equal to those of a manager. The assistant manager receives increasingly intensified training and special help from the manager and the district manager until a managership becomes available. Prior to the actual appointment to manager, the prospective manager is required to attend a seminar at Kresge International Headquarters in Detroit for one week. Each executive officer participates in the program, and seminar participants have an opportunity to raise questions and to discuss current topics concerning company policies with top executives.

Kresge's management proclaims that substantial autonomy exists for their store managers and that the return on investment is the individual manager's responsibility. Actual performance determines a manager's future progress.

Franchising. Numerous other retail employment opportunities have emerged because of the boom in franchising. Steak and Ale, McDonald's, and others routinely recruit and train assistant managers, pay well, and offer good chances for advancement into ownership or management.

EMPLOYMENT OPPORTUNITIES IN SMALL RETAIL ESTABLISHMENTS

As we have noted elsewhere in this text, almost 2 million retail establishments are in operation in the United States. Approximately two thirds of these have fewer than four employees. Overall, 90 percent are single-unit independent establishments.[10] Thus, most retail businesses are small by almost any definition. Many students choose to begin their retail careers with small establishments because of a desire to participate in and perhaps ultimately manage a family business.

---

[10] Paul L. Pleiffer, *Retailing,* Small Business Bibliography No. 10 (Washington, D.C.: U.S. Small Business Administration, 1975), p. 2.

Students who contemplate beginning their careers with a small retail establishment should probably do so only for the initial experience unless they will have the opportunity to buy into the business or unless the business is family owned. However, beginning in a small retail firm exposes a person to all aspects of the retail business almost immediately.

BUSINESS OWNERSHIP

Compared to other segments of the U.S. business structure, retailing offers far more opportunities for ownership than do other lines of business. Indeed, one has only to look at the classified ads in almost any newspaper to identify retail establishments which are for sale.

Many suppliers, wholesalers, and others will work closely with a person in establishing a retail outlet. Many lucrative opportunities also exist through franchising arrangements, though such arrangements place severe restrictions on the management. Increasingly, voluntary wholesale chains are working with independent supermarkets to help them buy land and build an outlet. The voluntary wholesale chains may also provide some of the financing.

The small retailer has some operating advantages which make it possible to compete very effectively with large-scale retail operations. Retailing is still largely local in nature despite the massive size of many of the chain organizations. A store trading area is relatively small, and all retail outlets tend to be regarded as local in nature. An independent retailer can offer tailor-made hours, products, and services which may be unavailable from a larger firm.

Risks of ownership

All of us are familiar with the going-out-of-business signs which we encounter in the windows of numerous retail establishments. It is the rare

TABLE 21–7
FAILURE RATE BY CATEGORY OF RETAIL TRADE
(first four months of 1976)

Category of trade	Number	Percent
Food and liquor	153	9.7
General merchandise	57	3.6
Apparel, accessories	219	13.9
Furniture and home furnishings	215	13.7
Lumber, building materials, and hardware	73	4.6
Automotive group	224	14.2
Eating and drinking places	307	19.5
Drugstores	41	2.6
Miscellaneous	285	18.1
	1,574	99.9

Source: Dun and Bradstreet, Business Economics Division, *Monthly Failures*, June 19, 1976, p. 2.

retailer who makes a conscious decision to go out of business. Even though the failure rate is high in retailing, individuals should not be discouraged from starting their own businesses, because the rewards, both monetary and psychological, can be substantial.

Failure by line of business. As noted in Table 21–7, eating and drinking places, automotive firms, furniture and home furnishings, and apparel and accessory stores have the highest level of failure among the general categories of retailing. General merchandise stores and drugstores have the lowest overall failure rates.

As shown in Table 21–8, the highest failure rate among specific retail lines is in men's wear, followed closely by women's ready to wear, infants' and

TABLE 21–8
RETAIL LINES RANKED BY FAILURE RATE

Line of business	Failure rate per 10,000 operating concerns
Men's wear	73
Women's ready-to-wear	62
Infant's and children's wear	57
Sporting goods	57
Furniture and furnishings	56
Cameras and photographic supplies	49
Gifts	45
Appliances, radio, and television	40
Department stores	38
Shoes	37
Books and stationery	34
Lumber and building materials	34
Auto parts and accessories	29
Dry goods and general merchandise	27
Bakeries	22
Automobiles	20
Drugs	20
Eating and drinking places	19
Jewelry	19
Hardware	17
Toys and hobby crafts	14
Groceries, meats, and produce	12

Source: *The Business Failure Record, 1974,* Business Economics Department, Dun and Bradstreet, Inc., New York, 1975, p. 6.

children's wear, and sporting goods. The lowest failure rates are in food stores, toy and hobby shops, hardware stores, and jewelry stores.

What are still other ways of viewing the record of failure in retailing? As shown in Table 21–9, the failures by size of debt are primarily in the $25,000–$100,000 category. Over half of total retail failures are in this group.

Early failure likely. The first five years in the life of a retail firm appear to be crucial. As shown in Table 21–10, approximately two thirds of all retail

TABLE 21–9
SIZE OF LIABILITIES IN RETAILING FAILURES
(first ten months of 1976)

Size of debt	Number	Percent
Under $5,000	55	1.6%
$5,000–$25,000	732	20.8
$25,000–$100,000	1,816	51.5
$100,000–$1,000,000	873	24.7
$1,000,000 and over	51	1.4
	3,527	100.0%

Source: Dun and Bradstreet, Business Economics Division, *Monthly Failures,* January 29, 1977, p. 1.

firms fail within the first five years of their existence. Survival for this period of time appears to significantly enhance the chances for future survival.

Causes of failure.   The most typical reasons for failure of retail firms, as shown in Table 21–11, are incompetence, unbalanced experience, lack of experience in the line of retailing in which the merchant is engaged, and similar experience-related categories. Failure because of neglect, fraud, or disaster is relatively rare. By analyzing the causes of retail failures, students interested in starting their own businesses will learn to place special emphasis on acquiring the management knowledge and skills necessary to prevent these types of problems from arising.

As a rule of thumb, you probably should make mistakes for others before investing venture capital in your own business. Four or five years invested in

TABLE 21–10
AGE OF FAILED RETAILING ESTABLISHMENTS

Age	Percent
One year or less	2.1%
Two years	16.1
Three years	22.3
Total three years or less	40.5%
Four years	15.6%
Five years	10.1
Total five years or less	66.2%
Six years	6.1%
Seven years	4.4
Eight years	3.1
Nine years	2.8
Ten years	2.0
Total six–ten years	18.4%
Number of failures	4,234

Source: *The Business Failure Record, 1974,* Business Economics Department, Dun and Bradstreet, Inc., New York, 1975, p. 10.

TABLE 21–11
CAUSES OF RETAIL FAILURES IN 1974

Underlying causes	Percent
Neglect	1.6%
Fraud	0.9
Lack of experience in the line	18.3
Lack of managerial experience	13.9
Unbalanced experience*	22.9
Incompetence	37.6
Disaster	1.1
Reason unknown	3.7
	100.0%
Number of failures	4,234
Coverage liabilities per failure	$252,635

* Experience not well rounded in sales, finance, purchasing, and production on the part of the individual in the case of a proprietorship, or of two or more partners or officers constituting a management unit.

Source: *The Business Failure Record, 1974,* Business Economics Department, Dun and Bradstreet, Inc., New York, 1975, p. 12.

working for a large retail establishment may help you to avoid many errors which can lead to the failure of your first business.

Think about franchising

Major benefits can accrue to the aspiring young retailer by becoming a franchisee for a well-established franchise system. Such systems provide a safer investment opportunity and also perhaps the opportunity to earn more money than would be possible through a nonfranchised arrangement. Among the advantages of the franchise route are assistance in location, the opportunity to buy merchandise through a centralized purchasing system, proven management procedures and training programs, and system-wide coordination of advertising and promotion.

In return for the above advantages, the franchisee will have to pay a franchise fee and perhaps a percentage of sales to the franchisor. In addition, the franchisee will have little opportunity to operate as an entrepreneur, since franchising is a system and the franchisee must operate as a part of the system. Thus, control over many activities may have to be given up.

Growth opportunities still appear to be good in franchising. Franchise sales in 1976 increased by approximately 18 percent over 1974. The most rapid franchise growth has been in the service areas—specifically, in such businesses as tax preparation, real estate sales and rentals, secretarial services, exercise clubs, and day-care centers. By 1980, "franchise sales are expected to reach $285 billion, reflecting an annual growth rate of 10 percent annually between 1976 and 1980."[11] If you are interested in further information about franchising, you may want to review Chapter 8.

AN OLD OR A NEW BUSINESS?

The aspiring owner-manager has the option of either buying an existing business or establishing a new one. This decision is subjective.

The possibility of purchasing an existing business depends on the availability of the desired type of business, its location, and whether population and purchasing power are large enough to allow a satisfactory return on investment. Moreover, a successful existing business has a large amount of goodwill in terms of community acceptance which may inflate the purchase price above the appraisal value. Entering business can be much quicker if an existing firm is purchased, since the equipment and merchandise inventory already exist, as do the bookkeeping system and contacts with suppliers.

Establishing a new business offers major advantages, including new stock, new fixtures, the possibility of employing the latest thinking in layout, and no payment for goodwill.

Determining the necessary investment is a rather straightforward process. The process includes an appraisal to establish a purchase price, attorneys' fees, inventory, cash flow contingencies, and living expenses until revenue is generated by the store. Funds may be secured from such conventional sources as a bank or perhaps through the Small Business Administration. Still, in the final analysis, the capital put into the business by the owner is probably the most important source of funds. Many suppliers may be willing to finance the initial inventory and perhaps store equipment. Many other questions have to be answered which are beyond the scope of this chapter. These include questions about the legal form of organization, the details of financing, accounting procedures, and similar matters. Most small business management texts discuss such problems in detail.

SUMMARY

Nearly 2 million small businesses are in existence in the United States. Most retail establishments are small and have fewer than four employees. However, most of us are also familiar with such giants of retailing as Sears, A&P, and Penneys.

Retailing probably offers more diversity in employment opportunities than does any other career path. Too often we think only in terms of sales when retailing is mentioned. However, numerous retail opportunities also exist in real estate, accounting, data processing, physical distribution, personnel management, and a host of other areas.

A career in retailing offers more job security than do other types of employment, the opportunity for employment in large and small communities,

---

[11] *U.S. News and World Report,* May 10, 1976, p. 10.

and opportunity for rapid advancement because of the large number and the diverse types of retail establishments. Starting salaries are low, but long-term earnings possibilities are good.

Training programs in retailing are rather well spelled out, particularly for the larger department and chain stores. These training programs may last from six months to three years and include extensive on-the-job training. At that point a choice can be made among numerous career paths within the firm.

Many students of retailing aspire to operate their own businesses. Numerous opportunities for success exist, but the likelihood of failure is also high. One of the safer approaches to operating one's own business is to become part of a franchise system. However, in this way one loses a degree of the control over the business which is present in a truly independent operation. In general, retailing requires a lower initial capital investment for getting started than does any other type of business.

KEY CONCEPTS

Career development	Training programs
Characteristics of retailing careers	Small business
Employment opportunities	Failure rates in retailing
Student views of retailing	Franchising

DISCUSSION QUESTIONS

1. Why do you think the social status of retailing appears to be low? What do you think can be done to improve the situation?

2. What are the employment possibilities for women in retailing? Why should women consider a career in retailing? Are the reasons different for women than for men? Why or why not?

3. What is the typical progression through a training program in a large department store?

4. What factors are likely to have an impact on the desirability of retailing as a career for the next several years?

5. If you are planning to own and operate your own retail business in the next few years, what types of experience do you think it would be best for you to obtain?

6. If you are thinking about opening a business, what are the advantages of becoming affiliated with a franchise system as opposed to owning your own business?

7. Why are starting salaries so low in retailing? Should salary be an important consideration in choosing a career?

8. What are the major categories of employment opportunities in retailing? What basic personality and skill characteristics are required for success in each of these major categories of employment?

PROJECTS

1. Write to a select number of different types of retail organizations, and ask for any "career information" which they have. From the information received, make up a summary chart comparing and contrasting the various "career components" which a potential management trainee (or merchandise trainee) in retailing would want to evaluate. Attempt to get information on such matters as entry salary, promotional opportunities, and career options.

2. Assume that you have been out of school for several years. You have been in a nonretailing position (assume any position you wish to), and you want to change career patterns. You want to investigate retailing as a career opportunity. Outline the process that you might go through to assist you in your information gathering. Then assume that you decide on retailing as a career. What sources are available in your job search? Do an inventory of the steps you will take and of the information you can accumulate. Then do a *marketing job* on yourself and prepare to offer yourself to the type of organization which you believe will offer you a good future.

3. In your local community, determine the different opportunities which exist in the retail field for college graduates. For each firm you investigate, find out about the entry level for college graduates, about the kinds and lengths of training programs, about promotional steps up the management ladder, and if possible, about entry-level salaries and promotion opportunities. Prepare a retail "career chart" for the community based on your investigation.

22

RETAILING AND THE FUTURE

*A*s retailers, we are in existence at the pleasure of our customers. We always have to ask ourselves, "What more am I offering or providing the customer than my competitors?" The degree to which we answer this question correctly for the benefit of the customer determines our success as individual retailers.

It is important, therefore, that the future wants, needs, and desires of customers be determined in order to better serve them. The size of the various customer segments must also be quantified and projected. Four trends in consumer behavior are particularly evident today. They are:

1. The increasing importance of value to the customer.
2. Consumerism.
3. The growing importance of life-style merchandise to the customer.
4. The equally important regard of the customer for a clearly focused marketing strategy.

These trends are expected to have long-term impact, and the more quickly we as retailers recognize and respond to them, the more effective we will be in serving customers.

Joseph L. Hudson, Jr.
Chairman and Chief Executive Officer
The J. L. Hudson Co.
Detroit, Michigan

607

The retailing management concept requires a close and continuous monitoring of the various environments facing retailers so they can adjust their management philosophy to reality. The benefit of such monitoring is that it enables retailers to respond aggressively to change. Given the rapid changes in our economy and our society during recent years, to do otherwise would simply be management by crisis. Early warning signs of eminent changes in the operating environments of the firm often exist, and the retailer must address these before they become too powerful to deal with. Among the changes which impacted retailing during the late 1960s and early 1970s were materials shortages, the oil crisis, rapid inflation, consumerism, air and water pollution controls, occupational health and safety legislation, and a host of other problems. Retailing is a dynamic sector of the economy and is subject to the impacts of many variables.

More than ever the management of change will be the key to successful retail management. Retailers are now adjusting to the need to assess the effects of their actions from the perspective of the environmentalist and the consumerist. Increasingly the monitoring of rapid social change will also be necessary. Within the next few years we are likely to see the futurist as a person who is important in the executive suite. This may sound a little farfetched, but ten years ago who would have thought that specialists in the environment or in social responsibility would be occupying executive positions?

MONITORING SOCIAL CHANGE

Professor George Cabot Lodge views the rapidly changing social dimensions of society as follows:

The United States is in the midst of one of the great transformations of Western civilization. What is happening is that the old ideas and assumptions which once made our great institutions legitimate, authoritative and confident are fast eroding. They are slipping away in the face of a changing reality and are being replaced by different ideas and assumptions which are as yet ill-formed, contradictory and shocking. This transition is neither good nor bad. There is the possibility of plenty of both. The point is simply that it is taking place.[1]

Indeed, as Ian H. Wilson of GE's business environment research operation has stated, "Identifying shifts in people's basic values is the single most important element in forecasting the environment in which organizations must operate in the future."[2]

Tracking shifts in people's attitudes, values, and behavior patterns is difficult and complex. We have as yet to develop the necessary tools to make this task part of standard operating procedure. However, retailers simply

[1] *Grey Matter*, vol. 47, no. 1, 1976, p. 1.
[2] Ibid., p. 2.

cannot continue to operate on the basis of intuitive judgments on these matters.

Florence R. Skelly, an executive with the consumer research firm of Yankelovich, Skelly, and White, has been conducting continuing research designed to monitor social changes which are likely to affect business during the next ten years. Let's take a look at some of her findings and predictions in order to better appreciate the nature of the changes which will affect retailing over the next several years.

The three American frontiers

Ms. Skelly points out that the United States has faced three frontiers in its 200-year history. The first, she states, lasted about 150 years, and covered the period when we opened the West, populated the country, and made a commitment to technology and the free enterprise system. The focus was on upward mobility and the Protestant ethic.

The second frontier, confronted most notably after World War II, was sparked by the American dream of upward mobility for all persons. We saw a conscious effort on the part of our government to provide a piece of the American dream for all persons. This gave us the civil rights movement, the women's movement, environmental legislation, consumerism, and a host of other issues, many of which were designed to redistribute the wealth of the nation.

Ms. Skelly indicates that we are now entering our third frontier, which is characterized by the possibility that growth and technology may not be unlimited and may not be the answer to the American dream. This raises the question of how we will adapt to shortages of energy, shortages of raw materials, and decreasing population growth. Most important from our point of view, to what changing social values of this newly emerging reality must retailers be alert? Ms. Skelly identifies a number of these, which we have simply listed below for your reaction:[3]

Consumer attitudes in the late 1970s

1. *Continued hostility toward both business and government.* Research has indicated, for example, that the public has a low level of trust in supermarkets and other business-related institutions.[4] Part of the problem lies with retailers who have not responded to the new realities of the marketplace. As has recently been noted: "Although social responsibility is frequently discussed by the business community and espoused by some leading corporations, the studies show that it has not

---

[3] The material in this section is based on Florence Skelly, "Changing Attitudes," *The Yankelovich Monitor,* 1975. Used with permission.

[4] Douglas L. MacLachlan and Homer Spence, "Public Trust in Retailing: Some Research Findings," *Journal of Retailing,* vol. 52 (Spring 1976), p. 3.

been incorporated into the operating plans and day-to-day actions of retailers. The main culprit appears to be the discount house, followed closely by the department store and then by the specialty store."[5] This statement should not be viewed as a general indictment of all retail establishments in these categories, however.

2. *A continued belief in the importance of self.* This means more self-fulfillment, self-expression, and self-development.

3. *A continued thrust in the changing role of women.* We are not likely to see a return of the supremacy of the homemaker role.

4. *Growing evidence of political conservatism.*

5. *A return to the work ethic.*

6. *A focus on cutting back expenditures in areas that have little emotional content.* This applies to the supermarket in particular.

7. *A continued commitment to simplification and convenience.*

8. *Less willingness to take risks.* This is a warning signal for retailers who are pushing private brands.

9. *Little mileage is likely to exist for a price-only store.* The nation is apparently sick of hyperbole and views talk about low prices with skepticism. An increased interest in high-end merchandise appears to be emerging.

10. *A chipping away at expenditures which are part of the good life.* Vacation trips, for example, are likely to be shorter and less luxurious in the future. However, no willingness seems to exist to cut out such expenditures altogether.

11. *Support will probably continue for the so-called consumerist movement.* This will occur because of an increased desire to know simply for the sake of knowledge. Thus, efforts on behalf of labeling, unit pricing, open code dating, and indeed anything that will make the consumer a more informed person will continue.

12. *Increased shame about waste.* This will have a major effect on consumption. Waste and leftovers in general will no longer be viewed as a source of pride.

The question that must be raised is, How will astute retailers adapt to these merging realities?

The environment from the business leader's perspective

How do the nation's top business leaders see the environment of 1985? Recently, 147 top executives of the *Fortune* directory of the 500 largest U.S. industrial corporations engaged in just this type of crystal gazing. They foresaw that social responsibility would continue to be an issue, as would the environment. Raw materials would remain high in price and somewhat

---

[5] Ronald J. Dornoff and Clint B. Tankersley, "Do Retailers Practice Social Responsibility?" *Journal of Retailing,* vol. 51 (Winter 1975–76), p. 42.

scarce, though major technological breakthroughs were anticipated. Prices would rise, but at a somewhat slower rate than in the past few years. The regulatory environment facing business would become increasingly complex.[6]

THE BUSINESS ENVIRONMENT OF 1985

The typical macroenvironment anticipated by industry in 1985, as indicated by a survey of 147 top executives, is as follows:

1. The issues of social responsibility confronting business will still be very much alive. Consumerism and its resulting pressures are likely to be even stronger than they are today.
2. The importance of protecting the environment and the importance of corresponding legislation will be more widely recognized, though the problems involved will be lessened somewhat because of ecological progress.
3. Scarcities of some natural resources will increase, and prices of resources will be somewhat higher. Though the rate of economic growth will be limited, most executives reject predictions of dire resource problems in the future.
4. Exciting technological developments are anticipated, but they will not be sufficient to solve many of the problems already confronting business and society.
5. The legal and regulatory environment of business will become increasingly complex and uncomfortable, with increasing jeopardy to the free market system.
6. Prices will continue to rise, and the national rate of economic growth will be slow. Marketing will be of somewhat increased importance in the struggle of businesses to earn an adequate rate of return.

Source: Jon G. Udell, Eugene R. Laczniak, and Robert F. Lusch, "Profiles of the Future: The Business Environment of 1985," *Business Horizons,* June 1976, p. 54.

SPECIFIC COMPONENTS OF CHANGE

Now let's examine on a more detailed basis some of the changes which may occur in the markets facing retailers.

Population growth rates

As noted in Figure 22–1, the proportion of the population 0–9 years of age declined consistently during the period 1960–75, whereas the proportion of the population 45–65 years of age and over increased consistently. These trends are forecast to continue in the future.

Population trends by age group are particularly important for retailers who are striving to appeal to specific age groups. Retailers who offer merchandise to college-age markets should anticipate a decline in the number of

---

[6] Jon G. Udell, Eugene R. Laczniak, and Robert F. Lusch, "Profiles of the Future: Business Environment of 1985," *Business Horizons,* June 1976, p. 54; see also William Lazer, "The 1980's and Beyond: A Perspective," *MSU Business Topics,* Spring 1977, pp. 21–35.

FIGURE 22–1
POPULATION TRENDS BY AGE GROUPS*

Population

Age	1960 (179.3)	'65 (193.8)	'70† (202.1)	'75 (211.9)
Under 5	20.3	20.4	17.1	15.8
5–9	18.7	20.5	19.8	17.2
10–14	16.8	18.9	20.7	20.3
15–19	13.2	17.0	19.0	20.8
20–29	21.7	24.5	29.1	35.6
30–44	36.0	35.3	34.8	36.5
45–64	36.0	39.0	41.6	43.4
65 and over	16.6	18.2	20.0	22.3

Share of total population (100.0%)

Age	1960	'65	'70†	'75
Under 5	11.3	10.5	8.5	7.5
5–9	10.4	10.6	9.8	8.1
10–14	9.4	9.8	10.2	9.6
15–19	7.4	8.7	9.4	9.8
20–29	12.1	12.7	14.4	16.8
30–44	20.1	18.2	17.2	17.2
45–64	20.1	20.1	20.6	20.5
65 and over	9.2	9.4	9.9	10.5

* Excludes Alaska, Hawaii, and armed forces overseas.
† Census data.
Source: "Change: An Asset or a Liability?" *Nielsen Researcher*, no. 2, 1976, p. 6.

potential consumers over the next ten years. On the other hand, we will see larger numbers of older consumers in the marketplace.[7]

The birthrate has continued to decline since 1958, with only small departures from this trend. This means a continuing decrease in average household size, with a resulting demand for smaller package sizes.

Howard L. Green, chief executive officer of a consulting firm specializing in site selection and land use studies, has offered the following observations about shifts in population.

The national population growth rate will continue to decline. The growth of metropolitan areas, which was so rapid immediately after World War II, has now stopped. We are likely to see some metropolitan areas actually losing population in the next few years. Birthrates will differ widely by regions and are forecast to be highest in the Southeast and the Southwest.

---

[7] "Change: An Asset or a Liability?" *Nielsen Researcher*, no. 2 1976, p. 6.

Small communities and rural areas are forecast to grow at a faster rate than metropolitan areas during the next several years. Already, food dollar sales have been growing faster in rural areas than in urban areas.[8]

Green also sees the continuing growth of small households consisting of young singles, empty nesters, senior citizens, and childless couples. The large growth in households in recent years has come from people living alone. This group has comprised over 40 percent of all household groups since 1970.

Single-family housing, according to Green, will decline because of rising construction costs, declining discretionary income, and the increasing numbers of people who will be relying on a government supplement of some kind, whether food stamps, welfare, unemployment compensation, Social Security, or whatever. Green foresees no major increases in productivity per worker. We can therefore expect an increase in the number of persons working in each family. The effects of these population shifts on retailing are depicted in Figure 22–2.[9]

FIGURE 22–2
AS POPULATION GOES, SO GOES RETAILING

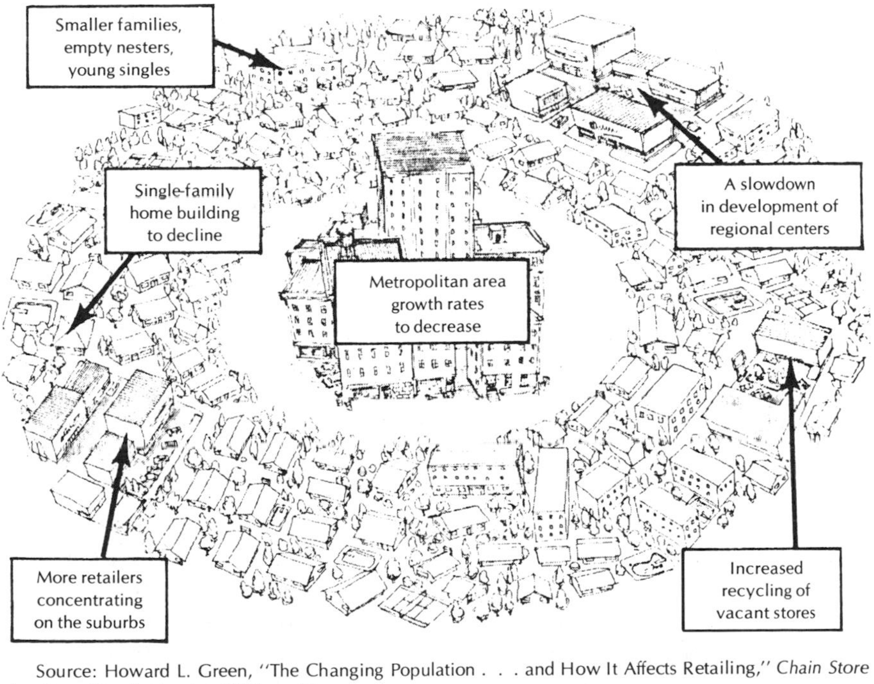

Smaller families, empty nesters, young singles

Single-family home building to decline

A slowdown in development of regional centers

Metropolitan area growth rates to decrease

More retailers concentrating on the suburbs

Increased recycling of vacant stores

Source: Howard L. Green, "The Changing Population . . . and How It Affects Retailing," *Chain Store Age Executive*, September 1975, p. 88.

---

[8] Ibid., p. 10.

[9] Howard L. Green, "The Changing Population . . . and How It Affects Retailing," *Chain Store Age Executive*, September 1975, p. 88.

Regional shifts

What specific shifts in population and per capita income within and among the various regions of the United States are likely to occur by 1985? The following projections have been offered:

1. In 1985, metropolitan areas will be the home of 75 percent of the population and 77 percent of the labor force, as well as the locus of much of the nation's expenditures.
2. Estimates show total U.S. consumption increasing 77 percent, from $544 billion to $961 billion (in terms of 1967 constant dollars). Consumption in metro areas will rise 71 percent, from $402 billion to $690 billion. Although this pace will be slower than that of the entire nation, metro areas will account for 72 percent of the total U.S. consumption in 1985.
3. The expected decline in the metropolitan share of total U.S. consumption is attributable to several factors:
    a. Per capita personal income will increase at a slower rate in metro areas than in nonmetro areas.
    b. The marginal tax rate for urbanites will be higher.
    c. People in metro areas will devote a larger proportion of their income to savings.[10]

As shown in Table 22–1, food sales in 1985 will comprise a smaller percentage of metro market sales than in either 1960 or 1970. Clothing sales will also be down slightly as a percentage of spending, as will personal care. Increased spending is forecast to occur in most of the other consumption categories.

Growth in metropolitan areas will vary widely by region between now and 1985. For example, the Southeast is forecast to experience the highest urban per capita income increase among all regions of the country and is also forecast to show the biggest spending jump, as shown in Table 1. This is good news for retailers planning expansions into this part of the country. The Southwest and mountain regions are forecast to show the largest increase in population.[11]

Table 22–2 concisely summarizes the foregoing statements plus additional information to yield a demographic profile of the population for 1980. As shown, the percentage of the population under 18 years of age will decline while all other age categories will increase. The level of education will increase as will employment in services and the percentage of working women. The percentage of families with incomes under $5000 (in 1975 dollars) will decline as incomes continue to increase in constant dollars. Our

[10] Joe Won Lee and Mark C. Kendall, "Metro Market Share of Consumption to Drop," *Chain Store Age Executive,* September 1975, p. 90.

[11] Ibid., pp. 90–94.

TABLE 22–1
METROPOLITAN AREA SHIFTS FOR 1985

Food's slice of metro spending will decline (in billions of 1967 constant dollars)

	1960		1970		1985	
	Dollars	Percent	Dollars	Percent	Dollars	Percent
Food	$ 71.3	26.2%	$ 87.8	21.9%	$134.3	19.5%
Clothing	28.3	10.4	40.3	10.0	63.2	9.2
Personal care	4.3	1.6	6.8	1.7	9.0	1.3
Housing	40.1	14.7	63.7	15.9	116.2	16.9
Household operation	37.0	13.6	56.9	14.1	107.0	15.5
Medical care	17.9	6.6	30.1	7.5	47.7	6.9
Personal business	14.2	5.2	21.3	5.3	41.5	6.0
Transportation	33.6	12.4	51.6	12.9	97.6	14.2
Recreation	16.0	5.9	28.1	7.0	44.9	6.5
Private education	4.1	1.5	7.0	1.7	13.5	1.9
Religious and welfare	4.2	1.6	5.8	1.5	8.6	1.2
Foreign travel, any other	0.8	0.3	2.0	0.5	5.9	0.9
Total consumption	$271.8	100.0%	$401.5	100.0%	$689.5	100.0%

Source: National Planning Association.

Urban per capita personal income to rise most in the Southeast
(in 1967 constant dollars)

	Personal income		Percent
Region	1970	1985	increase
Southeast	$3,233	$4,816	49%
Southwest	3,318	4,682	41
Mountain	3,423	4,817	41
Far West	4,005	5,522	38
Plains	3,704	5,384	45
New England	3,872	5,677	41
Great Lakes	3,866	5,569	44
Middle Atlantic	4,110	5,946	45
United States	$3,791	$5,431	43%

Source: National Planning Association.

Southeast metro areas targeted for biggest spending jump
(in billions of 1967 constant dollars)

	Consumption expenditures		Percent
Region	1970	1985	increase
Southeast	$ 54.2	$101.5	87%
Southwest	28.7	53.1	85
Mountain	6.9	12.7	84
Far West	68.3	120.1	76
Plains	24.3	41.3	70
New England	26.0	44.0	69
Great lakes	83.4	138.5	66
Middle Atlantic	109.6	178.3	63
United States	$401.5	$689.5	72%

Source: National Planning Association.

TABLE 22–1 *(continued)*

Southwest and mountain regions will experience largest urban growth

Region	Resident population in metropolitan areas (in millions)		Metropolitan population share (total regional population = 100 percent)		Percent increase, 1970–1985
	1970	1985	1970	1985	
Southeast	22.2	28.4	51%	53%	28%
Southwest	11.6	15.4	70	75	33
Mountain	2.7	3.6	54	55	33
Far West	23.1	29.8	85	91	29
Plains	9.0	10.7	55	60	19
New England	9.1	10.7	77	80	17
Great Lakes	29.9	34.8	74	78	17
Middle Atlantic	36.6	41.8	86	91	14
United States	144.3	175.3	71	75	21

Source: Joe Won Lee and Mark C. Kendall, "Metro Market Share of Consumption to Drop," *Chain Store Age Executive*, September 1975, p. 90.

central cities will be less important as places of residence while areas outside the central cities as well as nonmetropolitan areas will continue to increase in importance. On this point, it has been noted that rural American has disappeared "but in 1990 nonmetropolitan (under 50,000) America will account for the same share of the population as in 1974—roughly 27% ."[12]

PROJECTING THE RETAIL OPERATING ENVIRONMENT

Productivity increases

Let's look now at some of the specific impacts on retailing with an eye toward 1985. To offset constantly rising costs, retailers will have to invest increasing amounts of money in equipment and processes that will reduce the labor-intensive nature of retailing. Many experts feel that the only way to battle inflation is to increase productivity.

Productivity in the supermarket industry, for example, has been on the decline.[13] Productivity gains in the food industry will probably come from three major sources in the future: (1) improvement in the quality and utilization of manpower; (2) systems economies which require the cooperative efforts of firms; and (3) new technology.

---

[12] Juan de Torres, "The New Pattern of Urban Migration," *Conference Board Record*, vol. 13 (December 1975), p. 31.

[13] Gordon F. Bloom, "Supermarket Productivity Must Increase, or Else . . . ," *Chain Store Age Executive*, September 1975, p. 25.

TABLE 22–2
SELECTED MEASURES OF GROWTH, 1965–1980
(dollar figures in 1975 prices)

	1965	1970	1975	1980
Gross national product	$1,142.9	$1,336.8	$1,475.0	$1,930.0
Disposable personal income	762.6	937.5	1,085.0	1,390.0
Per capita disposable income*	3,925.0	4,575.0	5,080.0	6,240.0
Supernumerary income				
(after taxes)	45.5	77.0	90.0	170.5
Supernumerary income as				
percentage of DPI	6.0%	8.0%	8.5%	12.5
U.S. population	194.3	204.9	213.6	228.8
Persons by age				
Under 18	69.7	69.7	66.3	63.3
18–24	20.3	24.7	27.6	29.4
25–34	22.5	25.3	30.9	36.2
35–44	24.4	23.1	22.8	25.3
45–54	21.8	23.3	23.8	22.5
55–64	17.1	18.7	19.8	21.0
65 and over	18.5	20.1	22.3	24.5
Marriages	1.8	2.2	2.3	2.5
Births	3.8	3.7	3.2	3.9
Families	48.0	51.6	55.7	61.1
Households	57.4	63.4	71.1	78.2
Educational attainment†				
Elementary or less	34.0	30.3	27.0	23.5
Some high school	18.6	18.7	19.9	20.5
High school graduates	31.7	37.1	42.8	48.7
Some college	9.1	11.2	13.3	16.1
College graduates	9.7	12.1	15.1	19.3
Total employment‡	71.1	78.6	84.9	96.1
White-collar workers	31.9	37.2	42.1	49.2
Blue-collar workers	26.2	28.0	28.2	31.7
Service workers	8.9	10.4	11.6	12.7
Other	4.1	3.1	2.9	2.5
Working women as percentage				
of women 16 years and over	38.8%	42.8%	46.2%	48.5%
Place of residence§				
Metropolitan areas	128.6	137.1	143.3	150.4
Central cities	61.8	62.9	61.4	59.8
Outside central cities	66.9	74.2	81.9	90.6
Nonmetropolitan areas	61.0	62.8	66.6	70.8
Families by income class				
Under $5,000	8.6	7.5	7.8	7.3
$5,000–$10,000	13.4	12.4	12.5	12.5
$10,000–$15,000	12.9	13.2	14.2	14.5
$15,000 and over	12.9	18.6	21.2	26.9

Note: Dollar figures in billions; all other figures in millions, unless otherwise indicated.
  * Figures are in actual dollars.
  † Based on persons 25 and over.
  ‡ 1965 figures not strictly comparable with figures for later years.
  § Based on the civilian noninstitutional population.
  Sources: U.S. Departments of Commerce and Labor; The Conference Board, Reproduced from Fabian Linder, "The Second Half of the Seventies," *The Conference Board Record,* December 1975, p. 14.

Improvements in the use of labor will come first, since labor is the primary component of food marketing and distribution. This will call for better scheduling of hours, improved training, and cooperative efforts with unions to eliminate featherbedding.

Brown's Shoe Company has shown what proper space management can do to increase productivity. Historically, the company has been known as a three- or four-line family shoe store of about 2,500 square feet. However, because of rapidly rising rents and construction costs, the company switched to single-line specialty shops of 900–1,200 square feet. Whereas the older family stores had averaged $100 per square feet in sales and two stockturns per year, the new specialty shops now get three stockturns and $200 or more per square foot because of fewer markdowns, fewer returns, and more multiple purchases. Brown's also eliminated the display windows and streamlined the stockrooms. Historically, Brown's Shoe Company had featured space as follows: 20 percent display windows, 40 percent sales areas, and 40 percent stock. The new specialty stores feature 60 percent in the sales areas and 40 percent in stock.[14]

Energy

"If the 1960's were the decade during which industry added the word 'environment' to its organization charts, the 1970's will be remembered as the decade 'energy' made the list. For whether or not the world is ever again hit with an energy drought as sudden and dramatic as last year's Arab oil embargo, energy will remain a precious commodity."[15] In the future the problem will be not so much a shortage of energy as the rising cost of energy. This problem will bring numerous changes over the next ten years. Increasingly retailers will be seeking the most efficient and readily available fuel. Roof insulation will be upgraded; the use of glass will be reduced; and exterior building design will focus on reduced heat loss and the utilization of solar energy. "Studies on solar heat, recycling the heat of light and wastes, ideal lighting levels and sources, use of natural light through skylights, and countermeasures for brownouts and power shortages all are needed to be versatile in overcoming the effects of depleted resources."[16]

The environment

Government will probably continue to prescribe remedies for all manner of social ills. The consumerist and environmental movements of the 1970s caused the creation of a variety of tough agencies which will continue to monitor the environment. For example, the Environmental Protection Agency

---

[14] "Brown's Shoes Home Look Hikes Productivity," *Chain Store Age,* April 1974, pp. E30–E31.

[15] "Industry Braces for Energy Conservation," *Business Week,* September 14, 1974, p. 74.

[16] Charles R. Miller, "Energy and Materials Woes Can't Be Marked Down," *Chain Store Age Executive,* April 1975, p. 36; and Leon Winer and J. S. Schiff, "Rising Energy Costs Will Alter Marketing Patterns," *Marketing News,* May 6, 1977, p. 4.

and the Occupational Health and Safety Administration will remain active on a number of fronts, as will the Consumer Products Safety Commission, which sets standards for more than 10,000 consumer goods. Other agencies, such as the Equal Employment Opportunity Commission, are continuing to press forward with affirmative action programs which almost dictate the nature of the people who are hired. All of these programs will continue to add major costs to the retailing structure. Increasingly society will have to face the question of whether it wants these kinds of changes, which add little to the productive capacity of the various sectors of the economy but drive up consumer prices and deplete the supply of various raw materials.

Materials shortages

Probably no single development during the tumultuous 1970s caught so many business firms off guard as did the epidemic of materials shortages which first hit the United States in 1972–73. What are the long-run ramifications of this problem for retailing? Retailers are not typically involved in the acquisition of raw materials. However, they may decide to integrate backward as part of a vertical marketing system in order to have a more reliable supply of products. In addition, delayed deliveries may remain a problem. All of this simply means that retailers may have to reevaluate their growth goals during the latter part of the 1970s. Many retailers may have to curtail expansion.[17]

Smaller stores

Two quotations, one from an expert in real estate and the other from an expert in store planning, may illustrate the nature of store plans for the future. Foster Sears, a J. C. Penney vice president for real estate, has stated, "What it all adds up to is pressure for footage conservation, outboard or inboard. Stores of the 1980's are going to have to live with less space than they used in the 1960's and 1970's."[18]

Leonard S. Golden, assistant department head for store planning and construction and manager of corporate planning coordination of Federated Department Stores, has stated, "Mammoth stores are not going to be built in the midst of cornfields, 60 miles outside town. Gaps in the market are going to be filled with smaller stores. . . . Markets will be more narrowly focused for smaller stores. Department stores will move even further away from trying to be all things to all people."[19]

For example, the direction in men's specialty stores is clearly toward smaller units than could have been conceived of even five years ago. Each

[17] "I Can't Sell a Product if You Can't Make It," Business Week, September 14, 1974, p. 79.

[18] Foster Sears, "Smaller is the Word," Chain Store Age Executive, September 1975, p. 28.

[19] Leonard S. Golden, "From Quantity to Quality," Chain Store Age Executive, September 1975, p. 29.

National Shirt shop was formerly 3,000 square feet in area. Today these shops are 2,000 square feet in area, and the sales area of the new shops is almost equal in size to that of the older units.[20] The reasons for the change are that occupancy costs and construction costs have escalated, and that personnel problems have been getting worse. It is increasingly difficult to find competent persons to work in retailing, primarily because of the long hours and the Sunday openings of many outlets.

Remote retailing

"By 1985, remote retailing will be well advanced. Customers will make most routine retail purchases without leaving their homes. Retail outlets will offer only those products that the customer must feel or smell before making a buying decision."[21] Belden Menkus offers the following reasons why remote retailing will be upon us this quickly:

1. The introduction of smaller, more powerful, and less expensive computers, making their use as commonplace as today's pocket electronic calculators.
2. The expansion of cable television systems capable of two-way communication into a nationwide visual information transmission network.
3. Absorption of local store POS functions by an electronic funds transfer system that will eventually be nationwide.[22]

These possibilities are not farfetched. We just have to reflect for a moment to realize the tremendous advances which have been made in electronic calculators within the past two or three years. The same can be said of computers. In addition, cable TV offers an almost unlimited potential for growth since probably 40 to 50 of the channels are not now used for entertainment or information. Cable TV revenue growth is forecast to increase by 14–18 percent through 1980. Moreover, by 1985 5–7 million persons will be pay cable subscribers and 20–26 million persons will use the basic service.[23] As has been noted, "Retailers may purchase time to display and demonstrate selected products. Some retailers may choose to lease cable TV channels for their exclusive use. With one-way service, subscribers can place their orders by telephone. As two-way service arises, subscribers can use their home terminals to transmit orders in digital form upstream for recording in the central data terminal."[24]

---

[20] Robert Stone, "Specialty Change: If the Store Fits, Take It," *Chain Store Age Executive,* September 1975, p. 96.

[21] Belden Menkus, " 'Remote Retailing': A Reality by 1985?" *Chain Store Age Executive,* September 1975, p. 42.

[22] Ibid., p. 45.

[23] "Picture Phone Shopping Is Also a Distinct Possibility," *Marketing News,* July 2, 1976, p. 2.

[24] Jack M. Starling, "Cable Television: Prospects for Marketing Applications," *Akron Business and Economic Review,* Fall 1976, p. 31.

The era of electronic marvels is already upon us in retail banking. For example, Virginia National Bankshares announced that it was "opening 30 neighborhood branch banks in the state, and none will be staffed with people. . . . The system is designed to handle most consumer bank transactions: checking, savings, withdrawals, and transfer of funds from one account to another."[25]

Design changes for the future

Recently Edward Hambrecht, formerly chief architect for J. C. Penney, stated: "I think that this year [1975] begins the greatest era of revolution in merchandising and store design in this century. This notion will suggest a new vitality in merchandising and, through it, a new point of view in store design for the 80's."[26]

What are some of the changes we are likely to see? The idea seems to be that the shop or rigid plan in store layout will not be with us in the future. The move is toward an open landscape which allows movement and change. The one-shop plan can reduce energy use substantially.

We are also likely to see the replacement of the standard 4½-foot-high fixtures with fixtures that are at least 7 feet high. This is the so-called cube effect in merchandising.

The weak and perhaps costly categories of services in department stores will be readily dropped. For example, such services as beauty salons, watch repair, and travel agencies may not be present in the department store of 1980. In addition, selling space will be maximized by eliminating as many nonselling functions as possible. This will occur in conjunction with increased density of merchandise presentation. Thus, even more emphasis will be placed on style considerations. Permanent partitions are likely to go, as are partitions which reach to the ceiling. Increasingly changes in floor elevations will be used to separate the merchandise. High-intensity discharge lighting, such as mercury vapor lighting, will probably be installed in virtually every major specialty and department store by the 1980s.

FORECAST CHANGES IN VARIOUS CATEGORIES OF RETAILING[27]

It's probably worth a look to determine how various types of retailers are likely to adjust to the many changes we have outlined above. So let's look at some of the adjustments which some retailers are planning to make.

---

[25] "Marketing Observer," *Business Week,* August 9, 1976, p. 31.

[26] Edward C. Hambrecht, "Assess Social Patterns," *Chain Store Age Executive,* September 1975, p. 84.

[27] For further information, see Joseph Barry Mason, "Developing Marketing Institutions for a Steady State Economy," in *Science of Change and the Change of Science* (Washington, D.C.: Society for General Systems Research, 1977).

Drugstores

Ronald Gargano, director of store planning and design for Walgreens, indicates that the drugstore of the future will be smaller, typically around 8,000 square feet in area. The merchandise fixtures will be higher. Customers may be able to view merchandise on a television set which has a commercial channel featuring continuous advertising. This type of development will have basic impacts on the handling of merchandise, personnel, and space. In a sense, it would be a move to lower costs.[28]

Let's look further at some thoughts for the late 1970s and early 1980s as foreseen by Charles R. Walgreen III, president of the Walgreen Drug Company. For example, controversy is beginning to emerge as to whether pharmacists should become involved in health care by offering such services as blood pressure and eye examinations and diabetes tests. It is now legal for pharmacies to advertise prescription drugs. Thus, we are likely to see increased drug advertising. Private labels are becoming increasingly important, and for some drug chains they account for over 5 percent of total sales. Also, some drugstores are moving into food as a full-time promotional tool in retaliation against supermarket merchandising of health and beauty aids. Grocery volume in drugstores already accounts for approximately 1½ percent of chain drugstore sales.[29]

According to William F. Gagrra, chairman of the board and president of Payless Drugstores, computerized cash registers and electronic scanners will not make a heavy impact in the drugstore field for the next several years because the universal product coding of drugs still has a long way to go. Only 10 percent of drug products are marked with the universal product code as compared to over 50 percent of supermarket merchandise.[30]

Mass merchandising outlets

For mass merchandising, efforts to achieve higher productivity, including better use of store space, will be the key in the 1980s. Substitutes, technological innovation, and consumer conservation awareness will help offset some of the materials shortages foreseen for mass merchandisers. As has been noted by Donald V. Seibert, chairman of the board of the J. C. Penney Company,

There will be demands for longer-life products. Refurbishment, repair, and overhaul will become more commonplace and such services will prosper. Many products will be designed for re-use or made of material which can be recycled. . . . The population in 1990 will be more individualistic, self-reliant, better informed, and more

[28] Ronald Gargano, "The Changing Drugstore: Escaping from Giganticism," *Chain Store Age Executive,* September 1975, p. 39.

[29] Charles R. Walgreen III, "See Intensified Sales Effort," *Chain Store Age Executive,* September 1975, p. 63.

[30] William L. Gagrra, "Scarcer Sites, Rising Costs to Test Drug Chains," *Chain Store Age Executive,* September 1975, p. 38.

accepting of others. Conspicuous or ostentatious consumption will decline, to be replaced by spending patterns which relate to life experiments and self-expression.[31]

Seibert also sees improvements in high-speed communications, such as closed-circuit television, picture phones, and similar innovations. Electronic funds transfers will probably replace the checkbook. Some form of electronic shopping will also develop for the mass merchandisers.

Stewart Dychtwald, assistant director of real estate and store planning for Zayre Corporation, makes these predictions concerning fixtures:

Fixtures for basic merchandise will remain fairly stable in 1985, but will have greater flexibility for verticalization. The real change and impact will be in inexpensive point-of-purchase fixtures that are designed to do specific jobs for specific products. More POP fixturing will be manufactured to specifications of individual chains, with less reliance on those provided by individual vendors. This will permit mass retailers to have greater control over product presentation. Fixtures will have to be designed not to be labor-intensive, but flexible and to the point. Another phase of mass retailing to have an impact in 1985 will be interior graphics, signing and display. Simplicity and uniformity will be the key, and terms such as lightness, flexibility, warmth, inviting, easily identifiable, and freshness will be in great evidence.[32]

Discount department stores

Now let's look briefly at what Robert E. Dewar, chairman of the board and chief executive officer of the Kresge Company, has to say about the discount department store of the 1980s.[33] Once again, we see emphasis on greater productivity from people and distribution centers. Smaller markets will get increasing attention from discounters since they require less square footage.

Lead times for merchandise will remain a problem. The discount merchandisers, however, will be turning to automated distribution centers to insure prompt delivery by common, contract, or private carrier. These distribution centers may be shared by several different retailers.

Also, because of rapidly rising postal rates, the mass merchandisers are likely to be using private carrier services. This will allow more selective mailings at lower cost.

The food service industry

James W. McLamore, chairman of the board of Burger King Corporation, indicates that in the near future eating out will be an almost nondiscretionary

---

[31] Donald V. Seibert, "The Focus Is on Productivity," *Chain Store Age Executive,* September 1975, p. 65.

[32] Steward Dychtwald, "Mass Merchandisers Must Plan for Profitability," *Chain Store Age Executive,* September 1975, p. 37.

[33] Robert E. Dewar, "The New Growth for Discounters," *Chain Store Age Executive,* September 1975, pp. 67–70.

household expense. He foresees that in the 1980s one meal out of every two will be eaten away from home as contrasted to one out of every five during the 1960s.[34]

Further, McLamore foresees the increased use of salad bars, ice-cream bars, dessert bars, and soup bars to reduce labor costs without reducing the quality of the eating-out experience. Increasingly, the trend will be to limited menus and variable portions, with such items as steak and roast beef being sold by the ounce. Because of the rapid rise in energy costs per menu item, larger numbers of cold items may be sold.

Shopping centers

What does the future hold for the shopping centers which have been such a major part of the retailing scene since the 1940s? James Rouse, chairman of the board of one of the largest shopping center development companies in the nation, foresees that new regional centers will be both fewer and smaller. He sees an upgrading of older centers and "a surge of dramatically new and lively marketplaces in the center of older cities."[35]

Shopping centers will also be a part of comprehensive plans for developing multipurpose land use. Increased attention to public transportation, in Rouse's view, will make downtown a more dynamic and efficient marketplace. As has been noted by another executive, "Tomorrow's shopping center will more often be compact, multi-level, and multi-function. The old idea of clustering only retail stores will give way to the concept of creating a community center, with retailing mixed with other functions. In effect, the new form will be a new 'downtown' for a community."[36] Growing environmental awareness and regular guidance from government will shape the regional shopping center of the future at least as much as any other factors.

RETAIL STRATEGIES FOR THE 1980S

What, then, are some of the strategies which can be followed by retailers during the coming years as they adjust to the tumultuous environments of the 1980s?

Albert Bates and his associates have offered a series of tactics which can be followed by the retailer in adjusting to the environment of the future.[37] Similar

[34] James W. McLamore, "Upcoming: Fifty Percent Meals Eaten Out?" *Chain Store Age Executive,* September 1975, pp. 71–73.

[35] James Rouse, "New Retail Projects: Go Downtown, Young Man," *Chain Store Age Executive,* September 1975, p. 31.

[36] C. William Brubaker, "Tomorrow's Malls: Multi-Use and Better-Looking," *Chain Store Age Executive,* September 1975, p. 33.

[37] Albert D. Bates, David Kollat, and Cyrus Wilson, "Clearing Retailing's Upcoming Hurdles," *Chain Store Age Executive,* September 1975, pp. 24–25; also Albert D. Bates, "The Troubled Future of Retailing," *Business Horizons,* August 1976, pp. 22–28.

suggestions have been offered by specialists in the Distribution Research Program of the University of Oklahoma.[38] Let's look at what they suggest.

Store positioning.   Increasing numbers of retailers are positioning themselves to capitalize on various life-styles or demographic profiles. For example, "Byerly's, Handy Andy, and Treasure Island have positioned themselves to appeal to the upscale grocery shopper. Crate and Barrel and Pottery Barn also concentrate on the affluent consumer while Pier 1 focuses on the 'under 35' market and Radio Shack on the electronic enthusiast."[39] Table 22–3

TABLE 22–3
MAINSTREAM RETAILING STRATEGIES:
STORE POSITIONING, 1974–1975

Hardware/building materials retailing
    Convenience hardware stores (Mountview)
    Hardware supermarkets (Saxon)
    Super hardware stores (Central, Pascal)
    Paint and home decorating specialty stores (Sherwin-Williams)
    Paint and home decorating supermarkets (Standard Brands Paint)
    Home improvement centers (Beaver, Handy Dan)
    Home and leisure stores (Canadian Tire, Ole's)
Home furnishings retailing
    Decorative home accessories stores (Pier I, Crate and Barrel)
    Furniture specialty stores (Ethan Allan, Drexel/Heritage)
    Home furnishings clearance centers (W & J Sloane)
    Furniture warehouse showrooms (Levitz)
    Home furnishings showcase stores (Glick's)
    Home furnishings superstores (Kittle's)
    Home furnishings rental stores (Putnam)

Source: Bert C. McCammon, Jr., Robert F. Lusch, and Bradley T. Farnsworth, "Contemporary Markets and the Corporate Imperative: A Strategic Analysis for Senior Retailing Executives," paper presented at a seminar for top management in retailing, Graduate School of Business Administration, Harvard University, 1976, p. 24.

presents the successful positioning strategies in hardware/building materials and home furnishings during the 1970s.

Secondary markets.   Future expansion will focus more frequently on secondary markets in cities of under 250,000 population. This is because such investments are smaller and because wage rates are likely to be lower. Specifically, "Bi-Lo operates discount supermarkets in small rural communities; Pamida locates bantam discount stores in cities with a population of less than 10,000; and Wal-Mart operates discount department stores in

[38] Robert F. Lusch and James M. Kenderdine, "The Operating Dynamics of Chain Store Retailing in Recession and Recovery," Distribution Research Program, College of Business, University of Oklahoma, 1976, pp. 8–12.

[39] Albert D. Bates and Bert C. McCammon, Jr., "Reseller Strategies and the Financial Performance of the Firm," paper presented at the Structure, Strategy, and Performance Conference, Graduate School of Business, Indiana University, 1975, p. 15.

county seat towns throughout the Southwest."[40] By focusing on secondary markets, each of these organizations has been able to achieve a position of competitive dominance at a relatively low cost.

More institutional sales.   The consumption process is being increasingly institutionalized. Organizations rather than individuals are making final buying decisions. For example, "19.6% of all automobiles manufactured are fleet vehicles, 42.6% of all carpet produced goes into contract markets, and over 40% of all life insurance in force is in the form of group policies."[41] Further, career apparel and uniform sales to employers and rental organizations are growing twice as rapidly as the total ready-to-wear market. The furniture and equipment rental business is a $1 billion industry, and its projected growth rate is 15 percent a year over the next ten years.

Contract markets.   The fast growth of contract markets has important ramifications for distribution. Increasingly, retailers and wholesalers are reprogramming their operations to capitalize on this opportunity. Sears, Hudsons, and Marshall Field have strengthened their contract home furnishings divisions, and Hart, Schaffner, and Mark has become a strong factor in the career apparel market.

Market intensification.   The second option is market intensification, which involves clustering more stores in the same metropolitan area and in contiguous markets. This allows economies in promotion, better supervision, and similar advantages. As Edwin G. Roberts, Jr., president, J. L. Hudson Co., has stated, "We have to intensify our efforts in our existing units rather than look for endless expansion."[42]

Differences in store types.   Albert Bates and his associates suggest that in conjunction with this option retailers should develop a flexible portfolio of different-sized stores, depending on the size of the community and the existing retail competition. Further they suggest that retailers consider more use of secondhand space, since this can result in 30 percent or more savings in rent. Such companies as J. C. Penney, Sears, and Kresge have been following this approach.

Productivity increases.   Finally, Bates and his associates suggest the application of supermarket techniques (central checkout, self-selection, and low gross margins) to new areas. We have already seen the emergence of toy supermarkets, home decorating centers, and self-service shoe stores. Such applications of supermarket concepts allow retailers to keep operating expenses low and to maintain narrower margins on merchandise.

Fewer product options.   In the future, customers will have fewer product options. Product lines are being consolidated, and new product development is being cut back. This will have major impacts on retail offer-

---

[40] Ibid., p. 17.

[41] Bert C. McCammon, Jr., "Future Shock and the Practice of Management," in Phillip Levine (ed.), *Attitude Research Bridges the Atlantic,* (Chicago: American Marketing Association, 1973), p. 80.

[42] Edwin G. Roberts, Jr., "Department Stores Redefine Their Role," *Business Week,* December 13, 1976, p. 47.

ings. The emphasis will shift from the volume growth of the 1960s to a new stress on profit growth. Product line simplification will be a reality in the 1980s.

The growth of services.   Services retailing will continue to grow as a percentage of total retail sales. More and more products are in need of professional maintenance and service. In addition, increasing levels of discretionary income will give consumers more time for such services. It will also be possible to sell additional amounts of insurance and similar protective services.

More emphasis on research.   As has been noted, "Data on demographics, psychographics (measurement of attitudes), and life-style are being fed into retailers' computers so they can make marketing decisions based on actual spending patterns and estimate their inventory needs with less risk."[43] As retailers seek to increase market penetration or push to increase market shares by taking business away from competitors, they will need to know more about the buying characteristics of the consumer groups in whom they have the strongest interest. Research is the only viable basis for developing such information.

ENVIRONMENTAL UNCERTAINTIES

What are some of the specific variables which retailing management will have to face between now and 1985? *First* among these is economic uncertainty. Estimates of the future inflation rate vary widely, which necessitates the development of multiple management strategies that take account of the various possible contingencies. Increasingly, flexibility will be the key to avoid being trapped with the wrong strategies.

Second, price awareness on the part of consumers will continue to be a major issue. Shoppers will be increasingly price oriented because of pressures on consumer incomes. Such retail innovations as warehouse retailing will probably continue to have a marketplace advantage with consumers.

Third, labor cost pressures, translated into demands for greater productivity, will continue to be in evidence. During the past five years, productivity increases have been smaller in retailing than in any other sector, whereas increases in unit costs for labor have been greater in retailing than in any other sector. For example, between 1968 and 1972 real output per worker-hour increased only 0.8 percent per year in retailing as contrasted with a 4.5 percent increase for agriculture. Likewise, the annual increase in labor cost in manufacturing between 1968 and 1972 was 3.0 percent as contrasted to a 6.2 percent increase for retailing.[44] Pressures on labor costs can only be met by technological advances which will allow management to hold the line on payroll increases.

---

[43] Ibid.

[44] Bert C. McCammon, Jr., and William L. Hammer, "A Frame of Reference for Improving Productivity in Distribution," *Atlanta Economic Review*, vol. 24 (September–October 1974).

Fourth, the level of investment in retailing will have to increase sharply. Land and building costs have risen greatly, as have fixture and equipment costs. Management will face increasing financial difficulties because of the need to invest large sums of money in fixed assets. "Available forecasts vary widely, but the consensus suggests that the demand for additional capital will exceed new capital availability by approximately $500–$700 billion during the 1975–85 time period. If this proves true, all firms can expect to pay more for capital and many will be crowded out of conventional capital markets."[45] In these circumstances, retailers will try to minimize the necessary capital investments and to get profit levels up so as to project a more favorable image to the financial community.

Currently many retailers have leverage ratios of 2.5 times. This indicates that they have reached the limits of their borrowing capacity, particularly in an era of capital shortages and high interest rates.[46]

DISCUSSION

Beyond question, retailers will be faced with increasing governmental regulation, rising energy costs, periodic materials shortages, and changes in consumer spending patterns as they adjust to the new realities of the marketplace. It is not possible to say precisely what the store of the future will be like, but we can say that it will be whether the customer wants it to be.

In general, stores will be smaller, increasing emphasis will be placed on productivity in maintaining profit levels, multi-use shopping centers will probably emerge, and more self-service will appear as retailers strive to reduce labor costs. All of these changes will require increasing sophistication and ingenuity to avoid lowering the quality of merchandise offerings. The future will probably also include more telephone shopping, the routinization of electronic funds transfer, greater use of cable television for retailing purposes, television channels which carry advertising on a continuous basis, and similar electronic advances.

We have listed the retailers of the half-century below for your reaction. Each of the six retail industries listed was asked to cite the person who had done the most for its particular area of retailing since 1925. Use your imagination as to who will be awarded this honor at the end of the next 50 years. Perhaps their method of merchandising has not yet been introduced!

Man-of-the-Half-Century in the General Merchandise/Department Store field: the late James Cash Penney. ". . . among his contributions are the first profit-sharing programs. He was a pioneer respondent to consumerism before it was recognized by that name; not only a believer in but an ardent practitioner of the Golden Rule."

---

[45] Albert D. Bates, "The Superstores: Emerging Innovations in Food Retailing," in Robert Robicheaux et. al. (eds.), *Marketing* (Boston: Houghton Mifflin Co., 1977), p., 207.

[46] Bates and McCammon, "Reseller Strategies," p. 4.

Man-of-the-Half-Century in the Food Service field: Roy A. Kroc, chairman of the McDonald's Corp. ". . . for bringing to the restaurant industry the most advanced concepts of franchising and for the application of the most advanced marketing and operational techniques to the food service industry."

Man-of-the-Half-Century in the Supermarket field: Sidney R. Rabb, chairman of the Stop & Shop Co. ". . . reorganized the Super Market Institute into the kind of organization it is today. An industry leader in innovative merchandising and operations' techniques; renowned for introducing modern personnel relations concepts in the food field."

Man-of-the-Half-Century in the Discount Department Store field: Harry B. Cunningham, honorary chairman of the S. S. Kresge Co.". . . was the driving force behind the founding of K mart, which not only revolutionized his own company but set a model for industry leadership."

Man-of-the-Half-Century in the Chain Drug field: the late Charles R. Walgreen, Sr. ". . . the pioneer who envisioned a chain drug industry when there was none, then built his chain into that industry's leading retailer."

Man-of-the-Half-Century in the Home Improvement Center field: John A. Walker, executive vice president of Lowe's Companies, Inc. ". . . he introduced sophisticated marketing concepts to the lumberyard field, thereby creating a new retail apparatus, the modern home improvement center."[47]

At this juncture we are impelled to speculate about the "*People*-of-the-*Second*-Half-Century in . . ." We suspect that among the names we will find at least one or two women. Retailing provided middle-management positions for women long before this was fashionable. Top management is a reality for women in the 1970s, and as we approach the 1980s, is it not reasonable to predict that by the end of the next 50 years the honor in one or more particular areas will go to women?

More than ever retailing needs bright people to meet the many challenges of the 1980s which have been outlined throughout the text. You should consider sharing in the excitement of participation.

KEY CONCEPTS

The management of change	Energy management
Monitoring social change	Materials shortage
The environment in 1985	Remote retailing
Population trends	Market positioning
Shifts in growth areas	Market intensification
Productivity increases	

---

[47] "The Man of the Half-Century Awards," *Chain Store Age*, September 1975, pp. 76–77.

DISCUSSION QUESTIONS

1. What are the major environmental pressures which will impact retailing during the next few years?

2. Why is so much emphasis being placed upon increasing productivity in retailing? What are some of the more obvious ways in which productivity can be increased?

3. What major impacts will the increasing trend toward electronic merchandising have on conventional retailing? For example, what will the impacts be on labor costs, employment, and similar aspects of retail operations?

4. Do you believe that we will see an accelerated trend toward vertical integration in retailing during the next few years? Why or why not?

5. What impacts are smaller families, slowing levels of population growth, and more leisure time likely to have on retail merchandising?

6. Do the life-style projections for the 1980s outlined at the beginning of this chapter present more of a threat or more of an opportunity to the retailer? Elaborate on your answer, and give specific examples.

7. Where are the greatest opportunities for the expansion of retail sales likely to occur? Discuss this in terms of regional geography and community size and even in terms of areas within a community.

APPENDIXES

A. GOVERNMENT REGULATIONS
    AFFECTING RETAILING

B. GLOSSARY OF RETAILING
    TERMINOLOGY

APPENDIX A

GOVERNMENT REGULATIONS AFFECTING RETAILING

The *Sherman Antitrust Act* of 1890 was the first piece of federal legislation which provided a general statement of public policy in the matter of maintenance of competition. The act attacks two types of anticompetitive business behavior. One section declares that contracts, combinations, and conspiracies in restraint of trade or commerce among the states or with foreign nations is illegal. The activities which may constitute a contract, combination, or conspiracy in restraint of trade are limitless; however, generally speaking, agreements in restraint of trade cover such activities as price-fixing, pooling arrangements, division of markets along commodity or territorial lines, exclusive dealing, tying agreements, cornering of markets, and restriction of sales. A second section covers monopoly or attempts to monopolize any part of trade and commerce among the states and with foreign nations. The intent of this section was to render the monopoly firms impotent in order to restore competition.

The *Food and Drug Act* of 1906 was one of the first pieces of federal legislation designed to protect the consumer. The act forbade the misbranding or adulteration of food and drug products. Misbranding exists where the labeling or packaging is false or misleading or omits required information about harmful consequences of use.

The *Clayton Act* of 1914 was passed to supplement earlier laws against restraint of trade and monopolies. The act was passed "to arrest the creation of trusts, conspiracies, and monopolies in their incipience and before consummation," and to make the law relative to restraint of trade more specific. Practices specifically mentioned were discrimination in price, tying and exclusive agreements, the acquisition of another corporation's stock, and interlocking directorates. The act did not declare these activities to be illegal per se but only where their effect would be to substantially lessen competition or would tend to create a monopoly. Thus, the Clayton Act was more specific than the Sherman Act in declaring certain practices in commerce to be illegal if they might have an adverse effect on competition even if they were not in themselves contracts, conspiracies, or combinations in restraint of trade and even if they did not go far enough to constitute actual monopolization or attempts to monopolize. Further, the practices would not have to actually injure competition to be illegal. They were illegal if their effect *might* substantially lessen competition or *tend* to create a monopoly.

The *Federal Trade Commission Act* of 1914 created an independent agency, the Federal Trade Commission, to assist in the enforcement of the Clayton Act and other antitrust laws. The commission was given broad powers of investigation, jurisdiction over the enforcement of Section 5 of the act, which declares "unfair methods of competition" to be illegal, and the power to issue cease and desist orders. Business conduct in violation of any provision of the antitrust laws may be ruled illegal under Section 5 of the Federal Trade Commission Act. Further, anticompetitive acts or practices which fall short of transgressing the Sherman and Clayton acts may be restrained by the FTC as being unfair methods of competition.

The *Webb-Pomerene Export Trade Act* of 1918 exempts certain products and/or activities from federal antitrust legislation. Under this act, voluntary export trade associations are exempt from antitrust legislation as long as they are encouraging the extension of foreign trade but are not fixing prices in domestic trade or restraining the trade of a competitor.

The *Capper-Volstead Act* of 1922 allows persons engaged in farming to band together in associations established to process and market their goods. Thus, this act provides for an exemption to antitrust legislation.

The *Cooperative Marketing Act* of 1933 is another act which exempts certain products and/or activities from federal antitrust legislation. This act permits persons engaged in the production of agricultural products to act as a group in acquiring, interpreting, and disseminating crop and market information.

The *Fishermen's Collective Marketing Act* of 1934 permits fishermen or planters of aquatic products to form associations to permit more equal bargaining in selling to dealers and processors. The secretary of the interior, however, can issue cease and desist orders if prices become "unduly enhanced." This act provides for an exemption to federal antitrust legislation.

The *Wagner Act (National Labor Relations Act)* of 1935 was designed to protect the right of employees to organize and bargain collectively and to encourage the "friendly adjustment of labor disputes." Specifically, the act (1) outlawed certain conduct (defined as unfair labor practices) by employers which had the effect of preventing employees from organizing; (2) provided for the selection by employees of a union as their bargaining representative; and (3) created the National Labor Relations Board to administer the act and gave it power to issue cease and desist orders to employers engaging in unfair labor practices.

The *Robinson-Patman Act* of 1936, which amended Section 2 of the Clayton Act, was designed to control price discrimination. Since the act does not make price discrimination illegal per se, the exact provisions of its various sections are described here. Section 2(a) declares price discrimination to be unlawful only where the effect may be to substantially lessen competition or to tend to create a monopoly. This section permits price differentials where there are differences in the cost of manufacture, sale, or delivery resulting from the differing methods or quantities in which goods are to be purchased or delivered. Section 2(b) permits a seller to discriminate in pricing "in good faith to meet an equally low price of a competitor or the services or facilities furnished by a competitor." Section 2(c) requires that no discounts in the nature of brokerage payments be made except to intermediaries who are entirely independent of the buyer and the seller. Section 2(d) provides that payment to a customer for services or facilities furnished by the customer in connection with the processing, handling, selling, or offering to sell of the seller's goods is unlawful unless such payment is made available on proportionately equal terms to all other competing customers. Section 2(e) provides that any services or facilities furnished to a customer by the seller to aid the customer in handling or marketing the seller's goods be made available to all buyers on proportionately equal terms. Section 2(f) makes it unlawful to knowingly *receive* or *induce* a discrimination in price.

The *Miller-Tydings Resale Price Maintenance Act* of 1937 was passed to allow manufacturers of a brand or trade name product to have control over the retail price either for the purpose of creating a quality image or to protect their regular retail outlets from price-cutting competition. Thus, this act amended Section 1 of the Clayton Act to exempt from federal antitrust legislation resale price maintenance contracts under state fair-trade acts with respect to goods sold in interstate commerce. Exempting this form of vertical price-fixing from the antitrust laws made the act applicable to the Federal Trade Commission Act as well as the Clayton Act. However, the Consumer Goods Pricing Act declared that as of December 12, 1976, fair-trade pricing was illegal (and, in fact, was considered a felony) for goods sold in interstate commerce.

The *Fair Labor Standards Act* relates to federal government regulation of wages and hours. Originally enacted in 1938, it has been amended several times to increase the minimum wage, to decrease maximum hours worked, and to include workers not originally covered. The act also contains provisions regulating the employment of child labor.

The *Wheeler-Lea Act* of 1938 declares as unlawful the dissemination of false advertisements of foods, drugs, cosmetics, and therapeutic devices used in the diagnosis, treatment, or prevention of diseases. A false advertisement is an advertisement, other than labeling, which is misleading in a material respect, such as failure to reveal the consequences of the product's use. The act was actually an amendment to the Federal Trade Commission Act which granted the FTC jurisdiction over the false advertisement of foods, drugs, cosmetics, and therapeutic devices.

The *Wool Products Labeling Act* of 1939 was aimed at the misbranding of wool products. The act required that wool products bear a tag or label which indicates the percentage of wool and other fibers in the product. The name of the manufacturer or distributor must also be on the tag or label.

The *Taft-Hartley Act (Labor Management Relations Act)* of 1947 amended the Wagner Act. Its purposes were to ensure the free flow of commerce by eliminating union practices which hampered commerce and to protect the public in labor disputes which affected commerce. Its main provisions (1) outlawed conduct by unions considered as unfair labor practices, (2) created the Federal Mediation and Conciliation Service to aid in the settlement of labor disputes, (3) restricted the right of unions to insist on a union shop, and (4) provided for an eight-day cooling-off period in strikes which imperiled the national health or safety.

The *Celler-Kefauver Act* of 1950 amended the Clayton Act by prohibiting a corporation from acquiring the whole or any part of the *stock* or *assets* "of another corporation also engaged in commerce, where in any line of commerce in any section of the country the effect of such acquisition may be substantially to lessen competition, or tend to create a monopoly." The act broadened the Clayton Act by including assets as well as stock acquisition and broadened the Clayton Act's definition of the market.

The *Fur Products Labeling Act* of 1951 required that the fur content of fur products be clearly and properly identified in all respects.

The *McGuire-Keogh Fair Trade Enabling Act* of 1952 relates to nonsigners clauses of fair-trade legislation. Under a nonsigners provision, all retailers had to agree to the terms of a resale price maintenance agreement if it were signed by a single retailer. The act amended Section 5 of the Federal Trade Commission Act by providing that nonsigners provisions as a part of resale price maintenance are exempt from the federal antitrust legislation under state fair-trade laws with respect to goods sold in interstate commerce. This, along with fair-trade pricing, was later declared illegal for goods sold in interstate commerce.

The *Flammable Products Act* of 1953 prohibits the manufacture or sale of any article of wearing apparel or fabric which is so flammable that it is dangerous when worn by individuals. The law is enforced by the Federal Trade Commission, which develops the rules and regulations specifying various forms of misrepresentation. These rules have the effect of law, and the Commission has the power to apply to a district court for injunctive relief in cases arising under the act.

The *Textile Fiber Products Identification Act* of 1958 applies to textile fiber products sold to the ultimate consumer. The act requires that the percentage content of the various fibers in a textile product be identified. The name of the manufacturer or distributor and, if the product is imported, the name of the country must also be indicated. Disclosure of similar information, except for percentage breakdowns, must also be made in advertisements of these products.

The *Federal Hazardous Substances Labeling Act* of 1960 is designed to control the labeling of packages of hazardous substances intended or suitable for household use. The act, administered by the Food and Drug Administration, ensures that labels are affixed to toxic, corrosive, irritating, or flammable products which are in household use. These labels must state (1) the name and address of the manufacturer, packer, distributor, or seller; (2) the name of the hazardous substance; (3) the words *danger, warning,* or *caution* where applicable; (4) the principal hazard; (5) the precautionary measures to be followed and instructions for first aid; (6) any special handling or storage instructions; and (7) "Keep out of reach of children" or its equivalent.

The *Equal Pay Act* of 1963 amended the Fair Labor Standards Act by prohibiting employers from discriminating on the basis of sex in paying wages for the performance of equal work. The law applies only to employees who are covered by the minimum wage provisions of the Fair Labor Standards Act. An exception is provided in cases where it can be shown that the wage differential is based on a seniority system, a merit system, a system measuring wages by quantity or quality of production, or any other factor except sex. The act also prohibits labor organizations from causing any employer whose employees they represent to discriminate because of sex.

The *Civil Rights Act* of 1964, amended by the *Equal Employment Act* of 1972, relates to fair employment practices and is applicable to employers with 15 or more employees, labor unions with 15 or more members, all labor unions which operate a hiring hall, and employment agencies. The 1972 amendment extended coverage to all state and local governments, government agencies, political subdivisions and departments, and public and private educational institutions. The major purposes of the laws are to eliminate job discrimination (including discharge; refusal to hire; and compensation, terms, conditions, or privileges of employment) on the basis of religion, sex, race, color, or national origin. The Equal Employment Opportunity Commission was created as the agency which has primary responsibility for enforcing these laws.

The *Age Discrimination in Employment Act* of 1967 was passed to protect persons between the ages of 40 and 65 from job discrimination against them because of age. The law is enforced by the Labor Department or by private action.

The *Truth-in-Lending Act* (1968) is Title I of the Federal Consumer Protection Act. The act authorized the Federal Reserve Board to adopt resolutions to "assure meaningful disclosure of credit terms so that the consumer will be able to compare more readily the various credit terms available" and thus avoid uninformed use of credit. The act covers all transactions where (1) the lender is in the business of extending credit; (2) the debtor is a person, not a corporation or a business; (3) a finance charge may be imposed; and (4) the credit is obtained primarily for personal purposes. The act provides for full disclosure of credit terms in several ways. (Full disclosure is required whenever a buyer pays in four installments or more.) First, the law requires the lender to disclose the finance charge expressed as an annual percentage rate and to specify the method for making the computation. This information must be made known to the borrower by the use of a financing statement, given to the borrower before credit is extended. This statement also includes statements relative to (1) any default or delinquency charges resulting from late payment, (2) a description of any property used as security, and (3) the total amount to be financed (separating the original debt from the finance charges). The act further gives debtors the right to rescind or cancel certain transactions for a period of three days from the date of the transaction or from the date they are given notice of the right to rescind. The act also limits the amount of an employee's pay which can be garnisheed. Ordinarily the amount may not exceed *(a)* 25 percent of the employee's weekly take-home pay or *(b)* the amount by which the weekly take-home pay exceeds 30 times the federal minimum wage, whichever is less. The act also prohibits an employer from discharging an employee because his or her wages have been garnisheed for any one indebtedness.

The *Clean Air Act* (as amended in 1970) remedies many defects in air pollution statutes which date back to 1956. The act directs the Environmental Protection Agency to establish primary and secondary air quality standards and to see that these standards are met according to a definite timetable. The EPA must also approve state plans for the implementation of the standards and make sure that the plans are carried out. For control purposes, the act divides air pollution into stationary and mobile sources. An example of the act's control relative to stationary polluters is a requirement that factories, municipal incinerators, and power plants reduce emission levels sufficiently to bring down ambient air pollution to meet primary and secondary standards. Action taken relative to emission control by the automobile industry is an example of the standards set for mobile polluters.

The *National Environmental Policy Act* of 1970 was passed to establish a national policy which "will encourage productive and enjoyable harmony between man and his environment; to promote efforts which will prevent or eliminate damage to the environment and biosphere and stimulate the health and welfare of man; to enrich the understanding of the ecological system and control resources important to the nation; and to establish a Council on Environmental Quality." The act is divided into two titles. The first establishes broad policy goals and imposes specific duties on all federal agencies. The second establishes the Council on Environmental Quality, whose function is to gather and assess information, issue advisory guidelines, and make recommendations to the president on environmental matters.

The *Occupational Safety and Health Act* of 1970 was passed to assure safe and healthful working conditions for practically every employee in the United States. The act authorizes the Secretary of Labor to set safety standards for places of employment. It requires that employers furnish each employee a place of employment which is free from recognized hazards that are causing or are likely to cause serious physical harm or death. Thus, employers must maintain records relative to injuries and accidents and must allow inspectors to visit their establishments to see that standards are being maintained. The act also requires *employees* to comply with all safety and health standards. OSHA penalties may be civil and criminal.

The *Coastal Zone Management Act* of 1972 provides financial assistance to help states in protecting coastal zones from overpopulation and in preserving the natural resources of the coast.

The *Consumer Product Safety Act* of 1972 created the Consumer Product Safety Commission and established a Product Safety Advisory Council to impose safety regulations and standards relating to consumer products. Manufacturers of consumer products must furnish information about their products to the commission and must notify the commission whenever they learn that a product is defective or fails to meet standards. Manufacturers must also notify the general public, commission handlers, and known purchasers whenever it is found that a product is defective or in violation of a safety rule.

The *Federal Water Pollution Control Act* of 1972 was actually a comprehensive revision of legislation enacted in 1947 to deal with water pollution. Even though the states have primary responsibility for preventing, reducing, and eliminating water pollution, they exercise this responsibility within the framework of the new national program established by the act. The act extends federal pollution control to all waters in the United States, not just interstate waters. It authorizes the federal government to seek court injunctions against polluters when water pollution presents "an imminent and substantial endangerment" to public health. The act also increases federal aid to help local governments build sewage treatment facilities, makes financial aid available to small businesses to help them control water pollution, and provides more streamlined stringent enforcement tools than existed previously.

The *Noise Control Act* of 1972 is directed at controlling the noise emission of certain manufactured items rather than at limiting ambient noise levels. Under this act, the Environmental Protection Agency sets limits on noise emission for any product which is identified as a major source of noise or which falls into certain specified categories. A manufacturer subject to noise standards must maintain records and conduct, or permit the EPA to conduct, tests to determine whether the manufacturer is abiding by these standards.

The *Fair Credit Billing Act* of 1974 requires that a creditor take certain steps if a debtor, within 60 days of the receipt of a bill, complains that the billing is in error. The creditor must acknowledge the notice within 30 days and, within two billing cycles and within not more than 90 days, must either correct the error or send a written statement of clarification to the debtor. During this period, the creditor cannot close or restrict the debtor's account, or report or threaten to report the debtor to a credit rating organization. The law also contains provisions relating to the accounting practices of creditors (such as the prompt posting of all payments) and contains some restrictions on credit card issuers and their business practices.

The *Pension Reform Act* of 1974 relates to employee retirement, pension, profit-sharing, thrift, and savings plans and was enacted to control deficiencies and abuses which had occurred in these areas. The statute imposes much greater funding requirements on defined benefit plans, the effect of which is to give greater assurance to participants that the money will be available to pay them the benefits promised them upon retirement. The act also requires termination insurance coverage for all benefit plans, the idea being to require plans to remit annual premiums for insurance to pay the promised benefits to participants in the event that the plan is terminated or that its assets are not sufficient to do so. Strict rules were also established requiring that, in managing, investing, and depositing of a fund's assets, those managing benefit plans exercise the same degree of care that a prudent person would in handling his or her own affairs. The law also ensures the right of employees to benefits under a plan and places a limitation on the maximum retirement benefits which a participant may receive under a qualified defined benefits program. It also provides for rather strict record-keeping and reporting requirements.

The *Magnuson-Moss Warranty—FTC Improvement Act* of 1975 deals with written warranties covering products costing $5 or more. The act does not require manufacturers to give any warranty but states that if a warranty is given, its nature and extent must be in simple and readily understood language. Moreover, if a written warranty is given, there can be no disclaimer of implied warranties. If a product costs more than $15, the warranty must be labeled "full" or "limited." If a warranty is to be "limited," the limitations must be conspicuous so that buyers are not misled. Defective products covered by a "full" warranty must be repaired or replaced within a reasonable period of time at no cost to the consumer. Further, manufacturers cannot impose unreasonable requirements on consumers relative to obtaining repairs and/or replacements. The act also allows class action suits for damages if at least 100 individuals are affected by breach of warranty.

The *Energy Policy and Conservation Act* (1975) requires car dealers to make available "Gas Mileage Guides" in their showrooms. The 1977 guide is now available, and it has two important features that the 1976 guide did not include: (1) all vehicles are divided into classes according to their interior size; and (2) the average annual fuel cost for each car is given. The guide is made available through the joint effort of the Federal Energy Administration and the Environmental Protection Agency. It is hoped that this guide will aid consumers in selecting a vehicle that will meet their transportation needs and achieve fuel economies.

The *Consumer Leasing Act* of 1976 (effective March 23, 1977) requires that companies leasing merchandise make an accurate and detailed disclosure of all terms and costs to the customer. The purpose of the act is to protect the consumer against inadequate or misleading leasing information and thus enable the consumer to compare the various lease terms available and, where appropriate, to compare lease terms with credit terms. The law applies to the leasing of personal property (basically automobiles and other durable goods) for more than four months where the total cost of the transaction is under $25,000. The provisions of this act became additions to the Truth-in-Lending Act.

The purpose of the *Toxic Substances Control Act* of 1976 is to regulate commerce and protect human health and the environment by requiring testing and necessary use restrictions on certain chemical substances. Administered by the Environmental Protection Agency, the act requires the agency to test chemical substances and mixtures to develop data with respect to the risk of injury to health and/or the environment from their manufacture, distribution, processing, use, or disposal.

The *Equal Credit Opportunity Act* of 1977 was passed to open the way for married women to establish a credit history in their own name. It is an amendment to the Equal Credit Opportunity Act, passed in 1974, which prohibits discrimination on the basis of sex or marital status in granting credit. The 1977 amendment stipulates that for an existing account all lenders' reports to credit bureaus include both spouses' names if both use the account and if either requests dual reporting. The act required that notices be sent out between June 1 and October 1, 1977, to all account holders not classified as single to advise them of their new rights. The act makes dual-name reporting mandatory on credit accounts opened after June 1, 1977.*

* Most of the information in this section is taken from the following sources: Ronald A. Anderson and Walter A. Kumpf, *Business Law,* 10th ed. (Cincinnati: South-Western Publishing Company, 1976); Robert N. Corley, Robert L. Black, and O. Lee Reed, *The Legal Environment of Business,* 4th ed. (New York: McGraw-Hill Book Company, 1977); and Marshall C. Howard, *Legal Aspects of Marketing* (New York: McGraw-Hill Book Company, 1964).

APPENDIX B
GLOSSARY OF RETAILING TERMINOLOGY

Source: "Retail Terminology," a publication of NCR Corporation, Dayton, Ohio. The use of any material in this glossary shall be only with permission of the copyright owner (NCR) and not without its specific approval.

A

ABANDONMENT.   In transportation, cargo that has been damaged on a public carrier and refused at its destination.

ABATE.   Reducing an obligation in some manner, for example, a payment when made before due date.

ABSOLUTE SALE.   Buyer and seller agree to a transaction with no conditions or restrictions from either party.

ACCENT.   In fashion apparel, a description, such as emphasizing the French accent or the Italian accent. The design symbolizes a style of the country or other source of the accented idea.

ACCEPTANCE.   (1) Acknowledgment of responsibility by the drawee of an instrument, such as a draft or an invoice. (2) Favorable reception of a product or brand, or its promotion by the market. (3) Assent given by one to whom a legal offer is made.

ACCESSORIAL SERVICE.   In transportation, additional services given by a carrier to a shipper, such as assorting, precooling, heating, and storing.

ACCESSORIES.   Items that are offered in women's apparel stores and department and specialty stores carrying goods for women. Include gloves, hosiery, handbags, jewelry, handkerchiefs, and scarves, and perhaps shoes would be considered accessory items by some. Include items subsidiary to dress, coat, or suit.

ACCOMMODATION DESK.   A service area in a store for customer accommodation on such things as wrapping, buying stamps, or stamping parking permits.

ACCOUNT.   A formal record of a particular type of transaction expressed in money or another unit of measurement and kept in a ledger.

ACCOUNTING.   The art of recording, classifying, and summarizing business transactions in terms of money, and interpreting the results.

ACCOUNTING PERIOD.   The period of time for which an operating statement is customarily prepared; monthly and yearly are the most common accounting periods.

ACCOUNT OPENER.   A premium or special promotion item offered to induce the opening of a new account, especially in financial institutions and stores operating on an installment credit basis.

ACCOUNT PAYABLE.   A liability to a creditor, generally an open account, usually limited to unpaid purchases of goods and services.

ACCOUNT RECEIVABLE.   A claim against a debtor, generally an open account, usually limited to uncollected sales of goods and services and distinguished from deposits, accruals, and other items not arising out of everyday transactions.

ACCOUNT RECEIVABLE DISCOUNTED.   An account receivable that has been assigned or sold with recourse; until paid by the debtor, the amount is a contingent liability of the seller.

ACCOUNTS PAYABLE LEDGER.   This term is used to describe an account with an individual vendor, and to describe all vendors' accounts as a group. It may also be used to describe the accounts payable control account in the general ledger.

ACCOUNTS RECEIVABLE LEDGER.   This term is used to describe an individual customer's account, and to describe all of the customer accounts as a group. It may also be used to describe the accounts receivable control account in the general ledger.

ACCRUAL BASIS OF ACCOUNTING.   Under the accrual basis of accounting, revenue (sales) is reported in the income statement for the period when it is earned (regardless of when it is collected), and expenses are reported in the period when they occur (regardless of when the cash disbursement is made.)

ACRONYMS.   Words formed by use of initials, abbreviations, or parts of a name to identify a company or brand. Examples: "Texaco" for the Texas Company and "AMOCO" for the American Oil Company.

ACT OF GOD.   An action beyond the control of human beings. Examples: earthquakes and landslides.

ADDITIONAL MARKDOWN.   An increase of a previous markdown to further lower the selling price.

ADDITIONAL MARKUP.   The adding of another markup to the original markup; the amount of a price increase, especially in stores operating under the retail inventory method of accounting.

ADDITIONAL MARKUP CANCELLATION.   A downward adjustment in price that is offset against an additional markup.

ADD-ONS.   In charge accounts, purchasing additional merchandise without paying in full for previous purchases, especially in installment credit selling.

ADJUSTMENT.   (1) In selling, the settlement of a price misunderstanding or a refund. (2) In retail charge accounts, the correction of errors: overcharge, improper recording, wrong dating. (3) The handling of a customer's complaint to the satisfaction of both the customer and the store.

ADMINISTRATIVE OFFICES.   In Census of Business publications, locations, such as central offices, executive offices, and district offices, which are engaged in performing administrative functions for the retail stores within the same multiunit organization. Locations having other functions in addition to administrative functions are included in this group.

ADMINISTERED VERTICAL MARKETING SYSTEM.   A form of vertical marketing system designed to control a line or classification of merchandise as opposed to an entire store's operation. Such systems involve the development of comprehensive programs for specified lines of merchandise. The vertically aligned companies, even though in a nonownership position, may work together to reduce the total systems cost of such activities as advertising, transportation, and data processing. See Corporate Vertical Marketing System and Contractual Vertical Marketing System.

ADVANCE.   A down payment on the sale of a product; partial payment.

ADVANCE BILL.   A bill mailed to the buyer before receipt of goods or services; not common unless requested by the purchaser in order to include a payment within a certain period of the year.

ADVANCE DATING.   Arrangement by which the seller sets a specific future date when the terms of sale become applicable. For example, the order may be placed on January 5 and the goods shipped on January 10, but under the terms "2/10, net 30 as of May 1." In this case the discount and net periods are calculated from May 1. "Season Dating" is another name for terms of this kind.

ADVANCE ORDER. An order placed well in advance of the desired time of shipment. By placing orders in advance of the actual buying season, a buyer is often enabled to get a lower price because he gives the supplier business when the latter would normally be receiving little.

ADVERTISING. Any paid form of nonpersonal presentation and promotion of ideas, goods, or services by an identified sponsor, usually involving the use of such media as the following: magazine and newspaper space, motion pictures, outdoor (posters, signs, skywriting, etc.), direct mail, novelties (calendars, blotters, etc.), radio and television, cards (car, bus, etc.), catalogs, directories and references, programs and menus, and circulars.

ADVERTISING AGENCY. A service organization for preparing and placing advertising and related promotional and research activities, paid primarily out of commissions from media used in advertising and partly by advertisers served (clients).

ADVERTISING CAMPAIGN. A coordinated program of advertising activities covering a given period and directed at some specific objective.

ADVERTISING MEDIA. The vehicles or carriers through which an advertising message is conveyed to its intended audience. For example, newspapers, magazines, television.

ADVERTISING RESEARCH. Research primarily concerned with the effectiveness of advertising: copy tests by different methods (before and after publication); readership, recognition, and recall studies; measurement of radio and television audiences; analysis of coupon returns and other replies.

ADVICE OR LETTER OF ADVICE. Formal information from a shipper to a customer about a shipment, or from a banker on credits, drafts, and so on.

AFFILIATED BUYING. See Cooperative Buying and Buying Club.

AFFILIATED STORE. A store operated as a unit of a voluntary chain or franchise group. Also, a store controlled by another store but operated under a separate name.

AFFINITIES. Retail stores that have a natural tendency to be located in close proximity to one another. For example, furniture stores in a city may be located in close proximity to one another in order to facilitate consumer comparison shopping.

AGENCY. See Agent.

AGENT. (1) A business unit which negotiates purchases, sales, or both but does not take title to the goods in which it deals. (2) A person who represents a principal (who, in the case of retailing, is the store or merchant) and who acts under authority, whether in buying or in bringing the principal into business relations with third parties.

AGGREGATION. A concept of market segmentation which assumes that all consumers are alike. Retailers adhering to the concept focus on common dimensions of the market rather than uniqueness, and the strategy is to focus on the broadest possible number of buyers by an appeal to universal product themes. Reliance is on mass distribution, mass advertising, and a universal theme of low price. See Partial Market Segmentation, Extreme Market Segmentation, Benefit Market Segmentation, and Problem Market Segmentation.

AGING. (1) In retailing, aging is the length of time merchandise has been in stock.

(2) The aging of certain products is part of the curing—for example, tobacco, liquor, cheese.

AGING ACCOUNTS.   See Analysis of Accounts.

AIDED RECALL.   A method in testing memory of advertisements or radio-television programs by giving the reader or listener some clue, such as the campaign theme, to learn whether he knows the brand name, the advertiser's name, or some feature of the copy.

AISLE TABLE.   A table in a major store aisle, between departments, used to feature special promotional values.

ALLIED PRODUCTS OR LINES.   Products associated with one another in the same category—for example, associated products in the cosmetic category are lipstick, rouge, and cold cream.

ALLOWANCE FOR BAD DEBTS (Allowance for Doubtful Accounts).   A contra or valuation account to the accounts receivable. Credit entries are made each month to this account for the estimated loss on accounts receivable. In the same manner, actual losses are charged to this account.

ALLOWANCE FOR DEPRECIATION.   An account in the general ledger to show the accumulated depreciation taken. This is used to establish the net valuation of the assets.

ALLOWANCES.   Compensation by a wholesaler or manufacturer for certain services performed by the retailer, such as advertising, displays, or window showing, often granted as a percentage of the purchase price.

ALLOWANCES ON PURCHASES.   See Returns and Allowances from Suppliers.

ALL-PURPOSE REVOLVING ACCOUNT.   A regular 30-day charge account which has no service charge if paid in full within 30 days from the date of statement. But when installment payments are made, a service charge is made on the balance at the time of the next billing.

ALTERATION COST.   Net cost of altering goods for customers and stock repair. Includes labor, supplies, and all expenses, including costs for this service when purchased outside the store.

ALTERATION ROOM (Department).   A section, run in conjunction with one or more selling departments, that alters merchandise to customers' wishes, especially for men's and women's apparel.

ANALYSIS OF ACCOUNTS.   Classification of accounts receivable according to the period of time outstanding—for example, less than 30 days and 30–60 days. A useful method of determining the rate of collection and probable net loss on accounts receivable.

ANCHOR STORE.   Usually a large chain retail operation located in a shopping center and serving as the attracting force for consumers to the center.

ANCILLARY SERVICES.   Include layaway, gift wrap, credit, and any service that is not directly related to the actual sale of a specific product within the store. Some of these services are charged for, and some are not. See Services and Customer Services.

ANGEL.   A term used primarily in the world of the theater, but having similar connotation within retailing. Refers to a person who provides capital to a business venture in the expectation of making a return on his or her investment but who assumes no management role.

ANNIVERSARY SALE. A popular sales promotion theme observing the anniversary of a store's opening date, often observed annually.

ANTICIPATION. A discount in addition to the cash discount if a bill is paid prior to the expiration of the cash discount period, usually at the rate of 6 percent per annum—at this rate, for 60 days' prepayment, which is one sixth of an interest year, the anticipation ratio would be 1 percent of the face amount.

A1 CONDITION. Best or first-class condition.

AOG. Arrival of goods. Applicable to the cash discount period. Indicates that the discount will be granted if payment is made within the number of days specified, calculated from the time the goods arrive at the destination; used for the purpose of accommodating distantly located customers. Net payment period, however, is computed from the time of shipment. See ROG Dating.

APOTHECARY. In America, until recent times, the word referred to a compounder of drugs; predecessor of pharmacy or pharmacist.

APPEAL. Means used in advertising to create the prospect's favorable reaction; usually a plea to a desire that will be satisfied by the benefit bestowed by a product or service.

APPROVAL SALE. A sale subject to later approval or selection, the customer having unlimited return privileges.

APRON. A form attached to invoice or copy of purchase order in retail stores, containing details to check before payment; sometimes called "rider."

AR. All rail; the entire shipment is by rail.

ARCADE SHOPPING CENTER. Enclosed shopping area with a number of stores in lanes under archways and one roof overhead.

ARREARS. A charge account behind in its payments.

AS IS. Merchandise offered for sale without recourse to an adjustment or a refund. The goods may be "irregulars," shopworn, or damaged, but that is understood.

ASSEMBLERS. Establishments engaged primarily in purchasing farm products or seafoods in growers' markets or producing regions. They usually purchase in relatively small quantities, concentrate large supplies, and thus assemble economical shipments for movement into major wholesale market centers.

ASSET. Any owned physical object (tangible) or right (intangible) having a money value; expressed in terms of its cost, depreciated cost, or, less frequently, some other value.

ASSIGNMENT. Formal transfer of property, as for benefit of creditors, especially accounts receivable as collateral for a loan.

ASSOCIATED BUYING OFFICE. A type of resident buying office that is cooperatively maintained in a central market by a group of noncompeting stores. It is controlled and financed by the stores, each store paying its prorated share of the office expenses. See Resident Buying Office.

ASSOCIATED INDEPENDENT. A store owned, operated, and largely merchandised independently, but associated with other stores in the ownership of a merchandise buying organization.

ASSORTMENT. The range of choice offered to the consumer within a particular classification of merchandise. In terms of men's shirts, for example, the range of prices, styles, colors, patterns, and materials that is available for customer selection. The range of choice among substitute characteristics of a given type of article.

ASSORTMENT PLAN.   See Model Stock Plan.

ATMOSPHERICS.   Retail store architecture, layout, lighting, color scheme, temperature, access, noise, assortment, prices, special events, and so on, that serve as stimuli and attention attractors of consumers.

AT THE MARKET PRICE.   The selling price of a product as established by the active force of competition in a market. See Normal Margin Retailer.

AUCTION.   A market in which goods are sold to the highest bidder; usually well publicized in advance or held at specific times well known in the trade. Exchange is effected in accordance with definite rules, with sales made to the highest bidder.

AUCTION COMPANY.   Business establishment engaged in selling merchandise on an agency basis by the auction method.

AUDITED SALES.   Reconciliation of daily cash and charge sales against the recorded total on cash register. Accomplished in a back office procedure at the end of the day.

AUTHORIZED DEALER.   A dealer who has a franchise to sell a manufacturer's product. Usually the only dealer or one of a few selected dealers in a trading area.

AUTHORIZING.   The process by which credit sales are approved either through a telephone system from the selling floor to the credit office or through an automated system tied into a point-of-sale system.

AUTOMATIC MARKDOWN BASEMENT.   Low-price, downstairs area of store in which goods are transferred to sell at progressively lower prices the longer they stay in stock; a merchandising innovation of Filene's, Boston.

AUTOMATIC MERCHANDISING.   Selling by an automatic vending machine. See Automatic Selling.

AUTOMATIC REORDER.   The reorder of staple merchandise on the basis of predetermined minimum stock and specified reorder quantities without the intervention of the buyer except for periodic revision of items to be carried and the minimum and reorder quantities; can be handled manually by reorder clerks or automatically by computer methods.

AUTOMATIC SELLING.   The retail sale of goods or services through coin or currency-operated machines activated by the ultimate consumer-buyer.

B

BACKDOOR SELLING.   (1) Sales to ultimate consumers by wholesalers who hold themselves out to be sellers only to retailers. (2) A salesperson's practice of avoiding a purchasing agent by visiting departments in plants to obtain orders without authorization from the purchasing agent.

BACK HAUL.   Rerouting a freight shipment back over the route it has completed.

BACKLOG.   A reserve, especially with reference to unfilled orders or available funds.

BACK ORDER.   A part of an order that the vendor has not filled on time and that he intends to ship as soon as the goods in question are received, manufactured, or procured.

BAD DEBT.   An uncollectable receivable.

BAD DEBT ACCOUNT.   An account charged periodically with the estimated loss from uncollectable accounts, with an offsetting credit to Allowances for Bad Debts.

BAD RISK.   In the credit field, a classification indicating that a person or firm does not have the character or potential strength to honor debts.

BAIT ADVERTISING.   An alluring but insincere offer to sell; part of a plan or scheme whereby the advertiser does not intend to sell the advertised product at the advertised price; purpose is to increase customer traffic. Also called "bait and switch advertising."

BALANCE.   The difference between the total debits and the total credits of an account.

BALANCED STOCK.   The offering of merchandise in the colors, sizes, styles, and other assortment characteristics that will satisfy customer wants.

BALANCE SHEET.   A statement of financial position disclosing at a given moment of time the cost, depreciated cost, or other indicated value of assets, the amount of the liabilities, and ownership equity.

BANK CHARGE ACCOUNT PLANS.   The bank handles all credit responsibilities and opens charge accounts for customers of the participating stores. The stores are given a window decal or sign which identifies them as members of a particular bank plan. Stores send their charge sales checks to the bank at prearranged intervals, and receive credit for these sales, less a discount rate (usually 5–7 percent) in their own account, usually maintained at the same bank.

BANKRUPTCY (Involuntary).   The state of a debtor resulting from the legal filing of a request for bankruptcy by a creditor or creditors against him to at least partially recoup losses through legal means.

BANKRUPTCY (Voluntary).   The position of a debtor who realizes he cannot meet his obligations to his creditors and asks the court to declare him bankrupt.

BASEMENT STORE.   A department store division which is organized separately from the main store departments (not necessarily located in a basement), handles merchandise in lower price lines, features frequent bargain sales, purchases and offers considerable distress or job-lot merchandise, and usually offers a much more limited range of services and breadth of assortment than do main store departments.

BASIC LOW STOCK.   The lowest level of stock judged permissible for an item; indicates a conception of the smallest number of units that could be on hand without losing sales at the lowest sales period of the year or season.

BASIC STOCK LISTS.   An assortment plan for staple items which are continuously maintained in stock, usually for a period of a year or more.

BASING POINT.   A major producing point or one of several such points for such commodities as steel, cement, and lumber, where producers charge identical prices and no freight charges to buyers. For buyers elsewhere, transportation is included in the quoted price, as if from the basing point, regardless of actual origin of shipment.

BENEFIT MARKET SEGMENTATION.   A concept of market segmentation that seeks to segment markets on the basis of causal factors instead of descriptive factors. It assumes that the advantages people seek in a product are one of the basic reasons for market segmentation. A retailer following this concept is seeking a market segment that desires the benefits offered by the product line featured in his outlet. See Aggregation, Partial Market Segmentation, Extreme Market Segmentation, and Problem Market Segmentation.

BEST SELLERS. Items in each department or classification that sell in greatest volume.

BETTER BUSINESS BUREAU. A voluntary, nonprofit organization formed by responsible business companies to further and promote honesty and dependability in advertising, merchandising, and fair competition in trade, thereby increasing the confidence of the public in business.

BID. An offer.

BILLED COST. The price appearing on a vendor's bill before cash discounts have been deducted but after any trade and quantity discounts from the list price have been deducted.

BILL OF LADING. A document for shipments as evidence of carrier's receipt of the shipment, and as a contract between carrier and shipper. In air shipping called "air waybill."

BLACK MARKET. The availability of merchandise that is difficult or impossible to purchase under normal market circumstances; commonly involves illegal transactions.

BLANKET BRAND. See House Brand.

BLANKET ORDER. A general order placed with a manufacturer without specifying detailed instructions, such as sizes, styles, and shipping dates, all of which are to be furnished later, often in several orders for specific shipments.

BLIND CHECK. The checker counts and lists the items being received without the aid of the invoice.

BOLT. Compact package or roll of cloth.

BOM INVENTORY. Beginning of the month inventory.

BONA FIDE SALE. Sale made in good faith.

BONDED WAREHOUSE. A warehouse that is bonded to insure the owners of the stored goods against loss.

BOOKING. Order taking, especially for delivery at a later date; freuently the amount of production is based on the booking of advance orders.

BOOK INVENTORY. An inventory which is compiled by adding units and/or cost or retail value of incoming goods to previous inventory figures and deducting them from the units and/or cost or retail value of outgoing goods; or the units and/or cost or retail value of goods on hand at any time per the perpetual inventory records.

BOOK OF ORIGINAL ENTRY. An accounting record in which transactions are recorded in the sequence in which they occur; a journal. It serves as a point of origin for further recording in a ledger or book of account.

BOOK VALUE (or Cost). The net amount at which an asset appears on the accounting records as distinguished from its market or intrinsic value.

BOOSTER. Slang for a professional shoplifter.

BOOTLEGGER.   The seller of illegal merchandise.

BOUTIQUE.   In French the word means "little shop," but in American retailing the term has come to mean a carefully selected group of merchandise with unusual displays and fixtures; informal and attractive decor; and an atmosphere of individualized attention in the personalized manner of the image created in the operation. See Boutique Store Layout.

BOUTIQUE STORE LAYOUT.   A form of retail store layout pattern that brings together complete offerings in one department as opposed to having separate departments. For example, a tennis boutique in a department store will feature rackets, balls, shoes, and tennis outfits.

BRANCH HOUSE (Manufacturer's).   An establishment maintained by a manufacturer, separate from the headquarters establishment, and used primarily for the purpose of stocking, selling, delivering, and servicing the product.

BRANCH HOUSE WHOLESALER.   A national, regional, or sectional wholesaler who operates a number of branches to provide better customer service in all parts of the territory covered; differs from a chain wholesaler in that each branch is closely supervised as an extension of the main wholesale house.

BRANCH OFFICE (Manufacturer's).   An establishment maintained by a manufacturer, separate from the headquarters establishment and used as a regional or district sales office.

BRANCH STORES.   Units of a firm, usually administered by an operating executive of the company.

BRAND.   A name, term, sign, symbol, design, or a combination of these used to identify the products of one seller or group of sellers and to differentiate these products from those of competitors.

BRAND ASSOCIATION.   The ability of a consumer to associate a brand product with an advertisement, or vice versa, often measured in consumer marketing research.

BRAND IMAGE.   The total of all the impressions that the consumer receives from many sources: actual experience and hearsay about the brand, its packaging, its name, the company making it, the kinds of stores in which it is sold, the types of people the consumer has seen using or buying the brand, what has been said in the advertising, the tone and format of the advertising, the types of advertising media used.

BRAND LOYALTY.   Degree of consumer preference for one brand compared to close substitutes; it is often measured statistically in consumer marketing research.

BRAND MULTIPLICITY.   A product sold under different trade names; for example, a tire manufacturer who nationally advertises his own brand and also sells to other companies under different trade names.

BRAND SHARE.   The share of the market that one brand of a product has in relation to the whole market.

BREAD-AND-BUTTER ASSORTMENTS.   "Never-out" items within an assortment. Customers expect to find these items in stock, and the store has the obligation to assure that they are always in stock.

BREADTH OF MERCHANDISE OFFERING.   The assortment factors necessary to meet the demands of the market and to meet competition. See Width of Merchandise Offering.

BREAK-EVEN POINT.   The sales volume point at which revenues and costs are equal; a combination of sales and costs which yields a no-profit, no-loss operation.

BROKEN CASE-LOT SELLING.   To accommodate retailers who cannot afford to buy in full shipping case lots, many wholesalers break cases and sell smaller quantities.

BROKEN LOT.   Less than a standard unit of sale.

BROKEN-SIZED LOTS.   An assortment of sizes, but not a complete line of every size.

BROKER.   A middleman who serves as a "go-between" for the buyer or seller; assumes no title risks, does not usually have physical possession of products, and is not looked upon as a permanent representative of either the buyer or the seller.

BUILDUP METHOD OF SPACE ALLOCATION.   A method of determining space allocation for departments in a retail store. Is based upon an analysis of an ideal stock necessary to achieve projected sales volume, of how much stock should be displayed versus how much should be kept in reserve space, of how much physical space will be required to display the merchandise, and of how much physical space will be needed for any service requirements. See Model Stock Approach to Space Allocation.

BULK CHECKING.   Comparing the outside marking on a shipping carton or package with the invoice, without opening the package as a further check.

BULK FREIGHT.   Loose freight, such as coal.

BULK MARKING.   The practice of placing the price only on the original shipping containers or at least bulk packages; individual units are not marked until the merchandise is transferred from reserve to forward stock. Also referred to as deferred marking.

BUSHELMAN.   A repairer of garments, especially in the alteration room for men's clothing.

BUYER'S MARKET.   Such economic conditions as favor the position of the retail buyer (or merchandiser) rather than the vendor. In other words, economic conditions are such that the retailer can demand and usually get concessions from resources in terms of price, delivery, and other market advantages. Just the opposite of a Seller's Market.

BUYING CALENDAR.   A plan of a store buyer's market activities, generally covering a six-month merchandising season based on a selling calendar that indicates planned promotional events.

BUYING CHECKLIST.   A checklist to ensure that all pertinent questions are discussed before a purchase is authorized.

BUYING CLUB.   Any and all consolidations of orders by a number of stores or store buyers in separate stores.

BUYING COMMITTEE.   A committee that has the authority for final judgment and decision on such matters as adding or eliminating new products; especially common in supermarket companies and resident buying offices.

BUYING PERIOD.   The sum of the reorder period and the delivery period under the periodic stock-counting methods of unit control.

BUYING PLAN.   A breakdown of the dollar open-to-buy figure of a department or merchandise classification to indicate the number of units to purchase in different classifications and subclassifications.

BUYING POWER.   (1) The ability to buy in large quantities and thereby procure special price or other concessions. (2) The potential money or family income available for the purchase of consumer goods.

BX (Base Exchange).   A commissary operated for members of the Air Force.

C

CAF (Cost and Freight).   Includes cost of the goods and shipping charges. Neither insurance nor other charges are included.

CALL SYSTEM.   A system of equalizing sales among salespersons—for example, some stores rotate salespersons, giving each an equal opportunity to meet customers.

CANCELLATION.   A notification to a vendor that a buyer does not wish to accept ordered merchandise; also, merchandise declared surplus by retailers, often sold in broken lots to discount houses. (Out-of-style or slightly damaged shoes are frequently sold as "cancellation shoes.")

CANNED SALES TALK.   A prepared sales talk repeated from memory.

CAPITAL.   (1) That portion of the assets of a business which are owed to its owners. (2) In a corporation, the capital accounts represent the liability of the corporation to its stockholders and include capital stock, paid-in surplus, and retained earnings. (3) The liability of a business to its owner; the balance in the capital account of an individual proprietorship will reflect investments made in the business by the owner, less any withdrawals, plus any earnings of the business, less any losses incurred by the business. (4) The capital accounts in a partnership show the liability of the business to each partner, depending upon investment, the withdrawals, and the terms of the partnership agreement as to the division of profits and losses.

CAPITAL ACCOUNT.   An account showing the amount invested in a business by noncreditors, plus the amount of undistributed earnings (or less net losses). In the case of incorporated businesses, total capital is divided into contributed capital and undistributed earnings.

CAPITAL TURNOVER.   The number of times total capital investment is divisible into sales—the greater this figure, the smaller the net profit on sales required to meet a given return on investment.

CAPTIVE MARKET.   The potential clientele of retail or service businesses located in hotels, airports, railroad stations, and so on, where consumers do not have reasonable alternative sources of supply.

CAR CARD.   An advertisement on a laminated card in a public transportation vehicle, usually placed above side windows between strips of molding.

CARLOAD FREIGHT RATE.   A rate for shipping merchandise that is lower than less-than-carload rates because of the economies of the larger shipment.

CARRIAGE TRADE.   An old expression that refers to a wealthy class of patrons accorded special services.

CARRIER.   In transportation, a car, truck, vessel, plane, helicopter, train.

CARRYING CHARGE. The sum paid for credit service on certain charge accounts; interest usually charged on the unpaid balance.

CARRY-OVER MERCHANDISE. Goods left over from one selling season to the next season.

CARTAGE. In transportation, the charge for hauling cargo from pickup to destination.

CASH DISCOUNT. A premium for advance payment at a rate which is usually higher than the prevailing rate of interest; a reduction in price allowed the buyer for prompt payment.

CASH FLOW STATEMENT. A statement of the cash receipts and disbursements of any organization over a particular period of time, often stated in terms of the items appearing in balance sheets and income statements.

CASH REGISTER BANK. An assortment of change for the use of the salesperson. It is prepared at the end of the day by the salesperson operating a cash register or prepared by a cashier for the cash register operator.

CASH TERMS. The payment of cash for the purchase of goods, usually within a certain time period—for example, 10 to 14 days.

CATALOG BUYING. In store buying, the practice of chain store managers making selections and placing orders from merchandise catalogs prepared by the central buying office.

CATALOG SHOWROOM. A retail outlet that consumers visit to make actual purchases of articles described in catalogs mailed to their homes.

CAVEAT EMPTOR. Latin for "Let the buyer beware."

CBD (Cash before delivery). Terms in connection with a sale in which no credit is extended and no risks are assumed by the seller, chiefly because the credit standing of the purchaser is questionable or unknown.

CEASE AND DESIST ORDER. An order issued to a company by a governmental agency to stop what the agency considers an illegal or unfair practice.

CEILING PRICE. The highest price permitted by law on the sale of goods; generally a wartime measure.

CENSUS TRACTS. Small, fairly homogeneous metropolitan areas, usually with between 3,000 and 6,000 population. Detailed population characteristics for such areas are available at the time of decennial censuses. Planning commissions in many cities keep the census tract population figures up-to-date on an annual basis.

CENTER SPREAD. The two facing center pages of a publication.

CENTRAL BUSINESS DISTRICT (CBD). For statistical purposes, this area is specifically defined for individual cities. Because there are not generally accepted rules for determining what a CBD should include or exclude, the Census Bureau did not provide rigid specifications for defining the CBD but provided a general characterization of the CBD, describing it as an area of very high land valuation, an area characterized by a high concentration of retail businesses, offices, theaters, hotels, service businesses, and an area of high traffic flow, and required that the CBD should ordinarily be defined to follow existing tract lines—that is, should consist of one or more whole census tracts.

CENTRAL BUYING. A type of central market representation in which the authority and responsibility for merchandise selection and purchase are vested in the central market office rather than in the individual store units represented by the central office. Also referred to as consolidated buying.

CENTRALIZED ADJUSTMENT SYSTEM. A centralized office that handles complaints, whether placed by telephone, mail, or a personal visit to the store. Would not apply to routine matters, such as the return of merchandise in good condition and within the limits of the store's policy governing "approval" sales, exchanges, and so on.

CENTRAL MARKET. A place where a large number of suppliers are concentrated. The locations may be an area, such as a merchandise mart, or the same general section of a city. For example, New York is still the primary central market for many types of merchandise, especially women's wear.

CENTRAL PLACE. A center of trade or a cluster of retail institutions. It is distinguished from other communities because it is a source of goods and services for an area larger than itself.

CENTRAL PLACE SYSTEMS. Consist of a generalized pattern of subsystems or communities that are in the form of a hierarchy. Each subsystem is capable of performing a particular group of retail functions. Each larger central place, in addition to its own more specialized retail functions, also supports the same retail functions as the smaller central places.

CENTRAL PLACE THEORY. Developed by Walter Christaller in 1933, central place theory is the theory of the location, size, nature, and spacing of communities. The theory provides much of the conceptual basis for the geography of retail location.

CENTS-OFF COUPON. A promotional certificate (see Couponing) that entitles the customer to purchase a particular item of merchandise (or service) with the certificate in hand at a certain amount of money *off* the list price. Particularly popular in food stores as promotional efforts.

CERTIFICATION MARK. Any certified indication of a product's origin, quality, or license.

CERTIFIED PUBLIC ACCOUNTANT. An accountant who has met the requirements as to age, education, residence, moral character, and experience; has passed a uniform examination; and has been licensed by a state to practice public accounting. He uses the initials CPA after his name.

CHAIN (Chain Store System). An organization that consists of two or more centrally owned store units handling substantially similar lines of merchandise.

CHAIN DISCOUNT. A series of trade discount percentages or their total—for example, if a list (catalog) price denotes $100 and is subject to a 40–15–15 discount to dealers, the total or chain discount is $56.65—that is, $100 - 40\% = \$60, \$60 - 15\% = \$51, \$51 - 15\% = \$43.35$.

CHAIN STORE WAREHOUSES. Establishments that are operated by retail multiunit organizations primarily for the purpose of assembling and distributing goods and performing other wholesale functions for the stores of such organizations.

CHANNEL OF DISTRIBUTION. The route taken by the title to a product in its passage from its first owner, the agricultural producer or manufacturer, as the case may be, to the last owner, the ultimate consumer or the business user. Also, the structure of intracompany agents and dealers, wholesale and retail, through which a commodity, product, or service is marketed.

CHARGE ACCOUNT CREDIT.   Of a short-term nature, it is usually intended to be of 30 days' duration or less. It implies a continuing confidence on the part of the store that the buyer will be able to meet purchase obligations of a limited amount and to do this out of his current income. Also called *regular* charge account credit.

CHARGE PHONE SYSTEM.   Authorization given a salesperson by telephone to approve certain orders necessary to prevent the granting of credit to customers with a poor financial background.

CHART OF ACCOUNTS.   A list of accounts systematically arranged, applicable to a specific business, giving account names and numbers.

CHATTEL MORTGAGES.   When used in conjunction with installment sale contracts, title passes immediately to the buyer but the seller takes a mortgage upon the item to secure his extension of credit.

CHERRY PICKING.   Buyer selection of only a few numbers from one vendor's line, other numbers from another line, failing to purchase a complete line or classification of merchandise from one resource. With rapid development of multiunit stores, cherry picking from large numbers of resources becomes economically unsound.

CIA (Cash in Advance). Used interchangeably with "cash before delivery," and applies in the same instances as the latter.

CIRCULATION (Primary).   A figure including not only the buyer of the journal but members of his immediate family who also read the same journal—for example, if a man buys a paper, but his wife and son also read it, the primary circulation is three.

CL (Carload) FREIGHT RATES.   Freight rates that apply to full-carload shipments.

CLAIM.   In transportation, a statement of charges for damage to goods while in shipment or in possession of the carrier.

CLASSIC MERCHANDISE.   Merchandise not influenced by style changes, for which a demand virtually always exists.

CLASSIFICATION. A grouping of merchandise into a homogeneous category usually smaller than a department; useful for control purposes in particular. See Dissection Control.

CLASSIFICATION CONTROL.   A form of dollar inventory control where the dollar value of each classification of goods is smaller than the total stock of the department—for example, the sporting goods department may be divided into several classifications or dissections, such as golf, fishing, and active sports.

CLEARANCE SALE.   An end-of-season sale to make room for new goods; also "pushing" the sale of slow-moving, shopworn, and demonstration model goods.

CLIPPING BUREAU.   An agency which clips and files news stories, advertisements, and other forms of printed matter on a subscription basis for clients.

CLOSED DISPLAY.   Exhibit of advertised goods or promotional material under counter glass or in a case, as distinguished from "open display."

CLOSED-DOOR DISCOUNT HOUSE.   A discount store that sells only to consumers who purchase a membership card.

CLOSED STOCK.   Items sold only in sets with no assurance to the customer that the same pattern and quality can be bought at any later time. The merchandise is generally sold only in sets with no provision for replacing broken pieces (as opposed to *open* stock).

CLOSEOUT.   Offer at reduced price to clear slow-moving or incomplete stock; also, an incomplete assortment, the remainder of a line of merchandise that is to be discontinued, offered at a low price to ensure immediate sale.

CLOSING ENTRY.   A periodic entry or one of a series of periodic entries by means of which the balances in revenue and expense accounts and other accounts are adjusted for the purpose of preparing financial statements.

CLOSING INVENTORY.   The value of inventory on hand at the end of an accounting period, either at cost or at retail.

CLOSING THE BOOKS.   The process of transferring the balances of the income and expense accounts into the Profit and Loss account.

CLUB PLAN SELLING.   An arrangement in which a consumer is awarded prizes or granted discount buying privileges by getting new customers to join the "club." The "club" is the group of customers served by the selling organization, and one joins by making purchases.

COD (Collect on Delivery).   The buyer must make payment for purchase at time of delivery of goods; considered a poor substitute for "cash before delivery" (CBD) or "cash in advance" (CIA), because if the purchaser refuses the goods, the seller incurs return freight charges and any deterioration of the products in the process.

COG (Customer's Own Goods).

COLLECTION LETTER.   A letter sent to a debtor requesting payment, generally in a polite manner. The language becomes stronger with each additional letter and may reach the point where a suit is threatened.

COLUMNAR SYSTEM.   A system of bookkeeping whereby use is made of columnar records that permit continuous analysis and grouping of items, thus reducing the labor of posting.

COMMISSARY STORE.   Retail outlet owned and operated by one of the armed forces to sell food and related products to military personnel at special prices.

COMMISSION.   From the point of view of compensation, salespeople are paid a certain percentage of (usually) net sales as an incentive. See Straight Commission, Quota Bonus Compensation Plan, Salary plus Commission on Net Sales.

COMMISSION BUYERS OF FARM PRODUCTS.   Wholesale establishments primarily engaged in buying farm products on a commission basis from farmers for others.

COMMISSION BUYING OFFICE.   One that receives its remuneration in the form of commissions on orders placed from manufacturers rather than from retailers.

COMMISSIONAIRES.   A specialized type of buying agency that brings the domestic buyer in contact with proper vendors in foreign markets and acts as an interpreter for the domestic buyer; also facilitates the procedures of foreign exchange and shipping.

COMMISSION HOUSE (Commission Merchant).   An agent who usually exercises physical control over and negotiates the sale of goods. Generally enjoys broader powers as to prices, methods, and terms of sale than does the broker, although must obey instructions issued by the principal. Often arranges delivery, extends necessary credit, collects, deducts fees, and remits the balance to the principal.

COMMITMENTS. (1) Value of merchandise a selling department buyer is obligated to accept into stock during a given period. (2) Sometimes used to denote unconfirmed orders. In group buying a buyer may indicate intention of buying a certain quantity of an item. Until this plan is authorized by the merchandise manager, it is sometimes called a a commitment.

COMMITTEE BUYING. Whenever the buying decision is made by a group of people rather than a single buyer. A multiunit operation is usually the type of firm that uses this procedure.

COMMODITY EXCHANGE. An organization usually owned by the member-traders which provides facilities for bringing together buyers and sellers (or their agents) of specified standard commodities for promoting trades in these commodities—either spot or future, or both—in accordance with prescribed rules.

COMMON CARRIER. Individuals or transportation firms franchised by a government regulatory body that requires them to accept shipments from any party, maintain regular service over established routes, and move freight at published rates.

COMMUNITY SHOPPING CENTER. A type of shopping center usually having a gross floor area of 100,000 to 300,000 square feet, usually with a variety or junior department store as its anchor tenant, whose trading area normally does not extend beyond the community in which it is located.

COMPARATIVE BALANCE SHEET. Two or more balance sheets of the same organization with different dates, or of two or more organizations with the same date, customarily displayed in parallel columns to facilitate the observation of variances; supplementary columns are sometimes added to show differences.

COMPARATIVE PRICES. Statements in advertisements or signs comparing specific prices with previous prices, other prices, or price goods are estimated to be worth.

COMPARISON SHOPPING. Two major types of activity, namely merchandise shopping and service shopping, are involved. (1) Merchandise shopping activities rendered by an organized shopping bureau; include checks of new items being offered by competing stores, reports on advertised promotions of competitors, comparison price shopping, and so on. (2) Service shopping is normally performed by shoppers who pose as customers and report the quality of selling service on standard forms.

COMPLEMENT OF MARKUP PERCENTAGES. One hundred percent less markup percentage on retail.

COMPUTERIZED RETAIL SYSTEM. The utilization of computers in data collection and display for the purpose of decision making based on analysis of the information presented. Typically the integral part of an integrated point-of-sale system with terminals at the point of sale. The most sophisticated type of retail system, manual systems being the least sophisticated type.

CONCENTRIC ZONE THEORY. A theory of urban land use patterns, developed by William Burgess, which states that a city will assume the form of five concentric urban zones: the central business district, the zone in transition, the zone of working persons' homes, the zone of better residences, and the commuters' zone. Growth is accomplished by the expansion of each zone into the next zone.

CONCESSION.   Grant or lease of part of premises for a commercial purpose, as at a fair or amusement park; a leased department.

CONDITION.   An essential part of a contract, the breach of which discharges the contract. Method of shipment and merchandise specifications are conditions of a contract to deliver goods. If the vendor deviates from them, the buyer is under no obligation to receive goods unless he has been habitually receiving goods after the vendor has violated conditions.

CONDITIONAL SALE CONTRACT.   Agreement under which the title does not pass to the buyer until he has fulfilled his contract obligations. The buyer assumes complete responsibility upon delivery, must maintain the article purchased, and must make regular payments. If he defaults, the seller may repossess, use the proceeds of a sale of the item to satisfy the remaining obligation, and refund the excess, if any, above the cost of repossession and sale, to the buyer. If the proceeds of a sale are insufficient, the buyer is still technically liable to the seller for the remainder.

CONFIRMATION (of Order).   From the store's standpoint, the official order of a store for goods made out on the store order form and countersigned by the buyer and merchandise manager. It is distinguished from the memorandums that buyers often make out on vendors' order blanks that are not official orders and are not binding on the store. From the vendor's standpoint, the acknowledgment of a buyer's order by the vendor; his legal acceptance of the offer made by the buyer, generally in writing.

CONSERVATIVE RULE OF INVENTORY VALUATION.   Valuing ending inventory at the *lower* of cost or market. See Cost Inventory.

CONSIDERATION.   Something of value received or given at the request of the promisor in reliance on and in return for promise. It may be a payment of money, or merely an exchange of promises, as when a buyer orders goods and the vendor confirms the order. The buyer promises to buy and take the goods, and the vendor promises to sell and ship them.

CONSIGNEE.   Party or agent to whom the products are assigned and/or delivered.

CONSIGNMENT.   Products shipped for future sale or other purpose, title remaining with the shipper (consignor), for which the receiver (consignee), upon acceptance, is accountable. The consignee may be the eventual purchaser, may act as the agent through whom the sale is effected, or may otherwise dispose of the products in accordance with agreement with the consignor.

CONSIGNMENT PURCHASE AND DATING.   Very similar to memorandum purchase, except that the title to the goods does not pass at the time of shipment but at the expiration of a specified period, when the buyer is privileged to return any unsold goods. See Memorandum Purchase.

CONSIGNMENT SALE.   Title remains with the vendor until the goods are resold by the retailer; however, any unsold portion of the goods may be returned to the vendor without payment.

CONSIGNOR.   In traffic, the company or person shipping the products.

CONSOLIDATED BUYING. See Central Buying.

CONSOLIDATED DELIVERY SERVICE. A private business organized to deliver products for retailers. A fee is charged for every package delivered.

CONSULAR INVOICE. A copy of a foreign invoice signed by the American consul in the country of origin assuring that the invoice is genuine and the prices approximately correct.

CONSUMER. Individual, household, or family as purchaser and user of goods; distinguished from industrial user, from the buyer of industrial goods for remanufacture, and from the distributor who buys for resale. Sometimes called "ultimate consumer."

CONSUMER ADVERTISING. Promotion directed toward those who will personally use the product; distinguished from trade advertising, industrial advertising, professional advertising.

CONSUMER COOPERATIVE. A marketing organization owned and operated for the mutual benefit of consumer-owners who have voluntarily associated themselves for this purpose.

CONSUMER CREDIT. Credit used by individuals or families for the satisfaction of their own wants; also, the granting of credit by retailers, banks, and finance companies for this purpose.

CONSUMER (or Personal) FINANCE COMPANIES. Lending agencies licensed under state laws to engage in the business of lending money to consumers.

CONSUMERISM. A movement that expresses the concerns of the consumer for rights believed to be a natural expectation. The rights are the right to safety, to be informed, to choose, and to be heard. The "players" are the consumer, business, and government.

CONSUMER JURY. See Consumer Panels.

CONSUMER MOTIVATION. The study of what makes people act in a certain way when buying; an analysis of whether a customer's purchases are based on emotional or logical considerations.

CONSUMER PANEL. A consumer sample participating on a continuing basis in market research and product or service evaluation.

CONTAINERIZING. The practice in transportation of consolidating a number of packages into one container which is sealed at the point of origin and remains sealed until it reaches the point of destination.

CONTAINER PREMIUM. A container with a utility function after its contents have been removed, serving as an inducement to buy the product.

CONTINGENT LIABILITY. A potential obligation created by past events whose existence depends on future events. The associated dollar valuation may or may not be estimable.

CONTINUITY PREMIUMS. Sets or series of merchandise (china, table silver, etc.) given one at a time or one for a certain number of coupons. To get the entire set, the consumer must buy the advertised product continuously.

CONTRA ACCOUNT (Valuation Account). An offset account that is used to establish the net valuation of another account. Examples: Allowance for Depreciation, Allowance for Bad Debts.

CONTRABAND. Illegal merchandise.

CONTRACT.   An agreement enforceable by law. The essential ingredients are (1) a lawful promise, (2) competent parties, (3) an offer and acceptance, (4) a consideration, (5) a meeting of minds, and (6) in writing, if involving more than a certain amount ($50 in most states) or if extending for longer than one year.

CONTRACT CARRIERS.   Transportation companies that provide shipping service to one or various shippers on a contract basis. They do not maintain regularly scheduled service, and their rates are more easily adapted to specific situations than are those of the common carrier.

CONTRACT DEPARTMENT.   Unit in a department store set up to sell in quantity to institutions such supplies as food, bedding, and floor coverings; a department that arranges for the sale of goods in quantity to large buyers at special prices.

CONTRACTUAL VERTICAL MARKETING SYSTEM.   A form of vertical marketing system in which independent firms at different levels in the channel operate contractually to obtain economies and market impacts that could not be obtained by unilateral action. Under this system, the identity of the individual firm and its autonomy of operation remain intact. See Retailer-Sponsored Cooperatives, Wholesaler-Sponsored Voluntaries, and Franchising. See also Corporate Vertical Marketing System and Administered Vertical Marketing System.

CONTRIBUTION PLAN OR EXPENSE ALLOCATION.   Under this plan, departments are assigned only those expenses that can be charged directly to the department, that is, controllable expenses. The department is then evaluated on its contribution to storewide profits rather than on the profit of the department itself. Indirect, or noncontrollable, expenses are not allocated; thus, the contribution margin of the department goes toward covering total store indirect overhead costs.

CONTROL.   The process by which a person or an organization, operation, or other activity is made to conform to a desired plan of action.

CONTROL (or CONTROLLING) ACCOUNT.   An account whose balance equals the sum of the balances of a number of detail accounts. Example: accounts receivable control account.

CONTROLLABLE COSTS.   Costs which vary in volume, efficiency, choice of alternatives, and management determination; any cost an organizational unit has authority to incur and/or ability to change. See Direct Expenses.

CONTROLLED CIRCULATION.   Free distribution of a business magazine to a selected list of industrial or trade prospects for the magazine's advertisers.

CONTROLLER.   One of the vice presidential positions in most firms under whose purview fall all of the company's fiscal and accounting operations; in charge of the control division. Also known as "comptroller."

CONVENIENCE GOODS.   Articles which consumers purchase with a minimum of searching, measured either in terms of time or money spent in shopping, because the probable gain or satisfaction from making comparisons of alternatives is ordinarily slight.

CONVENIENCE STORE.   A retail institution whose primary advantage to consumers is locational and time convenience. These are high-margin, high-turnover retail institutions.

CONVERTER.   In the textile and paper trades, a wholesaling firm engaged in manufacturing activities to a significant degree; also, a firm (or merchant) that purchases gray cotton cloth (woven but not finished) and has it bleached, dyed, printed, or mercerized before sale.

COOPERATIVE.   An establishment owned by an association of customers. In general, the distinguishing features of a cooperative are patronage dividends based on the volume of expenditures by the members and a limitation of one vote per member, regardless of the amount of stock owned.

COOPERATIVE ADVERTISING.   A policy whereby a firm pays for the whole or part of advertisements of its product which are sponsored by a reseller in the firm's channel of distribution.

COOPERATIVE BUYING.   Any and all consolidations of orders by a number of stores or store buyers in separate stores. Also called "affiliated buying." See Buying Club.

COOPERATIVE CHAIN.   A group of retailers who on their own initiative have banded together for the purpose of buying, merchandising, or promoting.

COOPERATIVE DELIVERY.   Cooperative ownership and management of a single delivery system serving several retailers.

COOPERATIVE WHOLESALER.   A wholesale business owned by retail merchants. Typically, the wholesale establishment buys in its own name. Common in the food, drug, and hardware lines.

COOPTATION.   The inclusion of channel members at all levels in the decision-making apparatus so that channel members at all levels have a clearer understanding of common problems in the distribution of goods.

COPYRIGHT.   Legal protection for a writer or artist from having his work copied, plagiarized, or sold without permission for a 28-year period with a renewable right for another 28 years.

CORPORATE VERTICAL MARKETING SYSTEM.   A form of vertical marketing system in which all of the functions from production to distribution are at least partially owned and controlled by a single enterprise. Corporate systems typically operate manufacturing plants, warehouse facilities, and retail outlets. See Contractual Vertical Marketing System and Administered Vertical Marketing System.

COST CENTER.   A division, a department, or a subdivision thereof, a group of machines, people, or both, a single machine, operator, or any other unit of activity into which a business is divided for cost assignment and allocation.

COST CODES.   Item cost information indicated on price tickets in code. A common method of coding is to use letters from an easily remembered word or expression with nonrepeating letters corresponding to numerals. The following is illustrative:

youngblade
1234567890

COST DEPARTMENT.   A manufacturing or processing department within a retail store that is operated on the cost method of accounting; also, one of the independent departments selling merchandise or service (principally service) but carrying no inventories at retail value—for example, restaurant, barber shop, fur storage, and beauty parlor.

COST INVENTORY.   The actual cost or market value, whichever is lower, of the inventory on hand at any time. The term seldom refers to the original price paid for the merchandise, but rather to the present depreciated worth. If original price is to be designated, the term generally used is *billed cost of inventory*. See Conservative Rule of Inventory Valuation.

COST METHOD OF INVENTORY (Specific Identification of Retail Inventories). The determination of the cost of inventory on hand by marking the actual cost on each price ticket in code and computing inventory value using these unit cost prices.

COST MULTIPLIER.   The complement of the mark-on percent. This figure indicates the average relationship of cost to retail value of goods handled in the accounting period. Also referred to as the cost complement or the cost percent.

COST OF GOODS PURCHASED.   The purchase price of products bought plus the cost of transportation or delivery to the point where they are to be used. Does not typically include cash discounts.

COST OF SALES.   The difference between the opening inventory plus purchases at cost minus the closing inventory at cost, either before or after cash discounts have been deducted or alteration and workroom costs added. Other terms used: *gross cost of merchandise sold, total merchandise costs,* and *cost of goods sold.*

COST-PLUS.   Method of determining the selling price of goods or services whereby cost is increased in an amount equal to an agreed increment to cost.

COUNTER CARD.   A display card or poster placed on a counter to remind customers of the article for sale at that particular counter.

COUNTERSIGN.   A signature of a responsible person vouching for the reliability of the buyer. In a sale to minors, the seller may require the signature of a parent. In case of a default, the countersigner is legally responsible.

COUNTRY CLUB BILLING.   See Descriptive Billing.

COUPON ACCOUNT.   Coupons purchased for cash and used to make purchases in the store selling them.

COUPONING.   The distribution of certificates as a method of promotion that gives a customer the opportunity to buy a particular piece of merchandise (or a service) at a reduced price as stated on the certificate. See Cents-off Coupon, Store Coupon, Vendor Coupon.

COURTESY DAYS.   Days on which stores extend credit customers the privilege of making purchases at sale prices in advance of public sale.

COURTESY OR GRACE PERIOD.   The length of time beyond the nominal terms of sale that a customer may continue to make credit purchases without paying his account or making satisfactory arrangements for so doing.

CREATIVE SELLING.   A kind of selling of the highest level in retailing; involves knowledge of merchandise, ability to demonstrate, present product (or service) advantages, and also explain how and when the offering can and should be used. Just the opposite of "routine selling" or "self-service."

CREDIT.   (1) The power or ability to obtain goods, services, or money in exchange for a promise to pay later. (2) The right side of an account. A credit entry is an entry to the right side of any ledger. Credits will normally be increases to liability accounts and decreases to asset accounts. They may also be increases to income accounts and decreases to expense accounts.

CREDIT BUREAU. An organization that collects, maintains, and provides credit information to members or subscribers; sometimes cooperatively owned by users of the service. Maintains an up-to-date file containing a so-called master card (of credit information) for each consumer who has asked for credit from local merchants who use the service of the bureau.

CREDIT HISTORY CARD. A record maintained by the credit department on the payment history of credit customers for the purpose of extending additional credit and the like.

CREDIT INTERCHANGE. A system whereby merchants exchange credit information about a potential customer; performed by contacting a merchant, a trade association, or credit exchange offices (credit bureaus).

CREDIT LIMIT. The quantitative limit that indicates the maximum amount of credit that may be allowed to be outstanding on each individual customer account.

CREDIT TICKET. A form used by stores when a customer returns merchandise for a cash refund; usually filled out by the clerk and routed to the accounting department.

CREDIT UNIONS. Cooperative savings and loan organizations formed for the purpose of encouraging thrift among members and making loans to them at relatively low rates of interest.

CREDIT VOUCHER. In retailing, an authorization by a company official to grant a refund credit to a customer.

CROSS SELLING. The process of selling between and among departments to facilitate larger transactions and to make it more convenient for the customer to accessorize. See Interselling.

CUBE EFFECT IN MERCHANDISING. A concept in interior retail store design that utilizes display fixtures at least 7 feet high rather than the standard 4 foot 6 inch fixture.

CULL. Imperfect merchandise discarded because of inferior quality.

CUMULATIVE MARK-ON. The total of mark-on on the beginning inventory in any accounting period plus the aggregate purchase mark-on during the period, including additional markups, before any markdowns; the difference between the total cost and the total original retail value of all goods handled to date; commonly expressed as "percentage of cumulative original retail."

CUMULATIVE QUANTITY DISCOUNT (Patronage Quantity Discount). A price reduction or rebate based on the total amount of merchandise purchased over a predetermined period of time; does not consider the size or number of individual orders making up the total.

CURRENT ASSET. Unrestricted cash or other assets held for conversion within a relatively short period into cash or other similar asset or useful product, usually for a period of one year or less—for example, inventory, accounts receivable.

CURRENT LIABILITY. A short-term debt, regardless of its source, including any liability accrued and deferred, and unearned revenue that is to be paid out of current assets or is to be transferred to income within a relatively short period, usually one year or less.

CURRENT RATIO. The ratio of current assets to current liabilities.

CUSTOMER CONVERSION PROMOTION. A promotional activity designed to influence customers of a given product to switch from one brand to another. See Reminder Promotion, Market Positioning Promotion, Market Expansion Promotion, and Image Development Promotion.

CUSTOMER SERVICES.   Include layaway, giftwrap, credit, and any service not directly related to the actual sale of a specific product within the store. Some of these services are charged for, and some are not. See Services and Ancillary Services.

CUSTOM SELLING.   An outside salesperson calls on a customer in the home and measures, designs, or partially designs specifically for the customer a particular item of merchandise. A good example would be the outside sales approach of a drapery department or store wherein the merchandise is made to order for the customer rather than selected "off the rack."

CWO (Cash with Order).   The seller demands that cash covering the cost of merchandise and delivery accompany the customer's order. Cash before delivery (CBD) and cash in advance (CIA) apply similarly.

D

DATA BASE.   An available source of information from which a decision maker draws. For example, charge accounts can provide a data base for an analysis of where charge customers are located.

DATINGS.   The time limits governing payment for purchases. There are two principal types: (1) cash dating, the terms of which call for immediate payment; and (2) future dating.

DEALER IMPRINT.   Name and address of retail outlet, especially printed (added) on promotion material (dealer aids) furnished by a national advertiser; indicates where the advertised goods can be bought locally and seeks to add dealer's prestige to the manufacturer's.

DEALERSHIP.   The conventional type of franchise that grants a franchisee an exclusive marketing territory. See Service Franchise, Mobile Franchise, Distributorship, and Ownership Franchise.

DEBIT.   The left side of an account. A debit entry is an entry to the left side of any ledger. Debits will normally be increases to asset accounts and decreases to liability accounts. They may also be increases to expense accounts and decreases to income accounts.

DECAL.   A transparent, gelatinous film bearing an advertisement (trademark, product name, slogan) that can be affixed to a dealer's window, door, or showcase, usually to show that he is an outlet for the product thus advertised; a transparency."

DECENTRALIZED ADJUSTMENT SYSTEM.   Customers take their complaints directly to the selling department involved. Salespeople may make most of the adjustments, although the final approval of the department head or floor manager is often a requirement.

DEFERRED MARKING.   See Bulk Marking.

DELICATESSEN BUYING.   A store presents many different items in insufficient depth to satisfy customer demand for those sampled items. A highly questionable merchandising philosophy.

DELIVERED PRICE.   A quoted or invoice price that includes delivery costs to the f.o.b. point, the latter being a freight terminal, warehouse, or other location commonly accepted in the particular trade or specifically agreed upon between buyer and seller.

DELIVERY PERIOD.   The normal time between the placing of an order and the receipt of stock.

DEMOGRAPHICS.   "A picture of the population"—a description of the distribution of a target population in terms of age, sex, number of households, education, occupational level, income, and so on.

DEMURRAGE.   A transportation fee that is charged every day for goods stored in a car after the grace period (the time allowed for removing goods shipped in carlots after the car is delivered to the consignee).

DEPARTMENTIZED SPECIALTY STORE.   A term used to designate a concern organized in the same way as a department store but handling a narrower range of merchandise.

DEPARTMENTIZING.   The process of classifying merchandise into somewhat homogeneous groups known as departments.

DEPARTMENT MANAGER.   In a department or specialty store operation, this is likely to be the title for the buyer in the department, who is responsible for the selling as well. In a chain organization, it is more likely that this person is responsible for the sale of merchandise that has been purchased by the central buyer.

DEPARTMENT STORE.   A retail organization which carries several lines of merchandise, such as women's ready-to-wear and accessories, men's and boys' clothing, piece goods, small wares, and home furnishing, all of which are organized into separate departments for the purpose of promotion, service, accounting, and control. For census purposes, establishments normally employing 25 or more people and engaged in selling some items in each of the following lines of merchandise: furniture, home furnishings, appliances, radio and TV sets; a general line of apparel for the family; household linen and dry goods. An establishment with total sales of less than $5 million in which sales of any one of these groupings is greater than 80 percent of total sales is not classified as a department store.

DEPARTMENT STORE OWNERSHIP GROUPS.   Aggregations of centrally owned stores in which each store continues to merchandise and operate primarily as an individual concern with central guidance rather than central management or direction.

DEPRECIATED COST.   Cost less accumulated depreciation, if any, and less any other related valuation account having the intended effect of reducing the capitalized outlays to a recoverable cost.

DEPRECIATION.   Lost usefulness; expired utility; the diminution of service yield from a fixed asset or a fixed asset group that cannot or will not be restored by repairs or by replacement of parts; necessitated by wear and tear from use, obsolescence, or inadequacy.

DEPRESSION.   Lower phase of a business cycle in which the economy is operating with substantial unemployment of its resources and a sluggish rate of capital investment and consumption resulting from little business and consumer optimism.

DERIVED COST INVENTORY.   The market or wholesale value of goods on hand as determined from their value (retail) by applying the complement of the initial markup percentage.

DESCRIPTIVE BILLING.   A type of charge statement prepared for the customer in which a printout of the period's (usually a month) purchases appear on one statement with a description of the item purchased, the date, and the price, but the original sales check is not included in the statement. Country club billing is just the opposite.

DESCRIPTIVE LABELS.   Labels that carry terms descriptive of each significant characteristic of the product which is susceptible to objective measurement.

DETAILING.   Personal sampling and other promotional work among doctors, dentists, and other professional men done for pharmaceutical concerns in order to secure goodwill and possible distribution or prescription of their products.

DIALECTIC PROCESS THEORY.   A theory of retail institutional change. When challenged by a competitor with a differential advantage, an established institution will adopt strategies in the direction of that advantage. Also, the innovator makes changes in the direction of the "negated" institution. As a result of these mutual adaptations, the two retailers become quite similar or indistinguishable and constitute a new retail institution, termed the synthesis. This new institution is then vulnerable to "negation" by new competitors as the dialectic process begins anew. See Wheel of Retailing Theory, Retail Accordion Theory, and Natural Selection Theory.

DIRECT ACCOUNT.   A customer that is served directly, as contrasted with others that are sold through middlemen.

DIRECT ADVERTISING.   Mass or quantity promotion, not in an advertising medium, but issued from the advertiser by mail or personal distribution to individual customers or prospects; also, advertising literature appearing in folders, leaflets, throwaways, letters, and delivered to prospective customers by mail, salespersons, or dealers, or tucked into mailboxes.

DIRECT BUYING.   Buying directly from a manufacturer.

DIRECT CHECK.   Checking of the goods received against the vendor's invoice to determine whether the quantities received correspond with the amounts shown on the invoice.

DIRECT COST METHOD OF INVENTORY.   A system under which the cost value of each item sold is recorded along with the selling price so an accurate costing of sales may be obtained.

DIRECT EXPENSES.   Expenses that can easily be allocated to departments, branch stores, etc. These expenses are "direct" because they can be assigned to a specific area. Also called "controllable," as under control of a particular department. If the department were discontinued, the expenses would be discontinued. See Controllable Costs.

DIRECT SELLING.   Process whereby the firm responsible for production sells to the user, ultimate consumer, or retailer without intervening middlemen.

DIRECT SELLING ORGANIZATIONS.   Nonstore retailing establishments which solicit orders and distribute their products by house-to-house canvas.

DISCOUNT STORE.   Generally a large retail store open to the public which incorporates aspects of supermarket merchandising strategy to a high degree, attempts to price merchandise at a relatively low markup, renders only limited types of consumer services, usually on the basis of a specific extra charge. Can be distinguished from regular retailers only by its consistent emphasis upon "discount prices" and its self-designation as a discount store.

DISCRETIONARY BUYING POWER.   (1) Disposable personal income not required for the purchase of the basic necessities of life. (2) Disposable income not preempted by habitual purchases and contractual arrangements.

DISPLAY STORE.   A small store controlled by a mail-order house, containing samples of some of the best-selling lines in the catalog for display only.

DISPOSABLE PERSONAL INCOME.   Personal income minus income tax and other personal taxes paid to government units.

DISSECTION CONTROL. The subdividing of existing departments into relatively narrow groupings, then the establishing of dollar stock control records for each grouping. See Classification.

DISTRESS MERCHANDISE.   Merchandise marked down in order to make possible its rapid disposal; a situation brought about by a financial stringency or other emergency demanding a quick turnover; merchandise reclaimed by a manufacturer or wholesaler from a retailer for lack of payment.

DISTRIBUTION COST ANALYSIS.   A type of cost accounting that studies and evaluates income and outlays for different methods of marketing.

DISTRIBUTIVE EDUCATION.   A federally assisted program of education (augmented by state and local support) for workers in the distributive occupations at the high school and adult training level. Classwork in school facilities is combined with concurrent work experience.

DISTRIBUTIVE TRADES.   Establishments that are engaged principally in marketing products (wholesale trade, retail trade, and service industries).

DISTRIBUTOR.   Wholesale middlemen, especially in lines where selection or exclusive agency distribution is common at the wholesale level and the manufacturer expects strong promotional support. Often a synonym for *wholesaler.*

DISTRIBUTORSHIP.   A type of franchise system wherein franchisees maintain warehouse stock to supply other franchisees. The distributor takes title to the goods and provides services to other customers. See Service Franchise, Mobile Franchise, Dealership, and Ownership Franchise.

DIVERSION-IN-TRANSIT.   A change of direction from original destination while freight is in transit.

DODGERS.   Advertising circulars which are handed out on the streets or placed in doorways by carriers.

DOI DATING.   Denotes that the discount period begins with the date of the invoice. Both the cash discount and the net amount are due within the specified number of days from the date of the invoice.

DOLLAR CONTROL.   Control of sales, stocks, markdowns, and markups in terms of dollars rather than in terms of pieces or items.

DOMESTICS.   Classification of merchandise, including muslins, sheets, pillow cases.

DRAFT.   A written order to transfer a specified sum of money, usually domestic. Equivalent to bill of exchange.

DRAWING ACCOUNT.   An account from which an employee is permitted to draw commissions against future sales. Deficits are accumulated and subtracted from earned commissions in later periods when there is an excess over the drawing account limit.

DRAYAGE. Charges for hauling goods from one area to another, particularly to and from shipside.

DROP SHIPPER (Desk Jobber). A special type of wholesaler who deals in large lots shipped direct from the factory to the customer, takes title to the goods, assumes responsibility for the shipment after it leaves the factory, extends credit, collects the account, and incurs all the sales costs necessary to secure orders.

DUAL DISTRIBUTION. Under this type of distribution program, manufacturers sell directly to contractors and other large accounts at prices equal to or less than those available to independent retailers in the same market who are selling the manufacturer's products.

DUE BILL. A certificate for a stated monetary value that is valid at the store where issued. Stores issue due bills in lieu of cash for merchandise returns.

DUMPING. Selling low-price and/or low-quality products, especially in a foreign market, to meet competition or to unload a surplus on hand.

DUN. A demand for payment of a bill or account.

DUNNAGE. Protective materials, bracing, lining, flooring, and so on, for the protection of goods in shipment on a carrier.

E

EARLY MARKDOWN. A markdown taken early in the season or while the demand for the merchandise is still relatively active.

ECONOMIC CONCEPT OF RENT. A term reflecting the maximum amount that can be spent by a retail store for yearly rental expenses. Is calculated by subtracting from planned sales all projected operating expenses (except rent) and a projected or planned profit figure.

ECONOMY PACK. A merchandising phrase pointing out savings by including several products in one wrapping.

EDP (Electronic Data Processing). The application of electronic computers and other equipment to the classification and interpretation of information—a basic process in automation.

EFT (Electronic Funds Transfer). Utilizes a terminal at the point of service for credit authorization, credit card transactions, data capture, check verification, and funds transfer. Through use of the system customers can use their "instant transaction cards" to transfer funds automatically from their personal account to a retail merchant's account.

ELASTICITY OF DEMAND. Refers to the ratio of the percentage change in quantity demanded to the percentage change in price. The relationship may have unit elasticity (numerical value of the ratio equal to unity), be relatively inelastic (elasticity less than unity), or relatively elastic (elasticity greater than unity).

EMPLOYEE DISCOUNT. Most general merchandise retailers offer employees a certain discount from retail price. It is a kind of retail reduction from the point of view of accounting. Usually stores grant a larger percentage on personal wearing apparel than on gifts purchased by the employee.

END SIZES (Outsizes).   Those usually large, small, or extraordinary in some respect.

ENGEL's LAW.   Set of relationships between consumer expenditures and income. The relationships state that as a family's income increases, (1) the percentage it spends on food decreases, (2) the percentage it spends on housing and household operations remains about constant, and (3) the percentage it spends on all other categories and the amount it saves increase.

EOM (End of Month) DATING.   The cash discount and the net credit periods begin on the first day of the following month rather than on the invoice date. EOM terms are frequently stated in this manner: "2/10, net 30, EOM." Suppose an order is filled and shipped on June 16 under these terms. In such a case, the cash discount may be taken anytime through July 10 and the net amount is due on July 30.

EOM INVENTORY.   End of the month inventory.

EOM, ROG DATING.   End of month, receipt of goods. The net credit period applies as though the shipment were made at the end of the month, and the cash discount period begins upon receipt of the goods by the purchaser.

EQUITY.   The interest of an owner in property, business, or other organization subject to the prior claim of creditors.

ESCROW. Deposit of money or other valuables by one person for the conditional benefit of a second party, the deposit being entrusted to a third party with instructions to turn it over to the second party only on fulfillment of the conditions agreed upon.

ETHICAL DRUGS.   Drugs sold only by a physician's prescription.

EXCHANGE DESK.   A station within a store where customers take merchandise for exchange or credit, depending upon company policy. Usually more functions are performed at this station than just exchange. See Service Desk.

EXCLUSIVE AGENCY METHOD OF DISTRIBUTION.   The practice whereby the vendor agrees to sell his goods or services within a certain territory only through a single retailer or a limited number of retailers; may also apply to wholesalers.

EXPENSE.   Those assets expended or services used in order to earn income.

EXPENSE BUDGET.   A statement prepared by management that gives the planned commitments for operating expenses for a planning period (usually a season). (Compare with Merchandise Budget.)

EXPENSE CENTER.   A collection of controllable costs which are related to one particular area of work or kind of store service.

EXPENSE CENTER ACCOUNTING.   Expenses are grouped by their necessity in performing a particular kind of store service. Examples of expense centers are management, property and equipment, and accounts payable. Natural expenses are typically included as a part of the concept (e.g., payroll).

EXPENSE CONTROL.   Attempting to determine how operating expenses can be expended for more business or more profit or *profitable spending*. Even though expenses should be reduced where there is evidence that they are excessive in terms of a given objective, the primary purpose of expense control is not to see how *little* can be spent for operating expenses.

EXPERIENCE GOODS.   Products, such as soft drinks, that have to be purchased and tried before claims made about the products can be evaluated.

EXPLICIT COSTS.   Costs, generally of a contractual nature, for such items as wages, telephone bills, light bills, and supplies. These items are explicitly carried on the accounting records as costs and are charges against the operation of the business because they are obvious and definite in amount.

EXTRA DATING.   A form of deferred dating. The purchaser is allowed a specified number of days before the ordinary dating begins. To illustrate, in the sale of blankets the terms "2/10–60 days extra" may be offered by the vendor. This means that the buyer has 60 days plus 10 days, or 70 days, from the invoice date in which to pay the bill with the discount deducted.

EXTREME MARKET SEGMENTATION.   A concept of market segmentation which assumes that all consumers are unique and that differences among consumers make a standardized product unacceptable. A retailer following the concept is endeavoring to gain an excellent market position in a very limited number of market segments. See Aggregation, Partial Market Segmentation, Benefit Market Segmentation, and Problem Market Segmentation.

EYEBALL CONTROL.   A kind of nonperpetual stock control in which the responsibility for a certain grouping of merchandise is assigned to a person who visually inspects the stock level at periodic intervals. The assumption is that a concept of a model stock exists for an effective utilization of this stock control method.

F

FACTORING.   A specialized financial function whereby manufacturers, wholesalers, or retailers sell accounts receivable to financial institutions, including factors, banks, and sales finance companies, often on a nonrecourse basis.

FACTORS.   A special type of financial institution for the financing of accounts receivable. Factors usually make outright purchase of accounts receivable—that is, purchase without recourse, and thus assume all collection risks and responsibilities.

FAD.   A fashion of relatively short duration, accepted quickly and with exaggerated zeal and disappearing just as quickly.

FAIR TRADE.   Practice of resale price maintenance imposed by suppliers of branded goods under authorization of state and federal laws (now inoperative).

FAS (Free along Side).   In shipping, the shippper will pay transportation and other charges and assume full responsibility to the side of the vessel—that is, within reach of the vessel's loading tackle—but will not pay the costs of loading goods on the vessel or the shipping charges.

FASHION.   An accepted and popular style.

FASHION COORDINATION.   The function of analyzing fashion trends in order to ensure that the merchandise offered for sale in various related apparel departments is of comparable style, quality, and appeal.

FASHION CYCLE.   The tendency of all fashions to spread, rise, culminate, and decline.

FAST-FOOD OUTLET.   A food retailing institution with a limited menu of pre-prepared food, featuring takeout operations.

FET (Federal Excise Tax).   A tax levied by the federal government upon the manufacture, sale, or consumption of various commodities, or on the right, privilege, or permission to engage in a certain business, trade, occupation, or sport.

FIDELITY BOND.   Insurance against losses rising from dishonest acts of employees and involving money, merchandise, or other property; persons or positions may be covered.

FIELD WAREHOUSING.   An arrangement by which the owner of goods leases a portion of his storage facilities to a licensed warehouser who places a representative in charge, posts signs stating that a designated portion of the warehouse is in charge of the outside organization, and adds to or takes from stock as directed by the banker who has the stock as collateral.

FIFO (First In, First Out).   Method of assigning costs to inventory in which it is assumed that the oldest acquisitions are disposed of first, thus making the ending inventory a composite of the most recent purchase cost.

FIFTH SEASON.   An "in-between" season (assuming that the merchandising concept has the usual four-season structure) usually devoted to cruise work. Another connotation of the fifth season is the "slack season" when business must be encouraged by clearance sales of various kinds.

FILL-IN.   An order to complete stock or assortment on hand.

FINANCIAL STATEMENTS.   The Balance Sheet and the Profit and Loss Statement are generally spoken of as the financial statements. These reports reflect both the current financial status at the end of the accounting period and the change in financial status during the accounting period.

FISCAL YEAR.   Any accounting period of 12 successive calendar months, 52 weeks, 13 four-week periods, or a 12-month period ending with the lsat day of any month other than December, which is the calendar year.

FIXED ASSETS.   Those assets acquired for the purpose of providing the facilities needed to carry on the business. These assets are not bought to be sold. Examples: office furniture, trucks, buildings, and land.

FIXED COST (or Expense).   An operating expense, or operating expense as a class, that does not vary with business volume. Examples: interest on bonds, property tax, depreciation.

FLAGGING AN ACCOUNT (Restricting an Account).   The temporary suspending of an account until it is paid up; more commonly, making it a refer account, by which all charges are authorized at the office by a person charged with greater responsibility than the regular authorizer; done to keep the account more thoroughly under control.

FLAGSHIP STORE.   In a local department store organization, the main or downtown store, especially when large or dominant in relation to branch stores.

FLASH REPORT.   As soon as the day's sales figures have been "read" on whatever kind of register is in use, an "unaudited" report is released to give management the day's results for comparison with budget or perhaps last year's sales figure. It is tentative.

FLEXIBLE BUDGET.   A budget which is adjusted to reflect changes in sales, output, or some other measure of activity in order to provide a better measure of desired results at the activity level.

FLOAT.   The period of time between receipt of a check and the debiting of funds to the retailer's account.

FLOATER.   An applicant for credit who moves frequently from one address to another.

FLOOR AUDIT.   Involves the use of a floor sales register for all transactions, both cash and credit, so as to obtain from the register readings the total sales for each salesperson, department, and type of sale.

FLYER (Advertisement).   A handbill or circular distributed to persons or households.

FLYING SQUAD.   Essentially in the department store field, groups of well-trained and flexible salespeople available to be placed in any and all departments within the store when needed—hence they "fly" about the store from assignment to assignment.

F.O.B. DESTINATION.   A shipping term which indicates that the seller pays the freight to the destination. Title does not pass until the merchandise reaches its destination; thus the seller assumes all risks, loss, or damage while goods are in transit, except for the liability of the carrier.

F.O.B. ORIGIN.   Seller places merchandise "free on board" the carrier at the point of shipment (or other specially designated place); the buyer pays all freight charges from that point. Furthermore, the buyer takes title at the point of shipment and assumes all risks, loss, or damage while goods are in transit, except for the liability of the carrier.

FORCED DISTRIBUTION.   Advertisements or other promotional activity urging consumers to demand merchandise not handled by some retailers, seeking to compel them to order requested products.

FORCED SALE.   A sale of products at less than market price due to the urgent need for a merchant to liquidate his merchandise assets, generally to meet the demands of creditors; also, the sale of goods or property under order from the court; an ordered public auction sale.

FORWARD STOCK.   Merchandise carried on the selling floor rather than in a reserve stockroom.

FRANCHISE.   The privilege, often exclusive, granted a dealer by a manufacturer to sell the manufacturer's products within a specified territory. See Dealership, Distributorship, Mobile Franchise, Ownership Franchise, and Service Franchise. A franchise is an example of a contractual vertical marketing system. See also Retailer-Sponsored Cooperatives and Wholesaler-Sponsored Cooperatives.

FREE-FLOW PATTERN.   A store layout arrangement consisting of a series of circular, octagonal, oval, or U-shaped fixture patterns, resulting in curving aisles characterized by a deliberate absence of uniformity.

FREE-FORM STORE.   A retail institution that diversifies into other areas beside its "normal" retail function. For example, a conventional department store chain diversifying into discount operations, drugstore operations, life insurance operations, etc.

FREE GOODS.   A type of concession sometimes offered by direct suppliers in lieu of an extra discount—e.g., if the merchant buys a gross at a time, he may receive an additional dozen units free.

FREIGHT FORWARDER.   An organization that consolidates less-than-carload shipments from several manufacturers, distributors, or other shippers into carload lots.

FREIGHT POOL.   A group of manufacturers who frequently ship less-than-carload lots, finding it advantageous to cooperate in their shipments; thus, it becomes less costly to combine their less-than-carload shipments into one unit.

FRINGE SIZES.   These are the sizes that are either very large or very small and, if offered at all, are offered in very limited depth because of the thin market demand for them. See Outsizes. Some stores specialize in fringe or outsizes; for example, tall girls' shops; petite-size shops.

FRINGE STOCKS.   Those categories of merchandise from which a small percentage of sales come. For example, a rule of thumb is that 80 percent of sales come from 20 percent of merchandise. Merchants desire to reduce the amount of depth in fringe stock categories. (e.g., sizes and colors).

FRONT-END CHECKOUT.   Checkout lanes and registers are all located near the entrance to the retail store rather than being dispersed throughout the store.

FULL-LINE FORCING.   The practice of requiring that a retailer or wholesaler handle a full line of a manufacturer's goods.

FULL-LINE MARKETING.   Offering a full line of products relative to the number of related products successfully marketed by more important rivals.

FULL-LINE STORE (Retailer).   Any retail establishment that carries all of the merchandise varieties expected within that type of establishment. For example, a department store carries all apparel lines plus home furnishings and furniture.

FULL-SERVICE STORE (or Retailing).   The offering of an adequate number of salespeople and sales-supporting services to give customers the full range of expected services. Usually compared to *limited service,* which implies that some expected services are not offered, for example, credit.

FUNCTIONAL DISCOUNTS.   Those given to wholesale middlemen or others who act in the capacity of performing distributive services which would otherwise have to be performed by the manufacturer. These discounts prevail, regardless of the quantities involved (type of trade discount).

FUNCTIONAL EXPENSE CLASSIFICATION.   A type of expense classification system that identifies the *purpose* of an expenditure. The major functions promoted by the National Retail Merchants Association are (1) administration, (2) occupancy, (3) publicity, (4) buying, and (5) selling.

FUNCTIONAL MIDDLEMEN.   Middlemen who ordinarily assist directly in effecting a change in ownership but do not themselves take title to the goods in which they deal. They specialize in the performance of a single marketing function or a limited number of such functions, one of which is usually related to the transfer of title.

FUTURES.   Commodities bought and sold for delivery at a specified later date; contract or trading for such delivery is usually speculative.

G

GARMENT DISTRICT.   The leading textile center in the country located in New York City in the 34th Street area.

GARNISHMENT.   Generally refers to the allocation, by the courts, of the salary or other income of a debtor who fails to pay his bills; also applies to acquiring such debts which are owed to the debtor (defendant) as consideration for the creditor (plaintiff).

GENERAL LEDGER.   The summary of accounts which reflects the income and financial status of a business. This includes all operating and control accounts of the business.

GENERAL-LINE (or Full-Line) WHOLESALERS. Wholesalers who carry a complete stock of one type of merchandise, corresponding roughly to a substantial majority of the total merchandise requirements of customers in a major line of trade or industry classification.

GENERAL MERCHANDISE STORES. Establishments primarily selling household linens and dry goods, and either apparel and accessories or furniture and home furnishings. Establishments which meet the criteria for department stores, except as to employment, are included in this classification. Included are establishments whose sales of "apparel" or of "furniture and home furnishings" exceed half of their total sales, if sales of the smaller of the two lines in combination with "dry goods and household linens" account for 20 percent of total sales.

GENERAL MERCHANDISE WHOLESALERS. Those that carry a variety of goods in several distinct and unrelated lines of business.

GENERAL PARTNER. A partner who alone or with others is liable for the debts of a partnership.

GENERAL PARTNERSHIP. An association of two or more persons to carry on a business for profit.

GENERAL SALESPERSON. One who sells at wholesale an entire line of producer's goods; distinguished from specialty salesperson.

GENERAL STORES. Establishments primarily selling a general line of merchandise, the most important being food. The more important subsidiary lines are notions, apparel, farm supplies, and gasoline. These establishments are usually located in rural communities. In these establishments, sales of food account for at least one third and not more than two thirds of total sales.

GIFT CERTIFICATE. A certificate issued by a store upon payment by the customer; used as a gift by a recipient who brings the certificate into a store for merchandise in the amount of the certificate. Useful wherever size, taste, or unavailability are involved.

GMROI (Gross Margin Return on Investment). Shows for each dollar invested in merchandise inventory the equivalent dollars generated in gross margin.

GNP (Gross National Product). The total value of all final goods produced in the economy without allowance for capital depreciation.

GOODWILL. The present value of expected future income in excess of a normal return on the investment in tangible assets.

GRADE LABELS. Labels that imply quality specifications designated by a number, letter, or symbol.

GRADING. A process which tests the conformity of commodities to standards that have previously been set up. A service available from the U.S. Department of Agriculture that inspects and classifies (Grade A, B, C) canned and frozen fruits or vegetables.

GRAVITY MODELS. Retailers' primary source of ideas about the structure of market areas. The gravity model states that the volume of purchases by consumers and the frequency of trips to the outlet are a function of the size of the market areas and of the distance between the areas.

GREEN RIVER ORDINANCES. Municipal ordinances regulating or forbidding house-to-house selling, canvassing, or soliciting of business.

GRIDIRON PATTERN. A store layout of fixtures and aisles in a repetitive or rectilinear pattern, best illustrated by a variety store or the grocery department in a typical supermarket.

GROSS ADDITIONAL MARKUPS. The original amount of additional markups taken before subtraction of any additional markup cancellations to determine net additional markups.

GROSS COST OF MERCHANDISE HANDLED. The sum of the opening inventory plus purchases and additions at billed cost.

GROSS COST OF MERCHANDISE SOLD. The accumulated inventory at cost, plus additions at billed cost, less the closing inventory at cost. The gross cost and merchandise sold are subtracted from net sales to provide for maintained markup. Maintained markup is then adjusted by cash discounts and workroom cost to determine gross margin of profit.

GROSS MARGIN OF PROFIT. The difference between net sales and total cost of goods sold.

GROSS MARKDOWNS. The original amount of markdowns taken before subtraction of any markdown cancellations to determine net markdown.

GROSS SALES. Total sales before deducting returns and allowances but after subtracting corrections and trade discounts, sales taxes, and excise taxes based on sales; and, sometimes, cash discounts on sales.

GROUP BUYING. The consolidation of the buying requirements of individual stores.

GUARANTEE (Warranty). Assurance, expressed or implied, of the quality of goods offered for sale. Expressed guarantee, with definite promise of money back or other specific assurance, is often used as a sales aid, especially in mail-order selling in which merchandise cannot be inspected before purchase.

H

HANDBILLS. The term commonly used to identify all promotion pieces that are either handed out to shoppers at the store or distributed door-to-door by a messenger.

HAND-TO-MOUTH BUYING. Purchase by a business in the smallest feasible quantities for immediate requirements.

HARD GOODS. As compared with soft goods, which have a textiles base, these goods comprise mainly hardware, home furnishings, and furniture and appliances. More than likely, these goods are also durable goods.

HEAD OF STOCK. In departmentized stores, this individual is usually at the very first level of the training positions; an assistant to the buyer (or department manager) who is responsible for seeing that reserve and forward stocks are maintained properly for selection and reorder and replenishment; often performs routine control functions as well. Only large, highly specialized stores have this person, who usually reports to the assistant buyer.

HEART SIZES. The popular, middle-of-the-range sizes that are most demanded (e.g., in men's suits 40–44) and are carried in the greatest depth of all sizes.

HEDGE. A purchase or sale for the purpose of balancing, respectively, a sale or purchase already made or under contract to offset the effect of price fluctuation.

HOLDING COMPANY.   An organization that holds stock of another company (or companies) for purposes of control. In pure form, it does not operate for itself, but it does control subsidiaries in the same manner that majority stockholders control the affairs of a company—for example, by electing the board of directors.

HOODOO SITES.   Locations that apparently have all the factors necessary for the successful operation of a retail store but in which a successive number of merchants have failed.

HORIZONTAL COMPETITION.   Competition between two independent retailers of the same type, such as two drugstores.

HORIZONTAL MARKET.   The situation that exists when a product is bought by many kinds of firms in different industries.

HOUSE (or Blanket) BRAND   The practice of using one brand or trademark for all items in a line.

HOUSEHOLD.   According to the Bureau of the Census, those persons who live in "an apartment, or other group of rooms, or a room, that constitutes a dwelling unit." This includes a family, unrelated persons who live within the unit, or a single person within one dwelling.

HOUSEKEEPING.   A function that is essential for stores to stress as it involves keeping the stock in the most sales-presentable form possible. Everyone on the floor must be concerned with proper accomplishment of this function so that an attractive presentation of the merchandise is always in evidence.

HOUSE ORGAN.   An employee paper or magazine published by the employer.

HOUSE-TO-HOUSE (Door-to-Door).   Method of selling or sampling consumers by approaching each household or family; canvassing.

HYPERMARKET.   A combination discount store, supermarket, and warehouse under a single roof. Typically it sells both food and nonfood items at 10–15 percent below normal retail prices and stacks merchandise as high as ten feet. Hypermarkets are a European phenomenon.

I

IMAGE DEVELOPMENT PROMOTION.   A promotional activity designed to enhance and/or change a retail store's image. See Customer Conversion Promotion, Reminder Promotion, Market Positioning Promotion, and Market Expansion Promotion.

IMPLICIT COSTS.   The value of utilized economic resources which are not implicitly charged on accounting records of a firm—for example, interest on owners' capital investment.

IMPLIED WARRANTY.   Implicit assurance, without specification in writing, that a manufacturer or seller is responsible for the performance of the product and may be legally accountable for defects not caused by the purchaser or user.

IMPULSE GOODS.   Articles that are quite frequently bought on the basis of unplanned decisions.

IMPUTED COST.   Often used to indicate the presence of arbitrary or subjective elements of product cost which have unusual significance.

INCENTIVE MERCHANDISE.   Premiums used to stimulate sales.

INCENTIVE PAY.   Any compensation plan other than straight salary wherein the salesperson is given encouragement to sell more. Examples include straight commission (the strongest incentive) and a salary plus a small percentage of net sales.

INCENTIVE TRAVEL.   Form of sales promotional activity in which large companies reward their salespersons, agents, distributors, or dealers with trips to interesting places for attaining a specific objective, usually sales volume (or purchase commitments) in excess of some predetermined quota.

INCOME.   An increase in capital through earnings.

INCOME STATEMENT.   A financial statement that indicates the operating results of a period's operation. The format is to deduct from sales revenue the cost of sales; the resulting gross margin covers expenses and profit for the firm. See Profit and Loss Statement and Operating Statement.

INDEPENDENT STORE.   Retail outlet owned individually; not a chain or branch store.

INDEX NUMBER.   A measure, generally a statistical average, employed to indicate common qualities imputed to a group of items. A single number is often used as an index to compare an entire group.

INDEX OF RETAIL SATURATION.   A technique normally used in larger areas to aid retailers choose among possibilities for the location of new outlets. It offers better insight into location possibilities than a simple descriptive analysis of market potential since it reflects both the demand side and the supply side, that is, the number of existing outlets in the area and the number of consumers.

INDIRECT COMPENSATION.   Compensation received by retail employees as a form of tax-free income. The most common types of indirect competition are: (1) legally required benefits, such as Social Security, unemployment compensation payments, and worker's compensation (for accidents); (2) pension and retirement programs; (3) pay for time not worked, such as for vacation, leave, and holidays; and (4) insurance (life, health, and accident).

INDIRECT EXPENSES.   Those expenses that would exist whether or not a particular department were eliminated. Examples are rent for the building, heat and light, and administrative salaries. See Uncontrollable Expenses.

INDUSTRIAL DISTRIBUTOR.   A wholesaler who sells primarily to business or institutional customers who purchase items for business use rather than for resale.

INDUSTRIAL MARKETING.   The marketing of goods and services which are used in producing consumer goods, other business or industrial goods, and business or personal services or which facilitate the operation of a business enterprise.

INDUSTRIAL PRODUCTS.   Products purchased by business units (not for personal consumption) to assist in or to enter into the production of other goods or services.

INDUSTRIAL (or Business) USERS (Industrial Consumers).   Purchasers of goods and services for use in manufacturing establishments, offices, retail stores, wholesale houses, service businesses, financial organizations, and private and governmental institutions, and purchasers who buy for business purposes which may be conducted on a profit or nonprofit basis.

INFLATION.   A relative term for a situation in which the rate of increase in prices is generally greater than is considered "normal."

INFORMATIVE LABELS. Labels that supplement or, in some cases, replace descriptive and grade labels by providing information that goes beyond the characteristics of the product and can be stated in terms of objective measurements or designated symbols.

INITIAL MARKUP (Initial Mark-on). The difference between the merchandise cost and the original retail price placed on goods; expressed as a percentage of the retail value.

INSOLVENCY. Inability or failure to pay debts as they become due; also, the condition of an individual or organization in which liabilities exceed the fair and realizable value of the assets available for their settlement (federal bankruptcy law).

INSTALLMENT ACCOUNT. The resulting charge account of a customer who has purchased on an installment plan, that is, makes a down payment, and pays a specified amount per month, including a service charge. The customer has the use of the merchandise while paying. See Revolving Credit.

INSTALLMENT SALE. A sale of real or personal property for which a series of equal payments is made over a period of weeks or months; also, sale of goods on credit, often conditional (seller retaining title), with payments of the obligation in periodic portions.

INSTITUTIONAL ADVERTISING. Advertising effort channeled to the direct and exclusive identification and promotion of a store as an institution.

INSTITUTIONAL SALES. The selling of merchandise by a retailer, wholesaler, or manufacturer to such institutions as hospitals, prisons, schools, and restaurants.

INTEGRATED RETAILING. Retail outlets which not only conduct retail trade but also support that trade with other levels of business activity. For example, some large supermarket chains own and operate warehouses and manufacturing plants.

INTENSIVE DISTRIBUTION. The distribution of a product, for example, cigarettes to numerous retailers.

INTERSELLING. The process of selling between and among departments to facilitate larger transactions and to make it more convenient for the customer to accessorize. See Cross Selling.

INTERTYPE COMPETITION. This is competition between different types of firms selling the same product. For example, automobile tires may be sold through discount department stores; gasoline service stations; conventional department stores; tire, battery, and accessory dealers; and independent garages.

INTERURBIA. Large urban area resulting from the mingling and eventual uniting of close market areas into one large market area.

IN TRANSIT. A condition that exists when merchandise has been shipped from the vendor and has not yet arrived at the retailer's receiving dock.

INTRATYPE COMPETITION. Conflict (or competition) between firms of the same type—for example, a department store competes with another department store or a supermarket competes with another supermarket.

INVENTORY. Value of merchandise on hand at cost or retail. "Net inventory" generally refers to the market value after depreciation has been taken, either automatically under the retail method, or by comparison with current wholesale market prices under the cost method. "Perpetual inventory" marks day-to-day changes in inventory.

INVENTORY CUSHION.   The allowance in the inventory made for uncertainties in sales or deliveries, often added to the basic low stock to provide for conditions neither controllable nor accurately predictable.

INVENTORY OVERAGE.   Value of physical inventory in excess of the book value.

INVENTORY STOCK SHORTAGE.   Value of the book inventory in excess of the actual physical inventory, often expressed as a percentage of net sales. The amount of theft, breakage, sales in excess of amounts charged customers, and errors in record keeping. May be either clerical (caused by miscalculation), or physical (caused by misappropriation of goods).

INVENTORY TURNOVER.   See Stock Turnover.

INVOICE.   A document showing the character, quantity, price, terms, nature of delivery, and other particulars of products sold, including the amount due for payment.

INVOICE APRON.   An invoice with sufficient space for all who handle the incoming merchandise to make the necessary written entries.

INVOICE COST.   (1) Cost incurred by a buyer and reflected on an invoice which, unless otherwise specified, is net after deducting both trade and cash discount. (2) In retail accounting, billed cost less trade discount, but not cash discount.

ITEM MERCHANDISING.   The special planning and control effort employed to discover and take advantage of the sales opportunities afforded by items that are in greater consumer demand.

J

JOB ANALYSIS.   A study of a job to determine what duties are performed, what responsibilities and organizational relationships are involved, and what human traits are required.

JOBBER.   Earlier, a dealer in odd or job lots; now, a middleman who buys from manufacturers (or importers) and sells to retailers; a wholesaler.

JOB DESCRIPTION.   A summarized and organized statement containing the name of the job; its location; the operations, duties, and responsibilities involved; working conditions; and, in some instances, hours and wages.

JOB EVALUATION.   A program for measuring and comparing relative difficulties and required skills for various jobs for the purpose of establishing fair and equitable salary ranges, so that jobs with similar requirements are compensated in like manner and those with greater or lesser requirements are paid accordingly.

JOB LOTS.   A promotional grouping of merchandise through which some vendors dispose of end-of-season surpluses and incomplete assortments. For example, a blouse manufacturer may offer, in minimum units of three dozen garments, a miscellaneous selection of different sizes and styles at one half of the original or early season wholesale price.

JOURNAL.   A book of original entry in which transactions are recorded in chronological sequence prior to being entered in their respective ledgers.

K

KEY ITEMS.   Items that are in greatest consumer demand. Also Best Sellers.

KEYSTONE MARKUP.   The cost price is doubled, or a markup of 50 percent of retail is obtained. For example if an item is retailed at $20 and cost the retailer $10, then the keystone markup has been applied.

KEY VENDOR.   A resource that can be depended upon because of excellent past relationships. Every retailer should have a key vendor in each merchandise category for dependable delivery, price, and market information. See Prime Resource.

KICKBACK.   An unethical arrangement in which a payee returns some part of a payment or some gift in appreciation of patronage. Differs from the rebate in that it is pocketed by a salesperson or other representatives, whereas the rebate is usually returned to the purchasing firm.

L

LANDED COST PRICE.   The quoted or invoiced price of a commodity, plus any transportation charges.

LAYAWAY.   The purchase of an article with a down payment, the store retaining the article until full payment is made, often in a series of installments.

LCL (Less-than-Carload Lot).   Rates that apply to less than full carload shipments.

LEADER PRICING.   The practice of knowingly and intentionally marking a part of the stock at prices that will not yield the maximum profit return on these particular goods. The articles so selected for special price emphasis are identified as "leaders." See Loss Leaders.

LEAD TIME.   The amount of time determined by a merchandiser that is necessary to "add on" to the purchasing period in order to assure that sufficient merchandise will be on hand until the particular order is received. If delivery time is long, or if raw materials are in short supply, "lead time" may be longer than when conditions are "normal."

LEASED DEPARTMENTS.   Sections of a retail business managed and operated by an outside person or organization rather than by the store of which it is a physical part, whether leased by an individual or a chain.

LEDGER.   The final book of record in business transactions which contains all debits and credits from the journal. The word *ledger* is used to refer to both individual records (an asset, a liability, etc.) and to the whole group of ledger accounts.

LEVERAGE.   The extent to which a company utilizes debt rather than equity in financing its operations.

LIABILITY.   An obligation to pay a determinable dollar amount to another party, usually as a result of a contractual relationship.

LIEN.   The right of one person to satisfy a claim against another by holding the other's property as security or by seizing and converting the property under legal authority.

LIFO (Last In, First Out).   Method of assigning costs to inventory in which it is assumed that the most recent acquisitions are disposed of first, thus making the ending inventory (base stock) a composite of the oldest purchase costs.

LIMITED FUNCTION WHOLESALERS. Term applied to a variety of types of wholesalers that have placed emphasis upon reducing, eliminating, or modifying certain well-established functions ordinarily performed by regular wholesalers.

LIMITED PARTNER. An owner-investor who has limited his liability to the total sum he has actually invested in the partnership.

LIMITED SERVICE RETAILER. See Full-Service Store.

LINE OF CREDIT. Permission granted by a bank to borrow up to an established sum. Used sometimes to refer to the amount of credit which one company will grant another.

LIQUIDATION. The conversion of goods and other assets into cash. If forced, it is the obligatory conversion of assets imposed by need for cash or the insistence of creditors, and subject to legal action.

LIST PRICE. A printed price, as in a catalog, subject to trade and cash discounts.

LOADING. (1) The amount added to an installment contract to cover selling and administrative expenses, interest risk, and sometimes other factors. (2) The practice of increasing the amount of a purchase charged to a selling department by the difference between an arbitrary standard rate of cash discount set by the store and the cash discount actually obtained from the vendor.

LOCAL RATE. The lower rate charged by many newspapers for advertising of local origin.

LOCATION AFFINITIES. The clustering of similar or complementary kinds of retail stores.

LOSS LEADER. An item that is sold at a "loss" of markup which would normally be obtained on the particular item, for the express purpose of increasing store traffic. See Leader Pricing.

LTL (Less-than-Truckload Lots).

M

MAIL-ORDER HOUSES. Establishments primarily engaged in distributing merchandise through the mail as a result of mail orders received. For census purposes, organizations which operate both mail-order houses and other retail establishments are classified on the basis of their operations.

MAINTAINED ITEMS. Specific items that are continuously maintained in assortments.

MAINTAINED MARKUP (Maintained Mark-on). The differential between the cost of goods sold and net sales.

MALL-TYPE SHOPPING CENTER. A grouping of stores near the center of a shopping center plot, with a parking area surrounding the store concentration. All or most of the stores face a "mall," or pedestrian shopping area.

MANUFACTURERS' AGENT. A functional middleman who sells a part of the output of two or more client manufacturers in a specified territory.

MANUFACTURER'S SALES BRANCHES. Establishments maintained by a manufacturer apart from manufacturing plants and operated primarily for the marketing of the manufacturer's own products at the wholesale level.

MANUFACTURER'S STORE. Retail store owned and operated by a manufacturer, sometimes as an outlet for experimental products or publicity purposes.

MARKDOWN. A reduction in the original or previous retail price of merchandise. For comparative purposes, markdowns are stated as a percentage of net sales.

MARKDOWN CANCELLATIONS. Upward price adjustments that are offset against former markdowns. The most common example: the restoration of a price to original retail after the goods have been marked down temporarily for purposes of a special sales-event.

MARKDOWN CONTROL. Any system ensuring that every markdown taken is reported to the controller's office so that the book retail inventory may be kept in line with the actual physical inventory.

MARKET. The general population of people who spend their money for goods and services to satisfy needs and desires.

MARKET EXPANSION PROMOTION. A promotional activity designed to attract new customers either by encouraging consumers to shift from one brand to another or to try a totally new product. See Reminder Promotion, Customer Conversion Promotion, Image Development Promotion, and Market Positioning Promotion.

MARKETING. The process in a society by which the demand structure for economic goods and services is anticipated or enlarged and satisfied through the conception, promotion, exchange, and physical distribution of such goods and services.

MARKETING CONCEPT. A philosophy of management that includes the following components: (1) a consumer orientation, (2) a profit objective, (3) integration of the marketing functions under a key corporate executive, (4) a sensitivity to social trends and value changes, and (5) a sense of social responsibility.

MARKETING FUNCTION. A major economic activity inherent in the marketing process, which, through a continuous division of labor, tends to become specialized.

MARKETING MANAGEMENT. The planning, organizing, direction, and control of the entire marketing activity of a firm or a division of a firm, including the formulation of marketing objectives, policies, programs, and strategy. It commonly embraces product development, organizing and staffing to carry out plans, supervising marketing operations, and controlling marketing performance.

MARKETING MIX. The amount of relative emphasis placed upon different components of a firm's marketing program—for example, advertising versus personal selling.

MARKETING RESEARCH. The systematic gathering, recording, and analyzing of data about problems relating to the marketing of goods and services.

MARKETING STRATEGY. A complete plan for marketing a product over a long period of time with a flexibility which permits changes to fit unexpected situations.

MARKET INTENSIFICATION. Involves clustering more stores in the same metropolitan area and in contiguous markets.

MARKET POSITIONING PROMOTION. A promotional activity involving positioning or repositioning a product or store in the minds of consumers so as to broaden the customer base. A current example is promoting the use of baby shampoo for adult use. See Market Expansion Promotion, Image Development Promotion, Customer Conversion Promotion, and Reminder Promotion.

MARKET POTENTIAL.   A calculation of maximum sales opportunities for all sellers of goods or services during a stated period, often related to specific geographic markets.

MARKET SEGMENTATION.   A process of identifying and categorizing actual or potential buyers into mutually exclusive groups (segments) that have relatively homogeneous responses to controllable marketing variables. See Aggregation, Partial Market Segmentation, Extreme Market Segmentation, Benefit Market Segmentation, and Problem Market Segmentation.

MARKET SHARE (Other Potential).   The ratio of a company's sales to the total industry sales on an actual or a potential basis.

MARKET VALUE.   The actual price that prevails in a market at any particular moment.

MARK-ON.   See Markup and Cumulative Mark-on.

MARKUP (or Margin).   The difference between merchandise cost and the retail price. Also referred to as mark-on. See Initial Markup and Maintained Markup.

MARKUP PERCENTAGE.   The difference between cost and retail, expressed either as a percentage of cost or, commonly, as a percentage of retail.

MARKUP TABLE.   A tabulation giving markup percentages on cost price with the corresponding markup percentages on retail price. See Markup Wheel and Profit flashers.

MARKUP WHEEL.   A tabulation giving markup percentages on cost price with the corresponding markup percentages on retail price. See Markup Table and Profit Flashers.

MAT (Advertising).   A mat is an advertisement or portion thereof in mold form that the printer uses in reproducing the material for publication. It resembles "baked cardboard" in appearance and is easily mailed, stored, or otherwise handled.

MAXIMUM OPERATING STOCK.   The largest quantity that should ever be on hand during normal operating conditions; consists of merchandise to sell during the buying period, the cushion, and the basic low stock.

MAXIMUM SYSTEM OF STOCK CONTROL.   The system of setting, for each item of staple merchandise carried, an amount large enough to take care of probable demands of customers, and of periodically reordering the difference between the actual stock and the maximum set.

MAZUR PLAN.   The basic organization plan used in most department stores from the 1930s through the 1950s. The organization contained four functional areas: controlling, merchandising (buying and selling), publicity, and store operations.

MEMORANDUM PURCHASE AND DATING.   Indicates that merchandise shipped to a buyer is returnable within a specified period of time and that payment for goods kept longer or sold need not be made until this time, though legal title usually transfers at the time of shipment.

MEMORANDUM TERMS.   A special form of indefinite future dating under which the title of the merchandise passes to the buyer and he assumes all risk of ownership.

MERCANTILE CUSTOMER. One who buys for resale purposes rather than for his own consumption.

MERCANTILE TRADE CREDIT. The credit one business extends to another when selling goods on time for resale or commercial use.

MERCHANDISE AGENTS (Brokers). Wholesale establishments whose operators are in business for themselves and are primarily engaged in selling—or buying—goods for others. "Sales," in Census Bureau publications for agents and brokers, represent the selling, or purchase, value of the merchandise in the transactions negotiated. Functional middlemen who do not take title to the products they handle.

MERCHANDISE BUDGET. A statement prepared by management containing planned commitments for all the components of the merchandise mix (sales, reductions, stocks, margins, and purchases) for a planning period (usually a season). Compare with Expense Budget.

MERCHANDISE CHARGE. The customer purchases merchandise and the account is charged with the amount of the sale. It may be a regular, 30-day account; a 30–60–90-day account; or an installment account.

MERCHANDISE CLASSIFICATION. A subdivision of a selling department; a dissection of a department's inventory, purchase, and/or sales figures for the purpose of closer control.

MERCHANDISE CONTROL. The determination and direction of merchandising activities, both in terms of dollars (dollar control) and in terms of units (unit merchandise control).

MERCHANDISE COST. The billed cost of merchandise less any applicable trade or quantity discounts, plus inbound transportation costs if paid by the store.

MERCHANDISE DISSECTION. See Merchandise Classification.

MERCHANDISE HANDLED. The opening inventory plus purchases during a period. Under the retail method of inventory, it is computed at both cost and retail, the cost figure including transportation charges.

MERCHANDISE IN TRANSIT. Merchandise with its legal title passed to the retailer which has not been charged to a merchandise selling department.

MERCHANDISE MIX. Refers to the breadth of merchandise carried by retailing establishments.

MERCHANDISE PLAN. A plan, generally for a six-month period, by months, in which the chief elements enter into gross profit. The essentials are sales, markdowns, retail stocks at the first of each month, purchases, and markup percentage. Inventory shortages, cash discounts, and alteration costs may also be budgeted.

MERCHANDISE PURCHASES. Those items acquired by a business for purposes of resale for profit, as distinguished from those items needed for the conduct of the business or not intended for resale.

MERCHANDISE VENDING MACHINE OPERATORS. Establishments primarily engaged in the sale of merchandise through coin-operated vending machines which are generally located on the premises of other businesses.

MERCHANDISING. The planning involved in marketing the right merchandise, at the right place, at the right time, in the right quantities, and at the right price.

MERCHANT MIDDLEMEN.   Middlemen who buy goods outright and necessarily take title to them.

METROPOLITAN AREA.   Consists of a central city and usually one, two, or more counties which are socially and economically integrated with the central city. See Standard Metropolitan Statistical Area.

MIDDLEMEN.   Individuals, firms, or corporations that stand between prime producers and ultimate consumers, assume title, or assist directly in its transfer. They receive a profit for the risks assumed, are paid for the cost of services, and take whatever losses result from the assumption of an entrepreneur's functions.

MINIMUM AND MAXIMUM SYSTEM OF STOCK CONTROL.   A system whereby for each item of staple merchandise carried, a minimum quantity of inventory is established which, when reached, indicates a need to reorder. Maximum stock consists of the minimum and the predetermined reorder quantity.

MINIMUM ORDER.   The smallest unit of sales permitted by a manufacturer or wholesaler. Sometimes expressed in units or in dollar amount and sometimes in weight.

MINIMUM STOCK.   The sum of the basic low stock and the cushion.

MISSIONARY SALESPERSONS.   Those employed by a manufacturer to work with retailers to make store demonstrations, prepare window displays, or arrange for other sales promotional activity.

MOBILE FRANCHISE.   Is similar to conventional franchises; however, business is conducted from a vehicle that moves about. See Service Franchise Dealership, Ownership Franchise, and Distributorship.

MODEL STOCK APPROACH TO SPACE ALLOCATION.   A method of determining space allocation for departments in a retail store. Is based upon an analysis of an ideal stock necessary to achieve projected sales volume, of how much stock should be displayed versus how much should be kept in reserve space, of how much physical space will be required to display the merchandise, and of how much physical space will be needed for any service requirements. See Buildup Method of Space Allocation.

MODEL STOCK PLAN.   An outline of the composition of an ideal stock in terms of general characteristics or assortment factors, usually with optimum quantities indicated in an amount that reflects balance in relation to expected sales. Normally used in reference to type goods.

MODULAR FIXTURES.   Fixtures—e.g., showcases, counters, wall cases, wall shelving—constructed in standard widths and heights. Individual units are known as "modules."

MONOPOLISTIC COMPETITION.   A market structure of many firms selling similar but not identical products, without any dominant firms, and in which the rivalries of oligopoly are absent.

MONOPOLY.   A market structure with only one firm selling the product, and no other firms selling closely related products.

MOTIVATION RESEARCH.   The practice of finding out why people act or think the way they do; normally associated with psychological techniques used for this purpose.

MULTIPLE NUCLEI THEORY. A theory of urban land use patterns, developed by R. D. McKenzie, which states that a city develops a series of land use patterns or nuclei or similar activities that tend to group together. The following four factors explain the development of separate nuclei: (1) the interdependence of some activities because of a need for close physical relationships, (2) a natural clustering tendency of some activities, (3) a common need held by an otherwise unrelated group of activities, and (4) high rents or land costs which assert an attracting or repelling force on certain uses of land.

MULTIPLE-UNIT PRICING. The combination of several like-products as a unit of one, involving at least a slightly different markup than is obtained when individual items are sold.

MULTIUNIT ESTABLISHMENT. One of two or more establishments in the same general kind of business operated by the same firm.

N

NATIONAL (or Manufacturers') BRANDS. Brands or trademarks adopted and sponsored by manufacturers and having wide territorial distribution.

NATURAL EXPENSE CLASSIFICATION. A form of expense classification that identifies the *nature* of the expense rather than the *purpose* of the expenditure.

NATURAL SELECTION THEORY. A theory of retail institutional change, developed by A. C. R. Dreesman, which states that retailing institutions that can most effectively adapt to environmental changes are the ones most likely to prosper or survive. Is closely related to adaptive behavior theory. See Wheel of Retailing Theory, Dialectic Process Theory, and Retail Accordion Theory.

NEGATIVE AUTHORIZATION. In credit verification systems, the noting of only poor credit risks in the credit check. Any credit not negatively reported is assumed to be verified.

NEIGHBORHOOD CLUSTERS. Clusters of several stores scattered throughout the residential districts of cities.

NEIGHBORHOOD SHOPPING CENTER. Usually a small strip of stores and service establishments, predominantly of the convenience goods type, often with a single supermarket as the major tenant.

NET CREDIT PERIOD. The length of time for which mercantile credit is extended to businesses. For example, 2/10, net 30, provides a net credit period of 30 days.

NET OPERATING INCOME (Profit). Net sales less net cost of goods sold less operating expenses.

NET PROFIT PLAN, EXPENSE ALLOCATION. Under this plan, both direct and indirect expenses are charged to selling departments. Each department is viewed as a separate business to be evaluated on its profit showing.

NET PURCHASES. The cost of purchases plus freight in, less purchase returns, allowances, and cash discounts taken.

NET SALES. Gross sales less returns and allowances. In wholesaling, cash discounts allowed to customers are frequently deducted.

NET TERMS. Terms calling for the billed amount of the invoice. No cash discount is allowed.

NET WORTH.   The aggregate of the equities representing proprietary interests; the excess of the value of assets over liabilities.

NEVER-OUT LISTS.   "Key items" or "best sellers" listed separately from a model stock plan or basic stock list, or especially identified on the basic stock list by colored stars or other suitable means; sometimes referred to as a list of key items, checking-list items, or a best seller list.

NOMINAL CREDIT TERMS.   Terms applied to the date on which full payment of the account is due; in stores that bill customers on a monthly basis, full payment is usually due by the tenth day after billing.

NONMERCHANDISE.   Refers to offerings in stores consisting of services or intangibles versus typical tangible merchandise offerings. For example, fur storage, gift wrapping, and travel assistance.

NONPERPETUAL INVENTORY CONTROL SYSTEM.   An inventory system in which a physical count or visual inspection of merchandise must take place in order to determine inventory on hand. This system differs from a perpetual one in which an inventory is kept in continuous agreement with stock on hand by means of a detailed record-keeping system.

NONPRICE COMPETITION.   Competition between rival sellers who charge identical or comparable prices but differentiate their offerings in such items as quality, service, style, packaging, reputation, and prestige.

NONSALABLE.   Merchandise that is not for sale for one of several reasons—not up to quality standards, display only, damaged.

NONSELLING AREA.   Floor space other than the selling area used in the conduct of business in the main store building or in remote service or warehouse buildings, including entrances, show windows, vertical transportation facilities, offices, boiler and engine rooms, alteration rooms and workrooms, repair shops, receiving and marking rooms, and stockrooms.

NONSELLING DEPARTMENT.   Any department of a store engaged in work other than the direct selling of merchandise—for example, the receiving department.

NONSIGNER CLAUSE.   A provision whereby all retailers had to agree to the terms of a resale price maintenance agreement if it was signed by a single retailer.

NONSTORE RETAILING.   A form of retailing in which consumer contact occurs outside the confines of the retail store, such as telephone shopping, door-to-door selling, and catalog buying.

NORMAL MARGIN RETAILER.   A retailer who offers merchandise at prices comparable to those of competitive stores in the same market. The management attempts to be competitive but does not price below or above competition. See At the Market Price.

NOTES PAYABLE.   The name of a ledger account or balance sheet item showing separately or in one amount the liabilities to banks, trade, and other creditors evidenced by promissory notes.

NOTIONS DEPARTMENT.   In a department store that department, typically on the main floor, which carries small sundries which are usually considered as necessities of a small-ticket nature (e.g., ribbons and needles). The notions department is also found in drugstores today as well as in some superstores, variety stores, and discount operations.

O

OBSOLESCENCE.   The process of going out of use or out of style; loss in value of merchandise or other assets caused, not by deterioration, but by style changes or new inventions.

OCCUPANCY EXPENSE.   Expense relating to the use of property—for example, rent, heat, light, depreciation, upkeep, and general care of premises.

OCR—FONT A.   Optical character recognition—human-readable code—used in nonfood merchandising.

ODD LOT (Retailing).   Dealing with broken lots or unbalanced assortments reduced in price for quick turnover.

ODD PRICING.   Refers to the use of "odd prices," such as $9.95 rather than $10.00.

OFFER.   A proposal to enter into a binding obligation that is communicated orally or in writing to the one to whom it is made; an essential of a legal contract.

OFF-RETAIL PERCENTAGE.   The markdown as a percentage of the original price. For example, an item originally retails for $10 and is marked down to $5; the off-retail percentage is 50 percent.

OLIGOPOLY.   A market structure with a relatively small number of dominant firms, so that the actions of any one of these firms have a major impact on each of the others. The characteristic of an oligopoly situation is the existence of close rivalries and the necessity for each firm to consider potential reactions of its rivals in formulating its own policy.

ONE-CENT SALE.   A plan of selling two articles of a certain class at one cent more than the price of one.

100 PERCENT LOCATION.   The retail site in a major business district that has the greatest exposure to a retail store's target market customers.

ONE-PRICE POLICY.   At a given time, all customers pay the same price for any given item of merchandise.

ON ORDER.   When the retailer has ordered merchandise and it has not been received, it is considered to be "on order" and thus a commitment against a planned purchase figure. Thus, the open-to-buy figure is affected by the amount of the on-order dollars.

ON-PERCENTAGE.   The result of multiplying together the complements of a given series of discount percentages. To find the net merchandise price, the list price is multiplied by the on-percentage.

OPEN ACCOUNT (Open Credit).   The sale of goods on credit, the seller giving the buyer no written evidence of indebtedness; instead debits the buyer's account.

OPEN CODE DATING.   A date marked on food products to indicate the last day that the food can be sold in the store. See Open Date Labeling.

OPEN DATE LABELING.   A date marked on food products to indicate the last day that the food can be sold in the store. See Open Code Dating.

OPENING BALANCE.   The balance of an account at the beginning of a specified period, such as a month or a year.

OPENING INVENTORY.   The value of the inventory on hand at the beginning of an accounting period.

OPEN ORDER.   An order sent by a store to a market representative to be placed with whatever vendor the latter finds can best fill it. In department store buying, authority granted to a resident buyer to purchase merchandise required by the store.

OPEN STOCK.   Items kept on hand in retail stores and sold either in complete sets or in separate pieces—for example, china, glassware.

OPEN-TO-BUY.   The residual balance of current purchase allotments; total planned purchases for a period, less receipts and merchandise on order.

OPEN-TO-BUY REPORT.   Statement of existing or expected relations between inventory and sales, used to calculate open-to-buy amounts.

OPEN-TO-SPEND REPORT.   A periodic report summarizing actual expense commitments as compared to planned expenditures. This allows discrepancies to be noted and determination of expense monies remaining for the fiscal year.

OPERATING ACCOUNTS (Nominal Accounts).   Those accounts which include the income and expenses for an accounting period and are closed out at the end of the accounting period.

OPERATING INCOME.   Income derived from the primary operation of a business. Net Operating Income is determined by deducting all expenses from the gross profit.

OPERATING STATEMENT.   A financial statement that indicates the operating results of a period's operations. The format is to deduct from sales revenue the cost of sales; the resulting gross margin covers expenses and profit for the firm. See Profit and Loss Statement and Income Statement.

OPERATIONS MANAGER.   See Store Manager.

OPINION LEADERS.   Those individuals in a society whom the society as a whole considers knowledgable as to new trends, ideas, and information.

OPTION TERMS.   In credit, the choice granted the customer to select the terms best suited to his needs—for example, one month or several months in which to pay.

ORDER REGISTER.   A form on which orders placed with vendors are recorded; includes the date of each order, the name of the vendor, the total amount of each order, the month in which shipment is to be made, the amount to be delivered each month, and a serial number.

ORDINARY DATING.   Illustrated by such terms as "1/10, net 30" or "2/10, net 60." The two specified time elements are the cash discount and the net credit period. The cash discount may be deducted if the bill is paid within the discount period (10 days in both examples); otherwise, the full amount is due at the end of the credit period (30 and 60 days in the examples given). Both the cash discount and the net credit periods are usually counted from the date of the invoice, which, in most cases, is also the date of shipment.

ORGANIZED MARKET.   A group of traders operating under recognized rules in buying and selling a single commodity or related commodities; a commodity exchange.

ORIGINAL RETAIL.   The first price at which merchandise is offered for sale.

OTB.   Open-to-buy.

OUTLET STORE.   (1) A store specializing in job lots and clearance merchandise. (2) A store controlled by a vendor to dispose of surplus stocks.

OUT-SHOPPER.   A person from a smaller town who travels to a larger town in order to shop.

OUTSIZES.   These are the sizes that are either very large or very small and, if offered at all, are offered in very limited depth because of the thin market demand for them. Some stores specialize in fringe sizes or outsizes; for example, tall girls' shops, petite-size shops. See Fringe Sizes.

OVERAGE.   The amount by which a physical inventory exceeds the book inventory figure, as opposed to shortage; may also refer to cash excess.

OVERBOUGHT.   (1) A condition in which a store buyer has become committed to purchases in excess of his planned purchase allotment for a merchandising period. (2) The purchase of merchandise in excess of demand.

OVERHEAD.   Generally, the cost of materials and services not directly adding to or readily identifiable with the product or service constituting the main object of an operation; often used synonymously with fixed costs, or expenses that do not vary with the level of sales activity.

OWNERSHIP FRANCHISE.   A type of franchise system in which the franchisor has an ownership interest in the operation. See Service Franchise, Dealership, Mobile Franchise, and Distributorship.

P

PACKAGE-BAND PREMIUM.   One advertised in a strip wrapped around the package of the product that is promoted.

PACKAGING.   An element in a marketing program expected to perform at least three functions: (1) identify the brand, (2) identify the particular products of that brand, and (3) differentiate the brand favorably from competition.

PANTRY INVENTORY.   A survey of consumer use of products based on actual check and listing of items on hand in the home.

PAPER PROFITS.   A situation that results when, during periods of rising prices, a retailer values his ending inventory at current market value rather than the lower original cost value. (See Conservative Rule of Inventory Valuation.) On the income statement, cost of goods sold is understated, resulting in an overstated profit picture. The reason "paper" profits are referred is because the profits exist on the income statement; but the ending inventory, when carried over into the next fiscal year, may not be salable at current market value because of style changes, deterioration, etc.; thus, the profits which are anticipated may not actually be earned.

PARASITE STORES.   Those that live on existing traffic flow which originates from circumstances other than their own promotional effort, store personality, merchandising effort, or customer service.

PARTIAL MARKET SEGMENTATION.   A concept of market segmentation which recognizes that groups of consumers have varying demand curves. It recognizes a high degree of difference between segments and a high degree of similarity within segments. A retailer following this concept offers goods and services to most segments of the market but offers different products or services to each segment. See Aggregation, Extreme Market Segmentation, Benefit Market Segmentation, and Problem Market Segmentation.

PARTNERSHIP.   A contractual relationship based upon an agreement (written, oral, or implied) between two or more persons who combine their resources and activities in a joint enterprise and share in varying degrees and by specified agreement in the management and in the profits or losses.

PARTY-PLAN SELLING.   A practice in which salespersons arrange to have a party in a home at which merchandise is demonstrated to friends of the hostess.

PATRONAGE DIVIDENDS.   Any surpluses accrued from the spread between prevailing market prices and the cost of merchandise and store operation that are paid to members (of a cooperative) in proportion to their volume of purchases.

PATRONAGE MOTIVES.   Those motives which determine just where or from whom purchases will be made.

PAYEE.   The person receiving the payment; in contrast to the "payer," who makes the payment.

PERCENTAGE MARKDOWN.   The percentage markdown as a percentage of the marked-down price of an item. For example, an item originaly sells for $3, is marked down to $2; the amount of the markdown is $1. The percentage markdown is thus $1 ÷ $2 = 50 percent.

PERCENTAGE OF GROSS PROFIT.   The ratio of profit to sales expressed as a percentage.

PERPETUAL INVENTORY CONTROL SYSTEM.   An inventory kept in continuous agreement with stock on hand by means of a detailed record; may also serve as a subsidiary ledger where dollar amounts as well as physical quantities are maintained.

PERSONAL INCOME.   Net national income minus corporate income taxes, retained earning, and contributions for social insurance; plus interest paid by the government and business and government transfer payments—for example, Social Security benefits, veterans' pensions, relief payments, and unemployment compensation.

PERSONAL SHOPPING SERVICE.   A service provided by prestige stores to advise or assist customers in selecting merchandise.

PERSONAL TRADE.   A customer-salesperson relationship in which the same salesperson serves a particular customer over a long period of time.

PHANTOM FREIGHT.   The amount by which the allowance for freight delivery costs, as included in a seller's delivered price quotation, exceeds the actual cost for freight; commonly associated with basing point pricing systems.

PHYSICAL DISTRIBUTION.   The movement and handling of goods from the point of production to the point of consumption or use.

PHYSICAL INVENTORY.   An inventory determined by actual count and evidenced by a listing of quantity, weight, or measure; usually compiled in dollars as well as units.

PIECE GOODS.   Fabrics, generally sold by the yard.

PIGGYBACK SERVICE.   A form of coordinated local motor and long distance rail service in which loaded truck trailers are hauled on specially designed rail flatcars.

PILFERAGE.   The stealing of a store's merchandise. See Shoplifting.

PIN TICKET.   A price tag which may also include size, color, and style number, pinned or stapled to the product.

PLANNED STOCK.   The dollar amount of merchandise a buyer desires to have on hand at a given time in a certain department, merchandise classification, price line, or other control unit.

POINT-OF-PURCHASE ADVERTISING.   Advertising, usually in the form of window and/or interior displays, in establishments where a product is sold to the ultimate consumer.

POINT OF SALE.   Traditionally that point where the sale is consummated and where the merchandise is transferred to the customer. Most recently it has become modified for a type of data collection system used in retail stores. Also a modifier for a kind of advertising available where the sale is made.

POINT SCORING.   In credit application checking, a system of evaluation; to be approved, the applicant must reach a certain point score based on established criteria.

POLARITY OF RETAIL TRADE.   A projected trend in retailing which indicates that the predominant retailing institutions of the future will be on the one hand (pole) high-yield mass distribution outlets and, on the other hand (pole), high-yield specialty, single-line, boutique-type retail institutions.

POLICY ADJUSTMENT.   An exception to the usual complaint adjustment practice or policy which is made for the purpose of retaining the customer's goodwill.

POOLED BUYING.   The practice of independent merchants informally pooling their orders.

POSTAGE-STAMP PRICING.   Uniform delivered cost throughout the entire national market, with freight costs approached as unvarying, irrespective of distance; much like letter postage.

POSTING.   The process of recording in the ledger the debits and credits indicated by the journal entries.

PREMARKING.   Price marking by the manufacturer or other supplier before goods are shipped to a retail store. Also called "prepricing."

PREMIUM.   (1) Something given free or at a nominal price to induce a sale or to promote interest in a product. (2) The amount paid as consideration to the insurer.

PREMIUM STORE.   A store operated by a premium house, organized to exchange trading stamps (or coupons) for a premium (gift).

PREPACKAGED.   An item that is deliverable to the ultimate consumer in an unopened, factory-packed container.

PREPAID ASSET.   An expenditure for benefits yet to be received. This term usually describes an expense which has been paid for in advance, the cost of which will be spread over several accounting periods.

PREPRINTED ORDER FORM.   A form on which are listed the items stocked by a vendor.

PRERETAILING.   The practice of determining prices and placing them on a copy of the purchase order at the time that goods are bought (orders placed).

PRESS PUBLICIST.   A person assigned to the tasks of obtaining maximum publicity for educational and special interest events sponsored by a store and securing the placement of pictorial illustrations on women's pages for finer or more fashionable items of merchandise.

PRICE CODE.   A symbol placed on a price or bin ticket to indicate the cost price of an item.

PRICE DIFFERENTIAL.   The difference between the base price set by a vendor for goods of a certain size or quality and the price for similar goods of a different size or quality; may be expressed as a percentage of the base price or as a fixed amount on or off the base.

PRICE DISCRIMINATION.   The charge by a seller of varying prices to different customers under similar conditions of sale. It may be in violation of antitrust statutes if on the same level of distribution and if there is a tendency to create a monopoly and/or substantially lessen competition.

PRICE GUARANTEE.   The practice of vendors offering their customers guarantees against price declines.

PRICE LEADER.   (1) A firm whose pricing behavior is followed by other companies in the same industry. (2) An item of merchandise priced abnormally low for the purpose of attracting customers.

PRICE LEADERSHIP.   The practice in an industry of recognizing and adopting the price established by one or more members of the industry.

PRICE LINING.   A limited number of predetermined price points at which merchandise will be offered for sale—for example, $7.95, $10.95, $14.95.

PRICE MAINTENANCE.   The determination by the manufacturer of the price at which an identified item shall be resold by wholesalers and/or retailers.

PRICE ZONE.   A range of prices used in building a price structure—for example, $6.95 to $8.95.

PRIMARY BUYING MOTIVES.   Those motives which induce an individual to buy a certain kind or general class of article or service, as opposed to the selection of brands within a class.

PRIMARY PACKAGES.   Cans, drums, tubes, and other containers into which the product is initially placed; often the primary package is inserted into another container for protection or for additional sales appeal.

PRIME RESOURCE.   A resource that can be depended upon because of excellent past relationships. Every retailer should have a prime resource in each merchandise category for dependable delivery, price, and market information. See Key Vendor.

PRIVATE (or Distributor) BRANDS.   Brands that are the property right of middlemen in the channel of distribution; these brands may be sponsored by retailers, wholesalers, or cooperative buying groups.

PROBLEM MARKET SEGMENTATION.   A concept of market segmentation where the retailer, in offering goods or services for sale, focuses on ways of overcoming obstacles or problems of the consumers. See Aggregation, Partial Market Segmentation, Extreme Market Segmentation, and Benefit Market Segmentation.

PRODUCERS' COOPERATIVE MARKETING.   Type of cooperative marketing which primarily involves the sale of products of the membership. May perform only an assembly or brokerage function, but in some cases, notably milk marketing and citrus fruits, extends into processing and distribution of the members' output.

PRODUCT.   In a narrow sense, the physical thing marketed; but in a broad sense, consists of the satisfactions that may be derived from its use or consumption, including values added by middlemen.

PRODUCTIVITY.   A ratio of output, or the results of production, to the corresponding input of economic resources, both during a given period of time.

PRODUCT MANAGEMENT.   The planning, organizing, directing, and controlling of all phases of the life cycle of products, including the creation or discovery of ideas for new products, the screening of such ideas, the coordination of the work of research and physical development of products, packaging and branding, introduction on the market, market development, modification, the discovery of new uses, repair and servicing, and their elimination, if necessary.

PRODUCT MIX.   The composite of products offered for sale by a firm or a business unit.

PRODUCT PLANNING.   The practice of estimating the magnitude of potential markets and sales volume, of budgeting costs, and of considering other matters relating to the economics of modifying a product line.

PRODUCT POLICIES.   Policies concerned with the adding of new products and the dropping of old ones as well as the modification of existing products on a continuing or intermittent basis.

PROFESSIONAL DISCOUNTS.   Discounts granted to people in a specified professional field, especially those who are users of products in that field; for example, discounts given to physicians by drugstores, especially to those who favor the stores with prescription references.

PROFIT.   A general term for the excess of revenue, proceeds, or selling price over related costs.

PROFIT AND LOSS STATEMENT.   A financial statement that indicates the operating results of a period's operations. The format is to deduct from sales revenues the cost of sales; the resulting gross margin covers expenses and profit for the firm. See Operating Statement, Income Statement.

PROFIT FLASHERS.   A tabulation giving markup percentages on cost price with the corresponding markup percentages on retail price. See Markup Wheel and Markup Table.

PROFIT MIX.   The components that provide the return for a firm and may be manipulated for effective performance depending upon the merchandising philosophy of the firm. The components are: Price × Volume = Sales − Cost of sales = Gross margin − Operating expenses = Net profit before taxes.

PRO FORMA. (Latin, as a matter of form).   A preliminary and not precisely exact invoice of goods shipped or sold; also, an illustrative, hypothetical accounting sheet, price list, or similar statement.

PROGRAMMED MERCHANDISING.   The careful planning and concentration of purchases with a limited number of preferred, or key, vendors; usually for an entire line of merchandise and for extended periods of time, such as a year.

PROMOTIONAL ADVERTISING.   Intended to inform prospective customers of special sales; to announce the arrival of new and seasonal goods; and to feature, create, and maintain a market for the merchandise items in regular stock. See Image Development Promotion, Customer Conversion Promotion, Reminder Promotion, Market Positioning Promotion, and Market Expansion Promotion.

PROMOTIONAL ALLOWANCE (or Discount).   Given by a vendor to a retailer to compensate the latter for money spent in advertising a particular item in local media, or for preferred window and interior display space used for the vendor's product.

PROMOTIONAL STOCK.   Stock of goods offered at an unusually attractive price in order to obtain volume trade; generally represents special purchases from vendors.

PROPRIETARY DRUGS.   Drug products not requiring a physician's prescription; patent medicines.

PROPRIETARY STORE.   Establishment selling the same merchandise as drugstores, except that prescriptions are not filled and sold.

PROPRIETORSHIP.   Ownership of an unincorporated business by an individual.

PROTECTION DEPARTMENT.   The operating area of a retail store that is responsible for protecting the merchandise from pilferage (internal or external). Those working in the department may be store employees or outside people. See Security.

PROXIMO DATING.   Specifies the date in the following month on which payment must be made in order to take the cash discount—for example, terms of "2%, 10th Proximo, net 60 days" mean that the bill must be paid prior to the 10th day of the month following purchase in order to take the discount, but that a credit period of 60 days from the first of the month is allowed.

PUA (Production Unit Accounting).   A specific philosophy of making use of expense figures beyond their accumulation in expense centers. Involves utilizing the expense data through units of measure to determine productivity for the purpose of controlling expense; common in department store expense management.

PUBLIC MARKET.   A wholesale or retail market, primarily for foodstuffs, supervised or administered by a municipality which rents space or stalls to dealers; also municipal market, community market.

PUBLIC WAREHOUSE.   A storage facility, generally privately owned, that does not take title to the goods it handles; may issue receipts which can be used as security for loans.

PUFFERY.   Traditionally this term implied a slightly exaggerated claim which was not necessarily "believed" but was intended to place the product or service advertised in a favorable light. Today puffery might be considered an unsubstantiated claim and should be handled with care.

PURCHASE ORDER.   A document authorizing a vendor to deliver prescribed merchandise or materials at a specified price; becomes a contract upon acceptance by a vendor.

PURCHASE RETURNS AND ALLOWANCES.   See Returns and Allowances from Suppliers.

PURCHASING AGENT.   (1) An executive or other person (not strictly an agent) who is responsible for buying for his business concern and is paid a salary. (2) An independent middleman, buying broker for a principal or principals (usually wholesalers), paid a commission or fee for his services.

PUSH MONEY (PM).   A bonus that salespeople receive for each sale made of specially designated merchandise. See Spiff.

PX (Post Exchange).   A retail store operated by the armed forces primarily for the convenience of military personnel and their families.

Q

QUANTITY DISCOUNT.   A reduction in the cost of merchandise which is based on the size of the order.

QUOTA.   In compensation plans, salespeople are often given a goal figure above which they are paid a certain bonus. The term may also be used to indicate any goal to be achieved with or without a bonus. A quota may be used just for self-evaluation purposes.

QUOTA-BONUS COMPENSATION.   A plan which involves a basic salary and commissions paid on sales in excess of a predetermined quota.

R

RACK JOBBER.   A wholesale middleman operating principally in food stores, supplying certain classes of merchandise that do not fit into the regular routine of food store merchandise resources; commonly places display racks in retail stores, providing an opening inventory on a consignment or a guaranteed-sale basis; periodically checks the stock and replenishes inventories.

RACK MERCHANDISER.   See Rack Jobber.

RATED CONCERNS.   Companies that have been investigated with relation to their credit rating.

RATE OF RETURN PRICING.   A method of determining prices by adding a markup which will produce a predetermined return on investment.

REBATE.   An allowance; a deduction; a refund of a part of the price paid for a product, generally because of the large quantity of goods bought or shipped; under some circumstances, considered an ethically questionable and/or unlawful—for example, Robinson-Patman Act—practice.

RECESSION.   Downward phase of a business cycle in which the economy's income, output, and employment are decreasing, and a falling off of business and consumer optimism is reflected by a declining rate of capital investment and consumption.

RECIPROCAL SALES LEADS.   The exchange of the names and addresses of prospective customers by companies.

RECIPROCITY.   The practice of giving a company's customers preference when these customers are in the market for articles of the class sold by the company.

REDEMPTION COUPON.   Gives the holder the privilege of obtaining a free product or gift, or a product at a lower-than-regular price when it is presented to a retailer or mailed to the product's manufacturer.

REDEMPTION STORES.   Establishments operated by a trading stamp company at which stamps are redeemed for merchandise.

REGIONAL SHOPPING CENTER.   The largest class of planned shopping centers, usually with several major department store units and 50 to 100 stores, serving a very large trading area.

REGISTERED MARK.   A mark—trade, service, certification, collective—officially filed and registered with the Patent Office.

RELATED PACKAGING.   Package design or coloring which is the same for all merchandise produced by a company to assist in the identification of the company with its products.

RE-MARKING.   The practice of re-marking merchandise due to price changes, lost or mutilated tickets, or customer returns.

REMINDER PROMOTION.   A promotional activity designed to encourage consumers to stock products prior to seasonal increases in sales, in advance of anticipated product shortages, or in advance of anticipated price increases. See Market Positioning Promotion, Market Expansion Promotion, Image Development Promotion, and Customer Conversion Promotion.

REMOVAL SALE.   A sale advertised by a retailer who is moving from one store location to another.

REORDER UNIT.   The unit in which an item is reordered, the exact amount depending on trade practices—for example, dozen, gross, nearest hundredweight, or foot.

REPOSSESSION.   The recovery of merchandise by the store after delivery, owing to a customer's failure to complete payment.

RESALE PRICE MAINTENANCE.   The determination by the manufacturer of the price at which an item will be sold by wholesalers and/or retailers.

RESERVE SYSTEM OF STOCK CONTROL.   Method of controlling the amount of stock in the reserve stockroom by keeping records of all goods sent to the selling floor and all goods received from vendors; stock in reserve is determined without counting the goods by adding the number of pieces received to the past physical inventory and subtracting the number sent to the selling floor.

RESIDENT BUYING OFFICE.   Represents many retailers in the same line of business in the central market, providing information about market developments and guidance in purchasing for its clients.

RESOURCE FILE.   A brief compilation of facts and observations about vendors with whom the store has had dealings.

RESOURCE RATING.   The evaluation of resources through the statistical measurement and rating of vendors according to their respective contributions to store volume and profits.

RETAIL ACCORDION THEORY.   A theory of retail institutional change which suggests that retail institutions go from broad-based outlets with wide assortments to specialized, narrow-line stores and then back again to the wider assortments. Also referred to as the general-specific-general theory. See Wheel of Retailing Theory, Dialectic Process Theory, and Natural Selection Theory.

RETAILER.   Merchant middleman who is engaged primarily in selling to ultimate consumers. One retailer may operate a number of establishments.

RETAILER-OWNED COOPERATIVE.   An organization of independent retail stores which voluntarily join together as a group operating at the wholesale level to gain the advantages of cooperative buying and promoting.

RETAILER-SPONSORED COOPERATIVES.   A form of contractual vertical marketing system that is an example of backward integration. Independent retailers organize contractually to form a cooperative which gives cooperating stores greater market power in dealing with suppliers. See Franchising and Wholesaler-Sponsored Voluntaries.

RETAIL ESTABLISHMENT.   A single or separate place of business principally engaged in the performance of marketing functions, where in or out sales are made primarily to ultimate consumers.

RETAILING. The final part of the marketing process in which the various functions of the seller, usually a store or a service establishment, and the buyer, an individual consumer, are primarily oriented to accomplishing the exchange of goods and services for purposes of personal, family, or household use.

RETAILING (Defined as a Discipline). The study of the behavior of persons and their social institutions as they relate to the transfer of goods and services at the point of ultimate consumption.

RETAILING (Defined as a Science). The attempt to systematize knowledge through observation, study, and experimentation and to relate this derived knowledge to the discipline of retailing to establish principles.

RETAILING (Defined from a Managerial Perspective). The attempt to manage motivated human transactions at the point of ultimate consumption for the benefit of the business enterprise and society.

RETAILING MIX. Those variables that a retail store can combine in alternative ways to arrive at a strategy for attracting its consumers. The variables usually include product, price, promotion, place, operating policy, buying, and human resource considerations.

RETAILING THE INVOICE. The practice of writing the unit selling prices on vendors' invoices which serve as the market's authorization.

RETAIL METHOD (of Inventory). A type of accounting system whereby the closing inventory at cost is determined by the average relationship between cost and retail value of all goods available for sale during the period—for example, if the cumulative markup percentage is 40 percent, then the cost percentage is 60 percent. Assume a closing inventory at retail of $10,000. The closing inventory at cost would equal $6,000 ($10,000 × 0.60).

RETAIL REDUCTIONS. The total of markdowns, discounts to employees and other classes of customers, and stock shortages.

RETAIL SALE. One in which the buyer is an ultimate consumer, and the motive for buying is personal or family satisfaction stemming from the final consumption of the article being purchased.

RETAIL SPACE. The proximate environment that surrounds the retail shopper.

RETAIL STORE. A place of business open to and frequented by the general public, in which sales are made primarily to ultimate consumers, usually in small quantities, from merchandise inventories stored and displayed on the premises.

RETAINED EARNINGS. A term commonly used by corporations to show that portion of their capital which was derived from earnings and has not been paid out in the form of dividends.

RETURNS AND ALLOWANCES TO CUSTOMERS. The dollar sum of goods returned to the store and of reductions in the price allowed customers by the store; deducted from gross sales to get net sales. Also referred to as sales returns and allowances.

RETURNS AND ALLOWANCES TO SUPPLIERS. The sum of purchased goods returned to the supplier and unplanned reductions in purchase price; represents a reduction in the cost of purchased items or total purchases. Also referred to as purchase returns and allowances.

RETURN TO STOCK. When a customer returns merchandise to the store for an exchange, credit, or money back, the process of placing the merchandise into stock again must be accompanied by a transaction to "return to stock" so that the item and the dollar amount is added to inventory levels.

REVOLVING CREDIT.   A consumer credit plan which combines the convenience of a continuous charge account and the privileges of installment payment; commonly used for purchase of merchandise on a nonsecured basis. See Installment Account.

REWRAPS.   Merchandise repackaged because of damage to the original wrapper.

RIGID-LIMIT PLAN, REVOLVING CREDIT.   A form of installment charge account in which the customer's credit limit is established by the amount of the fixed monthly payment.

ROG DATING.   Receipt-of-goods dating; denotes that the discount period does not begin until the day the customer receives the shipment. See AOG.

ROTATED INVENTORY CONTROL.   A system of taking periodic inventories of different sections of a department's stock in order to obtain stock and sales information to be used in buying.

ROUTINE SELLING.   A form of personal selling involving the sale of nontechnical items, such as clothing, in which contact is made with the shopper prior to the shopper's decision to make a purchase.

ROYALTY.   A term with varying meanings within business, but which in retailing focuses on franchising; payment that a franchisee makes to a franchisor for services performed.

RUNNERS.   Styles, especially in fashion apparel, for which there are many repeat orders.

S

SALARY PLUS COMMISSION COMPENSATION.   A compensation plan in which the retail employee is paid a set salary but is also paid a certain percentage on sales made.

SALE.   (1) The exchange of property between one person and another for an agreed consideration. (2) In a legal sense a sale is a contract, once transfer of title takes place under agreed terms. (3) Also associated with the lowering of prices.

SALE AND LEASEBACK.   See Sell-and-Lease Agreement.

SALE MERCHANDISE.   Merchandise for a special sale, either bought expressly for that purpose or reduced in price from regular stock.

SALES BRANCH.   Local part of manufacturer's organization that carries stock, fills orders, and serves as headquarters for a local (territorial) sales force; a single manufacturer's substitute for a local wholesaler.

SALES FINANCE COMPANIES.   Firms principally engaged in financing consumer installment purchases of automobiles and other durable goods.

SALES FORECAST.   An estimate of sales, in dollars or physical units, for a specified future period under a proposed marketing plan or program and an assumed set of economic and other forces outside the unit for which the forecast is made; may be for a store, department, or smaller classification.

SALES GRABBER.   A salesperson who attempts to sell large quantities of goods at the expense of other salespeople in the department by waiting on customers out of turn or by neglecting small purchases in order to serve customers buying in large quantities.

SALES PLANNING.   That part of planning which is concerned with forecasting sales, devising programs for reaching the sales target, and deriving a sales budget.

SALES PRODUCTIVITY METHOD OF SPACE ALLOCATION.   Determination of the amount of space to allocate to a department based on sales per square foot of the department divided into the annual planned sales volume of the department.

SALES PROMOTION.   In a very broad sense, all activities and devices that are designed to sell more merchandise and create goodwill, directly or indirectly. Also, those activities and devices whose primary function is that of inviting, persuading, and otherwise encouraging and stimulating trade. In a more restricted sense, the selling activities that supplement advertising and personal selling, coordinate them, and render them more effective.

SALES QUOTA.   A projected volume of sales assigned to a selling unit or a person for use in the management of sales efforts; applies to a specified period and may be expressed in dollars or physical units.

SALES RECORD CONTROL.   A unit control system based on the analysis of sales records—for example, price ticket stubs, duplicate sales checks.

SALES RETAIL.   The price for which a product is actually sold.

SALES RETURNS AND ALLOWANCES.   See Returns and Allowances to Customers.

SALES TERMS.   The conditions under which a product is sold, involving such considerations as discounts, date of delivery, refunds, and methods of payment.

SATURATED MARKET.   The practical point of absorption of a product or service within a market.

SATURATION.   Complete coverage by advertising or by maximum retail representation.

SCANNING.   The process in complete point-of-sales (service) systems wherein the input into the terminal is accomplished by passing a coded ticket over a "reader" or by having a "wand" pass over the ticket. In the food business scanning is done by a non-human-readable bar code called the universal product code (UPC), and in general merchandise the proposed format is human-readable optical recognition characters.

SCRAMBLED MERCHANDISING.   A deviation from traditional merchandising which involves the sale of items not usually associated with a retail establishment's primary lines—for example, supermarkets handling nonfood items, drugstores selling variety goods and sometimes, hardware. Also scrambled retailing.

SD–BL (Sight Draft–Bill of Lading).   A sight draft is attached to the bill of lading and must be honored before the buyer can take possession of the shipment. Resembles COD terms and may be said to constitute one way of enforcing them.

SEASONAL DISCOUNT.   A special discount to all retailers who place orders for seasonal merchandise well in advance of the normal buying period.

SEASONAL MERCHANDISE.   Goods that have temporal shelf life and once a set time has passed, cannot be sold at regular prices. Examples are winter coats, Christmas cards, Easter candy. Seasonal merchandise must be carefully monitored to ensure proper decisions relative to actions taken during the season.

SEASONAL DATING. A form of advance dating allowed on merchandise of a seasonal nature, granted by a manufacturer to induce early buying of seasonal goods so as to keep his plant occupied in slack seasons.

SEASON LETTER. In the marking procedure of most general merchandise stores, part of the information on the ticket is a letter that indicates the season in which the merchandise came in (e.g., K is fall 1978); a number can also be included to indicate the *month* within that season. The information makes it possible to "age" inventories when physical counts are made and action must be taken on old stocks.

SECONDARY SHOPPING DISTRICTS. Clusters of stores that serve a population of several thousand people within a large city; similar in character to the main shopping districts of smaller cities.

SECOND-LINE MERCHANDISE. A brand-name product manufacturer who adds lower priced merchandise to his line of goods; not to be confused with "seconds," which are slightly damaged or handled goods.

SECRET PARTNER. An individual who contributes capital and has a voice in the management of a partnership but does not disclose his financial connection with the firm.

SECTOR THEORY. A theory of urban land use patterns which states that land users are arranged in wedges that radiate outward from the city and that rent patterns cause these shapes.

SECURED ACCOUNT. Any account against which collateral or other security is held.

SECURITY. The operating area of a retail store that is responsible for protecting merchandise from pilferage (internal or external). Those working in security may be store employees or outside people. See Protection Department.

SELECTIVE BUYING MOTIVES. Those which influence the decision to buy a particular item from among several possibilities within a product category.

SELECTIVE DISTRIBUTION (Selective Selling). Limiting the outlets (wholesale or retail) for one's product to those that will contribute most to profits and prestige, basing the choice on size of orders, credit standing, and the like; used mostly for specialty and shopping goods.

SELF-INSURANCE. Periodic expense deductions made from revenues and possible segregation of current assets to meet predictable, insurable losses; not to be confused with "assumption of risk."

SELF-LIQUIDATING DISPLAY. One for which there is a charge to the outlet that actually repays the advertiser what he spends for the display material at wholesale.

SELF-LIQUIDATING PREMIUM. Same as self-liquidating display, except that the consumer is charged instead of the outlet.

SELF-SERVICE. A type of operation where the customer is exposed to merchandise that may be examined without sales assistance, unless the customer seeks such assistance. Usually accompanied by checkouts or in some cases area wrap stations. Typical of supermarkets and discount stores. See Limited-Service Retailer and compare with Full-Service Store.

SELL-AND-LEASE AGREEMENT. A term applied to an arrangement whereby a business enterprise owning and occupying real estate sells it to an investor, such as an insurance company, and takes a long-term lease on the property and often, in addition, an option or agreement to buy, effective at the termination of the lease.

SELLER'S MARKET. A situation in marketing where the demand for goods tends to exceed the supply; the market that belongs to the seller.

SELLING AGENT. A functional middleman who serves his principals on a continuing basis, receives a commission for his services, does not take title to the goods, assumes responsibility for selling the entire output of his principal, gives advice on styles and patterns, furnishes financial aid, and assists in carrying or actually carries credits for the client.

SELLING AREA. Refers to the total departmental area used in selling, including clerk and customer aisles, fitting rooms, and forward stock areas contained within or contiguous to the areas used by merchandise departments for selling purposes; customer aisles that run between different selling departments are divided in calculating the selling area of each such department.

SELLING CALENDAR. A seasonal promotion plan giving specific dates for each important selling event.

SELLING EXPENSE (Cost). Any expense or class of expense incurred in selling.

SEMIDIRECT EXPENSES. Although not direct expenses, have an equitable basis upon which to allocate them to departments. An example is accounts payable, which could be allocated to departments based on the number of invoices charged to specific departments.

SEMI-JOBBER (Split-Function Wholesaler). A wholesaler who sells at retail as well as at wholesale.

SEND TRANSACTION. Retail sales of merchandise to be delivered to the customer.

SERVICE AREA. Any part of a store being used for sales-supporting (or nonselling) activities rather than for sales activities. Typically service areas occupy less valuable locations within the building, and if they require customer contact, are placed strategically for customer movement throughout the store.

SERVICE CREDIT. The credit extended by professional people—doctors, lawyers, accountants—for services rendered.

SERVICE DESK. A station within a store where customers take merchandise for exchange or credit, depending upon company policy. Usually more functions are performed at this station than just exchange. See Exchange Desk.

SERVICE FRANCHISE. A type of franchise system in which franchisors license franchisees to dispense a service under a trade name. See Ownership Franchise, Distributorship, Mobile Franchise, and Dealership.

SERVICE MARKS. Identifying signs or symbols of services or service organizations (distinguished from manufacturers of tangible products to which a trademark is attached) protected by federal trademark registration.

SERVICES. Include layaway, gift wrap, credit, and any service which is not directly related to the actual sale of a specific product within the store. Some of these services are charged for, and some are not. See Ancillary Services and Customer Services.

SERVICE SELLING.   Engaging a customer who wants to buy and knows what he wants; distinguished from creative selling.

SERVICE WHOLESALER.   See Wholesaler.

SHIPPERS' COOPERATIVES.   Nonprofit organizations that pool members' shipments so that they can be moved at low carload or truckload rates instead of the more expensive less than carload or less then truckload rates.

SHOPLIFTING.   The stealing of a store's merchandise by customers. See Pilferage.

SHOPPING CENTER.   A geographic cluster of retail stores collectively handling an assortment of goods varied enough to satisfy most of the merchandise wants of consumers within convenient traveling time, and thereby attracting a general shopping trade.

SHOPPING GOODS.   Those in which the consumer has a relatively large potential gain or satisfaction by making price, quality, or style comparisons among alternative sellers or among alternative items within a particular store before making a purchase.

SHOPPING RADIUS.   The distance or territory from which a store habitually draws customer traffic.

SHORTAGE.   See Inventory Stock Shortage.

SHORT DELIVERY.   A discrepancy in the amount of goods delivered, the number being less than that shown on the invoice. Also short shipment.

SHORT LINE.   A selection from a vendor's complete assortment of a few style numbers that a store buyer wishes to inspect; often done by a resident buyer to save the store buyer's time, thus making it unnecessary for the latter to inspect a complete line.

SHORT MERCHANDISE.   In a shipment from a vendor the complete order is often not received. The part of the shipment that does not come in is "short" and will normally be back-ordered.

SHRINKAGE.   The difference between actual stock on hand and the book inventory.

SIC.   Standard Industrial Classification Manual for U.S. government statistical purposes.

SILENT PARTNER.   One who is not generally known to the public as a member of a firm and who, by agreement among the partners, does not play an active role in its management; has unlimited liability for the debts of the firm.

SILENT SALESMAN.   (1) Direct mail literature. (2) Vending machine.

SIMPLIFICATION.   The elimination of superfluous variety.

SINGLE-DISCOUNT EQUIVALENT.   A single discount that is equivalent to a series trade discount. Assume a trade series discount of 30 percent, 10 percent, and 5 percent and a list price of $1,000. Based upon the series discount, the net price would be $598.50. To determine the single-discount equivalent, subtract $598.50 from $1,000, which leaves $401.50, and converts to a 40.15 percent single-discount equivalent to the series discount of 30 percent, 10 percent, and 5 percent.

SINGLE-LINE STORES. Those with an extensive variety of one line of merchandise that is related in sale or use.

SINGLE UNIT. An establishment operated by a firm which serves as the sole place of business in a particular kind of industry or trade.

SITUATION ANALYSIS. An organized way for a retailer to determine the strengths and weaknesses of the firm, to find out where the firm is today, how it became what it is, and where it is going if existing policies and organizational structures are not changed. The analysis focuses not only on matters internal to the firm but also on the total environment of the firm.

SIZE LINING. Related to concept of price lining; selection of predetermined size points at which merchandise will be offered. For assistance to customer selection, sizes should be according to customer behavior—for example, junior sizes together. If physical space is limited, *outsizes* are not practical.

SIZE SCALE. A chart of the proper quantity of an item to order in each size.

SKIP LOSS. Credit losses due to the disappearance of a customer who has purchases on a regular charge or installment basis.

SKUs (Stock-Keeping Units). The number of specific control items in a classification, for example, a dress, in size 9, in black is one SKU, while a red dress in size 9 is another.

SOFT GOODS. Merchandise basically of a textiles base and typically nondurable. Compare to Hard Goods.

SPAN OF CONTROL. A principle of organization addressing the question of how many persons should report to a supervisor. A supervisor's span of control depends on several factors: (1) the competence of the supervisor and the subordinates, (2) the extent to which the supervisor carries out nonmanagerial tasks, (3) the similarity of functions to be performed, (4) the degree to which procedures are standardized, and (5) the physical dispersion of persons and products.

SPECIAL ORDER. (1) One sent to a vendor for some item requested by a customer but not regularly carried in stock, or temporarily out of stock. (2) An order for specially manufactured merchandise which the retailer wishes to introduce, but which is not in the vendor's regular stock.

SPECIAL SALE. A sales promotion event usually using a "low price" or "special value" advertising appeal, which may last a single day or as long as a month and be storewide, departmental, or divisional in scope.

SPECIALTY ADVERTISING. Involves advertising by giving consumers an object (calendar, ball-point pen, key ring, ashtray, ruler, etc.) with the firm name and possibly other information printed on the item. The object of specialty advertising is to create goodwill. It also provides repetition for the advertising message since the item user is exposed to the message each time the article is used.

SPECIALTY GOODS. Consumer products with unique characteristics and/or brand identification for which a significant group of buyers are habitually willing to make a special purchasing effort—for example, specific brands and types of fancy foods, stereo components, certain types of sporting equipment, photographic equipment, and men's suits.

SPECIALTY STORES. (1) Stores which handle a limited variety of goods, as compared to single-line stores. (2) May be used to refer to departmentized apparel stores, as distinct from department stores.

SPECIALTY WHOLESALERS (Short-Line Distributors). Those who stock a narrow range of products.

SPIFF. A bonus that salespeople receive for each sale made of specially designated merchandise. See Push Money.

SPLIT SHIPMENT. A vendor ships part of a shipment to a retailer and back-orders the remainder because the entire shipment could not be shipped at the same time.

SPOT CHECK. Used particularly in receiving operations when goods come in for reshipping to branch stores in packing cartons. Certain cartons are opened in the receiving area of the central distribution point and spot-checked for quality and quantity.

SPOT SALE (or Purchase). The sale or purchase of a commodity for immediate delivery, often on a cash basis.

STANDARD. A measure generally recognized as having a fixed value.

STANDARDIZATION. The determination of basic measures or limits, including the process of conforming to such standards; the facilitating function of marketing concerned with these activities.

STANDARD MERCHANDISE. Merchandise generally branded that has no imperfections and meets the standard of quality set for it by its producer.

STANDARD METROPOLITAN STATISTICAL AREA (SMSA). An integrated economic area with a large volume of daily travel and communication between a central city of 50,000 inhabitants or more and the outlying parts of the area. U.S. Census of business areas, thus defined, are more restrictive than "market" or "trading" areas, though in each, except in New England, at least one entire county is included in the statistical complications.

STANDARD PRICE. The price of raw materials thought to be obtainable by the exercise of prudent procurement practices.

STANDING ORDER. An arrangement with a vendor to make shipments periodically in specified quantities in which the vendor may be authorized to ship a certain quantity each month or week for a set period.

STAPLE MERCHANDISE. That for which a fairly active demand continues over a period of years and which the retailer finds it necessary to carry in stock continuously.

STAPLE STOCK LIST. List of items that are to be carried in stock.

STATEMENT ANALYSIS. The analytic study of balance sheets, income statements, and other statements of a business enterprise, by themselves or in comparison with those of other dates or other enterprises; regarded as an aid to management or as a basis for measuring credit and investment risks; often prepared by employing accepted financial and operating ratios showing conditions and trends.

STOCK BALANCE. Concerned with planning and controlling merchandise investment so that it is balanced with expected sales. The three perspectives from which one can view stock balance are: (1) stock width (breadth), (2) stock support (depth), and (3) total dollars invested in stock.

STOCK BIN CONTROL. A system for maintaining assortments of staple goods by reordering periodically on the basis of empty spaces or of observed low stock conditions in bins or on stock shelves.

STOCK BOOK.   When a store has a unit control system, where goods are either perpetually or nonperpetually maintained, each item controlled is listed by number in a "stock book" on which daily additions and deductions are listed so that stock levels can be maintained.

STOCK CONTROL.   All the activities that are carried on to maintain a balance between inventories and sales.

STOCK DEPTH.   The number of units in individual merchandise items needed to meet sales of each assortment factor. See Stock Support.

STOCKOUT.   A situation in which a retail store does not have enough items of a particular kind to meet customer demand; thus, the product is not available when consumers come into the store for the purpose of purchasing the item.

STOCK-SALES RATIO.   The ratio between the stock on hand at the beginning or end of a period and the sales for the period; determined by dividing stock, preferably at the beginning of the period, by sales; distinguished from turnover in that the former yields a ratio at a given time rather than an average for a period of time.

STOCK SHORTAGES.   All unexplained or unrecorded shrinkages in the value of merchandise available for sale; the amount by which a physical inventory is short of a book inventory figure.

STOCK SUPPORT.   The number of units in individual merchandise items needed to meet sales of each assortment factor. See Stock Depth.

STOCK TURNOVER.   An index of the velocity with which merchandise moves into and out of a store or department. Formally defined, the "rate of stock turnover" is the number of times during a given period that the average inventory on hand has been sold and replaced; computed by dividing sales by average inventory, with both stated in comparable valuations, either cost or selling price.

STORAGE.   The marketing function that involves holding and preserving goods between the time of their production and their final sale.

STORE AUDIT.   A service usually purchased from a commercial marketing research organization that has field auditors regularly checking inventories of designated items to determine the unit sales of the client's brands, unit sales of each major competing brand, and other related information.

STORE COUPONS.   A store coupon is a print medium sponsored by the store itself and indicates a "cents-off" or "free deal" by the store. Compare to *vendor coupons* placed in an ad or the merchandise itself for redemption at time of purchase.

STORE LAYOUT.   Interior retail store arrangement of departments or groupings of merchandise. Should be organized to provide for ease of customer movement through the store and for maximum exposure and attractive display of merchandise.

STORE MANAGER.   In the classic department store organization, the "store manager" is the head of the operations division and typically at a vice presidential level. See Operations Manager.

STRAIGHT SALARY COMPENSATION PLAN.   A form of compensation plan in which the retail employee is paid a set salary that does not vary; based on sales productivity. Is often used in situations in which the retail employee performs many nonselling functions.

STRATEGY. The posture assumed by the management of a retail enterprise as it attempts to accomplish the objectives of the firm: namely, to make a profit by substantial satisfaction of customer markets.

STRING STREET LOCATION. A location on a major thoroughfare upon which various kinds of stores are strung for a number of consecutive blocks.

STRIP-TYPE SHOPPING CENTER. One in which stores are aligned along a thoroughfare, usually set back some distance from the street to permit front parking.

STUB CONTROL. A perpetual inventory system of unit control in which sales information is obtained from stubs of price tickets rather than from sales checks.

STYLE. John Fairchild of *Women's Wear Daily* says that style is an expression of individualism mixed with charisma. *Fashion* is something that comes after style—he feels that changes in fashion are created by the way people feel. A *fad* is a temporary fashion, and fashion is change; thus style is a fashion that is "here today and here tomorrow."

STYLE-OUT. A method of pinpointing the determinants of consumer demand for fashion merchandise whereby the buyer and merchandise manager physically inspect fast-selling and slow-selling items to determine their customer-attracting features.

SUGGESTED RETAIL PRICE. A recommended list price submitted by a manufacturer to a retailer.

SUGGESTION (or Suggestive) SELLING. Recommendation by salespeople of items related to those the customer asks about and expects to buy, of timely items, of special values, of new goods, and so on.

SUPERMARKET. A large departmentized retail establishment offering a relatively broad and complete stock of dry groceries, fresh meat, perishable produce, and dairy products, supplemented by a variety of convenience, nonfood merchandise, and operating primarily on a self-service basis. For some specific trade classifications, supermarkets are stated as having a minimum sales volume requirement—for example, $500,000 or $1,000,000—with variations by source of data.

SUPERSTORES. Very large stores that are typically outgrowths of supermarkets and offer all of the expected routine purchases of the mass market. (Compare to Hypermarkets, which do not offer all of the routine purchases but merely select those "winners" which can be sold in tremendous volumes.)

SUPPLY HOUSE. Middleman selling industrial goods to manufacturers; generally "wholesaler" or "jobber."

SYNDICATION. A form of mail-order distribution involving a merger of the mail-order selling technique with the extension of consumer credit through credit cards.

T

T-ACCOUNT. A skeleton ledger account which resembles the letter T. It is often used for demonstrating the effect of a transaction or a series of transactions or for solving short accounting problems.

TACTICS. To place in proper perspective, objectives of a company indicate where it wants to be; strategy indicates the intended route; and tactics indicate the particular vehicle that it will use. (Philip Kotler)

TAKE TRANSACTION.   Sale of goods that are turned over to the customer immediately upon closing the sale rather than through the delivery department.

TALLY (Card or Envelope).   Each salesperson receives a certain amount of cash for the "bank" for a given day. This amount is placed back into the tally at the end of the day so that a starting amount is ready for the next day. It is the minimum cash requirement anticipated to "open" the register.

TARE.   Weight of a container deducted from gross weight of package to determine net weight and allowance for freight.

TARGET MARKET.   The particular segment of a total population that a particular retail store focuses all merchandising expertise on to accomplish the profit objectives of the store.

TEAR SHEETS.   Advertisements torn from newspapers or magazines sent to an agency or advertiser as evidence of insertion.

TEN-PAY PLAN.   An installment selling plan often used in the clothing field whereby the customer completes payment in ten weekly installments, generally equal in amount.

TERM FILE.   Records showing the datings and cash, trade, and quantity discounts allowed by each vendor.

TEST MARKET.   Trading area selected to test a company's product, service, or promotion.

THEORIES OF RETAIL INSTITUTIONAL CHANGE.   Theories that provide insight into how retail institutions have evolved and adapted to environmental change. See Wheel of Retailing Theory, Retail Accordion Theory, Dialectic Process Theory, and Natural Selection Theory.

13-MONTH MERCHANDISING CALENDAR.   A calendar in which each of 13 "months" is always a standard four-week period.

TICKLER.   A file or record of maturing obligations or other items of interest maintained in such a manner as to call attention to each of them at the proper time.

TIME (Advertising).   The apportionment of the total advertising budget by months and perhaps by weeks or special promotion periods.

TIME BILL.   A bill of exchange due on a particular date.

TITLE.   Legal evidence of ownership or right of possession.

TOKEN ORDER.   Placing a small order with the possibility of a larger one in the future.

TOTAL COST OF GOODS SOLD.   Gross cost of goods sold plus alteration and workroom net cost, if any, less each discount earned on purchases.

TOTAL SYSTEMS COMPETITION.   The most sophisticated form of competition in retailing. Competition between systems in which each system links resources, manufacturing capability, distribution networks, and strong consumer loyalty.

TRACKING.   An effort to determine the possible causes of markdowns in order to avoid similar problems in the future.

TRADE ACCEPTANCE.   A non-interest-bearing bill of exchange or draft covering the sale of goods, drawn by the seller on, and accepted by, the buyer.

TRADE ACCOUNT PAYABLE.   A liability on open account for the purchase of commodities or services used in the regular course of business.

TRADE ACCOUNT RECEIVABLE.   In wholesale trade, an amount due from a business customer for products sold in the regular course of business; distinguished from a receivable resulting from other transactions.

TRADE ASSOCIATION.   A nonprofit organization, local or national in character, serving common interests of enterprises engaged in the same kind of business.

TRADE CARD.   Special card issued to the customer as successive purchases are made; entitles holder to a prize or purchase credit when a certain total is reached. Also punch card.

TRADE CREDIT.   Supplying goods (by wholesalers and manufacturers) on terms that are intended to permit sale by the retailer before payment is due.

TRADE DISCOUNT.   The discount allowed to a class of customers (manufacturers, wholesalers, retailers) on a list price before consideration of credit terms; applies to any allowance granted without reference to the date of payment.

TRADEMARK.   A brand or part of a brand that is given legal protection because it is capable of exclusive appropriation and is used in a distinctive way.

TRADE NAME.   The name by which a product is known in commercial circles; may or may not be registered as a trademark.

TRADE PREMIUMS.   Prizes, usually merchandise, given by jobbers' retailers for their cooperation in achieving sales.

TRADE PRICE.   The manufacturer's selling price to a dealer.

TRADE PUFFERY.   See Puffery.

TRADE REFERENCE.   In credit management, the business references with whom the applicant has had dealings and who can help determine the applicant's financial ability to pay a debt.

TRADING AREA.   A district whose size is usually determined by the boundaries within which it is economical in terms of volume and cost for a marketing unit or group to sell and/or deliver products. Also shopping radius.

TRADING STAMPS.   Stamps purchased by retailers from trading stamp companies and distributed to consumers—the number depending on the size of consumer purchases—for redemption in merchandise.

TRADING-UP.   (1) Seller's practice of handling and promoting more expensive or higher grade merchandise in order to elevate the prestige of his firm. (2) Salesperson's effort to interest customer in better-grade and more expensive goods than the customer expects to buy.

TRAFFIC.   When applied to retailing, refers to those people who frequent the store (or the shopping area) within a particular period of time. Traffice may be heavy, light, or medium.

TRAFFIC ITEMS.   Consumer products of high-replacement frequency which regularly bring traffic to a store or department.

TRANSACTION PROCESSING.   A type of personal selling in which retail employees function simply as checkout clerks or cashiers and engage in little personal selling. A typical example is a checkout clerk in a supermarket.

TRANSFERS (Interdepartmental Merchandise).   An intrafirm transaction accounting for the movement of merchandise from one selling department or location to another, which is a transfer-in for the department or other selling unit receiving the goods and a transfer-out for the department sending the goods.

TRIAL BALANCE. A listing or tabulation of the debit or credit balance of each account in the ledger to test that the debits and credits are in balance. A trial balance merely indicates that the debits and credits are in balance, not that the entries have necessarily been made correctly.

TUBE SYSTEM. An installation of pneumatic tubes to carry cash, sales checks, and other record forms from one part of a store to another.

TURNOVER. See Stock Turnover.

TWIG. Store (smaller than a branch) that specializes in a particular category or a few categories of merchandise. Usually established to combat some specific competition in an area where the firm does not believe an entire branch is reasonable (e.g., a home furnishings twig).

TYING CLAUSE. Limitation in a contract requiring price maintenance or exclusive purchase of certain products from one party by the other.

TYING CONTRACTS. Agreements which obligate the buyer or lessor to purchase supplementary goods or services in order to obtain desired items.

U

ULTIMATE CONSUMERS. Those who buy goods for personal or family use or for household consumption.

UNCONTROLLABLE EXPENSES. Expenses that would exist whether or not a particular department were eliminated. Examples are rent, heat and light, and administrative salaries. See Indirect Expenses.

UNEVEN EXCHANGE. An exchange of goods made by a customer when the value of the new goods received is different from that of the goods returned.

UNFAIR COMPETITION. Business practices which are not considered ethical in a trade or industry; according to federal and other laws, certain situations and/or practices which unduly injure competitors and work contrary to the public interest as interpreted in the business community and the nation's laws.

UNIT CONTROL. The control of stock in terms of merchandise units rather than in terms of dollar worth.

UNIT PACKING. Packing merchandise in selling units (by the manufacturer) so that it can be sold from sample and delivered to the customer without repacking at the store.

UNIT PRICING. Under unit pricing, products offered for sale include the price per unit, such as per pound or quart, in addition to the price of the product.

UNITY OF COMMAND PRINCIPLE. A principle of organization which states that no person should be under the direct control of more than one supervisor in performing job tasks.

UNIVERSAL PRODUCT CODE (UPC). A national coordinated system of product identification by which a ten-digit number is assigned to every grocery product sold through retail grocery channels in the United States. The UPC is designed so that at the checkout counter an electronic scanner will read the symbol on the product and automatically transmit the information to a computer which controls the cash register. The code is called OCR—font B.

UNSECURED CREDIT. A pledge to repay a loan with no collateral as backing against default. Also open-book credit.

V

VALUE ADDED.   The difference between the selling value of products shipped or delivered by a firm and the cost of materials, supplies, and containers, plus the cost of fuel, purchased electric energy, and contract work used by the firm.

VALUE ANALYSIS.   The use of formal analytic procedures in business purchasing relating the design and function of purchased products to cost with a view to reducing cost substantially through modification of design, change in specifications, different method of manufacture, change in source of supply, possible elimination of an item, or incorporation of a new item.

VARIABLE COSTS (Expenses).   Those that change as sales volume changes. Examples are salespeople's salaries, delivery expense, and receiving costs.

VARIABLE PRICE POLICY.   A policy of adjusting retail prices to different customers, depending on their relative purchasing power or bargaining ability.

VARIETY.   Has to do with the number of different classifications carried in a particular merchandising unit; implies generically different kinds of goods.

VARIETY STORE.   Establishments primarily selling a variety of merchandise in the low and popular price range, such as stationery, gift items, women's accessories, toilet articles, light hardware, toys, housewares, and confectionery. Frequently known as "five-and-ten" stores and "five cents to a dollar" stores, though merchandise is usually sold outside these price ranges.

VENDOR.   Any individual, firm, or corporation from whom purchases are made, whether manufacturer, manufacturer's agent, wholesaler, or commission merchant.

VENDOR ANALYSIS.   An analysis of sales, stocks, markups, markdowns, and gross margin by vendors.

VENDOR COUPONS.   See Store Coupons.

VERTICAL INTEGRATION.   Related to all the stages of an industry or channel of distribution from raw materials to distribution of finished products.

VERTICAL MARKET.   Situation in which an industrial product is used by only one or a very few industry or trade groups; the market is narrow but deep in the sense that most prospective customers in the industry may need the article.

VERTICAL MARKETING SYSTEM.   Consists of networks of horizontally coordinated and vertically aligned establishments that are managed as a system. Establishments at each level operate at an optimum scale so that marketing functions within the system are performed at the most advantageous level or position. See Corporate Vertical Marketing System, Contractual Vertical Marketing System, and Administered Vertical Marketing System.

VERTICAL MARKETING SYSTEM COMPETITION.   Competition between two vertical marketing systems. For example, the vertical marketing system of General Motors competing with that of the Ford Motor Company. See Vertical Marketing System.

VISUAL FRONT.   Open storefront design which has no vision barrier between the interior and the exterior.

VISUAL MERCHANDISING.   Places reliance upon the use of informative labels, descriptive signs, or a self-service type of display, as opposed to dependence upon a salesperson for information.

VISUAL SYSTEM OF STOCK CONTROL. Method of controlling the amount of stock on hand by systematic observation rather than by records. See Eyeball Control.

VOLUNTARY CHAIN (Group). A group of retailers each of whom owns and operates his own store and is associated with a wholesale organization or manufacturer to carry on joint merchandising activities, and is characterized by some degree of group identity and uniformity of operation. Activities generally included are cooperative advertising and group control of store operation.

VOLUNTARY GRADE LABELING. Grading by producer on his own system of classification as distinguished from mandatory or U.S. Department of Agriculture grading.

W

WAGON DISTRIBUTOR. A wholesaler whose inventory of merchandise is carried on trucks which are operated by driver-salespersons; retailer's requirements for merchandise are determined at the time of the sales call and orders are filled immediately from the stock carried on the truck.

WANT BOOK. A notebook in which store employees record the name of items called for by customers but not in stock.

WANT SLIP. A slip on which the salesperson records customer requests for items that cannot be supplied from stock.

WAREHOUSE RECEIPTS. Those which every public warehouse issues to depositors for goods placed in storage.

WAREHOUSE RETAILING. Retailing of certain types of merchandise, particularly food and furniture, in low-rent isolated buildings with a minimum of services offered and the consumer performing the bulk of the buying functions. This approach to merchandising allows profit margins to be maintained while offering low prices to the consumer.

WARRANTY. Subsidiary promise or collateral agreement, a breach of which does not discharge the contract but does entitle the buyer to make certain claims for damages against the vendor; may be expressed—arriving from specific agreement, or implied—from operation of law.

WAYBILL. For air shipments, the same as a bill of lading for rail or sea; shipments—a receipt from the carrier and a contract between carrier and shipper.

WEEKS' SUPPLY METHOD OF STOCK PLANNING. A method of stock planning whereby one plans for a certain number of weeks' supply. In utilizing this method, it is assumed that the same stock turnover can be maintained throughout the selling season; thus, inventory carried is in direct proportion to expected sales.

WHEEL OF RETAILING THEORY. A theory of retail institutional change, developed by Malcolm McNair, which explains retail evolution with a cycle concept. The cycle begins with a new, innovative institution initially offering lower prices than existing competitors. The innovator experiences a period of growth during which it takes business from existing competitors. However, at some point the innovative institution enters a period of maturity with an increase in gross margin, at which time the cycle begins again with another innovative institution initially offering lower prices. See Retail Accordion Theory, Dialectic Process Theory, and Natural Selection Theory.

WHOLESALE ESTABLISHMENT. A recognizable place of business that is primarily engaged in performing marketing functions, including the functions of exchange on the wholesale level of distribution.

WHOLESALE MARKET CENTERS. A concentration of vendors' sales offices or display rooms in one place, usually a city or an area within a city; sometimes identified by a concentration of production facilities as well as sales offices.

WHOLESALE MERCHANTS (Distributors). Establishments primarily engaged in buying and selling merchandise in the domestic market and performing the principal wholesale functions.

WHOLESALER. Merchant establishment operated by a concern that is primarily engaged in buying and taking title to goods, usually storing and physically handling them in large quantities, and reselling them (usually in smaller quantities) to retailers or to industrial or business users.

WHOLESALER-SPONSORED VOLUNTARIES. A form of contractual vertical marketing system which is an example of forward integration. A wholesaler induces many independent retail organizations to purchase from him. The wholesaler offers cooperating retailers standardized merchandising packages, programmed advertising, price marking, storage, central data processing, lower prices because of volume discounts available to the wholesaler, and other advantages. See Franchising and Retailer-Sponsored Cooperatives.

WHOLESALING. (1) All transactions in which the purchaser is actuated by a profit or business motive, except for transactions that involve a small quantity of goods purchased from a retail establishment for business use, which is considered at retail. (2) For U.S. Census of Business purposes, include business establishments primarily engaged in wholesale trade.

WIDTH OF MERCHANDISE OFFERING. The assortment factors necessary to meet the demands of the market and to meet competition. See Breadth of Merchandise Offering.

WILL-CALL. Products ordered by customers in advance of the time delivery is desired.

WORKROOMS. Service departments, such as the apparel alteration, drapery manufacture, furniture polishing and repair, and carpet workrooms.

X–Z

XL. In clothing, denotes extra large size.

ZONE PRICING. Delivered cost based on factory price plus averaged freight rate for section or territory to which goods are shipped (same delivered cost to all in the zone).

NAME INDEX

SUBJECT INDEX

This book has been set in 10 and 9 point Optima, leaded 2 points. Part numbers and titles and chapter titles are in 24 point Optima. Chapter numbers are in 72 point Caslon. The size of the type page is 27 by 46 ½ picas.

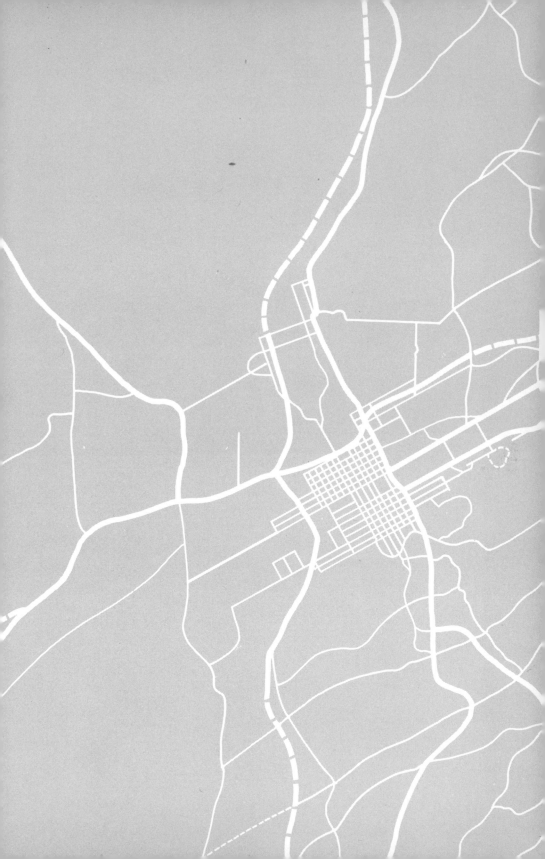